A New History of Modern Architecture

Laurence King Publishing

Published in 2017
by Laurence King Publishing Ltd
361–373 City Road
London EC1V 1LR
Tel +44 20 7841 6900
Fax +44 20 7841 6910
enquiries@laurenceking.com
www.laurenceking.com

A catalogue record for this book is available from the
British Library

ISBN 978 1 78627 056 6

Design: Allan Sommerville, Blok Graphic
Commissioning editors: Philip Cooper and Liz Faber
Senior editor: Gaynor Sermon
Copyeditor: Jonathan Wadman
Picture research: Claire Gouldstone
Index: Chris Dance

Printed in China

Front and back cover: allOver images/Alamy Stock Photo

A New History of Modern Architecture

Art Nouveau / The Beaux-Arts / Expressionism
Modernism / Constructivism / Art Deco / Classicism
Brutalism / Postmodernism / Neo-Rationalism
High Tech / Deconstructivism / Digital Futures

Colin Davies

Author's acknowledgments

It was Philip Cooper, then of Laurence King Publishing, who saw the need for a new history of modern architecture and was kind enough to commission me to write it.

Robert Harbison made many useful comments on a draft of the text, but more importantly set an example of excellence in his teaching, writing and thinking over more than 20 years. Brian Stater also commented usefully on the text and was stalwart in his support and encouragement. What I know about the theory and practice of history is mainly due to my teachers, Adrian Forty and Mark Swenarton, and before them the late Dalibor Vesely. Many journalistic and teaching colleagues helped to shape my view of modern architecture, among them Florian Beigel, John Burrell, Adam Caruso, Dan Cruickshank, Frances Holliss, Joe Kerr, Helen Mallinson, the late Martin Pawley, Peter St John, Helen Thomas and generations of students who repeatedly refreshed my thinking. Jonathan Wadman edited the text with great sensitivity and the staff at Laurence King were kind and tolerant as well as professional.

Finally I would like to thank my partner, Sue Wight, for her unfailing patience, moral support and practical suggestions.

CONTENTS

INTRODUCTION

This book aims to provide a useful and enjoyable history of twentieth- and twenty-first-century architecture. A history of architecture is not the same as a history of building. A history of building might strive for completeness, to 'cover the ground' systematically and objectively, assessing the relative importance of different building technologies or patterns of urbanization or government policies. Such a history might, for example, take the trouble to study popular housing – the 'Cape Cod' and 'ranch-style' homes of the American suburbs, perhaps – or the factory as building type, including the cheap portal-framed sheds that shelter manufacturing operations all over the world. A history of architecture, on the other hand, will pay scant attention to these numerous but anonymous buildings on the grounds that they are artistically uninteresting. Architecture is the design of buildings, but not of all buildings. And architectural history celebrates only a small selection from the minority of buildings that qualify as architecture.

The 'canon', in architecture as in any art, is an imperfect thing, full of distortions and injustices. But that doesn't mean it isn't useful. In fact it is essential to the progress of the art. Without it, architectural conversations – in books and exhibitions, in offices and conference rooms, and in schools of architecture – would be greatly impoverished. The canon is the pool of shared knowledge that unites architects all over the world and gives them their collective identity. When one architect mentions the Villa Savoye, another immediately sees a picture in his or her mind and is prepared to join in the discussion. A thorough knowledge of canonical buildings is essential to every serious architect and student of architecture, and this book is designed to help with the gaining of that knowledge.

In theory it would be possible to reject the canon completely and start again from scratch, reordering the evidence of the past in proportion to its artistic and social importance. In practice, however, such a history would probably be no less biased and selective than the histories it sought to supplant. And in throwing out the canon, one would be throwing out agreed standards of comparison and judgement that are the foundation of architectural culture. On the other hand, the canon must never be completely sacrosanct. Any new history has a duty to reassess it, to question the value of certain of its members and promote less familiar ones. That is what this book sets out to do. It is not revolutionary, but neither is it slavishly conservative.

In reassessing the modern architectural canon, one question has to be considered especially carefully: the relative

A typical cul-de-sac street. Architectural history pays scant attention to popular housing on the dubious grounds that it is artistically uninteresting.

(Opposite) Robie House, Chicago, Illinois, USA. Frank Lloyd Wright, 1910. Frank Lloyd Wright called his architecture 'organic' because it arose naturally from the circumstances of its creation.

importance of the style known as Modernism, which has often been seen, with good reason, as the characteristic style of the twentieth century. Histories of modern architecture have sometimes given disproportionate prominence to this style, becoming in effect histories of Modernism to which a few brief paragraphs on other styles have been added. In this book, the emphasis is adjusted somewhat, not in an aggressive or revisionist attempt to 'cut Modernism down to size' but simply to give representatives of other styles the respectful consideration that they deserve. The Beaux-Arts style of the pre-First World War years, the Art Deco style of the 1920s and 1930s, the Manhattan skyscraper, the classicism of the mid century in both fascist Europe and democratic America, the Chinese 'National' style – these modern but not Modernist architectures are often ignored or glossed over in surveys of this kind. They are included here not on ideological grounds but in order to paint a more complete picture and satisfy the curiosity of observant readers who would otherwise question their absence.

It is possible to imagine an ideal, geographically representative history of modern architecture that would choose examples from every region of the globe and allocate them on a democratic basis. This book falls short of that ideal. But then such a theoretically perfect coverage would be of limited use because it would ignore the fact that 'modern architecture' is essentially a field of western culture. We should recognize its limits, but also acknowledge its importance. To a large extent global architecture is western architecture. The traditional architectures of, say, China, India, South America, Japan, Malaysia or the Middle East have largely succumbed to western influence. In some cases, most notably Japan, western modern architecture has been fully adopted and taken forward in new directions. This book tries to describe that process with due sensitivity to the reciprocal influences of local traditions, but it also accepts that 'modern architecture' is a concept with a built-in bias.

How should a history of modern architecture be organized? There are perhaps six main possibilities: chronologically, geographically, typologically, biographically, technologically or stylistically. But there is a seventh possibility and it is the one that this book adopts, namely a judicious combination of all the others. Priority is given to chronology, both in the order of the chapters and within chapters, but otherwise the material is grouped according to the other five possibilities, for example: Houses (typological), Le Corbusier (biographical), Expressionism (stylistic), China (geographical) and Steel and Concrete (technological).

Galaxy Soho, Beijing, China. Zaha Hadid, 2012.
A futuristic vision, yet the urban spaces it creates are said to reflect the classical courtyards of old Beijing.

Chapters overlap chronologically, but are provided with a date-range in the heading (an idea stolen from Kenneth Frampton). The book is designed to be read either from cover to cover or as separate chapters in any order. Most chapters are provided with a short, boxed article which either introduces a new topic tangential to that of the main text, or provides additional material that would otherwise have interrupted the flow. The device recognizes that a broad survey of this kind is in any case bound to be discontinuous and episodic.

These ways of organizing the historical material suggest different kinds of connection with the world beyond architecture. Certain architectural historians lay great emphasis on political, socio-economic and cultural 'context', as if architecture had no ideas or principles of its own to contribute to wider culture. Contextual histories can sometimes seem to be about everything but the architecture that is their ostensible subject. This book acknowledges that forms and styles of architecture respond to ideas and practical developments in other fields. For example, Albert Kahn's factories are discussed in relation to Taylorism and Fordism, and the architecture of Zaha Hadid in relation to digital technology. Nevertheless the priority is to analyze and interpret projects and buildings in their own terms. There are, after all, numerous political, economic and technological histories available for cross-reference. Concentration on the products of architecture does not imply, however, that they should be judged purely on their formal qualities. This is not a guide book for connoisseurs. It is about architectural ideas rather than specific buildings, ideas that may find expression in imaginary projects, manifestos, books, exhibitions, buildings that no longer exist and buildings that never existed. A thorough understanding of the progress of architecture demands more than just a superficial acquaintance with preserved examples. Connections and comparisons must be made across the whole field.

What does it mean to say that a history is 'useful'? Useful to whom and in what way? If the past is to be represented truthfully then it must be understood on its own terms. Present-day preoccupations should, in theory at least, be suspended in order to arrive at accurate historical interpretations. But it would be foolish to deny that when we study the past we expect to learn something from it that will be of use to us in the present. This book explains certain formal and technical principles that remain relevant to the practice of architecture now, but above all it aims to be useful through its elucidation of architectural ideas with reference to specific examples. The hope is that it will help students, of any kind, to strengthen and deepen their own architectural thinking.

01 | ART NOUVEAU AND ADOLF LOOS 1881-1930

Architecture is more than just the design of buildings. It has other capabilities. For example it can give expression to the power and influence of a particular section of society – a ruling family, a religious institution or a commercial enterprise. It can also represent a whole community, even a whole civilization. Buildings are usually solid, enduring objects. They survive for long periods, sometimes hundreds of years, so when we look at them with curiosity we are, in a sense, looking into the past. In old buildings we find evidence of the way our ancestors thought. We can assess to what extent we differ from them and to what extent we have inherited their view of the world. When we look at a Gothic cathedral, for example, we see a world very different from our own, and yet the institution that sponsored the building still survives. When we ourselves build, we take on the responsibility of representing ourselves to posterity. Architecture therefore has a special, symbolic connection with the past and also with the future. Architecture and history are closely related disciplines.

In the nineteenth century this special connection between architecture and history was interpreted rather literally. Architects studied the buildings of the past not just to understand them but to recreate their spirit. The architects of the Gothic Revival, for example, filled their sketchbooks with details of medieval buildings and incorporated versions of them in designs for new buildings. Those new buildings were, in a sense, works of history. The 'classical' styles of ancient Greece and Rome had formed the basis of most western architecture ever since the Renaissance, but other historical styles were also studied and copied: Byzantine, Islamic, Chinese, Egyptian. This tendency to design new buildings in imitation of old ones is usually called 'historicism' and it was the prevailing orthodoxy of nineteenth-century architecture. The prevailing orthodoxy of twentieth-century architecture was Modernism. Modernism defined itself partly as non-historicism. It was thought of as a new style, a complete rethink, a return to basic principles. Modernism did not copy, it invented anew. Some architectural historians writing in the middle of the twentieth century saw the birth and rise of Modernism as inevitable because it was the expression of irresistible new technological and social forces – mass production, democracy and secularism. These had existed in

the nineteenth century too, of course, but architects had tried to ignore them. Historicism was an escape from the harsh realities of the modern world; Modernism embraced them and celebrated them, or at least that was how Modernist historians saw it.

Pevsner's 'teleology'
One of those Modernist historians was Nikolaus Pevsner, a German who lived in England for most of his life and made a special study of English art and architecture. He wrote the influential book *Pioneers of Modern Design*, first published in 1936, in which he traced the origins of Modernism in the work of certain late nineteenth- and early twentieth-century designers, especially those connected with the English Arts and Crafts movement led by William Morris. Pevsner wrote what is known as 'teleological' history, which means, roughly speaking, history written selectively as a justification of later developments. The work of those Arts and Crafts designers was being studied not for its own sake but in order to find the roots of the later Modernist style that would eventually, inevitably, emerge. For Pevsner, the late nineteenth century style known as Art Nouveau contained no such promising tendencies. 'Art Nouveau', he said, 'is outre and directs its appeal to the aesthete, the one who is ready to accept the dangerous tenet of art for art's sake.' He thought it was 'a blind alley' and 'completely lacking in a social conscience'.[1]

But if we examine Art Nouveau in its own terms, without the distorting effect of hindsight, we realize that its approach to design was revolutionary. It was revolutionary because it was non-historicist. Pevsner disliked Art Nouveau because it continued to use ornament, and absence of ornament would eventually become a defining characteristic of Modernism. But Art Nouveau ornament was of a new kind. It was inspired not by history or tradition but by nature. Of course, traditional ornament was also inspired by nature – think of the acanthus leaves on a Corinthian capital – but Art Nouveau ornament looked at nature afresh, trying to imitate not just the forms of plants and animals but the very forces of growth and resistance that produced them. Look, for example, at the back of the chair designed by Arthur Heygate Mackmurdo in 1881 – a very early example of Art Nouveau. Its frame is filled by a flat, profile-cut representation in wood of what seems

Chair, Arthur Heygate Mackmurdo, 1881. Ornament and structure: a plant drawn in profile-cut wood makes a beautiful, and functional, chair back.

to be a single plant, the stems of which writhe and intersect, asymmetrically, finally producing a row of five blossoms at the top. This is a functional part of the chair and it does its job very adequately, but it is also all ornament, inspired not just by the forms of a plant but by the way a plant grows to fill a space.

Art Nouveau, then, drew its inspiration from nature, not history. Its origins, however, were much more complicated and various than this simple formula might suggest. The designation 'Art Nouveau' was taken from the name of a gallery that opened in Paris in 1895, but by that time the style was already taking root in various European centres, including Brussels, Paris, Barcelona, Glasgow, London and Vienna. In Germany it was called *Jugendstil*, in Austria *Sezessionsstil*, in Catalonia *Modernisme*, and in Italy *Stile Liberty* after the well-known London home-furnishing shop that still exists. The greater part of the root system of Art Nouveau lay, however, in England, and arguably it was the painter, designer, craftsman and poet William Morris, foremost among Pevsner's 'pioneers', who sowed the first seeds. Morris was a medievalist and a socialist – anything but a believer in 'art for art's sake'. Nevertheless it was he and his colleagues, including the painters of the Pre-Raphaelite Brotherhood and architects such as Philip Webb and Norman Shaw, who took the first steps

away from historicist convention towards a new aesthetic freedom. Arthur Mackmurdo, whose chair we have already examined, set up the Century Guild of Artists in 1882 to produce hand-crafted home furnishings in friendly rivalry with William Morris's company, Morris and Co. According to Robert Schmutzler, an authority on Art Nouveau as a broad artistic movement, Mackmurdo's circle in the 1880s included the poets Laurence Binyon and William Butler Yeats, the playwright Oscar Wilde, the architect Charles Annesley Voysey and the painter James McNeill Whistler.[2] As an architect, Mackmurdo built very little but he and his circle were influential in developing the general aesthetic sensibility of Art Nouveau, which, as we shall see, soon spread beyond the shores of Britain. Meanwhile Whistler, an American living in England, introduced the Japanese element of this sensibility. He was influenced by the prints of Hiroshige, without which a painting like *Old Battersea Bridge: Nocturne in Blue and Gold* of around 1872 would have been inconceivable.

The primacy of ornament

In a sense Art Nouveau was the opposite of Modernism. Far from rejecting ornament, it based itself entirely on ornament. The style appears first not in functional artefacts or buildings but in wallpaper, posters, and especially book

Hôtel Tassel stairway, Brussels, Belgium. Victor Horta, 1893. Surface decoration on walls and floors turns into functional columns, steps and balustrades.

and in the mosaic floor. Only very occasionally does the gliding motion settle, like a butterfly, into a small symmetry, for example in a return panel of the otherwise swiftly flowing iron balustrade. Cast and wrought iron were by no means new building materials in the 1890s but they had mostly been used for conventional columns and beams in imitation wood or stone – the slender shafts of a Gothic arcade, for example. And here, perhaps, there is a link between Horta and his historicist predecessors. The influence of the great nineteenth-century French Gothicist, Eugène Viollet-le-Duc, is apparent. Viollet-le-Duc was intimately acquainted with medieval Gothic architecture through the many church and cathedral restorations that he conducted, including that of Notre-Dame in Paris. He saw Gothic as an efficient structural system, a way to make delicate frameworks out of masonry. But he also saw the potential of iron, and his book *Entretiens sur l'architecture* (Discourses on Architecture) of 1872 contains designs for Gothic structures that combine masonry with metal. Horta would certainly have been familiar with these designs.

Horta designed other large, luxurious houses in Brussels, including the Hôtel Solvay, the Hôtel van Eetvelde, and his own house and studio. In the House of the People, completed in 1899, now demolished, he proved that the Art Nouveau style could be applied to a large and relatively economical public building. Here the structure is steel, not iron, but in the day-lit auditorium the repeated frames that support the roof and balconies still managed to achieve an organic curvaceousness, like a dinosaur skeleton. But it is in the houses that the ambitions of Art Nouveau are most clearly expressed. The style is pervasive; it creates its own world. Every glazing bar and baluster, every light fitting and door handle is integrated into the whole.

illustrations like those of Aubrey Beardsley, Kate Greenaway and Heywood Sumner. These relatively ephemeral artworks exerted a powerful influence on architects looking for a way out of the nineteenth-century historicist museum. The first great master of Art Nouveau architecture was Victor Horta, who designed several important buildings in Brussels in the 1890s. In his Hôtel Tassel, completed in 1893, the style seems to appear all at once, fully developed. In the glass-roofed central staircase, stone, iron and glass are combined 'organically' as if they were the flesh, bones and membranes of a large animal. There are columns, beams and walls but they bend and merge into one another, creating a continuous flowing space. The distinction between structure and ornament is blurred. Thin, cast-iron columns sprout curling branches that might be purely decorative or might be forming a structural connection with the curved, perforated beams. These flowing, linear forms, like long ribbons flung into the air by a dancer, reappear as painted ornament on the walls

The best-known examples of Art Nouveau in Paris are the many Métro station entrances designed by Hector Guimard around 1900, and still in use. Whereas Horta was working for wealthy clients who could afford to pay for hand-crafted building components, Guimard was designing an economical standard product to be repeated all over the city. Cast iron was his chosen material because hundreds of casts could be made from a single mould. Columns, beams, brackets and perforated panels could be mass produced quickly and cheaply. This might logically have resulted in an articulated structure of separately expressed parts bolted together, but instead Guimard designed curving, branching components that could be combined to form continuous organic structures. Each seems to have grown like a plant or an animal skeleton. Glass canopies look like fan-shaped leaves, and lamp standards droop and nod like flowers. The spirit of Art Nouveau is cleverly preserved in an industrialized system.

Entrance to the Abbesses Métro station, Paris, France. Hector Guimard, 1912. Art Nouveau ornament realized in an assemblage of mass-produced cast-iron components.

Antoni Gaudí

Art Nouveau's chief representative in the Iberian peninsula was the Catalan architect Antoni Gaudí. His was the wildest and most fertile architectural imagination of the era. He drew inspiration from Gothic, especially as interpreted by Viollet-le-Duc, from the hybrid Christian-Islamic Mudejar architecture of Spain, and from the creative milieu of his father's ironworking business. But we only have to look at the iron gates of his first major building, the Casa Vicens in Barcelona, built in the early 1880s, to feel a more fundamental force at work: a spiritual and mythical vision of nature. Gaudí's patron was the wealthy industrialist Eusebi Güell, for whom he designed several important projects including the Palau Güell in Barcelona of 1890, the unfinished church of Colònia Güell, a workers' settlement in Santa Coloma de Cervelló begun in 1898, and Parc Güell of 1900 to 1914. Parc Güell, on a hillside to the north of Barcelona, was originally meant to be part of a housing development. The larger project was not realized but the park survives as one of the sights of the city and also one of the best places from which to view it. Its central feature is a large open platform raised on a forest of Doric columns creating a hypostyle market hall below. A continuous inward-looking bench, covered in coloured fragments of glazed pottery, snakes around the perimeter of the platform, accommodating the parental audience for children's games

that unfold on the level paving. Further up the hillside, rustic retaining walls arch back to form tunnel vaults over pathways following the contours. The columns that support these vaults lean into their load like raking shores, working both as columns and as buttresses.

This leaning-column idea became the structural basis of Gaudí's most famous building, the huge church of Sagrada Família that rears up like a weird geological excrescence in the middle of the panoramic view from Parc Güell. Construction started in 1882 and is still continuing more than 130 years later. The building was partly Gothic in its inspiration and indeed the first version of the design, by Francisco de Paula del Villar, was a conventional exercise in Gothic Revival. When Gaudí took over the project, however, he transformed Villar's synthetic, regular, historically sanctioned design into something organic that seemed to emerge spontaneously from the materials used and the forces acting upon them. In recent phases of the construction, Gaudí's forms have been realized in reinforced concrete, but this is a travesty. Gaudí did not simply create form to please the eye. Rather he collaborated with nature to find the forms that were natural to his chosen material, which was unreinforced masonry. His method was to imagine that the compressive forces acting on the building were tension forces, and to map them in an upside-down weighted-string

model. The weights were proportional to the gravitational forces in the actual building, so the strings automatically aligned themselves with the most efficient positions for structural members such as columns and vault ribs. In Gothic architecture columns are always vertical and the side-thrust of a stone vault is balanced by a flying buttress, but in Gaudí's system the side-thrust is balanced by leaning the column. It is a simple but transforming idea that is perhaps best exemplified in the much smaller crypt of the unfinished church at Colònia Güell. Here columns, some of brick, others of rough-hewn stone, refuse to conform to any consistent grid and lean in every direction as if desperately trying to hold up the twisted net of the vault ribs overhead. Inside it is like a gutted animal carcass; outside, teardrop-shaped windows look like the weeping eyes of a giant reptile.

Gaudí designed two apartment blocks in Barcelona's fashionable Passeig de Gràcia. The Casa Batlló, on the west side of the street, was a renovation of an existing building, which might explain its relatively conventional form. The six-storey facade is pierced by ordinary rectangular windows of uniform size on the upper levels. Everything else, however, is translated as if by magic into forms and substances that seem natural rather than man made, or if not natural then supernatural. The big first-floor windows seem to be made of animal bones, the wall itself shimmers and undulates like the bed of a shallow sunlit sea, the balconies are like pantomime masks and the writhing tiled roof is unmistakably a sleeping dragon. The whole composition has been interpreted as a symbol of Catalan nationalism.[3] If this was intended, then the dragon is not sleeping but dead, slain by the sword of St George, Catalonia's patron saint.

On the other side of the Passeig de Gràcia a prominent corner site is occupied by the building that is known locally as 'La Pedrera', the quarry, but known officially as the Casa Milà. It is a large apartment block with two inner courtyards and its most obvious characteristic is its curvaceousness. There is hardly a straight line in the whole building. The undulating facade was in fact chiselled from solid stone but looks more like something moulded in clay. Or perhaps it is some kind of jellyfish with skirts that ripple in gentle sea currents. Stragglings of iron seaweed on the balconies reinforce the underwater illusion. It is as if the building is floating. Gravity has finally been defeated.

(Opposite) Sagrada Família, Barcelona, Spain. Antoni Gaudí, 1882–. A new kind of Gothic architecture – ecstatically convulsive yet structurally rational.

(Below) Crypt of the Church of Colònia Güell, Barcelona, Spain. Antoni Gaudí, 1898–. Leaning columns and a twisted net of vault ribs create an interior like a gutted animal carcass.

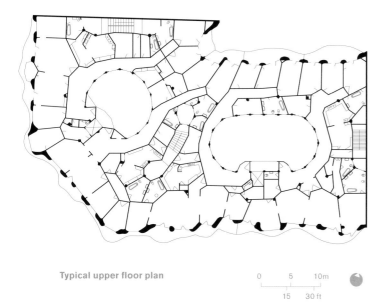

Typical upper floor plan

0   5   10m

15   30 ft

Gaudí's architecture is tougher and more vigorous than that of Horta or Guimard. The designation Art Nouveau begins to seem questionable. But there is no doubt that Gaudí was well versed in English architectural theory and fully aware of developments elsewhere in Europe. His architecture was truly original but he was associated with the wider 'Modernisme' style in Barcelona, represented by buildings such as the Palace of Catalan Music by Lluís Domènech i Montaner, completed in 1908. The building was technically advanced with a steel skeleton and what would later be called curtain walls of brick and glass, but it is also richly ornamented with mosaic and coloured ceramics. The huge stained-glass ceiling over the auditorium is a gaudy translation of Art Nouveau into the Catalan architectural language.

Mackintosh and Macdonald

The early work of the Scottish designers Charles Rennie Mackintosh and his wife Margaret Macdonald is more easily related to Belgian and French Art Nouveau. In 1898 the couple decorated Miss Cranston's tearoom in Buchanan Street, Glasgow, with a mural depicting elegant women and stylized roses set against large areas of flat colour. Aubrey Beardsley and Japanese prints were obvious influences. It was the beginnings of the Mackintosh style of interior design that, with his elegant high-backed chairs, has been popular ever since. What made Mackintosh's name as an architect, however, was his 1897 competition-winning design for Glasgow School of Art. Despite the simplicity of its plan, this is a complex and subtle building – the virtues of which lie more in its composition than its ornament. The site is a simple rectangle, sloping steeply from front to back, north to south. Mackintosh divided the building longitudinally by means of a long circulation spine, with high, north-lit studios ranged along the front and ancillary spaces at the back between recessed light wells. The subtlety is in the play of symmetry and asymmetry, repetition and uniqueness.

The moderately proportioned main entrance, powerfully emphasized by a window at first-floor level under a large segmental pediment, is exactly in the middle of the long north elevation. Its details are not traditionally classical but the general arrangement is formal and one would expect other elements to conform to the symmetry. This is not the case, however. The projecting balcony above the entrance, for example, has an extension on one side incorporating bay windows of a domestic scale at ground- and first-floor levels. Further up the facade there is another balcony, this time recessed and slightly offset with a little turret. Standing back to take in the whole elevation, one assumes at first that

Glasgow School of Art, Scotland. Charles Rennie Mackintosh, 1897–1909. An exercise in symmetry disruption. Industrial simplicity is humanized by domestic details.

these asymmetries are local occurrences within a larger symmetrical whole. But this is not the case either. There are four bays on one side of the entrance and three on the other, and the bays are of three different widths. A further subtlety is that the low wall marking the site boundary delicately restores the thwarted symmetry. But symmetry disruption is not the only game being played here. Those domestic-scale bay windows attract so much attention because they find themselves in a facade that is almost brutally factory-like. The enormous studio windows are plain, metal-framed rectangles with exposed concrete lintels. It is easy to see why later critics looking for the origins of functionalism have been attracted to this building. The game continues in the east and west elevations, where bay windows become multi-storey structures, and openings are formally dressed but informally arranged. The material is local granite, which suggests yet another layer of meaning: this is neither a house nor a factory, it says, but an important public building.

The west elevation is part of a later phase, added in 1906, which included a double-height library surrounded by a gallery. The wooden beams of the gallery extended out into the space, where they were supported on, or rather 'caught by', thin floor-to-ceiling columns. There may have been practical reasons for these offset supports – to position them over steel beams in the floor below – but spatially the effect was strikingly modern. It did not feel particularly Art Nouveau, however, except that it faintly recalled traditional Japanese construction. Once again, the Art Nouveau category had been stretched by a truly original designer. The library was destroyed by fire in 2014 but there are plans to restore it.

Mackintosh designed three important houses. Two were in Scotland, at Helensburgh and Kilmacolm, and the third was an unrealized design entered for a limited competition organized in Darmstadt – unrealized, that is, until 1996, when a version of the design was built in Bellahouston Park in Glasgow as a 'cultural attraction and tourist destination'. Hill House in Helensburgh is the best known of the three houses. It is both traditional and forward looking, borrowing forms from the Scottish tower-house tradition but simplifying them so that they become abstract sculpture. It is as if they have been sketched rather than constructed, and indeed the house looks best in Mackintosh's spare pen-and-ink perspective drawings. Mackintosh's closest English counterpart was Charles Harrison Townsend, the designer of two London museums, the Whitechapel Gallery and the Horniman Museum. The Whitechapel is almost exactly contemporary with the Glasgow School of Art and deals with the question of symmetry in a similar way. A front wall of solid stone extends upwards past a band of small windows to form two towers framing a large mural – except that the mural was never executed and the panel remained blank for more than a hundred years until 2012 when the artist Rachel Whiteread was commissioned to fill it with a gilded metal and terracotta frieze. This facade is composed symmetrically but the main entrance, dwarfed by a huge semi-circular arch, is placed to one side. At the Horniman Museum in south London, similar elements are combined in different proportions. This time the entrance is in the foot of an almost freestanding clock tower with rounded corners, which is crowned by a horizontal circular cornice and four turrets. These are bold, original buildings. They are not 'organic' in the manner of Horta or Gaudí, neither do they conform to any historical model, whether Gothic or classical, though they are vaguely reminiscent of medieval churches and fortifications.

(Above) Vienna Secession Building, Vienna, Austria. Joseph Maria Olbrich, 1898. The four turrets cradling the gilded openwork dome may owe something to Mackintosh and Townsend.

(Below) The Whitechapel Gallery, London, UK. Charles Harrison Townsend, 1899. The white panel, originally intended to contain a mosaic mural, now displays a sculpted frieze by Rachel Whiteread.

Vienna Secession

The work of Mackintosh, and to a lesser degree Townsend, was well known abroad and especially influential in Austria. Gustav Klimt, whose erotic, gilded paintings of human figures have since become world famous, was Vienna's leading

Art Nouveau artist. According to Nikolaus Pevsner, Klimt's style was influenced by the publication in 1897 of Mackintosh's Buchanan Street tearoom in *The Studio*, an English art magazine avidly read by Viennese artists and patrons. In 1898 the group known as the Vienna Secession, led by Klimt, began to publish its own magazine called *Ver Sacrum* (Sacred Spring), which was designed, says Pevsner, 'in a style strikingly similar to Mackintosh's'.[4] In 1899 the group commissioned a young architect, Joseph Olbrich, to design an exhibition hall. It is a symmetrical, articulated, cubic composition finished in white-painted stucco. From this description it would seem to have little to do with Mackintosh or Townsend, but there are resemblances – in the moulded stucco decoration, for example, and in the four turrets supporting the openwork gilded dome, which might have been borrowed from Whitechapel. The connection is confirmed by the fact that Mackintosh and his colleagues were invited to show their work at the annual Secession exhibition of 1900.

Olbrich was a disciple of Otto Wagner, the most influential Viennese architect of the early twentieth century. Though in his early career Wagner designed in a Renaissance style, he later, in Robert Schmutzler's words, 'liberated Viennese architecture from the shackles of historicism'.[5] He taught at the Vienna Akademie and wrote a book called *Modern Architecture*.[6] His architectural masterpiece was the Post Office Savings Bank in Vienna, completed in 1906. In its overall form it is rather conventional: a six-storey

Post Office Savings Bank, Vienna, Austria. Otto Wagner, 1906. The church-like banking hall, steel framed and glass roofed with a glass-block floor to light the spaces below.

office building occupying a whole city block with classically composed facades, including statues above the cornice. But there are two radically innovative features. The first is the external stone cladding. Thin sheets of marble (granite on the two lowest floors) are fixed to the structural walls with bolts, the heads of which are protected by aluminium caps. There is no attempt to conceal these fixings and pretend that the building is made of solid stone; instead they become a kind of functional decoration. The second radical feature is the steel-framed and glass-covered banking hall in the middle of the block. It has a church-like plan, with nave and side aisles, but there are no concessions to historicism. Ornament is completely absent, unless you count the rivets on the steel columns. The floor is innovative too, of glass blocks that borrow daylight for the rooms below. Such complete honesty seems to look forward to later, Modernist buildings, even perhaps to the High Tech style of the 1980s, but according to Richard Weston it is derived from principles established by the great nineteenth-century architectural theorist Gottfried Semper.[7]

Another of Wagner's associates, Josef Hoffmann, developed the Semperian cladding technique further in a large house in Brussels for a Belgian banker and art lover with Viennese connections. The Palais Stoclet, completed in 1911, has lost all sense of classical weight – of base, column and cornice. Its external walls are clad in thin sheets of marble, too big ever to be mistaken for loadbearing masonry. It is line and surface that matter, not volume or weight. To emphasize their weightlessness, the mostly cubic forms are outlined by continuous strips of gilded metal. It is as if the building has been drawn in three dimensions with a thick pen. Windows are treated as variations of the surface texture rather than as holes in the wall. On the top floor they project above the wall like dormers as if to draw attention to the absence of a classical cornice. The plan is, however, basically classical – symmetrical apart from service spaces on the ground floor and an off-centre tower that would not disgrace a town hall. Important internal spaces – entrance hall, dining room, music room, men's room, drawing room – are lined in coloured marble with murals by Gustav Klimt. Adolphe and Suzanne Stoclet were reputedly happy to submit themselves to the demands of Hoffmann's total design, though it was more like a public gallery than a house.

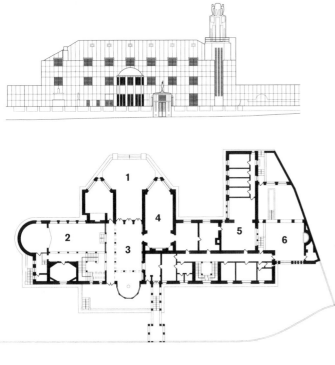

Ground floor plan

1. Terrace
2. Music room
3. Entrance hall
4. Dining room
5. Kitchen
6. Courtyard

0   5   10m
15   30 ft

Palais Stoclet, Brussels, Belgium. Josef Hoffmann, 1911.
The dining room, marble lined, with mosaic panels designed by
Gustav Klimt.

By 1910, Art Nouveau was already in decline. It seemed
that its very revolutionary nature, its lack of historical roots
or functional justification, weakened it and allowed it to be
seen as a mere passing fashion. The attempt to replace
historical ornament with natural ornament, and thereby give
expression to what was natural in the mind and body of a
human being, had been a failure. What would follow? A
return to historicism? Classical architecture did indeed enjoy
a revival in the early years of the century, but then it had never
really died among conservative architects and the privileged
institutions that they served. The question should perhaps
be: which way would progressive architects turn next? There
was one radical option: to do away with ornament altogether.
For the engineers who designed bridges and railway stations,
ornament, though often used, had never been essential. Why
shouldn't architects, who designed houses and museums,
follow the same logic? For one Viennese architect of those
years this seemed like an excellent idea and he set about
promoting it in forceful, sarcastic newspaper articles.

Ornament and Crime

Adolf Loos had spent three years in America. Perhaps it was that experience that gave him the courage to think new thoughts and state them fearlessly. One of his articles, 'Ornament and Crime', has become famous. In it he likens architectural ornament to erotic graffiti: 'as a general rule one can rank the cultures of different peoples by the extent to which their lavatory walls have been drawn upon'.[8] It followed that the man of taste, in his choice of clothes, furnishings and architecture, would always prefer the plain to the decorated. Loos hated Art Nouveau and attacked its practitioners by name in his articles. The architectural historian Reyner Banham called him a 'controversialist', happiest when stating the extreme, provocative view.[9] But his arguments were not unreasonable or merely destructive. For example, he ridiculed Art Nouveau's world-creating tendency as a form of cultural tyranny. In his view, clients like Adolphe Stoclet were paying to have their freedom restricted. They should at least be allowed to choose their own furniture. And Loos's attitude to history was sophisticated. A preference for the unadorned did not entail a forgetting of the past. Quite the reverse. Loos loved and respected vernacular architecture that had developed over centuries to serve settled societies in particular places

Loos House, Vienna, Austria. Adolf Loos, 1912. A mere grid of windows lights the upper floors but the main entrance is guarded by sober Doric columns.

without the assistance of professional architects. Kenneth Frampton states the position succinctly: 'Loos considered that all culture depended on a certain continuity with the past … He could not accept the romantic notion of the highly gifted individual transcending the limits of his own epoch.'[10]

Loos's buildings are consistent with his writings. The facade of his Goldman and Salatsch Building of 1912, a commercial building facing Michaelerplatz in Vienna (it is now known as the Loos House) seemed shockingly plain to contemporary critics – a mere grid of windows in a white stucco wall. Yet at ground- and first-floor level it is clad in grey, streaky marble and its entrance is graced by four sober Doric columns. The Kärntner American Bar in Vienna, fitted out by Loos in 1908 and still in existence, shows him to be a master of internal space. The bar is tiny – barely 6 metres (20 feet) long – but is made to seem almost monumental by the clever use of frameless high-level mirrors combined with a beamed and coffered ceiling. But it is houses for which Loos is best known. The Steiner House in Vienna of 1910 is

21

one of the first in which the typical Loosian characteristics are displayed. The exterior is perfectly plain – basically a stuccoed box with rectangular windows and a curved roof at the front to accommodate a height restriction. Externally it might be considered coldly functional, but inside the rooms are almost cosy, with parquet floors, wood-panelled dados, and ceilings with exposed beams. In the typical Loos house, windows are designed to admit daylight, not to look out of. There is no spatial flow from inside to outside as there might be, for example, in a Frank Lloyd Wright house. There is spatial flow inside, however. One room looks into another, often from a different level. This interlocking of the interior spaces has been given a name – 'Raumplan' – to distinguish it from the more familiar 'open plan' of later Modernist houses.

After a brief and turbulent period in charge of public housing in Vienna, Loos moved to Paris in 1924. There he made contact with the artistic avant-garde, including Le Corbusier and the Purists, who honoured him as a pioneer of the Modern Movement and republished his essays in their magazine, *L'Esprit Nouveau*. He designed houses for wealthy and famous clients, including the dancer Josephine Baker and the poet Tristan Tzara, and in 1930 he designed the Müller House in Prague, the definitive Raumplan house. By that time, however, his health, finances and personal life were in chaos and he died penniless in 1933.

Müller House, Prague, Czech Republic. Adolf Loos, 1930.
The living room, overlooked by the dining room and the lady's room on higher levels.

Upper ground floor plan

1. Living room
2. Dining room
3. Servery
4. Kitchen
5. Library
6. Lady's room

'Architecture' by Adolf Loos

'Ornament and Crime' is Adolf Loos's best-known polemical essay, which he delivered several times as a lecture, in Vienna, Berlin and Prague. But its tongue-in-cheek tone makes it hard to interpret. A better guide to his philosophy is the essay entitled simply 'Architecture', published in 1910. It begins with an unambiguous affirmation of the virtues of vernacular architecture – architecture without architects – describing an imaginary scene on the shores of a mountain lake in which the houses, farms and chapels seem as natural as the clouds, trees and mountains: 'it is as if they came straight from God's workshop'. But then a villa designed by an architect strikes a discordant note: 'Whether a good or bad architect, I don't know. All I know is that the tranquillity, peace and beauty have vanished.'

This favouring of tradition and craftsmanship over artistic invention is not what one would expect of a proto-Modernist. There is no talk of functionalism or the machine, no looking forward to a bright industrial future. The tone is conservative, not revolutionary. Loos's attack on ornament is not an attack on tradition, but an attack on the then modern concept of 'applied art'. For Loos, art cannot be 'applied' to anything, certainly not to craft. When the attempt is made, both art and craft suffer:

'People do not leave the artist free to do as he thinks fit because they are not in awe of him, and craftwork cannot develop freely because of the weight of aesthetic expectations that we place on it.' By implication, the architect should see himself not as an artist, but as a craftsman. Loos relates his own experience designing the Café Museum in Vienna: 'I did not approach the task like an artist, giving free rein to his creative imagination (as they doubtless put it in artistic circles). No. I went to the workshops, as timid as an apprentice, looked up respectfully to the man in the blue apron, and asked him to share his secrets with me.'

What exactly did Loos mean by 'ornament'? For us, a hundred years later, the word 'ornament' usually includes traditional classical motifs as well as the 'natural' ornament of the Art Nouveau designers. But for Loos, classicism was the essential ground of all western architecture. 'Our culture is founded on the recognition of the all-transcending greatness of classical antiquity.' Right at the end of the essay, we learn that the 'last great master' of classical architecture was the nineteenth-century German Karl Friedrich Schinkel. 'We have forgotten him. But the light of this great figure will fall on future generations of architects.' The future, then, will be classical, not modern; or perhaps classical *and* modern.

Steiner House, Vienna, Austria. Adolf Loos, 1910. The curved roof accommodates a height restriction but otherwise this is a plain stuccoed box. Material richness is reserved for the interior.

02 | HOUSES 1891–1911

In the previous chapter the roots of Art Nouveau architecture were found in the work of English architects and designers such as William Morris, Philip Webb, Norman Shaw and Arthur Mackmurdo. And yet, paradoxically, Art Nouveau in its pure, organic form, as represented by Horta or Guimard for example, was not popular in England. In England the offshoots of the Arts and Crafts movement travelled in a different direction and bore fruit in what W. R. Lethaby called English Free Architecture. It was based not on ornament but on a kind of humane practicality, not quite 'functionalist' yet seeming, in the eyes of later Modernist historians, to show the way to functionalism. This practicality owed something to the Gothic Revival of the middle years of the nineteenth century when the adoption of Gothic rather than classical models was justified in practical terms. Gothic plans were typically asymmetrical and informal, following the spatial requirements of the activities they accommodated rather than any abstract, formal rules. Gothic structure was functional too: buttresses that would have been screened from view in a classical building were openly displayed and enjoyed for their expressiveness.

Das Englische Haus

English Free Architecture flourished mainly in domestic architecture, where it was recognized and admired internationally. Hermann Muthesius, an attaché at the German embassy in London from 1896 to 1903, made a comprehensive study of English domestic architecture and published his findings in a book, *Das Englische Haus* (The English House), in which he paid tribute to pioneers such as Webb and Shaw, and celebrated the work of a younger generation, including C. F. A. Voysey, C. R. Ashbee, M. H. Baillie Scott and Edwin Lutyens. Muthesius's aim was to encourage his middle- and upper-class compatriots to follow the English example and live in simple, well-designed country houses rather than in showy urban apartments. 'English Houses', he wrote, 'are wisely reduced to essentials and adapted to given circumstances; the point, therefore, that is worth copying from them is the emphasis that is laid on purely objective requirements.'[1] This call for 'objectivity' was later absorbed and reinterpreted by the first German Modernists.

Of the younger architects admired by Muthesius, the most important historically are Voysey and Lutyens. But what does 'most important' mean here? It certainly does not mean that they were proto-Modernists. It is possible that they influenced Modernist designers. We know, for example, that Lutyens's work was admired by both Le Corbusier and Frank Lloyd Wright. But neither Lutyens nor Voysey, in their later years, held any respect for Modernism. 'I make no claim to anything new,' wrote Voysey in 1935, '… I followed some old traditions and avoided some others.'[2] Voysey and Lutyens are important for their own sakes, not as forerunners of any future movement. Their legacy lies more in the creation of an ideal vision of English rural domesticity than in any prescience of a future machine age.

14 **South Parade, London, UK. C. F. A. Voysey, 1891.** A plain exterior, asymmetrical with horizontal windows freely arranged. Is this a precursor of Modernism?

**Garden Corner, London, UK.
Interior by C. F. A. Voysey, c.1907.**
Voysey's cosy but elegant interiors
are arranged for practicality rather
than ceremony or display.

Voysey began his career as an assistant to the Gothic Revival architect John Seddon, setting up his own practice in 1882. In 1891 he designed a house in Bedford Park, the west London middle-class suburb developed under the direction of Norman Shaw. Looking at this house, it is immediately easy to see why Voysey should be thought 'modern'. It is a simple, box-like, three-storey tower, with extensions to the lower floors, including an off-centre bay window at the front. All of the windows are horizontal, divided by plain stone mullions, and freely arranged for convenience rather than to create an ordered facade. The walls are covered in lime-washed, rough-cast render and there is no ornament at all unless the slender iron brackets that support the roof overhang are considered to be ornamental. Even in this early work, Voysey's instinct for handsome proportions is evident. It is not, however, a typical Voysey house. He designed a few vertical town houses, but he is best known for low, spreading, cottage-like houses in rural or suburban settings. All are composed from a small set of similar, though not standardized, elements: rough-cast walls, often with tapered buttresses; sloping, stone-tiled roofs, both gabled and hipped, with generous overhangs; horizontal, stone-mullioned windows; and short, fat chimneys. The composition is always informal – a loose, asymmetrical assemblage rather than a geometrically integrated design. Inside the rooms are relatively small with very low ceilings, sometimes oak beamed. Plans are functional in the Gothic sense, typically L shaped with a narrower servants' wing and one-sided corridors. To English eyes these forms are very familiar

from debased versions in the small, suburban, detached and semi-detached houses that were built in their tens of thousands by speculative developers in the 1920s and 1930s. A common feature, for example, is the small gable that crowns and overlaps a semi-circular bay window. We find the originals in several Voysey houses, notably New Place in Haslemere and Norney in Shackleford, both in Surrey and built in 1897.

Voysey's masterpiece was Broad Leys, a summer retreat built in 1898 on the shore of Windermere for the son of a Yorkshire mine owner. Here we have all the usual features but with the addition of three very large, two-storey bay windows overlooking the lake. They are evenly spaced and the central bay, which lights a double-height hall and living room, is glazed from top to bottom. So here is Voysey adapting his design to the demands of both site and client – the beautiful view and the requirement for a hall-like billiard room. Also typical is the casual-seeming but actually carefully considered composition. The bay windows are symmetrically arranged but everything around them – roof, chimneys, flanking walls and a single porthole window – is asymmetrical. And note how the windows break through the roof eaves, asserting their separateness on the outside and disappearing upwards behind shallow-arched openings on the inside.

Voysey utterly rejected historicism. 'Our first duty', he wrote, 'must be to sweep away all shams and give up

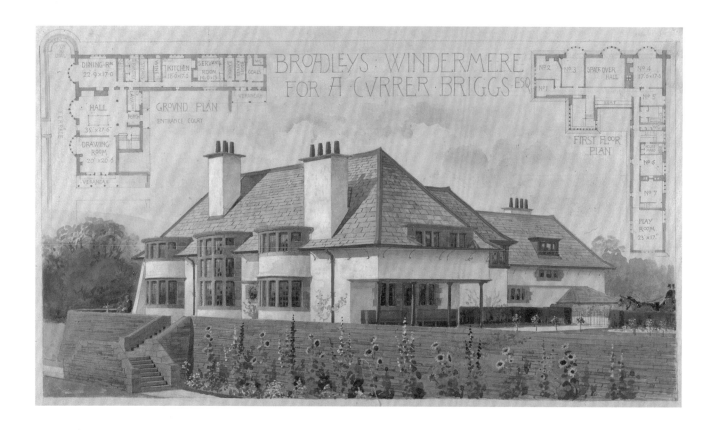

Broad Leys, Windermere, UK. C. F. A. Voysey, 1898.
Speculative developers of later years borrowed their repertoire of
rustic features from houses like this one, Voysey's masterpiece.

pretending to be Greeks or Romans in our architecture.'[3]
And yet his houses can hardly be called innovative, quietly
respectful as they are of the gentle character of the English
countryside and of the calm domesticity preferred by his
well-to-do clients. Throughout his career Voysey designed
simple wallpapers and elegant furniture that undoubtedly
exerted some influence on the later development of Art
Nouveau. But in spirit his work seems far removed from that
organic hothouse. His architecture emerges from 'a due
consideration of conditions and requirements'. To that extent
he can be called 'modern', but we also have to admit that
his work never developed or progressed and that he was
profoundly suspicious of any but the simplest of machines.
For Reyner Banham, writing in the 1960s, Voysey was a
frustratingly conservative figure who stubbornly refused to
acknowledge the historical importance of his own work.
His preference for hand-crafted rather than machine-made
masonry is dismissed by Banham as 'muddled thinking'.[4]
Voysey's true legacy, however, is to be found not in steel
and concrete Modernism but in the tastes and preferences
of ordinary English people. Domestic architecture has
long been a battlefield on which the conflicting visions of
architects and lay-people fight for power, but both sides
are satisfied by Voysey.

Edwin Lutyens also bridged that taste gap, though
he did it in a freer, more restless, more inventive style.

In his early Surrey houses of the 1890s, such as Munstead
Wood, which he designed for his lifelong collaborator, the
garden designer Gertrude Jekyll, he seems to want to do
no more than recreate the picturesque charm of sixteenth-
and seventeenth-century English vernacular architecture.
Orchards, just a mile from Munstead Wood, is so traditional
that it might be mistaken for an Elizabethan farmhouse.
Like Voysey's houses, its plan is basically L shaped but the
L forms two sides of a square courtyard that is completed by
a single-storey 'cloister' of big, round arches like a miniature
viaduct, and a studio for the lady of the house, who was a
painter. The entrance to the courtyard, under a tiled roof
embellished by a fake dormer window, lines up with the
porch on the other side, creating a moment of formality in
an otherwise informal composition. This plan makes the
house look bigger than it really is, and this is perhaps a
key characteristic of Lutyens's architecture. It has a playful,
theatrical quality. Whereas we could toy with the word
'functional' in relation to Voysey, it seems completely alien
to Lutyens. The two architects differ too in their attitude to
historicism. Voysey, as we have seen, frankly disavowed it,
whereas Lutyens loved historical details and incorporated
them into his buildings with joyous enthusiasm. In the early
houses, like the serenely romantic Deanery Garden in
Berkshire, built in 1901 for Edward Hudson, the publisher of
Country Life, these details are approximately medieval, like
the huge oriel window that lights the double-height hall, or
the Romanesque arched doorway and Elizabethan chimneys
that stand beside it. But Renaissance details were also
beginning to appear. Little Thakeham in Sussex, completed
in 1903, is soberly Elizabethan on the outside, but inside

its hall is provided with a screen, a fireplace and a balcony which might have been designed by Christopher Wren. The elaborate openings in the screen, with their rusticated jambs and segmental pediments, seem to take Lutyens's architecture in a completely new direction. He seems suddenly to have discovered the classical language. In a letter of 1903 to his friend and colleague Herbert Baker, he wrote: 'In architecture Palladio [i.e. Renaissance classicism] is the game. It is so big – few appreciate it now and it requires considerable training to value and realize it. The way Wren handled it was marvellous… It means hard thought all through – if it is laboured it fails … So it is a big game, a high game …'

Heathcote in Ilkley, Yorkshire was Lutyens's first complete exercise in the classical style. Completed in 1908, it was built, like most Lutyens houses, of the local stone, in this case Guiseley limestone. According to Lawrence Weaver, this stone showed a 'native hostility', to be overcome by 'subtlety of moulding, boldness of mass and rightness of line'.[5] The plan is like a Palladian villa, with a three-storey central block and two-storey wings, but the massing is condensed and solid, made more so by the steep-pitched roofs of red Roman pan-tiles. The front facing the road is classically proportioned but astylar and rather austere. The garden front is more cheerful with half columns and a continuous Doric frieze at first-floor level. Inside there are freestanding columns of green Siberian marble in the hall, Ionic pilasters in the stairway gallery, and a big pendentive dome over the billiard room.

Lutyens went on to play the 'high game' with consummate skill for the rest of his long career. He had originally found his inspiration in the vernacular architecture of the English Home Counties, in the Arts and Crafts movement and in the work of Shaw and Webb. But his discovery of classicism set his work in a larger historical context, and this is how it started to be seen by important clients in the years immediately before the First World War. As early as 1913 he was appointed architect of the Viceroy's Palace in New Delhi (see page 175). When the carnage was over he was called upon to provide the architecture of its commemoration.

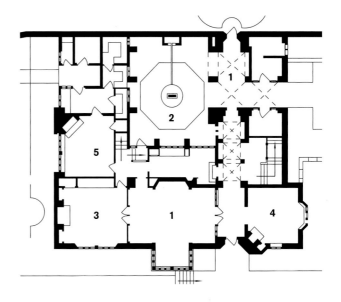

0   5   10m
    15   30 ft

Ground floor plan
1. Hall
2. Court
3. Dining room
4. Sitting room
5. Kitchen

Deanery Garden, Berkshire, UK. Edwin Lutyens, 1901.
The client was the publisher of *Country Life* magazine, then, as now, a conservative guide to style and taste.

Heathcote, Yorkshire, UK. Edwin Lutyens, 1908. Lutyens's first complete exercise in the classical style. Relaxed asymmetry gives way to imposing formality.

Thiepval Memorial, Picardy, France. Edwin Lutyens, 1932. A triumphal arch but with all of the triumph dissolved in dignified mourning.

With Herbert Baker and Reginald Blomfield, Lutyens was responsible for the design of hundreds of cemeteries in France and Belgium. The gigantic Memorial to the Missing of the Somme at Thiepval is hardly typical but nevertheless represents well enough the spirit of the whole architectural programme. Typologically it is a Roman triumphal arch but its altered purpose has changed it into a powerful expression of dignified mourning. A rigorous, inevitable geometry keeps emotion in check while at the same time magnifying and ennobling it. The memorial is monumental in every sense – massive and enduring – yet it is also a composition of voids. Criss-crossing tunnels rise in a four-step hierarchy from a base of 16 rectangular piers, culminating in a single arch that bears the burden of an apparently solid, stepped tower. This is a work of architecture, not sculpture, and it has a function to fulfil. The multi-arched form arose partly from the need to provide large areas of wall on which to inscribe the names of more than 72,000 missing men. Lutyens, the designer of playful country houses for the rich, rose magnificently to the solemn occasion, and it was classicism that enabled him to do so. No columns or entablatures adorn the Thiepval Memorial, yet it is unmistakably a classical building. To call it 'historicist' in the Victorian sense would be a misinterpretation. Lutyens did not reproduce a historical style; he worked creatively in an ancient tradition, bringing it back to life.

Frank Lloyd Wright

But this chapter is about houses, not memorials, and when an architectural historian thinks about the houses of the early twentieth century, one name stands above all others: Frank Lloyd Wright. Wright began his career in Chicago in the 1880s, working first for Joseph Silsbee and then for Adler and Sullivan. Louis Sullivan, whom Wright proudly acknowledged as his 'Lieber Meister', is well known as the inventor of the skyscraper (see Chapter 4) but his fame rests almost equally on his nurturing of the greatest American architect of the twentieth century. By 1900 the 33-year-old Wright's architecture had already reached a peak of maturity. Over the next ten years he produced some of his best work, though he was to go on designing with undiminished inventiveness until his death in 1959. In this early period he built several important non-domestic buildings that will be looked at in other contexts, but it is the houses that most clearly demonstrate the principles of his architecture. In his many books – he wrote 20 – he often used the word 'organic' to describe his buildings, by which he meant not that they resembled plants or animals in the manner of Art Nouveau ornament but that their designs emerged 'naturally' from the circumstances of their creation – the

Project by Frank Lloyd Wright published in *Ladies' Home Journal*, 1901. Space flows freely around a central hearth and reaches out to the surrounding landscape.

A Home in a Prairie Town

By FRANK LLOYD WRIGHT

This is the Fifth Design in the Journal's New Series of Model Suburban Houses Which Can be Built at Moderate Cost

A CITY man going to the country puts too much in his house and too little in his ground. He drags after him the fifty-foot lot, soon the twenty-five foot lot, finally the party wall; and the home-maker who fully appreciates the advantages which he came to the country to secure feels himself impelled to move on.

It seems a waste of energy to plan a house haphazard, to hit or miss an already distorted condition, so this partial solution of a city man's country home on the prairie begins at the beginning and assumes four houses to the block of four hundred feet square as the minimum of ground for the basis of his prairie community.

The block plan to the left, at the top of the page, shows an arrangement of the four houses that secures breadth and prospect to the community as a whole, and absolute privacy both as regards each to the community, and each to each of the four.

THE perspective view shows the handling of the group at the centre of the block, with its foil of simple lawn, omitting the foliage of curb parkways to better show the scheme, retaining the same house in the four locations merely to afford an idea of the unity of the various elevations. In practice the houses would differ distinctly, though based upon a similar plan.

The ground plan, which is intended to explain itself, is arranged to offer the least resistance to a simple mode of living, in keeping with a high ideal of the family life together. It is arranged, too, with a certain well-established order that enables free use without the sense of confusion felt in five out of seven houses which people really use.

The exterior recognizes the influence of the prairie, is firmly and broadly associated with the site, and makes a feature of its quiet level. The low terraces and broad eaves are designed to accentuate that quiet level and complete the harmonious relationship. The curbs of the terraces and formal inclosures for extremely informal masses of foliage and bloom should be worked in cement with the walks and drives.

Cement on metal lath is suggested for the exterior covering throughout, because it is simple, and, as now understood, durable and cheap.

The cost of this house with interior as specified and cement construction would be seven thousand dollars:

Masonry, Cement and Plaster	$2800.00
Carpentry	3100.00
Plumbing	400.00
Painting and Glass	325.00
Heating — combination (hot water)	345.00
Total	$6970.00

IN A HOUSE of this character the upper reach and gallery of the central living-room is decidedly a luxury. Two bedrooms may take its place, as suggested by the second-floor plan. The gallery feature is, nevertheless, a temptation because of the happy sense of variety and depth it lends to the composition of the interior, and the sunlight it gains from above to relieve the shadow of the porch. The details are better grasped by a study of the drawings. The interior section in perspective shows the gallery as indicated by dotted lines on the floor plan of the living-room.

The second-floor plan disregards this feature and is arranged for a larger family. Where three bedrooms would suffice the gallery would be practicable, and two large and two small bedrooms with the gallery might be had by rearranging servants' rooms and baths.

The interior is plastered throughout with sand finish and trimmed all through with flat bands of Georgia pine, smaller back bands following the base and casings. This Georgia pine should be selected from straight grain for stiles, rails and running members, and from figured grain for panels and wide surfaces.

All the wood should be shellacked once and waxed, and the plaster should be stained with thin, pure color in water and glue.

EDITOR'S NOTE — As a guarantee that the plan of this house is practicable, and that the estimates for cost are conservative, the architect is ready to accept the commission of preparing the working plans and specifications for this house to cost Seven Thousand Dollars, providing that the building site selected is within reasonable distance of a base of supplies where material and labor may be had at the standard market rates.

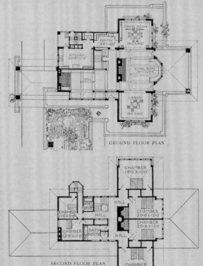

GROUND FLOOR PLAN

SECOND FLOOR PLAN

HALL, LOOKING TOWARD ENTRANCE

THE LIBRARY

LIVING-ROOM AND GALLERY

THE DINING-ROOM

INTERIOR VIEW OF THE FIRST FLOOR OF THIS HOUSE

17

accommodation required, the character of the surrounding landscape, the climate of the region, the available materials, and so on. Architecture for Wright was the 'human spirit' that combined these forces in a poetic act of creation. He always arrogantly insisted on the complete originality of his architecture, but there were identifiable influences. We know, for example, that he read Ruskin and Viollet-le-Duc, and that he was an admirer of the English Arts and Crafts movement. English ideas about functional planning, 'truth to materials' and belongingness in a landscape were absorbed and became second nature. Where he differed from Arts and Crafts thinking was in his attitude to the machine. C. R. Ashbee, having visited Wright in Chicago in 1900, wrote in his journal: 'He threw down the glove to me in characteristic Chicagoan manner in the matter of Arts and Crafts and the creations of the machine. "My God", said he, "is machinery, and the art of the future will be that expression of the individual artist through the thousand powers of the machine."'[6]

Japanese art and architecture, which had played such a large part in the creation of European Art Nouveau, was for Wright more than just an influence; it was a business. He was an important collector of, and dealer in, Japanese prints, sometimes making more money from this activity than from his architectural practice. He visited Japan in 1905 but long before that he had seen the Japanese temple at the 1893 World's Columbian Exposition in Chicago and had almost certainly studied Edward Morse's classic illustrated book, *Japanese Homes and Their Surroundings*. On the question of historicism, Wright, like Voysey, was uncompromising, but much more stridently so. Whereas Voysey was content to replace historical styles with the extension of a vernacular tradition, Wright set out to create a completely new, organic architecture. Renaissance architecture, which borrowed its forms from the ancient world, was for him an 'inglorious masquerade, devoid of vital significance or true spiritual value'.[7] One other influence should be mentioned: his mother and the gifts she gave him as a child. One of them was a set of geometrically co-ordinated wooden building blocks invented in the 1830s by the German educationalist Friedrich Froebel. Wright, so unwilling to acknowledge any specifically architectural influences, wrote in his autobiography of his Froebel blocks: 'All are in my fingers to this day.'

Wright called the houses that he designed in the Chicago area 'Prairie houses', perhaps to identify them firmly as products of the Midwest rather than of the culturally conservative east coast. Few of them, however, were built within sight of an actual prairie and the very first was designed for no particular location. 'A Home in a Prairie Town' was a project produced for publication in the *Ladies' Home Journal*. The heart of the plan is a symmetrical range

of three spaces, a living room, a library and a dining room, connected by wide openings. The central living room is double height, with a fireplace on one side and a big bay window opposite, both flanked by doors opening onto the entrance hall and a covered terrace respectively. A first-floor gallery overlooks the living room from above the fireplace. We can see immediately that a Prairie house has a free plan in which space flows from room to room, from inside to outside, and from ground floor to first floor. This is not a collection of boxes but a single, articulated space, free but also contained and controlled. It certainly isn't classical in the stylistic sense, like Heathcote, but it is nevertheless broadly classical in its symmetries and in the proportional relationships between its parts. When we look at the perspective external view, we see that the symmetry of the living spaces is a local occurrence and that the composition as a whole is asymmetrical. Low, hipped roofs on two levels predominate, stretching out over the terrace on one side and a porte-cochère on the other. Walls are secondary. Nowhere are they allowed to show their full two-storey height without some horizontal interruption from a roof, a string course, a cantilevered projection or a continuous ribbon of windows. This is a horizontal architecture, an architecture of wide open spaces, a prairie architecture. The house looks out on the landscape, but it is also anchored to its site by the hearth and its chimney, a symbol of home life and the family. Economy and practicality are not forgotten. A variant is shown in which the 'wasted' space of the upper living room is replaced by two extra bedrooms.

By 1902 Wright had built more than 40 houses in the Chicago area in various styles, constantly experimenting and developing his ideas, searching for a new American architecture. The Ward Willits House of that year is considered to be his first masterpiece. In it all of the characteristics of the Prairie style come together for the first time. Described simply, it is a two-storey house, cruciform in plan with a shallow-pitched hipped roof. The architecture, however, lies in the development of this basic parti into a cluster of forms and spaces that are individually purposeful yet belong together in an ordered and beautifully proportioned ensemble. In the centre stands the masonry chimney, serving fireplaces in both the living and dining rooms. As in almost all Wright houses, the hearth is the anchor, a fixed point, both physically and socially. But this is a hearth on the prairie, not a hearth in a cave. The house looks outwards, stretching itself towards the level horizon. A second low roof, the horizontal counterpart of the chimney, links the porte-cochère on one side to the dining terrace on the other, seeming to pass through the main spaces – entrance hall, living room and dining room – on the way.

The Ward Willits House is a timber-framed structure with a covering of textured plaster both inside and out. This is

Ward Willits House, Highland Park, Illinois, USA. Frank Lloyd Wright, 1902. The first fully developed Prairie house, showing a Japanese influence, though Wright always denied this.

apparent in the treatment of windows, such those of the living room and bedroom, which give the elevation facing the road a faintly Japanese character. But the Prairie style could also be adapted to solid, loadbearing wall construction. In the Robie House of 1909, on a narrow street corner lot in the Chicago suburb of Hyde Park, the main structural material is thin Roman bricks, which further accelerate the building's already extreme horizontality. Once again, symmetry and asymmetry are deftly combined. The low, secondary roof of the Ward Willits House has now become the dominant form, supported on the brick mullions of a continuous strip of windows, and cantilevered out to an improbable extent at both ends. This element is symmetrical but its symmetry is disguised by the off-centre chimney, which divides the living room from the dining room at first-floor level, and by the third, bedroom storey, which is itself like a small cruciform Prairie house. Inside, the ceiling of the main living space is divided by wooden strips into panels, each equipped with a pair of electric lights in glass globes. Windows are adorned by stained glass

in geometrical patterns. There is nothing coldly machine-like about this interior yet its ornaments are rectilinear and repetitive as if acknowledging the logic of the machine. Ashbee wanted to clothe Wright's buildings 'with a more living and tender detail'.[8]

Craftsman Style

So far in this chapter we have looked at houses designed for relatively rich people. The houses of the lower classes are rarely designed by architects, or at least not architects of the kind that call themselves artists. But there are sometimes channels of influence from 'high' architecture to 'popular' architecture and such channels can be traced at this time in both America and England. Gustav Stickley was the son of a stonemason who established a furniture factory at Eastwood in New York at the turn of the century. He called his furniture

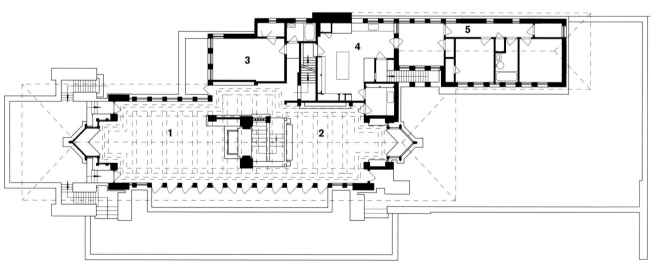

Robie House, Hyde Park, Chicago, USA. Frank Lloyd Wright, 1909. Thin Roman bricks, generous terraces and huge roof overhangs create a racy horizontality.

First floor plan
1. Living room
2. Dining room
3. Guest room
4. Kitchen
5. Staff quarters

0   5   10m
   15   30 ft

Robie House interior, Frank Lloyd Wright, 1909. Living and dining spaces share a hearth with a divided chimney.

'craftsman style' and it gained some popularity among home makers who liked its functional, durable, rustic character. In 1903 Stickley began publishing a monthly magazine called *The Craftsman*, which included articles about interior design and architecture. Soon, pattern books of designs for 'Craftsman Homes' began to appear. The architectural style was called 'Arts and Crafts' or sometimes 'Mission Style' after the old Spanish missions in California that Stickley admired. Some of these designs were by Stickley himself or his colleague Harvey Ellis, but others were contributed by architects and house owners sympathetic to the cause. And it was a 'cause'. Stickley was not merely a businessman. He had read Ruskin and was familiar with the philosophy of the English Arts and Crafts movement. His magazine published the work of several English architects, including Voysey and Lutyens. No Frank Lloyd Wright design ever appeared in *The Craftsman* but other members of the Chicago School, such as W. G. Purcell and George G. Elmslie, contributed articles. The typical Craftsman Home displayed many of the virtues of both English Free Architecture and the Prairie style. Plans were relaxed and open, designed as spatial sequences rather than clusters of boxes. There were Voysey-like low ceilings with wooden beams, cosy inglenook fireplaces and built-in window seats. 'First of all,' wrote Stickley, 'do away with any sense of elaboration and that a house must be a series of cells … Have a "living room" of the house that corresponds to the old "great hall" of ancient dwellings.'[9]

Eventually Stickley over-stretched himself financially and his business collapsed in 1916, but by then Craftsman had been established as one of the accepted styles of popular housing in America, to be included in the pattern books of later house builders and manufacturers such as Sears Roebuck who sold prefabricated house kits by mail order in the 1920s. The label even began to be applied, as it were against the flow, to the work of 'respectable' architects such as the brothers Charles and Henry Greene, who designed Japanese-influenced, shingle-clad, timber-framed mansions like the Gamble House of 1908 in Pasadena.

Among the contributors to Stickley's magazine was the English architect Barry Parker, who, with his partner and brother-in-law Raymond Unwin, successfully applied Arts and Crafts ideals to housing for ordinary people. In 1901 Parker and Unwin published a book called *The Art of Building a Home*, illustrated by their own designs. Voysey is an obvious influence on their larger houses. For example the Homestead of 1903 in Parker's home town of Chesterfield displays a pair of big bay windows that have obviously been borrowed from Broad Leys. But it was in the design of small houses that Parker and Unwin excelled. Their idea was simple: that the best form of dwelling for the English working class was neither the tenement nor the continuous terraces of so-called 'byelaw' housing but the country cottage with a garden. This seems like a patronizing idea today – dressing up an industrial working class as picturesque peasants –

but Parker and Unwin's own backgrounds were relatively modest and their Fabian socialist ideals were genuinely held. It was they who put architectural flesh on the bones of Ebenezer Howard's 'garden city' concept when they were appointed as architects and planners for the new town of Letchworth in 1904. Their plans for ultra-low-density residential areas, with two-storey linked cottages arranged freely among trees, lawns and meandering roads, was to influence the patterns of English suburban development for decades to come. In 1906 they were appointed planners for Hampstead Garden Suburb in north London, for which Lutyens designed two churches.

We have seen how the English Free Architecture was influential on progressive practice in America, and how its 'proto-functionalism' travelled to Germany in Muthesius's book. But there is another connection that completes the triangle. In 1911 a Berlin publisher, Ernst Wasmuth, published a lavish, two-volume folio of drawings of a selection of Frank Lloyd Wright's work since 1893. The book was massively influential in Germany, Holland, France, Switzerland and Austria. Historians have traced its influence especially in the work of early Modernists such as Ludwig Mies van der Rohe and Walter Gropius, and in the Dutch De Stijl movement. It is tempting to see this neat

Houses at Letchworth Garden City, Hertfordshire, UK. Barry Parker and Raymond Unwin, 1905. Country cottages with gardens: English Free Architecture for the working classes.

triangle of influences as the provider of all the necessary ingredients of Modernism: the rejection of historicism; the idea of functionalism and 'purely objective requirements'; the socialist ideals of William Morris; and Wright's acceptance of the machine as 'his God'. But hindsight is misleading. Opposing tendencies are also present in these examples. Voysey's architecture was essentially backward looking and not in any way progressive; Lutyens was a committed classicist; both Voysey and Lutyens hated Modernism in their later careers; none of the English Free architects showed any interest in new building technologies; and though Wright may have embraced the machine, ornament was nevertheless an essential part of his architecture. We could just as well argue that European Modernism emerged despite Voysey, Lutyens and Wright rather than because of them, and that Modernism came from somewhere else entirely. That doesn't mean, however, that these houses of the first ten years of the twentieth century are historically unimportant. The fact that they are still admired and enjoyed a hundred years later is sufficient proof of their worth and influence.

The balloon frame

Architecture, according to most dictionaries, is 'the design of buildings'. Does this mean that all buildings are architecture? In theory yes, in practice no. There is such a thing as 'non-architecture' – buildings designed by people society fails to recognize as 'proper architects'. Architectural history does not usually deal with 'non-architecture', which seems reasonable enough but can lead to a false perspective. The fact is that most buildings, and in particular most houses for ordinary people, are 'non-architecture'.

In the twentieth century a few architects, such as C. F. A. Voysey and Parker and Unwin, exerted some influence, indirectly, on the design of popular housing, but for the most part house builders conducted their business without the help of the architectural establishment. In the process they developed a simple, practical technology that revolutionized the craft of construction: the so-called balloon frame. Its invention, in the American Midwest in the 1830s, was prompted by the availability of two new building products: accurately sawn timber and mass-produced nails. The old 'post and beam' construction, using heavy timber members with handmade carpenter's joints, was quickly superseded by a system of lightweight panels, made from 5x10cm (2x4 inch) timber 'studs', closely spaced, nailed together and covered in clapboarding. It was cheap and fast, and it made a rigid, durable house.

In large parts of the world – the United States, northern Europe, Japan, Australia – the balloon frame, or its close relative the platform frame, became the standard method of house construction. Designs for balloon-frame houses were usually taken from pattern books compiled by draughtsmen rather than respectable architects. They were very cheap to buy or even free. You might pay a little more for a set of detailed working drawings. The balloon frame also lent itself to prefabrication and factory production. From before the First World War until the 1940s in the US, it was possible to order a prefabricated house by mail order from Sears Roebuck. 'Real' architects such as Walter Gropius and Le Corbusier repeatedly tried to break into the prefabricated house business, but with little success. Usually their designs were impractical or too expensive. The global impact of the balloon frame and its descendants – the products of non-architecture – has been greater than that of any architect.

1950s suburban housing project under construction.
The balloon frame is the basis of house-building technology in many parts of the world.

NATIONAL ROMANTICISM, THE NEW TRADITION AND THE BEAUX-ARTS 1893–1923

Architecture: Nineteenth and Twentieth Centuries, by the great American architectural historian Henry-Russell Hitchcock, was first published in 1958. It is a survey to which the adjective 'magisterial' is routinely, and justifiably, applied. The title of its penultimate chapter, number 24, is 'Architecture Called Traditional in the Twentieth Century'. There is a kind of hesitancy about that title, and the late appearance of the chapter in the book, as if the adjective 'traditional' and the architecture to which it is applied were in some sense suspect or inferior. Near the beginning of the chapter we read: 'The traditional architecture of the twentieth century is primarily an instance of survival; and cultural survivals are among the most difficult problems with which history has to deal. Their sluggish life, sunk in inertia and conservatism, is very different from the vitality of new developments.' There is more in the same vein about the 'static, not to say smug assurance' of survivals, and the 'generally accepted fact' of the 'dissolution' of traditional architecture. Then comes a faint relenting: 'Not all traditional architecture of the years 1900–1930 need be dismissed with scorn.' We get the idea. And yet, as Hitchcock freely admits: 'Whatever one calls it, this traditional architecture

includes the majority of buildings designed before 1930 in most countries of the western world.'[1] In 1958, Hitchcock's dismissiveness seemed almost reasonable. A revolution had occurred, Modernism had triumphed and the story of its rise seemed so much more important than any account of a mere 'survival'. But now, more than half a century later, Modernism itself is a survival and we can allow ourselves to view the architecture of the early twentieth century, including incipient Modernism, in a more sceptical light.

National Romantic Style

Hitchcock's taste and judgement are not in question, only the distorting influence of his historical circumstances. Those buildings that he thought 'need not be dismissed with scorn', many of them in Scandinavia, are still a good starting point for a brief survey of traditional architecture before the First World War. If we are to see them as 'survivals' then survivals of what? – of the Gothic and classical traditions, presumably, and of nineteenth-century historicism. But there was also a new ingredient, summed up in the stylistic label 'National Romantic'. The nation state, though challenged by globalization, is now taken for granted as a political norm.

Tampere Cathedral, Tampere, Finland. Lars Sonck, 1907. The big vaulted nave has no precedent in Finnish vernacular architecture.

Not so in 1900 when the unifications of Italy and Germany were well within living memory. In the Nordic countries, especially Finland, nationalism was a powerful cultural as well as political force. We must remember that Finland remained a semi-autonomous grand duchy of the Russian empire until 1917. The *Kalevala*, an epic poem reconstructed from the oral tradition in the early nineteenth century, was the focus of a revival of Finnish national culture in literature, the visual arts and music. The composer Jean Sibelius, for example, wrote his *Four Legends from the Kalevala*, including the well-known 'Swan of Tuonela', in 1895. National Romantic architecture was inspired by this cultural revival, but only indirectly. The architectural equivalent of the *Kalevala* was presumably the Finnish vernacular building tradition based on simple log construction, but it was hard to see how this could be adapted to the needs of a newly prosperous and rapidly urbanizing society. The fact is that Finnish architecture of the turn of century was remarkably open to influences from abroad. The small, tight-knit community of Finnish architects, most of them locally trained, were familiar with, for example, the writings of Ruskin and Morris, the rise of Art Nouveau (or its German version, *Jugendstil*) and the latest technical developments in steel and concrete construction. The work of the great American architect H. H. Richardson was particularly admired for its command of masonry and for its rugged strength, seen perhaps as a reflection of the Finnish national character.

Classicism, represented by Helsinki's Palladian cathedral designed in the 1830s as a tribute to Tsar Nicholas I, was associated with foreign domination, so it was natural that the first exercises in National Romanticism should have drawn on the Gothic tradition. The church of St John (now the cathedral) in Tampere, designed by Lars Sonck in 1899, is a picturesque, asymmetrical composition of spires and steep stone gables clustered around a roughly square, vaulted hall with galleries all round to accommodate the large Lutheran congregation. Such a hall had no precedent in Finnish vernacular architecture, yet it was a feature of several of those buildings associated with the National Romantic movement. The Finnish pavilion at the Paris Universal Exposition of 1900, for example, designed by Herman Gesellius, Armas Lindgren and Eliel Saarinen, adopted a church-like plan with a vaulted crossing under a tapering tower that wore its spire like a decorative hat. The impression is of a national style being invented from scratch rather than recovered from a folk tradition. Gesellius, Lindgren and Saarinen all lived together in a picturesque colony on the shore of Lake Vitträsk. Here they improvised and experimented with various architectural styles, including traditional log construction, Gothic vaulting and a version of Richardson's 'shingle style'. In 1902 the three architects won the competition to design the National Museum of Finland with a scheme that, once again, featured a Gothic-vaulted central hall with a varied collection of church-like, pitched-roofed forms grouped around it. Each wing was designed in response to the exhibits that it would contain. A tower and spire over the main entrance at one corner of the hall was strongly influenced by that of Copenhagen city hall by Martin Nyrop, one of the competition judges.

In 1904 Eliel Saarinen won another important national competition, for the main railway station in Helsinki. His design conformed to the picturesque Gothic norm, complete with tower and spire, but was severely criticized by disappointed rivals, especially Sigurd Frosterus, who

National Museum of Finland, Helsinki, Finland. Herman Gesellius, Armas Lindgren and Eliel Saarinen, 1910. The architects worked and lived together in a colony on the shore of Lake Vitträsk in Kirkkonummi.

called for a more modern design to suit the function of the building. The call was made in a newspaper article that reads today almost like a Modernist manifesto. Dismissing 'our modern Finnish style' as 'mindless romanticism', it goes on to argue that new materials and new building types call for new forms: 'We have more to learn about form from the construction of machinery, bicycles, cars, from battleships and railway bridges, than from historical styles.' However, it also shows a willingness to compromise with tradition that is characteristic of the time: 'Greek columns … with the intervals between the columns greatly multiplied, already constitute a more modern architecture than timid stone construction which imagines itself based on Gothic or Romantic styles.'[2] Frosterus's own designs – his unsuccessful entry for the railway station competition, for example – though progressive and formally inventive, would still be called 'traditional' by a modern historian. It may have been Frosterus's attack or it may have been a study trip to Germany and England in the summer of 1904 that persuaded Saarinen to modernize his design for the station. Its castle- and church-like forms were translated into a new language that combined basically classical rhythms with simplified ornament derived from *Jugendstil*. The most memorable feature of the building as it now stands is the monumental arch over the main entrance, which is guarded

by two pairs of frowning 'herms', 8 metres (26 feet) high, holding spherical lamps. Inside, the arch becomes a Roman barrel vault. The refreshment hall to one side is roofed by elegant portal frames in concrete, ornamented with plain stepped profiles that seem to anticipate the Art Deco style of 20 years later.

In Sweden the National Romantic style is best represented by Stockholm City Hall. In 1902 the city held a competition for the design of a new town hall and law courts. Six architects were shortlisted. Ragnar Östberg and Carl Westman were chosen to go on to the second stage. Then in 1908 the project was divided between them, Östberg taking the town hall and Westman the law courts. Westman's law court building, completed in 1915, was modelled on the seventeenth-century Vasa dynasty palace at Vadstena – a symmetrical, four-storey block with plain walls, steeply pitched roofs and a fat, domed tower. It is 'national' certainly, but perhaps too plain spoken to be called 'romantic'. Östberg's town hall, on the other hand, is romantic to a sublime degree. It stands right on the water's

Stockholm City Hall, Sweden. Ragnar Östberg, 1911–23.
A sublime tapering tower, right on the waterfront, is crowned by a dreamy belfry.

Stockholm City Hall interior.
The covered courtyard is extremely refined despite large areas of unadorned brickwork.

edge and announces its presence with a huge tapering tower crowned by a dreamy, copper-clad open belfry. Both the tower and the closeness of the building to the water are features borrowed from Westman's original competition design. The main part of the building is a rectangular block with two internal courtyards, one roofed, the other open and flowing out onto the waterside terrace through an arcade on squat columns. What looks from a distance like a fortification turns out to be an accessible and welcoming public building. It wants to look old, possibly medieval, but its precise style is hard to pin down. Brickwork is the main material, in large areas, mostly unadorned. There are tall, thin windows with cusped arches, corner turrets with onion domes and odd freestyle classical doorways and canopies. One is reminded of the stylistically mixed architecture of that other watery city, Venice. Part of the mysterious power of this building is surely due to its extreme refinement. Östberg is said to have continued altering the details of the design right through the long construction period. It was not finished until 1923.

Stockholm Court House, Sweden. Carl Westman, 1915.
The building was modelled on the seventeenth-century Vasa dynasty palace at Vadstena.

Denmark's best-known contribution to the National Romantic style has an even more other-worldly quality. Construction on Grundtvig's Church on the outskirts of Copenhagen began in 1921, but it had been designed in

1913 by P. V. Jensen-Klint. Its west front may have been inspired by the 'crowstep' gables of old Danish churches but this homely feature has been developed and exaggerated to become a soaring cluster of narrow brick piers like organ pipes. What seems at first like a two-dimensional composition is in fact one wall of a thick tower or 'westwork'. Inside, the church is Gothic of a very pure, abstract kind. The long nave, with side aisles, is entirely of pale yellow brick, including the floor and the ribbed quadripartite vaults high above. The only ornament is the plain, stepped profile of the piers and pointed arches – a Gothic version, perhaps, of Saarinen's railway station. A street of houses and ancillary buildings in the same stepped brick style leads up to the main entrance, providing a domestic foil to the heavenward-reaching church.

One other large brick building of this period should be mentioned, though it is often singled out from its National Romantic contemporaries because of the importance of its architect. Hendrik Berlage was the most influential Dutch architect of the early twentieth century. His work, and his ideas, formed a bridge between the traditional architecture of the nineteenth century and the Modernism of the younger generation. The Beurs or stock exchange in Amsterdam, completed in 1903, is his masterpiece. It is, to our twenty-first-century eyes, a completely traditional building with brick loadbearing walls and an iron-framed glass roof over its main trading floor. It is hard to see now what made it an inspiration and a constant reference point for younger architects for decades to come. It has been described as 'Romanesque' in style, which seems to imply that it is essentially a historicist or revivalist building. This is not really the case, however. For one thing, the designation 'Romanesque' does not quite fit. The arches that support the galleries around the trading floor, for example, are shallow and segmental – quite unlike the semi-circular arches that are typical of medieval Romanesque buildings. It may be that the comparison often made between Berlage and H. H. Richardson has led historians to transfer the historical references from the latter to the former, but it was not until 1911, long after the completion of the Beurs, that Berlage visited the United States and, though he certainly admired Richardson, it was Frank Lloyd Wright

Grundtvig's Church, Copenhagen, Denmark. Peder Vilhelm Jensen-Klint and Kaare Klint, 1940. The domestic scale of the church only emphasizes the unreal quality of the west front.

who impressed him most. Berlage's subsequent writings and lectures became one of the most important channels of Wright's influence in Holland and the rest of Europe. Perhaps for 'Romanesque' we should read 'non-classical' and 'non-Gothic'. Stylistic references mattered less to Berlage than abstract concepts such as the creation of space, truth to materials, and the repose that results from consistent proportional systems. Walls were especially important to him. 'Before all else,' he wrote in 1905, 'the wall must be shown naked in all its sleek beauty.'[3] This principle is well illustrated by the Beurs. Externally, the building is wrapped in one continuous, four-storey-high wall plane. There are no attached columns or cornices to articulate or embellish this wall. Doors and windows are plain openings with only sills and coping stones projecting. The clock tower at the corner of the building is a mere upward extension of the enveloping plane; compare this with Östberg's tower in Stockholm that steps forward and declares its formal independence. Inside the Beurs, the continuous-wall-plane principle holds true even in the arcaded galleries that surround the hall of the main trading floor. At ground-floor level, the wall is supported on granite columns whose bases and capitals, though clearly indicated in profile, have apparently been sliced off flush with

the wall plane. There are projections higher up, however, in the form of corbelled piers. Here again, though, there is smoothness and continuity in the way that the piers begin to curve inward as they rise, anticipating the curve of the iron arches that they support.

Berlage's Beurs is historically important because it perfectly illustrates an intermediate stage between style and abstraction, between tradition and modernity. Hitchcock called it 'the new tradition'. Ten years after the completion of the Beurs, on the eve of the First World War, Berlage designed a building in London that seems now startlingly prescient. Is it a harbinger of Modernism or simply a further development of those abstract principles that were Berlage's guarantee of architectural authenticity? The building in question is Holland House, an office block on what was then a very narrow street in the City of London. The client was Helene Müller, who, with her husband Anton Kröller,

Beurs van Berlage, Amsterdam, the Netherlands. Hendrik Petrus Berlage, 1903. Neither classical nor Gothic, it is sometimes described as Romanesque, though the arches are mainly flat, not rounded.

Holland House, London, UK. H. P. Berlage, 1916. An ill-informed architectural historian might easily misdate the building by 50 years.

owned a successful shipping and mining company. (It was for the Kröller-Müllers, incidentally, that Mies van der Rohe, in competition with Berlage, produced his now famous design for a villa and art gallery – see page 126.) Holland House is a very early example in Europe of a completely steel-framed building and it is clad in faience, or glazed terracotta, tiles. Louis Sullivan's Wainwright and Guaranty buildings (see pages 50 and 51), which Berlage visited on his 1911 trip to the US, undoubtedly influenced it. But whereas those early skyscrapers still honoured classical proportions in their base–shaft–capital form, the facades of Holland House are completely regular grids of thin, closely spaced mullions and identical square spandrel panels. There is a base, but of plain black granite, a negative rather than a positive form, and at the top the mullions are simply cut off without any terminating cornice. Such abstraction is very unusual for the time. An ill-informed architectural historian might easily date it to the early 1960s. Inside, the faience detailing continues, but in bright colours with geometrical patterns that anticipate Dutch abstract paintings of the 1920s.

Beaux-Arts

These 'National Romantic' or 'new tradition' buildings all commend themselves to history because they are

seen as progressive or 'transitional'. Transitional to what? To Modernism, of course. But this concept of architecture in transition is philosophically dubious and historically distorting. It singles out certain buildings because they display features that are characteristic of a later era. Their architects may in some cases – Walter Gropius, for example – have been consciously working towards a Modernist vision. But it is hard to claim this for architects like Sonck or Östberg or even Berlage, who, when he attended the Congrès International d'Architecture Moderne in 1929 declared that everything he stood for was being destroyed by his fellow delegates. It is necessary, therefore, to make some allowance for the distorting effect of hindsight. As well as searching for plausible examples of 'proto-Modernist' architecture, we should acknowledge the architecture that was actually predominant in these years. The fact is that, before the First World War, most important European and American buildings were designed in a traditional, classical style to which the name 'Beaux-Arts' is often applied. The name is borrowed from the school of architecture in Paris that, since before the time of Napoleon, had offered a methodical, project-based, competitive system of education favouring certain stylistic choices and methods of composition. Students typically produced enormous, beautifully rendered drawings of large, imaginary public buildings and submitted them to their tutors in the hope of winning the Prix de Rome, a scholarship for five years' study at the French Academy in that city.

In some histories of modern architecture 'Beaux-Arts' is used as a general term meaning simply 'pre-modern'. It is the dark, regressive background against which the emerging traces of bright, progressive Modernism are outlined. In this view, Modernist architecture was new, functional, technologically advanced and free of unnecessary ornament; Beaux-Arts architecture was therefore by contrast historicist, inefficient, technologically primitive and dressed in old-fashioned classical clothes. But if we lay Modernism to one side for a moment and look at Beaux-Arts architecture in its own terms we find that many of these characterizations are mere prejudices. Beaux-Arts buildings were in many ways as modern as Modernist buildings, and the development of Modernist theory owed a great deal to Beaux-Arts educational practice. From the 1890s until the Second World War the Ecole des Beaux-Arts set the pattern of academic architectural education throughout Europe and America. Many foreign architects attended the school, including several Modernist and pre-Modernist heroes. Louis Sullivan, Frank Lloyd Wright's mentor and the inventor of the steel-framed skyscraper, studied for a year at the Ecole in 1874; Auguste Perret, the French Modernist and pioneer of reinforced-concrete construction attended as a student in the 1890s and returned as a teacher in the 1940s; and Tony Garnier, author of the massively influential Cité Industrielle project of 1904, was a Grand Prix de Rome winner in 1899 (see Chapter 4). Equally important, however, were those Beaux-Arts architects who were later considered irrelevant to the history of Modernism but who were nevertheless responsible for the most important public buildings in cities like Chicago, New York, Washington, London and Paris.

In America, the popularity of the Beaux-Arts style was boosted by the 1893 World's Columbian Exposition in Chicago. The fair was centred on a vast formal court, half filled with a reflecting pool and surrounded by monumental classical buildings. Richard Morris Hunt, who had attended the Ecole des Beaux-Arts in 1846 and had lived in Paris for ten years, led an architectural team that included Louis Sullivan, Charles F. McKim, Charles B. Atwood and Daniel Burnham. McKim was another Ecole alumnus whose practice, McKim, Mead and White, was one of the biggest in America. Atwood did not attend the Ecole but nevertheless based his Fine Arts building on a Grand Prix de Rome-winning project of 1867. Burnham, who was responsible for co-ordinating the construction of the exhibition, would go on to apply its Beaux-Arts town-planning principles to his master plans for Chicago and Washington.

The exhibition buildings may have looked solidly monumental but in fact they were mocked up in hard plaster on relatively

World's Columbian Exposition, Chicago, USA, 1893. A Beaux-Arts stage set to prove American architecture's cultural respectability.

light frames. These architects were not merely playing with fantasy architecture, however. They were masters of the classical style and used it skilfully in their day-to-day practice. McKim, Mead and White's Boston Public Library is a version of the Sainte-Geneviève Library in Paris, designed by Ecole Grand Prix laureate Henri Labrouste and completed in 1851. If anything, the Boston library is even more solidly

Boston Public Library, Boston, USA. McKim, Mead and White, 1895. Influenced by the Sainte-Geneviève Library in Paris, but even more solidly monumental.

monumental, with a single, deeply coffered barrel vault over its main reading room in place of Labrouste's delicate, iron-framed original. Both McKim and his partner Stanford White had worked as assistants to H. H. Richardson, another Ecole alumnus, whose masterpiece, the Marshall Field Wholesale Store in Chicago of 1887, with its massively arcuated and rusticated stone walls, has been an example and constant reference point for American architecture ever since.

A library might be thought an appropriately traditional subject for an exercise in monumental classicism, but the Beaux-Arts style was applied with equal vigour to that prominent product of the machine age, the railway terminus. New York's Grand Central Station, completed in 1913, was designed by Whitney Warren, who had studied at the Ecole. For him there could be no better beginning to a railway journey than passage through a Roman triumphal arch, complete with giant Doric columns and a crowning

Pennsylvania Station, New York City, USA. McKim, Mead and White, 1910. Railway concourse or Roman baths? The building was demolished in 1963.

ensemble of baroque sculpture gathered round a large clock. McKim, Mead and White's Pennsylvania Station, New York, completed in 1910 and demolished in 1963, was even more grandly Roman, its central groin-vaulted waiting room modelled on the Baths of Caracalla.

Those architecture students who could not afford the sojourn in Paris could obtain their Beaux-Arts training at the University of Pennsylvania where, from 1903 well into the 1930s, the French architect Paul Cret (Ecole-trained, naturally) was a leading teacher. Cret also had a flourishing practice. His first major commission was the Pan American Union building (now the Organization of American States) in Washington, completed in 1910. Its front facade is another variation on the triumphal-arch form, with flat Corinthian pilasters. Cret later updated his style, suppressing ornament but maintaining a classical parti and sense of proportion. His Folger Shakespeare Library in Washington of 1932 is a good example. Louis Kahn (see Chapter 22) was one of Cret's assistants and is said to have worked on the design of this building.

The Beaux-Arts style was popular even in Britain, not normally welcoming to French cultural influence. We saw in Chapter 2 how Edwin Lutyens, who at first followed the Gothic-inspired Arts and Crafts tradition, later 'discovered' classicism. He was not breaking new ground, however, only placing his genius in line with the fashion of the time. Pre-war London was peppered with big new classical buildings as if it were trying to catch up with Paris. Admiralty Arch by Sir Aston Webb, completed in 1912, was a triumphal arch of a new kind, asymmetrical, concave on both sides and flanked by substantial five-storey office buildings. Its main function

Folger Shakespeare Library, Washington D.C. Paul Cret, 1932. The great Louis Kahn is said to have worked on the design of this building.

was to terminate London's only boulevard, The Mall, and at the same time resolve an awkward alignment with Trafalgar Square. Two years later, at the other end of The Mall, Buckingham Palace itself was given a new classical facade, also by Sir Aston Webb. It was built in only three months in order not to inconvenience the new king, George V.

Admiralty Arch, London, UK. Aston Webb, 1912. The plan cleverly resolves the awkward misalignment of The Mall with Trafalgar Square.

It would be wrong to think of these buildings as 'old fashioned'. They represented the latest renewal of an ancient style but, to their creators, they were buildings appropriate to the new century. They served modern purposes – railway stations, office buildings, department stores, hotels – and they used the latest structural and mechanical engineering techniques. The Ritz Hotel in Piccadilly, designed by the French architect Charles Mewès and his English partner Arthur Davis, somehow squeezed its eight above-ground storeys into the traditional classical format – base, column and entablature – to create a Parisian-style urban block. The top four form a mansard-roofed attic that is almost half the height of the building. Behind the fictitious classical structure figured in the Portland stone facade, a modern steel frame does most of the structural work. Opened in 1906, the Ritz was the first major steel-framed building in Britain. Methodist Central Hall in Westminster, designed by Lanchester, Stewart and Rickards and completed in 1911, was also structurally innovative. Its enormous steel-framed central dome is supported on wide, flat arches of reinforced concrete. These were designed with the help of an American consultant, Julius Kahn, the brother of the architect Albert Kahn (see pages 60–63). The main staircase is of a Baroque splendour to rival the Paris Opera itself. One more London example: the King Edward VII Galleries on the north side of the British Museum, designed by Sir John James Burnet,

a Scotsman trained at the Ecole. Its row of 20 attached Ionic columns follows the precedent of Robert Smirke's original early nineteenth-century building but invites comparison with the much more distinguished Altes Museum in Berlin by Karl Friedrich Schinkel. From our Modernist-dominated perspective, it is hard to believe that such a confident and accomplished classical building was finished on the eve of the First World War.

Emerging Modernism

We have become accustomed to the idea that Modernism was a radical alternative to the Beaux-Arts style, or indeed to any historically derived style. The gulf seems unbridgeable between, say, Burnet's galleries and Le Corbusier's Maison Dom-ino proposal of roughly the same date (see Chapter 4). And yet there are connections and continuities. Reyner Banham begins his classic work *Theory and Design in the First Machine Age*, first published in 1960, with an analysis of the writings of two Beaux-Arts professors, Julien Guadet and Auguste Choisy. Banham points out that these authors, who were writing mainly for the guidance of their students, do not talk directly about style in the classical

Methodist Central Hall, London, UK. Lanchester, Stewart and Rickards, 1911. Traditional forms built in reinforced concrete with advice from Albert Kahn's engineer brother, Julius.

sense. Guadet, in his *Eléments et théorie de l'architecture*, published in 1902, analyzes architecture in abstract terms. Buildings, he argues, are made from 'elements' of two types: 'architectural elements', like floors, walls, columns, beams and roofs, and 'compositional elements', like rooms, pavilions, towers or wings. The latter contain the former and are themselves contained by the whole building. Thinking about architecture in this way – as 'composition' rather than 'design' – gives rise to buildings that are complex and articulated, with different elements performing different functions. Much Beaux-Arts classical architecture is of this kind – look, for example, at the various porticos and pavilions that surrounded the central waiting room of McKim, Mead and White's Pennsylvania Station – but there is nothing intrinsically classical about such complexity. The form of a Greek temple is simple and unified, not complex and articulated. Elemental composition lent itself readily to a functionalist design method and is a characteristic of those buildings by Frank Lloyd Wright, Walter Gropius and Auguste Perret that are considered to be the very first examples of true Modernism.

Auguste Choisy, in his *Histoire de l'architecture*, published in 1899, seems similarly uninterested in stylistic questions. He was a rationalist who saw architecture as a direct consequence of building technology. 'It was in the suggestions of construction,' he wrote, 'that the architect of the great artistic ages found his truest inspiration.'[4] Choisy illustrated his book with worm's eye axonometric (or sometimes isometric) drawings that showed interiors

and exteriors at the same time, in three dimensions. The sumptuous drawings that students of the Ecole produced for their Grand Prix de Rome entries were mostly plans, sections and elevations, with every classical detail carefully coloured and shaded. But Choisy, their teacher, preferred his plain line drawings that suppressed ornament and emphasized the abstract rather than the visual aspects of the building. Le Corbusier, in the magazines and books that he published in the 1920s, reused Choisy's drawings to illustrate the new, rational approach to architecture.

There is really no need to set up an opposition between the Beaux-Arts style and emerging Modernism. It is true that the Modernist pioneers criticized the World's Columbian Exposition as a backward step in the journey of American architecture, but the tradition that it represented nevertheless aided their progress. Modernism and traditionalism were not mutually exclusive. Beaux-Arts architects like Sullivan and Cret adopted a functionalist approach (it was Sullivan who coined the hackneyed slogan 'form follows function'), used the latest engineering techniques and were prepared either to play down historical ornament or, in the case of Sullivan, invent ornamental systems of their own. On the other hand, Modernists like Tony Garnier and Auguste Perret designed symmetrical, articulated buildings that were not too different from the Beaux-Arts projects of their student days.

Edward VII Galleries, British Museum, London, UK. Sir John Burnet & Partners, 1914. Edwardian classicism on the eve of the First World War.

Selfridges Department Store

When, in 1906, H. Gordon Selfridge decided it was time to introduce American-style retailing to London, he had recently acquired (and almost immediately sold) a large department store in Chicago called Schlesinger and Mayer. The store was housed in a strikingly modern, 12-storey building designed by Louis Sullivan, a building known to architectural history by the name of its subsequent owners, Carson, Pirie and Scott. It is regarded as a fine example of Sullivan's style and of the progress of steel-framed architecture around the turn of the century. Its lower floors and street-corner entrance are floridly decorated but its upper floors present only a stark, glass-infilled, horizontally proportioned grid to the street.

When Selfridge came to London, therefore, he knew all about multi-storey buildings with steel frames and open floor plans. Architecture was an important part of his vision for retailing, which saw shopping as a leisure activity conducted in big flowing spaces, lavishly appointed and populated by an army of eager sales assistants. The local building regulations, however, were still based on old loadbearing wall technology and insisted on rigid compartmentalization to prevent the spread of fire. It was Selfridge's determination to realize his vision in a new department store on Oxford Street that led to the updating of those regulations and the passing of the so-called Steel Frame Act of 1909. Selfridges was not the first steel-framed building in London – that title is usually awarded to the Ritz Hotel – but it was the first to exploit the steel frame's potential to create continuous internal spaces and allow large areas of glass in facades.

Architecturally, those facades were traditional, though no-one would have thought them old fashioned. Daniel Burnham produced the earliest design in a Greek Revival style possibly inspired by John James Burnet's King Edward VII Galleries (see page 47), but another American architect, Francis Swales, 'updated' the classical order with a more fashionable, less severe 'Louis XVI' version. Three-storey-high Ionic columns stand on a Doric-pilastered ground floor and support a full-height attic with a stone balustrade. The reconciling of steel frame with classical order is achieved very simply by filling in the bays between widely spaced Portland stone-clad columns with large sheets of glass in cast iron frames. Even the attic storey is supplied with its full complement of 'Chicago windows', and the squat piers of the ground floor leave plenty of scope for the window dresser's art. Selfridges is a Chicago building dressed in French Beaux-Arts clothes. The combination is surprisingly successful, setting the tone of the now fashionable western end of London's main shopping street.

(Opposite) Selfridges Department Store, London, UK. Daniel Burnham, 1909–28. A classical facade but a thoroughly modern building.

Carson, Pirie, Scott & Co. Building, Chicago, USA. Louis Sullivan, 1904. Harry Gordon Selfridge's other department store and a landmark in the history of Modernism.

04 | STEEL AND CONCRETE: PIONEERS AND VISIONARIES 1891–1923

It is commonly assumed that the rise of modern architecture in the early decades of the twentieth century was partly due to the availability of new building materials, especially steel and concrete. These materials were not in themselves new – weapons and tools had been made of hand-forged steel for centuries and the ancient Romans had used concrete to construct large vaulted structures – but new technologies had been developed to exploit them and shape them to the needs of an industrial economy. From the 1860s onwards, after the invention of the Bessemer converter, steel production increased rapidly in Britain, Germany and the United States. The linear sections and flat plates produced in steel mills were first used for railways, steamships and bridges, but it was not long before American builders and architects recognized their potential for civic architecture.

Steel depends on investment in heavy industrial plant and is usually produced in standard profiles and sizes. Concrete is more craft oriented and site based. It can be cast 'in situ' in one-off wooden moulds. Most competent builders can, to this day, make a serviceable concrete lintel on site using only hand tools. In the history of architecture, steel and concrete are both firmly associated with modernity. While this is understandable in the case of industrially produced steel, it is, as Adrian Forty has pointed out, harder to see why concrete should have taken on this connotation.[1] It might just as easily have come to represent the primitive and the anti-industrial, as indeed it did in certain late works of Le Corbusier. It was steel reinforcement – the couple of steel bars cast into that site-made lintel to increase its tensile strength – that made concrete modern. Reinforced concrete was developed in several places at once and took many different forms, but by 1900 a settled methodology had emerged, especially in France, and its true potential was beginning to be realized. Because it was fluid in nature and mouldable to almost any shape, it began to be looked upon as a universal building material. Walls, floors, arches, domes and vaults could all be made of reinforced concrete, and with a new lightness and strength. The material seemed less appropriate for columns and beams, yet, surprisingly, these were the very elements for which it was most commonly used.

When we look for the architectural consequences of the arrival of steel and concrete we find that the most important innovation was common to them both: the multi-storey structural frame. The sheer strength of the new materials, so much greater than that of masonry, wood or iron, made it possible to build frames or skeletons that could bear the whole weight of a building, including floors, walls and roofs, and transfer it through vertical columns to the foundations. The structural frame was a force of architectural liberation; buildings could now be built higher, faster, cheaper and with more spatial flexibility.

Wainwright Building, St Louis, Missouri, USA. Adler & Sullivan, 1891. The building's steel frame is clad in brick and terracotta, with rich but contained ornament.

Guaranty Building, Buffalo, New York, USA. Adler & Sullivan, 1896. A new simplicity and repetitiveness but with classical overtones: base, shaft and capital.

Louis Sullivan

History has chosen two architects to represent the development of the structural frame in the two new materials: the American Louis Sullivan for steel, and the Frenchman Auguste Perret for concrete. Each has been looked upon as a pioneer of modern architecture, though neither ever questioned the traditional architectural virtues of uprightness, order, symmetry and proportion. Sullivan comes first. He was a leading figure in the so-called Chicago School, which included Daniel Burnham, John Root, William LeBaron Jenney, William Holabird, Martin Roche and Sullivan's partner, Dankmar Adler. The great Frank Lloyd Wright trained in the Adler and Sullivan office and acknowledged Sullivan as his mentor. For the purposes of this discussion, two Sullivan buildings are especially relevant, both quite similar in appearance and neither of them in Chicago. The Wainwright Building in St Louis, Missouri of 1891 is a ten-storey office building with shops on the ground and first floors. It was the first Sullivan building to use a true steel frame, clad externally in brick and terracotta.

The Guaranty Building in Buffalo, New York, designed in 1894, is three storeys higher and clad entirely in terracotta. Both buildings make good illustrative examples for a magazine article that Sullivan wrote in 1896, 'The Tall Office Building Artistically Considered'. The article discusses the relationship between traditional architecture and a new building type, the 'skyscraper', which was made possible by the invention of the steel frame and the high-speed elevator. It is a kind of ideological balancing act, calling for a new simplicity and directness in design while maintaining a respectful deference to traditional architecture. The general idea is that in nature form only changes when function changes, and so it should be in architecture: 'Whether it be the sweeping eagle in his flight or the open apple blossom, the toiling workhorse, the blithe swan, the branching oak, the winding stream at its base, the drifting clouds over all the coursing sun, form ever follows function, and this is the law.'[2] The implication for the tall office building is that if the function housed by every floor is the same then every floor should look the same. This was the principle adopted in the Wainwright and Guaranty buildings. The ground and first floors house shops and are therefore open planned with large windows. The top floor houses mechanical plant – lift motors, tanks, ventilation equipment – and has no need for large windows because it can be lit from above. The floors in between accommodate repetitive cellular offices formed by lightweight partitions, so their external walls are pierced by identical windows, repeated both horizontally and vertically to make a regular grid pattern.

Why should Sullivan feel the need to justify this straightforward design by an appeal to nature? Because other architects of the Chicago School, and even more so the architects of the eastern cities who favoured the French Beaux-Arts style, tended to break up the plain facades of their tall office buildings into smaller units. The classical tradition furnished no precedents for a tall building composed of 10 or 13 storeys, most of them identical. It was necessary therefore to treat the building as if it were several shorter buildings piled on top of one another.

Home Insurance Building, Chicago, USA. William LeBaron Jenney, 1885. Cornices appear at intervals over the height of the building in order to preserve classical proportions.

Sullivan does not mention any specific example of this desperate architectural ploy but he might have had in mind the Home Insurance Building in Chicago, designed by his old employer William LeBaron Jenney and completed in 1885. This ten-storey building (two more were added in 1890) was the very first to use steel as part of its metal frame, though most of it consisted of cast- and wrought-iron members. Like the Wainwright and Guaranty buildings, its base and its attic storey were differentiated architecturally from the main office floors, but in addition the seven floors in between were divided up into four groups by big horizontal cornices, as if each indicated the presence of a notional roof. It was the arbitrariness and dishonesty of this division that offended Sullivan. Architecture, it seemed to him, had become a pictorial fantasy rather than an expression of the true nature of the building.

While Sullivan first coined the slogan 'form follows function' it would be wrong to see his buildings as 'functional' in the Modernist sense. They did not reject architectural tradition; they adapted it to new purposes. Their tripartite vertical division clearly corresponded to the base–shaft–capital division of the Greek or Roman column, as Sullivan readily acknowledged in his article. What's more, they were always richly ornamented in a characteristic swirling vegetal style of Sullivan's own invention. The details of the ornament may not have been traditional but, for example, the top storey of the Wainwright Building, with its little round windows peeping through a moulded terracotta thicket, is a kind of classical frieze. The steel-framed skyscraper was to become one of the defining images of modernity in the twentieth century, especially when photographed in its natural habitat of Manhattan. Yet right up to the Second World War it maintained its allegiance to traditional architecture, both classical and Gothic (see Chapter 13). It was modern, but not Modernist.

Auguste Perret

Auguste Perret studied in the atelier of Julien Guadet at the Ecole des Beaux-Arts in Paris from 1891 to 1895. He was a devoted student of the history of French architecture and of the writings of the great Gothicist and structural rationalist Viollet-le-Duc. Dividing his time between the Ecole and the drawing office of his father's successful

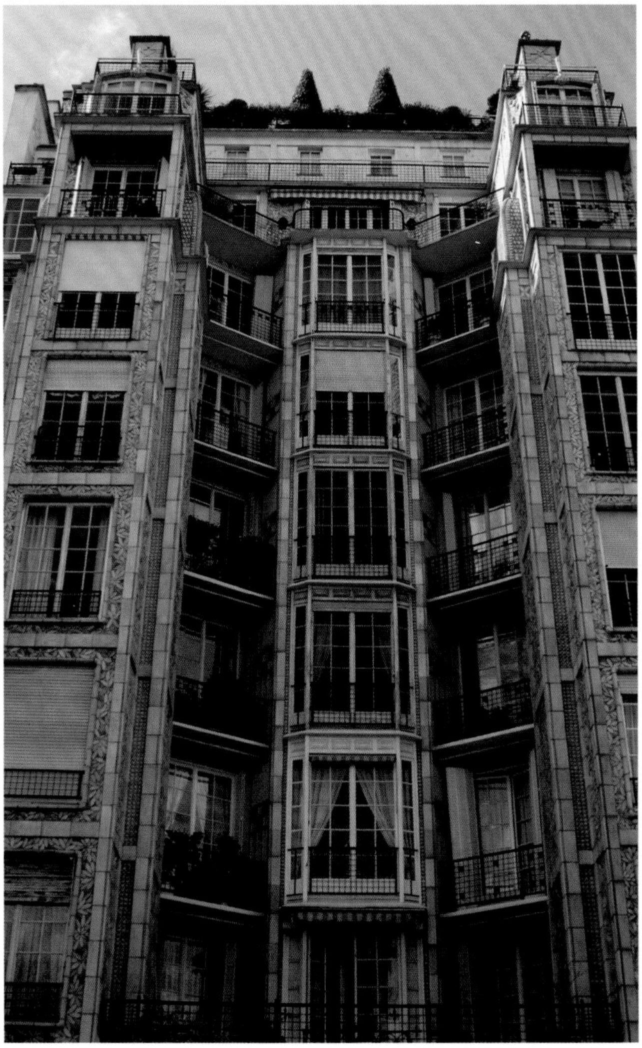

Rue Franklin Apartments, Paris, France. Auguste Perret, 1904. The indented front brings daylight into the middle of a plan with no light well at the back.

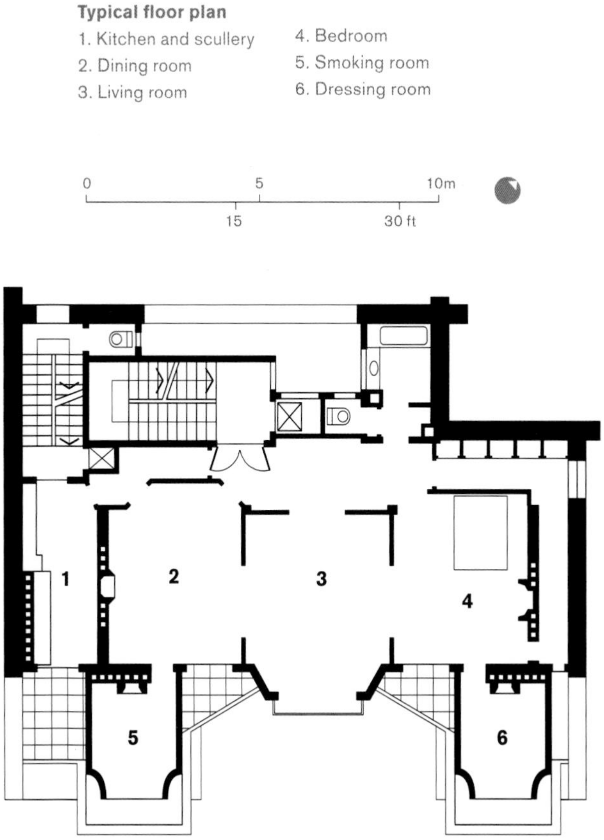
Typical floor plan
1. Kitchen and scullery
2. Dining room
3. Living room
4. Bedroom
5. Smoking room
6. Dressing room
0
5
10m
15
30 ft
1
2
3
4
5
6

contracting and property development company, Perret combined a grounding in the theory of architecture with a thorough knowledge of the practicalities, both technical and financial, of the building business. Around 1902 he became interested in reinforced concrete, possibly after reading a book by Paul Christophe, *Le Béton armé et ses applications*, about the Hennebique system. The famous flats at 25b Rue Benjamin Franklin in Paris, a speculative development built with family money, were completed in 1904. It was not the first apartment block to use a reinforced concrete frame but it was probably the first to give architectural expression to that frame. Though it is ten storeys high, nobody would ever call it a skyscraper, squeezed as it is onto a narrow plot in a continuous terrace. The plot is also shallow, with no space for a light well at the back, so the front wall is indented to let sufficient daylight into the apartments. Floor plans are spatially free flowing, with angled walls, wide openings between the main living spaces and large windows opening onto balconies. This is the liberating effect of the structural frame, which does away with the need for solid, loadbearing

walls. The external wall of the stairs at the rear is made of glass blocks set in a concrete honeycomb. In general form and outline the building is not so different from its more conventional neighbours, but it is clearly a frame in-filled with wall and window units rather than a solid wall pierced by openings. The frame is visible on the exterior, not as naked concrete but clothed in smooth ceramic panels that subtly alter the profiles of beams and columns, regularizing them and emphasizing their rationality. Solid in-fill panels are also clad in ceramic tiles, but textured with an Art Nouveau flower pattern. The fact that Perret chose to distinguish between frame and in-fill rather than covering both with the same ceramic tiles is possibly the building's most important innovation.

Sullivan's Wainwright Building and the Rue Franklin apartment block are very different buildings made of very different materials, but they both have structural frames and they both share a reluctance to stray too far from traditional architecture. Rue Franklin seems more Gothic than classical,

---

Garage Ponthieu, Paris, France. Auguste Perret, 1906. A reinforced-concrete frame but classically disposed with the suggestion of an attic storey.

Théâtre des Champs-Élysées, Paris, France. Auguste Perret, 1913. The sculptured frieze is by Antoine Bourdelle and made of marble, not concrete.

because of its verticality and its Viollet-influenced structural rationality, but classicism lay at the heart of Perret's architectural theory. He even found a theoretical connection between classicism and reinforced concrete, arguing that since the columns and beams of Greek temples were obviously stone versions of wooden originals, and wood was the material used to make the moulds in which concrete was cast, columns and beams were natural forms for concrete to adopt.

Perret's classicism is more evident in another Parisian street building, now demolished, a garage in Rue de Ponthieu, completed in 1906. This was an industrial building of a rather advanced kind – a small, three-storey, semi-automated car park. Lifts and gantries delivered the cars to their appointed spaces on shelf-like floors either side of a glass-roofed atrium. The structure was reinforced concrete and entirely functional, except for the street facade. Perret might have chosen traditional materials for this facade so as not to disrupt the street scene in this fashionable Paris district but instead he chose concrete, not clad in ceramic tiles this time but simply painted white. It was a composition of some subtlety. Its three bays echoed the arrangement of the garage within but were carefully proportioned, the central bay a little wider and emphasized by the projection of the full-height columns. Two columns of a minor order flanked the main entrance and the top floor was treated as an attic divided into eleven bays – three–five–three – by concrete mullions. This elegant, hierarchical frame was in-filled with metal-framed glass, including a modern version of a rose window in the centre. Though it displayed no traditional classical ornament, this facade was certainly classical in spirit. It pointed the way to a new style – 'classical modern' – and it did so in unadorned reinforced concrete.

One more Parisian building designed by Perret in the pre-war years must be mentioned: the Théâtre des Champs-Elysées on Avenue Montaigne. Several designers were involved in the genesis of this building, including the leading Art Nouveau designer of the day, Henry van der Velde, but when Auguste Perret and his brother Gustave were called in as consultants they promptly took charge of the whole job. The site was a difficult one, close to the bank of the Seine, and the painter van der Velde was not sufficiently experienced to deal with its structural implications. Perret was by now an expert in reinforced concrete construction and set about applying his knowledge to a complex brief that included a 2,000-seat main theatre and a smaller

auditorium placed over the entrance foyer. Louis Gellusseau was his consultant structural engineer. Their solution is complex in structural fact but simple in appearance. The main auditorium is basically cylindrical, with three galleries above the stalls level, yet the only visible structure is four pairs of full-height columns. Hidden above the ceiling is a rehearsal space suspended from two 21-metre (70-foot) segmental arches. The foyer is a plain rectangle, easy to navigate, with two straight flights of steps facing one another on either side of the stalls entrance. Ornament is minimal, confined to iron balustrades and understated friezes, but a tartan grid of columns and beams, echoed in the floor finish, gives scale and perspective to the space. At the time it was thought to be extremely austere. One critic called it 'unnecessarily brutal'. The front elevation is also rather plain, a stripped-down, marble-clad, classical composition framed by a giant order of double pilasters supporting a plain cornice over a deep sculptured frieze. The Théâtre des Champs-Elysées was based on a very advanced structure and was plain

Notre-Dame du Raincy, Le Raincy, France. Auguste and Gustave Perret, 1923. Concrete Gothic: an unusual style for Perret but nevertheless one of his most influential buildings.

enough to offend bourgeois taste in the Paris of 1913, but it was not revolutionary in the sense that, say, Stravinsky's *Rite of Spring*, which received its riot-provoking first performance in the theatre on 29 May 1913, was revolutionary.

Perret's architectural language was basically classical, and was to remain so for the rest of his career, but with one important exception. The church of Notre-Dame du Raincy, to the east of Paris, completed in 1923, might be described as concrete Gothic, with a basilica plan. Thin, fluted, tapering columns support a shallow longitudinal vault that changes direction over the side aisles, as it does in certain French Romanesque churches. The entire external wall is a perforated concrete curtain filled with stained glass – a monumental version of that glass block staircase wall at Rue Franklin. At the west end the stepped concrete tower, though huge, seems almost like an afterthought. The simplicity of this composition and above all the unashamed use of exposed concrete for both structure and enclosing wall seem truly modern, despite the Gothic overtones.

Perret used concrete arches in some industrial buildings, for example the Esders clothing factory in Paris of 1919, but mainly his was an architecture of columns and beams. What in traditional classical architecture were often merely ornamental representations of structure, Perret made real, in concrete. As his post-Second World War reconstruction of the city of Le Havre testifies, he continued to design concrete buildings in a plain classical style until his death in 1954. But by then his work looked decidedly old fashioned.

Younger architects like Le Corbusier had taken concrete in a new direction.

Concrete and form

We will see in other chapters how later architects exploited concrete's sculptural potential, but one pre-First World War building stands out as a daring feat of monumental concrete construction: the Jahrhunderthalle (Centennial Hall) in Breslau, Germany (now Wrocław, Poland) by Max Berg, completed in 1913. Built as the centrepiece of an exhibition to commemorate the hundredth anniversary of the defeat of Napoleon at the Battle of Leipzig, it was, and is, a multi-purpose assembly hall with seating for about 7,000 people. A ribbed saucer dome sits on a horizontal ring beam 65 metres (213 feet) in diameter, which is raised on just four mighty arches and braced all round by curved flying buttresses. Raked seating spills through the arches on four sides of a column-free arena. The general arrangement is similar to the traditional dome-on-pendentives form of a Byzantine or Renaissance church, except that the four arches are curved in line with the ring beam, creating an impression of plasticity appropriate to the fluid nature of concrete. Another innovation is the complete absence internally of any traditional architectural ornament. Functional structure creates its own aesthetic in a strikingly modern way, as if this were a piece of pure engineering like a bridge or a grain silo. Outside the impression is rather different. The stepped roof looks somewhat pedestrian, facetted rather than curved, and the main entrance is marked by a semi-circular portico of plain classical columns that might almost have been

Centennial Hall, Wrocław, Poland. Max Berg, 1913. Arches are curved in plan as well as elevation, creating a sinuous line that shows off the concrete's fluidity.

designed by Perret. Even a building as daring and original as this could not, it seems, completely dispense with architectural tradition.

Unique, freestanding buildings set in landscaped parks give opportunities for form-making that are denied to the compromised civic architecture of apartment blocks, garages, theatres and even churches. In the long run, the modest structural frame of reinforced concrete was more important to the future of modern architecture than the spectacular dome or the elegant bridge. Two younger architects shared Perret's vision of a new concrete architecture that would transform the city. They were Tony Garnier and Charles-Edouard Jeanneret, later known as Le Corbusier. Before 1914 their contributions were limited to theoretical projects, but these were to be more influential than even the most progressive built works of the time.

Tony Garnier, like Auguste Perret, studied in the atelier of Julien Guadet at the Ecole des Beaux-Arts in Paris. In 1899 he won the Prix de Rome and spent the next four years at the French Academy in the Villa Medici working on a visionary project called the Cité Industrielle. The project was exhibited in Paris in 1904, though it was not published comprehensively until 1917. Garnier was a socialist and his city is a kind of Utopia with a population of about 35,000. It is divided into two parts, a factory district close to the hydro-electric plant on the river, and a residential quarter on higher ground to the north. The plan is informal in outline and developed at low density but, unlike the first English garden cities, its streets and avenues conform to a rectilinear grid. What is most

interesting from an architectural point of view, however, is the style that Garnier invented to make his vision tangible not just in plan but in perspective and aerial views. It is modern and based on concrete construction. The population lives mainly in two-storey concrete houses set among trees in fenceless parkland. These houses are flat roofed with parapet walls in which a single groove is the only suggestion of a traditional cornice. Their windows are plain openings and their only ornaments are plant containers, canopies and pergolas. Public buildings in the Cité Industrielle exploit the structural potential of reinforced concrete to an extent that was probably not practical at the time. The forecourt of the railway station, for example, is sheltered by an impossibly thin concrete canopy cantilevered from a pair of slender columns, their mushroom capitals merging seamlessly with the soffit. Such futuristic images were to be an inspiration to Modernist architects for decades to come.

Jeanneret met Garnier in Lyons in 1907, just before taking up an appointment as a part-time assistant in Perret's Paris office. He absorbed the influence of both men and, with the help of an old structural engineer friend, Max Dubois, produced his own vision of a concrete future. He called it the Maison Dom-ino and summed it up in a small perspective drawing to which, for once, the over-used word 'iconic' seems applicable. Every history of modern architecture includes this drawing because, though simple, it seems to contain all the essential genetic material for the development of the Modernist style. It shows the naked concrete structure of a small two-storey house: three flat rectangular slabs – ground floor, first floor and roof – supported by six columns of square cross section, with a cantilevered double dog-leg

---

Cité Industrielle project. Tony Garnier, 1904. The architecture is modern, even Modernist, and based on concrete construction.

Concept sketch for Dom-ino House. Le Corbusier, 1914. A miniature manifesto to inaugurate the age of Modernism.

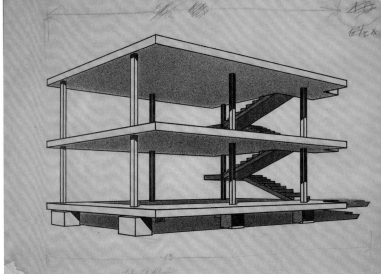

staircase in one corner. How can such a simple design be so important? The answer lies in the details. Jeanneret was familiar with the Hennebique system of reinforced-concrete construction but here he makes one crucial modification: he dispenses with beams. Perhaps he was inspired by that thin canopy on Garnier's railway station. Dubois would no doubt have pointed out the necessity for increased reinforcement at the column–slab junctions, but the modification was feasible structurally, and architecturally it opened up exciting possibilities. It meant, for example, that the positions of the columns were no longer fixed by the grid of the beams they supported. They could be moved around freely. In this case the move is a slight one, away from the edge of the slab, leaving a small cantilever, but it means that the external walls no longer have to accommodate the columns; they can simply sail past on the outside. Frame structures, whether of steel or concrete, always had a liberating effect on the plan of a building. In a 'flat slab' structure like this – not really a frame at all – that freedom is increased, suggesting a completely new architectural concept.

Jeanneret would later develop and codify this concept in his famous 'Five Points' (see Chapter 9) but for now the idea was simply to place these small, possibly mass-produced, units end to end on the site like dominoes on a table and in-fill them with blockwork walls and standard windows to make cheap, flexible housing. Jeanneret's sketches show a mixture of ordinary domestic windows and factory-style glazing, sometimes turning the corner of a block where in traditional loadbearing wall construction you would expect to find a solid pier. Garnier's influence is palpable, and a certain solidity and formality is still apparent. This is not yet a revolutionary new style but all the ingredients are present, encapsulated in that iconic image.

Garnier's comprehensive urban plan and Jeanneret's concise sketch both in their different ways illustrated the liberating potential of reinforced concrete. But more than that, they seemed to say that the ancient art of architecture had nothing to fear from modern technology; on the contrary, technology could reinvigorate architecture. In Italy a literary and artistic movement called Futurism, led by a wealthy poet, Filippo Marinetti, was saying something similar about art in general. In their foundation manifesto, published in *Le Figaro* on 20 February 1909, the Futurists declared their love of machines like automobiles, locomotives and power stations, and their hatred of all traditional institutions like museums, libraries and academies. Two more manifestos appeared, on painting in 1910 and sculpture in 1912. Politically, the Futurists were proto-fascist, glorifying war as 'the world's only hygiene'. Futurist artists included Carlo Carrà, Luigi Russolo, Giacomo Balla, Umberto Boccioni and Gino Severini. The painter and sculptor Boccioni is perhaps the best known. His set of three paintings called *States of Mind*, which attempts

to represent, in semi-abstract imagery, the emotions of people in a railway station, was strongly influenced by the Cubism of Picasso and Braque. His dynamic sculptural representation of a running figure, called *Unique Forms of Continuity in Space*, has come to symbolize the spirit of Futurism. In Milan in 1914, Antonio Sant'Elia, a young Italian architect as yet unconnected with the Futurists, exhibited a collection of his sketches of imaginary modern buildings under the title *Città Nuova* (New City). The accompanying text, or 'Messaggio', called for an architectural revolution: 'Architecture, exhausted by tradition, begins again, forcibly, from the beginning. Calculations of the resistance of materials, the use of reinforced concrete and iron, exclude "Architecture" as understood in the classical and traditional sense.'[3] Marinetti saw the exhibition and promptly recruited Sant'Elia to the Futurist cause, publishing an edited version of the Messaggio as yet another manifesto, *Futurist Architecture*.

But there are mismatches between Futurist words and Futurist images. 'We have lost the sense of the monumental, the massive, the static, and we have enriched our sensibilities with a taste for the light and the practical,' says the Messaggio at one point. In a later passage, added by Marinetti, the idea is developed further: 'Our houses

Unique Forms of Continuity in Space. Umberto Boccioni, 1913. Movement cast in bronze: the Futurists were iconoclasts but also strangely traditional.

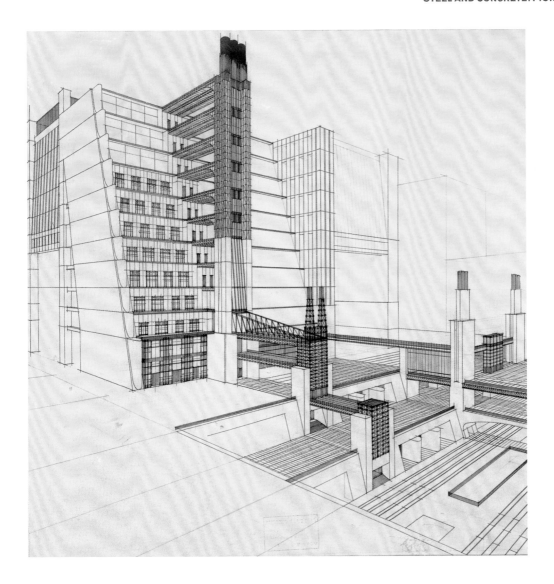

Apartment building, Città Nuova project. Antonio Sant'Elia, 1914. Stepped forms and gantry-like service towers would reappear in British architecture of the 1970s.

will last less time than we do and every generation will have to make its own.'⁴ Futurist buildings, we are led to believe, will be insubstantial, adaptable and disposable, creating a shifting, dynamic urban environment. But what we see in Sant'Elia's dramatically foreshortened perspectives is the very opposite: huge concrete structures for which the adjectives 'monumental', 'massive' and 'static' seem perfectly apt. Functional types are characteristically modern – power stations, transport interchanges, airship hangars, multi-storey apartment blocks – and traditional ornament has been banished, but compositionally these buildings are almost Beaux-Arts in their symmetry and articulation. Kenneth Frampton has pointed out that they owe something to the Italian Art Nouveau or *Stile Liberty* architect Giuseppe Sommaruga. Sommaruga's Faccanoni Mausoleum of 1907, for example, looks in retrospect like a Sant'Elia composition that has succumbed to an encrustation of ornament.⁵

And yet there is no doubting the prophetic power of Sant'Elia's vision. No overall plan is provided for the Città Nuova but it is evidently a city based on a multi-level high-speed transport system from which what would now be called megastructures of concrete and steel erupt to a height of 16 storeys or more. Tower-like forms taper upwards, emphasizing their verticality. A favourite type is the stepped-back apartment block served by vertical lift towers with gradually lengthening bridges. The usual material is plain concrete, sometimes giving way to steel frames at the upper levels. 'Dynamic' is the word most often used to describe this architecture, but it is a metaphorical rather than a literal dynamism. The cars and trains and lifts might be fast moving but the buildings are solid and permanent. Sant'Elia built very little but his 'paper architecture' was to be realized in American skyscrapers of the 1930s, in Brutalist megastructures of the 1960s, and in High Tech office buildings of the 1980s. Sadly he did not live to see these tributes to him. He was killed fighting in the eighth Battle of the Isonzo, near Monfalcone, in 1916 at the age of 28.

There can be no better refutation of the conventional historical opposition between Beaux-Arts and Modernist styles than the career of Albert Kahn. Kahn was a giant of twentieth-century architecture whom history has somewhat neglected. He was born the son of a rabbi in Rhaunen, Germany, in 1869 but his family emigrated to America in 1880 and settled in Detroit. At the age of 15 he took a job as an office boy in a local architectural practice, Mason and Rice, where his talents as a draughtsman, and then as a designer, were soon recognized and exploited. In 1891 he won a scholarship for a year's study abroad and went to Florence, where he met Henry Bacon, later the architect of the Lincoln Memorial in Washington, who was then working for McKim, Mead and White. The two toured Italy, France, Belgium and Germany, studying old buildings and recording them in their sketchbooks. It was probably through the influence of Bacon that Kahn adopted Charles McKim as his lifelong architectural hero.

When Kahn returned to the Mason and Rice office, he began to apply his now deepened knowledge of classical and Gothic architecture to designs for various houses and office buildings for local businessmen and industrialists. He left the practice in 1896, and eventually gained his full professional independence in 1902. Typical of Kahn's architecture of this period is the Temple Beth El at 3424 Woodward Avenue, Detroit (now the Bonstelle Theatre) – a miniature Pantheon externally, domed and porticoed, but internally decorated in the Louis XVI style. Kahn could create effective compositions in many different styles – Greek, Roman, Tudor, ecclesiastical Gothic, Italian and French Renaissance, even English Arts and Crafts. Such eclecticism was to remain a guiding principle throughout his career. He believed in the importance of history and precedent, and in an appropriate match of style to function. 'If, in re-employing older forms and applying them to our newer problems, we have done wrong,' he wrote, 'then all architecture of the past is wrong, for all of it is but a development of what was done before.'[1] Progressive modern

architects are not supposed to stick up for historicism in this way, so was Kahn's architecture just an irrelevant left-over from the nineteenth century? To argue this, we would have to ignore the aspect of his career on which his historical reputation almost entirely rests: his designs for factories.

First factories

Kahn was German born but Detroit was his home and he made an important contribution to the growth of that city's industrial power and fame. One of the first factories he designed was for the Burroughs Adding Machine Company. Completed in 1905, it consisted of a wood-and-iron production building with saw-tooth roof-lights, and a two-storey office building on the street front entered through a classical portico. Such a combination of the functional and the monumental was typical of Kahn, who could deliver both with equal skill. By 1905 he had already built nine utilitarian production buildings for the Packard Motor Corporation Company, using conventional construction methods with wooden floors. For Building No. 10 he decided to use a

Temple Beth El, Detroit, USA. Albert Kahn, 1903.
Stylistically, Kahn was a pluralist, as happy designing a miniature Pantheon as a utilitarian factory.

Packard Building No. 10, Detroit, Michigan, USA. Albert Kahn, 1905. Kahn's utilitarian style at its most basic. Reyner Banham called it 'cheap and nasty'.

reinforced concrete frame, because it was fireproof and allowed longer spans between columns. It was the first concrete-framed factory in Detroit. Kahn was helped by his brother Julius, who was a structural engineer and had developed a new type of steel reinforcement known as the 'Kahn bar'. The brothers were now well placed to provide architectural and engineering services for Detroit's fast-growing automobile industry.

In 1907, Henry Ford bought 53 hectares (130 acres) of land in the suburb of Highland Park, where he planned to build a new plant in which for the first time all the phases of car production would be combined in a single continuous process. Kahn got the job. The first Highland Park building, completed in 1909, was long and narrow, four storeys high, with a concrete frame and all-glass external walls, the steel frames of which were imported from England. Service towers containing stairs, lifts, toilets and changing rooms were placed outside the main volume so that the floor spaces were uninterrupted except by two rows of concrete columns. It was a factory but also a kind of laboratory in which Henry Ford could experiment with different arrangements of men and machines to achieve maximum production efficiency. This was the building in which mass production was born. Technically it was very advanced, yet it was still a piece of classical architecture. Its columns were clad in brickwork on the ground floor to form a visually solid base and there was a simplified concrete cornice at the top. On the drawing board, even

with these concessions to architectural decorum, the elevations must have seemed brutally monotonous, their extreme horizontality conflicting with the essentially vertical expectations of traditional classical architecture. Kahn therefore introduced tower-like brick panels with artificial stone dressings and decorative friezes, at the corners and at intervals in the facade along Woodward Avenue. Functionalism had not entirely supplanted tradition even in this stronghold of technological pragmatism.

Why did Kahn feel the need to apply traditional architectural ornament to this otherwise functional building? He had not, after all, considered it necessary in Packard Building No. 10, which was functional to the point of coarseness. (When Reyner Banham visited it in the 1980s he found it 'cheap and nasty'.)[2] Woodward Avenue was, and is, a major Detroit thoroughfare and the building was therefore on show in a way that the Packard plant was not. Perhaps the architecture was a kind of advertisement. It seems unlikely, however, that the arch-pragmatist Henry Ford would have seen classical architecture as in any way relevant to the promotion of his cheap, popular and technically advanced product, the Model T. The sense of tradition and decorum came not from the client but from his architect. In later factories, for Ford at the new River Rouge plant from 1917 onwards, and subsequently for many other vehicle and aircraft manufacturers, Kahn did eventually dispense with traditional ornament. But in attendant structures like the Ford administration building of 1925 or the engineering

(Above) Highland Park Ford Plant, Michigan, USA. Albert Kahn, 1910. A functional factory but with enough traditional architecture to keep it respectable.

(Left) Ford Engineering Laboratory, Rouge River Plant, Detroit, USA. Albert Kahn, 1925. Classicism pressed into industrial service. Four Doric columns 'in antis' mark the main entrance.

laboratory of the same year, he stayed loyal to his classical training. And when designing public buildings in the city centre, such as the Detroit Athletic Club of 1915 or the police headquarters of 1923, his classicism was undiluted. By 1928, when he designed Detroit's first skyscraper, the Fisher Building, Kahn had added Art Deco, arguably an offspring of the Beaux-Arts tradition, to his stylistic repertoire. Kahn's parallel allegiance to the functional and the traditional did not mean that he thought factories were unworthy of architectural attention. Later buildings like the Chrysler half-ton truck plant of 1938 or the B-25 bomber assembly plant, completed after his death in 1942, were supremely elegant architectural solutions in both the abstract and the visible sense. Kahn saw tradition as the essential basis of all modern architecture, whatever its purpose. In his own words: 'The attempt to continue a vital architecture and one relating to and enriching our own time instead of merely repeating old forms is, of course, proper.

Detroit Police HQ, Michigan, USA.
Albert Kahn, 1921. Away from the factory
Kahn returned to an utterly conventional
urban classicism.

What is wrong with the [modern] movement today is the throwing to the winds all precedent, the idea that the new style may be created by an abandonment of all old.'[3]

Kahn's connection with Henry Ford was more than just an accident of history. He may have had old-fashioned ideas about architectural style, but he was attuned to the rhythms of business and industry, and in this field if in few others the two men shared a vision. Kahn understood the importance of efficiency and economy and of what Frederick Winslow Taylor called 'scientific management'. Ford applied the principles of scientific management to the production of cars; Kahn applied them to the production of architecture. By the 1940s, Kahn's office was employing 450 architects and engineers, all participating in a co-ordinated hierarchical management system with Kahn himself at the top, supervising every major project. According to Henry Magaziner, who wrote a brief memoir of the Kahn office as it was in the 1940s, Kahn would meet his job captains one by one every Monday, each with a sheaf of blueprints representing the week's work. The drawings would be rapidly scanned, suggestions made on even the smallest details, and precedents in previous jobs pointed out.[4]

Kahn's oft-quoted aphorism 'Architecture is 90 per cent business and 10 per cent art' may be one of the reasons for the faintness of history's praise of him. Another reason might be his stylistic broadmindedness, which could not easily be accommodated in a story about the revolutionary fervour of Modernism. But there can be no doubt that Kahn was an extraordinarily successful and productive practitioner, that he was a superb designer both technically and artistically, and that his buildings were an inspiration to many of those architects to whom history has been more generous.

To trace one of the channels of Kahn's influence we must return to Europe, and in particular to Germany. In 1907 the German architect and diplomat Hermann Muthesius helped to found the Deutscher Werkbund, an association of architects, designers and industrialists who were dedicated to improving the quality of German industrial products. Muthesius had been a supplementary trade attaché in London, where he wrote *Das Englische Haus* (see Chapter 2). Werkbund meetings, in particular the congress of 1911, which took the 'The Spiritualization of German Production' as its theme, were attended by many architects who later became famous as pioneers of Modernism. They included Walter Gropius, Mies van der Rohe, Bruno Taut and Charles-Edouard Jeanneret, who later called himself Le Corbusier. In his keynote speech at the congress, Muthesius outlined a concept of design quality that is familiar now but was new then: that standardization could be a good thing, that a beautiful object (or a building) could be made of cheap materials, and that abstract form was more important than ornament.[5]

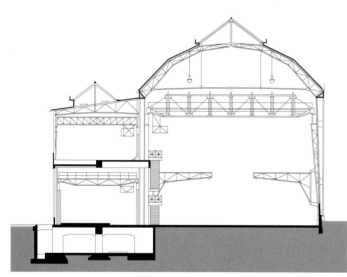

Section

```
0      5      10m
|——|——|——|
   15      30 ft
```

Peter Behrens

One of Muthesius's closest colleagues in the Werkbund was the architect Peter Behrens, a key figure in the history of Modernism, perhaps less for his own output, important though it was, than for the fact that Gropius, Mies van der Rohe and Jeanneret all worked in his office. In 1907 Behrens had been appointed design consultant to the Allgemeine Elektricitäts-Gesellschaft (General Electricity Company) or AEG. He was responsible for product design and what would now be called 'corporate image' as well as for the design of buildings. The best known of Behrens's buildings for AEG is the Turbine Assembly Hall, built in 1909

on a prominent corner site in the Moabit district of Berlin. It was essentially a housing for a travelling crane that moved the heavy generator turbines from one production station to another. Externally exposed steel portal frames, tapering to their visibly hinged bases, are in-filled with glass walls that lean slightly inwards. This visual lightness is contradicted at the corners, where there is no steel frame and the leaning glass in-fill is replaced by poured concrete with horizontal grooves in imitation of stone courses. These corner bastions also lean inwards but the glass end wall between them is vertical and appears, against all reason, to support a huge concrete gable or pediment with a facetted profile. This is very far from being a purely utilitarian industrial shed. Like Kahn's Highland Park building, it was designed to present a respectable face to passers-by on a busy street, and it does this by an appeal to architectural tradition. Clearly it is some species of classical temple. The fact is that, although he played his part in the development of Modernism, Behrens was essentially a classical architect. To confirm this we only have to look at his German embassy in St Petersburg of 1913 with its rank of tall, thin Doric columns and its bronze roof sculpture, 6 metres (20 feet) high, of the mythical twins Castor and Pollux with their horses. The building was much admired by Adolf Hitler's architect, Albert Speer (see Chapter 14).

Walter Gropius

Walter Gropius was one of the many ambitious and talented young architects who worked in the Behrens office around the time the Turbine Assembly Hall was being designed. He came from a cultured German family. His father was

an architect and his great-uncle, Martin Gropius, had
been a pupil of the great Karl Friedrich Schinkel. Walter
was himself to become a powerfully influential architect,
as founding director of the Bauhaus (see Chapter 8),
as a designer of innovative mass housing and, after his
emigration to the United States in 1937, as a Harvard
professor and head of a large multidisciplinary practice.
The conservative critic Tom Wolfe described him, not
without irony, as 'the silver prince' of Modernism.[6] In 1910,
when he was 27 years old and anxious to emerge from
Behrens's shadow, Gropius set up in practice with another
ex-Behrens employee, Adolf Meyer. The following year
they landed a sizeable industrial commission, to design a
factory at Alfeld, Lower Saxony for the Fagus company, a
manufacturer of wooden shoe lasts. The commission was
not, however, straightforward. Gropius and Meyer were to
collaborate with another local architect, Eduard Werner,
who had already prepared outline proposals. The company
was forward looking, with American connections, and
wanted the new factory to reflect their progressive
character. Gropius and Meyer would mainly be responsible
for the external appearance of the building. Despite this
limitation, the young architects seized their opportunity
and produced a truly original work of architecture.

The debt to Behrens's Turbine Assembly Hall is obvious, but
the differences between the two buildings are also crucial.
The most photographed, and therefore most influential,
part of the Fagus factory is the three-storey office wing. Its
external walls do not quite qualify as curtain walls because
they fill in the space between the structural brick piers rather
than enclosing them completely. But they are continuous over
the three storeys, with opaque lightweight panels instead of
glass to conceal the floor edges. There are no piers at the
corners. Floors and roof cantilever out and the glass wall
continues uninterrupted. A daring cantilevered concrete
staircase occupies the most prominent corner. In contrast to
all this suave airiness the main entrance is a solidly traditional
brick box with steps, door and clock all placed dead centre.
One subtle detail tells us that this building is a commentary
on, or perhaps a homage to, the Turbine Assembly Hall: the
brick piers lean slightly inwards so that they are recessed
from the line of the vertical glazing. This is a clear echo of the
way that solid and void change places between the side and
end walls of the Turbine Assembly Hall. And surely Gropius

and Meyer's glazed corners represent the logical step that Behrens, with his concrete bastions, was afraid to take. The Fagus factory is not a classical building; it is a Modernist building, one of the very first.

Gropius and Meyer's next important building was a model factory for the 1914 Werkbund Exhibition in Cologne. Once again, glass and brick are the main materials, used in provocative ways. Glass seems to have freed itself completely from its supporting structure and become an external walling material in its own right. In the office block at the front of the building, a solid brick centre is flanked by two spiral staircases completely enclosed by glass. The reverse arrangement – an open centre with solid wings – would be more conventional, which is perhaps why it was rejected. And yet, despite this demonstration of the spatial potential of new building technologies, in some ways this exhibition building re-establishes a connection with architectural tradition. It is an axial, elemental, almost Beaux-Arts composition that separates the futuristic office building at the front from the plain but elegant machine hall at the back. Whereas Behrens had dignified heavy engineering by clothing it in 'Architecture', Gropius and

Meyer still focussed their architectural attention on the clean, non-industrial part of the building.

These German buildings are historically important because they represent a fundamental change of attitude among progressive architects of the period. The English Arts and Crafts movement, led by William Morris, had rejected monumentality and stylistic eclecticism in favour of a more practical and functional approach to design. But the movement's hero had been the skilled artisan, not the factory worker, and it had deplored the social and urban consequences of industrialization. The steam-powered textile mills, the acres of cheap mass housing, the iron foundries, the great railway termini, not to mention the tacky, tasteless household trappings of bourgeois consumerism: these visible products of the Industrial Revolution had simply been ignored. In his novel *News from Nowhere* Morris dreamt that one day they would all be swept away and England would return to a state of pre-industrial harmony

Fagus Factory, Lower Saxony, Germany. Walter Gropius and Adolf Meyer, 1913. It was the glazed corners that decided this building's historical role as a herald of Modernism.

and tranquillity. Hermann Muthesius had recognized the forward step that Morris and his followers – architects like Philip Webb, C. R. Ashbee and C. F. A. Voysey – had taken, but he also recognized their blindness. He knew that the economic power of industry was not to be resisted, and that architects, if they were to maintain their status in society, must collaborate with it. In 1914 he made another speech to Werkbund delegates at the Cologne exhibition. The emphasis this time was on the importance of developing standard product types suitable for mass production. He declared his faith in large-scale industrial concerns that would mass-produce standardized but well-designed products for an international market. Artists, architects and designers must help industry to improve the quality of products. He clearly had Behrens's relationship with AEG in mind.[7] Such sentiments are commonplace today, but in 1914 the idea of an alliance between mechanized industry and the ancient art of architecture was new.

But what exactly was the relevance of mass production to architecture? Factories had to be designed to accommodate the production lines but were the factories themselves to be mass produced? It was hard to see how buildings could be made in factories. There was, however, one possible exception: popular housing. In 1910 Gropius wrote a memo to the management of AEG headed 'Programme for the Establishment of a Company for the Provision of Housing on Aesthetically Consistent Principles'.[8] In it he set out detailed proposals for the factory production of houses, or rather of a range of standard components that could be combined to make several different house types. Had the pitch been successful, it would have been the perfect example of a Muthesian collaboration between architect and manufacturer. But it was not successful. AEG was not ready to enter the housing market, and even if it had been it would not necessarily have welcomed Gropius's overture. The problem was not that the prefabrication of houses was impractical. Houses had been successfully prefabricated in large numbers throughout the nineteenth century, often for export to the colonies, and would continue to be so for decades to come. The problem lay in that phrase 'on aesthetically consistent principles'. The experience of the next hundred years would show that the prefabricated house industry could manage perfectly well without 'aesthetic principles'. Art needed industry but industry did not need art. Gropius's failed pitch is emblematic of a cultural blind spot that afflicts architecture to this day.

Gropius's approach to factory design was quite different from Albert Kahn's. Kahn was content to apply 'proper' traditional architecture to those parts of the building that required it, and to refrain from applying it where it would be an unnecessary expense. For Gropius this was a craven compromise. All historically derived ornament, even Behrens's austere classicism, must be swept away so that the beauty of efficient structure and plain materials could shine through. Architecture's new accommodation with industrial culture must be made apparent in pure abstract form. Unadorned industrial buildings were nothing new, of course. Mills, wharves and warehouses of loadbearing brick with cast-iron internal columns were commonplace. It was the new spatial and formal possibilities offered by steel and reinforced concrete that excited progressive young architects like Gropius and Meyer. They wanted to claim these technologies as the basis for their new architecture. When, in 1913, Gropius wrote an article about modern industrial architecture in the Werkbund yearbook he illustrated it with pictures of cylindrical concrete grain elevators in Buffalo and Minneapolis, and 'daylight factories' (to borrow Reyner Banham's term) in Cincinnati and Detroit. Albert Kahn's first Highland Park building for Ford was included, even though, as we have seen, it was traditionally ornamented because of its prominent position in the city.[9] These pictures of American buildings were to be recycled in later works of Modernist propaganda, most notably in Le Corbusier's famous book *Vers une architecture* (see Chapter 9). Le Corbusier felt the need to doctor the photographs, removing the Beaux-Arts ornaments that actually graced the buildings.

It is ironic that the work of a traditionalist like Kahn should be used to support the argument of a pioneer Modernist like Gropius. But perhaps there was also an influence in the other direction. Masterpieces of Kahn's later career, such as the diesel engine plant for General Motors in Redford, Michigan, were surely a realization of Gropius's ideals. The unadorned abstract style that had started as a crude expedient in the 1905 Packard Building No. 10 had by 1938. become Modernist architecture of the utmost purity.

Frank Lloyd Wright

Incipient European modernism, then, looked to American industrial buildings for inspiration, but it also looked to Frank Lloyd Wright. Historians have remarked how the office frontage of Gropius and Meyer's 1914 Werkbund pavilion is 'Wrightian' in its general profile. Wright did not design any factories but he came close to it in the administration block that he built in 1906 for the Larkin mail order company of Buffalo. Gropius would have been familiar with the design through Ernst Wasmuth's portfolio published in 1911. The Larkin Administration Building, which was demolished in 1950, was one of the masterpieces of Wright's early career. It was quite unlike his Prairie houses of the same period yet equally accomplished. Where the houses were wide and low, reaching out to embrace their leafy suburban surroundings, the Larkin Building, sited next to the company's factories and warehouses, was fortress-like and inward looking. It was five storeys high with open-plan floors surrounding a central top-lit atrium. Though not a factory, it resembled one in the openness of its floor plan, in the mechanistic layout of its

General Motors Diesel Engine Assembly Plant, Redford, Michigan, USA. Albert Kahn, 1938. Traditional architecture disappears and Kahn proves himself a master of Modernist purity.

purpose-made desks and in the production line sequencing of the clerical work carried out in it. Every bit as 'Taylorist' as Ford's Highland Park plant, it was also an architectural work of great conviction. Symmetrically ordered, tower-like forms contained the staircases and ducts necessary to service the single, multi-level working space. The main entrance was not symmetrically placed on the long axis as one might expect but slid into a generous reception area like the foyer of a theatre in a linked block to one side. Heroic figures and globes ornamented the building externally; inside, inspirational inscriptions encouraged diligence among the workforce. The structure was of steel and concrete but the main visible material was brick. In the Larkin Building Wright proved that he was more than just a domestic architect. When the occasion demanded it, he could command a complex industrial brief and invent a whole new style to accommodate it, one that has been influential ever since. This was one of the very first deep-planned, inward-looking, artificially ventilated office buildings in the world. Its top-lit atrium and attendant service towers were to become clichés of twentieth-century commercial architecture. Here we see them in their first freshness.

A couple of years later, Wright adapted this new vertical, articulated style to suit the requirements of a very different building type, a Unitarian church in the Chicago suburb of Oak Park. Smaller and lower than the Larkin Building, the Unity Temple is nevertheless composed of similar forms combined in similar ways. For example, the relationship

Larkin Administration Building, Buffalo, New York, USA. Frank Lloyd Wright, 1906. A forerunner of the 'atrium' office building, though no later version ever bettered it.

Ground floor plan
1. Office area
2. Reception
3. Light court
4. Entrance

0   5   10m
          15   30 ft

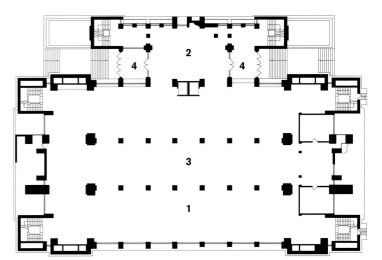

between the main worship space and the secondary 'church hall' is similar to that between the office block and the entrance block of the Larkin Building, though the proportions are different. Externally, the Unity Temple leaves its in-situ concrete walls exposed; internally it is richly but abstractly ornamented. The building is, of course, tangential to this discussion of transatlantic developments in industrial architecture but it is not completely irrelevant. What we see in these buildings by Kahn, Behrens, Gropius and Wright is the emergence of a new idea: that all of architecture, not just industrial architecture, might learn something from that lowly, practical building type, the factory. Historians have

sometimes used the phrase 'factory aesthetic' to sum up the peculiar beauty of plain, functional buildings. We have got used to thinking of it as a kind of cleanliness, a clearing away of the unnecessary clutter of the historical styles. But traces of the old ornament still cling to these buildings and perhaps architectural tradition runs deeper in them than we think. At that time, buildings were still judged by old-fashioned criteria such as scale, proportion, articulation and coherence, and they would continue to be so for decades to come. The factory exerted its influence but architecture was still architecture, a symbolic as much as a functional art.

Unity Temple, Oak Park, Illinois, USA. Frank Lloyd Wright, 1908. Another vertical composition though still showing a family resemblance to the 'Prairie' houses.

Taylorism and Fordism

In the 1880s Frederick Winslow Taylor began studying work processes and thinking of ways to make them more efficient. With the growth of mechanization, the old craft traditions were disappearing. Machines were tireless workers; how could the productivity of human workers be increased to match? The very word 'productivity' – production per person – was a Taylorist concept. Taylor's theories, summed up in *The Principles of Scientific Management*, published in 1911, were not as coldly inhuman as one might suppose. He recognized, for example, that it was necessary to motivate a workforce in order to improve its performance, which might mean better working conditions and higher wages, always provided that efficiency could be monitored, often by the introduction of piece-work. Management and workers were seen as part of a single system that by reasoned analysis could be improved for the benefit of all.

'Fordism' – Henry Ford's method for the efficient mass production of identical products through the division of labour – was similar to Taylorism, but seems to have arisen independently. Both concepts profoundly affected the development of Modernism in architecture. They represented a new scientific rationality that progressive architects were keen to emulate. Architecture was an old craft tradition. It needed to be modernized – Taylorized –

in order to survive in the machine age. Architecture could serve society by giving form to Taylorist ideas, not in public monuments but in ordinary buildings like factories and houses. Gropius's attempt in 1911 to persuade AEG to undertake the prefabrication of houses (see page 67) represents this ambition. Le Corbusier, writing about *maisons en série* (mass-produced housing) in his book *Vers une architecture* (see page 113), specifically acknowledges Taylor's influence. Le Corbusier's concept of the house as 'a machine for living in' was a call for the expansion of Taylorism into every aspect of daily life, even the sanctum of the family home. And in his urban projects, like the Ville Contemporaine or the Plan Voisin for Paris – named for and sponsored by a car manufacturer – we see the urban equivalent of the Taylorized factory. The site is cleared, like the shop floor of Albert Kahn's Highland Park factory for Ford, the buildings are laid out in functional zones like pieces of equipment, and every worker, from the captain of industry to the humble labourer, is allocated a place in the social and physical hierarchy.

Ford production line, Highland Park, Detroit, USA, c.1914.
Openness and flexibility – a Modernist feature that would later appear even in houses.

06 | EXPRESSIONISM
1914–1941

If this were a history of building then it would be necessary at this point to describe in some detail the political, economic and social consequences of the First World War. But this is a history of architecture, not building, and it is the cultural consequences of that global convulsion that are most relevant, in particular its effect on the minds of forward-looking architects. It is tempting to simplify the story in some such trite formulation as 'a completely new architecture emerged from the ashes of war' but history is not so neat and tidy. We have seen how the beginnings of a modern style can be traced in certain pre-war works, such as Gropius and Meyer's factories, Tony Garnier's Cité Industrielle and Le Corbusier's Maison Dom-ino concept, not to mention the Prairie houses of Frank Lloyd Wright. Immediately after the war there was what, in hindsight, seems like a hesitation or wavering among progressive architects in Europe, a reluctance to face the problem at hand and begin working out what contribution

architecture might make to the reconstruction of civic culture. The hesitation was, of course, partly the result of a dearth of opportunities to build, especially in Germany, but architecture does not entirely depend upon building. Visionary projects that never get further than drawings and models can sometimes be more important historically than conservative buildings. 'Hesitation' and 'wavering' are negative words; history has provided a more positive alternative: 'Expressionism'. Like most stylistic labels it is imprecise and to some extent misleading, but it was used at the time so its application is not entirely retrospective.

Bruno Taut

A key figure in the development of Expressionism was Bruno Taut, who had been, with Walter Gropius, a member of the Werkbund before the war. In Werkbund conference debates about the future of architecture, Taut tended to side with Henry van der Velde, who saw architecture as a spiritual and

Glass Pavilion, Werkbund Exhibition, Germany. Bruno Taut, 1914. What would later be called a 'geodesic dome' is raised on a plinth like a monument.

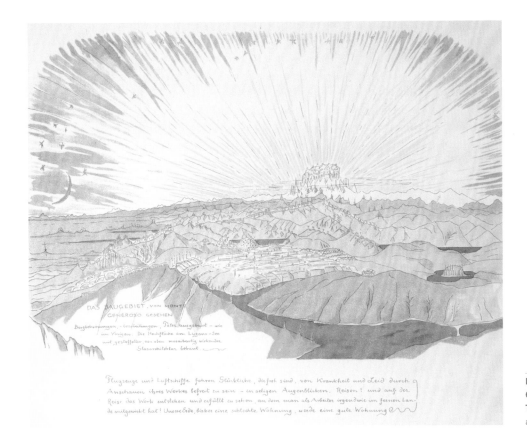

DAS BAUGEBIET. VON MONTE
GENEROSO GESEHEN

Building region seen from Monte Generoso. Drawing by Bruno Taut, 1919. A shining vision of hope after the dark horrors of war.

emotional art form, rather than with Hermann Muthesius, who aimed to reconcile architecture to the demands of manufacturing industry. Taut's Glass Pavilion, near the entrance to the 1914 Werkbund Exhibition in Cologne, was designed to show off the products of the German glass industry but it did so in a form inspired more by religion than commerce. A circular drum made of glass bricks was crowned by a pointed dome of coloured glass held in what would now be called a 'geodesic', reinforced concrete frame. The space inside was filled by winding, steel-framed glass staircases and an elaborate artificial waterfall. The visitor's journey up into the dome was a journey into light and spirituality. It was a Gothic creation to set against the basically classical compositions of Gropius and Meyer elsewhere on the site.

Taut was inspired by the vision of a poet, Paul Scheerbart, who wrote a book called *Glasarchitektur* in which he imagined building forms that would let light into people's minds as well as into interior spaces. It was a vision of hope after the dark horrors of the war. With nothing to build, it was time to dream. In 1919 Taut initiated the Glass Chain, a secret exchange of letters between like-minded artists and architects including Gropius, Hans Scharoun, Hermann Finsterlin, the brothers Hans and Wassili Luckhardt, and Taut's brother, Max. The correspondents adopted noms-de-plume and expressed their Utopian ideas about architecture and life in quasi-religious language. Taut also published three books in this period, *Alpine Architektur, Die Auflösung der Städte* ('The Resolution of Cities') and *Die Städtkrone* ('The City Crown'), which contained various projects for buildings in the form of flowers or phalluses or mountain peaks illuminated from within. They seemed to imply that the ills of the world could be cured by architecture alone if only it were sufficiently monumental and crystal-like.

Hans Poelzig

One post-war German building effectively sums up the Expressionist mood of the period: the Grosses Schauspielhaus in Berlin, designed by Hans Poelzig and completed in 1919. Poelzig, like Taut and Gropius, had made a reputation before the war as a progressive practitioner and an active member of the Werkbund. His chemical factory at Luban (now Lubon, Poland) of 1912 was, however, quite unlike the more famous Fagus factory of the same year (see Chapter 5). Where Gropius and Meyer's tight composition gave an impression of detailed forethought and total control, Poelzig's industrial complex seemed almost improvised, the result of an opportunistic design method in which occasions for characterful architectural expression were seized upon whenever they occurred. Repetition was the only unifying principle, repetition of small windows, semi-circular or square, in plain brick walls that followed the industrial process wherever it led, shifting in and out, stepping up and down. Repetition was also a prominent theme in the Grosses Schauspielhaus, a 'people's theatre' designed for the great impresario Max Reinhardt, and Berlin's first major new public building since the war. Actually a converted market building, its new external brick walls were enlivened by tall narrow recesses with elliptically arched tops so that they looked more like curtains than solid, ground-supported structures. Inside, the logic of this idea was triumphantly followed through in concentric fringes of wire-reinforced plaster that hung down from the ceiling like stalactites in a cave. Nothing about this building could be related to any stylistic tradition except perhaps the plaster *muqarna* vaults of medieval Islamic architecture.

What is 'Expressionism'?

So, given these few examples, what exactly does 'Expressionism' mean? When applied to painting or poetry it might be taken to mean simply the expression in an artwork of the artist's mental state. One theory about the origin of the term is that it was coined to serve as the opposite of 'Impressionism'. Whereas Impressionism strove to represent a scene accurately and objectively as it entered the consciousness of the artist, Expressionism strove to record the artist's emotional reaction to that scene. The former is 'incoming', the latter 'outgoing'. It is the difference between, say, Monet and Van Gogh. But how can this possibly apply to architecture, which is essentially non-representational and has a practical as well an artistic job to do? It would be

intolerable, surely, or at least irrelevant, for an architect to express his or her inner mental state through the medium of a building commissioned and paid for by other people to serve a quite different purpose. For this reason, some architectural historians have dismissed the term 'Expressionist' as meaningless. Yet it persists and is useful, and not only as a convenient way to group together certain buildings that are otherwise hard to categorize. One common feature of Expressionist buildings is their immediate impact. People are fascinated by them and like them without necessarily knowing anything about them. They are the opposite of an 'acquired taste'. It is not that they are beautiful; indeed they may well be ugly, but ugly in an attractive way. They have an innocence that appeals not to the prepared mind of the connoisseur but to an appetite for the unexpected that is in all of us. If Expressionist buildings express anything it is not the mental state of the individual architects at any particular time but an aspect of the mental state of most people all of the time.

Another common feature of some if not all Expressionist buildings has already been mentioned in relation to Poelzig: a spontaneous, improvised quality. This is well represented by a group of buildings not in Germany but in Holland, which had been a neutral country in the war and was therefore more able to build in its aftermath. The architects of the so-called Amsterdam School, including Michel de Klerk and

(Left) Sulphuric Acid Factory, Lubon, Poland. Hans Poelzig, 1912. Expressive form follows industrial function wherever it leads.

(Opposite) Grosses Schauspielhaus, Berlin, Germany. Hans Poelzig, 1919. Wire-reinforced plaster stalactites convert a market hall into a fantastic cave.

Spaarndamerbuurt development, Amsterdam, the
Netherlands. Michel de Klerk, 1916. Weird facades transform
otherwise straightforwardly planned mass housing.

Piet Kramer, were appointed by the city authorities to give
architectural respectability to the new estates of workers'
housing in the southern and western extensions of the city.
Their architectural 'godfather', Hendrik Petrus Berlage,
had drawn up a master plan for the southern extension in
1915. It was arranged not grid-iron fashion but with kinked
and angled streets creating unique picturesque vistas. The
two- to five-storey apartment blocks that lined the streets
were to be equally varied, avoiding uniformity even though
the apartments themselves might be modest and repetitive.
The architects' task was limited therefore: to dress up
traditional builders' structures in modern clothes. But as
the architect J. P. Mieras put it: 'Which is better – poor
houses with poor facades or poor houses with good
facades?'[1] And good facades they were, episodic and
inventive but unified by the almost exclusive use of
brickwork with occasional outbreaks of tile-hanging.

Michel de Klerk's Spaarndamerbuurt development on
the Eigen Haard estate in western Amsterdam is a good
example. On plan it looks simple enough: continuous
terraces of uniform depth defining streets and squares with
communal gardens behind. Some parts are five storeys high
and relatively plain with horizontally proportioned windows,
but at the corners of the blocks, for example at the junction
of Zaanstraat and Oostzaanstraat, a transformation occurs.
There is a step down to three, then two storeys, a tiled roof
suddenly asserts itself and the windows go mad, adopting
peculiar elliptical shapes or squeezing themselves into
horizontal bands thrust out over the street. At the other end
of the block there is an angled, re-entrant corner, only two

Erich Mendelsohn's sketch for Red Flag
textile factory in Leningrad, 1925. Typical
thumbnail sketch similar to those drawn in the
trenches of the Western Front.

storeys high, over which towers a weird, bulging obelisk, functionless and apparently without significance. These features may be seen as desperate attempts to overcome the dull logic of mass housing: if all the dwellings are basically the same, what justification can there possibly be to make them look different? How can one street be differentiated from another? How can the city be imbued with identity and meaning? The Renaissance and Baroque details that adorned the canalside houses of old Amsterdam belonged to the past. Modern equivalents had to be found. Expressionism, improvised and instinctive, was the answer. It filled, temporarily, the void left by the devaluation of traditional styles.

Erich Mendelsohn

Historians often include the German architect Erich Mendelsohn in the category 'Expressionist' for the negative reason that he does not easily fit anywhere else. In his early career, however, he did maintain connections with other Expressionist architects and was recognized by them as a kindred spirit. For example, in 1919 he lectured in Holland at the invitation of the local architectural association and its magazine *Wendingen* ('Turnings'), the mouthpiece of the 'Amsterdam School'. Later he would criticize the Dutch Expressionists for their 'overdrawn, emotional, romantic irrelevances'[2] but for the time being he was happy to have their support.

Mendelsohn's first architectural products were tiny freehand perspective sketches originally drawn in the trenches of the

Western Front but redrawn and exhibited in a Berlin gallery after the war. They bear some similarity to the sketches of the Italian Futurist Antonio Sant'Elia (see Chapter 4). The main difference is that Sant'Elia's imagined buildings soar vertically like rockets whereas Mendelsohn's more often crouch like predatory animals. They are given names that supposedly refer to their functions, often industrial ones – a silo, a vehicle factory, a blast furnace, a chemical plant. Plans are rarely provided, though, so the functions are notional. These are mostly isolated, symmetrical objects, without any indication of urban or rural context, yet they are not quite fantasies. They look usable and buildable in steel and concrete. The vehicle factory, for example, seems particularly well worked out, if this can be said of a sketch apparently dashed off in a moment of inspiration. An overhead gantry of steel girders, or possibly cables, is held in tension by two massive pylons that erupt from a continuous, moulded, ground-hugging base. Semi-circular clerestory windows, carved out of the concrete, light an interior that we can't see but can well imagine. Mendelsohn's sketches demonstrate a natural instinct for expressive architectural form. It is no surprise to learn that he was a keen admirer of Frank Lloyd Wright, whose work he studied in the famous Wasmuth editions, using the illustrations in his lectures. In 1924, he made a pilgrimage to the United States to view Wright's buildings in the flesh and meet the man himself.

Einstein Tower, Potsdam, Germany. Erich Mendelsohn, 1921. Apparently a seven- or eight-storeys-high building, the section reveals the truth.

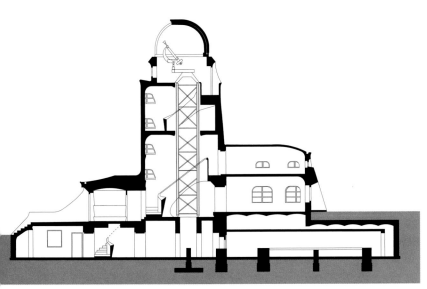

Mendelsohn's first major commission was for a very unusual building, an observatory and laboratory designed to test the predicted 'red shift' effect that was part of Albert Einstein's general theory of relativity. The client was a close associate of Einstein, Erwin Finlay-Freundlich, who conceived the project in 1917 – only six years after publication of the theory – and by 1919 had raised enough money to begin building on a site in Potsdam. It is tempting to read a cosmological significance into the form of this building, an architectural response to the new universe of 'space-time', but a simpler interpretation is that it is the built equivalent of one of Mendelsohn's wartime sketches. Here is the same fluidity of concrete form, the same symmetry, the same expressiveness. A stubby tower crowned by an observatory dome grows out of a ground-hugging base, the whole form continuous and freely modelled in concrete. (Actually, most of it is rendered brickwork in imitation of in-situ concrete.) The dome housed a telescope-like instrument called a coelostat, which directed light vertically down the inside of the tower into the basement where an angled mirror reflected it horizontally into a spectrograph. There are staircases, an entrance hall and facilities for the researchers including sleeping accommodation. All this might have been housed in a purely functional enclosure, but Finlay-Freundlich evidently wanted a piece of Architecture. What he got was a curiously ambiguous structure, both a monument to Einstein's achievement and a playful folly. The tower contains nothing but the coelostat and the staircase that gives access to it, yet externally it is treated as if it were a miniature apartment block. Four pairs of sculpted corner windows suggest four storeys but bear no relation to the staircase landings inside.

Hat Factory, Luckenwalde, Germany. Erich Mendelsohn, 1921. Mendelsohn creates satisfying form from an unpromising industrial brief.

Stuttgart. Partie a. d. Eberhardstraße

Mendelsohn went on to become a very successful architect, in both the artistic and the commercial sense. In the 1920s his big business clients included the publisher Rudolf Mosse, whose headquarters in Berlin he remodelled and modernized, the hat manufacturer Steinberg Herrmann, for whom he designed a factory in Luckenwalde, Brandenburg, and the Schocken brothers, for whom he designed several department stores. His office was large by European standards, at times employing as many as 40 assistants.

The Einstein Tower fits the Expressionist mould perfectly but Mendelsohn's later buildings are more controlled. Freehand curvaceousness has been regularized by the application of rule and compass. But they still have that quality of instant appeal, a dynamism that can be felt even in photographs. The Stuttgart Schocken Department Store of 1927 is a good example, though sadly it was demolished in the 1960s just at the time when the full importance of Mendelsohn's contribution to the development of modern architecture was beginning to be recognized. Its most prominent feature was its name, S C H O C K E N, spelled out in chunky, storey-height, widely spaced letters at first-floor level on the main street frontage. This was more than just a piece of necessary signage. It was part of the architecture and represented an important aspect of Mendelsohn's mature style: its flair for advertising, on behalf of clients but also on behalf of itself, its modernity and commercial confidence.

The building that formed the backdrop for the startlingly over-scaled sign was also an aid to advertising, its all-glass ground floor allowing maximum scope for the display of merchandise, especially at night. Though it bore little relationship to any established architectural tradition, it somehow evoked, in abstract form, a vision of a bright urban future. Mendelsohn's instinctive preference for horizontal rather than vertical forms might owe something to the influence of Frank Lloyd Wright, but whereas in Wright's Prairie houses (see Chapter 2) horizontality signifies repose and harmony with the landscape, in Mendelsohn's buildings it stands for the dynamism of the city, of traffic, pedestrian movement and the expansiveness of shared public space. A semi-circular glazed stair tower serves not to halt the progress of the horizontal facade but to accelerate it around the street corner. Louis Sullivan's Carson, Pirie, Scott store in Chicago of 1904 and Gropius and Meyer's Werkbund Exhibition building of 1914 (see Chapter 5) might be influences, but neither matches the sheer panache of Mendelsohn's form-making.

Mendelsohn was Jewish and in 1933 he was forced to leave Germany for England, establishing a practice

**De La Warr Pavilion, Bexhill on Sea, UK.
Erich Mendelsohn and Serge Chermayeff,
1935.** This is now a much-loved pre-war Modernist
building in what, at the time, was an architecturally
backward country.

Pavilion interior. Mendelsohn still revelling in the
formal freedom of reinforced concrete.

there in partnership with Serge Chermayeff. The seaside pavilion that they built in Bexhill on the south coast is a rare and much-loved jewel of early Modernism in a then architecturally conservative country. In 1935 Mendelsohn moved to Palestine where he successfully adapted his style to local climatic and cultural conditions in various buildings for the nascent Jewish state, including a house for Chaim Weizmann, the future president of Israel, and a government hospital in Haifa. Then in 1941 he went to the United States, setting up a successful practice once again after the war and designing several innovative synagogues. But it is in Germany, in the culturally tolerant era before the rise of Nazism, that his characteristic style was born and his place in architectural history established. Can that style reasonably be called 'Expressionist'? Perhaps not without extending the meaning of the term beyond reasonable bounds. But neither does it quite belong to the mainstream of Modernism, for three reasons: it was popular rather than elitist; it was commercial, paying its own way rather than relying on public or private patronage; and it was the product of an instinctive artistic talent rather than an intellectual programme.

Hugo Häring and Hans Scharoun

Another mode of architectural creation sometimes associated with Expressionism is represented in the architectural history of the 1920s and 1930s by two German architects, Hugo Häring and Hans Scharoun. Their buildings were fragmented and angular rather than composed and rectilinear. These formal preferences were justified by an objective analysis of function. Louis Sullivan had years before coined the phrase 'form follows function' (see Chapter 4). Häring and Scharoun took the slogan literally, believing that the forms of buildings should emerge naturally from the space requirements and movement patterns of the activities they housed. The idea seems very far from Expressionism, but as a young architect Scharoun was a member of Bruno Taut's Glass Chain and was deeply impressed by those post-war Utopian visions and the high-flown rhetoric that accompanied them. In a competition project for a cultural centre at Gelsenkirchen of 1920 he proposed a crystal 'Stadtkrone' of his own in the dome of the community hall at the centre of the complex. The buildings were otherwise mostly conventionally planned in a vaguely Beaux-Arts manner, but with some asymmetries and curved blocks that indicated the beginnings of a more flexible response to space and movement. Two years later, in a project for a stock exchange building in Königsberg (now Kaliningrad, Russia), movement has become a major theme. The plan now twists and turns, swells and shrinks like a diagram of the internal organs of the body. Attention has shifted from symbolism to functionalism, from imposition of a preconceived crystalline form to the search for what would these days be called 'emergent

form', form that grows organically, like plants and animals, from the building's purpose and circumstances. It was not until much later in his career, after the Second World War, that Scharoun's functionally responsive style fully matured. In the late 1920s and early 1930s, as we shall see, he came under the influence of the 'white architecture' of the Modernist mainstream.

For the clearest built example of the 'emergent form' approach in the 1920s we have to turn to Scharoun's good friend Hugo Häring. It was Häring who clarified the theory of this special kind of functionalism in an essay of 1925 entitled 'Approaches to Form'. We can see the theory in action in one of the strangest and least likely members of that select group of buildings called the 'historical canon'. It was built in 1924 but attained its canonical status rather late in life, in the 1960s, when enthusiasm for mainstream Modernism first began to wane. It is a farm at Gut Garkau, near Lübeck, built in 1925; more specifically the cow-shed on that farm. Cow-sheds very seldom attain the status of 'architecture' at all, let alone historic architecture, but

Cow-shed at Gut Garkau, Lübeck, Germany. Hugo Häring, 1925. Only a cow-shed, but a historic one, representing a special kind of functionalism.

Häring was an important figure among the architectural avant-garde of his day. He was a friend of Mies van der Rohe, with whom he shared an office for a while, and a co-founder of Der Ring (The Ring), a kind of private club for German Modernist architects. Even so, his 'alternative' view of modern architecture – he called it simply the New Building – did not gain general favour with his colleagues and was effectively forgotten for 30 years or more. The fact that its main built example was a cow-shed may not have helped.

The building, which still exists, is everything you would not expect of a 1920s Modernist design. Its structure is reinforced concrete but its main visible materials are wood and brick. It has an asymmetrical plan, somewhat church-like, with a main nave, where 42 cows gather to feed around an elongated horseshoe-shaped trough, and various side chapels, including a semi-circular one for calves and a Gothic-arch-shaped one in which root fodder is stored. Above the nave is a hay loft that supplies the stalls below via a trap door. A storage silo like a bell tower with a cat-slide roof completes the ensemble. This is not so much an articulated composition as a tight bundle of forms related to one another apparently without much regard for style or elegance. Mendelsohn would not, one imagines, have admired it. Yet it is undoubtedly a piece of architecture. Each form has been designed to fit its function like a glove and together they co-operate to support the various activities of animal husbandry in the most efficient way possible. The pear-shaped arrangement of the cows' stalls, for example, is a practical compromise between the circle that feeding cows would naturally form in the open and

an economical use of enclosed space. But is this purely utilitarian? One feature would suggest a symbolic purpose: the single bull of the herd has his own, much larger stall placed at the pointed end of the pear shape, almost as if he were the statue of a god in a temple. Häring was not simply responding to practical needs; he was creating a work of architecture, but one that started from function rather than from geometry, or tradition, or aesthetic theory. This is very different from mainstream Modernist philosophy represented, for example, by Le Corbusier, for whom abstract geometrical systems were a lifelong obsession. In his theoretical writings Häring often criticized Le Corbusier for what he saw as his neo-classicism. A battle between the two theories was fought behind the scenes of the 1928 CIAM conference. Häring lost and Le Corbusier's view has prevailed ever since in standard interpretations of the history of modern architecture.

In his pre-Second World War buildings, Hans Scharoun bridged the gap between Häring and Le Corbusier. The Schminke House of 1933 in Löbau, near Germany's border with Poland and the Czech Republic, mostly conforms to our idea of what a Modernist house ought to look like – flat roofed, open planned with big windows, and painted white. Its plan, though, is unusual. Two angled axes, one dictated by the main entrance to the south and the other by a long view to the north east, govern the orientation of the spaces and disrupt the expected rectilinearity. It is as if two differently oriented houses have agreed to occupy the same part of the same site. The geometry is impure but dynamic and, one might even say, expressive. Scharoun was brought up in the port city of Bremerhaven, which may account for

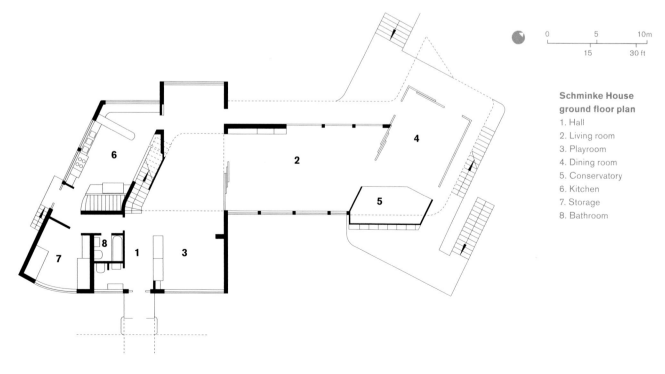

Schminke House ground floor plan
1. Hall
2. Living room
3. Playroom
4. Dining room
5. Conservatory
6. Kitchen
7. Storage
8. Bathroom

the nautical air of this building – its decks, its portholes and its external staircase like a ship's companionway. But it seems a long way from the Expressionist Utopian dreams of the years immediately after the First World War. Perhaps only a knowledge of Scharoun's later buildings (see Chapter 18) can justify its inclusion in the same chapter as Poelzig's Grosses Schauspielhaus, de Klerk's Amsterdam housing and Mendelsohn's Einstein Tower. Stylistic categories are never rigid and Expressionism is the least

Schminke House, Löbau, Germany. Hans Scharoun, 1933.
Angled axes disrupt the expected regularity. 'Deconstructivists' would take up the idea many years later.

rigid of all. It is an untidy cupboard rather than an organized showcase, but it serves at least one useful purpose: to remind us that the history of European architecture might very easily have taken a different path.

The connection between architecture and painting is not an obvious one. Architecture is a practical craft making functional objects for groups of people; painting is a luxury art making images to please the eye and mind of the individual. Yes, there are exceptions, but this is broadly true. Paintings are often figurative, imitating or 'picturing' things in the world, like people or places. The products of architecture, on the other hand, are mostly abstract. If a building imitates anything at all, it is usually another building. Yet despite these fundamental differences, the two disciplines have been closely allied in western culture ever since the Renaissance, when artists – painters and sculptors – took over responsibility for the design of important buildings from builders – masons and carpenters. An architect is an artist-builder and there is something of the painter in him or her. There is a kind of rivalry between painting and architecture, a fight over disputed territory. Architects envy the painter's relative freedom from obstacles to creativity like the need to accommodate a client's brief or to take account of gravity and the weather. Painters, on the other hand, envy the all-enveloping, three-dimensional, world-creating end-products of architecture. So there are architects who think they can be painters, and painters who fancy themselves as architects. In the early twentieth century a coincidence occurred that brought this rivalry out into the open and made it a central theme for both disciplines. What happened was that certain painters stopped wanting to represent the visible world and started wanting to make paintings of pure line and colour. At the same time, certain architects stopped liking traditional ornament and started wanting to make buildings with plain walls and flat roofs – buildings, that is, of pure line and colour.

Neo-Plasticism

One of the painters in question was Piet Mondrian. At first he had painted the landscape of his native Holland – views of land and sea, boats, cattle and windmills. But then he encountered the Cubism of Picasso and Braque, which encouraged him to emphasize abstract aspects of the objects and landscapes he painted. Gradually, those objects and landscapes dissolved into pure line and colour. A kind of destruction of reality took place. In early Cubist

paintings objects are looked at from several points of view at once and the space they occupy becomes distorted. Mondrian went further, deliberately destroying both objects and space. A typical Mondrian painting, such as *Tableau 1* of 1921, consists only of flat rectangles of colour separated by thick black lines. Does it represent anything? Possibly. Mondrian belonged to the Theosophical Society, whose members believed in the fundamentally spiritual nature of all material things. Perhaps the painting destroys the material world in order to make the spiritual world visible. Because of the purely 'plastic' – in the sense of real and physical rather than representational – nature of his paintings, Mondrian coined the term Neo-Plasticism to describe them and make them into a 'movement'.

Study for a Composition, Theo van Doesburg, 1923.
A black grid with primary colours: van Doesburg and Mondrian took abstraction to the extreme.

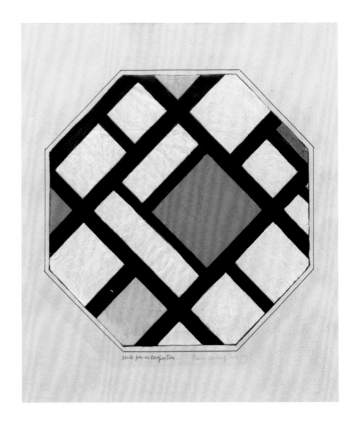

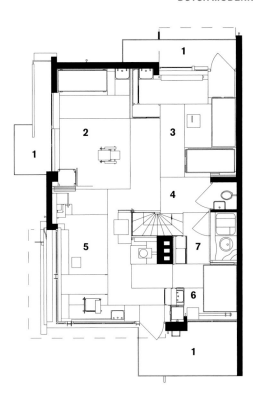

Schröder House, Utrecht, the Netherlands. Gerrit Rietveld, 1924. The house is a three-dimensional painting, open and extendable, as if it might one day take over the world.

In 1915 Mondrian met Theo van Doesburg, an ambitious and energetic designer and critic, who shared his urge to spiritualize painting by means of abstraction but who wanted to extend the process to the design of every aspect of everyday life, especially architecture. Van Doesburg collaborated with architects in the design of interiors. For example, when in 1918 the architect J. J. P. Oud, who later became a leading Dutch Modernist (see below), built De Vonk, a traditional, symmetrical classroom building for a summer camp in Noordwijkerhout, van Doesburg provided abstract, rectilinear designs for tiled floors and brick walls. They look now like miniature, repeating versions of Mondrian's later Neo-Plasticist paintings. Like Mondrian, van Doesburg was obsessed by lines, rectangles and primary colours. In 1917 he founded the periodical *De Stijl* ('The Style' – he almost called it 'The Straight Line'), for which Mondrian wrote many theoretical articles but that also included contributions from architects, including Oud, Jan Wils, Cornelis van Eesteren, Gerrit Rietveld and Robert van 't Hoff. Eventually, 'The Style' became a real, architectural style, a three-dimensional version of Mondrian's Neo-Plasticism. The best and most famous example of the style is a little two-storey dwelling in Utrecht called the Schröder House, built in 1924 by Rietveld.

De Stijl

But Rietveld was a furniture designer before he was an architect and we should first examine a chair that he designed in 1918. It is said to be more comfortable than it looks, but opportunities to test this theory are few because

(Above) Ground floor plan
1. Reading room
2. Studio
3. Hall
4. Work room
5. Bedroom
6. Kitchen/dining room

(Top) First floor plan
1. Balcony
2. Work room/bedroom
3. Work room/bedroom
4. Hall
5. Living/dining room
6. Bedroom
7. Bathroom

most examples are in museums. It is made of wood and its various components – seat, back, legs, arms – are all pure, straight forms that touch each other and overlap without any mitred or halved joints. Each element maintains its independence and its integrity. The parts are as important as the whole. The word 'Elementarism' was coined to describe this way of assembling forms. In its classic version the chair is painted red, blue, yellow and black, conforming to the De Stijl preference for primary colours.

Rietveld's Schröder House is an Elementarist composition for living in. Elementarist houses had been designed before, by van Doesburg and van Eesteren in 1920, and by the Ukrainian painter Kazimir Malevich, whose imaginary 'Planits' or 'Houses of the Future' of 1923–4 were realized only

Future Planits (Houses) For Earth Dwellers (People), **pencil on paper. Kizimir Malevich, 1924.** Malevich turned Elementarism into a mystical cult. See page 147.

Red and Blue Chair, Gerrit Rietveld, 1917. Rietveld was more a furniture maker than an architect, which is what made his architecture so original.

in drawings and models and seem more like suspended sculpture than architecture. It doesn't seem to matter which angle they are viewed from or which way up they stand. The Schröder House stands firmly enough on the ground but somehow manages to maintain this weightless quality. Its site is very ordinary – a left-over plot at the end of a terrace of unremarkable brick houses to which the Schröder House attaches itself like an over-elaborate book-end. Its walls and roofs are thin rectangular planes that seem to have been assembled not to contain usable space but simply to create a pleasing, balanced composition. There are subtle differences of monochrome tone, from pure white to mid-grey, enlivened by certain selected linear elements – columns, mullions and transoms – painted red, blue or yellow, the approved Neo-Plasticist colours. Windows are not holes in walls but membranes of glass stretched between the 'floating' planes. Hinged sashes can be fixed in only two positions: shut or open at 90 degrees. Materials can only be guessed at. All we see is paint. We might assume that the planes are made of reinforced concrete, and we may be meant to assume that. In fact they are mostly cement render on brickwork or a timber frame, with a steel column here and there to support an otherwise impossible overhang of roof or balcony. Inside, the space is not only enclosed and usable but designed to suit a rather specific functional programme. On the ground floor, rooms are of moderate size and enclosed by solid walls. There is a studio, a reading room, a study and a kitchen. Upstairs, though, the plan is completely open apart from a fixed central staircase and a chimney. An ingenious system of sliding partitions either subdivides the space for daily living or opens it up for entertaining. Much of the furniture

is built in and designed, naturally, in Rietveld's characteristic Elementarist style. This is more than just a three-dimensional painting. It is a fully functional house. Its client, Truus Schröder-Schräder, who at the time of its commissioning was a widow with three young children, went on living in it until her death in 1985.

A flat roof; plain, unbounded walls; reinforced concrete (or the imitation of it); large areas of glass; an open plan; a complete absence of traditional ornament or indeed of any ornament: here, for almost the first time, is full-blown Modernism. It is only a house and it was designed by a furniture maker, but it is also a work of art allied to painting and it conveys a message: that from now on the world is going to be different. The old architecture has been swept away in its entirety and a new spirit is at large. This assemblage of floating planes and linear elements that glide past one another seems to be only a fragment of a larger composition that might carry on extending itself until it covers the earth.

Was the Schröder House, then, completely unprecedented? Its connection with painting, in particular with Mondrian, is clear enough, but what were its architectural influences? A possible answer to this question is suggested by an earlier house, the Villa Henny in Huis ter Heide of 1916, designed by another member of the De Stijl group, Robert van 't Hoff. It is almost, but not quite, an Elementarist composition. It has a flat roof and mostly plain off-white walls, and this time both are of real reinforced concrete. The roof overhangs the re-entrant corners to a daring extent, and the windows, though divided by stout concrete mullions, are nevertheless treated

Villa Henny, Utrecht, the Netherlands. Robert van 't Hoff, 1916. We have seen these horizontalities before – in the Prairie houses of Frank Lloyd Wright.

as continuous horizontal ribbons. The wall planes do not 'float', however; there are definite corners, they are bounded top and bottom by strips of grey stone and they seem to stand firmly on the ground. Most importantly, the plan of the house conforms to a strict bilateral symmetry. We have seen this symmetry and this combination of solid concrete walls with overhanging flat roofs before: in the Unity Temple at Oak Park, Illinois by Frank Lloyd Wright (see Chapter 5). Van 't Hoff was born in Rotterdam and received his architectural education in England, where he designed several houses in the Arts and Crafts style. But in 1913 his father gave him a copy of the famous Wasmuth portfolio of Wright's work and the inspired young architect almost immediately sailed for the United States to see Wright's buildings in the flesh. He saw the Larkin Administration Building in Buffalo, the Robie House and the Midway Gardens leisure complex in Chicago, and many more, including the Unity Temple.

Wright's influence in Europe, and in Holland especially, was considerable. Hendrik Petrus Berlage, the godfather of modern Dutch architecture, boosted Wright's reputation in lectures from 1912 onwards. Of the other members of the De Stijl group, Wright devotees included J. J. P. Oud and Jan Wils. Another was one of the most productive and accomplished Dutch Modernists of the 1920s, Willem

Marinus Dudok. In his massively influential Modernist history *Space, Time and Architecture*, Sigfried Giedion mentions Dudok only once, describing his Wright-influenced architecture as 'sentimentalized'.[1] Reyner Banham, in *Theory and Design in the First Machine Age*, dismisses Dudok in a sentence as 'the hero figure of middle-of-the-road Modernists'.[2] There is a tendency in architectural history to value most highly the work of those architects, like Gerrit Rietveld and Theo van Doesburg, who produced little in the way of actual buildings. The law of supply and demand applies and scarcity raises the intellectual price of each precious project. Perhaps this is why historians have rather neglected Dudok, who devoted his life to public service in the city of Hilversum, first as director of public works, then as municipal architect, from 1915 to 1954, and was responsible for more than 200 completed buildings.

Dudok's best buildings, like those of Mendelsohn (and of Wright), have a certain suaveness of sculptural form that is immediately appealing but hard to explain. There are no comfortingly familiar traditional features like classical

Egelantierstraat School, Hilversum, the Netherlands. W. M. Dudok, 1927. Like Wright, who influenced him, Dudok was a practical builder, not just a project maker.

ÉCOLE BOSCHDRIFT
ARCH: W.M.DUDOK

colonnades or decorative friezes, no bilateral symmetries opening their arms to welcome us, no fanciness or folksiness. Indeed these buildings are rather austere in their choice of material, which externally is almost always fine-quality brickwork. Dr Bavinck School of 1921, Minchelers School of 1925 and Valerius School of 1930, all in Hilversum, show Dudok's style at work providing useful, elegant buildings for the community. His masterpiece, however, was the town hall, designed in 1924 but not completed until 1931. Unlike the schools, which are low, horizontally extended, even sprawling, the town hall is relatively compact, its central block pierced by a square courtyard. There is no formality in this arrangement. Box-like brick towers and slabs, rising to different heights and extending outwards to different distances, are brought together in a balanced composition not unlike one of Malevich's paper projects or a piece of furniture by Rietveld. But whereas Malevich's Planits are mostly symmetrical, Dudok's cluster of forms is asymmetrical. And whereas for Rietveld the point of the composition is to maintain the separateness of the various elements so that they glide past one another, in Dudok's version they collide and intersect. But it is misleading to talk about a town hall as if it were a piece of sculpture. This is a complex civic facility containing spaces of many different types – large and small, singular and repetitive, functional and ceremonial. Each of

Dudok's brick boxes has a functional as well as a sculptural job to do. The whole building represents the reconciliation of a complex brief with an artistic and symbolic vision. And the reconciliation extends further. Dudok was as much a town planner as an architect and his buildings respond sensitively to their surroundings. The town hall occupies a big island site with plenty of room to manoeuvre, but it is mindful of the quality of the spaces around it. Low wings extending from the central block create partially enclosed gardens with lawns and trees, and on the south side a huge rectangular pool reflects the building's 'best side', with a slender clock tower, itself an asymmetrical cluster of forms, standing proudly at the south-east corner.

One reason for historians' sniffiness about Dudok is perhaps that he never stirred himself to participate actively in theoretical debates about Modernism. One can hardly call a respectable and long-serving municipal architect a 'maverick' but he nevertheless followed his own instinct, confident in a technical and artistic skill honed over many years of practical design and construction. History favours van Doesburg

Hilversum Town Hall, the Netherlands. W. M. Dudok, 1931. Elementarist forms overlap and intersect in a balanced but asymmetrical composition.

because he dealt in the stuff of history – words and images;
he made projects, talked and wrote, argued and theorized.
Dudok was content to build. He absorbed influences –
Berlage, Wright, the Dutch brick-building tradition, and,
yes, the painters, furniture makers and interior designers
of the De Stijl group, but not for theoretical reasons or
on principle; rather because he found them useful in his
vocation as an architect.

J. J. P. Oud

Another Dutch municipal architect of the 1920s, Jacobus
Johannes Pieter Oud, has been better served by history,
possibly because he involved himself more wholeheartedly
in the De Stijl group. He wrote several articles for the
magazine and published theoretical projects in it, such as
a row of seafront houses with a stepped section, possibly
the first appearance of an idea that was to reappear
many times in following decades, notably in England in
the 1960s and 1970s. Oud would have been familiar with
the Expressionist housing projects of Michel de Klerk
and the other members of the 'Amsterdam School', but
he envisaged a rather different architectural future for the
rival city of Rotterdam, of which he was appointed chief
architect in 1918. His first public housing projects were
neither Expressionist nor Neo-Plasticist, but traditionalist.
The 1919 redevelopment of the Tusschendijken district, for
example, consists of four-storey apartment blocks with very

plain brick facades enlivened only by re-entrant corners
with shops on the ground floor and balconies above. The
Oud Mathenesse district of 1922 is even more traditional:
two-storey houses with steeply pitched roofs and thin,
rather picturesque chimneys.

By 1924 Oud was getting into his stride and beginning to
realize his Modernist ambitions. A small development at
Hook of Holland, consisting only of two straight terraces,
has become famous as one of the first truly Modernist public
housing schemes in Europe. The roofs are flat, the walls
are plastered and painted white, the windows are large
and horizontally proportioned, and the ends of the blocks
are rounded off by the curved windows of local shops,
shaded by thin concrete canopies. These are not houses
but single-storey apartments on two levels, very cleverly and
economically planned. What looks like an access deck is in
fact a continuous balcony shared by the upper apartments,
each of which has its own front door at ground level. In
1925, at Kiefhoek, on the southern outskirts of Rotterdam,
Oud applied his growing expertise to a larger scheme using
similar two-storey, flat-roofed terraces. This time the first-
floor windows are grouped into horizontal bands so that it is

hard to distinguish individual houses. Terraces are completely unified buildings, long and low, facing each other across straight, narrow streets.

These projects by Oud create a new image for workers' housing, an image not of traditional domesticity but of uncompromising modernity. They seem to say that from now on people are going to live in the present, not the past. At this time large estates of workers' housing were being built all over western Europe. In England, for example, the government sponsored a house-building programme called 'Homes Fit for Heroes'. It encouraged the development of new building methods such as light steel frames and ingenious precast-concrete systems to overcome the effects of the post-war labour and materials shortage. But the houses were all cottage-like in appearance and the site layouts were mostly cheapened versions of pre-war garden cities like Letchworth and Hampstead. Oud's Rotterdam housing followed no historic precedents, not even the common idea of what a house should look like. It is often assumed that this new domestic architecture arose from a rational analysis of the possibilities offered by a quantified brief and a limited budget, that the stark simplicity of Oud's long, straight terraces was the logical outcome of a scientific process. This is a misconception, however. Oud's designs were certainly efficient and economical, but then so were those supposedly traditional English cottages. The difference lay not in construction economics but in

Hook of Holland workers' housing, the Netherlands.
J. J. P. Oud, 1924. Each first floor flat has a front door at ground level. What looks like an access deck is a balcony.

architecture. Oud was a member of the De Stijl group, and though his budget would not stretch to floating planes and sliding partitions like those of the Schröder House, he nevertheless wanted his humble workers' housing projects to be equally forward looking.

Kiefhoek housing, Rotterdam, the Netherlands.
J. J. P. Oud, 1930. These are two-storey houses, their first floor windows grouped into horizontal bands.

Soon, in progressive German cities such as Frankfurt and Berlin, workers' housing became the proving ground of Modernism's social, indeed socialist, credentials. Previously 'Architecture', as an art form allied to painting and sculpture, had paid scant attention to social problems like the housing of the masses. In the nineteenth century, workers' housing had been designed by engineers and surveyors, not architects. But in the 1920s and 1930s an association began to form in the public mind between Modernism and workers' housing. Eventually they almost came to define one another. When in the early 1980s the right-wing journalist Tom Wolfe complained about the influence of European Modernism on post-war American architecture, it was its socialist overtones that he couldn't stomach: 'In short, the reigning architectural style in this, the very Babylon of capitalism, became worker housing.'[3] We shall learn more about workers' housing in Chapter 19.

Jan Duiker and Bernard Bijvoet

It is ironic that we look for the origins of Modernism in the pre-First World War factories of Walter Gropius or Albert Kahn – powerhouses of capitalism – yet a decade later we find its clearest expression in buildings to meet social needs: housing especially, but also hospitals and schools, of which Holland once again provides the best early examples. When Bernard Bijvoet and Jan Duiker set up a practice together in 1918 they quickly showed their talent in several competition wins, including an unexecuted design for a Royal Academy of Visual Arts in Amsterdam of 1917 that shows the influence

of Frank Lloyd Wright's Larkin Building. A few years later, however, in the buildings for which the partners, and Duiker in particular, became famous, all trace of Wrightian influence had disappeared. 'Machine-like' seems an apt description of the sanatorium at Zonnestraal, completed in 1926. It was a machine for curing tuberculosis, a disease that is transmitted on the breath of infected people and so thrives in over-crowded and ill-ventilated housing. In the 1920s, before antibiotics became the standard prescription, fresh air and sunshine were essential to the treatment. The machine therefore had to provide these commodities in abundance, by orientation and permeability to light and air. Its various components were arranged on the open site in optimum relation to one another and to the points of the compass. The arrangement was hierarchical and symmetrical, with a central service complex flanked by two (the original plan envisaged four) ward blocks or pavilions. These major components were divided into subcomponents, each with a well-defined function. So, the central service complex consisted of three parallel blocks – offices, kitchens and heating plant. On the upper level a fourth, cruciform block, containing an open dining and social space, formed a bridge link. The outlying pavilions were similarly articulated. Each had its own, smaller central complex, linked to a pair of narrow blocks in which wards were lined up on one side of a corridor and angled precisely to face either due south or south east. The realization of the plan in physical structure was also machine-like. A reinforced concrete frame was combined with external walls of metal, glass and cement-rendered blockwork in a

Design for Royal Academy of Visual Arts, Amsterdam, the Netherlands. Jan Duiker and Bernard Bijvoet, 1917. The design shows the influence of Wright's Larkin Building.

Zonnestraal Sanatorium, Hilversum, the Netherlands. Jan Duiker and Bernard Bijvoet, 1926–31. Functional, machine-like and designed specifically to help with the healing of tuberculosis.

shifting relationship that emphasized the independence of each element. The wall sometimes enclosed the frame and sometimes in-filled it; there were large areas of glass to admit sunlight but also cantilevered canopies to control it. The past tense is used to describe these features because, even though the building still exists and parts of it have recently been restored, its function has completely changed; and it was that original curative function that generated its architecture.

The Zonnestraal Sanatorium is a historic building because it exemplifies certain important characteristics of early Modernism: it is functional and machine-like, without a scrap of traditional architectural ornament; its structure and

materials, though not in themselves new, are new in the context of this building type; and it is 'healthy', not just because it was designed to help cure tuberculosis but because it is full of fresh air and sunshine and aims to promote well-being in a more general sense. The 'open air' school in Amsterdam that Duiker designed a couple of years later could be mistaken for a wing of a tuberculosis sanatorium. It stands in the courtyard of a residential urban block and is really no more than a four-storey stack of classrooms with a gymnasium on the ground floor, other functions being accommodated in a separate building. The plan is square, with a classroom at each corner around a central services and circulation core turned through 45 degrees. It is called an 'open air' school because the classrooms in the south-facing corner have no external walls. There is a kind of deliberate literal-mindedness about this design, a determination to provide what is needed as simply as possible, not letting aesthetic prejudice get in the way. It is almost ugly, though the cantilevered corners cut a certain dash. In the 1930s Duiker belonged to a group of functionalist architects called De 8 and edited its magazine. The group believed that 'for the time being it would be better to build something ugly and functional than to erect "facade architecture"'.[4] The Zonnestraal Sanatorium and the Amsterdam open-air school are fair representatives of this position. Hugo Häring and Hans Scharoun (see Chapter

6) held similar views but with very different architectural consequences – organic rather than machine-like.

This chapter began with a discussion about painting and architecture; it ends with a discussion of functionalism. They seem like opposite approaches and yet both are essential theoretical components of the style known as Modernism. They meet in the service of society, not of ruling elites or commercial interests but of ordinary working people. Modernism may not have been born in Holland, but it was in Holland that it differentiated itself from the Expressionism of the immediate post-war years and developed its own artistic, functional and democratic character.

Open Air School, Amsterdam, the Netherlands. Jan Duiker and Bernard Bijvoet, 1928. Aesthetic prejudice is not allowed to get in the way of functional design – yet the building looks handsome enough.

Karl Marx-Hof, Vienna

Supposed associations between architectural styles and political ideologies are always questionable and can usually be challenged by counterexamples. Modernism is commonly associated with socialism and in particular with publicly funded workers' housing of the inter-war years. Schemes by J. J. P. Oud in Rotterdam, Walter Gropius in Dessau, Ernst May in Frankfurt or Moisei Ginzburg in Moscow would seem to confirm the link. But one of the biggest and most successful socialist housing programmes of the inter-war period, the *Gemeindebau* (municipal building) of so-called Red Vienna, was largely innocent of Modernist functionalism. Conceived as part of a comprehensive welfare system, it produced more than 60,000 apartments in the city between 1918 and 1934.

The best known of the *Gemeindebau* projects is Karl Marx-Hof, a continuous, kilometre-long, six-storey-high apartment complex on the northern edge of the city. For most of its length, two parallel blocks flank long, landscaped courtyards running north–south in which social facilities such as a school, a library and a health centre are sited. Near the middle of the complex, the western block is interrupted to create a grand forecourt from which to view the eastern block, which at this point is boosted in scale and monumentality by six stepped and flagpoled towers, each straddling a wide, low, entrance arch more than a storey high.

Such monumentality cannot possibly be interpreted as Modernist but might nevertheless be taken as an expression of political power. That was certainly how it was interpreted by leaders of the right-wing Christian Social Party that ruled the rest of Austria. They saw it as an aggressive, even militaristic, symbol of proletarian resistance. But its architect, Karl Ehn, who had been a pupil of Otto Wagner, held no particular socialist allegiance and probably intended the towers as no more than an appropriate monumental flourish to adorn an otherwise plain and economical building. Whether intentionally or not, the building inevitably became symbolic when, in the 1934 civil war, Social Democrat supporters barricaded themselves inside while fascist forces bombarded it with light artillery. Many died, but the building survived, as did most other *Gemeindebau* projects, continuing to provide good-quality housing at affordable rents.

Karl Marx-Hof, Vienna, Austria. Karl Ehn, 1930.
A socialist architecture for workers' housing, but monumental rather than Modernist.

08 | GERMAN MODERNISM 1919–1933

What exactly is Modernism? The word has already appeared many times in this book without being properly defined. Its use is not, of course, restricted to the field of architecture. There are Modernisms in painting, music, theatre, cinema and literature. But it mainly applies to the arts. If we want to refer to other aspects of modern culture – industrialization, say, or the development of electronic communications – we use the more general term 'modernity'. It might be instructive to compare the use of the word 'Modernism' in different art forms. For example, does a Modernist poem written by Ezra Pound in 1913 have anything in common with a Modernist building designed by Walter Gropius in the same year? Well, yes, possibly. Most obviously, they both reject the authority of tradition. In poetry's case, tradition is represented by formal verse structures – metre and rhyme; in architecture's case, it is represented by something rather similar – the formal regularities and conventional ornaments of classical or Gothic architecture.

But if Modernism rejects tradition, what does it put in its place? In the case of music, Modernism replaced one formal system with another. The composer Arnold Schoenberg rejected the diatonic system that had been handed down over centuries and replaced it with a twelve-tone system that he invented himself. It is not so easy to say what replaced tradition in Modernist architecture (in truth, it isn't straightforward in music either) except in general terms: a revolutionary spirit, faith in the future, an eagerness to embrace change, both social and technological, and a new spatial openness symbolizing freedom of human action. Perhaps the most fundamental new idea was that architecture should reposition itself in society; that it should no longer be thought of as a special category of building restricted to certain monumental edifices like cathedrals, palaces and town halls but should include all buildings, even houses for ordinary people. Modernists wanted architecture to embrace the whole of the built environment. This was never a realistic aim. To this day most buildings are produced outside the cultural field called 'architecture'. But the expansion of the empire of architecture was a central, if unspoken, ambition of Modernist architects. It was part of their ideology.

This social repositioning had far-reaching implications for architectural practice. First, it meant that architects would have to catch up with developments in structural engineering. It had been engineers, not architects, who had designed the most technically advanced buildings of the nineteenth century, such as railway sheds, factories and greenhouses. Architects, who had hitherto been content to design within the limited field of knowledge of traditional craftsmen, would now be obliged to form alliances with engineers so as to realize the potential of new technologies like steel and reinforced concrete. Second, it meant that the function of a building would become more important than its symbolic meaning. One might forgive a lack of economy and convenience in a building whose main purpose is to glorify a monarch or an institution, but if its purpose is to house as many people as possible as comfortably and cheaply as possible then economy and convenience are paramount. The third implication was that Modernism would be an international enterprise, because modernity was international. Measurable efficiency, whether in functional or structural terms, would be judged objectively, without any reference to national or regional values based on tradition. Architecture was to be brought into line with the new, rational, scientific culture that was establishing itself all over the world.

But note that there is an ambiguity here. What exactly was being proposed? If architecture was to include edifices of all types, even barns and cow-sheds (see Hugo Häring in Chapter 6), what was there to distinguish it from ordinary building? Wasn't this like calling for the abolition of architecture? No. Architecture would remain an intellectual and artistic endeavour but it would be inspired by the progressive spirit of the new industrial age rather than by 2,000 years of architectural history. The phrase 'spirit of the age', or 'Zeitgeist' in its original, Hegelian form, has since become a cliché of architectural history, trotted out in lecture courses, television programmes and general surveys like this one. So the new architecture would be functional and efficient but it would also reflect the spirit of the machine age in its dynamism and informality. It would align itself with industry not just for practical reasons but for artistic reasons. Like Modernist painters –

Cubists, Purists, Futurists, Neo-Plasticists, Suprematists – Modernist architects would look afresh at form and space, exploring their potential to liberate daily life.

The Bauhaus and Walter Gropius

The headquarters of European Modernism in the 1920s was the Bauhaus. It was founded in Weimar by Walter Gropius in 1919, combining two older institutions, the Weimar Academy of Fine Art and the Grand Ducal School of Arts and Crafts, of which the Belgian Art Nouveau designer Henry van der Velde had been director before the war. The idea of combining fine and applied arts was an important principle of Gropius's educational method. He believed that artists and designers should also be craftsmen. Students therefore learnt about form and materials by making useful artefacts – furniture, light fittings, pots, textiles, tableware – with their own hands. Surprisingly, although Gropius was an architect and 'Bauhaus' means, roughly, 'house of building', the school did not offer an architecture course until 1927. In its early years, it seems to have seen itself as a kind of medieval guild or mason's lodge. The woodcut made by Lyonel Feininger for the front cover of Gropius's first 'proclamation' depicts a Gothic cathedral with three spires crowned by radiant stars. Clearly the intention was to evoke the creative spirit of medieval craftsmanship, not of twentieth-century mechanized industry. Expressionism, not Modernism, was the prevailing philosophy at this time. Even Gropius himself went through an Expressionist phase, designing a jagged concrete monument to the workers who died in the Kapp Putsch of 1920. Teaching was dominated by Johannes Itten, an Expressionist painter and follower of Mazdaznan, a quasi-religious cult derived from Persian Zoroastrianism. Other teachers included Gropius's partner Adolf Meyer and the painter Paul Klee.

Kathedrale (Cathedral). **Lyonel Feininger, 1919.**
A Gothic image for the front cover of Gropius's first Bauhaus 'proclamation'.

Monument to the March Dead. **Walter Gropius, 1922.**
An Expressionist work by an architect more commonly associated with the cold logic of industry.

Before the war, while working in the office of Peter Behrens, Gropius had written a long and detailed proposal, addressed to Behrens's client, AEG, for the establishment of a prefabricated-house factory (see page 64). At that time it had been clear to Gropius that architecture must form an alliance with manufacturing industry. It isn't hard to imagine how the disaster of the first mechanized world war might have cast a pall over this idea, forcing a retreat into Expressionism and medievalism. But by 1922 the trauma of war was fading, preparations were being made for the reconstruction of German cities, and Gropius turned again to the question of design for mass production. In a memo of that year he wrote: 'The teaching of craft is meant to prepare for designing for mass production … therefore the Bauhaus is consciously seeking contacts with existing industrial enterprises for the sake of mutual stimulation.'[1] Emphasis in teaching shifted from subjective expression to objective analysis, a shift that might have been triggered by the arrival in Weimar of Theo van Doesburg, representing the Dutch De Stijl group (see Chapter 7). Itten resigned and new teachers were appointed, including a brilliant ex-student, Josef Albers,

the Hungarian designer László Moholy-Nagy and the Russian painter Wassily Kandinsky. Holland, Germany, Hungary, Russia – the Bauhaus was becoming an international exchange for Modernist ideas.

When in 1925 the school moved from conservative Weimar to the more politically sympathetic industrial town of Dessau, Gropius designed a new building to accommodate it. With the possible exception of Duiker and Bijvoet's Zonnestraal sanatorium of roughly the same date (see Chapter 7), the new Bauhaus building was the first large-scale demonstration of a European Modernist architecture without compromise. Its plan is radically asymmetrical, a dynamic pinwheel arrangement of five rectangular blocks, one of which bridges over a road. There is no front or back and the main entrance is hard to find – something that Gropius was rather proud of. (In fact it has three main entrances, all inward looking.) The design is functionally determined in so far as each block has a specific use. The bridge, containing administrative offices with the director's office in the middle of the span, links the classroom block to the workshop block, which is in

The Bauhaus Building, Dessau, Germany.
Walter Gropius, 1926. One of the first large-scale demonstrations of uncompromising Modernism.

Ground floor plan
1. Laboratories
2. Classrooms
3. Physics room
4. Kitchen
5. Canteen
6. Stage
7. Auditorium
8. Display room
9. Cabinet-making workshop
10. Machine shop
11. Room for veneer work

First floor plan
1. Studios
2. Library
3. Administration
4. Conference room
5. Director
6. Waiting room
7. Lecture room
8. Classrooms
9. Staff room
10. Weaving workshop

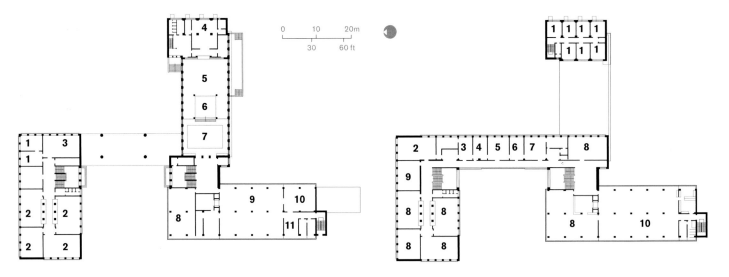

turn linked to a residential block by a low wing containing the canteen and the assembly hall. These elements are arranged on plan like a Neo-Plasticist painting but the composition can't quite be described as 'Elementarist'. The blocks are tight, self-contained boxes, not loose assemblages of floating planes like the Schröder House. All have reinforced concrete frames and therefore flexible plans, and the classroom block has continuous ribbon windows. In the workshop block columns are set back from floor edges and external walls are continuous curtains of glass, full length and three storeys high. The solid wall of a fire escape staircase at the end of this block displays the name of the school in a fat, round typeface. It has become a universal sign not just of progressive design education but of Modernism in general.

In the staff houses that Gropius designed for a site on a suburban street some distance from the school, we can see how the Modernist style adapted itself to a domestic brief. Two of these houses, including Gropius's own, were destroyed in the Second World War but five survive and have been restored. They look like miniature versions of the school building, an effect that is achieved by a kind of sleight of hand. Four of them are arranged in pairs, 'semi-detached', with standardized elements, but to avoid the repetition and symmetry that this would normally produce, the elements are oriented differently with different window arrangements. Materials are not quite what they appear to be either. What looks like reinforced concrete is actually cement render on loadbearing blockwork.

By 1927, the Bauhaus had gained an international reputation and its special combination of art, craft and technical teaching was beginning to be imitated in other schools. Gropius meanwhile was developing his own architectural practice. He had been commissioned by the municipality of Dessau to design an experimental estate of workers' housing at Törten. The houses were cheap, flat-roofed boxes grouped in terraces and arranged in rows on the site so as

Staff houses, ground floor plan
1. Hall
2. Living room
3. Dining room
4. Terrace
5. Kitchen
6. Storage

(Above) Housing at Törten, Dessau, Germany. Walter Gropius, 1927. An experimental estate of workers' housing, most of which was two-storey and arranged in terraces.

(Below) Staff houses, Dessau, Germany. Walter Gropius, 1931. Miniature versions of the Bauhaus building itself.

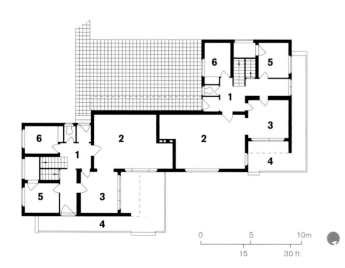

0   5   10m
    15   30 ft

to facilitate a production-line building method. The project perfectly suited Gropius's calling as a Modernist architect. He wanted to be free to do more of this kind of work. He therefore resigned as director of the Bauhaus, appointing the Swiss architect Hannes Meyer (not to be confused with Adolf Meyer) as his successor.

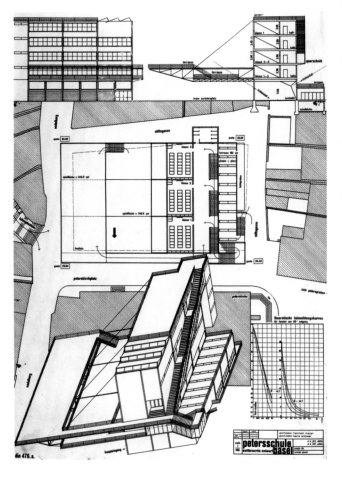

Hannes Meyer

Meyer strengthened the school's association with the *Neue Sachlichkeit* (New Objectivity) movement in German, Dutch and Swiss Modernism, which represented the complete opposite of the vaguely Expressionist philosophy that had dominated the school in its early years. *Sachlich* architects were politically left leaning, functionally oriented and opposed to what they saw as a growing 'formalistic' tendency among prominent Modernists such as Le Corbusier and Mies van der Rohe. Meyer himself was a Marxist who believed that architecture was a collective and technical, not an artistic and individual, discipline. 'Function multiplied by economics' was his rather bleak definition. His actual designs, however, such as his League of Nations competition entry, and a competition-winning scheme for St Peter's School in Basel, both designed with his partner Hans Wittwer, were functional in a rather sophisticated and imaginative way.

As director of the Bauhaus, Meyer appointed new teachers who were sympathetic to his way of thinking, including Wittwer, the Dutch architect Mart Stam and the German town planner Ludwig Hilberseimer. Stam was a brilliant designer who, having begun his working life as a joiner, travelled around Europe in the 1920s honing his architectural talent in various architectural practices. For a time he worked with El Lissitzky, the chief western ambassador for Russian Constructivism. Apart from his house at the Weissenhof Exhibition (see page 101), the building with which Stam is most associated is the Van Nelle tobacco factory in Rotterdam of 1931 by Johannes Brinckman and Leendert van der Vlugt. He is also said to have invented the principle of the tubular steel cantilevered chair, though its development is usually credited to another important Bauhaus teacher, Marcel Breuer. Ludwig Hilberseimer is best known for his extraordinarily austere vision of the city of the future in a

(Above) **Plan of St Peter's School, Basel, Switzerland. Hannes Meyer and Hans Wittwer, 1926.** Meyer believed in a pure form of functionalism – architecture as a collective, technical discipline.

(Left) **Van Nelle Factory, Rotterdam, the Netherlands. Johannes Brinckman and Leendert van der Vlugt, 1925–31.** Mart Stam, who had strong connections with Russian Constructivists, claimed authorship of this building.

project of 1924. Its wide roads, raised pedestrian decks, ranks of multi-storey slab blocks and complete absence of trees look now like a dystopic vision of the future, though in hindsight uncomfortably close to reality. He later emigrated to the United States, where he realized several less forbidding town planning projects.

Under Meyer the Bauhaus was both a respected teaching institution and a successful design business, but artists like Kandinsky and Klee resented the functionalist approach and there was much infighting. However, it was politics, not design theory, that finally defeated Meyer. He always maintained that his Marxism was a cultural orientation rather than a political affiliation, but it was nevertheless the underlying reason for his dismissal as director in 1930. He left almost immediately for the USSR, where he became a professor at the Moscow School of Architecture, returning to Switzerland in 1936. Mies van der Rohe succeeded Meyer as director, at Gropius's suggestion, but in 1932 a Nazi victory in local elections forced the school to move to Berlin. When Hitler came to power the following year, it was closed down.

The Werkbund and Mies van der Rohe

The fame of the Bauhaus helped to consolidate Modernism as a cultural movement, raising awareness of it among architects and intellectuals all over Europe. The movement was, however, still insignificant in the minds of the general public. It needed publicity of the kind that might follow from a big exhibition, something on the scale, perhaps, of the 1914 Werkbund Exhibition in Cologne. In the years immediately after the war, the Werkbund had remained an inclusive organization in which progressive and conservative designers alike could meet and discuss the relationship between art and industry. It was a reforming rather than a revolutionary body. But by 1924 a Modernist faction had begun to infiltrate its hierarchy. It was in this year that Mies van der Rohe, a leader in the Berlin-based group of avant-garde architects who called themselves Der Ring (The Ring), decided to join the Werkbund as part of what he called a 'transfusion of new blood'. The following year he was appointed by the Stuttgart branch of the Werkbund as artistic director of a proposed exhibition of Modernist housing. It would not just be a display of drawings and models, it would be a real *Siedlung* or estate of permanent dwellings. A mixture of single-family houses, row houses and apartment blocks was to be built on a hillside to the west of the city centre. The sloping site was not ideal, but it gave Mies the opportunity to place his own contribution to the exhibition, a long, four-storey, steel-framed apartment block (see Chapter 10), in a dominant position at the top of the hill. Lower down, the mostly two-storey buildings were arranged in a compact group like a Mediterranean hillside village. Many of them still exist, either preserved or rebuilt as historical monuments. Le Corbusier, J. J. P. Oud, Mart Stam, Peter Behrens, Walter Gropius, Ludwig Hilberseimer, Bruno Taut, Hans Poelzig, Hans Scharoun – the list of contributors is like the index to a history of modern architecture.

The style of the buildings is far from uniform. Behrens's apartment block at the north end of the site hardly seems Modernist at all with its thick walls and vertically proportioned windows, whereas Le Corbusier's houses at the other end of the site are racy white cubes lifted above the ground on pilotis, with roof gardens, ribbon windows and free plans. There are more modest row houses, a group of five by Oud and a group of four by Stam. Scharoun characteristically introduced a couple of organicist curves into his single-family house, but for the

most part the buildings are cubic and flat roofed. A pitched roof would have been unthinkable on this site. Despite the name of the exhibition – 'Weissenhof Siedlung' (Weissenhof Settlement) – its houses were painted a variety of colours. Stam's row houses were blue, Taut's single house was red, and other buildings were off-white rather than pure white. In the early stages of the planning of the exhibition it had been decided that rationalization and standardization should be major themes. The rationalization of the building process and the standardization of building components in order to facilitate mass production were thought to be intrinsic to the whole idea of *Neue Bauen* or modern architecture. Gropius, who as we have seen had been interested in factory-made housing since before the war, took the proposal seriously and designed two houses, one traditional in construction, the other prefabricated, so that their relative performance could be assessed. Mies, however, seems to have had different ideas. In an official publication issued at the opening of the exhibition he said: 'The problem of the modern dwelling is an architectural problem in spite of its technical and economic aspects … I therefore felt it necessary, despite our current slogans such as "Rationalization" and "Standardization", to keep the tasks set for Stuttgart free from a one-sided and doctrinaire approach.'[2]

Weissenhof Siedlung Exhibition, Stuttgart, Germany, 1927.
Mies van der Rohe was director of the exhibition and designed the long apartment block at the top of the site.

House, Weissenhof Siedlung. Hans Sharoun, 1927.
White and Modernist but with expressive curves and subtle articulations.

In these rather evasive sentences, the two terms that had originally represented the exhibition's main purpose have become mere 'slogans'. Mies realized that there was no necessary connection between Modernist architecture and the idea of efficiency. Nobody was yet prepared to describe Modernism as a 'style' – that would come later – but it was beginning to be justified on artistic rather than technical grounds. It was coming of age and developing a degree of self-knowledge. A contradiction lay at its heart: that it was the product of an intellectual and artistic elite yet its basic philosophy demanded that it be universally accepted. The only way that contradiction could be resolved was by stepping back from the role of producer to the role of advisor. Modernism could not solve all of society's problems but it could at least illustrate some future possibilities.

The Weissenhof exhibition in the end did almost the opposite of what it set out to do: it disentangled the idea of Modernism from the idea of efficiency. It demonstrated that efficiency had nothing to do with flat roofs, white walls and large windows. Traditional houses with pitched roofs could be just as efficient and were usually cheaper. Of the

many German housing exhibitions that followed and were inspired by the Weissenhof, several were promoted and designed by traditionalist architects. For example, in 1927 the prominent traditionalist Paul Schmitthenner planned a direct riposte to the Weissenhof on a nearby site at Am Kochenhof. One of the aims of Schmitthenner's exhibition was to demonstrate the greater economy and practicality of traditional, pitched-roofed, wooden-framed houses in both site-built and prefabricated versions. Ironically, in view of the later association of Modernism with the political left, the project was supported by the Communists and Socialists on the city council but rejected by the Nationalists and the People's Party on the grounds that it would compete with private enterprise. The project went through many bureaucratic and architectural chicanes over the next five years but by the time it was completed the question of political meaning had been settled: in 1933 the new Nazi mayor of Stuttgart insisted that it be built in the *Heimatstil* or 'homeland style' with no technical experiments. It was one of the first examples of Nazi intervention in an architectural project and it confirmed the regime's opposition to Modernism.

Modernism versus traditionalism
A similar polarization was illustrated by the juxtaposition of two adjacent housing estates in Berlin-Zehlendorf: the Onkel

Weissenhof Estate exhibition house, Stuttgart, Germany. Mies van der Rohe, 1927. The only built version of the Maison Citrohan that made its first appearance as a project in 1920.

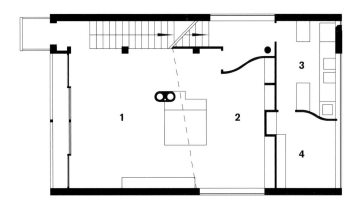

First floor plan
0   5 m
            15 ft
1. Living room
2. Dining room
3. Kitchen
4. Maid's room

Toms Hütte Siedlung, designed by Bruno Taut, Hugo Häring and Otto Rudolf Salvisberg, built in 1926, and the Siedlung am Fischtalgrund designed by Heinrich Tessenow, built in 1928. The former was Modernist with flat roofs; the latter traditionalist with pitched roofs. It was a 'war of the roofs'. Tessenow was a well-established designer of housing in a plain but refined style and was respected by Modernists and

traditionalists alike. He had been invited to participate in the Weissenhof exhibition but had turned down the opportunity, perhaps in the knowledge that his homely pitched roofs would not be acceptable. Now he found himself on the opposite side of a stylistic and eventually a political divide. Tessenow was never a Nazi but his historical reputation has suffered because of his association with Nazi-approved traditionalism.

What the general public thought about the emerging Modernist–traditionalist dichotomy is uncertain, but some light might be shed on the question by the fate of the Weissenhof houses themselves. When the exhibition closed, the various political factions in the city council generally agreed that it had been a public-relations success, helping to improve Stuttgart's progressive image. They also agreed, however, that the houses were mostly failures for a variety of reasons: they were too expensive, unsympathetic to common taste, badly planned and technically flawed. They were eventually let to mainly middle-class tenants. The apartments were the most popular, especially those designed by Mies van der Rohe; Le Corbusier's houses were the last to go, at much-reduced rents. One might tentatively conclude that outward appearance was less important to potential tenants than internal planning, which was straightforwardly room based in the apartments but comprised radically open-plan double-height living spaces in Le Corbusier's villas.

Mies van der Rohe was aware of the tenuous nature of Modernism's relationship to rationalization and standardization, but Walter Gropius was still committed to the idea of Modernist efficiency. In his 1928 plan for a housing estate at Dammerstock in Karlsruhe, designed in collaboration with Otto Haesler, he arranged his austere flat-roofed houses and apartment buildings in parallel rows running north–south, spaced to maximize the penetration of sunlight. This so-called *Zeilenbau* or ribbon-like planning principle is associated with early Modernist housing but it had a long history and was often used in projects that would be considered traditional. In later phases of the Dammerstock development, for example, the houses became completely traditional, with pitched roofs, but the layout remained the same. The *Zeilenbau* principle saw town planning as a diagrammatic, mechanistic procedure that ignored traditional forms such as streets and squares and any idea of picturesqueness. It was certainly a modern, but not necessarily a Modernist, idea.

One of Gropius's collaborators at Dammerstock was Ernst May, who in 1925 had been appointed city architect of Frankfurt. With the full support of the city's progressive mayor, Ludwig Landmann, May set up a house-building programme that would eventually produce a total of 15,000 units. In reality this was only a relatively small part of the

Siedlung am Fischtalgrund, Berlin, Germany. Heinrich Tessenow, 1928. Tessenow was well respected but too traditional to participate in the Weissenhof exhibition.

Onkel Toms Hütte Siedlung, Berlin, Germany. Bruno Taut, Hugo Häring and Otto Rudolf Salvisberg, 1926. Simple, repetitive, flat-roofed row houses designed by the sometime Expressionist, Bruno Taut.

Stadtteil Heddernheim, Römerstadt
Estate, Frankfurt, Germany. Ernst
May, 1928. Curved streets follow the
contours of the river valley site in an
almost picturesque manner.

Weimar Republic's national house-building programme, but architectural history has given it prominence for two reasons: because May was a determined publicist who conveniently recorded his department's successes in a journal called *Das Neue Frankfurt*, and because he was a committed Modernist. He had not always been so, however. Before the First World War he had worked in England with Raymond Unwin, designing cottage-style dwellings for Hampstead Garden Suburb (see Chapter 2). He later applied this garden city experience to small rural developments for a non-profit-making housing association in Silesia.

The best known of May's Frankfurt housing estates are Römerstadt, designed in 1926, and Westhausen, designed in 1930. The two are very different. At Römerstadt long linear blocks, two and four storeys high, follow the contours of the river valley site, creating contained, curving, picturesque streets. The influence of May's garden city training is evident. At Westhausen, however, the layout is pure *Zeilenbau*, with identical four-storey apartment blocks

arranged on the flat site in rank and file like freight containers. The apartments are small, incorporating space-saving devices such as fold-away beds and concertina partitions. Kitchens are consummate exercises in compact, activity-based planning. Their designer, Margarete Schütte-Lihotzky, must be credited with the invention of the worktops-and-wall-cupboards arrangement that is standard in small kitchens to this day.

In 1929, at May's suggestion, Frankfurt was chosen as the venue for the second meeting of the Congrès International d'Architecture Moderne, or CIAM. The first meeting had taken place the previous year in La Sarraz, Switzerland in the chateau of a wealthy art lover and benefactor, Madame Hélène de Mandrot. Le Corbusier and the historian Sigfried Giedion were the chief instigators. There were 28 delegates including Hendrik Petrus Berlage, Hugo Häring, Hannes Meyer, Gerrit Rietveld, Mart Stam and El Lissitzky. The meeting seems to have been occasioned by the controversial judging of the League of Nations headquarters competition, in which Le Corbusier's Modernist entry had been passed over in favour of a neo-classical design. So CIAM was initially a defensive organization, a kind of trade union of Modernist architects founded, in Giedion's words, 'to establish contemporary architecture's right to existence against the antagonistic forces of official architectural circles who controlled the major building enterprises'.[3] This statement reveals two important ideological aspects of Modernism in the 1920s: its self-image as a beleaguered, even persecuted, minority movement, like a revolutionary political party; and the implied assumption that it would eventually, inevitably, prevail over those 'antagonistic forces'. Low-cost, or *Existenzminimum*, housing was the topic for the Frankfurt meeting. Delegates toured May's new *Siedlungen* and exhibited their own designs in plans, sections and elevations, all drawn to the same scale – an analytical, comparative method that became standard in subsequent CIAM meetings. At the third congress in Brussels in 1930 housing was again the main topic for discussion, this time with the emphasis on rational site planning. The fourth meeting was to have been held in Moscow but was cancelled when it became clear that the Soviet state was antagonistic towards Modernist architecture. Undoubtedly the rejection of another Le Corbusier competition entry, this time for the Palace of the Soviets, was a factor in the decision. It was Marcel Breuer who suggested that the meeting should take place on a cruise ship. The SS *Patris II*, sailing from Marseille to Athens, was duly booked. By now the scope of Modernism's ambition had arrived at the scale of the whole city and the topic for discussion was nothing less than the future of town planning. Plans of 33 cities, including London, Paris, Rome, Berlin, Athens, Los Angeles and Detroit, were drawn up to the same scale and exhibited for comparison. The results were later summarized in two publications, *Can Our Cities Survive?* by Josep Luis Sert, published in 1942, and *The Athens Charter* by Le Corbusier, published in 1943. The latter was a rather free interpretation of the actual discussions, more definite and more dogmatic. Its influence was enormous, creating a new orthodoxy that sought to divide the city into separate zones for living, working and recreation, and a connective zone for transport. It was a functionalist view of the city that would hold sway among progressive architects and planners until the 1970s.

Although its leading light, Le Corbusier, was far more an artist than a technician, nevertheless CIAM's early discussions were more practical than poetic in their tone

---

Westhausen Estate, Frankfurt, Germany. Ernst May, 1930.
The abstract, *Zeilenbau* layout contrasts with Römerstadt's picturesque, 'contextual' plan.

and subject matter. The assumption was that Modernism had a duty to answer problems of mass housing and urban planning with rational, economical designs. Architecture, with a capital A, was a secondary concern. This created a tension in the movement between those who saw architecture as a purely functional discipline and those who saw it as an art. The functionalists argued that if a building served its purpose well and had been built for a reasonable cost then it was a good building no matter what it looked like. Architects such as Mies van der Rohe and Le Corbusier, who looked upon their buildings as works of art, were criticized as 'formalists'. It took the intervention of a couple of Americans, the architectural historian Henry-Russell Hitchcock and the young dilettante director of architecture at the Museum of Modern Art in New York, Philip Johnson, to resolve the conflict, at least on a theoretical level. Both had travelled widely in Europe and were familiar with the latest examples of Modernist architecture. In 1932 the fruits of their research were gathered together in MOMA's first ever architecture exhibition. Forty-eight Modernist architects were represented, most of them from Germany, the Netherlands and France, plus a handful of Americans. Le Corbusier, Mies van der Rohe, Walter Gropius, Alvar Aalto, Erich Mendelsohn – all the big names were there, and a few more obscure ones like the Austrian Lois Welzenbacher and the Czech Ludvík Kysela. The exhibition was called 'The International Style'. The word 'international' was uncontroversial. All Modernists saw themselves as part of an international movement. It was the word 'style' that was provocative. Surely, the Europeans

argued, Modernism was more than just a style; it was an architectural revolution. But as Hitchcock and Johnson were at pains to explain in their catalogue, 'style' was meant not in the nineteenth-century sense of one style among many, but in the deeper sense of a new tradition. They saw Modernism as a style comparable to the classical or Gothic styles, not the neo-classical or Neo-Gothic styles. The Modernist style, they argued, embodied three main principles: volume (as opposed to mass), regularity (as opposed to symmetry) and absence of ornament. These principles arose from the nature of modern construction – the replacement of the solid loadbearing wall, built stone by stone or brick by brick in a continuous mass, by the steel or concrete frame bounded by a lightweight skin. Building according to these principles had become an art form; more than that, it had become a style.

Hitchcock and Johnson approached their examples with a critical eye, not hesitating to point out, in their exhibition captions, what they considered to be stylistic errors. They were nevertheless fervent supporters of European Modernism, anxious to bring it to the attention of their conservative compatriots and equally anxious to point out the dangers of the purely functionalist view. If Modernism was nothing more than good building, then architecture was redundant. But it was more than good building, it was a potentially noble style and should be recognized as such. The very last sentence in the catalogue summed up their argument succinctly: 'We have an architecture still.'[4]

The cantilever chair

For ardent Bauhaus Modernists of the 1920s the urge to build was strong but the opportunities few. Teaching and project-making were important for the progress of the cause but ultimately the challenge of the real material world had to be met. Furniture design offered a limited, affordable field in which to experiment. And there was a real need for a new kind of furniture – light, practical and mass produced – to complement open-plan, light-filled interiors. Le Corbusier, in early showcases like the Pavillon Esprit Nouveau (see page 114), had favoured the ubiquitous bentwood 'café' furniture made by Thonet, an Austrian company founded in the 1850s. It was time for Modernism to see if it could do better.

Marcel Breuer was probably the first Bauhaus teacher to explore the potential of nickel-plated tubular steel frames. Around 1925 he designed a very simple cube-shaped stool that was later adapted to become a set of four nesting tables. Later, stacking versions of his Model B5 upright chair of 1926 or 1927, with its canvas seat and back, have become familiar in schools and village halls in the decades since. A more elaborate 'club' armchair proved that tubular steel and canvas could also support a more relaxed sitting position. Breuer set up a small company to make and market these chairs, in the process falling out with Walter Gropius, who wanted to keep all of the Bauhaus's manufacturing enterprises under his own control.

Most tubular steel chairs rested on runners rather than legs so that they could easily be slid around the floor. It was almost certainly Mart Stam who, contemplating this feature, came up with the idea of a chair with only two upright members – a 'cantilever' chair. The story goes that he sketched the idea at a dinner attended by Le Corbusier and Mies van der Rohe, and Mies copied it for use in his block of flats at the Weissenhof exhibition. When Stam's own version appeared its frame was rectilinear and utilitarian whereas Mies's was elegantly S-shaped and available in various finishes, including an expensive chrome-plated version with a leather seat and back. Breuer's cantilever chair, designed in 1928 and designated B32, was also chrome plated but with a cane seat and back in wooden frames. By now, Breuer's little company had been taken over by Thonet, who, for patent reasons, attributed the design of B32 to Mart Stam. Of all the cantilever chairs, B32 is the one that has best stood the test of time, perhaps because of Breuer's willingness to soften the machine aesthetic with natural materials. It is still in production, its true authorship now properly acknowledged.

Cesca side chair (Model B32), Marcel Breuer, 1928.
Mart Stam, Mies van der Rohe and Marcel Breuer all designed cantilever chairs. This one is still in production.

LE CORBUSIER PART 1
1906–1932

In 1987 the Hayward Gallery in London staged a centenary exhibition of Le Corbusier's work and gave it the nicely ambiguous title 'Architect of the Century'. Not everyone would agree with the implication that Le Corbusier was the most important architect of the twentieth century – Americans would probably reserve that title for Frank Lloyd Wright – but it is at least an arguable proposition. Whether we can go further and claim that Le Corbusier was 'architect of the century' in the sense that it was he who decided what the century should look like is more questionable, but he was the undisputed leader of the Modern Movement in the 1920s and 1930s, his creativity and originality remained undimmed in the post-war years right up to his death in 1965, and his influence on architects of his own and later generations was enormous. The number of his finished buildings is small by the standards of the giant international practices of the twenty-first century, but there is hardly a city in the world that has remained untouched by his ideas, transmitted at second and third hand. The signs of his presence can be discerned

Charles-Edouard Jeanneret (Le Corbusier).
Born in La Chaux-de-Fonds, Switzerland, 1887.
Died in Roquebrune-Cap-Martin, France, 1965.

wherever there is an estate of tower blocks, a flat-roofed house on stilts or a wall of naked board-marked concrete. Non-architects who know his name will sometimes blame him for what they see as modern architecture's inhumanity. But among architects, to this day, he is simply 'Corb', their teacher and their hero.

Villa Fallet

Charles-Edouard Jeanneret was born and brought up in La Chaux-de-Fonds, a small town in Switzerland, close to the French border. He attended the local art school, at first with the intention of becoming a watch engraver like his father, though his personal ambition was to become a painter. His teacher, however, saw the architect in him and guided his studies accordingly. By 1905, with the help of a local architect, he had designed and built his first house, the Villa Fallet, on the north side of the town. He was 18 years old. The house still exists, in good repair. It is a chalet of a kind, richly ornamented in the Art Nouveau manner, with a steep-pitched roof. Jeanneret designed four more houses in La Chaux-de-Fonds over the next five years, including one for his parents. They are all traditional in style and owe their place in architectural history solely to the identity of their author and his later achievements.

While designing these houses, Jeanneret began to travel and make the personal contacts that would help him in the career to which he was now committed. In 1907 he visited Florence and Vienna, where he contacted Josef Hoffmann and became familiar with the work of Wagner and Olbrich. The following year he arrived in Paris, where he got a part-time job in the office of Auguste and Gustave Perret – the best possible place to learn the technology of reinforced concrete (see Chapter 4). When he was not reading Nietzsche's *Also Sprach Zarathustra* and imagining himself as the famous artist he would surely become, he took history classes in the Ecole des Beaux-Arts and studied the textbooks of Choisy and Guadet. In 1910 he went to Berlin, where he worked for the great classicist and proto-Modernist Peter Behrens (see Chapter 5). It is tempting to imagine him working alongside those other Modernists-to-be, Walter Gropius and Mies van der Rohe, who also worked in Behrens's office, but unfortunately the dates don't quite tally. Then in 1911 he set off in an easterly direction, to Budapest, Bucharest, Athens and Istanbul, where he filled his sketchbooks with vigorous drawings of ancient temples and mosques. More than a hundred years later, those sketchbooks are still available in facsimile editions for architecture students to admire and emulate. The later Le Corbusier would refer to this journey as the *voyage d'Orient*, as if it were a pilgrimage during which the future of architecture was revealed to him.

Villa Schwob

We catch a glimpse of that revelation in the Maison Dom-ino project of 1914 (see Chapter 4) but there was a further distance still to travel before anything like a coherent Modernist style emerged. In 1916 Jeanneret designed another house in La Chaux-de-Fonds, the Villa Schwob, for friends of his parents. It is modern in that it is made of reinforced concrete – one of the earliest examples of the use of that material in a private house – but it is certainly not Modernist. A two-storey box, almost square on plan, is intersected symmetrically by a church-like form with apsidal ends. A big stepped cornice unites these forms and a set-back 'attic' storey reinforces the basically classical parti. History would certainly have ignored this building had its author not later become famous, but that author himself retained an affection for it and was happy to include it in later publications of his work. While the Villa Schwob

(Top) **Villa Fallet, La Chaux-de-Fonds, Switzerland. Le Corbusier, 1905.**
Le Corbusier's first house, designed when he was 18 with the help of a local architect.

(Right) **Villa Schwob, La Chaux-de-Fonds, Switzerland. Le Corbusier, 1916.** Le Corbusier retained an affection for this early house, though it shows no signs of incipient Modernism.

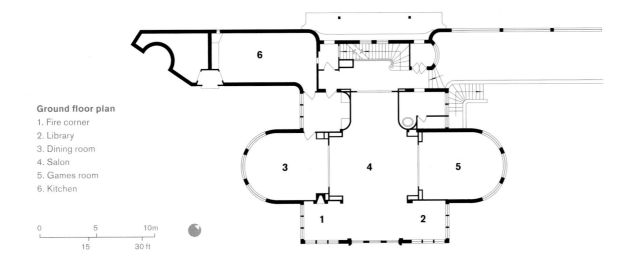

Ground floor plan
1. Fire corner
2. Library
3. Dining room
4. Salon
5. Games room
6. Kitchen

0   5   10m
15   30 ft

was being built, Jeanneret moved to wartime Paris where his old boss, Auguste Perret, introduced him to Amédée Ozenfant, a painter and critic and the owner of a high-class fashion shop. The two soon developed a close professional relationship, with Ozenfant at first the dominant partner. Jeanneret's old ambition to be a painter was revived and he began a routine of painting every morning, leaving afternoons free to develop his architectural ideas. Later he would say that the two activities were inseparable, the former a necessary preparation for the latter. Ten years earlier the Cubism of Pablo Picasso and Georges Braque had taken western painting down a new road into a world in which the unity of vision that had prevailed ever since the invention of perspective in the fifteenth century had been broken. Cubism had replaced the assumption of a single viewpoint and a single moment in time with a looser, more dynamic framework in which objects could be viewed simultaneously from different viewpoints in both time and space. It had been a conceptual breakthrough and it had revolutionized modern art, but for Ozenfant and Jeanneret its decorative and Expressionist tendencies were out of tune with the austere and orderly character of the new machine age. In 1918 they published a manifesto called *Après le Cubisme*, which called for the restoration of the 'plastic continuum' of objects, in other words their integrity in time and space. In Ozenfant's and Jeanneret's own still-lifes, objects are accurately represented not as they appear to the eye, the way an Impressionist might represent them, but objectively in the manner of a design drawing. Jeanneret's *Still-life with a Pile of Plates* of 1920 is typical. The pile of plates is cylindrical, yet the top plate is depicted as a circle, as if seen in plan. Other objects in the painting include an open book, two bottles, two pipes, a tobacco jar and a guitar. The choice of objects is revealing. One might have expected

something more obviously modern and machine-like – a typewriter, perhaps, or an electric fan – but instead they are all traditional, crafted artefacts. Jeanneret called them *objets-types*. They represent the perfect alignment of form and function, fine tuned over centuries and uncorrupted by style or authorship. In this sense they are 'pure', and the style of painting that celebrates them is therefore called Purism.

It is paradoxical that two believers in the ultimately benevolent spirit of the machine age should find their inspiration in the anonymous products of centuries-old craft traditions. These objects perhaps represented an ideal to which mass production should aspire, but in the end it was their sensual qualities, their profiles and proportions, that Ozenfant and Jeanneret, as painters, admired. For Jeanneret in particular, the 'research' that he was conducting in his paintings was research not into the logic of mass production but into the artistic possibilities of form. We shall see soon how those *objets-types* began to appear, transformed, in his early Purist architecture.

Becoming Le Corbusier

In 1920, after the success of *Après le Cubisme*, Ozenfant and Jeanneret decided to publish a monthly magazine to promote their Utopian vision of a new society in which humanity and the machine would be reconciled. They called it *L'Esprit nouveau* and it eventually ran to 28 issues. In it the artistic and architectural implications of their vision were explored by a variety of contributors including Paul Dermée, Jean Cocteau, Louis Aragon and Auguste Lumière. Articles written years earlier, such as 'Ornament and Crime' by Adolf Loos (see Chapter 1) and Theo van Doesburg's De Stijl manifesto (see Chapter 7) were reproduced and brought to a new audience. Many of the essays, however, were written by Ozenfant and Jeanneret themselves under pseudonyms. Ozenfant called himself 'Saugnier', his mother's maiden name. Jeanneret revived an old family name, Lecorbésier, but detached the 'Le' and changed the 'é' to a 'u'. We can only guess what kind of subtle alteration the adoption of this pseudonym effected in Jeanneret's self-image, but from then on the architect in him became Le Corbusier, though the painter remained Jeanneret and it was not until 1928 that Le Corbusier finally prevailed.

One by-product of the *Esprit nouveau* publishing enterprise was to become far more influential than the magazines themselves. In 1923 Ozenfant and Jeanneret (or Saugnier and Le Corbusier) combined several of their *Esprit nouveau* essays into a book called *Vers une Architecture*, a book

Still-life with a Pile of Plates. Le Corbusier, 1920.
Common objects, or *objets-types*, depicted objectively: the essence of Purism.

that is still in print and is still sometimes found on reading lists of first-year architecture students. In the first English edition of 1927, the title was translated as *Towards a New Architecture*.[1] It is a rather disjointed work with short, inwardly repetitive chapters on a variety of themes connected only by their general relevance to architecture. It is copiously illustrated by photographs and drawings, some of them pirated from other books and magazines. Its readers tend to remember most vividly the pictures of cars, ships and aeroplanes, because they convey a simple but powerful message: that modern architecture should be as functional and beautiful as modern engineering. Pictures of American grain silos and car factories were recycled from Walter Gropius's Werkbund yearbook of 1913 (see Chapter 5) but doctored to remove any vestiges of traditional architectural ornament. In other parts of the book, illustrative examples are taken from conventional architectural history. The chapter called 'Regulating Lines', for example, analyzes the proportions of the Senatorio Palace in Rome, the Petit Trianon at Versailles and the west front of Notre-Dame in Paris, as well as Le Corbusier's own Villa Schwob. There is a chapter called 'The Lesson of Rome' in which the power and simplicity of monuments like the Pantheon and Colosseum are celebrated. In the third of a trio of chapters called 'Eyes Which Do Not See', ancient and modern examples are juxtaposed to illustrate the process of progressive refinement in design. The relatively primitive Greek temple known as the 'Basilica' at Paestum is compared with a Humber motor car of 1907, while on the opposite page the Parthenon – the epitome of refinement – is compared to a racy Delage Grand-Sport of 1921. For Le Corbusier the products of engineering are beautiful because they are plain and simple, like the *objets-types* in his Purist paintings. Engineers, he argues, design functionally but also geometrically, combining simple shapes like cylinders, cubes and spheres, and architects should do the same. History has proved Le Corbusier

wrong in this analysis. When certain dynamic functions – streamlining, for example – are fed into the functional design equation, the simple shapes disappear and are replaced by continuous flowing surfaces. What Le Corbusier called 'the engineer's aesthetic' was really the architect's aesthetic all along, but stripped of its traditional ornamental clothes.

Mass-market housing

In the last but one chapter of *Vers une architecture*, called 'Mass-Production Housing', Le Corbusier takes the opportunity to publicize his own house designs. First comes the Maison Dom-ino concept developed during the First World War (see Chapter 4), then the Maison Monol house-building system of 1919, with asbestos-cased rubble walls and curved concrete roof. It is not until we come to the Maison Citrohan that the idea of a standardized popular house type comes fully into focus. 'Citrohan' is a slightly obscure pun on 'Citroën', the car maker, so this is a house like a car, a product for a market rather than a piece of architecture. 'Mass-production' is, however, a misleading translation of *Maisons en Serie* because it implies prefabrication and factory production, which Le Corbusier never seems to have envisaged. The house is designed for rationalized, economical, site-based construction, with loadbearing flank walls of a material to suit the locality, concrete floors and a flat roof. Its most important feature is spatial rather than technical: a double-height main living space, which seems to have been inspired by a bistro in Rue Godot de Mauroy that Ozenfant and Jeanneret frequented. It was to become a standard feature of Le Corbusier's domestic designs right down to the Unité d'Habitation apartments of 1952.

Maison Citrohan project. Le Corbusier, 1922. A version of this house type was built at the Weissenhof exhibition of 1927 (see page 104).

The idea of a standard, architect-designed, mass-produced, possibly factory-made house for the popular market – a house like a car – had been a Modernist ideal ever since Gropius's unsuccessful pitch to AEG of 1911 (see page 67). It was to remain an ideal, largely unrealized, throughout the twentieth century. Although millions of prefabricated houses were built in developed countries like the USA, Sweden, Japan and Australia, very few were architect designed and even fewer could be described as Modernist. Most used lightweight timber-framed panels of the kind pioneered in the American west in the 1830s, and adopted traditional classical or Gothic styles. Modernism's total failure to break into the field of popular housing – the real test of its claim to universality – is an important but neglected theme in the history of architecture. The Maison Citrohan is an early instance of the architect-designed mass-production house prototype, a category of architectural project that has attained a certain historical prominence but that had very little direct effect on the built environment.[2]

Only one permanent Maison Citrohan was built, at the Stuttgart Weissenhof exhibition of 1927 (see Chapter 8),

by which time it had acquired a reinforced concrete frame and pilotis or columns that lifted it off the ground. Another, more interesting, version was built as an exhibition pavilion at the 1925 International Exhibition of Decorative Arts in Paris. It was named the Pavillon de l'Esprit Nouveau, after the magazine, and took the form of a stark concrete cube containing an L-shaped two-storey house and a roofed patio garden. The living room of the house was double height and lit by a huge industrial steel-framed window, just like the Citrohan prototype, but the idea had developed into something quite different. The concrete cube, though presented as if it were a detached suburban house, was conceived as an apartment to be mass produced and stacked up in eight-storey blocks known as Immeubles Villas. These blocks were in turn components in a plan for a whole city for three million people called the Ville Contemporaine, drawings of which were presented in an extension to the pavilion.

Pavillon de l'Esprit Nouveau, Paris Exhibition of Decorative Arts, France. Le Corbusier, 1925. The 1925 Paris Exhibition inaugurated Art Deco; Le Corbusier's contribution, however, was pure Modernist.

Immeubles Villas project. Le Corbusier, 1925. Pavillons de l'Esprit Nouveau stacked up to form an apartment block, with a garden for every apartment.

The breathtaking sweep of Le Corbusier's vision now becomes clear. The Pavillon de l'Esprit Nouveau represented nothing less than a whole new way of life incorporating *objets-types* at every scale, from the mass-produced Thonet chairs that furnished the house to the whole rationally planned and functionally zoned city. Voisin, the aeroplane and car manufacturer, had been persuaded to sponsor a special version of the Ville Contemporaine that envisaged the building of eighteen 60-storey skyscrapers in the district of central Paris known as the Marais. Was the 'Plan Voisin' a serious proposal? If so, by twenty-first-century standards, it would have been an act of civic vandalism. Or was its intention purely polemical, an electric shock to wake up the world to the true nature of modernity? This ambiguity has always accompanied discussions of Le Corbusier's urban projects, including the later Ville Radieuse, first exhibited at the third CIAM meeting in Brussels in 1930. But there is no doubt that in the years after the Second World War planners and architects took these projects seriously and were profoundly influenced by them. They thought that the old European city, with its multifunctional streets and squares carved out of a solid mass of stone buildings, was obsolete and must be replaced by the sunny openness of a park in

which buildings stood proudly and nakedly like grain silos. It was not until the late 1960s, after various fragmentary built versions of the Ville Contemporaine had proved to be social and technical failures, that urbanists began to look again at the traditional city and note its virtues.

Villa La Roche and Villa Stein

But in the mid-1920s Le Corbusier's comprehensive urban vision had no hope of realization. His actual buildings continued to be one-off houses commissioned by wealthy patrons. Their style, however, had changed beyond recognition. The traditional chalets and villas of La Chaux-de-Fonds were left behind and Modernism was embraced wholeheartedly. The Villa La Roche–Jeanneret of 1925 was a far from straightforward commission for two houses, one for Le Corbusier's brother Albert and the other for Raoul La Roche, a banker who also needed a gallery in which to display his collection of modern paintings. With a complicated brief and an awkward site at the end of a cul-de-sac in the Paris suburb of Auteuil, it was never going to be a simple, standardized design like the Maison Citrohan. Le Corbusier nevertheless did his best to stick to Purist principles. The two single-aspect houses are of different sizes but the street facade is arranged to create the impression that they are a mirrored pair. Their walls are white, their windows plain and steel framed, and their gardens are on the roof. The gallery stands at right angles to the houses

Ville Contemporaine project. Le Corbusier, 1922. Le Corbusier's cities of the future look more appealing than those of, for example, Ludwig Hilberseimer (see page 101).

at one end and takes the form of a double-height, clerestory-lit hall raised on pilotis, with one curved wall and an internal ramp rising to a library at second-floor level. A ramp is an inefficient and time-consuming way to move from one level to another on foot, and on this occasion there is no staircase to provide a short cut, but by creating what Le Corbusier called an 'architectural promenade' it converts a cluster of static spaces into an internal landscape to be enjoyed as one might enjoy a garden.

'A house is a machine for living in': the hackneyed quotation from *Vers une architecture* is often cited as evidence of Modernism's supposed inhumanity. But the Villa La Roche is not remotely machine-like, and neither is the Villa Stein–de

Monzie of 1927. It might be argued more convincingly, as Colin Rowe did in his famous essay 'The Mathematics of the Ideal Villa', that the Villa Stein is essentially a classical building, possibly modelled on the sixteenth-century Villa Foscari by Andrea Palladio.[3] The two buildings share the same overall proportions – eight units long by five and a half units deep by five units high – and the same ABABA pattern of single and double structural bays. The house is set far back on a narrow site in Garches, 12 kilometres (7½ miles) from the centre of Paris. Its front facade is very obviously

Plan Voisin project for Paris. Le Corbusier, 1922. A shining new city was envisaged, but also the destruction of one of Paris's most loved districts.

a thin, non-loadbearing screen, like an abstract painting on canvas. There is a drawbridge-like canopy over the front door and a top-floor balcony that seems to have been cut out of the canvas and folded down. Two narrow ribbons of window extend across the full width of the facade, right up to the outer edges. The other, private side of the house is more relaxed and open, with generously proportioned windows and a double-height covered terrace that extends outwards and lowers a gangway-like staircase into the garden. This is a large luxurious villa with a complicated plan designed to accommodate two families and their servants, but it is also recognizably a relation of the Maison Citrohan and the Pavillon de l'Esprit Nouveau.

Villa Savoye

The Villa Savoye at Poissy of 1931 is the best known of Le Corbusier's 'Purist' villas and is now a busy pilgrimage destination for architecture students from all over the world. It sits in the middle of a large site unconstrained by neighbours, trees or property boundaries. A shallow box, roughly square on plan, is raised on pilotis over a recessed ground floor that contains an entrance hall, a garage and servants' accommodation. All the main living spaces, including an open terrace, are at first-floor level, inside the box. On the roof, a second terrace or solarium is semi-enclosed by a curved, freestanding wall. These spaces are linked together by an architectural promenade that starts as soon as the car that brought us the 24 kilometres (15 miles) from Paris has entered the site. The driveway takes it under the building where it turns left and drops us at the main entrance before continuing to follow the curved wall round into the garage. We meanwhile find ourselves at the foot of a ramp in a glass-walled entrance hall. There is a spiral staircase to the left for the use of servants but we must ascend the ramp, which delivers us, in two flights, to the 'piano nobile' where we find the main 'salon' opening onto the terrace through full-height glass sliding doors. The terrace is open to the sky but is nevertheless a room with walls that have openings like windows. We are reminded of the terrace of the Pavillon de l'Esprit Nouveau, which is also a room but with a missing

Villa La Roche, Paris, France. Le Corbusier, 1925. The pedestrian ramp was one of Le Corbusier's favourite devices: a dynamic element to set space in motion.

Villa Stein, Garches, France. Le Corbusier, 1928.
Colin Rowe argued that this was essentially a classical
building, a version of a villa by Palladio.

wall rather than a missing roof. But this is not the end of the
promenade. The ramp, now external, rises another two flights
to the rooftop solarium where we can settle in deckchairs or
enjoy the view over the valley of the Seine, perfectly framed
by a window-like opening in the freestanding wall.

Five Points of a New Architecture

The Villa Savoye has come to be regarded as the exemplary
masterpiece of high Modernism, and rightly so because it
illustrates all the important features of the style. Le Corbusier
himself summed them up in what he called the 'Five Points of
a New Architecture':

1   Pilotis. Modern buildings should be raised off the ground
    on columns allowing space to flow freely underneath.
2   Roof gardens. Roofs should be flat and the space should
    be used.
3   Free plan. The supporting structure of a Modernist
    building will be a steel or concrete frame, not loadbearing
    walls, so partitions can be placed anywhere and space
    can flow freely.

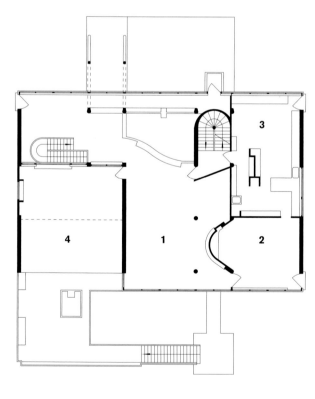

First floor plan
1. Living room
2. Dining room
3. Kitchen
4. Terrace

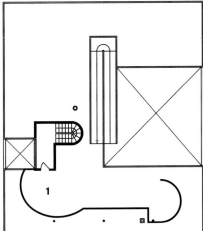

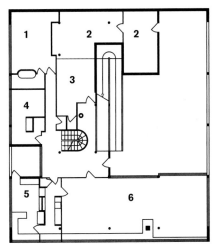

Villa Savoye, Poissy, France. Le Corbusier, 1931.
A three-dimensional Purist painting in which stairs,
ramps, windows and windbreaks become *objets-types*.

4 Free facade. Similarly, if the external walls are not
   loadbearing, then openings can be placed to suit the
   views or the day-lighting without worrying about arches
   or lintels.
5 Long windows. If there are no arches or lintels, then
   why not have the widest windows possible, continuous
   'ribbon windows' like those on the entrance side of the
   Villa Stein and on all four sides of the Villa Savoye's
   shallow box?

The Villa Savoye is exemplary in another way. It illustrates
that Modernism means more than just Functionalism. If the
building were to be assessed only on the grounds of function
and economy it would be found wanting. It is a large house,
yet the area of enclosed space is rather small. This is partly
because of changes made during the design process to
reduce the cost – the rooftop solarium, for example, was
originally meant to be a suite of bedrooms – but mainly it is
because nobody is measuring the efficiency of the design. It
is a work of art, a three-dimensional Purist painting in which
space is manipulated like paint on a canvas – contained and
freed, shifted and balanced, held still and set in motion. The
normal distinction between inside and outside is abolished.
Gardens become rooms, roofs become floors, windows
become balconies. If it is a machine for living in, then that
machine is an ocean liner, an image perhaps deliberately
evoked by the funnel-like profile of the solarium wall.

Public commissions

In 1927 Le Corbusier, in partnership with his cousin Pierre
Jeanneret, entered the competition for the design of the
League of Nations headquarters building in Geneva. It
was to prove a turning point in his career, not because he
won the competition but because he lost it in controversial

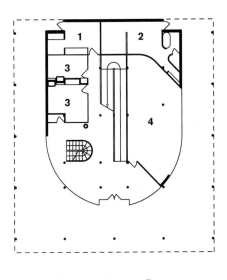

0   5   10m
|_____|
   15   30 ft

Second floor plan   5. Kitchen
1. Sun terrace   6. Salon

First floor plan   **Ground floor plan**
1. Son's room   1. Laundry
2. Madame's room   2. Chauffeur's room
3. Bathroom   3. Maid's room
4. Guest room   4. Garage

circumstances. The ensuing public row made his name and confirmed his position as the leader of the Modern Movement. His leadership was not unchallenged, however. The 'functionalist' wing of the movement, led by the critic Karel Teige, criticized the monumental turn that Le Corbusier's architecture had taken, both in the League of Nations design and in a project for a 'Mundaneum' or world centre of cultural co-operation sponsored by the Union of International Associations in Brussels. For Teige and his followers, including architects such as Hannes Meyer and Hans Wittwer who had also entered the League of Nations competition, Modernism's task was purely social and functional; it had no business glorifying government institutions with outmoded devices like colonnades and grand axes. Le Corbusier was more pragmatic. He agreed that functional efficacy was the first priority of a Modernist architect, but saw no reason why the symbolic power of Modernist forms should not be exploited. His League of Nations design is firmly Modernist in its details – its flat-roofed, piloti-supported and ribbon-windowed administration blocks, for example – but monumental in the symmetry of its auditorium block, which faces a *cours d'honneur* dominated by an equestrian statue.

Le Corbusier's growing reputation brought him new commissions, not for single houses now but for large public buildings. In 1928 he won a competition for the design of the Tsentrosoyuz building in Moscow for the Union of Co-operatives in the USSR. Its combination of office blocks and an auditorium was similar to the League of Nations design, but on a more restricted urban site. A change of client during construction, and much cost-saving and corner-cutting, meant that it never functioned very satisfactorily, though Le Corbusier's inflexibility over certain features of the design, like the ramps that were the only link between the entrance hall and the first floor, was undoubtedly a factor. His entry for the Palace of the Soviets competition in 1931 was on a different scale. It was to be an assembly rather than an administrative building, with two gigantic auditoriums, the larger seating 15,000 spectators, the smaller a mere 6,500. They share an axis and a vast ceremonial forecourt, but it is the externally exposed structure that declares most forcefully the architectural intentions and allegiances of the

Design for the League of Nations Headquarters. Le Corbusier and Pierre Jeanneret, 1927. Modernist details combined with a new, controversial monumentality.

whole project. Both auditorium roofs are suspended from deep beams in fan shapes, like the bones of hands. Those of the larger auditorium are in turn suspended from a huge parabolic arch. The boldness and clarity of the concept was clearly inspired by the spirit of Russian Constructivism. Le Corbusier did not win the competition but with hindsight we can see that he was never going to. Stalinism was turning against Modernism and the judges chose a traditional classical design by Boris Iofan, later to be developed into an absurd wedding cake surmounted by a gigantic statue of Lenin (see Chapter 14). It was never built.

Back home in Paris, Le Corbusier received two important commissions, both of which he saw as opportunities to develop residential prototypes for the city of the future. The first was from the Salvation Army for a Cité de Refuge, a hostel for the homeless, mainly destitute bachelors but also mothers and babies. The site is cramped and steeply sloping, forcing the building into a tight cluster of overlapping forms and spaces. Visitors first mount a flight of steps to the tall, open-sided box of the entrance porch. From here they cross a canopied footbridge over a sunken service road to reach the reception area, housed in a squat drum. Next in this short architectural promenade comes a rectangular hall, the heart of the social-services wing, with access to a large lecture theatre in its basement. The backdrop to this collection of Purist objects is an eight-storey slab containing private rooms and dormitories. Its big flat facade, originally all glass apart from a double attic storey with a saw-tooth plan, faces a little west of due south. During the first spell of hot weather after the opening of the building in 1933,

the residents fried and the folly of the glass wall became apparent. The story of this failure is an important episode in the history of the relationship between modern architecture and environmental engineering. Le Corbusier thought he had invented an effective system for what we would now call airconditioning. His idea was that the air inside the building should be constantly recycled. A central plant would filter it, clean it and keep it at a temperature of 18 degrees Celsius (64 degrees Fahrenheit). This was called 'exact respiration'. To control heat loss and heat gain a separate system, called the 'neutralizing wall', would pass heated or cooled air through the broad cavity between two layers of glass. Cost cutting meant that the double glazing was never installed and the central plant had no cooling capability, but the probability is that the system would never have worked anyway. Various remedies were tried, including ordinary opening windows. Eventually, years later in the 1950s, the whole facade was rebuilt with a reduced area of glass and projecting concrete sunshades.

This episode is important because it highlights Le Corbusier's belief in a universal Modernist architecture. He thought that buildings all over the world, from the Arctic circle to the equator, should maintain an internal temperature of 18 degrees and should use similar means to achieve this uniformity. It was a prophetic vision, though it was the spread of the much simpler American system of air conditioning,

Tsentrosoyuz Building, Moscow, Russia. Le Corbusier and Nikolai Kolli, 1933. Le Corbusier was both influenced by, and an influence on, Russian Constructivist architects.

of which Le Corbusier seems to have been unaware until his trip to the US in 1935–6, that made it a reality. But he was adaptable. The development of his architecture followed a zig-zag line and this was one of its sharp changes of direction. By 1936, advising Lúcio Costa and Oscar Niemeyer on their design of the Ministry of Education and Health building in Rio de Janeiro (see Chapter 20), he was recommending what he called *brises-soleil* – sun breakers – to shade the facades. This would now be described as a shift from active to passive climate control. Arguably, Le Corbusier was a pioneer of both. But it was also a larger, ideological shift, from the idea of a universal architecture to a greater awareness of regional differences in climate and culture. It is typical of Le Corbusier that, rather than tinkering with a technology, gradually improving it, he should replace one big idea with another.

The other important Paris commission of the 1930s was also for a hostel, this time to accommodate Swiss students at the Cité Universitaire on the south side of the city. The main elements of the Pavillon Suisse are similar to those of the Cité de Refuge, but smaller and simpler: a four-storey slab containing the student rooms is lifted up on pilotis and connected to a single-storey reception and refectory wing by a tower containing staircase and lift. The almost mechanical rationality of this arrangement, with straight rows of identical rooms along single-loaded corridors, was probably influenced by the communal housing schemes that Le Corbusier saw on his trips to Moscow in connection with the Tsentrosoyuz project. As at the Cité de Refuge, the extensive glazing of the south-facing rooms caused over-heating. On the other side of the building, however, there are signs of a new acceptance of heavyweight construction and natural materials. The north and end walls of the block are clad in smooth stone panels, and the curved north wall of the refectory is of rough, uncoursed masonry. It is as if that tendency of early Modernism to abolish the solid wall

in favour of the ever-lighter in-filling of a structural frame has reached its limit and changed direction. The Pavillon Suisse is a pivotal project in Le Corbusier's oeuvre. It looks back to the Purist villas and the Five Points, and it looks forward to a new, richer, more inclusive, more emotional style that would reach maturity in the 1950s and 1960s.

Charlotte Perriand

Le Corbusier's interiors were not furnished; they were 'equipped'. And the equipment, like the architecture, had to be designed from first principles. In 1927 he appointed Charlotte Perriand to take charge of this aspect of his practice. Their first meeting had not been a success. She had showed him her work, the outcome of her traditional training at the School of the Central Union of Decorative Arts in Paris, and he had dismissed her, saying 'we don't embroider cushions here'. But he had under-estimated the depth of her intellect, not least the extent to which she had been influenced by his own theoretical writings. He soon realized his mistake and for the next ten years she worked with him and his cousin and partner Pierre Jeanneret on now famous designs such as the Chaise à Dossier Basculant or 'sling chair', the Grand Confort armchair and the Chaise Longue. Shown here is Perriand herself demonstrating the Chaise Longue at full recline in the famous publicity still. These steel-framed items of equipment were designed not to conform to traditional types of chair and couch but to support the sitting, lying, sprawling and slumping postures that people actually adopt in domestic interiors. And they were conceived with industrial mass production in mind, though in practice they were handmade in small numbers for exhibitions and for houses like the Villa Church and the Villa La Roche.

Perriand would probably not have become famous without Le Corbusier, yet in hindsight it now seems that her time with him was only a preparation for a more interesting subsequent career. She continued to collaborate with Pierre Jeanneret and with the influential designer and metalworker Jean Prouvé (see page 361) until 1940. Then, on the very day that German troops marched into Paris, she left for Japan to become a design consultant to the government. One result of this cultural encounter was a version of the Chaise Longue made of bamboo, which sounds like a bad joke but was in fact part of an intelligent reassessment of the relationship between western and Japanese design – how Japanese attempts to reproduce western forms represented a missed opportunity for a mutually respectful cultural dialogue. She left Japan in 1943 and, unable to return to Paris, went to what is now Vietnam, where she married a military officer and became a mother. Back in France after the war she briefly worked again with Le Corbusier, designing the first prototype for the kitchens in the Unité d'Habitation (see page 224), and collaborated regularly with Prouvé on exhibitions and research projects. But she also had her own clients, including Air France, whose London premises in Bond Street she fitted out in the early 1960s. In the 1980s architectural scholars rescued her reputation from Le Corbusier's shadow and in 1985 she was the subject of a major retrospective at the Musée des Arts Decoratifs in Paris. She died in 1999 at the age of 96.

Chaise Longue, Charlotte Perriand and Pierre Jeanneret, 1929. Charlotte herself reclining on her most famous creation.

MIES VAN DER ROHE IN GERMANY
1907–1938

Ludwig Mies van der Rohe was unquestionably one of the form givers of modern architecture. The typical Modernist house with its flat roof and free plan, and the typical Modernist office block with its glass curtain wall, are both Miesian inventions. It was Mies, far more than, say, Le Corbusier or Frank Lloyd Wright, who carried the cleansing of traditional architecture to its logical conclusion, banishing all figurative ornament and allowing the basic elements of the building to speak for themselves. The phrase 'less is more', now become an advertising cliché, was coined by Mies and neatly encapsulates his philosophy. One must not, however, jump to the conclusion that Mies was a mere functionalist, that he was interested only in solving practical problems in the most efficient way with the latest technology. Far from it. He often talked about architecture in spiritual terms. For example: 'Let us not give undue importance to mechanization and standardization. Let us accept changed economic and social conditions as a fact.

Ludwig Mies van der Rohe. Born in Aachen, Germany, 1886. Died in Chicago, Illinois, USA, 1969.

All these take their blind and fateful course … One thing will be decisive: the way we assert ourselves in the face of circumstance. Here the problems of the spirit begin.'[1] Neither should we assume that he was ignorant of the architecture of the past or unwilling to learn from it. As we shall see, his architecture was in a sense a continuation of a tradition that stretched back to the Romantic classicism of the early nineteenth century and beyond that to the temples of ancient Greece and Rome. Mies was no dry academic. He never went to university and never underwent any formal architectural education. Above all, he was a craftsman and a builder who had worked with his hands and knew the weight and working properties of building materials.

Ludwig Mies (he added the 'van der Rohe' later, using his mother's maiden name) was born in Aachen in 1886. He was the son of a monumental mason and as a child he sometimes helped in his father's yard, where his speciality was marking out the lettering on the gravestones. As a teenager he studied at the local trade school where he learnt how to draw, and when he left school at the age of 15 he took a one-year building apprenticeship that included bricklaying. After working for a while as a draughtsman in Aachen, in 1905 he set off to make his fortune in Berlin, taking up a post in the office of the furniture designer Bruno Paul. In 1907, while working in Paul's office, he designed and built his first building – a house for the philosopher Alois Riehl and his wife. This was a brave act of patronage – the would-be architect was only 21 – but the Riehls were pleased with their house and Mies remained a friend for years to come. The house was completely traditional but very competently executed and its success must have given Mies enormous confidence. One feature was particularly striking: the way that the long retaining wall that terraced the sloping site was integrated with the house so that, when viewed from the lower garden, it looked like a temple portico. Perhaps it was this feature that persuaded Hermann Muthesius to publish photographs and plans of the house in the second edition of his book *Landhaus und Garten*.

Apprenticeship
In 1908 Mies joined the office of Peter Behrens, one of the most important German architects of the period and

Riehl House, Potsdam, Germany. Mies van der Rohe, 1907. A brave act of patronage on behalf of the philosopher Alois Riehl and his wife. Mies was 21.

Monument to Bismarck (unbuilt). Mies van der Rohe, 1910. The influence of Schinkel is clear, and arguably persisted in Mies's later Modernist works.

a pivotal figure in the history of modern architecture. Le Corbusier (then Charles-Edouard Jeanneret) and Walter Gropius also worked for Behrens at this time. Behrens is now thought of as a proto-Modernist. His most famous building is the AEG Turbine Assembly Hall in Berlin of 1909 (see page 64), which is modern in its structure and materials but traditional in its monumental, temple-like form. In the three years he spent with Behrens, Mies learnt as much about the classical tradition, in particular the work of the great nineteenth-century German architect Karl Friedrich Schinkel (see page 135), as he did about new materials and new technologies. We shouldn't be surprised, therefore, that when, in 1910, he entered a design competition for a monument to Bismarck, he should produce an austere neo-classical composition that gives no hint of the Modernist transformation to come.

In 1912 Mies designed a large villa and art gallery for the shipping magnate A. G. Kröller and his wife Helen Kröller-Müller, who collected paintings. Mies had worked on the project in Behrens's office but had been asked by the client to produce his own design. He proposed a low, articulated, asymmetrical composition with flat roofs and long colonnades, firmly neo-classical in spirit.

After setting up his own practice in 1912 Mies designed several more neo-classical houses, many of which were built and some of which, such as the Urbig House at Potsdam-Neubabelsberg of 1917, survive in good condition. One thing that these houses all have in common is the careful way that they relate to their sites through secondary structures such as porches, pergolas and terraces. In the Urbig House, for example, the dining room, reception room and parlour all open onto a raised terrace, actually the roof of a basement, which is like another, external room. House and garden are combined in a single work of architecture. The influence of Behrens is clear and, beyond him, of Schinkel, but perhaps we can also see here the beginnings of that overlapping of internal and external spaces that is such an important feature of the later, Modernist designs. In 1925 Mies was still developing his domestic neo-classical style. The steeply pitched hip roof of the Mosler House, also in Potsdam-Neubabelsberg, rests on plain walls relieved only by minimal abstract ornament in the form of grooves and stepped reveals around finely proportioned windows. The local building inspector at the time was worried that it would look like an army barracks, but to modern eyes it looks suave and sophisticated.

**Glass skyscraper (unbuilt). Mies van der Rohe,
1921.** One of two glass skyscraper schemes –
a conceptual advance that would not be fully realized
until the 1950s.

A change of direction

But the Mosler House was a last, late example of Mies's
neo-classical style, for in 1922 he had changed his name,
left his wife Ada and their three children, and devoted
himself to a new kind of architecture. In the standard
historical accounts, this new architecture is represented
not by finished buildings but by a group of five theoretical
projects. We must remember that after the First World War
the Weimar Republic was in a parlous economic state and
opportunities to build were scarce. Perhaps the lack of
work was itself a spur to creative rethinking, an opportunity
for Mies to pause and change direction. The five projects
are: two glass skyscrapers of 1921 and 1922, the Concrete
Office Building of 1923, the Concrete Country House of
1923 and the Brick Country House of 1924.

At this time Mies was influenced by the Expressionism
of Bruno Taut and the fantasy glass architecture of Paul

Scheerbart (see page 73). His two projects for glass
skyscrapers are not fantasies, however, but practical
proposals, the second of them a competition entry for
a corner site in Berlin's Friedrichstrasse. Mies seems
to have been fascinated by the unpredictable visual
effects created by a large facetted glass building – the
elusiveness of shadows, and the way that transparency
and reflectiveness were combined. The charcoal drawings
he made to study these effects were more like abstract
art than representations of buildings. But in hindsight the
conceptual advance made in these projects was more
important than their visual qualities. A free-form floor plan
supported by a steel or concrete frame is stacked up
to skyscraper height and sheathed in a continuous skin
of glass. This was a prophetic vision. It took the typical
skyscraper of New York or Chicago and rationalized it,
stripping it of its traditional architectural clothes and
revealing its true nature.

The other urban project of this period, the Concrete Office Building, was also an experiment in construction. Mies, ever the practical builder, worked with the characteristics of his material, using its strength, its structural efficiency and its monolithic nature to create a new form. Floors like trays are stiffened by downstand beams and supported on columns with cruciform capitals that merge into the beams. The floors are cantilevered all round the building with upstand walls at their edges. Gaps between these walls and the floors above are filled with continuous ribbons of glass. It could almost be some kind of purely functional storage system, but there is architecture in the details – the way the cantilevered beams are allowed to penetrate the glass, for example, or the way that a section of floor is removed to create a double-height entrance with a grand flight of steps.

Concrete Country House and Brick Country House

The ideas represented in these commercial and urban projects would have to wait 30 years to be realized in actual buildings. They re-emerged not in Germany but in America. For the time being, we must put them to one side in order to concentrate on the two house projects. They are so different from the neo-classical houses that it is hard to believe they are by the same architect and designed at about the same time. Both are loose, asymmetrical compositions of flat planes and cubic volumes. The plan-form of the Concrete Country House is like a three-legged swastika; the Brick Country House is indistinct in outline, seeming to consist of a rectilinear cluster of freestanding walls of different thicknesses and lengths. Three of these walls are extended to the edge of the drawing as if they might go on to infinity. It is hard to be more precise in the description of these projects because all that survives of them are two model

Concrete Office Building (unbuilt). Mies van der Rohe, 1923. The entrance is formed by simply omitting a section of solid wall to reveal a flight of steps.

photographs with two perspective views in the case of the concrete house, and a sparsely annotated plan with a single perspective view in the case of the brick house. But there is enough information for us to see clearly that they announce the arrival of a new architectural system. Certain features have since become commonplace: the long ribbon windows and cantilevered flat roofs of the concrete house, for example, and the free plan of the brick house, which is composed not of separate rooms but of loosely defined spaces that overlap, flow into one another and are only notionally contained by glass external walls. We have seen these things in many a subsequent twentieth-century Modernist house; here they are appearing for the first time.

But nothing in architecture is completely new and these projects also have traditional aspects. One is apparent in their titles. They are not insubstantial visions or purely aesthetic creations like the various Expressionist projects of the period; they are houses designed to be built in specific materials, concrete and brick, and their forms arise from the nature of those materials. Reinforced concrete is an enormously strong, monolithic material that can span long distances and overhang its supports. Brick, on the other hand, is best for solid walls with small openings – or in this case no openings at all. There are later versions of the brick house plan, prepared in Mies's office in the 1960s, in which every single brick is drawn. This is Mies the bricklayer, respecting the dimensional discipline that brick imposes.

Concrete Country House (unbuilt). Mies van der Rohe, 1923. The building's relationship to its site applies lessons learnt in more traditional designs.

It is a respect that we can see very clearly in the beautiful traditional brickwork of, for example, the Mosler House. We can also detect here the influence of Hendrik Petrus Berlage, Peter Behrens's Dutch counterpart, whom Mies met when working on the Kröller-Müller House. Berlage, whose most famous work is the Beurs in Amsterdam of 1903 (see page 41), was a committed believer in the nineteenth-century idea of truth to materials. It is an aspect of Berlage's architecture that Mies greatly admired and referred to regularly throughout his career.

There is another traditional feature that links these designs to Mies's neo-classical houses: the way that they relate to their sites. In the Brick Country House, the long extended walls lock the building into its location and orientate it with the precision of a sundial so that the site and surroundings actively participate in the design. The building seems to have grown here rather than been placed here. And in the stepped terraces of the Concrete Country House, with its tucked-in lower floor taking advantage of the slope, we see the careful modelling of the site to receive the building that is such a satisfying feature of Mies's traditional houses, going right back to the Riehl House.

But where does the new, modern system come from? At this time, Berlin was an important European centre of modern art. Both Theo van Doesburg, the leader of the Dutch De Stijl movement, and El Lissitzky, chief promoter of Russian Constructivism and Suprematism, were frequent visitors to Berlin in the early 1920s. Mies knew them well and collaborated with them in the publication of the magazine *G*, in which Mies's glass skyscraper projects were first published. A superficial resemblance between two works of art does not prove that one influenced the other, but when we look, for example, at van Doesburg's painting *Rhythm of a Russian Dance* of 1918 it is hard not to believe that we are looking at the inspiration for the plan of the Brick Country House. In the early 1920s Mies the builder opened his mind to the spatial possibilities suggested by the work of painters like Piet Mondrian and Kazimir Malevich. Abstract painting did not supplant the traditions of craftsmanship and classical restraint in Mies's mental makeup, but joined with them to quicken and strengthen a new creative impulse.

Brick Country House (unbuilt). Mies van der Rohe, 1923. The Elementarist plan shows the influence of Dutch and Russian painters that Mies met in Berlin.

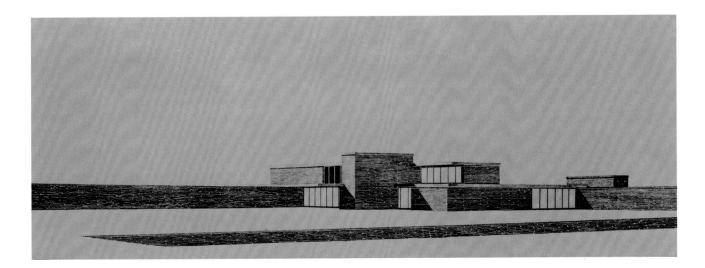

Influence of Wright

There is no doubting the influence on Mies of De Stijl and Russian Suprematism, but we should not forget another, underlying influence that Mies shared with many progressive European architects of the time: Frank Lloyd Wright. The Wasmuth portfolio (see page 34) had been published in Berlin in 1910 and had had a profound effect on the work of architects attached to the De Stijl group, especially Robert van 't Hoff (see page 88). Wright was mostly antagonistic towards European Modernism and neither did he have much respect for the classical tradition represented by Schinkel. But from his feeling for materials and his deft disassembly of the old room-based domestic plan, Mies learnt a fundamental lesson. This is what Mies wrote in later years about his early encounter with Wright's work: 'The more we were absorbed in the study of these creations, the greater became our admiration for his incomparable talent, the boldness of his conceptions and the independence of his thought and action.'[2]

The country house projects marked a turning point in Mies's architecture. But they were only projects. In the buildings that followed, such as the Wolf house of 1927 and the Lange and Esters houses of 1928, we see that new creative force struggling to impose its will on real clients, real budgets and real sites. The results are impressive and intriguing, but not yet fully mature. The Wolf House, for example, built in Gubin (now in Poland) for a wealthy factory owner and collector of modern art, was clearly a compromised version of the Brick Country House. On the main floor, there were discernible, traditionally designated rooms – study, music room, living room, dining room – but they were not completely defined because

each shared a wall plane with its neighbour. Space was encouraged to flow between them and out onto the large terrace, which was another partially defined room. This was a version of the Urbig House plan, but more dynamic and abstract. Brick was the main external material. Sadly the Wolf House was destroyed in the Second World War but if it had survived, to judge from the photographs, it would stand now as a model of perfection in the art of laying bricks, both conceptually and physically.

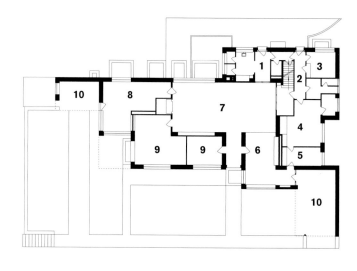

Ground floor plan

1. Entrance
2. Service entrance
3. Maid's room
4. Kitchen
5. Servery
6. Dining room
7. Living room
8. Study
9. Day room
10. Covered terrace

Lange House, Krefeld, Germany. Mies van der Rohe, 1928. Ideas developed on paper at last face the discipline of real clients and real sites.

Mies was never a very socially conscious architect. He accepted economic and social conditions as given and interpreted them as an artist, not as a politician. Perhaps it was because of his political neutrality that in 1927 he was called upon by the Deutsche Werkbund to co-ordinate an ambitious exhibition of modern housing in Stuttgart. The Weissenhof exhibition is so important to the history of Modernism that it must be treated separately (see page 101) but Mies's own contribution, a long, four-storey apartment block at the top of the sloping site, dominating the estate, represents an important development in his architecture. Like most of the rest of the houses in the exhibition it is covered in smooth stucco, but the almost continuous bands of windows betray its true, steel-framed nature. This was Mies's first steel frame. Its effect was more conceptual than visual, allowing flexibility in the planning of apartments. In later buildings, as we shall see, it was to break cover and assert its architectural value.

Tugendhat House

History has chosen two buildings to represent the period of Mies's artistic maturity – the Tugendhat House in Brno, Czech Republic, completed in 1930, and the so-called

Apartments, Weissenhof Siedlung, Stuttgart, Germany. Mies van der Rohe, 1927. The steel frame, so characteristic of Mies's later works, as yet remains hidden.

Barcelona Pavilion, actually the German pavilion, at the 1929 International Exposition in Barcelona. Both buildings develop ideas that appear first in the country-house projects, but there is a major difference: the main structural material is now neither brick nor concrete, but steel, steel made visible in cruciform columns sleeved in shiny chromium-plated casings. The columns are so slender that in some versions of the plans they are hard to see, and in the buildings themselves they can hardly be said to dominate the scene. What is more, there is some doubt, in the case of the Barcelona Pavilion at least, as to whether they are structurally necessary. It might have been possible to have supported the roof on the walls. Nevertheless, these columns are the keynote of both designs. Their function is as much symbolic as structural. They symbolize two related ideas: first that the internal space is freed from the discipline imposed by loadbearing walls, and second that a more subtle discipline is present nevertheless in the regular grid to which the columns conform. In these

Tugendhat House, Brno, Czech Republic. Mies van der Rohe, 1930. Sections of the glass wall can be lowered into the floor by electric motors.

columns we see a reconciliation of opposites: discipline and freedom, classicism and Expressionism, the collective and the individual, tradition and invention. They are perhaps the keynote not just of these particular buildings but of the whole of Mies's architecture.

Greta Tugendhat was an intellectual, an early follower of the philosopher Martin Heidegger, and she knew exactly what she was doing when she commissioned Mies to design a house for herself and her husband Fritz. In plan and section the house is rather complex, three storeys high on a steeply sloping site with the entrance on the top floor. Its architectural heart, however, is the main living room on the middle floor, which geometrically is not much more than a simple slice of space between level floor and flat ceiling. Walls of glass on adjacent sides offer either a long view over the garden to the south or a close-up view of pot plants in a narrow winter garden to the east. Other walls are complicated by informal set-backs and alcoves, but there are local symmetries in the middle of the room where two extraordinary full-height objects, a flat screen of solid onyx and a dark, ebony-veneered partial cylinder, stand side by side facing the garden. The first provides the backdrop for a sitting area and the second is wrapped round a circular

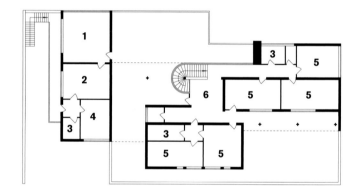

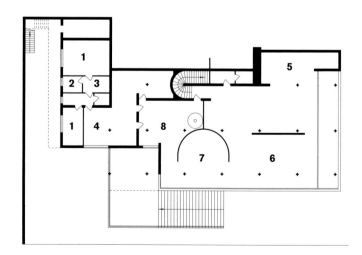

Second floor plan	**First floor plan**	7. Dining area
1. Garage	1. Staff room	8. Servery
2. Storage	2. Bathroom	
3. Bathroom	3. Storage	
4. Chauffeur's room	4. Kitchen	
5. Bedrooms	5. Study	
6. Main entrance	6. Sitting area	

dining table. Each is assisted in its space-defining by a pair of chrome-clad columns aligned with mullions in the glass south wall. Panels of glass between the mullions can be lowered into the floor by electric motors. Dining and sitting, whether as solitary or group activities, were never before so minimally yet so sumptuously supported by architecture. A door at the west end of the south wall opens onto a paved terrace from which a broad flight of steps descends to the garden. When the house was new, a willow tree stood near these steps, exactly opposite the dining area.

Barcelona Pavilion

It is some measure of the prominence that Mies had attained in Germany that he should have been chosen to design the national contribution to the Barcelona Exposition. As well as the pavilion itself, he was responsible for various industrial exhibits in the main exhibition halls. These he entrusted to his friend and collaborator Lilly Reich. We should not infer from this that the exhibits were unimportant to Mies or that Reich was a mere assistant carrying out the master's wishes. She was a designer of vision and her influence on Mies was considerable, especially in matters such as colour, texture, materials and lighting. It was a sensible division of responsibility and it allowed Mies to concentrate on the most important commission of his career. He saw its potential and he eagerly grasped the opportunity.

History has sanctified the Barcelona Pavilion. It has come to be regarded not just as Mies's masterpiece but as the epitome of modern architecture. It was not a house but we can see in it all of the themes that Mies had been developing in his domestic architecture for 20 years. Here is the raised podium that first appeared in primitive form in the Riehl House; here is the concept of garden and house combined in a single composition that we have seen in the Urbig House and many others including the Kröller-Müller House and the Concrete Country House; here is the free-flowing plan of the Brick Country House, the flat roof, the floor-to-ceiling glass and the straight unbuttressed walls of indefinite length; here is the builder's love of materials – the travertine paving and the figured marbles of the heavy yet seemingly weightless walls; and here is classical discipline represented by the eight shining columns and the plain rectangle of the roof that they support. The building

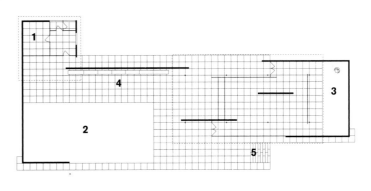

Plan
1. Office   4. Bench
2. Pool   5. Entrance steps
3. Sculpture

0   5   10m
15   30 ft

German Pavilion, Barcelona Exposition. Mies van der Rohe, 1929, reconstructed 1986. The Pavilion was lovingly rebuilt on its original site by modern-architecture enthusiasts.

has been analyzed many times in many ways. One of the most interesting interpretations is the idea that specular reflection is a prominent theme; that the mirror-like surfaces of marble and glass are as important as the arrangement of horizontal and vertical planes. The building also mirrors itself horizontally, the horizon being a continuous joint in the marble at approximately the eye height of a standing person.

The Barcelona Pavilion had no specific function other than to accommodate its own opening ceremony. When the King and Queen of Spain came to sign their names in a golden book they sat on chairs specially designed by Mies. Those chairs of chromium-plated steel with leather-covered cushions are still in production and can be seen in architects' living rooms and the foyers of office blocks all over the world. But they were originally thrones for a king and queen. In the Barcelona Pavilion Mies proved that Modernism could mean more than mere functionalism, that it could be symbolic, honorific, spiritual. When the exhibition was over, the building was torn down but it was not forgotten by architects. They mourned its passing and in 1986 they rebuilt it, reproducing it lovingly from drawings and photographs. It became a monument to Modernism. In 1929 Peter Behrens, Mies's old mentor, had said: 'The Pavilion will someday be called the most beautiful building of the century.' It must have seemed mere hyperbole at the time, but he was right.[3]

The Barcelona Pavilion and the Tugendhat House represent the pinnacle of Mies's achievement in the European phase of his career. He remained in Germany for another nine years, but they were years of increasing frustration. In 1930 he took over the directorship of the Bauhaus School in Dessau where he remained for two years until the growing influence of Nazism in the local authority forced its closure. Mies reopened it as a private school in Berlin, but it lasted

only a few months. Meanwhile, his career as an architect stagnated. He built very little apart from an impressive demonstration house at the Berlin Building Exhibition of 1931, but he continued to refine his ideas in paper projects. For example, he designed a series of court houses that demonstrate with complete clarity the balance of freedom and discipline that had become a hallmark of his work. The House with Three Courts of 1934 can be seen as a version of the now familiar open-plan house adapted for an urban site. The basic ingredients – cruciform columns, flat roof and glass external wall – are handled with great assurance, but the whole composition, including the three external courtyards, is bounded by a continuous wall like the frame of a picture. Ten years earlier, in the Brick Country House, walls reached out into the surrounding landscape. Now the house had become a self-contained world.

For a time after Hitler's accession to power in 1933, the Nazis' attitude to modern art and architecture was ambiguous. Mies still hoped to build and tried several times to secure government commissions. The question was to what extent his artistic principles would have to be compromised. His shortlisted entry for an extension to the Reichsbank in Berlin took the form of an enormous, symmetrical, three-pronged block clad in austere and monotonous curtain walling. The project did not go ahead. His design for the German pavilion at the 1935 Brussels World Fair included an imposing symmetrical hall of honour. Mies had refused to display any national symbol other than a flag on the Barcelona Pavilion, but in the drawings of the Brussels pavilion we can see, tentatively sketched, an eagle and a swastika. Again the project was aborted. Tempting invitations began to arrive from American institutions and individuals. Finally, in 1938, this German who had lived in Germany all his 50 years chose unsettling freedom over ignoble compromise and sailed for America.

Design for the German pavilion for the Brussels World Fair. Mies van der Rohe, 1925. Eagles and swastikas were tentatively sketched.

Karl Friedrich Schinkel

Karl Friedrich Schinkel was the greatest German architect of the nineteenth century. He began his career as a painter and stage set designer and worked briefly as an independent architect, but in 1810 he dedicated himself to the service of the Prussian state and monarchy. The city of Berlin was transformed by the major public buildings that he designed, such as the Neue Wache (guardhouse), the Schauspielhaus (theatre) and the Altes Museum, all executed in a beautifully proportioned classical style derived from his teacher, Friedrich Gilly, from the French architectural theorist J. N. L. Durand and from the architecture of ancient Greece. The style came to be known as Romantic classicism. Schinkel was, however, capable of designing equally skilfully in the Gothic and Italianate styles and after a trip to England in 1826 he became interested in the functional architecture of factories and commercial buildings, applying what he learnt in buildings such as the Neue Packhof (new customs house) and the Bauakademie (architecture school) in Berlin.

Twentieth-century German architects such as Mies van der Rohe's mentor Peter Behrens venerated Schinkel, both for his superb handling of form and for his progressive attitude to building technology. In the years before the First World War, Behrens would make tours of the Schinkel buildings around Berlin with his young assistants, including Mies. The influence of Schinkel is obvious in Mies's early

traditional houses and in the Bismarck Memorial project of 1910 but critics have also felt it in his later, Modernist works. Crown Hall at the Illinois Institute of Technology, for example, has been compared to the Altes Museum for its simplicity and poise. Certain details too, such as the carefully considered corner treatment of the Seagram Building in New York, recall the refinement of Schinkel's classicism.

Philip Johnson, who championed Mies in the late 1930s and helped smooth his passage to America, saw parallels between Schinkel's picturesque Italianate designs and Mies's free, abstract style of the late 1920s and early 1930s. The Gardeners' House at Charlottenhof, designed in the 1830s, might at first seem a world away from the Barcelona Pavilion of 1929, but the two buildings share certain features, such as the asymmetrical disposition of the basic elements, the use of sculpture, the raised podium with steps parallel to the wall rather than perpendicular to it, and the relationship between house (or pavilion) and garden. The Barcelona Pavilion is uncompromisingly modern but in its spatial effect, according to Johnson, it is 'Schinkelesque'.

Altes Museum, Berlin, Germany. Karl Friedrich Schinkel, 1830. The influence of Schinkel is more obvious in Mies's later, more monumental works.

RUSSIAN CONSTRUCTIVISM
1917–1936

Modernist architecture is as much Russian as western European. History has traced its origins in Germany, Holland and France but its character would have been very different without the injection of revolutionary fervour that it received from Russian artists and designers after 1917. Progressive architects in Russia were impressed by western developments and keen to learn from them. Le Corbusier, Ernst May, Hannes Meyer and Erich Mendelsohn were all invited to carry out projects in the USSR in the 1920s. But the flow of ideas was not all in one direction. The influence of Malevich's and El Lissitzky's Suprematism, for example, had already been absorbed in the development of De Stijl and Elementarism (see Chapter 7). And as theoretical projects began to be translated into actual buildings, it was in Russia that the most impressive examples were to be found.

Moisei Ginzburg's Narkomfin communal housing block, completed in 1930, clearly shows the influence of Le Corbusier, but there is nothing to match it among Le Corbusier's own built works until the Unité d'Habitation of 1952. The progressive educational programme of the Vkhutemas art and architecture school, established in Moscow in 1920, was comparable to that of the Bauhaus. It has even been suggested that it was the influence of Vkhutemas, and in particular of the painter, sculptor and photographer Aleksandr Rodchenko, that woke Walter Gropius and his colleagues from their Expressionist trance and encouraged them to adopt a more practical, industry-based curriculum.

Ideological groups

'Vkhutemas' is only one of a confusing array of acronyms for the various artistic and ideological groupings of the post-revolutionary years. Inkhuk (the Institute of Artistic Culture), founded in Moscow in 1920, was not a specifically architectural association but it set the tone of avant-garde artistic debate. Asnova (the Association of New Architects) was set up by Nikolai Ladovsky in Moscow in 1923.

Beat the Whites with the Red Wedge,
poster by El Lissitzky, 1919.
Constructivists thought that art should serve society – a principle readily transferred to architecture.

Wassily Kandinsky, Kazimir Malevich and El Lissitzky were members. The group took a basically rationalist view of the craft of architecture, taking into account psychological as well as objectively measurable criteria. OSA (the Union of Contemporary Architects), founded by Moisei Ginzburg in Moscow in 1925, took a different view, arguing that functional requirements and available technical resources were sufficient to determine the form of any building. Architecture was seen as the servant of the state, solving social and technical problems by developing new building types and new methods of construction. It was Ginzburg and his colleagues in OSA, including the three Vesnin brothers (Aleksandr, Leonid and Viktor), who developed the architectural wing of the artistic movement known as 'Constructivism'. It is a term (like its opposite, 'Deconstructivism', coined 60 years later) that sits awkwardly in an architectural context. Its central principle – that art should serve a useful social purpose – is already taken for granted in architecture. And the idea that works of art could be 'constructed' from premade components, like the printed text in Lissitzky's poster *Beat the Whites with the Red Wedge* or the metal rings in one of Rodchenko's 'Spatial Constructions', is commonplace in the art of building. Constructivism seems to say little more than that art should be more like architecture. The term has nevertheless established itself firmly in architectural history and is often used to refer to Russian Modernist architecture as a whole.

In the years immediately after the revolution, modern artists served the state mainly through the graphic art of posters, film, theatre and other propaganda media. Architects had to be content with theoretical projects like Vladimir Tatlin's Monument to the Third International (an international communist organization founded in 1919). It would have been about 100 metres (330 feet) taller than the Eiffel Tower but in the Russia of 1920 it had no prospect of being built, although many scale models of it have since been made for display in exhibitions of Russian art. Its spiralling iron frame leans over like a gun firing long-range missiles of communist ideology into distant countries. Inside the spiral, three pure geometrical solids – a cube, a pyramid and a cylinder – contain, respectively, auditoriums, offices and a communications centre. The cube rotates once a year, the pyramid once a month and the cylinder once a day. On a smaller scale but hardly less impractical, Lissitzky's 'tribune' for Lenin is another leaning, open-framed tower, this time supporting an Elementarist pulpit perched on the end of an impossibly cantilevered platform. In the drawings, Lenin leans even further forward as if projecting his message to the whole world.

Monument to the Third International. Vladimir Tatlin, 1920. 100 metres (330 feet) taller than the Eiffel Tower but with no chance of realization in 1920s Russia.

Lenin Tribune. El Lissitzky, 1920. A dynamic architecture to reflect the ambitions of the new communist state.

At least one of these early Constructivist projects was a prophetic masterpiece. The Vesnin brothers' design for a building to house the Moscow branch of the newspaper *Leningradskaya Pravda* is a six-storey building but so small on plan that it looks like a soaring skyscraper. An exposed steel frame is in-filled with glass, lifts are clearly visible in their articulated glass shafts, there is what seems to be a revolving news bulletin board at high level on the street frontage, and above that a digital clock. A searchlight on the roof looks to modern eyes like a satellite dish. It could be a High Tech building of the 1980s, perhaps by Richard Rogers (see Chapter 26). The Vesnins began their career in pre-revolutionary years designing mainly in a traditional, neo-classical style, but by the early 1920s they had become leading Constructivists. Their entry for the Palace of Labour competition of 1923 accommodates its vast auditorium in an oval drum connected by a high-level bridge to a stepped administration block possibly inspired by Walter Gropius's entry for the Chicago Tribune tower competition. Bridge

girders and roof trusses are exposed to view and the whole ensemble is crowned by an enormous, elaborate radio antenna like the rigging of a sailing ship.

Konstantin Mel'nikov was not a Constructivist. Trained first as a painter he was loosely connected with Vkhutemas and Asnova but maintained his independence and developed his own style. His Soviet pavilion at the 1925 Decorative Arts exhibition in Paris was completely unconventional, avoiding the fashionable Constructivist symbolism of exposed steelwork and radio antennae. It was made of wood and rectangular on plan but sliced in half diagonally by an external staircase that rose and fell from corner to corner. A canopy of interlocking panels and an open, freestanding tower played further variations on the angled theme. Though its geometry was unusual, its construction was simple and cheap. It is said to have been built in less than a month by only ten men. Such ingenuity and practicality was to be put to good use in more permanent buildings later in the decade.

(Left) Leningradskaya Pravda Building project by Leonid, Viktor and Aleksandr Vesnin, 1924. A High Tech project before its time. It even appears to have a satellite dish on the roof (actually a searchlight).

(Below) Soviet Pavilion, Paris Exposition of Decorative Arts. Konstantin Mel'nikov, 1925. Mel'nikov invented new forms and techniques independently of his Constructivist contemporaries.

One of the first major public buildings to be built in Moscow after the revolution and civil war was the headquarters of the newspaper *Izvestiya*, designed by Grigori and Mikhail Barkhin. It still exists and looks now like a routine Modernist office block with shops at street level. When it was completed in 1927 it must have looked far more assertive. Old photographs show it dwarfing the classical facade of the monastery next door, now demolished. Projecting balconies and a storey-height sign at roof level give it a vaguely Constructivist air, although the row of circular windows, suggesting a classical 'attic', was criticized at the time in the OSA magazine *SA* (short for *Sovremennaya Arkhitektura* or 'Contemporary Architecture') for being too traditional.

Lingering traces of the classical tradition can be seen even in engineering structures such as those connected with the vast project to electrify the whole country. The river frontage of Ivan Zholtovsky's Moscow city power station,

designed in 1926, is clearly the work of a classically trained architect. There is no pure ornament, but a row of plain pilasters between arched windows supports a vestigial cornice with a glazed attic above. The rear of the building is more adventurous with large areas of glass in tall projections like multi-storey bay windows. When, in 1929, Viktor Vesnin entered the competition to design the hydro-electric power station associated with the Dnieper dam in the Ukraine he refused any such compromise. The dam was the biggest of its kind in the world and the first fruit of Stalin's drive to establish the USSR as a fully developed industrial power. It was a huge propaganda opportunity and the architecture of the power station was therefore a matter of national importance. Vesnin's building has been rebuilt in an altered form since its destruction in the Second World War, but originally it was a long, stark, flat-roofed concrete box with two continuous horizontal ribbon windows stretching from end to end. If anything, it is the dam itself, with its row of vertical piers and buttresses, that looks vaguely classical.

Izvestiya headquarters, Moscow, Russia. Grigori and Mikhail Barkhin, 1927. One of the first major buildings to be completed in Moscow after the revolution.

139

Classicism vs Modernism

Classicism is traditionally associated with social elites and this was as much the case in communist Russia as in the capitalist west. If the Barkhins' Izvestiya building is Modernist with a lingering trace of classicism, certain apartment blocks in Moscow originally designed for prominent party members are classicist with a nod to Modernism. Boris Iofan was the architect of the Government House building in Moscow, sometimes called the 'House of Ghosts' because so many of its occupants disappeared in Stalin's purges. Designed in 1928 and completed in 1931, this eleven-storey-high complex fills a whole urban block on the Moskva River, facing the Kremlin. It includes various communal facilities, including a cinema in a separate, functionally designed building with a semi-dome roof, but the main residential wings are classically inspired. The river frontage, for example, is a symmetrical composition with Sullivanesque towers at each end and a four-storey-high hexastyle portico in the middle, stripped of ornament.

In 1933 it was Iofan who eventually won the Palace of the Soviets competition (see pages 146 and 184) with a monumental design that confirmed the triumph of the officially approved classicism over Modernism/ Constructivism. History naturally favours progressive trends in the development of architecture, sometimes creating the impression that these trends were dominant in practice as well as in theory. Government House and many buildings like it are reminders that most Soviet architecture of the 1920s and 1930s blended Modernist austerity with the symmetries and regularities of the classical tradition.

Russian Modernists were well aware of developments in western Europe and sometimes helped to secure official commissions for famous foreigners. Le Corbusier's well-known Tsentrosoyuz complex in Moscow (see page 120) was not an isolated example. In 1925 Erich Mendelsohn was invited to design a large textile factory in Leningrad (now St Petersburg). His master plan for the whole site was altered by production engineers, but his design for the power plant was built as he intended. It occupies a prominent site on a street corner and is typically Mendelsohnian in its arrangement of horizontally banded, semi-circular forms. Jealous local Modernists, writing in *SA* magazine, were critical of its dynamic expressiveness, considering it insufficiently 'functional'.

(Below) Government House, Moscow, Russia. Boris Iofan, 1931. A blending of Modernism with classicism. Note the four-storey-high plain hexastyle portico.

(Opposite) Power Plant, St Petersburg, Russia. Erich Mendelsohn, 1927. A typically racy Mendelsohnian composition, though local architects thought it insufficiently functional.

In 1930 Ernst May, Modernist city architect of Frankfurt since 1925 (see Chapter 8), was invited to Moscow to work on the development of a new city in the southern Urals called Magnitogorsk. It was to house workers at a new steelworks built with the aid of American advisors – a flagship project in Stalin's five-year plan. May's team, or 'brigade', included Margarete Schütte-Lihotzky, Hans Schmidt and Mart Stam. At the time, before the cruel consequences of Stalin's development drive became apparent and disillusionment set in, May wrote in glowing terms of the regime and the architectural opportunities it offered. Hannes Meyer, Gropius's successor as director of the Bauhaus, was another western Modernist who, fleeing from fascism in Germany, found for a short time a sympathetic client in the Soviet state. But perhaps the most important foreign architect to work in Russia in the 1930s was the American Albert Kahn (see Chapter 5), who in 1929 signed a contract with the Soviet government to design a tractor factory in Stalingrad (now Volgograd).

Kahn had been recommended by his long-standing client, Henry Ford, who had been selling motor vehicles to the Russians since 1919. More commissions followed over the next three years, including another tractor factory in Chelyabinsk, the aforementioned steelworks in Magnitogorsk, and a car and truck factory at Nizhny Novgorod based on the design of Ford's River Rouge plant in Dearborn, Michigan. Kahn established a large design office in Russia, managed by his brother Moritz, which employed, and effectively trained, hundreds of Russian architects and engineers. The venture was short lived, however, coming to an end in 1932 when the Russians insisted on paying Kahn in local currency. By this time opinion formers in America, approving at first, had begun to question the strategic wisdom of the relationship.

Visions of a new domestic architecture

But Russia had its own leading Modernists, among them Moisei Ginzburg, founder of OSA and author of *Stil' i epokha* ('Style and Epoch'), the Russian equivalent of Le Corbusier's *Vers une architecture*. Ginzburg was a believer in social as well as political revolution, in the restructuring of family life and the emancipation of women. A new kind of family meant a new kind of home, not the traditional multifunctional group of rooms but a rational allocation of space for individual and collective activities. Ginzburg thought, for example, that the apartment of the future would have no need of a kitchen since cooking and eating would be communal activities taking place in a separate wing of the building. Communal creches and kindergartens would allow mothers to work full time, for the benefit of the state as much as for their own social standing.

The Narkomfin apartment block in Moscow, designed by Ginzburg with Ignaty Milinis and completed in 1932, is as close as Russian domestic architecture came to realizing that vision of the future. It still exists, half ruined and with no immediate prospect of restoration, though its historical importance is widely acknowledged. 'Narkomfin' refers to the People's Commissariat of Finance, whose bureaucrats were the building's first tenants. The main block is six storeys high and contains 54 apartments of two main types: two-bedroom, two-storey; and one-bedroom, one-storey. Access is via long, straight corridors. The smaller flats, for single people and childless couples, were originally provided with very basic, theoretically temporary kitchens on the assumption that tenants would eventually learn to eat their meals communally.

This description might suggest a mean and minimal provision but in fact the apartments are well lit and quite generously proportioned. Each has windows on both sides of the block and a double- or one-and-a-half-storey-height living room. Even the corridors are pleasant spaces, lit by continuous ribbon windows with freestanding concrete columns to measure out their length. These architectural bonuses are the result of an ingenious section with corridors only on alternate levels – an arrangement much imitated by later Modernist housing designers, including Le Corbusier himself. But there is give-and-take here, because there can be no doubt that the overall form of the block – concrete framed, raised on pilotis, with ribbon windows and a garden on the roof – conforms knowingly to Le Corbusier's 'Five Points'. A second, cube-shaped wing, connected to the main building by an enclosed bridge at first-floor level, contains most of the necessary communal facilities, including a dining hall and kitchen, a gymnasium and a library. A separate kindergarten block was designed but never built. Ginzburg himself lived, with his family, in one of the larger apartments.

Narkomfin Building, Moscow, Russia. Moisei Ginzburg, 1932. Le Corbusier, honoured in Russia as a Modernist master, was himself influenced by buildings such as this.

The communal housing complex on Ulitsa Ordzhonikidze, Moscow, designed in 1929 by the 28-year-old Ivan Nikolaev to house students of the State Textile Institute, also seems to have influenced, and been influenced by, Le Corbusier. It was if anything even more radical than the Narkomfin building. A straight, narrow, 200-metre- (650-feet-) long, eight-storey slab contained 1,000 tiny, identical two-bed rooms. Communal facilities, including a dining room, a reading room and a sports centre, were grouped in an (almost) parallel three-storey block. A sanitary block linked the two, with bathrooms, exercise spaces and vertical circulation in the form of a spiral ramp, triangular on plan. So the students' basic needs were all supplied but in a rationalized, collective form, as if each were either a sleeping individual or an active member of a 2,000-strong cohort, with nothing in between. Time was as regimented as space.

Communal housing for the State Textile Institute, Moscow, Russia. Ivan Nikolaev, 1929. Bedroom block on the left, sanitary block on the right. This was collective living without compromise.

All students were expected to go to bed at ten, rise at six and follow a strict daily routine. Unsurprisingly, this regime and others like it were unpopular and soon collapsed, leaving their architectural analogues washed up like rusting hulks in an ideological backwater. The Textile Institute building survived nevertheless and was recently refitted to suit a more relaxed lifestyle.

The ingenious Mel'nikov owed no debt to Le Corbusier but went his own way, inventing new forms and new styles. The house that he built for himself in Moscow in 1929, and lived in until his death in 1974, looks like a small chapel. A pair

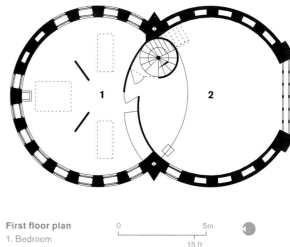

First floor plan
1. Bedroom
2. Living room

0   5m
15 ft

Mel'nikov House, Moscow, Russia. Konstantin Mel'nikov, 1929. Bizarre yet logical. Lozenge-shaped windows need no lintels and cylinders are self-buttressing.

of interlocking cylinders is perforated by a discontinuous grid of small, lozenge-shaped windows. Some critics have read mystical meanings into this strange configuration but in fact it was designed as an experimental prototype for low-cost workers' housing. The cylinder is a logical shape for loadbearing brickwork since it requires no buttressing, and the lozenge-shaped windows, formed by stepped and corbelled bricks, obviate the need for steel or concrete lintels. The floors of the house are innovative too, using a primitive stressed skin structure to span the 9-metre (30-foot) diameter of each cylinder. Not that Mel'nikov was an entirely rational designer. He had strange views about sleeping and hygiene, for example. The bedroom of the house was equipped with three fixed, symmetrically arranged, tomb-like sleeping platforms, one double and two singles for parents and two children, with no other furniture. Clothes were stored in a communal dressing room on the ground floor.

Mel'nikov was equally unconventional in public commissions. His Rusakov Workers' Club, built in Moscow in 1928, was one of many 'social condensers' designed to extend the cultural and educational reach of the communist state. It is an exercise in adaptability. A 1,200-seat auditorium with raked seating is divided into three segments that can be further subdivided at both stalls and balcony levels. This is not a single theatre, therefore, but a cluster of theatres of different sizes nested within one another. Externally the three main segments are expressed as separate forms radiating from a common stage, their upper tiers boldly cantilevered. The whole building has an industrial look, like a machine for handling grain or gravel, with no concessions to architectural respectability.

The slightly earlier Zuev Workers' Club, designed by Ilya Golosov in 1927, manages to look less utilitarian, more urbane, without resorting to explicit classical references. Its complex exterior form plays concrete against glass, often using one where you would expect the other. For example, a fat but fragile glass cylinder on the street corner interpenetrates and seems to support a heavy rectangular concrete mass at high level. Such sophisticated form-making might have been influenced by Mendelsohn. Mel'nikov could also enjoy form for its own sake, and in an unlikely building

Rusakov Workers' Club, Moscow, Russia. Konstantin Mel'nikov, 1928. A cluster of auditoriums that can be used individually or in different combinations.

type. He designed several purely functional garages and car parks for Moscow in the 1920s and 1930s, but in the Gosplan Garage of 1936 he and his co-designer, V. I. Kurochkin, allowed themselves a degree of Expressionist freedom. The office wing has fluted external walls like the radiator of a car. Beside it a two-storey-high circular window of uncertain function is set in a dynamic spiral of concrete like a piece of Futurist sculpture.

Zuev Workers' Club, Moscow, Russia. Ilya Golosov, 1927.
Golosov plays concrete against glass, often using one where you would expect the other.

Paper architecture

Architectural history remembers projects as well as buildings, and 'paper architecture' can be just as influential as the concrete kind. Ivan Leonidov built almost nothing yet had a profound influence on later inheritors of the spirit of Modernism, especially the 'Deconstructivists' of the 1990s (see Chapter 28). In the mid-1920s Leonidov was a student at Vkhutemas, where his prodigious talent was soon recognized by teachers such as Aleksandr Vesnin and Moisei Ginzburg. It was Ginzburg who, in 1927, ensured that Leonidov's final year project for a Lenin Institute and Library in the Lenin Hills just outside Moscow was displayed at the Exhibition of Contemporary Architecture and published in

SA. Here was a student project of a new kind, not a mere exercise, a 'dummy run' for a real-life building project, but a truly creative exploration of architectural possibilities. Perhaps it was precisely at this point in history that the student project, as a category, won its independence from the practical and professional concerns of 'real architecture' and became a mode of artistic creation in its own right. Architectural education has lived with the consequences, both positive and negative, ever since.

The Lenin Institute project is typical of Leonidov's compositional method, which owed something to Kazimir Malevich's Suprematist paintings. Separate, geometrically simple objects are arranged in measured, rectilinear juxtaposition on an open site. A glass sphere, raised off the ground like a golf ball on a tee, shares a flat, circular base with a tall, slim tower, stiffened by tension cables and struts. From this node point, ground-scraping versions of the tower of 1928 divides the accommodation between two simple elements – a vertical slab and a horizontal bar on pilotis. It almost certainly influenced the development of Le Corbusier's winning entry, which was complicated and confused in comparison. Many common Modernist design strategies found their first clear expression in Leonidov's projects. The office floors of the Tsentrosoyuz slab, for example, are open plan and landscaped in the manner of the 1950s Bürolandschaft movement; and the external envelope of that building, with its glass curtain-walled sides and solid ends, was to become a familiar form in post-war Modernist towers such as the United Nations building in New York and Oscar Niemeyer's government buildings in Brasília. Leonidov was also an innovator at the scale of town planning. His proposal for a linear city extending outwards from the industrial centre of Magnitogorsk balances the rigid order of a traditional grid-iron plan with variety and choice in the arrangement of the 'superblocks'. Low-rise communal dwellings in a chequerboard pattern alternate with high-rise towers and landscaped blocks providing parks, allotments and sports fields. Again one thinks of later projects, both real, like Milton Keynes, and imaginary, like Bernard Tschumi's Manhattan Transcripts.

Model for the Lenin Institute and Library. Ivan Leonidov, 1927. Leonidov built almost nothing, but projects such as this were to be an inspiration to the avant-garde of the 1980s.

reach outwards to an indefinite extent. The sphere contains a subdividable 4,000-seat auditorium, the tower contains the library and the horizontal blocks contain 'research institutes'. These are not just elegant, static forms but components in a dynamic, connected whole. The auditorium, for example, can be subdivided by suspended partitions, cut in half by rotating one semi-circle of seating under the other, or converted into a planetarium. It was envisaged that radio and telephone links would enable the various research institutes to form a single collective, possibly even working on a single project – an idea that seems prophetic now, in the internet age. But communication devices are symbolic as well as functional. The whole complex was to have been connected by high-level monorail to the centre of Moscow.

Leonidov's projects have a dream-like or sci-fi quality. His Palace of Culture of 1930, for example, is usually represented by an elevation drawing showing a few big, simple objects – a pyramid, a dome, an impossibly slender tower – in a desert landscape over which floats an enormous dirigible like a visiting alien spaceship. And yet he was also capable of producing practical proposals for real buildings. His entry for the Tsentrosoyuz competition

Leonidov built only one significant work of architecture, in 1939: a cascade of steps with theatre-like landings, part of the Kislovodsk sanatorium complex on the Crimean coast designed by Moisei Ginzburg. It is more classical than Constructivist and utterly unlike Leonidov's usual style. But by then all forms of Modernism had effectively been banned by a political regime that demanded a return to populist neo-classicism. 'Leonidovism', meaning visionary but unbuildable architecture, became a term of abuse. Even the younger generation, in particular the founders of Vopra, the All-union Association of Proletarian Architects, called for a return to traditional styles. The decisive turning point was the conclusion of the Palace of the Soviets competition in 1933, when Boris Iofan's colossal monument surmounted by a statue of Lenin 100 metres (330 feet) high – a different kind of visionary but unbuildable architecture – was preferred over all Modernist entries, including Le Corbusier's. The truth is, however, that neo-classicism had never really gone away. Old-timers like Ivan Fomin and Aleksei Shchusev were still on hand to lead the new 'Post-Constructivist' style. They had continued to practise through the 1920s and 1930s but the neo-classicism of their youth had always been visible beneath the surface of their diluted Modernism. Even a few exemplary Constructivists, like Ilya Golosov, designer of the Zuev Workers' Club, were able to adapt themselves to the new climate. Historians differ about the demise of Russian Modernism. According to Selim Khan-Magomedov it died of natural causes – ideological changes internal to the architectural profession.[1] The majority view, however, is that it was killed by politics, fear and self-censorship.

Kazimir Malevich and Suprematism

In December 1915, Kazimir Malevich, a Ukrainian artist of Polish extraction, exhibited a small painting called *Black Square* at an exhibition in Petrograd (now St Petersburg). The title of the painting describes it accurately enough, except that the black square is surrounded by a white margin; or is it painted on a white background? Immediately, there is room for interpretation even in this painting that seems to be as simple as a painting could possibly be. The story goes that when Malevich had completed *Black Square* he did not eat or drink or sleep for a week. He was obsessed. He thought that he had done something completely new, dangerously new, and he might have been right. Here was abstract art of an extreme kind. It 'represented' the end of all representation, all figuration, all meaning, all beauty. But to Malevich its importance stretched far beyond the world of painting. It meant nothing less than the obliteration of reality itself as perceived by human beings. Two years earlier he had designed the set for an avant-garde opera called *Victory over the Sun*. Now he redesigned that set with a black, square backdrop. He also began to use the phrase 'total eclipse'. *Black Square* would blot out the sun, the source of light and therefore of all representation. Malevich the painter became Malevich the mystic. According to his 'vision' (the word seems inappropriate) the universe was abstract and the world inside the human skull was made of pure, objectless sensation.

But what about that white border? Malevich realized that it implied a simple kind of representation. If the border could be read as a background then the black square was an object on display. The aim to establish 'objectlessness' was frustrated. So he painted two more paintings. One, called *Four Squares*, is like four squares of a chessboard. Black and white are equal

and it is impossible to say which is foreground and which background. The other, called *White on White*, abolishes black altogether and with it any possibility of figuration.

But the question of foreground and background, and the boundaries or edges that divided them, was dealt with in other ways in other paintings. Malevich called them 'Suprematist', because in them the concept of 'object' was overcome by pure colour. In paintings like *Dynamic Suprematism* of 1916, coloured lines and rectangles are arranged apparently randomly on a white background. For Malevich they represented nothing but themselves. They were not representations of real things but real things, or 'beings', in their own right. In 1922 he began to make three-dimensional versions of them called 'architectons', composite cubic forms that look like models of Modernist buildings except that they have no ground on which to stand. Perhaps they are spaceships. The idea is not as fanciful as it seems. Malevich was obsessed with outer space and is said to have always carried a telescope in his pocket. He wrote, in a mystical rather than a scientific vein, about the possibilities of interplanetary travel and was the first to call a satellite a *sputnik* ('travelling companion'). '*Planit*' was his name for what we might now call a space station.

Malevich was well known in his own lifetime, in Russia, among the Dutch De Stijl artists and at the Bauhaus. But he became famous once again in the 1960s, when his space travel prophesies were beginning to come true, and in the 1990s when his paintings, and perhaps also his total rejection of tradition, inspired 'Deconstructivist' architects like Zaha Hadid, Bernard Tschumi and Rem Koolhaas.

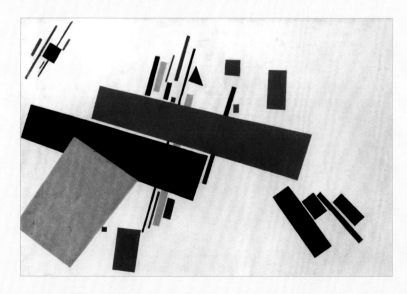

Dynamic Suprematism. **Kazimir Malevich, 1916.**
The coloured shapes are meant to represent nothing but themselves.

12 | WRIGHT, SCHINDLER AND NEUTRA 1911–1938

In 1909 Frank Lloyd Wright left his wife Catherine and their six children to spend almost a year in Europe with his lover, Martha 'Mamah' Borthwick Cheney. Soon after his return, he built a house on a hilltop near Spring Green in rural Wisconsin where he could live with Mamah. But it was more than just a house; it was also a studio, a farm, a nascent school of architecture and, most importantly, a symbol of future happiness and fulfilment. Wright called it Taliesin, after a sixth-century Welsh bard, invoking both the spirit of poetry and the patrimony of his Welsh forefathers.

Tragedy at Taliesin

Architecturally, Taliesin was recognizably a Wrightian composition, but calmer, freer, quieter than the Prairie houses. A collection of simple domestic forms on the brow rather than the top of the hill ('Taliesin' means

Frank Lloyd Wright. Born in Richland Center, Wisconsin, USA, 1867. Died in Phoenix, Arizona, USA, 1959.

'shining brow') drew attention not to itself but to the views of the surrounding hills and the valley of the Wisconsin River. The household was soon established, including a handful of architectural assistants and servants, supervised by Mamah whenever Wright was away on business in Chicago. It was on one of those occasions that tragedy struck. At lunchtime on 15 August 1914, Wright received news that there had been a fire at Taliesin. On the train home that evening he learnt the full horror from newspaper headlines. The house had been destroyed and Julian Carlton, a servant Wright had taken on three months earlier, had butchered seven people, including Mamah and her two visiting children, with a hatchet. Wright wrote of his despair in his autobiography: 'Something strange had happened to me. Instead of feeling that she, whose life had joined mine there at Taliesin, was a spirit near, she was utterly gone.'[1]

What effect this trauma had on Wright's later architecture is a matter of speculation and interpretation. Perhaps the most remarkable fact is that it did not put an end to his creativity altogether. He rebuilt Taliesin and he rebuilt his career, eventually finding new clients and new sources of inspiration in the sunshine and intellectual freedom of southern California. At the time of the tragedy he had been supervising the construction of Midway Gardens in Chicago and preparing the first designs for the Imperial Hotel in Tokyo – both large, formal, rigidly symmetrical and highly decorated public complexes, quite different in spirit from Taliesin. In October 1918 he left for Japan with his new partner, Miriam Noel, and stayed there for most of the next four years, supervising the construction of the hotel. He was already an expert in, and lover of, Japanese art, and traditional wooden Japanese architecture had been an inspiration to his Prairie style of house-building. The Imperial Hotel would, he thought, teach the Japanese about masonry, and in particular how to make masonry structures earthquake-proof by floating them on rigid but articulated foundations. In this he was triumphantly successful. On 1 September 1923 the building stood firm against one of the most powerful earthquakes ever recorded in Japan. According to Neil Levine, 'Wright interpreted the construction of the Imperial Hotel as evidence of his own ability to survive catastrophe'.[2]

Aline Barnsdall

Wright's sojourn in Japan was not continuous. He became a wanderer, crossing and recrossing the Pacific, dividing his time between Tokyo, Taliesin, Chicago, Arizona and Los Angeles. In 1915, soon after the Taliesin disaster, he had met Aline Barnsdall, a rich oil heiress with a passion for avant-garde theatre. She had commissioned him to design a new theatre for the Players Producing Company in Chicago. The project had not progressed far before Barnsdall decided that Los Angeles would be a more sympathetic setting for her theatrical ambitions. She bought Olive Hill, a large square 'superblock' between Hollywood and Sunset boulevards, with the intention of developing it as a theatre community. In 1920 Wright drew up a master plan that included a large public theatre, a cinema, a row of shops and various houses

for artists and theatre people, all arranged around the perimeter of the site. Barnsdall's own house would dominate the scene from the top of the hill. In the event only the main house and two smaller residences were built. Barnsdall called her house Hollyhock House after the flowers that grew wild on Olive Hill.

The whole scheme was a romantic conception appropriate to its location among the dream factories of Hollywood that were just then establishing themselves. Wright, now no longer a suburban family man but a wandering artist, was happy to join in the escapist mood. Hollyhock House is as much a stage set as a functional building. The drama for which it was created was a story about man and nature, specifically American man and the landscape of America.

Taliesin, Wisconsin, USA. Frank Lloyd Wright, 1911 (rebuilt in 1914 and 1925). A collection of simple domestic forms on the brow of a hill.

Imperial Hotel, Tokyo, Japan. Frank Lloyd Wright, 1923. The building survived one of the most powerful earthquakes ever recorded in Japan.

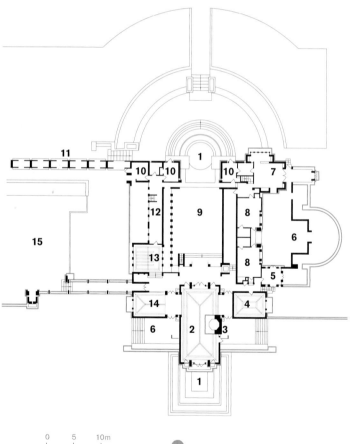

Ground floor plan

1. Pool	8. Bedroom
2. Living room	9. Garden courtyard
3. Fire	10. Staff rooms
4. Library	11. Kennels
5. Conservatory	12. Kitchen
6. Patio	13. Dining room
7. Nursery	14. Music room
	15. Car court

Hollyhock House, Los Angeles, California, USA. Frank Lloyd Wright, 1921. Battered roofs look like solid concrete but are actually framed in wood. Wright himself designed the relief over the fireplace.

Olive Hill, a 'Mount of Olives' with long views of mountains to the north and ocean to the west, had long been a gathering place for Easter Day sunrise services. Its spiritual nature shows itself in the architecture of the house, though in pre-Christian terms. Unusually for Wright, this is an explicitly historicist composition, borrowing its basic formal language not from the European classical tradition but from Pre-Columbian American architecture, such as the eighth-century Mayan palace complex at Palenque in southern Mexico. It is there that we find the ancestors of Wright's squat, massive forms, with their upright walls and battered roofs separated by a frieze of stylized stone hollyhocks. The inward-looking plan is also unusual for Wright. It seems inappropriate for such an elevated, essentially outward-looking site, until we realize that the flat roofs that surround the courtyard are all accessible viewing platforms. And the courtyard is more than just a quiet, sheltered space. There is no evidence that it was ever used as a theatre, but it is not hard to imagine an audience gathered in it, spilling over onto the surrounding roofs. The bridge of bedrooms in the east wing forms a kind of proscenium arch. Or perhaps the theatre was meant to work the other way round, the audience climbing the hill from Vermont Avenue and gathering outside the courtyard in the miniature Greek auditorium with the circular pool under the bridge boarded over to form the stage or 'orchestra'.

So the house is a palace, a theatre and perhaps a temple. The hollyhocks themselves are like religious symbols, especially where they become freestanding sentinels guarding entrances and flights of steps. Inside, the hearth is the heart of the house. It stands on the long side of the double-square living room, leaving the short west side free for big glass doors that open onto the terrace and the ocean view. Over the hearth, a big abstract relief in cast concrete, designed by Wright himself, is open to many possible interpretations but seems to tell the story of a vast inhabited landscape under a Californian sun. The actual sun shines down on it through a roof-light of wood-framed stained glass. In front of the hearth lies a pool of water, part of an artificial stream that flows through the house and courtyard. Earth, air, fire and water are thus combined in a symbolic landscape. The shallow-pitched ceiling, springing from a little above door height, is a surprise when we remember the external form. And here the stage-set nature of the building becomes apparent. It looks like a massive, concrete edifice, similar perhaps to the Unity Temple over a decade earlier, but in fact it is a mixed structure of cement-rendered blockwork supporting a wood-framed roof. It is impure and imperfect, and Wright knew it. Perhaps that's why he called it his 'Californian Romanza' – something not quite real and therefore not completely satisfying. In his own words: 'Soon began the gnawing of the old hunger for reality ... Always the desire to get some system of building construction as a basis for architecture was my objective – my hope. There never was, there *is* no architecture otherwise, I believe.'[3]

'Woven' blocks

The system of building construction that he had in mind was based on the humble concrete block, which he described as 'the cheapest (and ugliest) thing in the building world'. He would raise it up from 'the architectural gutter' and acknowledge its true worth. It was a modern material in that it was simple and repetitive, lending itself easily to mass production by machine. But for Wright the elegance of the architectural concept was more important that any quantitative measure of efficiency or productivity. The blocks would be serial works of art, each 400 millimetres (16

inches) square, made of local sand and gravel so they were one with the site and the region. There would be different types, some impressed with abstract designs, some plain; some solid, some perforated. A blockwork wall is an unstable structure, particularly in an earthquake region, so they would have to be reinforced by thin steel rods laid into the joints. If they were 'stack bonded' the vertical joints could also be reinforced. Wright likened the process to weaving, echoing, perhaps deliberately, an old idea about the origins of architecture formulated 70 years earlier by Gottfried Semper.

The brave client who volunteered to commission the first prototype was Alice Millard, a dealer in antiques and rare books, for whom Wright had built a Prairie-style house in Highland Park, Illinois in 1906. The site, chosen by Wright, was a small, watery, eucalyptus-shaded ravine on Prospect Crescent, Pasadena. It was a difficult project, with many a disagreement between architect, contractor and client, but in the end Millard came to love her house and lived in it until her death in 1938. It is called La Miniatura though it has a large, double-height living room at first-floor level, overlooked by a gallery and opening onto a balcony, as well as all the

La Miniatura (Millard House), Pasadena, California, USA. Frank Lloyd Wright, 1923. Despite its name this is a big house with a double-height living room on the first floor.

usual attendant spaces including three bathrooms. Its fairly compact, flat-roofed, vertical form has led some historians to compare it with Le Corbusier's roughly contemporary Maison Citrohan, but it could hardly be more different in surface character. Conceptually, the blockwork is cheap and austere; sensually, however, it is warm toned and richly textured both inside and out. Wright built three more 'textile block' houses in Los Angeles, the largest of which is the Ennis House of 1923, on a commanding site in the hills above Los Feliz Boulevard. Its walls are stepped and battered in Mayan profiles reminiscent of the Hollyhock House, which would seem to go against the essentially vertical, loadbearing nature of the material.

To assist him in his Californian practice, Wright employed two young Viennese architects, Rudolph Schindler and Richard Neutra. Both had been brought up in the proto-Modernist tradition of Otto Wagner and Adolf Loos. They were friends and had come to the USA hoping to learn from the author of the designs they had so much admired in the Wasmuth portfolio (see page 34). They therefore represent an important historical juncture: the coming together of the European and American Modernist traditions. Schindler was the first to arrive, in 1914. In 1917 he joined Wright's studio at Taliesin, where he worked on the designs of the Imperial Hotel in Tokyo. Then in 1920 he moved to Los Angeles where he was largely responsible for the supervision of the Olive Hill project, including Hollyhock House. In 1922 he built a double house for himself, his wife and their friends, Clyde and Marion Chace, on Kings Road in West Hollywood.

A house like a camp

If the Schindler–Chace House combines American and European Modernist strains it shows no obvious characteristics of either of its parents. It has none of the decorative richness of Wright's Los Angeles houses and is more relaxed and open than the houses of Adolf Loos or even Le Corbusier. Said to have been inspired by a camping trip that Schindler and his wife made to the Yosemite Valley, it is more like a temporary shelter than a permanent house. It is also very Japanese. There are three main wings, one for each family and one for a guest. The family wings are L shaped, with concrete outer walls and glass inner walls facing onto gardens. Concrete is not a material we associate with temporary shelters, but here it is used in such a way that its ponderousness is dissolved. Plain, flat, storey-height panels were cast on the ground and then lifted into position to make a wall, leaving gaps between each panel to be in-filled with glass. Schindler did not invent this method. It was first patented in 1908 and was used in several buildings by the pioneer Californian Modernist Irving Gill, whose work Schindler knew well. But this house was an important demonstration of its potential. 'Tilt-up' would later become a common construction method on the west coast, despite

concerns about its earthquake resistance. The inner, garden walls of the house incorporate big, sliding glazed doors. These are external walls but since the gardens themselves are like roofless rooms, complete with fireplaces, the walls recall traditional Japanese *shoji* space-dividing screens. The split-level flat roof with its exposed redwood frame also has a Japanese look. Glass panels between the two levels reinforce the impression of openness and permeability. Two small staircases lead up to the roof, which is equipped with wooden sleeping shelters – a camp on top of a camp. This house for the Californian climate and the Californian way of life was to be an inspiration to the architects of the classic Case Study houses of 30 years later, by which time Modernism had become the new orthodoxy (see Chapter 15).

Lovell Beach House and Lovell Health House

The other canonical Schindler house of this period is the Lovell Beach House, completed in 1926, and here the client is as important as the architect. Philip Lovell was the high priest of healthy living. A physician from New York, he got rich in California by promoting fitness exercises, vegetarianism and nude sunbathing. He would have approved of those sleeping shelters on the roof of the Schindler–Chace House. The beach is, of course, where fitness and beauty show themselves off, so it was natural Lovell should want to live on a beach. But how could a house be built on a beach without spoiling it? Schindler's solution was to lift it off the ground on what Le Corbusier would have called 'pilotis'. In this case, however, the pilotis take the form of five portal frames like parallel concrete walls pierced by very large openings and with cantilevered extensions. Wooden floors and roofs span simply between these main structural elements. The main living space is on the first floor, double height and overlooked by a gallery that gives access to bedrooms facing west over the ocean. Each bedroom has a sheltered balcony big enough to sleep on.

But Philip Lovell is best known to architectural history as the client of another house, the so-called Lovell Health House, completed in 1929 and designed by Schindler's friend Richard Neutra. Neutra had worked for Erich Mendelsohn in Berlin before emigrating to America in 1923, eventually finding employment in Wright's Taliesin studios a year later. It is possible that he effectively stole the Lovell Health House commission from Schindler. If he did he made the most of the opportunity. Lovell often wrote articles on healthy living for the *Los Angeles Times* and occasionally included hints on the building of healthy houses, so when he built a house for himself and his family in the Hollywood Hills it was inevitably going to be seen as a demonstration of his ideas. What would a healthy house look like? There is no obvious link between healthy living and architectural style but it seems that for Lovell a healthy house meant a modern

Lovell Beach House, Newport Beach, California, USA.
Rudolph Schindler, 1926. Perforated concrete cross-walls
provide the basic structure.

house – spacious, open, full of light and air, and without
ornament. This cultural association between Modernism and
healthy living was already established in Europe; the Lovell
house brought the idea to America. Stylistically modern, the
house was also modern in its construction. A rectangular,
three-storey, lightweight steel frame with lattice trusses and
perimeter columns at very close centres was assembled
in just a few days at right angles to the steep slope of the
site. Solid walls were of concrete sprayed onto metal mesh
('Gunite'), but large areas of the external envelope were
of glass in steel subframes. The house is well preserved
and is now a Los Angeles Historic-Cultural Monument. Its
distinctive complex form, with many recesses, overhangs
and double-height spaces, is achieved by 'subtracting'
volumes and planes from a notional box-like whole.
Balconies are suspended from cantilevered roof beams.
The main entrance is on the top floor, which also

Lovell Health House, Los Angeles, California, USA.
Richard Neutra, 1929. A basic box from which elements are
'subtracted' stands at right angles to the steep slope.

accommodates the bedrooms with their screened sleeping balconies. A wide staircase descends in a big, sunny, glass-walled hall to a long living room with a slightly incongruous rustic fireplace that might have been borrowed from Frank Lloyd Wright. It is one of the most photographed interiors in the history of Modernism. When the house was finished, Lovell trumpeted the fact in his newspaper column and invited his readers to come and look. Thousands turned up to be either impressed or appalled by this vision of a new, healthy world.

In 1924, while Schindler and Neutra were making their reputations in Los Angeles, Frank Lloyd Wright left the city, deciding that it did not after all offer the opportunities for personal and artistic renewal that he had envisaged. His domestic life was once again in trouble. He had married Miriam Noel in 1923 but she had begun to show signs of mental instability. Then there was a second fire at Taliesin in 1925. In 1927, he divorced Miriam and a year later married Olgivanna Lazovich, a Montenegrin dancer and theosophist. She was to remain his companion and advisor for the rest of his life.

Professionally, the late 1920s and early 1930s were lean times for Wright. With the coming of the Depression he concentrated on teaching, writing and lecturing, finding a receptive international audience for his ideas. In 1932 he set up his own school of architecture known as the Taliesin Fellowship, and in the same year wrote his autobiography. Many more books followed, including *The Disappearing City*, in which he presented his prophetic vision of a new urban, or anti-urban, environment – dispersed, low rise, individualistic

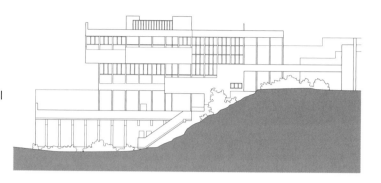

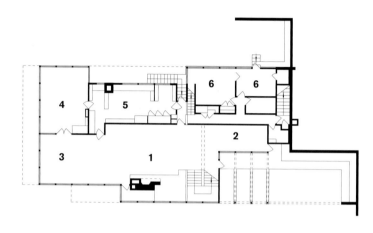

First floor plan
1. Living room
2. Library
3. Dining room
4. Porch
5. Kitchen
6. Guest room

Lovell Health House interior. Living room, showing the stairway descending from the entrance level above.

Fallingwater, Bear Run, Pennsylvania, USA. Frank Lloyd Wright, 1939. Wright's design co-operates with the site's natural features – a slope, a rocky outcrop and a waterfall.

and designed for car ownership. The project was called Broadacre City. It could hardly be more different from the work of European near contemporaries, such as Le Corbusier's Ville Radieuse (see page 252) .

Fallingwater

In 1934 Wright received a commission from the department store magnate Edgar J. Kaufmann for a weekend retreat in the woods of western Pennsylvania. Kaufmann and his wife had already built a little cabin there. It was their habit to fish and swim from a rock by a waterfall on a stream called Bear Run. Wright decided to build the house on that very rock. It must at first have seemed a self-defeating idea – the destruction of the house's own *raison d'être*. The sort of house Wright had in mind, however, would not destroy its setting but complete it harmoniously. The rock was extended upwards in walls and piers of rough local stone

from which reinforced concrete terraces cantilevered out over the waterfall like giant bracket fungi. Wright named the house Fallingwater. History has decided that it is one of the greatest houses of the twentieth century. In some respects it is very different from his earlier houses; there is no ornament or localized symmetry and its main material – reinforced concrete, daringly engineered – was never before used so expressively. And yet in its outward-looking, centrifugal plan, it still bears a certain family resemblance to the Prairie houses of 30 years before. It is as if Wright stole all the drama of European Modernism – the fantasy projects of the Constructivists or the painterly assemblages of De Stijl – and heightened it with a new, American vigour. In the European

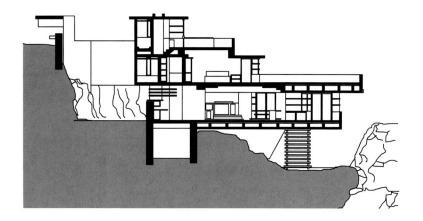

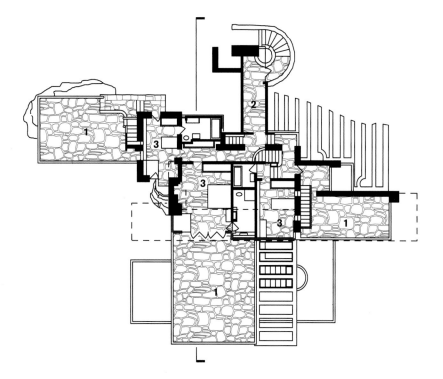

**Fallingwater, section
and first floor plan**
1. Terrace
2. Entrance
3. Bedroom

0   5   10m
15   30 ft

version of this compositional method, the man-made and the natural are opposed; in Wright's version they are united. Of all Wright's buildings, this is the most 'organic'. Fallingwater inaugurated a new, fertile phase in Wright's career, though he was now in his late sixties.

Johnson Wax

In 1936 the Johnson Wax company commissioned him to design their new administration building on an industrial site in Racine, Wisconsin. The design was proof that Wright's powers of invention were undimmed. It has sometimes been associated with the 'streamline' branch of the Art Deco style because of its horizontality and rounded corners, but the logic of the form is too rigorous to be merely 'stylistic'. Like its predecessor, the Larkin Building of 1906 (see page 69), it is a unified, inward-looking, open-plan office building. The roof of the double-height main 'workroom' is supported

by columns on a grid 6 metres (20 feet) square. This is a true statement but a woefully inadequate description of a completely new structural arrangement. The reinforced concrete 'mushroom' column, with a spreading 'capital' to strengthen the junction between the column and the slab it supports, was at that time becoming a common form, mainly in industrial buildings. Wright took this form and transmuted it, extending the circular mushroom caps, linking them together to form a discontinuous slab and letting daylight in between the circles. The metaphor switches from mushrooms to floating lily pads, their column shafts like stems, elegantly tapering to their bases as if they were suspended rather than supporting. Local building inspectors were sceptical and called for tests. A sample column was erected and loaded up until it failed – at many times the allowable safety margin. The evenly lit, subaqueous environment of the room is comfortable to work in, with a

spaciousness that more than compensates for lack of any view out. Red brick is the main walling material, both inside and out. It easily accommodates the rounded corners that arise naturally from the lily pad structure. Roof-lights were less successful technically. Wright devised a strange glazing system using stacks of Pyrex tubes to fill in the gaps between the lily pads and between the external walls and roof. Sealed joints between the tubes quickly failed and let in the rain. Eventually the tubes were replaced by fibreglass sheets with lines drawn on to give the effect of tubes. Wright designed all the furniture for the building, including desks with rounded ends and a famously unstable three-legged office chair.

Johnson Wax Headquarters, Racine, Wisconsin, USA. Frank Lloyd Wright, 1939. Columns seem to hang from concrete discs that float like lily pads in a pond.

Usonian houses

One more building designed by Wright in the late 1930s deserves mention not for its individual importance but because of its influence on ordinary American domestic architecture. The Jacobs House in Madison, Wisconsin was the first of the so-called Usonian houses. 'Usonia' was Wright's name for the USA – or perhaps for a future USA designed by himself – so the Usonian house was a modest dwelling for a typical middle-class American family. At that time most suburban family houses were adaptations of traditional Colonial or Cape Cod prototypes – two-storey, box-like and plonked in the middle of the site. Wright rearranged the accommodation in a single-storey L shape that embraced the garden rather than dividing it up.

Twenty years earlier a family like the Jacobses would have employed a maid and the kitchen would have been tucked away out of sight. But by 1938 the kitchen had become the domain of the lady of the house, equipped with labour-saving devices like an electric cooker and a refrigerator, so it takes a commanding position at the centre of gravity of the plan. Space flows from kitchen to dining alcove to living space and on out into the garden through a whole wall of wood-framed

glass doors. A split-level flat roof incorporates clerestory windows that further deconstruct the usual domestic box. The technology of the house was revolutionary too. External walls that were not glazed were either brick or a special sandwich construction of plywood sheets (then a new material) faced on both sides with alternating softwood and hardwood strips. A simple ground-bearing concrete slab incorporated an early form of under-floor heating. This was not a prefabricated house in the normal sense of the term. Wright never envisaged setting up a factory to mass-produce Usonian houses. But its industrially processed materials and its standardized construction details made it relatively cheap. A moderately prosperous professional family (Herbert Jacobs was a journalist) could now afford a house designed by America's greatest architect.

Jacobs House, Madison, Wisconsin, USA.
Frank Lloyd Wright, 1936. The 'lady of the house', now without help from a maid, supervises daily life from her kitchen command post.

Plan
1 Living room
2 Kitchen
3 Dining room
4 Bedroom
5 Bathroom
6 Car port

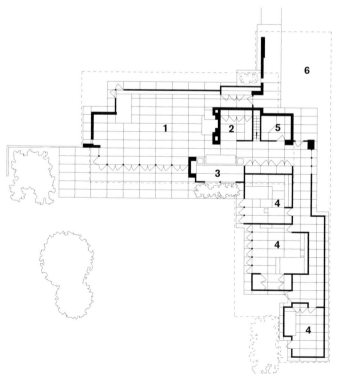

Taliesin West

In 1932 Frank Lloyd Wright established an apprenticeship scheme called the Taliesin Fellowship. Its educational motives were no doubt genuine but the fees were a useful source of income in otherwise lean times and the students formed a willing workforce, both in the drawing office and for the day-to-day maintenance of Taliesin itself, its house, farm and studio. The Wisconsin winters were harsh, however, and the complex was heated only by open fires, so in 1937 Wright and his wife Olgivanna decided to build winter quarters, Taliesin West, in the Arizona desert 40 kilometres (25 miles) north east of Phoenix.

Taliesin West had a predecessor or prototype. Almost ten years earlier, Wright had been commissioned to design a resort hotel to the south of Phoenix. He needed to be close to the site during the detailed design and construction phases of the project. Rather than rent accommodation in the city, he set up a desert camp for his family and his architectural assistants. He named it Ocotilla after a type of cactus. Temporary buildings were made with low walls of boxwood and roofs of canvas on angled wooden frames. The camp, and the hotel project that occasioned it, were abandoned after the 1929 Wall Street crash but Wright later wrote fondly of Ocotilla, of its resemblance to a fleet of sailing ships, and of the gentle, diffused light under its canvas roofs.

Taliesin West would be bigger, more unified and more permanent but no less camp-like, with similar angled roofs of canvas on wooden frames. Walls, however, would be of stone, thick and heavy with sloping or 'battered' faces. Wright was as creative in construction as he was in form or space, and the Taliesin West walls are a good example. Big, pink stones gathered from the surrounding desert were stacked with their flat sides against the outer case of a wooden formwork. Smaller boulders and rubble filled the gaps behind and between. Cement was then poured in, binding the stones together and creating a kind of coarse concrete. It was a cheap and simple construction method making use of relatively unskilled labour and the material of the desert itself.

The original building accommodated about 30 people. Its various wings – drafting studio, kitchen, dining room, private living quarters, apprentices' rooms, Wright's own office and a small theatre – were all composed as variations on the basic stone, wood and canvas theme. Pergolas, gardens, pools and stepped terraces married the building to its site, informally and asymmetrically, but following a triangular geometry in both plan and section. The Taliesin Fellowship still operates and Taliesin West still exists, though now much extended and altered, its canvas replaced by glass and its open fires by central heating and air conditioning.

Taliesin West, Scottsdale, Arizona, USA. Frank Lloyd Wright, 1937. Canvas roofs (originally) in wooden frames stand on walls made from desert boulders.

13 | ART DECO AND THE SKYSCRAPER 1925–1939

Most histories of early twentieth-century architecture are dominated by the rise of Modernism in its various national guises – Dutch, German, French and Russian. But this is a kind of favouritism. Modernism gets all the attention for two reasons: because it benefited from the most articulate and culturally sophisticated spokespersons, among them Walter Gropius, Le Corbusier, Henry-Russell Hitchcock and Sigfried Giedion; and because it was destined to capture the orthodox mainstream of western architecture after 1945. A more objective survey of the 1920s and 1930s would find that, in purely quantitative terms, Modernism was no more than a sideshow, a project of interest only to a specialist intellectual elite. Most architects in those decades adapted the classical and Gothic traditions to suit modern purposes and modern technologies, feeling no necessity for a stylistic revolution. Sometimes the adaptation was minimal. The American architect Ralph Adams Cram, for example, specialized in the 'Collegiate Gothic' style, designing university chapels, libraries and residences that look like time travellers from the Middle Ages. The chapel at Princeton University in New Jersey, completed in 1928, is a good example. And classical architecture was still very much alive, especially for national monuments like Henry Bacon's Lincoln Memorial, completed in 1922, an exercise in Greek Revival that might have been built 100 years earlier or even, in a different place, 2,000 years earlier. But as well as these literal reproductions and revivals, there were stylistic developments that broke new ground without engaging in the moralistic and socialistic debates that gave Modernism its intellectual authority. These developments did not constitute a self-conscious movement and had no name until the 1960s when certain commentators, in particular the British critic Bevis Hillier, decided to call them 'Art Deco'.[1]

1925 Paris Exhibition

The term was not entirely new. In the 1920s Le Corbusier had written a series of articles about the International Exhibition of Modern Decorative and Industrial Arts (in French, Exposition Internationale des Arts Décoratifs et Industriels Modernes), held in Paris in 1925, and had given them the title *1925 Expo: Arts Déco*.[2] Here, however, the stylistic label was no more than a convenient abbreviation implying a disdain for the contents of the exhibition (not

including, of course, Le Corbusier's own contribution, the Pavillon de l'Esprit Nouveau (see Chapter 9), which represented the Modernist alternative). The purpose of the government-sponsored exhibition, which had been many years in the planning, was to re-establish France's pre-eminence in the design and manufacture of luxury goods – furniture, textiles, ceramics, metalwork and interior design generally. It set out to prove that traditional French craftsmen could produce modern artefacts as well as traditional reproductions. Pavilions were typically freestanding, temporary structures, the interiors of which represented the drawing rooms of wealthy families. The great designer Jacques-Emile Ruhlmann, for example, designed the interior of the House of a Connoisseur, including several items of supremely elegant furniture: a black lacquered cabinet decorated with silver inlay, a delicate occasional table of ebony and bronze, a pair of armchairs with scarlet upholstery enlivened by tapestry pictures of peacocks. This was not design for the masses. Architecturally the pavilions were novel but, with a few exceptions like Konstantin Mel'nikov's Soviet pavilion (see page 138), not so novel as to upset the conservative elite which was assumed to be their main audience. The pavilion representing the Paris department store Galeries Lafayette, for example, was a two-storey hexagonal structure, painted to look like marble, with fat, fluted, sculpture-crowned columns at the corners. The upper part of its high entrance portico was filled by a huge stained-glass sunburst – a common motif of early Art Deco. Lafayette's rival, Printemps, built an even more exotic pavilion, with a conical, domed, ceramic-clad roof fringed by trailing plants. Structures like these were traditional only to the extent that they were symmetrical, upright and richly ornamented, but they were certainly not Modernist.

Wider Influences

In a narrow sense, 'Art Deco' may be said to have originated in the 1925 exhibition, but its root system is wider and deeper and its definition more vague. Influences included 'Cubist' painting (sometimes used as a shorthand for avant-garde painting in general), African art, Egyptian archaeology (Howard Carter's discovery of the tomb of Tutankhamun in 1922 started a craze for Egyptian decorative motifs), Pre-Columbian American art, Japanese interiors, streamlined

Galeries Lafayette Pavilion, Paris, France. Georges Beau, Joseph Hiriart and Georges Henri Tribout, 1925. A fake marble monument to luxury taste with a sunburst entrance – a common Art Deco motif.

Printemps Pavilion, Paris, France. Henri Sauvage and Georges Wybo, 1925. Lafayette's rival relied on lavish planting rather than fake marble.

vehicles, and the early products of Modernism. Its immediate ancestor was Art Nouveau, which also combined the modern with the decorative, but more politely and less gregariously. Art Deco imagery includes the mechanistic as well as the natural. Architecturally, it is allied to those early twentieth-century styles that were modern but do not fit comfortably into Modernism's narrow canon: Poelzig's Expressionism, Mendelsohn's dynamic urbanity, Dudok's translations of Frank Lloyd Wright, even late Mackintosh. The architectural historians Tim and Charlotte Benton and Ghislaine Wood have usefully suggested that Art Deco architecture be divided into two main streams: 'modernized classicism' and 'decorative Modernism'.[3] In the 1925 exhibition, the first was exemplified by Josef Hoffmann's Austrian pavilion, with its fluted walls and simplified classical porch, and the second by Robert Mallet-Stevens's Tourism Pavilion with its elegant, abstract clock tower.

If we adopt Bevis Hillier's loose definition of Art Deco then it includes almost every architect-designed building of the 1920s and 1930s that was not either Modernist or out-and-out traditional. Art Deco buildings are to be found all over the world, in Johannesburg, Sydney, Shanghai and New Delhi as well as Paris, London, New York and Los Angeles. Art Deco was the architecture of the early twentieth century as Baroque was the architecture of the early seventeenth century, except that it was applied not just to churches and palaces but to every modern building type: houses, factories, office buildings, railway stations and entertainment buildings, not forgetting purely monumental structures like the Anzac

(Above) Tourism Pavilion, Paris, France. Robert Mallet-Stevens, 1925. 'Decorative Modernism' was represented by this small clock tower.

(Below) Austrian Pavilion, Paris, France. Josef Hoffmann, 1925. 'Modernized classicism' by the architect of the Palais Stoclet.

war memorial in Sydney or the colossal statue of Christ the Redeemer in Rio de Janeiro. Art Deco was, and is, popular – something that cannot be said with any conviction of Modernism. There were perhaps two main reasons for this: first that its basic architectural instincts were traditional and familiar, were drawn, in fact, from a century or more of Beaux-Arts architectural training; and second that its ornament and imagery were drawn from popular culture.

Cinemas

It was cinema more than any other medium that shaped and reflected popular taste in this period, and it is in design for cinema, both the sets of Hollywood movies and the buildings in which they were shown, that Art Deco is seen in its full glory. Artificial worlds created on film – the future city in Fritz Lang's *Metropolis*, the opulent night clubs in which Fred Astaire and Ginger Rogers danced, or the extravagant dreams of Busby Berkeley – were reflected in the design of the cinemas themselves. In Britain, the Odeon cinema chain, founded in 1928 by Oscar Deutsch, comprised more than 250 cinemas by 1939. Many of them were designed by Harry Weedon, but it was Weedon's assistant, Cecil Clavering, who designed the first thoroughly Art Deco Odeon, in the Birmingham suburb of Kingstanding in 1935. It is a symmetrical composition with a facade of smooth faience tiles worn like a mask on the brick skin of the auditorium. A central three-bladed tower rockets upwards from the curved bay of the main entrance. Corners are rounded as if in acknowledgement of the influence of Erich Mendelsohn, designer of the De

Odeon cinema, Birmingham, UK. Cecil Clavering, 1935.
A functional brick box wears a mask of smooth faience tiles.

La Warr Pavilion in Bexhill, one of very few Modernist buildings in England at the time. It was the Kingstanding cinema that established the Odeon house style – Art Deco in its streamlined, 'Moderne' mode. The tower, the rounded corners, the faience facade, the bold lettering, the stripy ornament inside and out – these basic components were combined in different ways to suit different sites. In the Yorkshire seaside town of Scarborough, for example, Weedon and Clavering rearranged the basic elements of

Odeon Leicester Square, London, UK.
Harry Weedon and Andrew Mather, 1937.
Cinema interiors were not unlike the sets of Busby Berkeley or Astaire and Rogers films.

Kingstanding asymmetrically for a corner site. Biggest if not best of the whole oeuvre is the Odeon Leicester Square, by Weedon again, with Andrew Mather. This time the faience is black and the tower a solid modern campanile. The walls and ceiling of the 1,600-seat auditorium (originally holding 2,000) are a single, wrap-around ribbed surface with concealed lighting, refusing any reference to conventional architectural elements like columns and beams. It is perhaps a distant descendant of Poelzig's Grosses Schauspielhaus (see page 73).

Charles Holden

Cinemas provided a dream-like escape from the hardships of everyday life in the Depression years, but workaday buildings also benefited from the imaginings of architects who were beginning to question the traditional rules in which they were trained. One such was Charles Holden, whose career was a steady progress, without obvious turning points, from Edwardian Arts and Crafts to a kind of modernism with a small 'm'. In 1908 he designed the British Medical Association building (now Zimbabwe House) in London, which is mannered and slightly awkward in its classicism. The naked male figures by Jacob Epstein that adorn its facade were thought shocking at the time. The 1914 dormitory block for Sutton Valence School, high on a ridge overlooking the Weald of Kent, is formal and rather gaunt, in red brick with tall chimneys, a lead-clad clock tower and simplified classical entrances. The school hall, originally groin vaulted with thermal windows like a Roman bath, now contains a modern theatre. Holden's most important client, however, was Frank Pick, the boss of London Underground and an enlightened patron. Their long association began with facades for various stations, then, in 1929, the commission to design the organization's headquarters building near St James's Park. The building has more sculpture by Epstein but traditional classical elements have almost disappeared. In 1930, Pick and Holden toured the Netherlands, Scandinavia and Germany to examine European Modernism in the flesh and decide on its appropriateness or otherwise for London Underground buildings, in particular the stations of a planned extension to the Piccadilly line. Judging from the results, their enthusiasm was muted. The only obvious influence is Gunnar Asplund's non-Modernist Stockholm city library, the drum-like central reading room of which is reinterpreted in the ticket hall of the station at Arnos Grove.

With the Piccadilly line stations, Holden's architecture arrived at a sublime compromise between tradition and modernity. Like Weedon's Odeons, they were composed from a few geometrically simple elements: a tall ticket hall – round (Arnos Grove), rectangular (Turnpike Lane) or octagonal (Bounds Green); a low, spreading base containing ancillary accommodation; and a slim ventilation tower carrying the distinctive London Underground symbol. Inside, from the edge of the ticket hall, the escalators plunge in their plastered, up-lit chutes to the platforms far below. There is very little ornament and none of it traditional, yet the fundamental Beaux-Arts virtues are observed – the

Arnos Grove underground station, London, UK. Charles Holden, 1932. Abstract forms retain a certain classical bearing. Note the simplified cornice.

Zimbabwe House, London, UK. Charles Holden, 1908. Holden's almost-Modernism should be seen in the light of his earlier Edwardian Mannerism.

elemental composition, the geometrical clarity, and a sense of classical containment in the plain friezes and cornices. There are large areas of steel-framed glass wall but the main solid walling material is brick, not concrete.

Holden certainly didn't think of himself as an Art Deco architect. It is only in the distant view of history that his buildings appear to lie close to that stylistic territory. And yet how else are we to characterize a building like his Senate House in Bloomsbury, the library and administrative centre of London University? At 19 storeys high it is hardly a skyscraper yet it bears a certain family resemblance to its New York cousins (see below), with a symmetrical stepped-back profile. Clad in white Portland stone – a familiar London material – it rises like a shining vision of the future as it must have looked in 1938, including anxieties about the rise of fascism. It is said to have been the architectural inspiration for the Ministry of Truth in George Orwell's *Nineteen Eighty-Four*, first published in 1949.

If Holden's architecture hovers on the fringes of Art Deco, the work of Thomas Wallis, of Wallis, Gilbert and Partners (Gilbert and the other partners were probably inventions to make the practice sound bigger), lies at its heart. His Hoover factory, built in 1933 on the main road west out of London, is the building that defines the style in Britain. Wallis had established his practice in 1916 as a British outpost of 'Kahn-crete', an advanced American concrete reinforcement technology developed by the Detroit architect Albert Kahn and his engineer brother Julius (see Chapter 5). It was natural, therefore, that Hoover, an American company making domestic vacuum cleaners, should choose Wallis to design its British factory, spending a little more than usual on the architecture in order to advertise its presence in the country. It is probably because of this building that to British eyes

Senate House, London, UK. Charles Holden, 1938. Said to have been the model for the Ministry of Truth in George Orwell's *Nineteen Eighty-Four*.

Art Deco, despite its French origins, always looks vaguely American. Some have even seen Native American patterns in the coloured glass and faience ornament – the obligatory sunburst over the main entrance might conceivably be a quiver of arrows – but a more certain influence is, once again, Erich Mendelsohn. The quadrant-shaped corner windows of the towers that flank the long front facade, for example, seem to have been lifted from Mendelsohn's Einstein Tower of 1921 (see page 77).

The foregoing examples have been British but they might just as well have been American or Australian, Indian or Chinese. The Art Deco hotels and condominiums of South Beach in Miami, Florida are well preserved and justly celebrated. Less well preserved but no less excellent examples can be found mouldering in the back streets of New Delhi or Mumbai. The Hungarian architect László Hudec carried out his best Art Deco work in that Paris of the Far East, Shanghai, including the Park Hotel and the Grand Theatre (see page 459). Art Deco was far more an international style than the 'International Style' of Modernism. There is, however, one especially important branch that must be examined in some detail: the architecture of the American skyscraper.

(Right) Art Deco houses, New Delhi, India. Art Deco was far more an international style than the International Style.

(Below) Hoover factory, London, UK. Wallis, Gilbert and Partners, 1933. An American company proclaims its modernity on the main route west out of London.

The American skyscraper

The skyscraper is the characteristic building type of the twentieth century, yet architectural history has never been quite sure how to deal with it. It seems somehow above and beyond architecture. Its form arises not from a deliberate design intention but as it were automatically from a geographical and economic equation. The usual determinants of building design – function, budget, site context, and so on – apply differently to the skyscraper, especially the Manhattan skyscraper. The street grid of the island seems to have its own generative power. It is as if the planners who established it in the early nineteenth century already knew that it would eventually be populated by skyscrapers. What would the skyscrapers be for?

Business? Industry? Housing? Recreation? The question was of secondary importance. The grain of the grid, the containment of the island and the concentration of population dictated that available floor area must be increased to accommodate every mode of daily life – living, working and playing. The skyscraper would be a type defined by its form, not its function.

How was it to be built? Not by a positive creativity but rather by a release of restraint. Five or six storeys had always been the maximum height of urban buildings. It was what gave them 'scale' and made them human. The combined inventions of the steel frame and the electric elevator lifted this restriction. Buildings could now be superhuman. And what would the skyscraper look like? Would it be necessary to invent a new architecture to suit this extraordinary new form? Strangely, the answer is no. The old Gothic and classical architectures, carried forward by the Beaux-Arts educational tradition, would do just fine, but with one proviso: the traditional correspondence between the inside and the outside of a building, between its enclosed spaces and its external forms, its construction and its expression, must be broken. Skyscrapers would wear their architecture like loose-fitting clothes. The purpose of the clothes was to disguise reality, not reveal it. Skyscrapers would wear togas or cassocks, not leotards or swimsuits. The Modernist skyscraper was a latecomer that did not assert its authority until after the Second World War.

The old Fuller Building on Madison Square, better known as the 'Flatiron', designed by Daniel Burnham and completed in 1902, illustrates perfectly the cold logic of the skyscraper. Its site is unusual for Manhattan – a triangle, not a rectangle – and its form is simply an upward extrusion of this shape to a height of 21 storeys. It was designed mainly for business use, but with retail space on the ground floor and a large basement restaurant. Its 'architecture', or rather its clothing, executed in limestone and terracotta, is basically classical, both in detail and in overall treatment. Burnham, a Chicago architect, borrowed Louis Sullivan's idea that a tall building should be treated like a classical column, with a rusticated base, a relatively plain shaft and an elaborate 'capital' like a separate building raised high in the air. In the Woolworth Building, designed by Cass Gilbert and completed in 1913, the Manhattan skyscraper found a more appropriate model. At 241 metres (792 feet), it was the tallest building in the world. Gilbert's master stroke was to choose the Gothic rather than the classical style. The Sullivanian base–shaft–capital idea had its limitations, tending to make a large building look like a grossly inflated small building. Gothic, as Augustus Pugin, the pioneer of the Gothic Revival, had long before pointed out, was more flexible. It could accommodate different

forms at different scales, grouping them and unifying them in a hierarchical composition. And of course Gothic was a vertical architecture; it could soar to an unlimited height. What could be more appropriate for a skyscraper?

In the Woolworth Building the forms to be accommodated were a tall, U-shaped block and a soaring tower rising in several stages and substages from the middle of the street frontage. Horizontals are suppressed and verticals emphasized, continuing upward onto the tower, which is crowned by an ornate, copper-clad pinnacle. The Woolworth Building made earlier attempts to civilize the skyscraper –

Fuller Building (Flatiron), New York City, USA. Daniel Burnham, 1902. Unusual for Manhattan because triangular, but nevertheless a typical upward extrusion of the site plan.

the neo-classical Municipal Building by McKim, Mead and White, for example, or the Metropolitan Life Tower, which imitated the campanile of San Marco in Venice – look clumsy and over-inflated. But if it was tamed by its Gothic garb, it was still a very big beast. Some 14,000 people worked in the building, travelling to their comfortable, electrically lit offices in 29 lifts, including two 'expresses' rising 54 floors non-stop. The lobby was and is Gothic in detail but spatially Byzantine, with a central, mosaic-clad pendentive dome.

Skyscraper-building was becoming an art. One of its pioneers was Hugh Ferriss, who, though trained as an architect, worked mainly for other architects, including Cass Gilbert, as an architectural 'renderer'. Ferriss developed his distinctive graphic style in response to an unexpected stimulus: the 1916 New York zoning laws, which restricted the volume and height of buildings so as to limit the overshadowing threat to neighbours. The rules were geometrically complicated and architects badly needed a graphic guide to what was permissible. In 1922, Ferriss provided that guide in the form of a sequence of four Conte crayon perspective drawings illustrating the development of a theoretical skyscraper, beginning with the abstract and impractical form allowed by the regulations and ending with a buildable and usable building. That final image, a night view of a mountainous triple tower with set-backs,

dramatically floodlit and silhouetted, was to be an inspiration to skyscraper architects for the next two decades. It is here that the story of Art Deco and the story of the skyscraper merge. Ferriss's plain, massive forms shared in, and contributed to, the sensibility of Art Deco, taking it forward to a new simplicity and dynamism.

Of all the architects influenced by Ferriss's vision, the greatest was Raymond Hood, though at first he was more influenced by Cass Gilbert's Gothic. Like Gilbert, he had studied at the Ecole des Beaux-Arts in Paris before the war, but by 1922, aged 41, he was still struggling as a one-man-band architect in an office he couldn't afford on 42nd Street. Then he happened to bump into his friend John Mead Howells, who had been invited to enter an international competition for the design of a new building to house the *Chicago Tribune* newspaper. Howells had no time to complete a design, so he suggested that Hood should enter in his place. This was no small undertaking. History has recognized the Chicago Tribune competition

Woolworth Building, New York City, USA. Cass Gilbert, 1913.
Unprecedented height is tamed by an older architecture of verticality: Gothic.

Set-back principle perspective sketch, Hugh Ferriss, 1922.
An intermediate stage in a sequence from zoning laws diagram to recognizable building.

as a turning point in American, and indeed in world, architecture. Unsuccessful entries from Walter Gropius (the first truly believable Modernist skyscraper), Adolf Loos (the skyscraper as a single Doric column) and the Finn Eliel Saarinen (a supremely elegant stepped composition) have since become famous.

But it was Hood's Gothic tower, complete with flying buttresses at the top, that won the competition and that now stands at 435 North Michigan Avenue, Chicago. His reputation was made and commissions for skyscrapers in New York soon followed. The first of these is, in skyscraper terms, a little gem: the American Radiator Building (now the American Standard Building), built in 1924 on West 40th Street, opposite Bryant Park. It is clad in black brick with gold-glazed terracotta ornament and rises a modest 22 storeys from its perfectly proportioned base. Though vaguely Gothic in form and detail, it also partakes of Ferriss's dynamism and drama.

By 1930 Hood was finding less need to dress his buildings in traditional costumes. The vertically striped form of his Daily News Building is stepped, but subtly and elegantly, and without any decorative embellishment of bases or summits – more like a single form from which slices have been cut than an additive cluster of distinct elements. It might almost be

(Above) **Tribune Tower, Chicago, USA. Raymond Hood and John Mead Howells, 1925.** The competition winner: a Gothic tower complete with flying buttresses.

(Far left) **Tribune Tower competition entry by Adolf Meyer and Walter Gropius, 1922.** If realized, it would have been the first Modernist skyscraper.

(Left) **Tribune Tower competition entry by Adolf Loos, 1922.** Loos betraying his classical preferences in the most obvious way.

(Left) American Radiator Building, New York City, USA. Raymond Hood and André Fouilhoux, 1924. Hood's little gem opposite Bryant Park with the later Empire State Building looming behind.

(Opposite) McGraw-Hill Building, New York City, USA. Raymond Hood, 1931. The plain, almost Modernist cladding is embellished with Art Deco motifs.

mistaken for a European Modernist production but for the Art Deco ornament in the spandrel panels and the pictorial low-relief, complete with sunburst, over the main entrance. The 1931 McGraw-Hill Building on West 42nd Street, designed by Hood and his French partner André Fouilhoux, is more obviously Art Deco, though this impression is created more by the lettering of the signboard on its sculpted summit than by its almost factory-like flat cladding of green terracotta with horizontal windows. Henry-Russell Hitchcock and Philip Johnson thought it Modernist enough to include in their 'International Style' exhibition. But for most New York architects of the 1930s, European Modernism was

an irrelevance. The Chrysler Building, best beloved of all New York skyscrapers, is one of the buildings that defines the Art Deco style. It was designed by William Van Alen and completed in 1930. Conventionally stepped at its lower levels, it soon gathers vertical thrust and becomes an elegant, slender tower of grey and white brick. Then, at about the 68th floor, it sprouts a set of eagle-headed, stainless steel gargoyles, like the chrome bonnet ornaments of contemporary Chrysler cars. Above gargoyle level, the tower narrows, then transforms itself into a multi-layer, three-dimensional sunburst, 61 metres (200 feet) high, tapering to a spike. That spike was a late addition designed

to steal the title 'world's tallest building' from 40 Wall Street, a 66-storey skyscraper designed by Van Alen's former partner, H. Craig Severance. The title was not held for long, however, for already the Empire State Building – 102 storeys and 381 metres (1,250 feet) high – was under construction.

Despite its size and its perfect proportions, like a well-dressed woman standing alone and calmly poised on its midtown site, the Empire State is essentially a practical, money-making, developer's building. Its designer, William F. Lamb, described the brief that he was given in unromantic terms: 'A fixed budget, no space more than 28 feet [8.5 metres] from window to corridor, as many storeys and as much space as possible, an exterior of limestone, and completion by May 1931, which meant a year and six months from the beginning of sketches.'[4] It was to hold the 'tallest building' title for 40 years, for a simple reason: it did not make financial sense to build higher. The Empire State Building was the supreme New York skyscraper, fitting itself precisely into the shape determined by zoning laws, construction costs, the proliferation of space-consuming elevators and that 28-foot optimum depth for day-lit offices. No fewer than 80,000 people worked in it. Its mostly open-plan floors were laid out and equipped like clean factories, with telephones, telegraphs, adding machines, typewriters and Roneo copiers.

But it would be wrong to see the skyscraper as a designed response to the need for more office space. The development of Manhattan had its own logic – Rem Koolhaas, in his 1978 book *Delirious New York*, called it 'Manhattanism' – by which the size and shape of a building were determined first and the uses to which it might be put were decided later. The best example of this, and arguably the high point in the early history of tall buildings, is Rockefeller Center, a huge multifunctional complex occupying three whole city blocks between Fifth and Sixth avenues, and 48th and 51st streets. It was entirely financed by John D. Rockefeller Jnr., designed by a large team of

Chrysler Building, New York City, USA. William Van Alen, 1930. The supreme Art Deco skyscraper with eagle gargoyles and a sunburst spire.

Empire State Building, New York City, USA. William F. Lamb, 1931. The answer to a developer's equation but elegant enough in its midtown isolation.

RCA Building, Rockefeller Center, New York City, USA.
Raymond Hood, 1939. Its suave laminated, stepped, subtractive
form turns zoning regulations into modern art.

architects and engineers in which Raymond Hood played a
key role, and built in the Depression years between 1930 and
1939. In functional terms it was several projects combined:
an underground concourse of shops and restaurants entered
from a sunken plaza and a subway station; a series of deep-
planned, ten-storey-high quasi-industrial blocks containing
radio and television studios; a fully landscaped rooftop
park; a 6,000-seat theatre, the famous Radio City Music

Hall; and a cluster of soaring office towers dominated by
the suave 70-storey slab of the RCA Building (now the
Comcast Building), the design of which can safely be
attributed to Hood. Formally, the RCA Building is similar
to the Daily News Building – a subtractive, laminated form,
but higher, more slender, more weightless-seeming. In it
the architectural potential of the New York skyscraper, first
indicated by Hugh Ferriss, is at last fully realized.

MODERN CLASSICISM
1923–1942

In histories of the architecture of the 1920s and 1930s, Modernism usually stands for democracy, and classicism for totalitarianism. It is an over-simplified interpretation and can readily be refuted. Nevertheless, the progress of architecture itself has been deeply affected by it. It perhaps arose from two important political/architectural events: the closing of the Dessau Bauhaus by the Nazi Party in 1931, and the deciding of the Palace of the Soviets competition in favour of Boris Iofan's gigantic 'wedding cake' in 1933 (see page 184). Both Hitler and Stalin, it is assumed, hated Modernism and loved classicism. Progressive Modernists like Walter Gropius and Mies van der Rohe left Germany for democratic America, taking their Modernism with them, and the dichotomy was fixed.

One effect of the classicism–totalitarianism link was to enhance the prestige of Modernism, which after the Second World War became almost the only respectable style for progressive, socially responsible architects. There was also a retrospective effect. History has tended to look with a jaundiced eye on the classical architecture of the early twentieth century, viewing it as an embarrassing survival and a stylistic dead end. But classicism is an ancient and deep-seated tradition in western architecture and its temporary association with two evil but relatively short-lived regimes

is not sufficient reason to ignore its pervasive influence. It is an important ingredient of Modernism itself. We must remember that Gropius, Le Corbusier and Mies van der Rohe all began their careers in the office of Peter Behrens, whose fundamentally classical instincts live on in their later Modernist creations.

A more objective history might correct the tendency to suppress classicism; it might even permit a study of German or Russian classical architecture on its own terms rather than as the dark alternative to Modernism. A few anti-Modernist critics, notably Léon Krier, have even been prepared to declare an admiration for Nazi architecture, in particular the architecture of Albert Speer. The arguments are shrilly presented and sometimes incoherent, but a few palpable hits are scored. Why, for example, should Nazi architecture be rejected as irretrievably corrupt when the regime's industrial achievements – autobahns, Volkswagens, domestic product design, rocket science – were all eagerly copied by western democracies after the war and are still much admired?[1]

Lutyens in India

Perhaps the best way to see Nazi architecture more clearly is to look first at roughly contemporary classical architecture elsewhere in the world. England's greatest contribution to

Secretariat Building, New Delhi, India. Herbert Baker, 1927. Palace-like secretariat buildings flank the approach to the Viceroy's Palace.

Gardens of the Viceroy's Palace. Guard post in the form of a *chhatri* or cupola.

Viceroy's Palace, New Delhi, India. Edwin Lutyens, 1929.
Western classical rhythms with Mughal details: an Englishman dressed for the climate.

mid-twentieth-century classicism is in India: the Viceroy's Palace in New Delhi, now called the Rashtrapati Bhavan or President's House, by Edwin Lutyens. It was designed before the First World War, when the British Empire was still a viable political entity, but not inaugurated until 1931 when Indian independence was already in prospect. A wide, low, symmetrical composition with a central dome, it is statistically smaller than the palace of Versailles but no less majestic. A pair of secretariat buildings, themselves large palaces, designed by Herbert Baker, flank the approach road, adding to an impression of calm authority. But 'approach road' hardly captures the vastness of the broad, tree-lined mall that starts its journey 3 kilometres (2 miles) away at the India Gate, a triumphal arch and war memorial, also designed by Lutyens. This vista caused Lutyens and Baker, who had been old friends, to fall out. Lutyens wanted the east front of his palace to be continuously visible throughout the whole journey but Baker, given responsibility for fixing the levels, pushed it some way back from the brow of the hill on which it sits so that it disappears from view as one draws near. It was a blunder that Lutyens never forgave.

The Rashtrapati Bhavan is a western classical building, notionally single storey with two basement levels. But it is also an Indian building with traditional Mughal features like the thin, projecting *chhajja*, taking the place of a cornice,

which casts black shadows on the main elevations, and the *chhatris* or cupolas that punctuate the skyline. Deep, shady loggias in the main facades are screened by columns with hybrid Mughal/Corinthian capitals. It is as if the classical style has found a sympathetic Indian relative and borrowed certain features from it, especially those that have evolved to suit the local conditions. 'Build as an Englishman dressed for the climate' was Lutyens's formula.[2] The details may be Mughal but the rhythms and proportions of the composition are western. Inside, 340 rooms are packed, neatly, precisely, hierarchically in proportions and juxtapositions to suit their domestic or ceremonial functions. On the main level there are staterooms, dining rooms, drawing rooms and ballrooms served by domically vaulted corridors and wide, shallow staircases. At the centre lies the domed Pantheon of the Durbar Hall where the viceroy and his consort sat on thrones either side of that 3-kilometre (2-mile) axis to welcome important visitors entering through the big east door.

Is this a totalitarian architecture? Perhaps. Yet its author, earlier in his career, had been the creator of idyllic country houses of the kind that English people now love to visit on

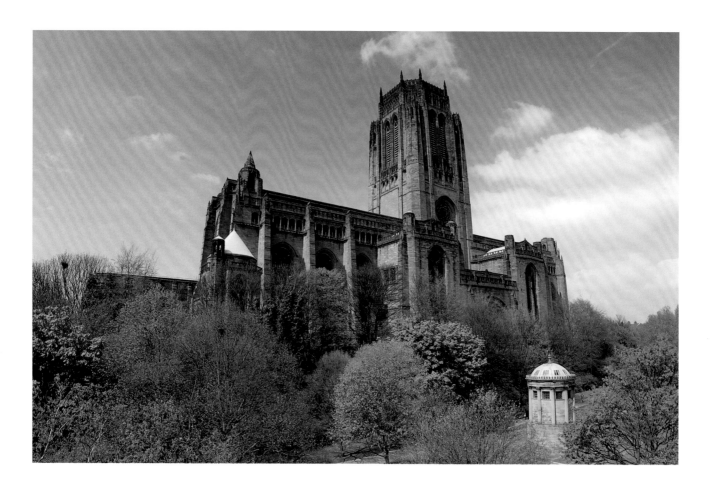

(Above) Liverpool Anglican Cathedral, UK. Giles Gilbert Scott, 1903–78. Aged 22 when the project started, Scott had been dead for 18 years when it was completed.

(Right) Cambridge University Library, UK. Giles Gilbert Scott, 1934. Both Gothic and classical but rather austere, like Scott's later power stations.

Sunday afternoons. The Viceroy's Palace was Lutyens's masterpiece. It might have been surpassed had his design for a new Roman Catholic cathedral in Liverpool, commissioned in 1929, been fully realized. Only its massive vaulted crypt was built, now serving as an occasional exhibition venue. But Liverpool already had a twentieth-century cathedral of great architectural importance: the Gothic Anglican cathedral, the first version of which was designed in 1903 by the 22-year-old Giles Gilbert Scott, grandson of the great Victorian church architect George Gilbert Scott. It was not to be completed until 1978. Nevertheless, it made Scott's reputation and he went on to become, in the eyes of some non-Modernist historians, the most important British architect of the mid-twentieth century.

Unlike Lutyens, who in his mature years was married to classicism, Scott was stylistically uncommitted. Certain of his buildings, such as the Memorial Court at Clare College, Cambridge, designed in 1923, are definitely classical, in this case a domestic Neo-Georgian in brick with sparse stone details. But in the nearby University Library, completed in 1934, Gothic, classical and perhaps even Art Deco of an understated kind are combined in a rather bleak brick

building with a soaring central tower. This semi-abstract style was later applied to buildings of a very different type: power stations. The one at Battersea, built in two phases, in the 1930s and the 1950s, and now half ruined, became a well-loved landmark because of the boldness of its form, with a chimney at each corner. The one at Bankside, right opposite St Paul's Cathedral, has a central chimney like an attenuated version of the Cambridge University Library book stack. It was completed in 1963 and over 30 years later converted into one of London's biggest tourist attractions: Tate Modern.

Scott could produce the occasional competent exercise in European Modernism. A watercolour drawing of 1932

depicts a white house with a stepped and curved plan
and a fully glazed spiral staircase in the manner of Erich
Mendelsohn. But public buildings in England at this time –
town halls, banks, libraries, office blocks – were almost all
traditional, usually bearing some reference to classicism.
Lutyens's colleague Herbert Baker, for example, completely
rebuilt the Bank of England, piling it up to eight storeys
and crowning it with a huge, inaccessible twelve-columned
portico. In the process the elegant single-storey domed halls
built by John Soane in the early nineteenth century were
destroyed. Nikolaus Pevsner called it 'the worst individual
loss suffered by London architecture in the first half of the
twentieth century' in spite of the Second World War.[3]

Scandinavia

In Scandinavia, twentieth-century classicism took a
different form – lighter, gentler, less pompous. Columns
and beams were seen not as symbols of authority but simply
as graceful ornaments or, even more straightforwardly,
as functional structures. The concert hall in Stockholm
by Ivar Tengbom, completed in 1926, is equipped with
a huge ten-columned Corinthian portico occupying most
of the street facade. In Berlin or London this would be
an assertion of stern orthodoxy but here it seems almost
frivolous. Its columns are tall and elegant and it is far too
shallow to have any kind of practical function. There are
classical columns inside the auditorium too (it is here that
Nobel Prize ceremonies are held) but they are so slender
that they have been likened to the fantasy architecture of
Pompeian wall paintings. This might be seen as a failure
to take classicism seriously, but in other Swedish buildings
of the period, such as Gunnar Asplund's Woodland
Chapel at Stockholm's Woodland Cemetery, lightness
and seriousness go together.

(Above) Bank of England,
London, UK. Herbert Baker,
1925–1939. Of John Soane's single-
storey multi-domed original, only the
perimeter wall survived.

(Right) Stockholm Concert Hall,
Sweden. Ivar Tengbom, 1926.
A purely symbolic classical portico,
frivolous rather than authoritarian.

Half of a steep hipped roof covered in shingles is supported on wooden, Tuscan columns forming an open portico with a plain boarded soffit and no visible beams. The other half of the roof covers the enclosed part of the chapel. From the primitive character of the portico one anticipates a dark, rustic interior, so the white, hemispherical dome, lit from above, comes as a complete surprise. Eight columns – Doric this time and fluted – support the rim of the dome, but there are still no beams. This is a deeply traditional building both in its form – domes have been associated with funeral buildings since Roman times – and in its structure, which is like a recreation of the origins of classicism.

The chapel was part of a competition-winning master plan for the cemetery, designed by Asplund in collaboration with Sigurd Lewerentz. Both architects had studied with Ivar Tengbom and with Ragnar Östberg, the designer of Stockholm City Hall (see Chapter 3). Lewerentz's Resurrection Chapel, in another part of the cemetery, takes a different, but equally unorthodox approach to the classical tradition. A tall, plain, stuccoed, barn-like building with a single window is classicized by the addition of various ornamental features applied like clothing to a naked body. The window, which is placed high up and off centre in the south wall, is given full 'aedicule' treatment externally and big consoles internally to support its architrave. Most impressive of these garments, however, is the hefty portico, placed not, as one might expect, at the axial west entrance, which is left plain, but at a side door in the north wall. It is deliberately over-scaled, a fortissimo chord in an otherwise quiet composition. Twelve columns, a thick Greek entablature and a fully sculptured pediment form a complete temple, not just a porch. Strangest of all, it stands at a slight angle to the

Woodland Chapel, Stockholm, Sweden. Erik Gunnar Asplund, 1920. Like a recreation of the origins of classicism.

chapel itself, perhaps accommodating some slight irregularity in the site layout but in the process breaking an unwritten law of classicism: that all parts of a building should conform to the same geometrical logic. A similar relaxed attitude to geometry and order can be seen in an early house by Asplund, the Villa Snellman of 1918, the two wings of which collide at an odd angle. Inside, corridors taper and every room is different, one of them made into an almost circular upper hall. This kind of freestyle classicism was to be an inspiration to Postmodernists of the 1980s (see Chapter 24).

Resurrection Chapel, Stockholm, Sweden. Sigurd Lewerentz, 1925. The porch stands at a slight angle to the body of the chapel.

Asplund eventually adopted the international Modernist style effortlessly and with great skill in his buildings for the Stockholm Exhibition of 1930. However, his greatest and best-known work remains the thoroughly classical Stockholm Public Library, completed in 1927. Its overall form is easy to describe: a tall cylinder, about as high as its circumference, sits in what would otherwise have been the central courtyard of a relatively low, roughly square perimeter block (one side of which was added later). The square block is subdivided internally to accommodate reading rooms, offices and ancillary accommodation, but the cylinder contains a single space: the main public lending hall, surrounded, amphitheatre fashion, by three stepped tiers of bookshelves.

How should one enter such a space? 'Near its centre' is the answer, having climbed a long, shallow staircase from an entrance hall in the perimeter block. In an earlier version of the design, the main space was covered by a dome, perforated to admit daylight. It would have been an elaborate and expensive structure. The drum that takes its place is comparatively cheap and simple, with its ring of ordinary rectangular windows and its steel roof structure hidden by a ceiling, but it is perhaps more impressive than the dome would have been. There is an architectural lesson here: that simplicity and economy can be more effective than complexity and expense. One might argue, even so, that the drum is an extravagant provision: after all more than half of its volume, above the level of the top tier of bookshelves, has no practical function. But it is essential to the composition, unifying it both internally and externally. That characteristic lightness of Scandinavian

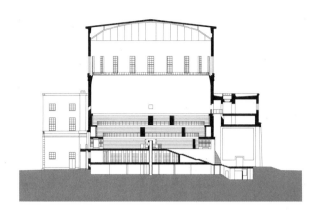

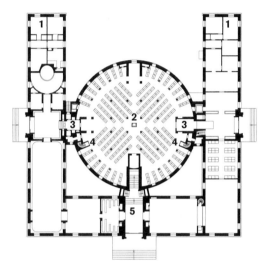

0   5   10m
15   30 ft

Ground floor plan
1. Offices/reading rooms
2. Main rotunda
3. Entrance to reading rooms
4. Stairs to upper galleries
5. Main entrance

**Stockholm Public Library, Sweden.
Erik Gunnar Asplund, 1927.**
The plain cylinder is perhaps more impressive than the elaborate dome originally proposed.

classicism is here achieved by the avoidance of any visible loadbearing elements or representations of them; no columns or entablatures, in other words. We recognize the building's classical allegiance by its symmetry, its regularity, and its carefully balanced proportions.

Asplund never entirely abandoned classicism even after he had adopted Modernism. In 1935 he returned to the Woodland Cemetery site to design a crematorium with three linked chapels. The chapels are low, rather bunker-like and basically Modernist but the big open portico that they share is more ambiguous. Its perimeter columns and beams are plain and stone clad with no ornament, yet this is obviously some species of classical temple. It might be described as 'abstract classical' – a style that was to become common in public buildings of subsequent decades that wished to be modern while retaining a degree of formality; one thinks, for example, of Lincoln Center in New York or Kennedy Center in Washington D. C. (see Chapter 15).

Italy

In Italy the ideological allegiances of Modernism and classicism are even less clear cut than in Scandinavia. Italian classicism of the 1930s is best exemplified by a project, originally known as E-42, to build a new town 7 kilometres (4½ miles) south west of Rome. The first designs were drawn up in 1935 with the intention of providing the context and infrastructure for a universal exposition to be held in 1942 – the 20th anniversary of the inauguration of the fascist state. The expo never took place because of the Second World War, but the development was nevertheless partially completed in the 1950s as an outlying business and government district of the capital. It is still known as EUR (Esposizione Universale Roma). The style of its buildings, laid out along monumental axes, can best be described as 'stripped classical' – symmetrical, often with columned porticos but without traditional ornament.

For example, the Museo della Civiltà Romana (Museum of Roman Civilization), much visited by architectural historians wishing to view its vast scale model of ancient Rome, has windowless grey stone walls rising to an uninterrupted plain cornice. For visual relief it relies entirely on full-height, purely cylindrical columns standing guard at the entrances and carrying the cornice over a covered way to link the two identical but handed wings. It achieves a certain grandeur of a cold, mechanical kind. Pietro Aschieri, Domenico Bernardini, Cesare Pascoletti and Gino Peressutti were the architects. But the building most often used to represent the architecture of the EUR, and pre-war Italian classicism in general, is the Palace of Italian Civilization by Giovanni Guerrini, Ernesto Lapadula and Mario Romano. It takes the form of an almost perfect cube of white stone, pierced, like a coarse cheese grater, by regular grids of plain arched openings on all four sides. It looks like a purely monumental structure – some kind of columbarium perhaps – but in fact it is a functional six-storey building with stone-vaulted open loggias at every level shading glass-walled exhibition spaces.

These buildings at EUR are both modern and classical, the result of a compromise between traditionalists led by Marcello Piacentini, the most experienced and best-connected Italian architect of those years, and modernists led by Giuseppe Pagano, editor of the magazine *Casabella*. The compromise eventually gave way under the strain. In 1941 Pagano decided that he had made enough concessions to classicism and denounced the plan that he had at first supported both as a designer and in the pages of his magazine. In the early war years this was a brave position to adopt, but would not necessarily have been

(Left) **Chapel of the Holy Cross, Woodland Cemetery, Stockholm, Sweden. Erik Gunnar Asplund, 1935.** Classical in spirit despite the absence of traditional details.

(Opposite) **Palace of Italian Civilization, Rome, Italy. Giovanni Guerrini, Ernesto Bruno Lapadula and Mario Romano, 1937.** The vaulted loggias shade glass-walled exhibition spaces.

politically dangerous had not Pagano gone further, declaring himself an anti-fascist and joining the resistance. He was eventually deported to Germany and died in the Mauthausen concentration camp in 1945.

Pagano's fate should not be taken, however, as confirmation of the classicism = totalitarianism equation. The fact is that many Italian Modernists, or 'Rationalists' as they were called, were wholehearted supporters of the fascist regime and, unlike their Futurist predecessors (see Chapter 4), were always at pains, in this cradle of classicism, to declare their respect for tradition. The most brilliant of their number was Giuseppe Terragni, and his most famous building, the Casa del Fascio (Fascist Party headquarters) in Como, completed in 1936, has become their chief representative in architectural history. It is a work of geometry as much as of architecture – a perfect square on plan, with elevations that are double squares. The central courtyard that appears in early versions of the design has become an atrium in the finished building, covered by a roof of glass lenses set in concrete and surrounded by galleries that give access to offices and meeting rooms. The atrium is as much a public

Casa del Fascio, Como, Italy. Giuseppe Terragni, 1936.
In Italy at this time the conventional association of fascism with classicism did not apply.

space as the piazza outside, onto which it can be opened instantly by means of a rank of automatic doors to disgorge or admit political demonstrations or military parades.

Piacentini, Pagano and Terragni were all, in a sense, collaborators in the design of the Italian pavilion at the 1937 Paris International Exposition. Architecturally it was one of the most progressive pavilions in an expo better known for its traditional monumentalism. Piacentini was the lead architect, Pagano designed some of the interiors and Terragni's Casa del Fascio was the acknowledged inspiration. Here was a thoroughgoing exercise in abstract Modernism not merely being tolerated by a totalitarian regime but being called upon to represent it. The only bombastic element of the design was the statue by Georges Gori of a naked man on a stout stallion riding confidently forward from an asymmetrically placed plinth. It was supposed to represent the triumph of Mussolini's invasion of Ethiopia.

Paris Exposition

International expos are useful signposts in the history of architecture because the ideological messages that their buildings convey are consciously intended and carefully gauged. What the Paris expo indicates is that in 1937 classical architecture was winning the contest with Modernism. There were exceptions: the Spanish pavilion,

for example, was designed by the young Josep Lluis Sert, who in subsequent decades became the father figure of Spanish Modernism. Commissioned by the Republican government, the pavilion housed Picasso's *Guernica*, that huge, epoch-making representation of the horrible slaughter of innocent civilians in an aerial bombardment ordered by General Franco. Most of the important expo buildings, however, were classical. The tone was set by the enormous Chaillot Palace, by Jacques Carlu, Louis-Hippolyte Boileau and Léon Azéma, taking the north-western end of the site in its long curved arms terminated by solid pavilions. Baroque in plan and silhouette but with stripped-down details, it was a deliberate rejection of the Modernism of Le Corbusier, who was a runner-up in the design competition. Part of the palace now houses a museum of architecture. The other permanent classical monument associated with the expo was the Musée d'Art Moderne, also known as the Tokyo Palace. This has since seemed like a mismatch of building and contents – a conflict that the building of the Centre Pompidou in the 1970s was meant to resolve – but the classicism of the building is of a modern kind, radically simplified, with large areas of plain wall, cylindrical columns and a thin cornice; the effect is similar to that of the later Museo della Civiltà Romana, which might have been influenced by it.

Classicism, then, is as much in evidence in French as in English, Scandinavian or Italian architecture of the inter-war years. We have seen how in these countries its political meaning was variable: sometimes conservative, sometimes progressive. It was in the USSR and Germany that the association of classicism with authoritarianism was established. Conveniently, a good illustration of this is to be

found at the centre of the Paris expo where the German and Soviet pavilions confronted one another across the main axis of the site. The confrontation was deliberate and it sounded a harsh warning note in an exhibition otherwise dedicated to the promotion of peace and harmony. On one side stood a huge metal statue, by the French-educated sculptor Vera Mukhina, of a pair of workers, male and female, triumphantly brandishing a hammer and a sickle to form the emblem of the USSR. Directly opposite stood a tight cluster of fluted columns supporting a stepped cornice on which perched an eagle with a wreathed swastika in its claws. It is said that Albert Speer, the designer of this monument and Hitler's favourite architect, had secretly been allowed to view in

(Above) Musée d'Art Moderne, Paris Exposition, France, 1937. A mismatch of building and contents? The Centre Pompidou was realized in order to resolve this very conflict.

(Left) Palais de Chaillot and the pont d'Iéna, Paris Exposition, France, 1937. The Russian pavilion (left) by Boris Iofan is confronted, deliberately, by Albert Speer's German pavilion (right).

**German Pavilion, Paris, France. Albert Speer,
1937.** The products of German industry displayed
in a classical interior with chandeliers.

advance the design of the Soviet pavilion, and that his taller,
more massive structure was intended to symbolize a halt to
the advance of communism.

The architect of the Soviet pavilion was Boris Iofan, whose
winning 'wedding cake' entry in 1933 for the Palace of the
Soviets competition had signalled the defeat of Modernism
in Stalinist Russia. His Paris pavilion was similar, in concept
if not in scale – its surmounting statue so dominant that
it reduced the building itself to a mere plinth. But in both
cases the plinths deserve closer scrutiny. The Palace of the
Soviets, of which many versions were created in the years
before the project was halted in 1941, conformed loosely to
classical expectations in its symmetry and monumentality.
Yet it was also a skyscraper, not so different in spirit from the
pre-Modernist skyscrapers of New York. And, of course, its
colossal statue of Lenin inevitably called to mind the Franco-
American Statue of Liberty. The Paris pavilion was even more
American looking, and this was no coincidence. Iofan had
visited, and much admired, Raymond Hood's Rockefeller
Center in New York and copied its main compositional idea:
a 'laminated' mass, with vertical strata that rise to different
heights and extend to different lengths, all disciplined by a
strict bilateral symmetry.

In short it was modern, or 'modernistic', not classical.
Inside the pavilion there were more references to American
modernity, including a Ford automobile (produced under
licence in Nizhny Novgorod, by now renamed Gorky)
placed like a piece of sculpture centrally on a landing of the
grand staircase. The German pavilion showed a car too, a

futuristically streamlined Mercedes with a swastika badge,
looking out of place among traditional pilasters, cornices and
chandeliers. If the contest between the USSR and German
pavilions had been purely architectural, then the former
would have won. Its speeding, horizontal form, so much more
dynamic than Speer's stolid stump, was much admired. Frank
Lloyd Wright himself described it as 'a master architect's
conception' and 'the most dramatic and successful exhibition
building at the Paris fair'.

Russia

'Socialist Realism' is the name given to the artistic style
officially approved in Stalin's Russia. If Iofan's Paris
pavilion plinth somehow managed to evade Socialist
Realist prescriptions, Mukhina's statue – representational,
monumental and triumphalist – illustrates them well enough.
Can there be a Socialist Realist architecture? Not in any
obvious way, since architecture is mainly an abstract art;
buildings rarely represent anything in the figurative sense
except other buildings. But then what is the classical tradition
if not a chain of successive representations, sometimes
inventing new versions of traditional features, sometimes
returning to the ancient originals? In this sense classicism
and Socialist Realism belonged together. It was logical that a
totalitarian regime, allowing no dissent or disagreement even

**Design for the Palace of the Soviets. Boris Iofan,
1937.** A plinth for a statue, yet not so different in spirit
to the pre-Modernist skyscrapers of New York.

among its artists, should insist on classicism as the 'correct' style. Several traditionally trained Russian architects had remained in practice since pre-revolutionary years. One of the most prominent was Vladimir Shchuko, who had achieved success in the early years of the century as an architect and stage designer working mainly in the neo-classical style. But he was prepared to turn his hand to almost any style, including Constructivism. The plinth that he designed in 1925 for the statue to Lenin at the Finland station in St Petersburg, for example, is an abstract composition with echoes of Malevich and van Doesburg. When Shchuko and his junior partner Vladimir Gelfreikh entered the design competition for the Lenin Library in Moscow, they first submitted a modestly Constructivist scheme. In the second stage it was 'classicized', but still retained its asymmetrical plan. By the time the building was completed in 1941 its austere colonnades had taken on the appearance of 'modern classical' buildings elsewhere in Europe, such as the Musée d'Art Moderne in Paris.

The Lenin Library might be seen as transitional between Constructivism and Socialist Realism, except that these categories were not really well defined. In certain buildings of the 1920s, such as Ivan Zholtovsky's Moscow city power station (see page 139) classicism was never far below the

Constructivist surface. In 1934 Zholtovsky revealed his true colours in the facade of an apartment block on Ulitsa Mokhovaya in Moscow. Its giant Corinthian columns are an almost literal copy of Palladio's Loggia del Capitano in Vicenza of 1565. It was buildings like this one and the Lenin Library, on prominent sites in Moscow, that relegitimized classicism and indicated the way forward for a Socialist Realist architecture. Very soon, however, their relatively restrained manner was overtaken by the megalomaniac monumentalism typified by the Palace of the Soviets. Shchuko and Gelfreikh were assigned to the project, against Boris Iofan's will, supposedly to help with technical and administrative aspects but actually to ensure that Stalin's personal taste was satisfied.

Among the best-known and most loved products of Socialist Realist architecture are the underground stations of the Moscow Metro. In the 1950s they became almost oppressively Baroque with marble-clad columns, barrel-vaulted ceilings and elaborate chandeliers (Komsomolskaya station, designed by Aleksei Shchusev, is a good example), but some of the earlier stations of the 1930s are elegant and well proportioned. Passengers on the main platform of Mayakovskaya station, designed by Alexei Dushkin, promenade beneath pendentive domes crowned by elliptical cupolas. Detailing is Art Deco rather than classical, with fluted stainless steel casings to the columns and flattened arches. Mosaic ceiling panels depict sky scenes with aeroplanes. Typical of the late, post-war Stalinist style are the so-called

Mokhovaya Building, Moscow, Russia. Ivan Zholtovsky, 1934. Giant Corinthian columns seem to have been borrowed from Palladio.

Seven Sisters, Moscow's answer to the skyscrapers of New York. Functionally, they are of various types – government buildings, hotels, apartment blocks, a university – but their main function was to save Stalin's embarrassment at the absence of high buildings in the capital. Gothic in profile but Baroque in plan, all are bilaterally symmetrical with a tall central block flanked by lower wings, sometimes with subsidiary towers. The differences between the typical Moscow skyscraper and its New York counterpart are rather subtle. Both were designed from the outside in rather than functionally from the inside out, but for different reasons. In the American case it was to maximize the development of expensive land; in the Russian case it was to create a freestanding landmark confirming the prestige of a political regime. Stylistic differences are even less distinct. Stalin is said to have been a lover of spires, which might explain why every one of the Seven Sisters is provided with at least one spire. But take away the spires and the buildings begin to look like cousins of Rockefeller Center.

Germany

In Germany, as in Russia, traditional, monumental architecture was chosen for the most important symbols of state power. This does not mean, however, that all Nazi

Mayakovskaya station, Moscow, Russia. Alexei Dushkin, 1938. Flattened arches and pendentive domes with elliptical cupolas: more Art Deco than classical.

Moscow State University, Russia. Lev Rudnev, 1953. One of the 'Seven Sisters', Moscow's answer to the skyscrapers of New York City.

architecture was classical. Other styles were represented, including a kind of Modernism. The architect Herbert Rimpl, who had been an associate of Walter Gropius, designed an aircraft production facility for Heinkel in three distinct styles: stripped-down classical for the offices, functional Modernist for the factory buildings, and folksy vernacular for the workers' housing. Architecture was exploited for propaganda purposes, the most important projects being illustrated repeatedly in state-sponsored magazines and exhibitions to demonstrate the creative capabilities of the regime. Yet there was no logic or consistency in the relationship between style and meaning. In housing, for example, an anti-urban, anti-industrial, arts-and-crafts style predominated, illustrating the 'blood and soil' aspect of Nazi ideology. But a rather similar style, with pitched roofs and 'agricultural' plans, was also applied to modern building types such as broadcasting stations and autobahn garages. For Party buildings such as the *Ordensburgen* or leadership schools, in which healthy and racially 'pure' young men were indoctrinated, a simplified Romanesque style, evoking a medieval past of chivalric duty, was considered appropriate. The Sonthofen Ordensburg at Allgäu in Bavaria is typical – something between a monastery and barracks with accommodation blocks of heavy timber and stone construction and a castle-like tower. Its architect was Hermann Giesler, who would later prepare a plan for the city of Munich to rival Speer's

plan for Berlin. On a smaller scale, many provincial buildings such as clinics and schools were plain, functional structures that in another context would be described as Modernist were it not for their pitched roofs.

Hitler himself favoured the neo-classical style for those buildings in which he took a personal interest. The first of these was the House of German Art in Munich, built between 1933 and 1937 and still in use as an art gallery. Its main facade is dominated by a 22-columned portico clearly meant to recall Karl Friedrich Schinkel's Altes Museum in Berlin but simplified and modernized, with rather mechanical Doric columns supporting a plain entablature. Its architect was Paul Ludwig Troost, who was a close friend of Hitler and had been a National Socialist since 1924. Hitler, an architect manqué, associated himself completely with the building, ordering elaborate ceremonies and lavish publicity to celebrate every stage of its construction. It set the stylistic pattern for all of Hitler's pet building projects, which, after Troost's death in 1934, were designed by his successor as official architect of the Reich, Albert Speer.

Speer had been a pupil of Heinrich Tessenow, who combined the arts-and-crafts and classical traditions in a distinctive, humanistic style. The theatre at Dresden-Hellerau is a good example. Though he had great respect for Tessenow, Speer's architecture was to take on a completely different character once he had come to Hitler's notice as an ambitious and hard-working servant of the Nazi Party. His major project as chief architect of the Reich was the design of the architectural setting for the huge militaristic rallies and ranting Hitlerian speeches that have since become so familiar from endlessly replayed old newsreels. The Zeppelinfeld, part of the Nazi Party congress grounds in Nuremberg, was an almost-square parade ground given direction and monumental significance by a straight grandstand or tribune, 360 metres (395 yards) long, on the north-east side. This was the backdrop of a political theatre. Hitler's uniformed figure was part of the architecture, the focal point of its perfect symmetry, with ranks of square columns extending on either side, far beyond the bounds of reasonable human proportion. Among Speer's many talents was a gift

for theatrical display, the architectural equivalent of Leni Riefenstahl's stirring propaganda films. At the Nuremberg rally on the evening of 11 September 1937 he arranged more than 100 searchlights around the perimeter of the Zeppelinfeld and pointed them at the sky so that their beams formed 'a cathedral of light'.

More conventional, but equally theatrical, was Speer's design for the New Reich Chancellery in Berlin, completed in 1939. Its public frontage, extending along the whole 450-metre (490-yard) length of Voss-Strasse, was almost polite – moderate in its proportions, with plinths, cornices and attics conforming to the conventional classical pattern. Columns occurred only at the full-height recessed entrances to the flanking administrative blocks. The true nature and purpose of the building was revealed inside. According to Speer's later account, Hitler wanted 'grand halls and salons which will make an impression on people, especially on the smaller dignitaries'.[4] In other words its purpose was to intimidate visitors. Diplomats alighted from their cars in the perfectly

(Left) **House of German Art, Munich, Germany. Paul Ludwig Troost, 1937.** A form clearly meant to echo Schinkel's Altes Museum in Berlin.

(Above) **Zeppelinfeld, Nuremberg, Germany. Albert Speer. 1934.** The architectural setting for huge militaristic rallies.

(Left) New Reich Chancellery, Berlin. Albert Speer, 1939. Details were classical but columns appeared only at recessed entrances.

(Above) Interior of the New Reich Chancellery. The architecture of intimidation. Visitors walked the length of the gallery to their meeting with Hitler.

proportioned roofless room of the Cour d'Honneur. Then began the long nervous walk to their meeting with Hitler via a top-lit mosaic-lined hall, a domed rotunda and a gallery 150 metres (165 yards) long, its floor, its architraves and the deep reveals of its 19 tall windows all dressed in marble. 'They'll get a taste of the power and grandeur of the German Reich,' said Hitler. The building was demolished by the occupying Soviet power soon after the war.

Speer's plans for the reconstruction of Berlin, drawn up between 1937 and 1940, were no different in general form from eighteenth-century plans for Washington, nineteenth-century plans for Paris or twentieth-century plans for New Delhi. In scale, however, they crossed the line that divides ambition from megalomania. A new north–south axis was proposed, culminating in a Great Square, big enough to hold a million people and dominated by a domed People's Hall (Volkshalle) 220 metres (720 feet) high that would have been the largest single enclosed space in the world. Like the sublime visions of the eighteenth-century French architect Etienne-Louis Boullée, Speer's Berlin plan shows an impressive command of traditional architectural form but

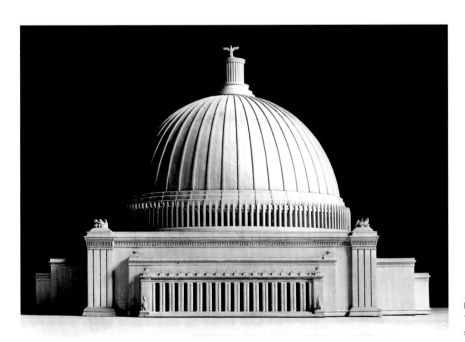

Design for the Volkshalle. Albert Speer, 1940. This would have been the largest single enclosed space in the world.

a flagrant disregard of economic and political realities. By 1942, Speer's talents were required elsewhere. He became armaments minister and one of the most powerful men in Hitler's inner circle. After the war he was convicted of war crimes and spent 20 years in Spandau prison.

As we have seen, Speer's polished but hard-faced style had its equivalents all over Europe. Modernized classicism was not exclusive to National Socialism nor to any other political ideology. It was common in America too, where Beaux-Arts-trained architects like Paul Cret and Albert Kahn continued to design formal, symmetrical buildings for government and business clients well into the 1930s. Cret's Federal Reserve headquarters in Washington D. C. for example – symmetrical and stone clad, its simplified Doric portico crowned by an eagle – would not have looked out of place in Speer's

Berlin. But the catalogue of Washington architecture in the 1930s also includes a classicism of a different kind, not modernized or simplified but served straight, Roman style. And here perhaps a political meaning is explicit. The new government office buildings of the so-called Federal Triangle on the north side of Constitution Avenue almost all put on utterly traditional and rather dull classical suits. The Internal Revenue Service Building, by Louis A. Simon, is typical. John Russell Pope was the master of this literal-minded style, never hesitating to grace his buildings, such as the National Archives Building, completed in 1935, and the National Gallery of Art, completed in 1941, with full-blown octastyle porticos, Corinthian and Ionic respectively. His last building, completed in 1943, was the Pantheon-like Jefferson Memorial, a monument to a founding father of American democracy who was also a classical architect.

(Above) Eccles Building, US Federal Reserve HQ, Washington D. C., USA. Paul Cret, 1937. Washington, not Berlin, but the architectural language is similar.

(Left) Thomas Jefferson Memorial, Washington D. C., USA. John Russell Pope, 1943. Pope was the master of full-blown classicism, here in the form of a Pantheon to commemorate an architect-president.

Classicism – the basics

Western classical architecture was born in ancient Greece when wooden temples modelled on chieftains' houses began to be reproduced in carved stone and thereby monumentalized. The Parthenon, a now ruined temple to the goddess Athena on the Acropolis in Athens, is often taken to be the perfect example, though its proportions are untypical with porticos of eight rather than the more usual six columns. Its main internal function was to house a statue of the goddess. Public religious rituals took place outside the building. A blank-walled 'cella', a surrounding 'peristyle' of closely spaced columns supporting a thick stone beam or 'entablature', and a shallow-pitched roof with triangular gables or 'pediments': these are the essential components of the Greek temple and of classical architecture in general – standard parts combined in standard proportions, irrespective of scale. Temple builders could choose from three different systems or 'orders': Doric (like the Parthenon), Ionic and Corinthian. They are usually identified by their distinctive column capitals, but the order governs the proportions and ornaments of the whole system, including the 'frieze', 'architrave' and 'cornice', which make up the entablature. What these ornaments originally signified – Doric triglyphs, Ionic volutes and Corinthian acanthus leaves, for example – is unknown, which makes their survival into the modern age all the more remarkable.

Ancient Rome inherited the Greek orders but altered them slightly and introduced two more, the Tuscan and the Composite. They were, however, put to quite different use, becoming ornaments of an imperial architecture based not on columns and beams but on arches, domes and vaults made of concrete and brick. It was from the 'arcuated' palaces, baths and amphitheatres of Rome and its colonies that medieval Romanesque architecture derived its formal and structural principles, later to be refined in the pointed arches and ribbed vaults of the Gothic. Classical architecture receded. But then, in fifteenth-century Italy, it was revived in a new configuration based on Roman precedents, including round arches and domes. It now took on a new meaning, representing the rebirth of a half-remembered golden age.

For the next three centuries classical principles governed the form of most royal and religious buildings in western Europe. Different styles and fashions were identified and named by later historians – Mannerism, Baroque, Palladian, Neo-Classical – but all were based on versions of the ancient orders. In the nineteenth century, other styles were revived, especially Gothic, which was preferred for its Christian rather than pagan associations and for the purity and honesty of its forms. It was from contemplation of the Gothic that Modernist architects of the twentieth century derived their doctrines of truth to materials and honest expression of structure. Classicism in contrast seemed shallow and artificial, its forms imposed upon the materials of its construction rather than emerging from their intrinsic nature. But always the Gothic was a reaction against a classical orthodoxy, which survived and thrived in the Beaux-Arts educational tradition and in the conservative instincts of rich and powerful patrons. Modernism may have been the characteristic style of the mid-twentieth century, but important buildings were still more likely to speak the language of classicism.

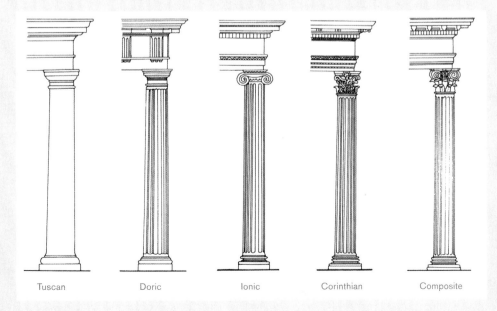

Tuscan Doric Ionic Corinthian Composite

The five Roman orders. These are based on Sebastiano Serlio's sixteenth-century treatise on architecture.

MODERNISM IN THE USA
1932–1972

'The International Style', Henry-Russell Hitchcock and Philip Johnson's epoch-making 1932 exhibition at the Museum of Modern Art in New York (see page 108), was mainly dedicated to European Modernist architecture, with only a handful of American examples.[1] Walter Gropius was represented by the Bauhaus buildings and the Törten Siedlung in Dessau; Mies van der Rohe by the Weissenhof apartments, the Barcelona Pavilion, the Lange House and the Tugendhat House. By the early 1940s both of these Modernist 'form givers' were installed as professors in American architecture schools – Gropius at Harvard, and Mies at the Illinois Institute of Technology (IIT). Other Modernist emigrés included Marcel Breuer, who joined Gropius at Harvard, and Ludwig Hilberseimer, who joined Mies at IIT.

Case Study houses

America was ready to receive Modernism and adapt it to the middle class, suburban, car-owning way of life. Rudolph Schindler and Richard Neutra, who could by now be regarded as 'home-grown' Modernists, had indicated the possibilities in their Los Angeles houses of the 1920s (see Chapter 12). In 1945 John Entenza, the editor of a progressive Californian architectural magazine called *Arts and Architecture*, decided that the best way to promote Modernist domestic architecture was to sponsor the building of actual houses and invite the public to come and look at them. Twenty-six so-called Case Study houses were built between 1945 and 1966, making the reputations of several west coast architects, including Craig Ellwood, Raphael Soriano, Pierre Koenig and the husband-and-wife team Charles and Ray Eames. These houses became world famous, partly through Julius Shulman's photographs in which well-dressed young people relax stylishly in open-plan living rooms and on poolside patios. His night view of Koenig's Case Study House No. 22 of 1959 – flat roofed and glass walled, perched high above Los Angeles, with two full-skirted girls posed just so and the glittering carpet of the city stretched out below – seems to promise a future of unlimited freedom and prosperity.

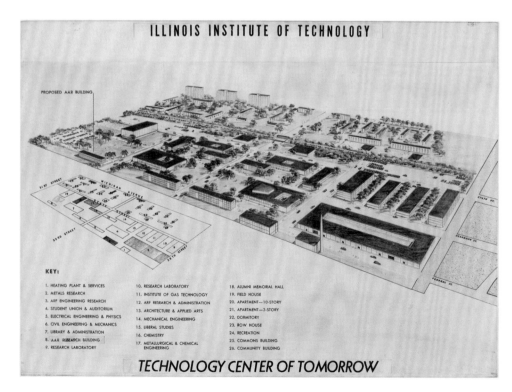

Plan for Illinois Institute of Technology, Chicago, USA. Mies van der Rohe, 1940. A modular grid for the free placement of buildings, but with some symmetry surviving from earlier versions.

Case Study House No. 22, Los Angeles, California, USA.
Pierre Koenig, 1959. Julius Shulman's famous photograph from
1960 seemed to promise a future of freedom and prosperity.

Eames House, Pacific Palisades, California, USA. Charles and Ray Eames, 1949. Industrial components softened by colour, planting, wood-block floors and timber boarding.

and clad informally with brightly coloured panels and steel-framed windows. Internally, the lightweight steel frame and metal decking are exposed but combined with warm, natural materials such as a wood-block floor in the studio and a timber-boarded wall in the living room. Over the years, many myths have arisen concerning the design and construction of this house, for example that it took only a few days to build and that all the components were ordered as standard from manufacturers' catalogues. The stories are at best only partially true, but the idea of a house quickly assembled from mass-produced metal components was to be an inspiration to architects in years to come, in particular the British High Tech architects of the 1970s and 1980s. The Hopkins House of 1976 (see page 352) is essentially a homage to the Eames House.

Ironically, the Case Study houses had little influence on the mass market, which preferred traditional styles and tried-and-tested structural forms such as the wooden 'platform frame', an updated version of the old nineteenth-century 'balloon frame'. There was, however, at least one commercial house-builder prepared to commission Modernist architects. From 1950 onwards for more than 20 years, Joseph Eichler built high-quality middle-class housing subdivisions in northern California, often working with the architect Archibald Quincy Jones. A typical Eichler house is single storey with a flat or very shallow-pitched roof and a freely articulated plan. Living rooms flow out onto patios or courtyards, which are sometimes covered and become 'atriums'. Steel frames are rare, but their place is taken by

The house and studio that the Eameses built for themselves in Pacific Palisades in 1949 was part of the Case Study series but has since been singled out as especially prophetic. An early design for a bridge-like glazed structure lying across the contours of the hilltop site was rejected as too assertive, too 'Miesian'. Ray Eames was a painter, not an architect, and it may have been her influence that suggested a less strenuous arrangement of two-storey boxes, one for the house and one for the studio, placed along the contours,

Eichler House, California, USA. Joseph Eichler, 1950s. Eichler's modernity was unusual. Most housing developers stuck to traditional styles and methods.

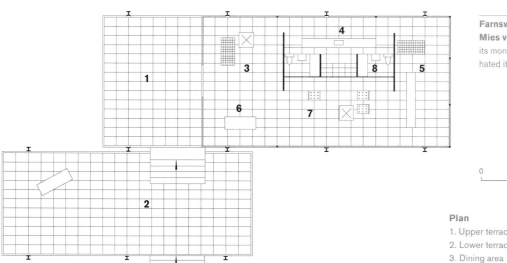

Farnsworth House, Plano, Illinois, USA. Mies van der Rohe, 1951. Architects love its monumental simplicity but the client hated it.

Plan
1. Upper terrace
2. Lower terrace
3. Dining area
4. Kitchen
5. Sleeping area
6. Office area
7. Living area
8. Bathroom

plain wooden posts and beams, left undecorated. This is the kind of 'good design' that the Case Study houses were meant to promote. Eichler made money, but not as much as rival developers like William Levitt in New York, who mass-produced hundreds of thousands of the inexpensive 'little boxes' mocked in the 1963 Pete Seeger song, and set the norm for American suburbia.

Mies van der Rohe and Johnson

The Case Study houses and their offspring are Miesian only up to a point. In them one senses an American impatience with European formality and intellectualism. In 1945 Mies himself designed an American house, at Plano, Illinois, for a Chicago academic, Dr Edith Farnsworth. The

Farnsworth House is flat roofed and glass walled, just like its Californian cousins, but unlike them it is a miniature monument. Its steel frame is a twentieth-century classical order – formal, symmetrical and finely adjusted. Mies insisted that the name of the steelworks, embossed on the webs of the ordinary H-shaped columns, should be ground smooth (or so the story goes). It is the epitome of Mies's style, what Kenneth Frampton has called 'the monumentalization of technique'. Mies built it to please himself, not his client, who hated it. It was too hot in summer when mosquitoes made the porch unusable, and in winter the glass walls streamed with condensation. Nevertheless, architects have long loved it for its purity and perfection.

Foremost among Mies's American admirers was Philip Johnson, who in 1947 compiled a comprehensive exhibition of Mies's work at the Museum of Modern Art, accompanied by a scholarly monograph. Johnson had himself only recently qualified to practise architecture, studying at Harvard under Walter Gropius and Marcel Breuer, and graduating in 1943 at the age of 37. He was a rich man and could afford to be his own client. The house that he built at New Canaan, Connecticut is a tribute to Mies and a version of the Farnsworth House, though it is far from being a copy. Whereas the floor plane of the Farnsworth House is lifted 1.5 metres (5 feet) above the flood-prone site, the floor plane of the Johnson House is a brick carpet laid on the ground. From it rises a brick cylinder containing the bathroom and the fireplace. The house is therefore anchored rather than floating, and in this respect more like Wright than Mies. The walls are glass, of course, but there is no celebration of structure. Columns are subsumed into the framing of the glass, not expressed separately. In a sense, this is only half a house because guests are accommodated in a separate structure like a negative version in solid brick. Its interior is graced by false, shallow domes inspired by the breakfast room of John Soane's early nineteenth-century house in London. Johnson may have admired Mies, but architecturally he was his own man. In the guest house at New Canaan we see the seeds of his later Postmodernism (see Chapter 24).

Architects often use houses as test-beds for architectural ideas and it is tempting to see the Farnsworth House as a prototype for Mies's later urban buildings. The fact is, however, that Mies's first American urban commission, the layout of the new IIT campus on a 50-hectare (125-acre) cleared site on the south side of Chicago, preceded Farnsworth by at least six years. The layout went through several versions, broadly symmetrical at first but finally becoming a modular grid in which individual buildings could be placed more freely. In these buildings, added over almost three decades from 1942, Mies and his local collaborators systematically explored the possibilities of space and structure, monumentality and technique, scale and proportion, but always in the same austere, basically classical language. Usable space was generally conceived as 'universal' rather than functionally specific, and structure was almost always a regular steel frame. If the frame had to be encased in concrete for fire protection, then its steel nature would be reasserted in a cladding of welded angles and I-sections, the Modernist equivalent of classical pilasters.

Glass House, New Canaan, Connecticut, USA. Philip Johnson, 1949. Johnson was a champion of Mies, but this is by no means a slavish copy of the Farnsworth House.

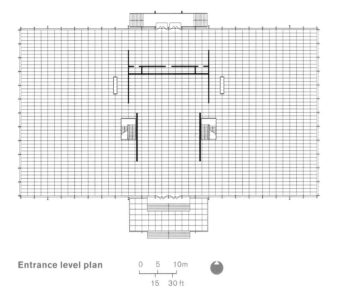

Entrance level plan

0   5   10m

15   30 ft

steps up to the main entrance pauses at an intermediate
floating platform. This is unmistakably a larger version of the
Farnsworth House, so perhaps there is something in the test-
bed theory after all.

The architectural language developed by Mies at IIT proved
to be a versatile medium, applicable to many building
types. Eventually, architects all over the world would learn
to speak it, especially in its high-rise version. In 1946, Mies
was commissioned by the developer Herbert Greenwald
to design a 22-storey apartment block in the Hyde Park
neighbourhood of Chicago. It is concrete, not steel, with a
double T-shaped plan. At a time when skyscrapers were still
expected to display traditional architectural ornament, the

Structure is paramount in these buildings. It is the discipline
to which space submits. In the Barcelona Pavilion and the
Tugendhat House, Mies's European masterpieces (see
pages 133 and 131), structure appears as a chrome-clad
cruciform column that allows space to flow freely around
it. In the IIT buildings, the American I- or H-section takes
charge, asserting its directional authority. The best example
is Crown Hall, completed in 1956, a glass-and-steel temple
that has been compared with Schinkel's Altes Museum
in Berlin. It actually houses the architecture school but
nothing about its plan betrays this fact. There are rooms
in the semi-basement, but the entrance level is conceived
as a single, high, completely uninterrupted slab of space.
All of the structure is on the outside: I-section columns
supporting beams 2 metres (6½ feet) deep above roof level.
External walls are all glass, in very large sheets. A flight of

**Lake Shore Drive Apartments, Chicago, USA. Mies van der
Rohe, 1951.** The apparent relationship between the two blocks is
carefully judged.

absolutely regular grid of its frontage facing Lake Michigan must have seemed starkly functional. Yet it was also rather refined, combining a few elements – projecting columns, window mullions and brick spandrels – in a handsomely proportioned whole. In the Promontory Apartments, simplicity and refinement took the place of ornament, and changed the rules of skyscraper design. Five years later the same developer commissioned a similar development on nearby Lake Shore Drive. This time there were two towers, both simple rectangles on plan, placed casually at right angles to one another. And they were steel, not concrete, with all-glass walls. The steel that did the structural work was encased in concrete for fire protection but faced externally in flat steel sheets to which relatively small steel mullions – dummy columns, in effect – were welded. Critics have sometimes seen this as a weak deception but Mies was never a strict functionalist. His classical upbringing had taught him that columns played a representational as well as a structural role.

Mies's triumphant architectural entrance into the city of New York came with a commission from the Seagram whiskey company to design a new headquarters building on Park Avenue. The Seagram Building is a descendant of the Lake Shore Drive apartments but raised to a new level of quality and refinement. In most photographs it looks like a perfect prism, a tall, handsome, 42-storey monolith, monumental in character by virtue solely of its proportions. In fact its form is rather more complicated: T-shaped on plan with a high ground floor recessed behind columns and a wide, five-storey block at the back of the site. What gives the Seagram Building its special air of authority is the fact that it is set back from the site frontage, creating an open plaza, a rare if not unique occurrence in the congested grid of Manhattan. The plaza has no function other than to provide a space in which to pause and admire the building (or alternatively the building opposite, McKim, Mead and White's Racquet and Tennis Club, a handsome Renaissance palace built in 1918). Whereas at Lake Shore Drive the outlines of

Seagram Building, New York City, USA. Mies van der Rohe, 1958. Apparently a simple monolith but actually T-shaped on plan with a five-storey block behind.

structural columns are clearly visible through the regularly spaced, painted steel mullions, in the Seagram Building structural members are hidden behind a continuous, uniform curtain of bronze-tinted glass. Transparency and reflection are evenly balanced and we are reminded of Mies's glass skyscraper projects of 30 years earlier. Here they are realized at last, but taking on an unexpectedly weighty, formal character.

Corporate Modernism

Completed in 1958, the Seagram Building provided a model for corporate office buildings all over the world for at least the next 20 years. But it was not the only glass-walled skyscraper in town. A little further down Park Avenue, Gordon Bunshaft of Skidmore, Owings and Merrill (SOM) had already completed a smaller but equally elegant US headquarters building for Lever Brothers, the British soap-manufacturing company. Bunshaft was a committed Modernist who had travelled in Europe and

was undoubtedly familiar with Mies's work, but he brought a typically American energy and optimism to the practice of architecture. Though a brilliant designer, he was also attuned to the growing corporate culture and saw the practice of architecture itself in corporate terms. By the time of his retirement in the early 1980s, SOM had grown to be the biggest architectural practice in the world, employing more than 2,000 people. Lever House was the seminal SOM building: a slim 24-storey rectangular tower clad in the simplest possible curtain wall, just an aluminium grid filled with glass, either transparent or opaque. In form it was similar to the Seagram Building but in character completely different – light and airy rather than weighty and monumental. There are no bronze mullions to remind us of the classical past, and instead of a ceremonial open plaza, Bunshaft provides a useful podium, covering the site but raised on pilotis, a mediator between skyscraper and sidewalk. This combination of tower and podium was perhaps even more influential internationally than Mies's monolith.

Lever House, New York City, USA. Skidmore, Owings and Merrill, 1952. The designer, Gordon Bunshaft, was influenced by Mies, though Lever House was completed before the Seagram Building.

General Motors Technical Center, Detroit, USA.
Eero Saarinen, 1955. Modernism pressed into the
service of corporate industrial culture.

In the late 1950s Mies collaborated with his old colleague
Ludwig Hilberseimer to design a large social-housing
development in Detroit known as Lafayette Park. It combines
two 22-storey towers with low-rise town houses in a carefully
landscaped setting designed by Alfred Caldwell. The towers
are simple slabs raised on pilotis, not very different in overall
form from contemporary European examples such as the
Alton Estate in west London, but clad in the sort of curtain
walling that is more often associated with office buildings.
Town houses adapt the language of the IIT campus, with
walls of either brick or glass in exposed steel frames. It
does not sound like a recipe for homeliness. There are no
concessions to traditional domesticity such as pitched roofs
or porches or picket fences. And yet, in a city now virtually
ruined, both socially and physically, Lafayette Park survives
as a mature and peaceful environment with a mixture of low-
income and professional residents.

Back in the corporate world represented by Seagram
and Lever, the wealth and power that were celebrated on
Park Avenue could also find expression in more expansive
settings. Out-of-town industrial and business parks were
mostly undistinguished architecturally, but a few were
conceived as 'campuses' and designed to project a
consistent, co-ordinated image. General Motors' Technical
Center on the outskirts of Detroit is a good example. Its
architect was Eero Saarinen, the son of Eliel Saarinen, who
had emigrated to the US from Finland in 1923 and built a

distinguished reputation as an architect, town planner and
teacher. Father and son worked together on the General
Motors design until Eliel's death in 1950. Eero's architectural
philosophy was pluralistic, not unlike his great predecessor in
the business of architecture for motor manufacturing, Albert
Kahn. He could design in concrete or steel, using rectilinear
or curvilinear geometries, sometimes uncompromisingly
Modernist, sometimes following a traditional form. It hardly
seems possible, for example, that the bird-like TWA airport
terminal (see page 212) came out of the same architectural
mind as the General Motors complex, which is distinctly
Miesian.

The tone is set by the big rectangular lake in the middle of
the site, in which stands an egg-like stainless steel water
tank on a tripod tower. Nearby lies the shallow silver Styling
Dome with its big central oculus designed to show off the
gleaming Cadillacs and Chevrolets to best advantage. The
overall layout is vaguely reminiscent of the IIT campus, with
mostly three-storey rectangular buildings, but cleaner and
slicker than the Mies originals. Saarinen was a creative
technician who saw the artistic opportunities offered by the
industrialization of building construction. General Motors
cars of the time were flashy and colourful – it was the age
of the fin and the fairing, with a new model every year – but
Saarinen learnt much from the basics of car construction –
the chassis, the metalwork and the glazing. His curtain walls
were steel framed, using rectangular sections, not I-beams,
and in-filled by thin, insulated panels of porcelain-enamelled
metal. Windows and panels were fixed into the frame with
neoprene gaskets, just like car windows. It was an example
of what would later be called 'technology transfer' and it
was to have a profound influence on the British architects
Richard Rogers and Norman Foster. Twenty years later,
when Rogers was designing the Centre Pompidou (see
page 350) he surely had in mind the Technical Center's plant
room with its colour-coded pipes and ducts arranged like an
abstract painting. High Tech was still in the future, however,
and the interiors of the main GM buildings are palatial rather
than industrial. Foyers are settings for grand staircases like
pieces of modern sculpture: in the Styling Building, a slow,
shallow double flight suspended over a pool; in the Research
Administration Building, an operatic spiral. All elements of
the office interiors – walls, partitions, ceilings, furniture – are
thoroughly co-ordinated on a 1.5-metre (5-foot) grid. It is a
symbol of almost military control but with a smooth face and
a luxury finish.

Mention of the military is not inapt. The phrase 'military-
industrial complex' entered common parlance after it was
used by President Dwight D. Eisenhower in his 1961 farewell
address. In these Cold War years, the American public
was made acutely aware of the importance of defence,
and architecture had a part to play in the propaganda. The

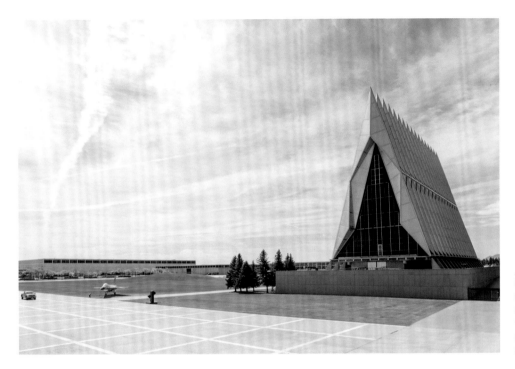

US Air Force Academy Cadet Chapel, Colorado Springs, USA. Skidmore, Owings and Merrill, 1962. Vaguely Gothic, as befits a chapel, but also subtly evoking the technology of flight.

US Air Force Academy in Colorado Springs, designed by SOM and built between 1957 and 1962, was a milestone in the progress of American Modernism. If it had been built before the Second World War it would almost certainly have conformed to a Beaux-Arts norm. It was inevitably going to be compared with the Military Academy at West Point, New York and the Naval Academy at Annapolis, Maryland, both rebuilt at the turn of the century in traditional styles, the former mainly Gothic, the latter mainly classical. Now, 50 years later, Modernism was considered to be the appropriate style in which to mark the Air Force's entry into the military educational establishment. Even the choice of site in Colorado Springs – a level platform set against a mountainous backdrop – seemed to convey subtle messages about community and individuality, formality and freedom.

The main Cadet Area is a campus of three- and four-storey rectangular buildings with gridded facades, surrounding a vast lawn and parade ground. There is plenty of glass but also a measure of marble facing, no doubt as a concession to traditionalist elements of the client body. The overall composition is non-axial yet somewhat classical in its formality. The same cannot be said of its centrepiece, the chapel, which is Gothic, of a cleverly abstracted kind. Designed by SOM's Walter Netsch, it takes the form of a row of 17 triangular frames, like 17 spires, assembled from 100 identical aluminium-clad tetrahedrons. Stained-

Lincoln Center, New York City, USA. Wallace Harrison, 1966. Modernist but formal enough to appeal to the opera-, concert- and theatre-going public.

201

glass strips divide these components and light the soaring interior. Though essentially a simple, repetitive assemblage, it manages to overlay an image of piety and togetherness on an alternative image of advanced technology and perhaps even of flight itself.

In the 1950s and 1960s Modernism asserted itself in every field of American building, but it was a characteristically American Modernism, undogmatic and ready to make concessions to traditional expectations. When New York decided it needed a multi-auditorium performing-arts complex and at last found a site for it in a poor district of Manhattan known as Lincoln Square, the new Modernist orthodoxy was required to rise to a monumental challenge. An opera house, a concert hall and a theatre suitable for ballet were to be the main ingredients. Wallace Harrison was a safe choice as master planner. Beaux-Arts trained, he had played a part in the building of Rockefeller Center (see page 172) and had chaired the international committee, including Le Corbusier and Oscar Niemeyer, that had designed the United Nations headquarters. His plan for Lincoln Center aimed high on the monumental scale, arranging the main buildings on three sides of a piazza, thereby inviting comparison with Michelangelo's Campidoglio on the Capitoline Hill in Rome.

Such formality was anti-Modernist in spirit but it was too late now for a revival of full-blown classicism so there would have to be a compromise. All three buildings were provided with classical/modern porticos clad in travertine stone: five tall arches for the opera house, designed by Harrison himself; four pairs of columns and a plain entablature for Philip Johnson's theatre; and an unconventional nine

columns, tapered elegantly, for Max Abramovitz's concert hall. In all cases internal arrangements are conventional and competently planned. None of these buildings is particularly distinguished as architecture, but the whole ensemble, including the fountain in the middle of the piazza, creates a suitably sumptuous setting for an evening's traditional entertainment. Architectural purists prefer the smaller Vivian Beaumont Theater round the corner, designed by Eero Saarinen. It has no columned facade, just a simple stone-clad bridge over a fully glazed foyer – a direct expression of the spaces within.

Edward Durrell Stone

The Beaux-Arts style, which had survived into the 1930s, sometimes morphing into Art Deco, had suited the American taste for monumentality and decorative display and remained an influence not far below the surface of post-war Modernism. Architects like Edward Durrell Stone and Minoru Yamasaki were Modernists, certainly – pioneers, even – but their buildings were formal and decorative enough to satisfy popular taste. Progressive intellectuals in the profession considered them frivolous. The Museum of Modern Art in New York – strictly Modernist, almost Corbusian – was one of Stone's earliest commissions (with Philip L. Goodwin) but the US embassy in New Delhi, completed in 1959, is more typical of his style. A low box, with a water garden inside it, is raised on a plinth like a Mughal tomb, complete with reflecting pool. Delicately swelling columns, painted gold, support a thin flat roof overhanging generously on all sides. External walls are perforated concrete screens, continuous apart from the glazed main entrance at the top of a grand flight of steps. These features can be seen as responses to local culture and climate but 12 years later and 11,000

John F. Kennedy Center for the Performing Arts, Washington D. C., USA. Edward Durrell Stone, 1971. Slender columns measure out a stately promenade along the Potomac riverfront.

Conservatory of Music, Oberlin College, Ohio, USA. Minoru Yamasaki, 1963. A typical example of Yamasaki's 'concrete origami'.

World Trade Center, New York City, USA. Minoru Yamasaki, 1972. Destroyed by terrorist air attack in 2001.

kilometres (7,000 miles) away many of them were recycled in Washington's answer to Lincoln Center, the John F. Kennedy Center for the Performing Arts. Here is the same box, long and relatively low, with overhanging roof and slender columns. It is a far larger building than the embassy yet equally simple. Its three auditoriums – concert hall, theatre and opera house – are simply lined up side by side, with grand halls – the Hall of Nations and the Hall of States – to divide them and a high foyer running the whole length of the building to unite them. From the audiences' point of view, all the complicated service and backstage functions are magicked away. Nothing is allowed to interrupt the stately promenade along the Potomac riverfront.

Minoru Yamasaki

If Edward Stone's style might be described as fundamentally classical but superficially modern, Minoru Yamasaki's style was fundamentally modern but superficially Gothic. The facades of his buildings, and not just the skyscrapers, are almost always insistently vertical, using repeated precast concrete or metal profiles. Several university buildings display variations on this theme. For example, the Conservatory of Music at Oberlin College in Ohio, completed in 1963, has an absolutely regular and repetitive three-storey facade like a folded and cut-out concertina of white paper. Its monotony is relieved somewhat by the unusual lozenge-shaped windows and by a delicately frilly parapet. More examples of this 'origami' style can be found at Wayne State University, Detroit (the Education Building), Butler University, Indianapolis (the

Irwin Library) and Princeton University (Robertson Hall). But the biggest and most famous example no longer exists: the twin towers of the World Trade Center in New York, completed in 1972 and destroyed in the terrorist air attack of 11 September 2001. Yamasaki was an unlucky architect. At the beginning of his career he had designed a very large public housing project consisting of 33 eleven-storey blocks in parallel rows on a 23-hectare (57-acre) site in St Louis, Missouri. It was named Pruitt-Igoe after an African-American fighter pilot and a US congressman. Almost as soon as it was occupied in 1954 it suffered social problems and by the mid-1960s it had become a dangerous, semi-ruined slum. In 1972 the decision was taken to demolish it. Later in the decade, the critic Charles Jencks would choose the explosive destruction of Pruitt-Igoe as the event that marked the death of Modernism (see Chapter 24).

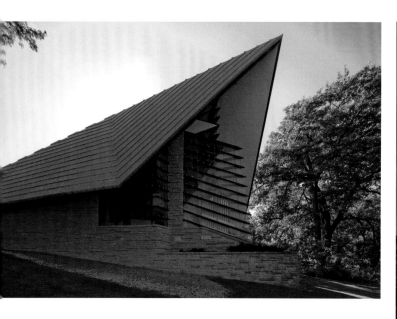

First Unitarian Church of Madison, Wisconsin, USA. Frank Lloyd Wright, 1951. Wright's late style is less organic, more mathematically formulaic.

Late Wright

European Modernism, faintly flavoured by admixtures of the old classical and Gothic ingredients, cannot account for the whole of American architecture in the 1950s, if only because Frank Lloyd Wright, the native genius, was still alive and working, now in the seventh decade of his career. Wright had never taken much notice of either European Modernism or the Beaux-Arts tradition but there had been a certain internal consistency of style in his work, even in buildings as different as, say, the Robie House and Fallingwater. After the Second World War his buildings became less 'organic', more mathematically formulaic. Circular and triangular forms appeared, especially in public buildings for assembly or worship. The rhomboidal nave of the First Unitarian Church of Madison, Wisconsin, designed in 1947, is covered by a tilted, double-pitch roof, its gable-end filled by angled and sloping glass walls. At the Beth Sholom Synagogue in Elkins Park, Pennsylvania, completed in 1959, the idea is developed further and on a larger scale. A tall, tent-like roof of translucent fibreglass rises over a 1,000-seat hall with a basically triangular plan. At night the whole building glows like a beacon. In Wright's only really tall building, the 19-storey Price Tower at Bartlesville, Oklahoma, completed

(Above) Price Tower, Bartlesville, Oklahoma, USA. Frank Lloyd Wright, 1956. Adapted from an unrealized project of 1930 for the Bowery district of Manhattan.

(Left) Marin County Civic Center, San Rafael, California, USA. Frank Lloyd Wright, 1962. Setting for the 1997 science fiction film Gattaca.

in 1956, a triangular grid orders an intricate plan, mixing offices with two-storey apartments. Structurally it is a tree, its lift-shafts forming a concrete trunk and its floors cantilevered like branches. The design was adapted from an unrealized project of 1930 for three apartment towers at St Mark's in the Bowery district of New York City. It might have looked more at home there than in the Oklahoma prairie.

Wright's circular buildings of the period have sometimes been dismissed as so much meaningless form-spinning. In the Annunciation Greek Orthodox Church at Wauwatosa, Wisconsin, designed in 1956, a shallow dome is balanced on top of a vaguely cruciform plan, perhaps trying to reinvent the ancient Byzantine dome-on-pendentives form. Eye-like openings around the shallow drum, shaded by a scalloped fringe, give it a comical, cartoon look. Wright's last major building, the Marin County Civic Center at San Rafael, California, seems to have escaped from a 1950s fantasy magazine.

Two long, straight, bridge-like, three- and four-storey administration wings are connected at an angle by a circular library and cafeteria building under a shallow dome. Circulation is by means of linear atriums with galleries, originally open to the sky but later glazed over. It is a simple, not to say simplistic, building plan made into architecture by

its curved blue roofs (Wright originally wanted them to be gold) decorated with circles and scallops, and its external walls that look like tiers of arches on the principle of the Roman aqueduct but are in fact suspended screens of metal and stucco. It is hard to imagine anything less 'organic' but it serves well as a setting for science fiction films such as Andrew Niccol's *Gattaca* of 1997.

But there is one circular building that, despite its wilfulness and illogicality, has become one of Wright's best-loved works. In theory, the Guggenheim Museum in New York fits neither its function nor its site. An inverted circular ziggurat of plain white concrete is the last thing one expects to find on a rectangular Fifth Avenue lot facing Central Park; and a continuous spiral ramp, borrowed from a 1925 scheme for a drive-up mountaintop observatory (the Gordon Strong Automobile Objective and Planetarium), seems an awkward setting for the quiet contemplation of European abstract paintings by Piet Mondrian, Wassily Kandinsky or Kurt Schwitters.

Solomon R. Guggenheim Museum, New York City, USA. Frank Lloyd Wright, 1959. An inverted circular ziggurat on a rectangular Manhattan lot.

Wright's organic architecture, ultimately derived from natural forms, had little in common with what Solomon R. Guggenheim and his artistic advisor Hilla Rebay called 'Non-objectivity'. (The term was perhaps meant as a challenge to the New Objectivity or *Neue Sachlichkeit* movement in pre-war Modernist architecture.) There is a kind of contradiction in the very idea of an art gallery designed by Frank Lloyd Wright. No-one admired Wright's genius more than Wright himself and showing off the work of other geniuses was not for him an important aim. So it is the building that visitors come to see and it is the building that they remember when they leave. In functional terms there is nothing right about the gallery environment: a continuous, low-ceilinged space with a concave hanging wall, a sloping floor and a horizontal strip of glass that seems designed to maximize unwanted glare. But looking down from the top of the ramp into the fountain at the foot of the swirling, top-lit, funnel-shaped atrium is one of the unmissable architectural sights of New York. The first designs for the Guggenheim were prepared in the early 1940s, but the building was not opened until October 1959, six months after Wright's death at the age of 91.

Guggenheim Museum interior. Not an ideal environment for viewing modern art. It is the building that visitors remember.

West–east section

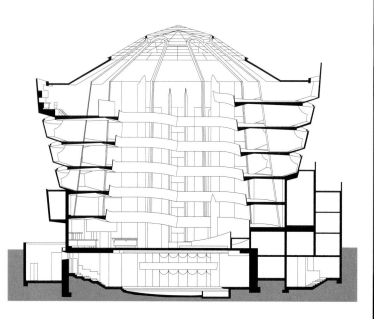

Bruce Goff

Bruce Goff's architecture was neither backward nor forward looking. He acknowledged no tradition and claimed no foresight but was content to design in what he called 'the continuous present'. 'Any idea that can be conceived in our time', he wrote, 'can be created in our time.' It was not so much a philosophy or theory of design as a justification for complete originality and freedom of expression.

Born in 1904 of a poor family in Alton, Kansas, Goff was apprenticed at the age of twelve to a firm of architects, Rush, Endacott and Rush, in Tulsa, Oklahoma. He quickly attained a mature competence in design and in his early twenties was already in charge of important projects such as the Art Deco Boston Avenue Methodist Church in Tulsa, with its elegant, soaring tower. The artists of the Vienna Secession, especially Gustav Klimt, and the Prairie style of Frank Lloyd Wright were early influences. But it is his later houses, designed after 1942 when he began teaching at the University of Oklahoma, for which he is best known, and they show no obvious influence other than, occasionally, the colours and patterns of Native American art.

The Bavinger House in Oklahoma, designed for a couple of art teachers, is the best known. A spiralling roof, like the skin of a continuously peeled apple, hangs by stainless steel cables from a single steel mast, and a rough stone wall, also a spiral, rises from the ground to meet it. Ribbons of glass complete the enclosure, but conceptually there is no enclosure; the inside is like the outside – a paved and planted garden complete with fish pond. It is possible to climb up the spiral on hanging steps to reach upper levels, but there are no floors or enclosed rooms. Instead, rounded platforms hang freely in the spiralling space like shells or saucers, each accompanied by a revolving cylindrical closet. At the top of the spiral, where it tightens to a single point, the highest saucer breaks out like the turret of a castle. In plans of the building saucers are given conventional names such as 'parents' sleeping area' or 'play area', and sunken parts of the ground floor are reserved for lounging and dining, but this is a slice of natural landscape, a playground in which anything can happen anywhere. An architectural historian coming across it for the first time would find it hard to date. In fact it was built over a five-year period between 1950 and 1955 by the clients under Goff's inspiring guidance.

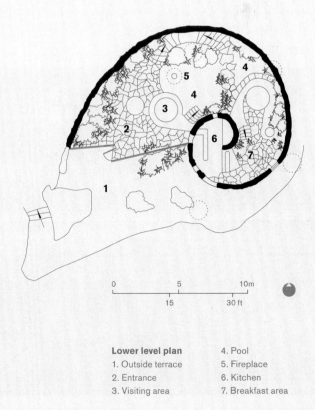

Bavinger House, Norman, Oklahoma, USA. Bruce Goff, 1955.
Platforms hang freely in the spiralling space like shells or saucers.

Lower level plan
1. Outside terrace
2. Entrance
3. Visiting area
4. Pool
5. Fireplace
6. Kitchen
7. Breakfast area

16 | DOMES, SHELLS AND TENTS
1952–1973

The ancient Romans built shell-like structures in concrete, many of which survive, such as the dome of the Pantheon and the groin vaults of the Baths of Diocletian. Traditionally it is the arch that distinguishes Roman from Greek architecture, but it was these transformations of the arch, by rotation and extrusion, that made possible the monumental interior spaces of Roman public buildings. Concrete was used as a strengthening material, often in combination with brickwork. It was strong in compression but relatively weak in tension, which made it suitable for geometrically regular arch forms. Western medieval church architecture inherited the groin vault but relied entirely on masonry, at first sticking to a semi-circular geometry but later introducing pointed arches. This freed the plan, allowing rectangular as well as square bays, and gave rise to the supremely elegant vaulting of High Gothic cathedrals like Chartres and Amiens. In the Eastern empire, the architecture we call Byzantine adopted the dome rather than the vault, placing it on a square bay and filling in the open corners with curved triangular 'pendentives'. Hagia Sofia, in what is now Istanbul, is the prime surviving example of an architecture that combined hierarchies of domes and semi-domes to create exultant interiors.

What could the twentieth century offer to match these consummate achievements of the ancient and medieval worlds? There was certainly no lack of demand for large, unified public interiors, including parliament buildings, opera houses, sports halls, transport interchanges and cathedrals, not to mention everyday buildings like markets and factories. The ancient precedents could be imitated, of course, in traditional buildings of Roman scale like the Viceroy's Palace in New Delhi or the gigantic unbuilt People's Hall in Berlin (see Chapter 14), but to Modernists this seemed a cowardly expedient. In former ages technology and form had progressed in step with each other, and so it should be in the modern age. New materials and new methods were at hand. The structural properties of reinforced concrete – strong in tension as well as compression – were now well understood by engineers. Mathematical modelling was opening up a new world of formal possibilities. Max Berg's 1913 Jahrhunderthalle in Breslau (see page 56) indicated

Airship hangars, Orly, France. Eugène Freyssinet, 1916–23. These paraboloid-arched enclosures were as technically advanced as the airships they housed.

Brynmawr Rubber Factory, Wales, UK. Architects Co-Partnership with Ove Arup, 1952. The building's high reputation among architects and critics could not save it from demolition in 2001.

the potential of the reinforced concrete dome, but was still recognizably a kind of Pantheon – circular and arcuated, with a ribbed dome and a traditional classical portico. New, stranger forms were possible and were beginning to be explored in structures designed by engineers rather than architects – the bridges of Robert Maillart and the airship hangars of Eugène Freyssinet, for example.

Development of shell domes

The first architectural applications of this new concrete geometry were actually rather pedestrian. In the late 1920s, a group of German structural engineers, including some who had worked on Berg's Breslau dome, carried out research into concrete shells of different shapes and thicknesses. Their favoured form was a thin, square, shallow-domed shell, supported on its corners, rather like the ceilings of early-nineteenth-century houses by John Soane. Domes of this kind were first applied to large but architecturally unpretentious market buildings in Leipzig, Frankfurt and Basel. After the Second World War, the form came to Britain where nine such domes were used to roof the Brynmawr Rubber Factory in south Wales, designed by Architects Co-Partnership with the engineer Ove Arup and completed in 1952. Though widely admired by Modernist architects and critics (Reyner Banham called it 'one of the most impressive interiors in Britain since St Paul's') and listed as a building of special architectural interest, it was demolished in 2001.

Unusual concrete shell domes – round, square and triangular on plan – appeared throughout the 1950s. That most formally adventurous of American Modernists, Eero

Kresge Auditorium at MIT, Cambridge, Massachusetts, USA. Eero Saarinen, 1955. Supreme economy of enclosing form: just four curved planes.

Saarinen, designed the shell dome of the Kresge Auditorium at the Massachusetts Institute of Technology, completed in 1955. It is hard to imagine a simpler external form for a building. It has just four main surfaces: an eighth of a sphere resting on the ground at three points, with vertical but curved glass curtain walls to fill the three outward-leaning arches. A larger, more complex and less elegant version of this form was built in 1958 at La Défense on the outskirts of Paris to house the Centre of New Industries

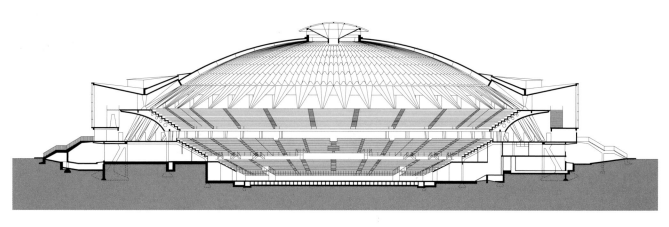

Interior and section of the Palazzo dello Sport, Rome,
Italy. Pier Luigi Nervi and Marcello Piacentini, 1959.
The 'double saucer' form, with no columns, creates an intense
focus on the sporting contest.

and Technologies (CNIT). Here the curves of the dome
depart from the spherical ideal so that the three arches are
straightened and made vertical. As a result the overall form
is more like a triangular cross-vault than a true dome. The
chief designer was Robert Camelot.

Two of the most beautiful domes of the period were
designed for the 1960 Olympic Games in Rome by
the great Italian engineer/architect Pier Luigi Nervi in
collaboration with Marcello Piacentini and Annibale
Vitellozzi. Nervi had been experimenting creatively with
reinforced concrete since the early 1930s and had already
produced several masterpieces in the medium, including a

series of aircraft hangars for the Italian air force, in particular
the one at Orvieto – a shallow pointed barrel vault stiffened
by a diagonal lattice of concrete ribs. These buildings
seemed proof of the Modernist proposition that purely
functional structure was intrinsically beautiful. The two domes
for the Rome Olympics – the Palazzo and Palazzetto dello
Sport – are traditional in that they are circular, but otherwise
far removed from Roman or Renaissance precedents. Each
is like a saucer inverted over a second saucer containing the
circular rows of seating. The larger Palazzo dome is stiffened
by radial ribs that intensify an already extreme concentration
of attention on the drama of the ball game or boxing match.
However, the Palazzetto has the more handsome exterior

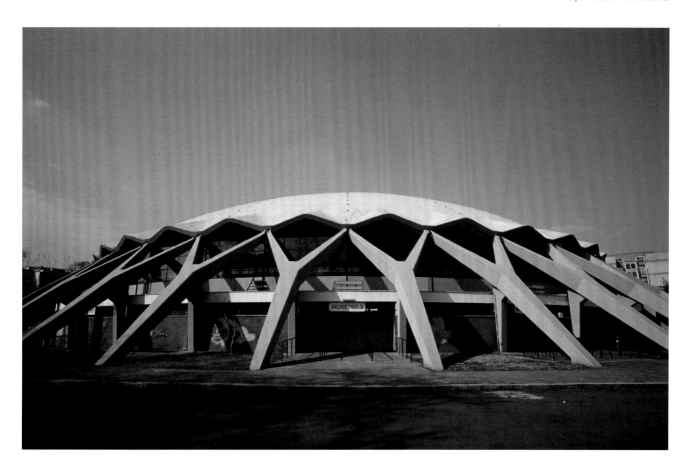

(Above) Palazzetto dello Sport, Rome, Italy. Pier Luigi Nervi and Annibale Vitellozzi, 1957. Smaller than the Palazzo but with the more expressive external structure.

(Left) Airport terminal, Lambert–St Louis, Missouri, USA. Minoru Yamasaki, George Hellmuth and Joseph Leinweber, 1955. Hardly Gothic in character, but these are traditional groin vaults nevertheless.

with its fringe of Y-shaped buttresses like gymnasts joining hands to hold up – or perhaps hold down – the billowing dome.

But these are single forms covering single spaces. It is when shell-like forms are repeated and combined, as they were in medieval buildings, that architecture begins its real task. Scale, proportion and spatial sequence come into play. It was Minoru Yamasaki and his partners George Helmuth and Joseph Leinweber who first thought of applying shell technology to an airport terminal. The terminal at Lambert–St Louis airport in Missouri, completed in 1955, is a consciously Gothic-inspired building, though it is long and low rather than tall and soaring, as if the groin vaults of a wide four-bay nave had been sliced off and lowered to the ground.

This truly innovative structure is sometimes thought to have been inspired by the work of Félix Candela (see page 214) but in fact the influence was in the other direction. More famous, though technically less pure, is the TWA terminal at John F. Kennedy airport in New York by Eero Saarinen. It created a sensation when it was completed in 1962, a year after the architect's death. Where Yamasaki's terminal is repetitive and earthbound, each of its vaulted bays standing squarely on four feet, Saarinen's almost takes flight. The image of a bird – an eagle that has just landed and has yet to fold its wings – is irresistibly called to mind. Four pointed barrel vaults – two wings, a tail and a head – stretch out from freely sculpted, talon-like feet. Glass curtain walls are sharply raked outwards as if making their own aerodynamic

contribution. Inside, the simile changes: concrete staircases and walkways flow like volcanic lava in the mouth of a cave. A low, flat-roofed, boomerang-shaped base, hardly noticed by photographers, accommodates the workaday functional spaces. Virtually unextendable, the building eventually proved inadequate to accommodate increased traffic but nobody could bear to tear it down so it is preserved as the grand entrance of a new terminal.

Sydney Opera House

Mention of shell-like, cantilevered forms, sculpturally composed, inevitably calls to mind the Sydney Opera House. It was designed in the late 1950s by the then almost unknown Danish architect Jørn Utzon. Sydney Harbour Bridge, built by British engineers in the 1930s, had in not much more than 20 years become the symbol of the city and of the whole country. The Opera House was to match it, symbolizing the cultural as opposed to the economic health of the nation. It would be built on the narrow peninsula called Bennelong Point, facing the full width of the bridge. The story goes that, during the judging of the design competition, Utzon's scheme was rescued from the reject pile by none other than Eero Saarinen. Two auditoriums were required, a concert hall and an opera house. Utzon decided to place them side by side on a raised public podium reached by a flight of steps 90 metres (98 yards)

TWA Flight Center, John F. Kennedy International Airport, New York City, USA. Eero Saarinen, 1962. Concrete vaults stretch out like the wings of a bird that has just landed.

Sydney Opera House, Sydney, Australia. Jørn Utzon, 1959–73. Sail-like shells successfully match the scale of the Harbour Bridge.

Section through opera theatre

0   10   20m
30   60 ft

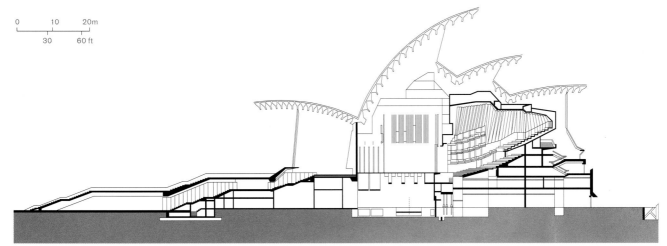

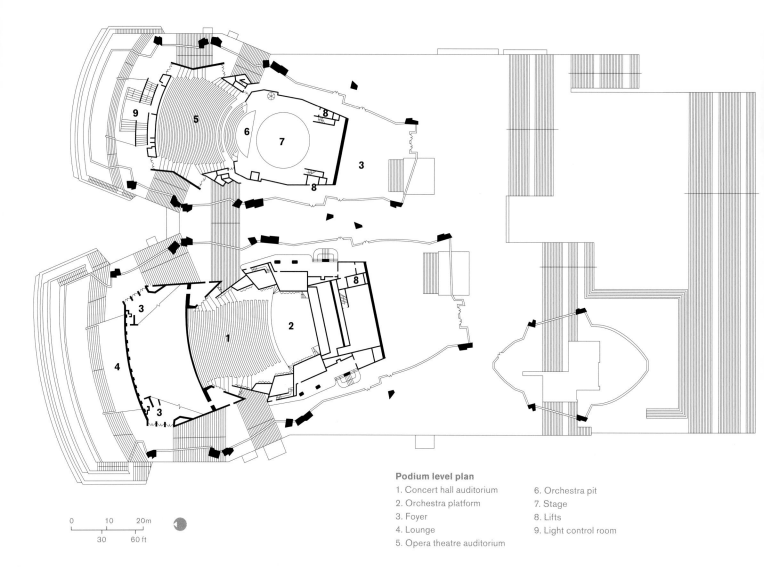

Podium level plan
1. Concert hall auditorium
2. Orchestra platform
3. Foyer
4. Lounge
5. Opera theatre auditorium
6. Orchestra pit
7. Stage
8. Lifts
9. Light control room

0   10   20m

30   60 ft

wide. This was unusual enough; what caught Saarinen's eye, however, were the concrete shell roofs that would tower above the podium like the multiple spinnakers of a huge yacht. They seemed to do the job perfectly – the job, that is, of matching the symbolic power of the bridge. Utzon thought they could be built using the new thin-concrete-shell technology but he was wrong. His sail shapes were intrinsically unstable and would need some hefty thickness to make them stand up. This highlights an important truth of the art of engineering: a structural form that looks right will not always be efficient or economic, or even feasible. But those sails were essential to the concept. Somehow the engineers would have to make them work. Eventually, after years of struggle, Ove Arup and Partners arrived at a solution. Utzon insisted that, if the sails were to be made of heavyweight concrete, then that concrete should be in precast pieces that could be made accurately off site. A degree of standardization was therefore essential. In these days before computer-controlled machines, making all the components different would have been prohibitively expensive. It seemed an insuperable problem until Utzon realized that all of the sails, large and small, could be

derived geometrically from a single sphere 75 metres (246 feet) in diameter. Symmetrical pairs of tapering ribs, each made of smaller precast components, would rise to different heights at different angles in each sail, but their curvature would remain constant. This was no place for visible rough concrete so ceramic tiles would cover the whole surface, making it appear weightless. Utzon resigned from the job before the building was finished, in protest at political interference. Other architects modified his designs for the auditorium interiors and for the big glass walls that fill in the gaping voids of the sails. But nothing could diminish the power of that original symbolic gesture, and the building has become perhaps the most famous and best loved of the twentieth century. It was finally completed in 1973.

Félix Candela

The Mexican architect and self-taught engineer Félix Candela did not approve of the Sydney Opera House or, for that matter, of the TWA terminal. To him they represented a betrayal of the potential of thin-shell construction. When shells were shaped correctly, he thought, following their inner structural logic, they could be miracles of lightness

Cosmic Rays Pavilion, Mexico
City, Mexico. Félix Candela, 1951.
The roof had to be thin enough to
allow the penetration of cosmic rays.

Sagrada Família School,
Barcelona, Spain. Antoni
Gaudí, 1909. Possibly the earliest
application of the 'hypar' principle.

and strength. If they happened to resemble bird wings
or sea shells or flower petals, it was only because these
products of nature themselves followed an inner structural
logic. One type of geometrical figure was of particular
interest to Candela – the hyperbolic paraboloid, or 'hypar'.
Hypars have the useful characteristic that although, like
domes, they have double-curved surfaces, unlike domes
they can be formed from straight, linear components. They
are both cheap to build and enormously strong because
the saddle-like shape is almost a diagram of the forces
acting within it. Candela was sometimes able to reduce
the thickness of his reinforced concrete hypar shells to
less than 25 millimetres (1 inch).

In the Cosmic Rays Pavilion, built in 1951 for the atomic
physicists of Mexico City University, the thinness of the
concrete had another benefit: it allowed rays from outer
space to pass through it. This little building, really just a
housing for a scientific instrument, is often described as the
first hypar building (actually it's a double hypar), but there

are rival claims. One is from the 7,000-seat J. S. Dorton Arena at Raleigh, North Carolina, which has a steel-cable-supported roof stretched between giant concrete parabolic arches. It was designed in 1950 but not built until 1952, after the death in a plane crash of its Polish-born architect, Matthew Nowicki. Half a century earlier, Antoni Gaudí was working with hypars in a less mathematical, more instinctive way. The clearest example is the school that he built in 1909 for the children of construction workers on the site of the great church of Sagrada Família. This charming little three-room building, which now houses the church administration, has a wavy roof and wavy walls of thin Catalan brick. It is the special form of the waves – alternating on either side of the

roof so that they form a straight and level line in the middle – that qualify it as a hypar building. But there are hypars to be found in many Gaudí buildings, including Sagrada Família itself. They arise from his habit of allowing the pattern of forces in a building to create its form – form-finding rather than form-shaping. It was a principle that would be adopted a century later by architects harnessing the modelling power of computers (see Chapter 32).

Los Manantiales restaurant, Xochimilco, Mexico. Félix Candela, 1958. The theory that efficient engineering is automatically beautiful sometimes needs help from an architect.

Candela's buildings show none of Gaudí's frenzied creativity. They are calm and beautiful in a flowers-and-sea-shells kind of way. The Los Manantiales restaurant in the Xochimilco township, south of Mexico City, is a pavilion formed of four hypars intersecting to make an octagonal groin vault. Inside, the joints between the arches are sharp lines, as they would be in a Gothic or Romanesque vault, but outside, careful details create the illusion of a single sheet of concrete, extremely thin, waving like the skirt of a jellyfish. It was built in 1958. Old photographs show it filled with straight rows of square tables stubbornly refusing to get the spirit of the free-flowing form overhead. This is the opposite of 'form follows function'; here form follows a structural and geometrical logic, and function, in the sense of conventional patterns of human use, has to fit in as best it can.

Tents

When does a shell become a tent? The distinction is not clear cut. For example, is Nowicki's arena at Raleigh a hypar shell or does its tension cable roof make it a tent? Tensile and compressive forms mirror one another. Gaudí's upside-down hanging models were just a means to find the right

form for a right-way-up full-size compressive structure. But hanging, tent-like forms can also be used in real, permanent buildings. The simplest structure of this kind is called a 'catenary': imagine a blanket draped between two washing lines. Once again, the restlessly creative Eero Saarinen provides a good example: the main terminal at Washington D. C.'s Dulles airport, completed in 1962.

It may have been inspired by the Healy Guest House in Sarasota, Florida, designed by Paul Rudolph in 1948, the 'drooping blanket' roof of which is supported by flat steel strips fixed to wooden posts, which are in turn anchored to projecting floor beams by external steel rods. It is an elaborate arrangement for such a small span, but the thinness of the roof and the faint resemblance to a tent pitched on a lawn make it seem perfectly appropriate. Saarinen's version is vastly bigger but the principle is the same. Dispensing with tension rods, instead the supporting columns lean outwards and taper upwards, as if straining

Dulles International Airport, Washington D. C., USA. Eero Saarinen, 1962. Tent or shell? A simple catenary roof, like a hanging blanket, but in reinforced concrete.

to bear the weight of a concrete blanket strengthened
by hidden steel cables. The architectural success of this
building is due largely to its finely judged expressiveness.
Its overall form seems exactly right for its function, lifting
itself up higher on the landward side to invite departing
passengers in under its soft, welcoming canopy. Details are
equally expressive – the way, for example, that the raking
columns penetrate the blanket through visible holes and
reach over the top to grasp its edge. Even the concave glass
curtain walls seem to participate in the muscular effort. As
we have seen, satisfying sculptural form and ideal structural
form do not always coincide, but in this building they seem to
have reached a happy agreement.

Dulles's catenary roof was influential on several later
buildings, including Jørn Utzon's National Assembly Building
in Kuwait of 1982. But an earlier tent-like Saarinen building,

the ice hockey rink that he built for Yale University in 1958,
was arguably even more influential. It looks (to further
extend the repertoire of similes) like an inverted Viking
ship. Its keel is a concrete parabolic arch, 90 metres (98
yards) long, with upturned ends, and its gunwales follow
the same profile but laid flat as ground beams. Steel cables
span between keel and gunwales to support the wooden
boards of the 'hull'. The David S. Ingalls Rink, as it is known
(the building was completely renovated in 2009 by Roche-
Dinkeloo, the practice formed in 1966 by two of Saarinen's
associates), certainly influenced two sports halls in Yoyogi
Park, Tokyo, designed for the 1964 Olympics by the great
Japanese architect Kenzo Tange.

**Olympic sports halls, Yoyogi Park, Tokyo, Japan. Kenzo
Tange, 1964.** Nervi's stadiums for Rome are simple circles on
plan; Tange's equivalents for Tokyo are more like swirling dresses.

The larger of the two halls, which originally housed the swimming and diving events, follows the same structural principle as Saarinen's rink except that the concrete 'keel' is replaced by a pair of cables stretched between vertical masts and the 'gunwales' become the rim of the circular concrete dish containing the seating and performance area. So this is essentially a circular building with two masts placed symmetrically on its circumference. What gives it its special dynamism, however, is the pair of tangential roof extensions that reach out beyond the masts to form entrances. The smaller hall is a single-masted version of the same idea, with only one roof extension. But both halls are enormous, the smaller seating about 4,000 and the larger more than 13,000. It is a common misconception that structural forms work the same way however big or small they are – that, for example, a scale model of a bridge will behave just like the full-size version. This is not the case. The Yoyogi stadiums are actually too big to work as prestressed tents; their main roof surfaces are in fact semi-rigid steel shells.

Frei Otto

The acknowledged master of tent structures was the German architect Frei Otto, who in 1964 founded the Institute for Lightweight Structures at the University of Stuttgart. His earliest buildings were simple shelters and pavilions but in 1967 he rose to international prominence

Olympic sports hall (swimming and diving), Yoyogi Park, Tokyo, Japan. Kenzo Tange, 1964. The roofs may look like tents but are in fact semi-rigid steel shells.

when, with Rolf Gutbrod, he designed the German pavilion at Expo 67 in Montreal. The pavilion's exhibitions were accommodated in a multi-level cluster of steel-framed structures conceived as a man-made landscape, but the main exhibit was the free-form tent overhead that seemed by comparison almost natural. It was made of four main elements: a steel cable net, a translucent waterproof membrane, eight supporting masts and 28 perimeter ground anchors. Prefabricated in Germany and erected on site in about three weeks, it was a perfect example of design by form finding, a structure that co-operated with rather than resisted the force of gravity. It seemed to open up a new vista of architectural possibilities – except that Bedouin Arabs had thought of it centuries before.

At the Munich Olympics of 1972, Otto's tents faced a bigger challenge: to provide shelter for the main stadium and also for the nearby athletics and swimming arenas – not just a tent but a whole encampment, on a huge scale. This was to be the first colour-television Olympics, so camera-friendliness was important. The tents must not cast black shadows. For this reason it was decided that, instead of a translucent fabric membrane, the cable net should be covered by rectangular transparent plastic panels joined together with neoprene gaskets. It was an awkward clash of geometries, made worse by the need to accommodate thermal and wind movement, and there were other ugly details, mostly caused by the inevitable acceleration of the construction programme as it approached an immovable completion date. The 1972 Olympics are now remembered not for the tent, nor for colour television, but for a terrorist attack. Eleven members of the Israeli team and one policeman were taken hostage and killed by a group calling itself Black September.

Buckminster Fuller

Richard Buckminster Fuller was an inventor, not an architect, but an inventor of an unusual kind. It might be said that he invented a way of looking at the world – the physical rather than the human world, though for him the two were inseparable. He believed in human progress, but measured that progress in terms of cold efficiency. He began his working life as a salesman in his father-in-law's company, which manufactured a new type of concrete block. It was a tough assignment, which might explain

his later contempt for architects and the traditions of their profession. Architecture, he said, was a mere 'restraint of trade' preventing any progress in building technology. In 1927 the struggling concrete block business was sold to another owner and Fuller lost his job. He was 32 years old. This failure, and the death in his arms of his four-year-old daughter, caused him to suffer a kind of mental breakdown. It is said that he remained silent for a whole year, immersing himself in technical books and journals. When at last he broke his silence, it was to pour out ideas and inventions in torrents of verbiage for which he later became famous, and in clumsy sketches annotated with childish lettering. These ideas all shared a single aim: to optimize the efficiency of technology; to do more with less. 'Dymaxion' was the brand name he gave to these projects. There was, for example, a Dymaxion house, hexagonal on plan, its floor and roof suspended from a central mast. In it was to be found a Dymaxion bathroom, a forerunner of the prefabricated

Olympic Stadium, Munich, Germany. Otto Frei, 1972. Transparent tent roofs suited the cameras at the first Olympics to be screened on colour television.

bathroom 'pod' now common in cheap hotels. There was also a Dymaxion car that looked like the fuselage of an aeroplane, streamlined and steered by a single tailwheel. Fuller developed these ideas and others like them over the next 20 years with some success but no decisive breakthrough. After the Second World War, he designed a prefabricated house, based on the Dymaxion House, to be mass produced in the Beech Aircraft Company's factory at Wichita, Kansas. Architectural history has gazed admiringly on the Wichita House but the truth is that in business terms it was an embarrassing failure. Once again Fuller found himself searching for a purpose in life. He found it in a new obsession: domes.

In 1949 Fuller taught at an architectural summer school at the progressive Black Mountain College in North Carolina. He got the students to build a dome 15 metres (50 feet) in diameter out of old venetian blinds. It collapsed, but it began a programme of development and improvement in dome construction that was to continue for the rest of his life. More dome prototypes followed, at first as student projects but later sponsored by industrial investors and the

military establishment. There were cardboard kit domes, plywood domes, corrugated iron domes and domes made from aluminium tubes. The US Marine Corps was a good customer, commissioning a variety of 'radomes' and storage domes that could be lifted in one piece by helicopter. The first major commercial application came in 1953 when the Ford Motor Company asked Fuller to design a dome with a 28-metre (92-foot) span to cover the circular courtyard of its 'courtesy building', known as the Rotunda, in Dearborn, Michigan. By 1958 the maximum dome diameter had reached 117 metres (384 feet) in a structure to accommodate the repairs department of the Union Tank Car Company at Baton Rouge, Louisiana.

These were all geodesic domes. 'Geodesic' is a surprisingly old word meaning simply 'pertaining to a sphere', in particular the globe of the earth, but it has come to refer specifically to the forming of spheres from simple

Wichita House, Kansas, USA. Buckminster Fuller, 1948. Designed for mass production in an aircraft factory, but only two were actually built.

geometrical figures, such as triangles and hexagons. For example, the Ford Rotunda dome was formed of flat, triangular facets, each of which was a space-frame made of tetrahedrons – the simplest possible three-dimensional figure. A geodesic dome is many times lighter and stronger than a conventional masonry dome. This is because it makes use of the tensile as well as the compressive strength of its components. But there is a particular type of geodesic dome for which Fuller reserved a special term: 'tensegrity'. A tensegrity dome combines tension-resisting cables with compression-resisting rods that are not contiguous; that is, the compression rods do not touch each other but are joined only by the tension cables. It seems at first impossible that such an arrangement could result in a rigid structure, but it can, and with a further improved strength-to-weight ratio.

The high point of Fuller's dome-building career came in 1967 when he designed the US pavilion for the Montreal Expo – the same Expo for which Frei Otto's tent served as the German pavilion. Fuller's pavilion was a tensegrity dome 76 metres (250 feet) in diameter, clad in transparent acrylic panels. More than a hemisphere, it sat on its site like a golf ball. Its constituent hexagons were fitted with computer-controlled 'irises' that opened and closed like a camera shutter, tracking the sun to provide shade when necessary. The building still exists in skeletal form, having lost its acrylic panels in a fire. It now forms part of a museum known as the Montreal Biosphere.

The US pavilion was a big building, but not in the mind of its creator, who always thought on a global scale. His biggest dome was never built, but it was buildable. Fuller and his colleague, Shoji Sadao, realized that the tensegrity principle removed the normal weight constraints on very large structures. In 1960 they proposed – and calculated – a dome 3 kilometres (2 miles) in diameter to cover the whole of mid-town Manhattan, skyscrapers and all. It would weigh only 4,000 tonnes (4,400 tons) and would be built in sections by helicopter in three months. Its main purpose was the same as that of most buildings: to control the internal environment and keep out air pollution. Real buildings on this scale are still far in the future, and may never come to pass, but Fuller and Sadao proved that, in theory at least, they are possible.

US Pavilion, Montreal Expo, Canada.
Buckminster Fuller, 1967. The building that gave worldwide currency to the geodesic dome concept.

Design for a dome over Manhattan. Buckminster Fuller and Shoji Sadao, 1960. Theoretically possible but yet to be realized: a geodesic dome 3 kilometres (2 miles) in diameter.

Robert Maillart

It was Sigfried Giedion, in *Space, Time and Architecture*, who first introduced the Swiss engineer Robert Maillart to the pages of architectural history; 26 pages, to be exact – a surprisingly generous allocation for a non-architect known mainly as a bridge builder. Giedion rightly locates Maillart's genius in the recognition that the humble floor slab or deck had taken on a new, active role since the invention of reinforced concrete. It was no longer merely a dead weight to be supported by a separate frame; it was capable of making its own contribution to a monolithic structure in which all elements co-operated, strengthening and supporting each other. Early in his career Maillart worked with François Hennebique (see page 54), whose standard method was to translate traditional masonry and timber structures into reinforced concrete. Maillart was more radical, developing the 'mushroom column' technique and doing away with beams altogether. Giedion includes a picture of a warehouse in Zurich of 1910, designed by Maillart, which he claims was the first of its kind in Europe. Similar developments were taking place in the United States.

But it was Maillart's bridges that most impressed Giedion, setting him off on a rapturous commentary that compares engineering with painting and Maillart's concrete with Picasso's Cubism. This is far fetched and no longer seems convincing, yet Maillart's bridges did represent a liberation from old ways of thinking. He used two main types of arch: 'three hinged' and 'deck stiffened'. The first is best illustrated by the Salginatobel Bridge, completed in 1930,

which leaps effortlessly across a steep-sided river valley in Schiers, Switzerland. Its level road deck is supported on a shallow arch, U shaped in section, that tapers to almost nothing at its crown and springings where the three hinges accommodate dynamic live loads and thermal movement. There were two versions of the design and the contrast between them illustrates precisely the moment of liberation from conventional form. In the first version the approach roads were to be supported by masonry viaducts with round arches of the old Roman kind; in the second version, as constructed, the arches have been replaced by a row of vertical concrete supports that simply carry on marching up the arch as it rises over the ravine below. In the deck-stiffened type, the arch is a two-dimensional curved or facetted plane, just a few centimetres thick, connected to the deck of the bridge by straight, vertical fins. The Schwandbach Bridge near Berne of 1933 is a good example that seems even lighter and more agile than Salginatobel because it follows a bend in the road, curving on plan with apparent ease, without strain or distortion.

That Maillart was an artist in the medium of concrete is not disputed. But what precisely was it from which these bridges were being liberated? The solidity and verticality of masonry construction, certainly, but also all ceremoniousness and formality, the traditional wish to mark the passage from road to bridge, from solid ground to suspension over a river or ravine, with buttresses, towers and gateways, suitably ornamented. In other words, they were being liberated from architecture, of the old, classical kind.

Salginatobel Bridge, Schiers, Switzerland. Robert Maillart, 1930. A dramatic leap over a steep-sided Alpine valley.

17 | LE CORBUSIER PART 2
1932–1965

Unité d'Habitation in Marseille, completed in 1952, is one of the great buildings of the twentieth century – radical in concept, bold in execution and enormously influential. It is an apartment block with communal facilities, and as such owes something to Russian housing projects of the 1930s by Moisei Ginzburg and Ivan Nikolaev (see Chapter 11). But whereas they were designed to promote a communist reordering of society, the Unité, as Le Corbusier was at pains to point out, was designed to support traditional family life. Its apartments are like houses – most of them two storeys high, facing in two directions, with double-height living rooms, and balconies on both sides of the block. It is an idea that goes back to the Immeubles Villas project of 1925 (see page 114). Fitting such dwellings into an economical 18-storey slab was not easy. They are rather narrow, their bedrooms like minimal ship's cabins, and the access corridors have no daylight. But these sacrifices were necessary to achieve double height and double orientation – the key features that make these apartments feel like individual homes rather than mere allocations of horizontal space. Each enjoys both morning

Le Corbusier, c.1947. Le Corbusier contemplates a model of the Unité d'Habitation roof.

and evening sun, and a sense of orientation in relation to the distant hills and the sea. A cross-section through the block shows how this is possible, with interlocking apartments and wide access corridors on every third floor. It is ingenious, though not entirely original. Ginzburg made a partial version of it in the Narkomfin Building (see page 136).

The Unité, then, is a vertical stack of houses, a village for 1,600 people, and like a village it provides for other aspects of daily life. There is a row of shops on the seventh floor, and a small hotel. The roof is like a park with a paddling pool, an exercise area and two freestanding communal buildings, one of them like an upturned boat, all surrounded by a running track. Engineering necessities like air vents and lift motor rooms are treated like concrete sculpture. There is continuity here with Le Corbusier's earlier architectural and urban ideas – for example the flat, usable roof and the pilotis, which are now thick and muscular, like a weightlifter's thighs – but a transformation has taken place. Whereas the Purist villas were abstract compositions of uncertain material constitution (were they reinforced concrete or plastered blockwork?) the Unité is made of coarse concrete, marked for ever by the grainy wooden boards against which it was cast. What architects often call 'materiality' is now the most important determinant of the building's character. Le Corbusier called his concrete '*béton brut*', which means simply 'raw concrete', but the phrase was later anglicized and incorporated in the name of a stylistic movement: 'New Brutalism' (see Chapter 21). The surface texture of the material is matched by the larger, formal texture of the building's exterior. Elevations are gridded like crates, the glass walls of the apartments set well back in balconies that serve as *brises-soleil* or sun breakers. Later Brutalist concrete buildings were criticized for their dull greyness but the Unité is painted in primary colours, albeit carefully framed and limited to the flank walls of the balconies.

The Unité had its origins in pre-war visionary projects like the Ville Contemporaine and the Ville Radieuse, and in more specific proposals such as Le Corbusier's post-war plan for the reconstruction of Saint-Dié in eastern France.

Unité d'Habitation, Marseille, France. Le Corbusier, 1952.
An enormously influential building, though it owes something to Russian housing projects of the 1930s.

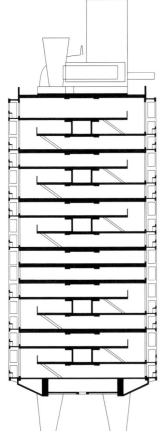

Section: two typical units

Typical unit plans

```
0        5        10m
|--------|--------|
        15       30 ft
```

A larger urban plan is implied – not one Unité but several Unités standing in parkland like a fleet of ships on the ocean – but the idea was never realized. Other Unités were built – three elsewhere in France and one in Berlin – but always as single buildings. It was left to Le Corbusier's followers to realize the Utopian vision in a thousand

watered-down versions, many of which were technical and social failures. The original Marseille Unité, however, is well preserved, the fame of its architect guaranteeing its appeal to artistic and professional tenants – painters, photographers, academics, journalists and, of course, architects. In a word, it has been 'gentrified'.

There is another, half-hidden characteristic of the Unité that reveals Le Corbusier's almost limitless artistic ambition: the building was designed according to a proportional system called the Modulor, which he invented and made available to architects all over the world. Once again it was the continuation of an old preoccupation. In *Vers une architecture*, his best-selling book first published in 1923, photographs of old buildings such as the Cathedral of Notre-Dame in Paris and the Petit Trianon in Versailles appear overlaid with diagonal lines indicating repeated proportions. Proportion in architecture is a complicated subject. Theorists distinguish different types of proportional system – commensurate (using whole numbers) and irrational (using figures like the so-called Golden Section), arithmetical and geometrical, relative and absolute. Le Corbusier's system combines all of these to arrive at a set of standard dimensions (actually two sets, designated Red and Blue) that, when used by a sensitive architect, would in theory result in beautiful, perfectly scaled buildings. The system was symbolized by the figure of 'Modulor Man' (Le Corbusier's answer to Leonardo's 'Vitruvian Man') embodying three special dimensions: 1.13 metres, 1.629 metres and 2.26 metres (3 feet 8½ inches, 5 feet 4 inches and 7 feet 5 inches) – the heights respectively of his navel, the top of his head and his upstretched hand. The system was only ever adopted by a handful of Le Corbusier's most fervent admirers, and there were fundamental objections to it (where is Modulor Woman?). Nevertheless, it possibly accounts for the confident poise of the Unité, combining roughness with precision, and order with a kind of calculated casualness.

Objets à réaction poétique

In a cursory view of Le Corbusier's career it seems obvious that the shift from a rational to a poetic approach was caused by the Second World War, but in fact the Unité is only the consolidation of a change that had taken place at least 20 years earlier. In his paintings, for example, the *objets-types* of Purism had been supplanted by what he called *objets à réaction poétique* – natural objects like shells, bones, pebbles and tree bark as well as the human figure, especially the naked female human figure. His unbuilt Plan Obus for Algiers of 1933, with its continuous, curvaceous, inhabited viaduct sweeping along the coast, reflects this new freedom. In 1934 he built a little weekend house at La Celle-Saint-Cloud, 16 kilometres (10 miles) west of Paris, for the director of a bank. Single storey, with rubble walls and an arched concrete roof covered with turf, it is the opposite of pure or machine-like. More than 20 years later this primitive style was revived in a pair of houses called the Maisons Jaoul at Neuilly-sur-Seine in the Paris suburbs. The houses stand at right angles to one another and are similar but not identical. Their coarse brick walls – discontinuous, with small windows, often full height – support concrete floors and roofs cast on traditional Catalan vaults of clay tiles. A spine wall divides the space unequally, allowing a variety of room proportions, and ends are in-filled with panels of plywood and glass. The materials are natural (if plywood can be considered natural) and the technology adapted from vernacular traditions, but the flow of space internally and the open-ended, indeterminate forms are modern, and modern in a new way. Le Corbusier's architect followers found it hard to adapt to this new primitive modernity. It seemed a betrayal of the principles that had originally inspired their loyalty. The British architect James Stirling, for example, who was later to become a leading Postmodernist (see Chapter 24), said it was 'disturbing to find little reference to the rational

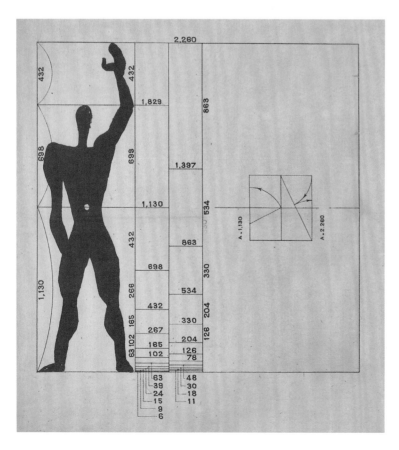

Modulor Man, Le Corbusier, 1943. A system that combines the Fibonacci Series with the proportions of the (male) human figure.

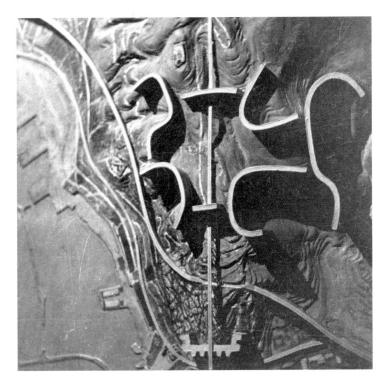

(Left) **Plan Obus for Algiers. Le Corbusier, 1933.** Visionary project for a serpentine inhabited viaduct sweeping along the coast.

(Below) **Maisons Jaoul, Neuilly-sur-Seine, France. Le Corbusier, 1955.** A new acceptance of natural materials and traditional form: brick and wood with 'Catalan' vaults.

Maisons Jaoul interior. Traditional materials but modern space – open-ended and indeterminate.

principles which are the basis of the Modern Movement'.[1] The disturbance was evidently a creative one. Rough brickwork walls and exposed concrete floors showing an obvious influence of the Maisons Jaoul soon appeared in his own small housing scheme at Ham Common in west London.

Ronchamp

The chapel at Ronchamp, in eastern France near the Swiss border, completed in 1954, was not so easily absorbed. Stirling's article about it in the *Architectural Review* of March 1956 offers a hesitant description followed by a brief, baffled analysis, weakly concluding that it is a 'Mannerist' work. The building still seems weird and inexplicable, yet it has a kind of logic and even conforms to certain traditional patterns: the entrance is on the south side at the west end, there is a nave with an altar to the east, there are side chapels for quiet contemplation and worship, and there are towers, the tallest of which is visible from afar. There is stained glass too, in the deep-set, apparently randomly distributed windows

in the south wall, and though the symbols in the colourful enamelled steel panels that adorn the main door (clouds, a river, an open hand, a pyramid) seem more personal than conventional, they are nevertheless open to religious interpretation in the broad sense.

This is a pilgrimage chapel on top of a hill. According to Le Corbusier, its forms respond 'acoustically' to 'the four horizons'. It is as though the three towers and the welcoming concave surface of the south wall are transmitters and receivers of spiritual messages heard faintly in the surrounding countryside like the sound of bells. With this in mind, the physical forms of the architecture begin to make sense. On the east side of the building, where a concave wall and overhanging roof shelter an outdoor altar and a pulpit to address a hillside

Notre-Dame du Haut, Ronchamp, France. Le Corbusier, 1954.
Inexplicable to contemporary critics. Stirling called it 'Mannerist'.

Chapel interior. The slot between roof and wall betrays the
presence of a frame.

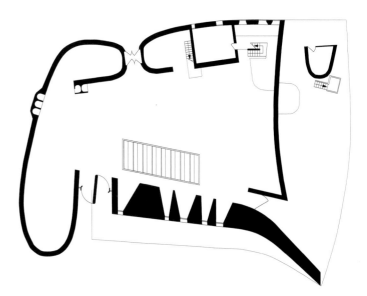

Ground floor plan

congregation, the acoustic analogy becomes literal. And there is yet another dished receiver/transmitter in the concrete roof like an inverted crab shell or, when viewed from inside, a sagging tent. In the hands of a more rational architect – Eero Saarinen, perhaps – this roof would be recognizable as an engineering solution, but Le Corbusier treats it like a natural object of mysterious origin, separating it slightly from the walls to admit a narrow beam of daylight. More than a mere shelter, it lies ready to receive the blessing of rain, which it gathers and pours forth through a two-nostrilled gargoyle into a sculpted concrete basin.

The construction of the building is irrational too. The original intention had been to erect a steel-framed mesh and spray it with concrete, like a sculptor's plaster maquette, but in the event a mixture of materials was used, including reinforced concrete and loadbearing masonry covered in rough-textured, white-painted render. This willingness to abandon the Modernist principle of 'truth to materials' was another reason for general scepticism and bafflement in the Modernist architectural community. Such was Le Corbusier's prestige, however, that his followers eventually accepted the building, cautiously admiring it but without ever absorbing it into any developing tradition. It remains a unique and inexplicable work of art.

Monastery of La Tourette

Le Corbusier's second major commission from the Catholic Church was for a new monastery, Sainte-Marie de La Tourette, at Eveux near Lyons. The brief called for 100 cells, a church, a library, a refectory and all the ancillary accommodation necessary to support a community of Dominican friars. There was, however, another element to the brief. The client's representative, Father Marie-Alain Couturier, had visited the medieval Cistercian abbey at Le Thoronet, near Toulon, and had especially admired its secluded cloister.

A similar element was therefore to be included in the proposed new monastery. Such requests often fall on deaf architectural ears and so it was at La Tourette. Le Corbusier's first move was to choose a steep hillside site, which would make a traditional cloister prohibitively expensive. The 'cloister', he decided, would be a rooftop walkway. This was part of a bigger idea: to turn the conventional monastery upside down. Instead of a level

Monastery of La Tourette, Lyons, France. Le Corbusier, 1957. An inverted composition: walls and columns descend from a level roof line.

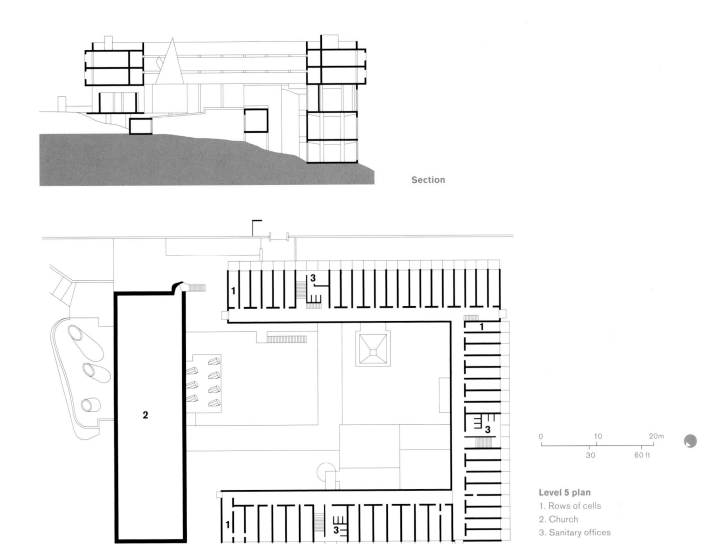

Section

Level 5 plan
1. Rows of cells
2. Church
3. Sanitary offices

0   10   20m
    30   60 ft

groundline from which buildings rose to different heights, the buildings would instead 'hang', conceptually if not structurally, from a level roofline, leaving the sloping ground relatively undisturbed. The result in the finished building is an aggressively assertive form, more like a fortification than a religious community. Two floors of monks' cells are ranged along three sides of a square, their heavily concrete-framed windows staring out over the landscape as if on the look-out for approaching enemies. The fourth side of the square is occupied by the plain concrete box of the church. Further accommodation – the refectory, the library, the oratory, conference rooms and so on – is slotted in under the beetling brow of the cell ranges. Circulation across what, on a level site, would have been the courtyard is made possible by a cross-shaped corridor, ramped to accommodate changes of level. The client having unsurprisingly rejected the rooftop cloister idea, this corridor is designated 'the

cloister', though it hardly deserves the name. Contemporary critics showered praise on La Tourette, assuming it to be mature work by an acknowledged master. However, its authorship has been called into question.[2] There is nothing unusual in this. The attribution of large buildings to single authors, though normal in architectural histories (including this one), is always questionable. Often it is the titular head of an architectural practice rather than the actual designer whose name appears in the credits. There is ample historical evidence that Le Corbusier closely supervised the development of the design of La Tourette, but it is equally clear that many of its most striking features were the product of a different mind, that of Iannis Xenakis, a Greek refugee who later became a world-famous composer. By his own account, Xenakis was responsible for the invention of the 'ondulatoires', a glazed curtain-wall system used on the lower floors of the building, with concrete mullions spaced according to the geometrical equivalent of shifting musical intervals. The array of roof lights called '*mitrailleuses*', or machine guns, which light the sacristy can also be confidently attributed to Xenakis, as can the grand-piano-shaped chapel with its 'cannons of light' on the other side of the church. Critics often see what they want to see and make their interpretations accordingly. It is often said, for example, that the rough concrete that is the main visible material at La Tourette is the architectural equivalent of a friar's coarse woollen habit. The fact is, however, that the original specification of smooth cement to cover the concrete was cut for cost reasons. The same applies to Xenakis's plan to improve the acoustics of the church by fitting pyramid-shaped sound absorbers to the walls and ceiling. La Tourette is of mixed authorship and is nobody's masterpiece. Nevertheless, it has become a place of architectural as well as religious pilgrimage.

Chandigarh

One reason for Le Corbusier's rather loose hold on the design of La Tourette might have been that he was preoccupied by an even bigger and more important project in India: the new city of Chandigarh, state capital of the eastern Punjab. It was a project of enormous political importance, symbolizing post-independence India's determination to become a modern industrial power. Prime Minister Nehru took a close interest and himself suggested that the American architect Albert Mayer should draw up the master plan. Mayer was very ably assisted by the Polish-

born architect Matthew Nowicki. Since 1946 Nowicki had worked in the United States, where he designed what is now the J. S. Dorton Arena at Raleigh, North Carolina (see page 216) and acted as Polish representative on the United Nations headquarters project (see page 235). His death in a plane crash in 1950 forced a rethink in the constitution of the Chandigarh design team. British Modernists Maxwell Fry and Jane Drew were approached to join the team and they in turn suggested Le Corbusier. Nowicki had himself been an admirer of Le Corbusier and this may have added weight to the suggestion. In February 1951, Le Corbusier travelled to India with his cousin and collaborator Pierre Jeanneret and for the first time saw the full potential of the project. Here was a chance to realize his ambition to design a government centre and align his architecture with the prestige of political authority. The League of Nations, the Palace of the Soviets, the Mundaneum and the UN headquarters had all been disappointments. Chandigarh promised satisfaction at last.

Mayer's master plan drew on the garden city tradition, with curving, picturesque streets. Le Corbusier's first task was to straighten it out, make it less domestic and supply it with a grand axis. It could never be as grand, or as traditional,

Plan for Chandigarh, Le Corbusier, 1951. The master plan, though based on Mayer's design, was nevertheless influenced by the Ville Radieuse plan of 1933.

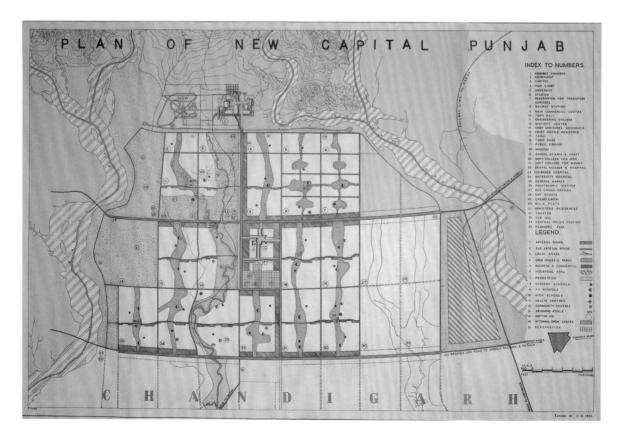

as Lutyens's New Delhi but the comparison was inevitable and Le Corbusier accepted the challenge. Surprisingly, the most distinctive feature of this new plan – the siting of the Capitol complex of government buildings on the north-eastern edge of the city, 1½ kilometres (1 mile) from the centre – had already been established by Mayer and Nowicki. But this may be a case of Le Corbusier influencing himself through Nowicki, who would certainly have been familiar with the Ville Radieuse plan of 1933, which shows a similar arrangement.

The point of a grand axis is usually to focus visual attention on a single building – the Viceroy's Palace in Delhi, say, or the Arc de Triomphe in Paris. This is not the effect at Chandigarh, partly because the governor's palace that might have dominated the Capitol complex was never built. Nehru considered its symbolism inappropriate to the new democracy. So this is an incomplete plan. Even so, its composition seems so loose as not to be a composition at all. There are three main buildings: the Palace of Assembly and the Secretariat, which are close enough to engage in a formal dialogue, and the High Court, which is fully half a kilometre (550 yards) away to the south east – too far to walk even in a temperate climate. The siting of

these buildings seems to obey some mysterious sacred geometry, like the pyramids of Egypt, rather than ordinary human convenience. A security fence now divides the vast, featureless plain on which they stand. Individually, however, the buildings are more powerful than anything else that post-war Modernism has to offer. They express simple architectural ideas bluntly and loudly, but in a strange, haunting accent.

The High Court, for example, is a shoe box when viewed from a distance (from the Secretariat Building, perhaps). Closer up it turns out to be a giant canopy, like the remains of a viaduct, under which the courtrooms shelter from the sun. But as in so many Le Corbusier buildings, the appearance of functional design is more important than actual effectiveness. The courts are entered not via the full-height entrance hall as one might assume, but directly from the plaza, and here there is no protection from the sun. An additional low, flat canopy had to be built to shelter the queues.

Secretariat Building, Chandigarh, India. Le Corbusier, 1953. The facade is episodic, changing its character abruptly to suit different internal functions.

The Secretariat Building is simple and unified in outline, like the High Court, but extraordinary in its proportions: eight storeys high and more than 250 metres (275 yards) long. Le Corbusier's first proposal was for a tower, a recycling of his 1942 design for an office block in Algiers, but there were some doubts about the quality of local concrete and the client insisted on a relatively low building. Its facade is episodic, changing its character to suit different functions. For example, the location of the ministers' double-height offices is signalled by an abrupt change of facade pattern over all floors, almost as if it were a different building. It is, however, a variation on a theme, the standard version of which consists of fixed glazing with separate fly-screened ventilators set well back in crate-like concrete *brises-soleil* with freestanding, sill-height upstands. It is an arrangement that Le Corbusier used on other Indian buildings including ordinary office blocks in the centre of Chandigarh. The long facades are further enlivened by projecting stacks of enclosed switch-back concrete ramps. Le Corbusier loved ramps – we only have to think of the ramp at the heart of the

Villa Savoye (see page 117) or in the entrance hall of the Tsentrosoyuz building (see page 120) – but in a large office building they are an architectural indulgence. Conventional corridors, lift lobbies and escape stairs are provided for everyday use.

Of the three realized Capitol buildings, the Legislative Assembly is the strangest and most radical. Its full-width entrance canopy is both an enormous gutter to collect the monsoon rain and a symbolic sculptural form, a formal echo, perhaps, of the nearby 'Open Hand' monument. Three- and four-storey administrative offices with regular *brises-soleil* form the other three sides of the perfectly square plan. The courtyard that one might reasonably expect to find inside turns out to be a hypostyle (many-columned) hall with a flat concrete roof. In it stands the great 'cooling tower' of

Legislative Assembly, Chandigarh, India. Le Corbusier, 1963. The canopy is both an enormous gutter to receive the monsoon rain and a symbolic sculptural form.

the General Assembly chamber, bursting up through the ceiling, and the smaller, pyramid-roofed Governors' Council chamber, raised on pilotis. If building plans can have political meanings, then the meaning of this plan is that the decision makers in the two enclosed chambers must eventually emerge and face the people who surround them in the free space of the atrium. In practice, circulation in the atrium space is carefully controlled but the symbolism is powerful nevertheless, and equally visible in the distant view, when cooling tower and pyramid rise above the flat roof into the sunlight. There is political but also cosmic symbolism in this building. The path of the sun is depicted in the brightly coloured enamel picture on the big, pivoted main door, and up on the sloping top of the cooling tower there is an array of mysterious solar tracking devices calling to mind the eighteenth-century astronomical observatories at Delhi and Jaipur. On another symbolic level, the cooling tower might represent the technological and industrial ambitions of the new democracy. As a debating chamber, unfortunately, it is an acoustical nightmare.

Last years

Le Corbusier's work is not well represented in the United States, a country that fascinated but also disappointed

him. Arriving for the first time in Manhattan in 1935 he declared that its skyscrapers were 'too small'. He was excited by their picturesque effect but could not approve of the unplanned commercialism that produced them. Immediately after the war he hoped to dominate the design team for the United Nations headquarters, but his disciple Oscar Niemeyer produced a better scheme and ultimately he was side-lined by the project co-ordinator, Wallace Harrison. It wasn't until 1963 that Le Corbusier at last built an important building in the US, the Carpenter Center for the Visual Arts at Harvard University in Cambridge, Massachusetts. It is like a catalogue of all the architectural devices he ever invented. In it the contrasting pre-war and post-war styles are reconciled. The Five Points are all present, including the pilotis, the roof garden and the free facade, but the *ondulatoires* and the *brises-soleil* also make an appearance. There is a ramp, naturally, that rises and falls, passing right through the building. Not all the ideas are recycled. The curvaceous, lung-like studio wings, for example, bulge out of their rational, rectilinear container in a new way, and the exposed concrete is smooth, not rough and board marked. It is as if Le Corbusier, at last invited to build in a country to which he felt hostile, decided to go in with all guns blazing.

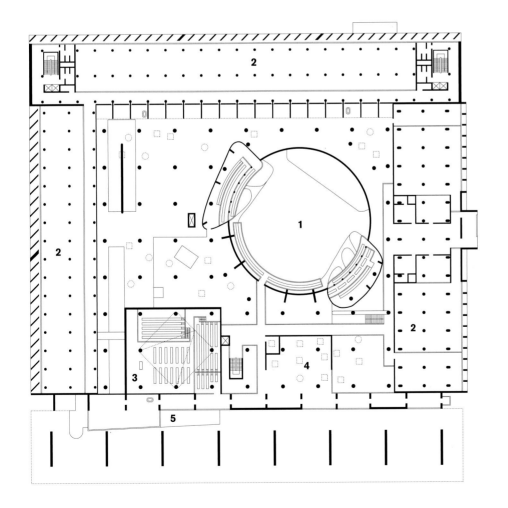

Second floor plan
1. Assembly chamber
2. Office
3. Senate chamber
4. Journalists' lounge
5. Balcony

**Ceremonial door of the Legislative Assembly,
Chandigarh, India. Le Corbusier, 1963.** Earth and sky,
nature and astronomy – Le Corbusier's themes were never
less than universal.

Le Corbusier was an artist of strong will and boundless ambition. But he was also obsessive and insecure. A strange story might offer some insight into the nature of the man and the source of his creativity. When he visited Algiers for the first time in 1931 he was taken to the Casbah, where he met two beautiful young girls and made sketches of them nude in their room. According to the architectural theorist Beatriz Colomina he continually traced and retraced these sketches at intervals for the rest of his life.[3] In 1938 his friend the architectural critic Jean Badovici allowed him to paint a series of murals in the now famous house known as E1027 on the coast at Roquebrune-Cap-Martin in the south of France. The house had been designed by Badovici's ex-partner, the pioneer Modernist architect Eileen Gray. One of the murals was based on the Algiers sketches. According to Le Corbusier it depicted Badovici and Gray with their unborn child. When Gray found out about the painting of the murals, she was furious, regarding it as a symbolic act of rape. In 1952, Le Corbusier built a little cabin for himself – Colomina describes it as an 'observation platform' – on the site immediately above E1027, effectively destroying its privacy. In 1965, while swimming in the sea close to the house, Le Corbusier suffered a heart attack and died.

Carpenter Center for the Visual Arts, Harvard University, Cambridge, Massachusetts, USA. Le Corbusier, 1963.
Le Corbusier's only building in the USA is a catalogue of his formal inventions: pilotis, ramps, *brises-soleil*, *ondulatoires* and so on.

18 | ALVAR AALTO AND HANS SCHAROUN
1924–1971

Consistency is usually considered to be a virtue in architecture. We expect one end of a building to be consistent with the other, perhaps using the same materials or the same structural principle. In the case of a Modernist building, we expect consistency between form and function, and if the building houses more than one function – a factory with offices, say, or a theatre with a restaurant – we expect the architect to resolve the differences by a consistent process of adaptation or articulation. But where does one set the boundary of an architect's responsibility? A university campus might be designed by several architects in several different styles or by a single architect in a single consistent style. Which is better? The choice seems arbitrary. Why shouldn't each function in a building have its own architectural expression, like adjacent but different buildings in a city? The architect and historian Demetri Porphyrios gave this idea a name: 'heterotopia', from *hetero-*, meaning 'different' and *topos*, meaning 'place' – so, roughly, 'a place of difference'. Its opposite is 'homotopia', 'a place of sameness [or consistency]'.

Hugo Alvar Henrik Aalto Born in Kuortane, Finland, 1898. Died in Helsinki, Finland, 1976.

A heterotopic architect is therefore one who creates places of difference. The specific architect Porphyrios had in mind was Alvar Aalto.[1]

Look, for example, at the plans of Aalto's 1962 Cultural Centre in Wolfsburg, Germany (home of the Volkswagen car factory). It is as if three different buildings have collided and fused into a single mass. The first is a conventionally rectilinear set of community rooms of different sizes accessed by corridors; the second is a cluster of small auditoriums arranged in a fan shape; and the third is a trapezoidal library on two levels. The section is as radically inconsistent as the plan. This is a two-storey building but its upper floor is like a new groundline dividing one architectural system from another. Community rooms on the upper level at the south end are grouped under a pitched roof as if they had been designed as a separate single-storey building. Elevations are equally episodic and unco-ordinated. The auditoriums facing the market square are clad in vertical strips of marble as if wearing their best suits, but as the facade turns the corner into Porschestrasse, marble immediately gives way to ordinary white-painted stucco with a Corbusian strip of windows.

At first the overall effect seems naive, perhaps the work of an architectural student not yet taught the principle of consistency. But of course, it is deliberate and purposeful. It is an anti-system and it has a social meaning. In 1940, Aalto wrote an essay called 'The Humanizing of Architecture' in which he said: 'But architecture is not a science … Its purpose is still to bring the material world into harmony with human life.'[2] So the inconsistency of Aalto's buildings has something to do with the humanizing of architecture. Human activities, he thought, have their own peculiar logic and should not be subject to any abstract system.

Functionalism

It took Aalto some years to develop this principle into a design method. He was born and brought up among the forests and lakes of central Finland and his earliest buildings are to be found in and around the small city of Jyväskylä. They are mostly in a traditional classical style that owes something to the influence of Gunnar Asplund (see

Cultural Centre, Wolfsburg, Germany. Alvar Aalto, 1963.
A 'heterotopic' plan seems to fuse together a group of conceptually different buildings.

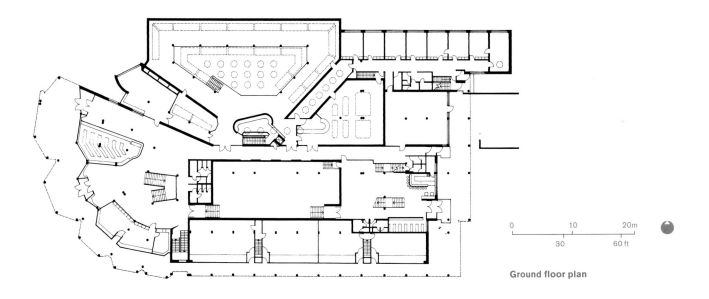

Ground floor plan

Chapter 14). For example, the workers' club of 1924, on a street corner in the centre of Jyväskylä, lifts a mostly blank-walled theatre up onto squat, widely spaced Tuscan columns with glass walls in between. The main entrance is at one end of the long side, but otherwise a strict bilateral symmetry reigns. His church at Muurame of 1929 is even more conventional: an Italian-style, white-stuccoed temple with a broken pediment over the west entrance and an attached campanile. But like Asplund, Aalto soon became aware of exciting developments in Germany, France and Holland and began to explore the possibilities of 'functionalism'. The

building that best represents this shift is the tuberculosis sanatorium in Paimio, in the far south west of Finland, completed in 1932. Sigfried Giedion considered it one of the three most important Modernist institutional buildings of the pre-war years, the others being Gropius's Bauhaus and Le Corbusier's project for the League of Nations. There is nothing remotely classical about the Paimio Sanatorium. At first glance it might almost be a Constructivist housing project by Ivan Nikolaev or an industrial building by Mart Stam. A more direct influence might be Duiker and Bijvoet's sanatorium at Zonnestraal, completed in 1931 (see page

93), which we know Aalto visited. Fresh air and sunlight was then the standard prescription for tuberculosis. All wards therefore face south west in a long, narrow, seven-storey block with an open terrace on the top floor. For more intensive sunbathing, a linear extension, hinged at a slight angle, was originally completely open like an empty bookcase, its shelves cantilevered out from a single row of tapering reinforced concrete columns.

The main entrance hall, with lifts and main staircase, projects at right angles from the corridor side of the ward block. Beyond it, four smaller blocks of varying height, containing social spaces, offices, kitchens and plant, are loosely arranged and connected according to no obvious functional or geometrical logic. It is here, perhaps, that we see the beginnings of Aalto's 'heterotopic' method of composition. In the library at Viipuri (now Vyborg, Russia), which Aalto began designing in 1927 but which was not completed until 1935, the arrangement of spaces is apparently more logical: two simple box-like volumes are juxtaposed in a sliding, asymmetrical relationship. Inside, however, the spaces they contain relate to one another in a very complex way, combining, overlapping, bridging and interpenetrating. The top-lit, split-level lending library and reading room, with its broad flights of steps and cleverly placed handrails controlling the pattern of circulation, has been an inspiration to library builders ever since. Also worth noting is the undulating wooden ceiling of the lecture theatre. It was designed to improve acoustics, but its organic form and natural material anticipate later stylistic developments.

Villa Mairea

One other pre-war Aalto building must be mentioned: the summer house at Noormakku in western Finland that he designed for his wealthy industrialist clients Harry and Maire Gullichsen. Known in architectural circles as the Villa Mairea, it was completed in 1939 and is usually taken to represent the first full flowering of Aalto's mature style. This is surprising given its hesitant beginnings. Construction work had already started when, encouraged by his clients to be experimental, Aalto decided to rethink the design completely. But instead of starting afresh, he kept the basic outline of the original design, as if it were an archaeological trace that must not be erased. The main two-storey, L-shaped part of the house is linked by a flat roof and a rubble wall to a traditional sauna, with a plunge pool in the space between. This 'space between' is important. Like Frank Lloyd Wright, whose roughly contemporary Usonian houses adopted similar L-shaped plans, Aalto always tried to avoid designing buildings as unified forms surrounded by open space, preferring instead to wrap them around courts or gardens. It was important that these semi-enclosed spaces be inhabited, not just looked at. Kenneth Frampton

(Above) Church at Muurame, Finland. Alvar Aalto, 1929. An Italian-style white-stuccoed temple with an attached campanile.

(Below) Library at Viipuri, Vyborg, Russia. Alvar Aalto, 1935. Spaces may overlap and interpenetrate but circulation is cleverly controlled.

calls them 'spaces of human appearance'.[3] (In the Wolfsburg Cultural Centre, the space of human appearance takes the form of a roof terrace at first-floor level, hidden from the surrounding streets.)

Paimio Sanatorium, Finland. Alvar Aalto, 1932. This was Aalto's first big Modernist composition, influenced by Dutch and Russian precedents.

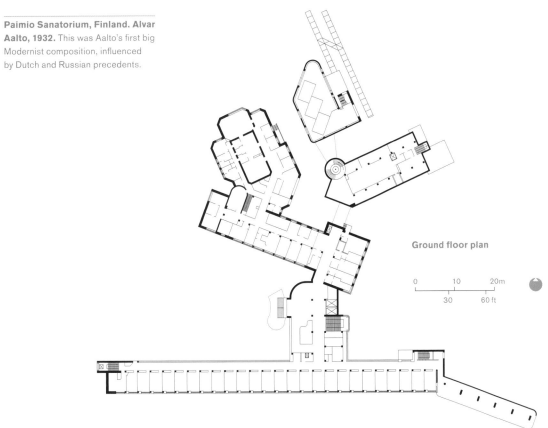

Ground floor plan

0	10	20m
	30	60 ft

Villa Mairea, Noormarkku, Finland. Alvar Aalto, 1939.
A house in a clearing that borrows something of the forest's natural, given character.

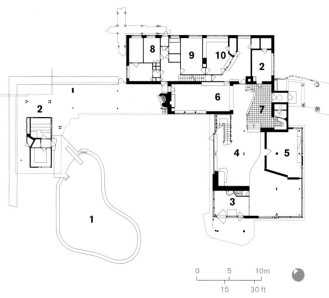

Ground floor plan

1. Swimming pool
2. Sauna
3. Winter garden
4. Living room
5. Library
6. Dining room
7. Entrance hall
8. Staff rooms
9. Office
10. Kitchen

The Villa Mairea is an exceptionally rich building, hard to represent in drawings and almost impossible to describe in words. Nevertheless in order to illustrate the heterotopic design method it is worth analyzing the main living part of the house, which occupies the wing to the left of the main entrance. Surprisingly, this wing is perfectly square on plan, and subdivided structurally into nine smaller squares. This looks suspiciously like an abstract system, though in material reality it is barely perceptible. On the ground floor, the space is divided by different means into different functional zones.

A serpentine line in the floor finish separates painted tiles from varnished wood, the first denoting a sitting area focussed on a corner fireplace and the second a south-facing room for music and entertainment. In the other two corners of the square, a library is defined by casually placed bookcases, and a 'winter garden' is walled in by painted brickwork. This functional division does not correspond to the geometrical or structural division of the square, so columns, all of them different, appear in the middle of spaces.

Upstairs, we seem to be in a completely different house. There is a very generous landing with its own fireplace, and two bedrooms – Harry's and Maire's. But these spaces fail to fill up the square outline of the enclosure below, so there are large areas of flat roof left over. As if to compensate for this, Maire's organically shaped, timber-clad studio bulges out over the south-west corner of the square and has to be supported by a couple of non-matching supplementary columns. The main columns continue upwards from the floor below, which is structurally sensible, but they bear no relation whatever to the dividing walls, which means that, once again, they appear as random obstructions in usable spaces. Described in this way it all seems rather disorganized – undesigned, even. But the effect, if not exactly 'calculated', is nevertheless carefully composed. This is a house in a forest clearing and it has borrowed something of the forest's natural, given character. Columns are trees, the plunge pool is a miniature lake, and timber-boarded walls recall old Finnish farmhouses. There is brick and stone and white render, and there are steel columns, but wood is the dominant material – natural, warm and sensuous.

Living room of the Villa Mairea. Columns seem to bear no relation to walls. Relaxed inconsistency is the rule.

Säynätsalo town hall

It is sometimes said that this town hall, Aalto's most famous building, was inspired by Italian hill towns. This may be true at some deep, unconscious level, but superficially it is hard to see any connection between this cluster of brick structures on an island in Lake Päijänne and, say, the towers of San Gimignano, which Aalto first visited in 1924. Säynätsalo is a small, dispersed forest settlement dominated by a timber factory. Aalto's building is called a 'town hall' but its wooded site is anything but urban. When it was completed in 1952, Aalto's choice of brick rather than concrete or steel or glass as the dominant material signalled a decisive break with what had already become the conventions of Modernism. There was no hint of a return to classicism or National Romanticism, however, so this was Modernism of a new kind.

It is a small building, but seems determined to make the most of its limited bulk, building up to three storeys at the highest point and wrapping a U-shaped block round a 'space of human appearance', with an apparently freestanding public library on the fourth side. The brick box of the council chamber, with its one big window and upward-stretching mono-pitch roof, is raised up high above the domestic, commercial and office accommodation, symbolizing, as it should, the primacy of the democratic process. Lettable shop units were included in the brief in an attempt to increase the volume of the building and enhance its public importance,

but they were not commercially viable and have long since been converted into offices. Aalto dealt with the mismatch between spatial resources and symbolic ambition in an ingenious way: by using the earth dug out for the foundations to raise the courtyard up to first-floor level. Left at ground level it would have been too small – little better than a light well – but raised up it enjoys a happier proportional relationship with the now effectively single-storey buildings surrounding it. And perhaps there is something in that hill town comparison after all, because it is necessary to climb up into the courtyard to find the building's main entrance. There are two possible routes: a straight, formal flight of stone steps on one side, and an informal cascade of crooked, grass-covered steps on the other. We can see now why the shop units were added: to provide the substructure necessary to create the 'hilltop'. The lower storey in fact completely surrounds the 'hill', incorporating a continuous retaining wall, but the flights of steps create the illusion of discontinuity. The library is therefore only *apparently* freestanding.

But it was not this ingenious design strategy that impressed those post-war architects who were dissatisfied with the purely instrumental tendencies of mainstream Modernism. For them it was the softness, the crookedness, the colours, the textures and the thoughtful details that seemed to show a new way forward. Windows were big and bright but they were wood framed and placed only where they were needed,

Säynätsalo Town Hall, Finland. Alvar Aalto, 1952. The building makes the most of its limited bulk, wrapping itself around a grassy courtyard at first-floor level.

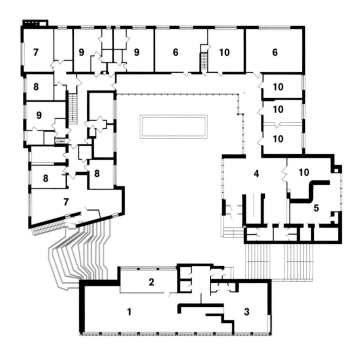

0   5   10m
15   30 ft

Courtyard level plan

1. Adults' library
2. Reading room
3. Children's library
4. Entrance hall
5. Cloakroom
6. Meeting room
7. Living room
8. Bedroom
9. One-room apartment
10. Office

not where an abstract system dictated. Brickwork was allowed inside the building, in both walls and floors, creating a fashion for so-called fair-face brickwork in institutional buildings that would last for decades. The roof of the council chamber was supported on a pair of madly irrational trusses like many-fingered hands. Even the door handles – bronze wrapped in leather – seemed to escape the harsh rule of the machine-age. Säynätsalo Town Hall was part of a larger town centre development that was never built. Its importance to the local community was therefore limited. Its influence on the course of modern architecture, however, was pivotal.

The project was pivotal also in Aalto's private life. His first wife Aino, herself an architect and his professional as well as personal partner for 25 years, had died of cancer in January 1949, casting him into a deep depression and causing him to abandon his teaching career in the United States. He had been appointed research professor of architecture at MIT in 1946 and in 1948 had completed the Baker House dormitory on the Charles River in Cambridge, Massachusetts. Its six-storey, brick-faced wall of student rooms, all facing south over the river, would be monotonous and mechanical – all that Aalto hated – were it not for its serpentine kink. Even more unusual is the north elevation, which is almost a circulation diagram made real. Single-loaded corridors are served by continuous enclosed flights of steps slung off the building like the companionways of an enormous ship. It is bold and original, but unsubtle to the point of ugliness.

Baker House dormitory, MIT, Cambridge, Massachusetts, USA. Alvar Aalto, 1948. The perforated brick wall facing the river is saved from monotony by a serpentine kink.

A few months after Aino's death, perhaps relieved to be back in Finland and to have given up any ambitions to teach or establish a practice abroad, Aalto was working happily on the Säynätsalo project with its 'job architect' Elissa Makiniemi. In 1952, Elissa became his wife.

Just a few kilometres south of Säynätsalo lies Muuratsalo, another island in Lake Päijänne, on which Aalto built what he called an 'experimental' summer house for himself and Elissa. In 1952 the island was inaccessible except by boat, so Aalto designed his own small craft that might be thought of as part of the house. Set back a little from shore, among the trees, the house seems at first like a ruin or a fragment, certainly nothing luxurious or ostentatious. Its footprint is a perfect

square, about half of which is an open courtyard, itself a perfect square, with a perfectly square fireplace at its centre. We are reminded of the notionally square living wing of the Villa Mairea. The ruin-like and fragmentary aspect is the means by which this geometrical perfection is disrupted and 'humanized'. Standing in the courtyard and looking up at the tall, brick, slope-topped walls it seems obvious that this was once a large room, the mono-pitch roof of which has fallen in or been removed. On plan it is about the same size as the council chamber of Säynätsalo Town Hall, which also has a mono-pitch roof. And like the chamber, the courtyard has a single large 'window', unglazed but with vestigial mullions. These resemblances can't be accidental. We are looking at the imagined ruin of a building designed by Alvar and Elissa and completed on a neighbouring island only a few months earlier. Perhaps it is a kind of monument, playful rather than mournful, to commemorate the start of their relationship. The walls of the enclosed part of the house, on two adjacent sides of the courtyard, look like an exhibition of apprentice bricklayers' samples. Different combinations of brick, bond and joint are displayed in small areas stitched together like a quilt. This may have been Aalto's (unsuccessful) attempt to avoid paying tax on the house by arguing that it was a test-bed for construction methods. Or it may be a work of art.

Experimental House, Muuratsalo, Finland. Alvar Aalto, 1954. Squares within squares on plan but irregular in section and elevation, like a ruin or a fragment.

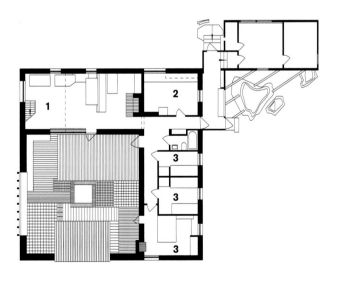

Ground floor plan
1. Living room
2. Kitchen
3. Bedroom

0   5   10m
   15   30 ft

Aalto's style is distinctive but in no way uniform or repetitious. Some of his best buildings are sober and upright, like plain modern versions of his early classical works. The Festival Hall, for example, completed in 1957, turns a deadpan face towards the town, refusing all display and rhetoric. The glass doors of the foyer, which is tucked under the rake of the auditorium, are welcoming enough, but there is no portico, not even a simple canopy. Above them a slightly facetted expanse of brick wall cries out for ornament of some kind, perhaps just an identifying sign, but remains blank and uncommunicative. Inside, however, the space is expansive and cheerful. Between a pale grey marble floor and a perforated and stepped suspended ceiling, partially fluted columns rhyme playfully with the straight trunks of the trees outside, visible through the full-height glass walls.

The quality of this space, one realizes, was fully imagined from the start. It is a notionally outdoor public gathering place – a clearing in the forest – made comfortable for the snowy Finnish climate. A canopy might well have destroyed the whole effect. To the right of the foyer, a second, everyday entrance sidles into the space between the hall and a teaching block. This time there is a canopy, a useful one in which bikes can be parked. From this entrance, a high, wide, top-lit, street-like space passes through the building to the campus beyond. This space contains a subtly satisfying

combination of simple elements: to the left, a high brick wall lifted up on stout round columns to allow passage through to the foyer; to the right, another brick wall, this time standing solidly on the ground and forming the balustrade of a straight stair that rises three storeys in five flights. The floors to which this stair gives access are given a Corbusian, Maison Domino treatment. We see their edges and the widely spaced round columns that support them, with lightweight metal balustrades between. A flat ceiling is enlivened only by a row of oval roof-lights, placed where they are needed, over the stairs. All this is simple and obvious seeming, but nicely judged in massing, light, detail, colour and texture.

The Festival Hall auditorium adopts a conventional concert hall plan apart from one practical feature: the upper and lower tiers of seating can be closed off from one another, giving a choice of formats. In the Church of the Three Crosses at Imatra, completed a couple of years later, this idea becomes the mainspring of a design that is otherwise very different. Here, sobriety and uprightness are abandoned in favour of a free moulding of form and space. Reyner Banham describes it best: it seems, he says, 'to turn from the viewer and hide, humping its copper roofs defensively against the sky and lifting cautious windows, like watchful alligator eyes, above the white substructure in which it seems to burrow'.[4] It's a brilliantly vivid image. He is, however,

(Left) Festival Hall at Jyväskylä University, Finland. Alvar Aalto, 1957. A subtly satisfying combination of simple elements.

(Opposite) Finlandia Hall, Helsinki, Finland. Alvar Aalto, 1971. Technically problematic marble cladding seems the cold hard opposite of the materials normally associated with Aalto.

describing the back of the building, where it faces the edge of its woodland clearing, which most users will see only from an oblique angle.

A slim tower, now looking uncomfortably like a concrete mobile phone mast, marks the main public entrance, or rather entrances, for there are three, corresponding to the three sections of the nave. There is a fourth, ceremonial entrance on the far corner of the building. Inside, the weirdness is intensified. It turns out that the 'alligator eyes' light the nave only indirectly through a second set of stepped, inward-sloping and randomly divided windows. These are part of a kind of inner lining tailored by folds and tucks and pleats to fit the three-in-one nave. The double wall provides an interstitial parking space for two curved concrete mobile partitions that trundle out into the nave when needed to divide the space. With these in position, each of the three sections becomes a cave-like room rather than just a slice of a something larger. At the (liturgically) east end (actually the north end – the building is not orientated conventionally) the undulating ceiling dives down to the floor behind the altar and the three crosses that give the church its name. This is Aalto's answer to Mies van der Rohe's 'universal space'. Flexibility, he seems to say, need not destroy the special qualities of special places.

Finlandia Hall

Aalto's last major building was the Finlandia Hall in Helsinki, completed in 1971. It is a technically flawed work and opinions differ about its architectural quality. Throughout his career Aalto was an enthusiastic but somewhat unscientific acoustician. In the main Finlandia auditorium his idea was to provide an unusually high space but to install a lower, perforated ceiling that could be used to adjust the reverberation time. It didn't work and major alterations had to be made. The white Italian marble external cladding was also problematic. Finnish frost and sunshine warped the panels, creating an interesting but unintended woven effect. In 1999 it was all replaced with higher-quality marble and a different fixing system but it warped again, this time in the other direction. White marble is the cold, hard opposite of the kind of materials we normally associate with Aalto, and there is something mechanical about the repetitive bays of the long, straight east facade, which, though it is effectively the back of the building, is nevertheless visible from a distance. The west side of the building, facing the narrow park along the major road called Mannerheimintie, is more welcoming, especially since the later addition of the conference centre with its playful, crinkly facade. For some critics the three-level foyer is a masterpiece of 'internal landscape'; for others it is just the space left over when a fan-shaped but asymmetrical 1,700-seat auditorium

**Philharmonie Concert Hall, Berlin, Germany.
Hans Scharoun, 1963.** Concert hall as landscape:
a valley of small terraced vineyards was the
architect's own metaphor.

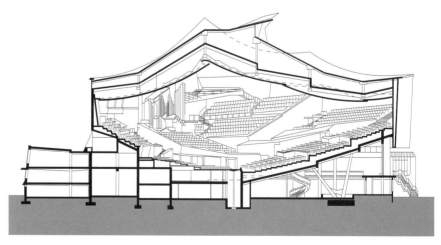

Section

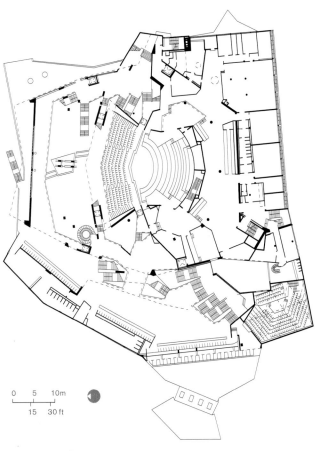

0 5 10m
15 30 ft

Lower level plan

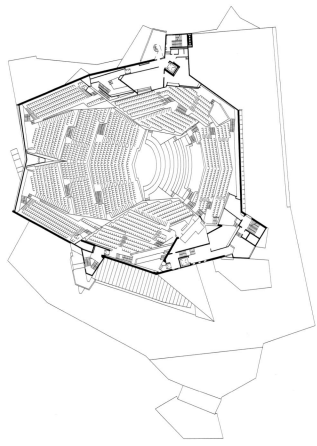

Upper level plan

is placed inside an angular site boundary. But the smaller, 340-seat chamber music hall, also asymmetrical, has its own appropriately scaled foyer, opening off the main foyer, and the whole ensemble works well enough. Richard Weston goes so far as to call it 'one of the great spatial sequences in modern architecture'.[5]

Alvar Aalto's mode of architectural creativity was unique and inimitable. Though it was influential and came to represent the human face of modern architecture, it did not inaugurate any movement or style. There were, however, contemporary architects with similar aims and methods, most notably Hans Scharoun, whom we last encountered as the designer of the Schminke House in Löbau of 1933 (see page 82). It may be invidious to compare an architect brought up in the Nordic classical tradition with one who began his career as a German Expressionist, yet there is an apparent convergence of their careers, if only in the negative sense that they both represented alternatives to mainstream Modernism. Scharoun's best-known building is the Philharmonie Concert Hall in Berlin, built for the Berlin Philharmonic Orchestra in the early 1960s when its musical director was the great Herbert von Karajan.

Philharmonie

Unlike the Finlandia Hall, the Philharmonie has excellent acoustics, so the first functional requirement is satisfied. But it is very far from being a scientifically determined design. Like Aalto, Scharoun believed that human experience should be architecture's guiding principle, in this case the experience of listening to music in an audience of more than 2,000 people. For him this was a worryingly large number, likely to prevent any concentrated involvement with the music. On the other hand, listening to a live performance with other people, rather than listening to a recording at home, was the essence of concert-going. Scharoun therefore set about dividing the audience up into smaller groups, giving each a little subauditorium of its own in order to create, if only for the duration of the concert, a sense of identity with a more intimate gathering. The result is a tiered terrain that the architect himself compared to a valley of small terraced vineyards, each clearly defined and uniquely angled. Rather surprisingly, these vineyards are arranged symmetrically but this is only perceptible from the concert platform. So it is a space tailored to a precisely defined function, though no-one would call it 'functionalist'. The foyers under and around the auditorium are also functional in this sense, but

New National Gallery, Berlin, Germany. Mies van der Rohe, 1968. A close neighbour of the Philharmonie but architecturally its opposite.

without any trace of a geometrical ordering system. Stairs, passageways, bridges and balconies are angled and shaped to follow the natural flow of arriving concert-goers, leaving their coats in the cloakrooms and pausing in small groups before finding their seats in the inner landscape of the auditorium. Externally the building is an ungainly lump made no lovelier by gold-coloured metal cladding and weakly profiled parapets that echo the convex suspended ceilings inside. It is sited in what used to be called the Kulturforum on the edge of West Berlin, near the Wall, an area once rather isolated but now easily accessible from Potsdamer Platz. Mies van der Rohe's temple-like, steel-framed New National Gallery, completed in 1968, is a close neighbour – a juxtaposition that architectural theorists and historians find convenient. One could hardly wish for a more starkly illustrative contrast between the abstract, geometrical, universal space of the gallery and the romantic, untidy but human space of the concert hall.

Aalto's furniture

The design of furniture was not a side-line in Alvar Aalto's architectural career but a field of experiment and a source of formal inspiration. His conversion from classicism to functionalism had come with a refusal to be ruled by any abstract geometrical order. Even in the Paimio Sanatorium, his Modernist masterpiece, the various wings of the building are eccentrically angled. Then in the Viipuri Library and the Villa Mairea curved forms begin to appear – a wavy ceiling, an angled and rounded canopy, a bulging and overhanging studio – with a preference for natural materials, especially wood. These were as much social statements as practical schemes. They asserted the priority of human desire over scientific authority, of man over machine. Space was being shaped to support human activities in the same way that a comfortable piece of furniture might be shaped to support the human body. We expect furniture to be curvaceous and made of materials that are warm to the touch; why should buildings be any different?

In his early attempts at furniture-making, Aalto worked with two important collaborators: his first wife Aino and Otto Korhonen, the manager of a joinery firm in Turku who showed him what could be done with plywood, how it could be bent and moulded and how it lent itself to mass production. The first chairs were similar to those being produced at the same time in Germany, with shaped plywood seats on tubular steel frames. But then in 1932 a new range appeared, designed for the Paimio Sanatorium, which included an armchair with a seat-and-back like a continuous scroll of plywood slung between closed plywood loops. The loops combine straights, curves and angles in a single figure quite unlike the regular, geometrical profile of, say, Mies van der Rohe's cantilevered chair. They could almost be plans of buildings or parts of buildings. Another armchair in the Paimio set is cantilevered, as if Aalto wished to prove that he could do anything the Germans could do but in warm wood rather than cold steel. His design for a simple, stackable, round wooden stool with bent plywood legs has been endlessly imitated in both three- and four-legged versions. He also designed other domestic items such as screens, light fittings and glassware, often tracing that characteristic sinuous line derived from natural landscape, from hills, lakes and forest edges. His famous Savoye vase, for example, with its flat 'floor' and vertical, serpentine 'walls' is like a miniature glass room.

International exhibitions in London and Zurich opened up new markets for Aalto's furniture in the early 1930s. He needed a more sophisticated marketing operation and a more reliable manufacturing base. In 1935, Maire Gullichsen, member of a wealthy industrial family and eponymous client of the Villa Mairea, joined with Alvar and Aino Aalto, Otto Korhonen and an art critic, Nils-Gustav Hahl, to found a new company called Artek. The company still exists and still includes many original Aalto designs in its catalogue.

Birchwood chair by Alvar Aalto for the Paimio Sanatorium, 1933. Loops and scrolls emerge from bent plywood technology but might also be echoes of landscape features.

19 | MASS HOUSING 1949–1968

Architecture is concerned with more than just the solving of a local accommodation problem. It strives for a more general relevance, inviting comparisons, developing and extending traditions, and breaking new theoretical ground. Above all, it sees itself as an art, not merely a practical craft. Nikolaus Pevsner made this point succinctly when he declared that Lincoln Cathedral was a work of architecture, but a bicycle shed was just a building.[1] In the nineteenth century, architecture was responsible for important buildings like churches, art galleries and town halls, while completely ignoring factories, railway sheds and urban housing for the poor. But in the twentieth century, the clear line of distinction between architecture and ordinary building became blurred, not because ordinary building aspired to the status of architecture but rather the reverse: because a new breed of Modernist architects burned with a desire to bring architecture to the masses and reconcile their ancient art with the realities of a new industrial society. The design of mass housing now became architecture's most important task. Pioneers like Tony Garnier, Ludwig Hilberseimer and Le Corbusier created visions of a new kind of city in which ordinary housing was more important than monumental public buildings. Le Corbusier experimented with various housing forms designed for healthy, ordered twentieth-century living and for efficient machine production. For example, his 'à redent' or 'set-back' housing in the Ville Radieuse project of 1930 took the form of continuous linear blocks raised on pilotis over a freely accessible terrain, in effect a public park. Later, in his 1935 project for Zlín in Czechoslovakia, the continuous blocks were abandoned in favour of freestanding slabs, foreshadowing that great post-war built manifesto, the Unité d'Habitation in Marseille (see page 224).

Post-war Europe

After the Second World War, the reconstruction of ruined European cities presented a golden opportunity to realize this new urban vision. The vision had three main elements. First, a whole city, or at least a substantial part of one, could be designed from scratch by a single design agency, perhaps even a single architect. The old city that grew and changed gradually over a long period of time – the buildings renewing themselves but the streets and public spaces mostly remaining in place – would be superseded by a functional design that swept away the remains of the past and treated the site as a tabula rasa. Second, the city would be machine-like, with different components, or zones, for different functions – residential, commercial, industrial and cultural – linked by rapid transport systems. Daily life would be planned and managed like a business operation and the old multifunctional city quarter would be cleared away. Third, urban space would be transformed. In the old cities, streets and squares were enclosed and contained by a solid accretion of building, like canyons carved out of rock. In the new city, buildings designed optimally to serve specific functions would stand free in the fresh air and sunshine of a landscaped park.

The Ville Radieuse and the Unité d'Habitation fixed the image of the new city, and architects all over Europe set about making it a reality. In the Pimlico district of London, for example, a large area of nineteenth-century terraced housing bombed in the Blitz was replaced by 32 apartment blocks, seven to eleven storeys high, designed by Powell and Moya and built between 1949 and 1962. The development, known as Churchill Gardens, was cautious in its interpretation of Corbusian precedent. Linear slab blocks were not raised on pilotis over continuous parkland but aligned with conventional streets, and though their structural frames were concrete, their external walls were of brick. Nevertheless, these ship-like buildings, complete with fat funnels on the roof to house water tanks and lift motors, were a symbol of Modernist optimism to brighten the post-war economic gloom. A novel technical development was the district heating system, which used waste heat from Battersea Power Station on the other side of the river. Further west at Roehampton on the outskirts of the city, London County Council's architects' department designed a housing development called Alton West, which mixed low-rise terraced housing with 12-storey towers and 11-storey slab blocks, all in a park-like setting with mature trees. In architectural photographs of the estate, completed in 1958, it is the five slab blocks that feature most prominently because they were so obviously influenced by the Unité d'Habitation, though each is barely half the size of its model. The design team, led by Colin Lucas, included Bill

Alton West, Roehampton, UK. London County Council Architect, 1958. Slab blocks obviously influenced by Le Corbusier's Unité, but on a smaller scale.

Howell and Colin St John Wilson, who, with Philip Powell and Hidalgo Moya, would go on to become prominent practitioners of British Modernism in the years to come.

The new architecture of mass housing appealed in different ways to different constituencies: tenants liked the generous space standards, the central heating, the bathrooms, the fitted kitchens and the views from high windows; politicians saw an opportunity to accelerate the long and tedious process of building, making its political impact more immediate; architects enthusiastically promoted it because it seemed the fulfilment of the Modernist dream, an architecture at last in tune with the spirit of the age. But it was new building technologies that gave it its progressive impetus. For almost a century architecture had been learning how to use engineered materials, mainly steel and reinforced concrete, adapting them to a new formal and spatial conception: the structural frame with lightweight in-fill (see Chapter 4). Easily transported components such as doors and windows were now routinely standardized and mass produced, and in mostly non-architectural popular housing, simple technologies such as the American 'balloon' or 'platform' frame had been adapted for prefabrication to varying extents.

Box-frame construction

The question now was: could mass housing, in multi-storey towers and slabs, be made in factories? The reinforced concrete frame did not lend itself either to prefabrication or to the division of large buildings into smaller self-contained units. Columns and beams, which might easily be absorbed into the open plan of an office building, were awkward intrusions into domestic interiors. Solid, soundproof internal walls between dwellings were a fixed and inevitable feature of mass housing; could they perhaps be used as structural members, in effect as thin planar columns? And since the spans between them would be relatively short, might it be possible to get rid of the beams, relying only on the strength of a flat slab? These thoughts gave rise to a new conception: 'box frame construction'. It was an idea that arose in many places simultaneously in the years immediately before and after the Second World War. One version of it was developed by the great structural engineer Ove Arup, father of what is now the biggest engineering consultancy in the world.

Arup worked in England where, before the war, he collaborated with the Russian (or, strictly, Georgian) emigré architect Berthold Lubetkin, a committed Modernist who had worked in Paris in the 1920s with, among others, Konstantin Mel'nikov and Auguste Perret. Moving to England in 1931, Lubetkin set up a collaborative architectural practice called Tecton. He and Arup together designed what is now considered to be an early masterpiece of British Modernism, the Highpoint I flats in Highgate, north London. The building is of reinforced concrete construction with freestanding columns in a spacious foyer on the ground floor. In the upper storeys, however, floors are supported by the flat planes of the concrete external walls and by a central spine which is a kind of hybrid panel/frame – either a panel with very large openings or a flattened beam and columns. In the later Highpoint II next door, loadbearing concrete walls are arranged at right angles to the external walls, leaving the facade to be in-filled freely with glass and lightweight panels. These were early experiments in what, after the war, Arup developed into the fully fledged box frame. The eight-storey Spa Green estate in central London, designed by Tecton and Arup and completed in 1949, is probably the earliest example in Britain.

A structural form had been found that suited multi-storey housing and lent itself readily to rationalized construction. Formwork used to cast the concrete walls could be standardized to a degree and recycled, but the concrete was still being poured on site. A further stage of development beckoned: to move the casting process off

site into a factory. Complete panels could then be delivered to the site by truck and placed carefully onto the growing house of cards (a metaphor that would eventually prove tragically apt). With the arrival of the tower crane on British building sites around 1950, all the elements of the construction kit were in place and mass production of mass housing could begin.

Precast concrete

This was not exclusively, or even mainly, a British idea. Very similar technical developments were taking place in France, Sweden and Denmark, of which Ove Arup, himself a Dane, was well aware. In 1949, the French minister of reconstruction and urbanism, Eugène Claudius-Petit, declared that it would be necessary to build 240,000 dwellings a year for the foreseeable future to deal with a desperate housing shortage. It was taken for granted that such a target would be impossible to meet without a thorough industrialization of the French building industry. In 1952, the year of the completion of the Unité d'Habitation, Petit's ministry launched a specific programme to build 4,000 dwellings on various sites around Paris using a precast-concrete system that had been patented in 1948 by the engineer Raymond Camus. Precast concrete had long been a French speciality but had hitherto been limited to relatively small components such as lintels and facing panels. Camus's system was much more ambitious, producing whole structural walls and floors on the box frame principle. Marcel Lods, a committed Modernist and a strong supporter of industrialized building, was appointed to lead a team of

Highpoint I, London. Berthold Lubetkin, 1935. A masterpiece of early British Modernism designed by an architect who had worked in Paris in the 1920s.

architects in the design of a range of standard blocks either five or nine storeys high. A new factory to produce the panels was built at Montesson in the western suburbs of Paris, and by September 1955 the building campaign was ready to go: 72,000 panels of 185 different types produced by 165 specially trained workers plus 20 truck drivers. Eighteen months later the first blocks were ready for occupation and the programme was being hailed as a success. According to Camus's efficient publicity machine, his system was faster, cheaper and of higher quality than conventional site-based construction.

Architecturally, the results were ambiguous. To progressive Modernists like Lods and his colleagues, these housing estates were a stage in the realization of the Ville Radieuse dream. They provided all the essentials for comfortable

living, but more than that they represented a new freedom and a new healthy way of life. They also had artistic qualities, though of a severely abstract kind. For example, the site plan designed by Bernard Zehrfuss (architect of the CNIT building in Paris, see page 209) for the massive 3,850-dwelling estate, or *grand ensemble*, at Nanterre was an elegant Elementarist composition, like a painting by Mondrian or Malevich. An architect might also find satisfaction in the proportions of the facades with their alternating recessed and cantilevered balconies. But these qualities were of little importance to the politicians and civil servants, who saw only the impressive production figures and cost savings, or to the residents, who, though they may have appreciated the modern conveniences, saw only plain, uninteresting boxes disposed in meaningless open space. Before long there were other things to be unimpressed by. The surfaces of the external walls quickly decayed and the joints between the precast concrete panels started leaking. It seemed that the famed accuracy of Camus's manufacturing process was more theoretical than actual. These problems were eventually solved and the estate survives, now called Cité Marcellin Berthelot, part of the town's university quarter. Camus was the first and biggest of the French systems, but there were many others. Zehrfuss worked with one of them, the Balency post-and-slab system, in the design of three enormous 13-storey slab blocks on

another site in Nanterre, completed in 1956. Here, though, the external walls are of ordinary rendered concrete block.

These Nanterre estates are typical of hundreds of similar projects initiated in western Europe in the 1950s and 1960s. In Denmark, for example, a distinguished team of architects, including Povl Hoff and Bennet Windinge, created a powerful architectural statement at Høje Gladsaxe to the north west of Copenhagen by lining up five 16-storey slab blocks end to end on top of an embankment. Schools, nurseries, a shopping centre and other facilities were built nearby, creating a self-contained town, completed in 1966. Equally uncompromising, the Albertslund development further west demonstrated the application of precast-concrete technology to low-rise housing, creating a uniform carpet of 1,000 identical single-storey courtyard houses. Surprisingly, the extreme, almost brutal rationality of these projects seems to have served reasonably well socially in the years since.

Albertslund used a version of the Larsen-Nielsen system, which, as licensed to contractors Taylor Woodrow-Anglian,

Slab blocks at Nanterre, France. Bernard Zehrfuss, 1956. Prefabrication on a grand scale but with architectural aspirations in the site layout and facade modelling.

(Above) Høje Gladsaxe housing, Copenhagen, Denmark. Povl Hoff and Bennet Windinge, 1966. Unashamed modernity: five 16-storey slab blocks lined up on top of an embankment.

(Right) Albertslund development, Copenhagen, Denmark. Viggo Møller-Jensen, Tyge Arnfred and Mogens J. Pedersen, 1963. 1,000 identical single-storey precast concrete houses laid out like a carpet.

had a high reputation among British architects and local authorities, particularly London County Council. The Morris Walk estate in Woolwich, south London, built between 1962 and 1966, was one of the earliest collaborations, with the architect Martin Richardson in charge. Ten-storey towers are mixed with parallel three-storey blocks linked by bridges to freestanding enclosed stairways. Joints between the roughly square, storey-height exposed aggregate panels are clearly visible, creating an insistent, rather coarse pattern, but landscaped spaces between the buildings are of a tolerably human scale. Richardson's influence on the design is clear enough, though he was working in a tight political space between the client's cost limits and the contractor's desire to make the most of the economies the system offered.

In Britain, as in France, there were many rival systems competing for a slice of the public housing pie, including Laing's Jespersen, from Sweden, Shepherd's Spacemaker and, most prolific of all, Concrete Ltd's Bison Wall Frame.

Morris Walk Estate, London. Martin Richardson, 1966. The Danish Larsen-Nielsen system adapted to the British preference for mixed developments.

All over the country, local authorities were beginning to turn not to architects but to system builders to satisfy their housing targets.

American public housing

In the United States, there were few attempts to systematize housing in this way, though many high-rise estates were built in eastern and Midwestern cities. Architectural history tends to assume that publicly funded housing was a negligible category in a country where private enterprise was the unquestioned basis of economic life. The private real-estate lobby was fiercely opposed to government-sponsored housing (though not to government support for private mortgages) and the political climate was generally hostile. The Truman administration made some attempt to tackle the housing shortage in the 1949 Housing Act, which included a target of 810,000 new units by 1955, but ten years later only 125,000 units had been built. Public housing meant housing for the poor, and the poor must never be allowed to live in better conditions than citizens who paid their way in the world. From a conservative political point of view, therefore, architectural quality in

public housing was an ambiguous concept, something of which to be suspicious rather than something to celebrate.

Nevertheless, there were some early attempts to apply European Modernist ideas to American public housing – 'Le Corbusierism' as it was known at the time. For example, the Chicago Housing Authority (CHA), under the leadership of a pioneer advocate of public housing, Elizabeth Wood, employed progressive local architects such as Harry Weese and Skidmore, Owings and Merrill to design early post-war projects. SOM's Ogden Courts, completed in 1949, borrowed its details from Mies van der Rohe's Promontory Apartments (see page 198), with an exposed concrete frame and brick in-fill, though its overall form – two long seven-storey T-shaped blocks – was very different. At Loomis Courts, completed in 1951, Harry Weese experimented with open-access galleries, similar to the 'streets in the sky' favoured by British Brutalists of the time (see page 280). Wood and her supporters, such as Catherine Bauer, author of the classic *Modern Housing*, first published in 1934, eventually became disillusioned with the European, high-rise model, partly on the grounds that it was unsuitable for families with children, but also, perhaps, because it played into the hands of conservative administrators in the federal Public Housing Administration (PHA) who saw it as a way of cutting costs to the bone.

In the late 1950s, the CHA fought a losing battle against PHA cost limits, which effectively ruled out anything but the simplest and most austere high-rise layouts. Examples include Robert Taylor Homes (4,400 units) on the South Side of Chicago, Washington Park Homes nearby (1,400 units), and William Green Homes (1,000 units), an extension to the massive Cabrini estate on the Near North Side. These estates consisted entirely of unlovely, freestanding 16-storey slab blocks. British and European attempts to introduce scale and variety by mixing low-, medium- and high-rise buildings were rejected as wasteful and inappropriate.

Pre-war public housing schemes in New York, such as First Houses (so called because they were the first-ever publicly funded housing) and Harlem River Houses in Manhattan, had been built specifically to rehouse African-American slum dwellers. By the 1960s, segregation had become unofficial but the high-rise projects became de facto ghettos anyway. To what extent their rapid descent into gun crime and gang culture was due to the nature of the physical environment – the architecture, in other words – is debatable, but there is no doubt that residential towers became stigmatizing symbols of urban poverty. Minoru Yamasaki's Pruitt-Igoe development in St Louis (see page 203) was the first public housing estate to be blown up, in 1972, but it was far from the last. With the exception of Loomis Courts, none of the

(Above) **Robert Taylor Homes, Chicago, Illinois, USA. CHA, 1962.** In American public housing, architectural quality was an ambiguous concept.

(Below) **Harlem River Houses, New York City, USA. Archibald Manning Brown, 1937.** Pre-war public housing built specifically to rehome African-American slum dwellers.

Chicago estates mentioned above still exists. They were all eventually abandoned and demolished, their displaced residents given vouchers to buy or rent property in the private sector.

Khrushchev's initiative

Meanwhile, on the other side of the world, and of the Cold War conflict, an equally debased form of 'Le Corbusierism' was being promoted vigorously by the new Soviet premier, Nikita Khrushchev. In the Stalinist era, Russian architecture had abandoned its Constructivist ambitions and returned to a conservative monumentality. Investment in housing was neglected in favour of the production of armaments and agricultural machinery. By 1955, the year of Khrushchev's rise to power, most Soviet city dwellers lived either in over-crowded slums or in dormitory hostels. The sixth Five Year Plan (1956–60) included a commitment to double the rate of production of housing units, which actually rose from 1.5 million in 1956 to 2.7 million in 1959. By the late 1980s, Khrushchev's house-building programme had delivered a total of almost 70 million dwellings. The key to this success was a simple principle – quantity, not quality – which Khrushchev justified in a blunt question: 'Would a citizen rather settle for an adequate apartment now, or wait 10 or 15 years for a very good one?'

Architecture, in the traditional sense, could only be an obstacle to such a policy and, by definition, the urban environment was bound to suffer. But even if these distractions were discounted, the technical challenge was formidable. Khrushchev and his advisors, like Eugène

Claudius-Petit before them, came to the conclusion that industrialization of the building industry was the only way. The new, western European, precast-concrete large-panel systems, in particular the French Camus system, provided a ready-made model that was duly copied. System building was well suited to a command economy that could insist on thorough standardization, locate factories for optimum efficiency and allocate vast tracts of land for development. Standard apartment plans were designed, as well as standard plans for the factories that would make them. By 1965 no fewer than 2,305 precast-concrete production plants were operating in the USSR. Some of the more advanced operations followed what would now be called lean manufacturing principles, minimizing warehousing by delivering components to sites 'just in time' and lifting them directly from trucks to the building itself. Building sites themselves became factories, their layouts governed more by the logic of the production process than the spatial coherence of the final product.

A key figure in the development of industrialized Soviet housing was the engineer Vitaly Lagutenko, who designed the infamous and ubiquitous K-7, a four- or five-storey walk-up block containing tiny two-room apartments. Square mile after square mile of peripheral urban land was covered with K-7s and their later, nine-storey successors. They were known as *khrushchyovki* ('Khrushchev buildings'), which very soon became *khrushchoby*, a pun on *trushchoby* ('slums'). Early estates, or 'mikrorayons', such as the Novye Cheryomushki and Belyayevo districts of Moscow, were provided with schools, shops and other communal facilities, but were often

K-7 block at Novye Cheryomushki, Moscow, Russia. The K-7 standard precast concrete block designed by Vitaly Lagutenko.

1960s apartments in Belyayevo, Moscow. Later, nine-storey versions of the K-7. Construction was notoriously shoddy.

badly located in relation to local employment, leading to long commutes on crowded public transport. As the system developed, every normal measure of good planning was sacrificed to the quantity-not-quality principle. Construction defects were rife. Gaps between panels, water penetration, poor insulation and leaking drains were so common they were regarded as normal. Local construction agencies struggling to meet targets often handed apartments over before they were properly finished. One consequence of the drive to meet targets and cost limits was that apartments got smaller and smaller, falling from 16 square metres (172 square feet) per inhabitant in the early 1960s to just 12 square metres (129 square feet) at the end of the decade. Communist East European countries such as East Germany, Hungary, Romania and Czechoslovakia all submitted to similar prefabricated house production regimes. In purely quantitative terms, it was a phenomenal achievement, the greatest public housing programme the world had ever seen. Looked at another way, it was an architectural, urban and environmental disaster on a continental scale.

A tarnished vision

In western Europe, the impact of the Corbusian urban model allied with industrialized building was less devastating. It was not long, however, before the vision became tarnished here too as the estates sank into social decay, the general public began to regret the loss of the old domesticity, and the technology started to reveal its hidden flaws. In Britain the turning point can be precisely dated: 16 May 1968, when a gas explosion caused the partial collapse of a newly completed 22-storey tower block in east London called Ronan Point. It had been built by Taylor Woodrow-Anglian using the Larsen-Nielsen system. There was an 'overshoot' of production into the early 1970s, but effectively the Ronan Point collapse brought precast-concrete system building to an end. By the 1990s, its development had not just ceased but had gone into reverse, as demolition of tower blocks by controlled explosion became a popular public spectacle all over Europe.

Intellectual opinion had shifted too. In 1961 the journalist and urban theorist Jane Jacobs had published *The Death and Life of Great American Cities*, an impassioned critique of Modernist planning, calling for a halt to the destruction of the old multifunctional streets and urban quarters. The logic of functional zoning and comprehensive redevelopment was called into question and interest in the virtues of the traditional city began to revive. Then in 1972 Oscar Newman, an architect and urban planner, published *Defensible Space*, which provided ammunition for those who saw a causal connection between crime and built form. It seemed that tower blocks really did cause social breakdown. With hindsight it seems obvious that the seeds

Ronan Point, London, UK. Taylor Woodrow-Anglian, 1968.
This progressive collapse caused by a gas explosion signalled the end of the precast-concrete era.

of decline were present in the Modernist mass-housing model right from the start. The abstract rationality of its forms, which avoided any dialogue with tradition, whether in the site and surroundings, in the way of life of its inhabitants or in the language of architecture itself, eventually proved a fatal weakness. Such rationality had been foreshadowed in the pre-war German *Zeilenbau* estates of Walter Gropius and Ernst May (see Chapter 8) but after the war it became an unquestioned orthodoxy that dazzled and seduced its creators. Though it was architects themselves who first proposed the model, in doing so they were exposing their art to judgement by shallow, instrumental criteria, and thereby jeopardizing their own *raison d'être*. Le Corbusier's 'magnificent play of forms in light' soon dissolved into a pure productionism – 'quantity, not quality'. The vision had always been vulnerable and in the end the ordinary people, who had struggled to accept its demands, insisted on its destruction.

20 | LATIN AMERICAN MODERNISM 1932–1982

In the 1950s, North American architecture took only what it wanted from European Modernism, developing a smooth, superior style suitable for an advanced industrial economy. It was less interested in the socially transforming potential of new materials and the overthrow of architectural tradition. The old Beaux-Arts respectability lay not far beneath the surface. This selectiveness might be expressed in shorthand form as a preference for Mies van der Rohe over Le Corbusier. But in the other America, south of the Mexican border, where poverty and political instability prevailed, it was Le Corbusier who was honoured as the prophet of modernity.

Mexico

As early as 1924, Juan O'Gorman, then a third-year student at the architecture school in Mexico City, was reading and rereading the recently published *Vers une architecture*, and beginning to rebel against his traditional teachers. He believed in an extreme and perhaps naive

functionalism – the idea that the form of a building could emerge automatically from the activities it was to house and the materials available to build it without any reference to tradition. To prove his point he built a house for himself in the fashionable San Angel district of the city, with a reinforced concrete frame, plain blockwork walls and an unscreened water tank on the roof. The house was noticed by Diego Rivera, the great muralist, who asked O'Gorman to build a house and studio nearby for him and his wife, the painter Frida Kahlo. The Rivera–Kahlo House was completed in 1932 and still stands, preserved as a museum. It is really two houses, one for Diego and one for Frida, connected by a high-level bridge. The former is painted red and white, the latter blue, but both are thoroughly Corbusian and strongly influenced by the Ozenfant studio in Paris built ten years

Rivera–Kahlo House, Mexico City, Mexico.
Juan O'Gorman, 1932. The houses are connected by a high-level bridge, just visible.

Mexico City University Library (left), Mexico. Juan O'Gorman, 1953. The windowless walls of the library book stack are covered in murals made with coloured tiles.

earlier. Mexico had seen nothing like them before. Rivera introduced O'Gorman to the minister of education, which resulted in commissions to design 24 cheap, functional schools built to a simple quantitative recipe without any claim to architectural distinction in the traditional sense.

It was the muralists who constituted the main thrust of Mexican Modernist art in the 1920s and 1930s. Rivera himself established an international reputation and was called in to decorate Rockefeller Center in New York with politically controversial pictures. An alliance with Modernist architects seemed inevitable – there can be no murals without walls to paint on – but the openness of Modernist architecture, its preference for glass over solid walls, made this problematic. By the 1950s functional Modernism had been accepted as an appropriate mode for low-cost housing and hospitals,

but in the building of the Ciudad Universitaria (University City) in Mexico City it took on a special, symbolic role, representing the progress made in the social and economic development of the country since the revolution of 1910. The site was a vast field of volcanic rock known as El Pedregal to the south of the city. Some of the sports buildings on the campus, in particular the handball courts, borrowed their truncated pyramidal forms from remains of the ancient city of Teotihuacán 48 kilometres (30 miles) away, but the teaching and administration buildings mainly conformed to Corbusian principles – slabs and towers, raised on pilotis with ribbon windows and flat roofs. Murals were incorporated rather awkwardly in most cases. For example, the glass curtain wall of the rectorate building, a 15-storey tower by Mario Pani and others completed in 1952, is interrupted at fifth- and sixth-floor levels by a concrete lecture theatre pushed outwards, the better to display David Alfaro Siqueiros's colourful outsize version of the university crest. All over the campus figurative murals fight for space in abstract Modernist grids. The battle is decided in the library building, where the windowless walls of the book stack tower are completely covered by a riotous representation of the legendary origins of Mexico City executed in coloured tiles. Surprisingly, that once fiercely committed functionalist Juan O'Gorman was both architect and muralist. Félix Candela's little Cosmic Rays Pavilion (see page 215) adds a more rational, scientific ingredient to the university's rich architectural mix.

Luis Barragán

El Pedregal was also the site of a select residential development designed by Luis Barragán with the painter and sculptor Mathias Goeritz. Barragán was not involved in the mainstream, government-sponsored, development of Modernist architecture in Mexico but has nevertheless come to be regarded as the greatest Mexican architect of the period. He began his career in the late 1920s designing elegant, neo-colonial private houses in Guadalajara. Then in 1932 he visited Paris, where he attended lectures by Le Corbusier. The result was a clutch of Corbusian houses and apartment buildings in Mexico City built between 1936 and 1940. But it was in the Jardines del Pedregal, begun in 1945, that his mature style emerged. The elemental strangeness of 'the gardens of stones' was his inspiration. He wanted to preserve its beauty but 'humanize' it by the addition of simple elements such as walls, pavements, steps, pools, fountains and cacti. Houses, some of them designed by Barragán himself, were subject to strict guidelines to maintain the gentle, respectful treatment of the landscape. In the decades since, the plots have been subdivided and the guidelines ignored. Barragán's vision is preserved only in the black-and-white photographs of Armando Salas Portugal.

Barragán House, Mexico City, Mexico. Luis Barragán, 1948. An inward-looking house, experienced room by room, with a garden that is also a room.

Ground floor plan
1. Garage
2. Kitchen
3. Hall
4. Dining room
5. Library
6. Living room
7. Vestibule
8. Office
9. Office
10. Workshop
11. Garden

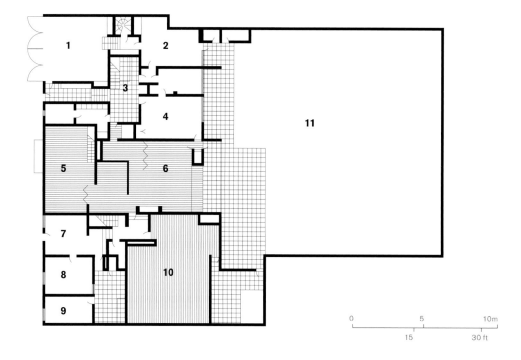

Brazil Pavilion, New York's World Fair, USA.
Lúcio Costa and Oscar Niemeyer, 1939.
An L-shaped Corbusian block on pilotis brought
to life by a sweeping entrance ramp.

Critics use words like 'contemplative', 'mystical' and sometimes 'surreal' to describe Barragán's style, which is best represented now by the house he built for himself in Mexico City in 1948. Externally it is unremarkable. Plain stuccoed walls, with a sparse scattering of square windows, step up from one to three storeys according to no discernible system. Inside, all contact with the surrounding city is cut off. This is an inward-looking building, experienced room by room, with a walled garden that is also a kind of room. The garden and the double-height main living room must be considered a single spatial experience,

connected as they are by the house's most photographed feature: a large square window, its glass set framelessly into walls, floor and ceiling but quartered by glazing bars that are obviously meant to represent a Christian cross (Barragán was a devout Catholic). Materials are natural and hand crafted: walls of plain plaster, wooden-beamed ceilings, and floors of wide wooden boards or terracotta tiles. The inward-looking character is maintained even on the roof, which is enclosed by high walls and chimneys painted in shades of cream, orange, green and purple. There are no cornices or coping stones so the composition is completely abstract, faintly recalling Dutch De Stijl interiors of 30 years earlier. Barragán took the traditional Spanish/Mexican house-building tradition, removed its conventional ornament and discovered a powerfully simple architecture, modern but without any of Modernism's pretensions and affectations.

Brazil

In Brazil, Le Corbusier's influence was even more powerful and direct. He visited the country in 1929 when, with characteristic immodesty, he sketched a proposal for the complete reshaping of the city of Rio de Janeiro. Like his later Plan Obus for Algiers (see Chapter 17), it included a huge megastructure in the form of an inhabited viaduct snaking along the coast. Seven years later he was called in as a consultant in the design of a new building for

Sketch plan for Rio de Janeiro. Le Corbusier,
1929. A characteristically bold scheme for the
complete remodelling of Rio de Janeiro.

the Ministry of Education and Health (MES). It was to become a landmark in the development of South American Modernism. The lead architect was Lúcio Costa, who had become a fervent admirer of Le Corbusier after establishing a partnership with Gregori Warchavchik, a Ukrainian-born architect credited with designing the first Modernist house in Brazil.

Costa entered the design competition for the new building in 1935 only to be disqualified on the basis that his architecture was too radical. But the minister of education, Gustavo Capanema, was determined that the new building should become a symbol of the government's progressive social policies. He overruled the judges and appointed Costa directly. Costa invited other radical young architects to join his team, including Affonso Eduardo Reidy and Oscar Niemeyer. All were Modernists and admirers of Le Corbusier, who arrived in person in July 1936 and stayed for six weeks, advising, encouraging and lending legitimacy to the radicalism of the young Brazilians. The resulting design is a clear demonstration of Corbusian principles but reinterpreted for Brazil. A 14-storey slab is lifted on pilotis over its city centre site, leaving the street level open except for an entrance lobby and a two-storey auditorium and exhibition block. It is an abstract composition, the final choice of many alternative configurations, yet it also responds to particular local conditions. The south-facing, shady side of the slab is completely glazed but the north side is covered in a concrete egg-crate incorporating adjustable louvres or *brises-soleil*. End elevations are blank walls, like the deep frame of a painting.

Oscar Niemeyer

The United Nations building in New York, to the design of which Oscar Niemeyer made an important contribution, is a more famous example of the form, but designed a decade later. Climatic adaptations were not the only Brazilian feature. As in Mexico, mural art and decoration were considered essential to represent the visual culture of the nation. Seahorses, starfish, crabs, sailing ships and other maritime motifs swim among cloud-like forms in the blue and white ceramic tiles, or *azulejos*, that adorn most of the solid walls at ground level. Candido Portinari was the artist. Roof gardens too – an important component of the Corbusian formula – were designed with characteristic Brazilian vigour and freedom by the great landscape architect Roberto Burle Marx. Their combination of serpentine paths with boldly sculptural planting was to become an important ingredient in later Brazilian Modernism.

Of the young architects in Costa's MES team, it was Oscar Niemeyer who rose to international prominence. His and Costa's design for the Brazilian pavilion at the 1939 New York World's Fair made North American architects aware that European Modernism had truly become an international style and could no longer be ignored. Its basically Corbusian form – an L-shaped block raised on pilotis – was brought to life by a new curvaceousness. A sweeping entrance ramp landed in

Church of São Francisco de Assis, Pampulha, Belo Horizonte, Brazil. Oscar Niemeyer, 1943. Freely expressive forms: a parabolic arched roof and a tower that tapers the wrong way.

Pedregulho development, São Cristóvão, Rio de Janeiro, Brazil. Affonso Eduardo Reidy, 1947. The serpentine block may have been influenced by Le Corbusier's sketch for the remodelling of Rio.

an open-sided 'esplanade' at the upper level, its thin flat roof carved away at the back as if by the spontaneous wielding of a knife. Visitors proceeded into the main exhibition hall in the longer arm of the L, which waved slightly on plan as if moved by an underwater current. Overhead a gallery with a serpentine edge faced a glass wall overlooking a naturalistic pond in the garden below.

This new free-form Modernism was developed further in an ambitious lakeside development at Pampulha in Belo Horizonte. It was promoted by Juscelino Kubitschek, then mayor of Belo Horizonte but later to be president of the republic. Key leisure and cultural buildings – a casino, a yacht club, a dance hall and a church – were positioned at strategic points along the lake shore to encourage high-class residential development. Roberto Burle Marx was the landscape architect, working closely with Niemeyer. In these buildings, basically cubic Corbusian forms share space with a variety of unruly bulges, waves and wiggles. In the casino,

for example, a double-height foyer, many columned and flat roofed with straight ramps up to a gambling gallery, sprouts a roughly elliptical extension over the lake shore containing a restaurant and night club. On the opposite side of the lake, the more down-market dance hall, nearly circular on plan, is linked to an external stage by a meandering concrete canopy like a Burle Marx footpath raised up on a single row of columns. Most freely expressive of all is the church of São Francisco de Assis, in which Niemeyer's characteristic flat, beamless sheets of concrete are bent and folded to form simple parabolic arched roofs. The freestanding campanile avoids any reference to traditional precedent by tapering downwards rather than upwards. This was the early 1940s, before Brazil entered the Second World War on the side of the Allies. Le Corbusier had already begun to loosen his machine-like repertoire of forms and allow himself to be inspired by nature, but always with a certain serious-mindedness. There is nothing in Corb to match Niemeyer's playful spontaneity.

The bourgeois playground of Pampulha was hardly a shining example of Modernism's social programme. Rehousing the poor who lived in Rio's rickety hillside favelas had been a problem repeatedly shelved because of its sheer intractability. But Affonso Eduardo Reidy, who had been a member of the MES design team and had built a hostel for homeless people in Rio in 1930, nursed a vision of a comprehensive state-sponsored housing development for the poor. The opportunity to realize this dream came with the Pedregulho development in the São Cristóvão industrial quarter of Rio de Janeiro, the first large-scale public housing project in Brazil. Reidy knew that once the housing was built there was a risk, almost a certainty, that the communal facilities he considered essential to the concept would be cut. He therefore ensured that a primary school, a dispensary, a gymnasium, a shopping centre and various other social facilities were built first. Although the project was started in the late 1940s, the main residential block remained unfinished until the early 1960s. It is long and thin, seven storeys high and raised on pilotis with an open deck at third-floor level serving as a meeting place and playground. What brings it to life, however, is its snake-like plan-form, following that vigorous curve that might have originated in Le Corbusier's 1929 Rio sketch but that by now had become characteristically Brazilian.

In 1955 moving the capital of Brazil from Rio to a new city in the central highlands was already an old idea. US advisors

Palácio da Alvorada, Brasília, Brazil. Oscar Niemeyer, 1958. Designed before the Brasilia master plan but setting the architectural tone of its public buildings.

had surveyed the territory and a design team including Reidy and Roberto Burle Marx had fixed the precise site at the confluence of two rivers. All that was lacking was the political will. Then Juscelino Kubitschek, standing in that year's presidential election, made the building of 'Brasília' the central plank of his political platform. It would be the symbol and measure of his promise to make 'fifty years' progress in five'. Once elected and inaugurated he was anxious not to let the initiative lapse. Almost immediately he commissioned his old friend Oscar Niemeyer to design a new presidential residence for Brasília even though there was as yet no master plan for the city. The Palace of the Dawn (Palácio da Alvorada) is both monumental and Modernist; that is its peculiarity and its strength. It avoids specific reference to the classical tradition while somehow managing to steal some of its dignity and authority.

It is a simple three-storey box with high, ceremonial spaces on the raised ground floor, service functions in a semi-basement, and private accommodation in a kind of attic. This is, of course, a conventional classical arrangement, and there is even a temple-like peristyle of columns on either side. But there the classicism ends, because these columns are more like graphic devices than solid supports, tapering where one would expect them to thicken and merging like viscous liquid at their bases. It turns out, on closer inspection, that these 'columns' do relatively little structural work. They support only the upward-curving roof overhang; the main roof is supported by straight, round columns set just inside the glass external walls.

Niemeyer suggested holding a design competition for the master plan of Brasília, but this was a political ploy rather than a serious attempt to find the optimum solution. The competition was open only to Brazilian architects and planners and Niemeyer himself was a member of the international jury. The announcement in March 1957 that Lúcio Costa had won came as no surprise. His plan consisted of little more than a crude sketch and a vaguely worded report. It was, he said, the beginning rather than the end of a planning process. But this suited Kubitschek because the inevitable complications and delay of a properly considered plan had been bypassed. Work could start immediately and proceed quickly. The city might even be established before the end of his presidency. Costa's sketchy plan has since become an icon of urban planning history. It is essentially a cross, the simplest possible marker of a precise location, but its north–south axis is curved like

a bow to accommodate the form of the land and to nest more neatly into the triangle formed by the river confluence. It is a spontaneous gesture rather than a developed solution, yet it seems purposeful and functionally balanced. For example, the relationship between the city centre and the curved matrix of ordinary streets seems more integrated than in Le Corbusier's plan for Chandigarh, where the government buildings are sparsely grouped in a capitol to the north of, and remote from, the static, rectangular street grid (see page 232).

Niemeyer was the architect of most of Brasília's major government buildings, including the presidential offices, the supreme court and the National Congress building, which are arranged in a triangle at the end of the monumental west–east axis to form the Praça dos Três Poderes (Plaza of the Three Powers). The first two face one another across the axis. Both are variations of the Alvorada theme, with raised ground floors and tapering columns on their long sides. It is as if the Alvorada columns have been split down

---

Master Plan of Brasília. Lúcio Costa, 1957.
Original plan, as presented in the New Capital of Brazil design competition. This is little more than a crude sketch, a cross to mark the city's location.

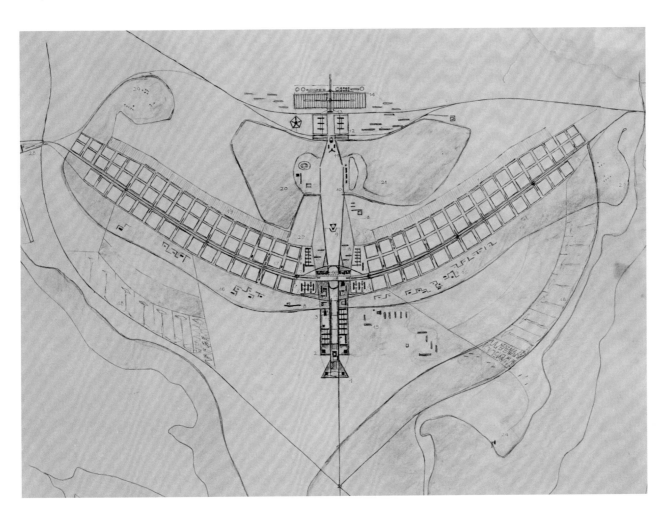

National Congress building, Brasília, Brazil.
Oscar Niemeyer, 1960. A dish, a dome and tower: the
building still symbolizes the country as a political entity.

their centre lines and turned through 90 degrees like gates
opening to admit the masses.

The presidential offices turn their side to the plaza, but the
supreme court is end on, showing off the elegant curves
of its columns. The National Congress building, at the
third point of the triangle, has come to symbolize the whole
city – its optimism, its futurism and its Latin sense of style.
This is the focal point of the whole composition, axial yet
asymmetrical. A long, low base building, rectangular like
its sister palaces, fills in the space between the highway
embankments so that its roof becomes an artificial ground
level. Two white circular forms, a dome and a dish, appear to
rest on this rooftop esplanade. A huge split ramp links both
roof and floor of the base building to the sunken lawn on the
west side. And on the east side, in a reflecting pool, stands
a slender double tower, off centre, closer to the dome than
the dish to balance the composition. It seems appropriate to
describe this complex without reference to its use because
it is as much sculpture as architecture. But the base building
contains a double-height entrance hall flanked by offices and

committee rooms; the dish contains the 648-seat Chamber
of Deputies; the dome contains the 265-seat Senate; and the
27-storey tower contains the offices of the secretariat. These
buildings were designed for specific uses but they were
also designed to symbolize the progress of the nation, and
this latter function was more important. Niemeyer was well
aware that they would soon be too small to accommodate the
growing bureaucracy, but their monumentality could not be
compromised by allowance for expansion. That would have
to take place on other sites.

There are many other exuberant monumental buildings in
Brasília, such as the concrete crown of the cathedral, which
seems to have been assembled from more supple versions
of the Alvorada columns, or the Museum of the City, with its
impossible-looking one-sided cantilever. But the everyday
parts of the city, the curved grid of residential 'superquadras',
are equally inventive and futuristic. Each block, 280 metres
(306 yards) square, was designed as a landscaped, inward-
looking, traffic-free zone with local shops, recreation areas,
a primary school and a population of about 3,000 living
in six-storey apartment blocks raised on pilotis. Larger
amenities such as secondary schools and churches served
groups of four blocks while garages, cinemas and larger
shopping centres were located along the highways and
service roads. It was clearly and consciously an interpretation

(Above) Museum of Contemporary Art at Niterói, Brazil. Oscar Neimeyer, 1996. Even more futuristic and formalistic than Niemeyer's classic early works.

(Right) Interior of the Museum of Contemporary Art, Niterói. Like many modern art museums, the building is more important than its contents.

Communist Party headquarters, Paris, France. Oscar Niemeyer, 1972. The stalactite ceiling recalls Poelzig's 1919 Grosses Schauspielhaus in Berlin.

of CIAM planning doctrine – the city as an inhabited, freely accessible park. Gradually, however, the traditional street form reasserted itself. Shops that were meant to face the landscaped interiors were turned round to face the service roads. The superquadras were meant to allow for a degree of social 'gradation' without making sharp distinctions between classes. In practice, however, their apartments were far out of reach of the poorest people, including the workers who built the city. The great arc of the Corbusian city became in effect an exclusive civil-service quarter.

As a construction project, Brasília was an astonishing success, fulfilling President Kubitschek's dream that it might be inaugurated before the end of his term of office. The building of a new capital city in just four years sent a clear message abroad that a new Brazil had arrived on the world stage. Architectural critics were at first intrigued by Niemeyer's new, confident Modernism but quickly changed their minds as a different Brutalist version of Corbusian doctrine gained influence and Brasília's monuments began to look shallow and formalist. Niemeyer carried on regardless, however, designing many more sculptural, futuristic monuments such as the Communist Party headquarters in Paris, completed in 1972, and the flying-saucer-like Museum of Contemporary Art at Niterói in Rio de Janeiro, completed in 1996. He died in 2012 at the age of 104.

Lina Bo Bardi

We can see something of that emerging Brutalist tendency in the work of Lina Bo Bardi, an Italian designer, architect and journalist who emigrated to Brazil in 1946. Her first Brazilian building was a house for herself and her husband in what was then the remnants of the original rainforest surrounding São Paulo but is now a wealthy suburb. Its large, open living room, glass walled on three sides, looks out over the tamed jungle from the brow of a hill. Sandwiched between beamless concrete slabs and lifted up on pilotis, it might be a version of Le Corbusier's Maison Dom-ino project except that the roof slopes gently. Bedrooms and servants' rooms are built on the solid summit of the hill at the back. Completed in 1951, the house is delicate rather than Brutalist. However, in the building for which she is best known, the São Paulo Museum of Art, the Brutalist influence is clear. Built between 1960 and 1969, it takes the form of a huge two-storey inhabited bridge, apparently suspended from a pair of longitudinal portal frames of rough, board-marked concrete. It bridges over nothing other than an open plaza, actually the

Lina Bo Bardi House, São Paulo, Brazil. Lina Bo Bardi, 1951. A slice of space sandwiched between thin concrete slabs and raised on pilotis.

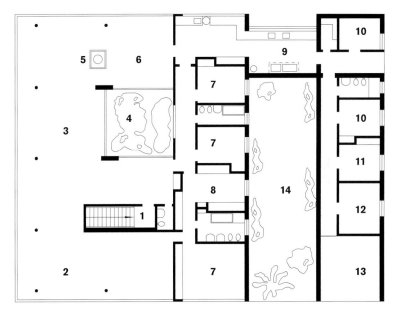

First floor plan

1. Entrance
2. Library
3. Living room
4. Courtyard
5. Fireplace
6. Dining room
7. Bedroom
8. Clothes cupboard
9. Kitchen
10. Staff bedroom
11. Staff living room
12. Wardrobe
13. Veranda
14. Patio

(Above) São Paulo Museum of Art, Brazil. Lina Bo Bardi, 1960–69. Evidently a bridge, but structurally not quite what it seems.

(Below) Museum of Art interior with Lina Bo Bardi glass easels. The inaugural exhibition, designed by Bo Bardi to be non-hierarchical.

roof of an underground civic hall but conceived as a public square, a stage for the everyday social drama of the city. In fact the structural principle of the building is not as simple as it seems.

The long exposed beams support only themselves and the relatively light load of the pleated concrete roof. Most of the work is done by a second pair of beams, lower down inside the building, which supports the two floors, the lower one suspended by rows of closely spaced thin steel rods. Only the upper storey is therefore free of obstruction. When the building was inaugurated, Bo Bardi made full use of this open floor with an exhibition of Brazilian paintings mounted separately on sheets of frameless glass and arranged in straight rows facing the entrance. It was an inspired piece of exhibition design meant to convey a political message: that paintings, like people, were individuals of equal standing to be judged on their merits, not on their position in a hierarchy.

The full force of Bo Bardi's social and architectural vision is felt in her last major project, the SESC Pompéia leisure centre in São Paulo, completed in 1982. SESC (Social Service of Commerce) was, and is, a philanthropic organization originally set up by business interests to prevent social unrest by the provision of community facilities. In 1971 it acquired a large disused refrigerator

SESC Pompéia leisure centre, São Paulo, Brazil. Lina Bo Bardi, 1982. Ball-game courts are stacked in a square block with a separate service tower.

factory on the north-west side of the city, intending to demolish it and build a leisure centre. When the project proved to be too expensive, Bo Bardi was called in to advise. She proposed keeping the old brick-and-concrete factory sheds and converting them to social use. A library, a restaurant, exhibition spaces and a theatre were created by the insertion of simple structures such as fixed furniture, concrete reading galleries, bleacher seating and an internal reflecting pool.

The original access road between the sheds became a busy pedestrian street. Sport was the other major social activity to be accommodated, but a protected stream running through the southern part of the site left very little open space. Bo Bardi's solution was bold and simple: to stack up four ball-game courts in a square tower of rough concrete with a swimming pool on the ground floor. Lifts, stairs, changing rooms, offices, medical facilities and the like occupy a

separate 11-storey tower on the other side of the stream, now covered by a boardwalk. The two towers are linked by angled concrete bridges at the levels of the four courts. A slim, cylindrical water tower completes the group, strengthening the impression that these are industrial structures of some kind. It is as if Bo Bardi was so pleased with the idea of converting the factory sheds that she created more half-ruined structures to convert. Openings for ventilation and day lighting (one can hardly call them 'windows') are rough-edged holes that might have been made by missiles or a wrecking ball, though inside they can be screened by rectangular sliding wooden grilles. This is what Bo Bardi called '*arquitetura pobre*' or 'poor architecture'. It has some similarities with Brutalism, but its social message is quite different. Where Brutalism was essentially elitist, ignoring the taste and culture of the ordinary people, *arquitetura pobre* gave the ordinary people a dignity beyond the shallow flattery of growing consumerism.

Stylistic labels are never very precise. Once issued, they lead lives of their own, ranging far beyond their issuer's imaginings, getting stuck to buildings that don't really deserve them. The label 'Brutalist', not always meant pejoratively, is these days applied to almost any big concrete building of the 1960s and 1970s, anywhere in the world. Its main function is to mark the boundary between the self-confident but generally unpopular form of Modernism initiated by Le Corbusier's Unité d'Habitation at Marseille (see page 224), and the less demanding kind represented by architects like Edward Durrell Stone and Minoru Yamasaki (see Chapter 15). However, it is possible – and useful – to define 'Brutalism' rather more precisely and to trace its origins in 1950s Britain. The critic and historian Reyner Banham nurtured it and wrote a book about it, *The New Brutalism*, in 1966, but it was his young friends and colleagues, the architects Alison and Peter Smithson, who provided its first representative example, a secondary school at Hunstanton in Norfolk, completed in 1954. Surprisingly, the building is only two storeys high,

rather formal and symmetrical in its plan, and made of steel and brick, not concrete. It owes a debt not to Le Corbusier but to Mies van der Rohe, specifically his buildings on the IIT campus in Chicago (see page 192).

New Brutalism

Such a building as Hunstanton would not now be called Brutalist. Evidently the term meant something different in 1954. It was first coined as 'New Brutalist' by Hans Asplund (son of Gunnar) in 1950 to describe, jokingly, the Villa Göth in Uppsala by Bengt Edman and Lennart Holm – a two-storey, flat-roofed brick box with a radically simplified plan. Asplund subsequently used the phrase in conversation with a group of English architects visiting Sweden, who took it home to England and incorporated it in the shorthand of their office banter. It soon spread like a meme among progressive young English architects, not as a joke but as a stylistic label with positive connotations.[1] The Smithsons were happy to have it applied to their Miesian school for two reasons:

Secondary school at Hunstanton, Norfolk, UK. Alison and Peter Smithson, 1954. The rule was to leave structure and services exposed rather than to conceal or bury them.

because it was likely to provoke controversy and therefore enhance their reputation, and because it clearly distinguished their architecture from the gentle, decorative Modernism that prevailed in England at that time. No doubt they also liked the idea that their very first major building might go down in history as the initiator of a whole new style.

But as usual in Modernist debate, the word 'style' was problematic. New Brutalism, said the Smithsons, was 'an ethic, not an aesthetic'. The whole point of it was that buildings should be direct functional and material adaptations of the human habitat. What they looked like was irrelevant. It was an old idea that went back to nineteenth-century arguments about the superiority of Gothic over classical architecture and, more recently, to the formalism-versus-functionalism debates among 1930s Modernists, and it was riddled with contradictions. Hunstanton School was more than just a practical arrangement of materials and spaces; as much as any Renaissance church or palace, it was a work of art. The Smithsons themselves talked about the importance of its 'purely formal' qualities. They insisted, for example, on a heavy steel frame even though it meant delaying completion for several months because of a steel shortage caused by the Korean War. Other, more practical, architects of the time, such as those developing prefabrication methods for schools in the county of Hertfordshire, used lightweight steel components to get round the problem. For the Smithsons it had to be Miesian steel for aesthetic, not ethical reasons, and the same applied to the internal brickwork, the bare soffits of the precast concrete floors, the exposed plumbing and the standard sectional water tank on its freestanding steel-framed 'campanile'.

Nevertheless, historians, led by Reyner Banham, have chosen Hunstanton School as the marker of a change of direction in

British architecture, and with some justice. What preceded and provoked New Brutalism was a style inspired by Swedish housing estates like those designed by Sven Backström and Leif Reinius. These estates, though conceived in Modernist terms, were largely traditional in form and material. At the Gröndal estate of 1946 in Stockholm, for example, four-storey apartment blocks, called 'star houses' because of their Y-shaped plans, were rendered and coloured, with small, square windows and tile-covered, shallow-pitched roofs. They could stand alone as point blocks or be linked together, necklace-like, around landscaped parks, as they were at the later Rosta estate in the industrial town of Örebro. Projects like this appeared frequently in the pages of the *Architectural Review* and in books such as *Sweden Builds* by G. E. Kidder Smith, published in 1950. To the public-sector architects of the new British welfare state, especially those working for London County Council (LCC), they represented a new kind of Modernism, in tune with the socialist post-war spirit – reasonable, undogmatic and willing to compromise with public taste. 'New Empiricism' was the *Architectural Review*'s name for it, but 'Contemporary' was the term most people used.

The showcase of the style was the 1951 Festival of Britain, a nationwide event but focussed on a South Bank site in the centre of London. The original intention had been to celebrate the centenary of the Great Exhibition but the Festival's real purpose was to lighten the gloom of post-war economic austerity. It was to be, in the words of its director, 'a tonic to the nation'. Architecturally it was relatively unadventurous, though its one permanent building, the Royal Festival Hall, was to become, and still is, a much-loved symbol of the nation's middlebrow culture. The fact that it was designed by a team of LCC architects, including Robert Matthew, Leslie Martin and Peter Moro, rather than an

Royal Festival Hall, London, UK. Robert Matthew, Leslie Martin and Peter Moro, 1951. Showcase of the 'New Empiricist', or simply 'Contemporary' style.

individual, was in tune with the prevailing collaborative and anti-heroic ethos. Hugh Casson held overall responsibility for the architecture of the rest of the exhibition, co-ordinating the work of then little-known architects such as Maxwell Fry and Jane Drew, Philip Powell and Hidalgo Moya, Wells Coates and H. T. Cadbury-Brown. Their architecture was Modernist, but light hearted, colourful, almost pretty. To the eyes of Banham and the Smithsons it was utterly feeble, and a betrayal of the movement's revolutionary spirit. A few miles downstream in Poplar, a demonstration housing estate, called the Lansbury Estate after a Labour Party leader of the 1930s, was built for the Festival under the direction of Frederick Gibberd. From the Smithsons' point of view, this was even worse – fragmented, picturesque, mostly traditional and Swedish influenced.

Brutalism, then, defined itself as the tough, principled alternative to Contemporary. But what its principles were exactly is hard to pin down. At an early point in its development it was noticed that the French for raw concrete was *béton brut*, and since this was the term that Le Corbusier himself used to describe the concrete of the Unité d'Habitation (see page 224), rough concrete, and the Unité, could be claimed for the Brutalist camp. Indeed the Unité is the first building to be given comprehensive illustrative treatment in Banham's book. But there is no *béton brut* at Hunstanton, which is stylistically remote from the Unité, so right from the start there was uncertainty as to what Brutalist architecture actually looked like. The Smithsons' artistic allegiances were clear enough, however. They and Banham were members of the Independent Group, which met regularly at the Institute of Contemporary Arts in London and included artists such as the painter Richard Hamilton, the sculptor Eduardo Paolozzi and the photographer Nigel Henderson. In exhibitions such as 'Parallel of Life and Art' of 1953, and 'This Is Tomorrow' of 1956, the group tried to reconnect art with the realities of modern life, including American consumer culture. In a brief manifesto written in 1954 the Smithsons mentioned Japanese traditional architecture, which had been an inspiration to Modernists since Frank Lloyd Wright's Prairie houses. The point was that Brutalism, like Japanese architecture, was 'the direct result of a way of life'. Well, one might possibly trace an indirect connection between the wood frame of the Katsura Palace and the steel frame of Hunstanton, but in the next paragraph the latest Cadillac convertible, its bodywork fantastically finned but mostly functionless, is also mentioned with approval.[2] It begins to seem that the Smithsons were magpies who indiscriminately stole appealing ideas and images with which to decorate their ideological nest. The only unifying factor, as Banham remarked, was a certain 'bloody mindedness', an arrogant confidence that followed its own desires and saw no reason to take account of the opinions of non-architects.

Lansbury Estate, London, UK. Frederick Gibberd, 1951. Corbusian pilotis combined with patterned English brickwork. Balfron Tower can be seen at the far right.

The Smithsons' best-known built works are actually rather varied in character. The Miesian manner of Hunstanton was never repeated. In 1959 they began designing a new building for *The Economist* magazine in the smart St James's district of London. It is cleverly planned, sensitive to its historic surroundings and anything but Brutalist. Four apparently freestanding buildings share an inhabited plinth that covers most of the roughly square, three-way-facing site, creating a raised artificial ground level. One of the four is an elegant eighteenth-century house occupied by a gentlemen's club. Next to this, on the street corner, a commercial building containing shops and a bank matches the scale of the old buildings on St James's Street. The other two corners of the site are each occupied by a tower, one 16 storeys high containing offices for *The Economist*, the other an 11-storey block of flats. This ensemble might almost have been composed for purely pictorial effect. The three new buildings are all basically square on plan with chamfered corners and clad in the same combination of glass and Portland stone with pressed metal flashings to control weathering. But there are subtle variations. The footprint of the residential tower is half that of the office tower, so the spacing of the stone-clad mullions is also halved, creating an adult-and-child effect. Even the old club building has been admitted to the family by being provided with a new chamfered bay window. Neither the plans nor the elevations of these buildings show much sign of responding to internal functional pressures and there is not a square inch of *béton brut* to be seen. They stand like well-dressed attenders at some formal ceremony, doing their very best not to upset their more elderly neighbours. It is all very far from the bloody-mindedness of Smithsonian Brutalist rhetoric.

Economist Building, London, UK.
Alison and Peter Smithson, 1964.
A central London gathering of office and residential buildings that is more polite than brutal.

Robin Hood Gardens

This housing estate in east London, completed in 1972, occupies a very different site, among miscellaneous post-war public-sector housing projects and next to an urban motorway. The Smithsons' design combined 20 years of theorizing and project-making in mass housing, beginning with their entry for the 1952 competition for Golden Lane, also in east London, which proposed a configuration of 11-storey linear blocks linked by continuous open walkways or 'streets in the sky' at every third level. These blocks were conceived as components of a larger system that would spread like a net all over the city. A photomontage shows a fragment of just such a net under construction in the blitzed city of Coventry, dwarfing the old medieval centre and the remains of its cathedral. The Golden Lane project is well known to architectural history, though it did not win a prize (the competition was won by Chamberlin, Powell and Bon with a more conventional Modernist scheme) and was not particularly original. The Narkomfin Building in Moscow of 1929 (see page 142) used a similar system of circulation and may have been brought to the Smithsons' attention by the emigré Russian architect Berthold Lubetkin.

Robin Hood Gardens is a clearly a descendant of Golden Lane. Two long, kinked blocks, seven and ten storeys high, stand either side of a grass-covered mound. Apartments vary in size but most are two storeys high, with entrances at either the upper or lower level from open-access decks on every third floor. Living rooms face onto the

noisy surrounding roads while bedrooms overlook the quiet, sheltered green space. Floor areas conform to the minimum standards of the time, which now seem generous, and there are garages tucked under the buildings at lower-ground level. It all sounds perfect; the problem is its scale and forbidding greyness, which a rather busy pattern of precast concrete mullions does nothing to soften. There was anti-social behaviour and vandalism among the residents right from the start, which of course was not necessarily the fault of the architecture, but the architects got the blame anyway and it isn't hard to understand why. The Smithsons had apparently thought carefully about the social use of the building – how, for example, the open decks would encourage neighbourliness and the little alcoves beside each front door would 'offer themselves naturally for potted plants, flower boxes etc – the normal paraphernalia of domestic outside show'.[3] But they were blind to the bigger picture and the certainty that these vast brutal, or Brutalist, walls of grey concrete would be hated by their working-class tenants. There were attempts to improve the situation by controlling access to the decks and prettifying the communal areas, but in March 2012, despite attempts to get the estate listed as a historic building, the local authority decided to demolish it.

Robin Hood Gardens, London, UK. Alison and Peter Smithson, 1972. Thoughtful details were lost in the general oppressiveness of the vast grey walls.

Park Hill

In architectural terms, Robin Hood Gardens was out of date before it was completed. The biggest and best example of the 'streets in the sky' idea had been built ten years earlier at Park Hill in Sheffield, designed by Jack Lynn and Ivor Smith. The Smithsons' Golden Lane project is sometimes cited as a key influence on Park Hill, but in fact Lynn and Smith had been working on the idea since 1945 and had entered the competition with a deck-access design of their own. Built on sloping land near the centre of the city, replacing a notorious slum known locally as Little Chicago, Park Hill slots 1,000 apartments into what is in effect a single building. From most angles it looks like a castle or a citadel, a simile that was even more apt before the slightly later Hyde Park estate, towering over it higher up the hill, was demolished. Castles built to terrify become picturesque in more peaceful times, an effect that perhaps has something to do with turreted and crenellated skylines.

There are no such poetic concessions at Park Hill, the roofline of which is level across the whole site. Closer

inspection reveals that the monolithic impression is false; the building is in fact a kind of branching train of tall, narrow slabs, which vary from four to 13 storeys to take up the slope of the land. The continuous sky-streets, famously 'wide enough for a milk float', occur at every third level, all but the highest eventually meeting the slope of the ground. The estate suffered its share of social problems but unlike Robin Hood Gardens was saved from demolition and completely renovated in 2011 by architects Hawkins\Brown working for developers Urban Splash. Only the exposed concrete frame was preserved, its brick in-fill replaced by coloured aluminium panels and enlarged windows. The Brutalist label no longer seems entirely appropriate. The renovation was publicly subsidized but two-thirds of the apartments were offered for private sale.

Park Hill, Sheffield, UK. Jack Lynn and Ivor Smith, 1961.
The roofline is level across the whole site and most of the 'streets in the sky' meet the ground at some point.

Ernö Goldfinger

'Streets in the sky' did not necessarily imply a medium-rise, linked-slab format. Trellick Tower, in west London, designed by Ernö Goldfinger and completed in 1972, is more like a singular monument than a fragment of a network. The slab has grown tall – 31 storeys – but the circulation system is similar: walkways (now enclosed) at every third level serving mostly two-storey dwellings. In most high-rise residential blocks, lifts, escape stairs and vertical service ducts are accommodated in a central core, invisible from the outside. At Trellick Tower the 'core' has escaped its confinement to stand alone to one side, a thin concrete shaft linked by bridges to the walkways in the main block. Separating the lifts from the dwellings in this way might have been justified on grounds of acoustic insulation, but its real purpose was formal and symbolic. The building looks like some kind of industrial processing plant. It is the very opposite of 'domestic' and its early tenants hated it but its generously sized apartments were well planned and once a 'concierge'

Trellick Tower, London, UK. Ernö Goldfinger, 1972. The articulated service tower might appear to be part of some industrial processing plant.

had been installed to supervise the entrance it became a desirable address, especially among artists and architects. It is not hard to trace the origins of this expressive concrete aesthetic. Goldfinger, originally from Hungary, had studied in Paris in the 1920s with that pioneer of architectural concrete, Auguste Perret (see Chapter 4). Never a 'white box' Modernist, his main preoccupations were exposed structure, honestly expressed materials and fine proportions. Trellick Tower and its slightly older brother Balfron Tower in east London, not far from Robin Hood Gardens, may be hard to live with, but as pure sculpture they are rather beautiful, perhaps owing something to the Futurist visions of Antonio Sant'Elia (see Chapter 4).

Board-marked concrete

Concrete was the typical material of Brutalism. In the late 1960s and early 1970s, almost all of Britain's important works of public or commercial architecture made at least some passing reference to the *béton brut* of Le Corbusier's Unité d'Habitation. In a few cases, board-marked concrete was almost the only visible material. The cultural complex completed in 1968 on London's South Bank is a good example. Two concert halls and an art gallery, linked to the earlier Royal Festival Hall by a raised walkway, were moulded and shaped in rough concrete then left naked to defend themselves against onslaughts from conservative critics and the general public. The complex was designed by a team in the Greater London Council architects' department including Warren Chalk and Ron Herron, who later became members of the Archigram group (see Chapter 26). As late as 1976 Denys Lasdun was still using board-marked concrete, inside and out, for the National Theatre, on the other side of Waterloo Bridge where it commanded a bend in the river. The building was generally well received by architects who especially admired its stratified terraces and free-flowing foyers, but the Prince of Wales gave voice to public opinion when he likened its bare concrete fly-towers to a nuclear power station. That board-marked concrete should have been accepted as a suitable face for these essentially communicative and celebratory functions is some measure of Brutalism's prestige at the time and of public clients' willingness to accept the advice of their architects. Attempts have since been made to cheer these buildings up with neon sculpture, electronic sky signs and ordinary paint, but without much success.

(Opposite, top) Hayward Gallery and Queen Elizabeth Hall, London, UK. GLC Architects Department, 1968. Members of the South Bank design team later joined the Archigram group.

(Opposite, below) National Theatre, London, UK. Denys Lasdun, 1977. Lasdun's masterpiece is sternly untheatrical but admired for its terraces and foyers.

American 'Brutalism'

It was probably in the United States that the term 'Brutalist' began to be applied to almost any big and, in the eyes of the general public, ugly concrete building of the 1960s. The Art and Architecture Building at Yale University in New Haven, Connecticut, designed by Paul Rudolph and completed in 1963, is a good example – a burly, confident building made of rough concrete, inside and out. 'Brutalist' sounds about right, but the label covers up more than it reveals. For example, one might expect a Brutalist building to be brutally direct in the relationship between its form and its function. This is a building to accommodate art and architecture students. Surely all they need is some flexible, well-lit studios and drafting rooms. Yet what is provided is a complicated collection of Elementarist, interpenetrating forms and spaces nested into a seven-storey-high structure with no fewer than 36 floor levels. It is like a less strictly ordered version of Frank Lloyd Wright's Larkin Building (see page 69). And that rough concrete is not as brutal as one might suppose. Almost all of it has been cast in multiply grooved formwork then bush-hammered to expose the aggregate, creating a texture that, from a distance, is rather delicate, like the hatched shadows in a lithograph. Rudolph was a brilliant draughtsman who tried to convey in drawings the sensual as well as the abstract qualities of his buildings. Ridge-hacked concrete was his way of transferring this urge to the building itself, making it subtly responsive to the play of light and shade. As a postgraduate student at Harvard he had studied

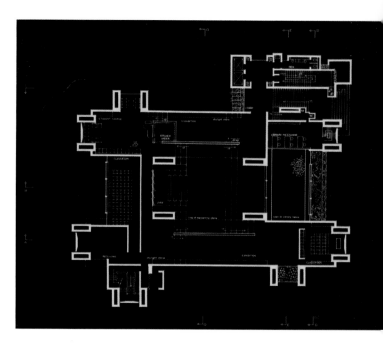

under Walter Gropius, who encouraged a collaborative and scientific approach to design. The Art and Architecture Building represents Rudolph's resistance, as an individual artist, to Gropius's worthy scientism. The 'Brutalist' label begins to look less appropriate.

Not long after its completion the functional shortcomings of the A&A Building, as it was known, became clear. Painting

(Above and left) **Art and Architecture Building, Yale University, New Haven, Connecticut, USA. Paul Rudolph, 1963.** A wilfully complex, many-levelled building where one might have expected open, flexible spaces.

and sculpture students complained about cramped studios, the atrium-like open spaces designed for the architecture students were hard to work in, and the multi-level layout was totally inflexible. Modifications were made that ruined the original spatial concept and in 1969 there was a fire said to have been started by a frustrated student. Meanwhile, architectural opinion was turning against it as the new empire of Postmodernism (see Chapter 24) gained ascendancy. Eventually, however, the wheel of taste turned again and a new generation recognized the building's artistic and symbolic value. In 2008 it was completely renovated and renamed Rudolph Hall.

Brick

Not all Brutalism was concrete. There was an equally uncompromising brick version and once again Le Corbusier was the main source of inspiration – not the Unité this time but the Maisons Jaoul (see page 226). James Stirling and James Gowan's flats at Ham Common are a good example (see page 228). The British university building boom of the 1960s provided ideal conditions for the flourishing of progressive architecture – cultured clients, greenfield sites and government money to spend – and in many cases a species of brick Brutalism was the built result. At the University of Sussex, by Sir Basil Spence's practice, dozens of three-storey Jaoul Houses seem to have been gathered together around loosely defined quadrangles. The effect is tamely picturesque rather than truly Brutalist, for the

brickwork is smooth and regular and the concrete 'Catalan' vaults, though board marked in the approved manner on their exposed faces, are actually precision precast units. This is a Brutalism of style rather than principle. At Churchill College, Cambridge, by Richard Sheppard, Robson and Partners, concrete vaults are dispensed with altogether apart from three thin shell vaults over the central dining hall. In the linked residential courts, a Jaoul-like combination of brown brick walls and board-marked concrete floors is enlivened by recessed balconies and teak-framed bay windows. Its Brutalist allegiance is clear enough but, like Sussex, it is tame and civilized.

For full-strength Brutalist brickwork we must turn to the Swedish veteran Sigurd Lewerentz, whom we last encountered in 1925 designing the classical Resurrection Chapel at the Woodland Cemetery in Stockholm (see page 178). In the late 1950s Lewerentz designed the church of St Mark at Björkhagen in Stockholm. It was built of the roughest, coarsest brickwork imaginable, with deliberately messy mortar joints almost as thick as the bricks themselves. Reyner Banham included it in his book *The New Brutalism* but was aware that this was a cheeky presumption. Lewerentz, who had trained with Östberg and Tengbom before the First World War and was about the same age as Le Corbusier, could hardly be bracketed with the 'dissident young architects' like the Smithsons, yet his Björkhagen church was more Brutalist than anything they ever produced.

Falmer House, University of Sussex, Brighton, UK. Sir Basil Spence, 1962. The language of Le Corbusier's Maisons Jaoul applied to a large institutional building.

A few years later, in St Peter's Church, Klippan, his last major work, Lewerentz went even further, combining wild, free brickwork with a rusty steel frame to create a dark sacred cave. Irregular, shallow brick vaults are supported on a single T-shaped steel column that stands like a cross just off centre of the perfectly square nave. Daylight creeps in through plain rectangular openings sealed by unframed single sheets of glass fixed to the outer face of the wall. The brick floor slopes down to the brick altar 'to help the doubtful to communion', in Lewerentz's words. It is said that he made few drawings, communicating construction details by word of mouth on daily site visits. Of all the buildings of the 1960s and 1970s to which the label Brutalist might be attached, this is the purest, the least stylistic, perhaps the only true illustration of the 'ethic, not aesthetic' principle.

Brick Brutalism also made its mark in the United States, for example in Paul Rudolph's married students' housing at Yale of 1962, and here another aspect of the style emerges. The site slopes quite gently but Rudolph made it appear steeper by building three storeys at the top, two storeys lower down and a single storey at the bottom. Blocks are stepped and staggered horizontally too, creating a complex cluster of brick boxes interspersed with courtyards, terraces and footpaths. The materials and details are Brutalist and the apartments themselves are standardized, but the general fragmented form is human scaled and inviting. Versions of this proliferating, cellular manner of composition appeared all over Europe and America in the 1960s, especially on sloping sites.

The Siedlung Halen at Berne in Switzerland, designed by Atelier 5 and completed in 1961, is a classic of the type, though here the rows of narrow, three-storey houses mostly remain in line as they step down the slope. The picturesque, hill-village effect is due mainly to a compacted site plan, strict control of vehicles and the absence of any left-over open space apart from a central public square complete with campanile in the shape of a tall chimney. Yet again Le Corbusier is the chief source of inspiration, this time through an unbuilt project of 1949 known as Roq et Rob for a hillside at Roquebrune-Cap-Martin on the Côte d'Azur.

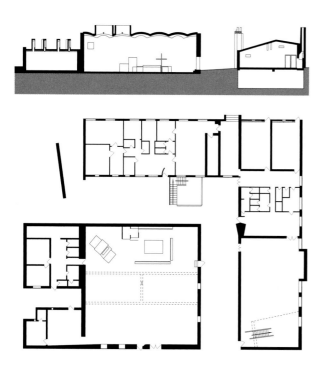

Section and plan   0   5   10m
                        15   30 ft

St Peter's Church, Klippan, Sweden. Sigurd Lewerentz, 1966. Lewerentz's rough brickwork and rusty steel was more Brutalist than anything the Smithsons ever imagined.

If no hill happened to be available, then cubic forms could be piled up to make artificial hills, like the well-ordered 'ziggurats' of Denys Lasdun's student accommodation at the University of East Anglia in Norwich, completed in 1968, or the free-form brick and concrete aggregation that is Darbourne and Darke's roughly contemporary Lillington Gardens development in Pimlico, London. The epitome of the style, however, must be Moshe Safdie's Habitat 67 housing complex in Montreal, built for Expo 67, in which ideas about the 'volumetric' (box-like) prefabrication of standard concrete housing units combined with the fashion

for proliferating clusters to create what now, since the freight-carrying revolution, looks more like a stack of shipping containers than a permanent building.

'Structuralism'

Where did this 'crumbly' aesthetic originate? When the Smithsons attended the ninth CIAM conference at Aix-en-Provence in 1953 they began to forge links with like-minded architects elsewhere in Europe who wished to find a way round the ideological impasse of the Athens Charter (see page 107). Gradually they undermined the CIAM organization

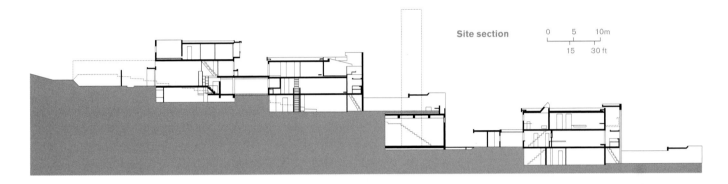

Site section

0   5   10m
15   30 ft

(Above) Siedlung Halen, Berne, Switzerland. Atelier 5, 1961.

(Left) Married students' housing, Yale University, New Haven, Connecticut, USA. Paul Rudolph, 1962. Domestic Brutalism: a cluster of brick and concrete boxes define courtyards and terraces.

until it was finally abandoned in 1959 and replaced by a younger, more informal, more exclusive group known as Team X ('Team Ten'). Among its members were the Italian Giancarlo De Carlo, the American Shadrach Woods and the Dutchman Aldo van Eyck. Brutalism was a continuing Team X theme, but van Eyck introduced another -ism into the discussion, 'Structuralism', the built manifesto of which was an orphanage completed in 1960 on the south side of Amsterdam.

The site is completely flat and the building mainly single storey; nevertheless, the square grid that governs its plan contains the seeds of all those crumbly housing schemes. It is a building full of contradictions. Its sprawling plan responds freely to functional requirements, with many an open courtyard and perimeter set-back, but the modules of which it is composed are uniform and symmetrical: each a 3.6-metre (12-foot) square, roofed by a single shallow dome. Here and there modules combine to form nine-square groups with larger domes, and some of these rise to two storeys, but always the 3.6-metre grid remains firmly in control. The layout is unified by its regularity, but also divided into

separate 'houses' in which the orphans, segregated by age group, lived as quasi-families. Free but controlled; unified but divided – one can appreciate the subtleties of the design and yet, despite playful details like shallow pools, built-in seats and circular play pits, this seems a strangely cold architecture for such an essentially homely institution.

The biggest contradiction, however, lies in that designation 'Structuralist'. Van Eyck was a keen student of anthropology and was especially interested in the part that architecture played in the symbolic life of so-called primitive peoples – the way, for example, the physical layout of a village might reflect its social structure. The term Structuralism, borrowed from linguistics, was at that time being applied to the theories of Claude Lévi-Strauss, who believed that in all cultures at all times, language and art conformed to abstract structures of 'difference'. To apply the term to architecture was bound

Halls of residence, University of East Anglia, Norwich, UK. Denys Lasdun, 1968. If the site does not slope then it is sometimes necessary to create artificial slopes.

Habitat 67 housing, Montreal, Canada. Moshe Safdie, 1967. The ultimate 'proliferating' forms, suggesting exciting urban possibilities.

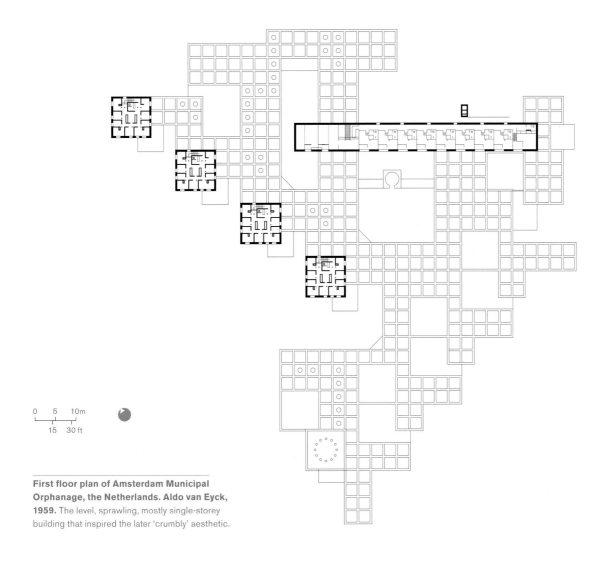

0 5 10m
15 30 ft

First floor plan of Amsterdam Municipal Orphanage, the Netherlands. Aldo van Eyck, 1959. The level, sprawling, mostly single-storey building that inspired the later 'crumbly' aesthetic.

to cause confusion. Most architects assumed that it had something to do with real, physical structure – columns, beams and domes – when it was actually meant to apply to less tangible relationships between social conventions and spatial use. (A similar confusion was to arise 20 years later over the term 'deconstruction'.) But even setting this confusion aside, it is hard to see how an anthropological approach gave rise to such a mechanistic design. It seems to have more to do with the myth of mass production than the social realities of childhood and family. In the early 1960s, the care of orphans in large institutions was being replaced by foster-parenting in real families. The building was soon abandoned and fell into disrepair until rescued by architects and converted into offices for the Berlage Institute.

This did nothing to diminish architects' interest in square grids, however. In 1967 van Eyck's follower, Herman Hertzberger, applied a similar method to the design of an office block for the insurance company Centraal Beheer in the Dutch town of Apeldoorn. Here the grid is more complicated – a multi-storey 'tartan' woven from square platforms, each sized to accommodate four workstations, surrounded by continuous top-lit circulation paths. Stacked up to a maximum of four storeys, the platforms are mostly open sided, with cantilevered corners and narrow bridges in between, creating an internal landscape like a three-dimensional maze. It is flexible on the small scale of the platforms, but solid and immutable in its totality, like a city perhaps, but a city with a single, obsessive spatial theme.

Centraal Beheer office block, Apeldoorn, the Netherlands. Herman Hertzberger, 1967. A 'tartan' grid, four storeys high, creating a three-dimensional maze.

Megastructure

Reyner Banham did not coin the term 'megastructure' – credit for that should probably go to Fumihiko Maki (see page 368) – but it was Banham's 1976 book *Megastructure: Urban Futures of the Recent Past* that clarified the concept, marshalled the illustrative examples and ultimately consigned it to its historical niche. In his introduction, Banham dutifully quotes other people's definitions, including Maki's, but then, almost inadvertently, provides a better one of his own in an elegantly concise phrase: 'a permanent and dominating frame containing subordinate and transient accommodations'. The very first megastructure, he says, was Le Corbusier's 1930 Plan Obus proposal for Algiers, which envisaged a serpentine multi-storey support system on which individual families could build houses in the architectural style of their choice. Note that this was an unrealized project, as were more obvious examples from the 1960s such as Archigram's Plug-in City (see page 344) and the 'Metabolist' visions of Kenzo Tange and his followers (see Chapter 27). Actual buildings that fit the definition are hard to find except in international expositions – Moshe Safdie's Habitat 67 in Montreal, for example, or Tange's 1970 Festival Plaza at Osaka.

But the megastructure was an aesthetic as much as a technical idea and it is possible to trace its influence in many buildings of the 1960s and 1970s that don't strictly conform to the definition. For example the raised pedestrian decks that appeared in parts of London – on the South Bank, in the Barbican development and along the street known as London Wall – were fragments of a future multi-level city in which accommodation and infrastructure would combine in new ways. Buildings standing on the ground with streets in between seemed hopelessly old fashioned. Schemes for other London districts such as Covent Garden and Fitzrovia envisaged a similar complete rethink but were prevented from realization by public outcry. Banham is prepared to call Denys Lasdun's student housing at the University of East Anglia a megastructure (see page 287), not because its dwellings are 'subordinate and transient' (they are not) but because of its proliferating ziggurat form. Patrick Hodgkinson's Brunswick Centre in Bloomsbury, London, designed in 1962, is included for the same reason. Its concrete service towers and stepped banks of flats were surely derived from Antonio Sant'Elia's Città Nuova (see page 59), a source of megastructural imagery that Banham's

first book, *Theory and Design in the First Machine Age*, helped to popularize.

Surprisingly, Banham does not mention either Aldo van Eyck's Amsterdam orphanage (see page 288) or Herman Hertzberger's Centraal Beheer offices at Apeldoorn (see page 290), perhaps because he wished to avoid border disputes with other 'isms' such as Brutalism (in which he held a personal interest) and Structuralism. These buildings nevertheless display a similar obsession with the infinitely extendable, cellular structure, whether as ground-hugging mat or labyrinthine cluster. Banham's final example, the Centre Pompidou, was still under construction at the time, yet he was in no doubt that he was writing the history of an architectural idea that had come to an end.

Why did the megastructure die? Because there was a flaw at the heart of the concept. In Banham's words: 'The logical solution to the problem was to leave so much liberty for the self-housing and self-determining intentions of the inhabitants that they had the liberty also to destroy the megastructure itself.' And once the concept had fallen, the formal vision necessarily fell with it.

Book cover for Reyner Banham's *Megastructure*.
Megastructures immediately became history upon the publication of Banham's book.

LOUIS KAHN – MONUMENTAL MODERNISM 1953–1982

We have seen how the Beaux-Arts tradition in American architecture continued to make its presence felt in the post-war years. Public buildings such as Lincoln Center in New York and Kennedy Center in Washington D. C. demanded a monumentality that European functionalism could not provide. Traditional classicism was in decline but modern or even Modernist forms were subjected to a classical discipline that made them acceptable to a prevailing conservatism in civic life. Progressive architectural culture found the results uninspiring. But there was one architect who gave fresh thought to the Beaux-Arts tradition in which he was thoroughly trained, and created a vigorous new style that was both monumental and functional, both traditional and modern. Born in modern-day Estonia, he was brought to the United States at the age of five and spent his childhood in a poor district of Philadelphia. But his family was cultured and his aptitude both as a visual artist and as a musician

Louis Kahn. Born in Kuressaare, Estonia, 1901. Died in New York City, USA, 1974.

was recognized. In 1920, at the age of 19, he entered the University of Pennsylvania to study architecture under Paul Cret. His name was Louis Kahn.

Inherent form

Kahn questioned the Modernist idea that architectural problems could be analyzed in abstract terms and solved by the invention of new forms. According to Kahn's theory, this process is of secondary importance because form is already inherent in human society. The architect's first job is to identify the relevant aspect of that inherent form. Take, for example, the habit of sitting round a table with friends and family to eat a meal: here is a piece of architecture ready made. All that is necessary is to support it and contain it without damaging it. Kahn's Esherick House of 1961, built for a single woman in a northern suburb of Philadelphia, illustrates this and other aspects of his philosophy in a simple, summary form. Unlike the Modernist houses of Le Corbusier or Mies van der Rohe, or even Frank Lloyd Wright, in which space is a flowing continuum, the Esherick House is a compact arrangement of static, well-defined rooms to suit different uses: a double-cube living room with a fireplace in the centre of the long wall; a dining room the same on plan but half the height with a bedroom and study over; and between them a strip of space containing the entrance hall, the staircase and front and back porches with balconies above. Kitchen, bathrooms, storerooms and the like are similarly grouped in a rectangular strip beside the dining room, perfectly illustrating one of the most influential aspects of Kahn's theory: the clear distinction between 'served' and 'servant' spaces.

Kahn disliked the tendency of modern building to solve heating and cooling problems by mechanical means. But the machines – boilers and chillers, pipes and ducts, or in this case cookers and washers – could not be ignored. They had to be allocated sufficient servant accommodation to prevent them from spoiling the human, served spaces. And that servant space must have its own architectural identity. Architecture, so to speak, remained in charge. This idea was to become almost a cliché among architects such as Norman Foster and Richard Rogers, though in the latter case (see page 350) it became a way to flaunt

Esherick House, Chestnut Hill, Philadelphia, USA. Louis Kahn, 1961. Not flowing, flexible space but static, well-defined rooms to suit different uses.

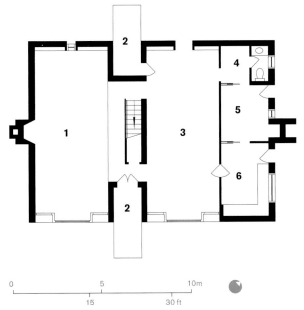

First floor plan
1. Living room   4. Lobby
2. Porch   5. Laundry
3. Dining room   6. Kitchen

upright stance and carefully judged proportions give it a dignified bearing. Perhaps it was his Beaux-Arts training under Cret that instilled in Kahn a respect for architecture's formal public duty.

The influence of Rome

One of Kahn's favourite buildings was 30th Street Station in Philadelphia, designed by Graham, Anderson, Probst and White and completed in 1933. Its massive Corinthian portico and grand arrival and departure hall show not a trace of Modernist influence. But Kahn always insisted whenever possible on returning to his home town by rail rather than by road or air so that he could participate once more in the formal drama of arrival. At first this monumental instinct was suppressed in the straight Modernist housing schemes of his early career, but then in 1950, at the age of 49, he was appointed architect in residence at the American Academy in Rome. He had spent a year travelling in Europe in the 1920s but this time his programme of visiting and sketching was more focussed. What particularly impressed him were the ruins of ancient buildings such as the Pantheon, the Forum of Trajan and the Baths of Caracalla. These vaulted brick and concrete carcasses, long ago stripped of their marble facings and delicate

rather than contain the machinery on which most modern buildings depend. We can see another aspect of this idea in the detailing of the windows of the Esherick House. Rather than spoil the simplicity of the full-height glazed openings with subframes of hinged or sliding sashes, Kahn provides separate wooden ventilation shutters on either side. And glare from the large areas of glass is controlled not by adjustable blinds but by the balancing light of the other windows in the room; in other words by architectural rather than mechanical means. Finally, the Esherick House illustrates Kahn's love of monumentality. Though this is a small building, plain and box-like, nevertheless its formal, ornament, presented a powerful image of solidity and spatial clarity. Kahn was deeply impressed. Could modern architecture somehow partake of this massive strength? The answer came in the design of a new art gallery for Yale University, the commission for which was confirmed on Kahn's return from Rome. When the building was completed three years later Reyner Banham immediately enlisted it in the Brutalist cause (see Chapter 21).

The Yale University Art Gallery is a simple four-storey box with a narrower bay to link it to the existing Neo-Gothic gallery of 1928, the height and alignment of which it respects. External walls are either all brick or all glass, never brick and glass combined to form conventional windows. Inside, concrete columns divide the main volume into three bays. The narrower middle bay is notionally the servant space, containing a massive cylindrical, top-lit stair tower. The quality of the served gallery spaces is determined less by their shape or by the daylight from the all-glass north wall than by the ceilings, which are exposed concrete space-frames. Kahn's original idea had been to cover the soffits and service runs with concave suspended ceilings – a faint echo of Roman vaulting, perhaps – but his new love of solidity and strength led him to devise this ingenious structure, almost 900 millimetres (3 feet) deep, through which pipes and trunking could be threaded. It may have been inspired by Buckminster Fuller (see Chapter 16),

Bathhouse at Trenton, Ewing, New Jersey, USA. Louis Kahn, 1955. Modest, dignified, even monumental spaces, created with simple means.

Kahn's faculty colleague at Yale, who regularly joined him on part of his rail commute from Philadelphia. It is ironic that Fuller, the supreme advocate of lightness in buildings, should have inspired a structural form chosen for its monumental weightiness. Another Yale colleague, Anne Tyng, was interested in Fuller's ideas and worked with Kahn on the art gallery. Later they would collaborate on many projects, including the City Hall Tower project for Philadelphia, a three-dimensional space-frame skyscraper.

Bathhouse at Trenton

But in hindsight, space-frame structures – lightweight, universal, all enveloping – seem antithetical to Kahn's architectural instincts. In the bathhouse at Trenton, New Jersey, the only built section of a proposed Jewish community centre, we see his basic intentions more clearly. The building contains the changing rooms for an open-air swimming pool. Its plan is a cross made of five square bays, four of them roofed by wooden pyramids, the central bay unroofed, like the atrium of a Roman house. Braced by steel rods, the roofs are supported at their corners on hollow, plain blockwork piers, 2.4 square metres (8 square feet). These create notional strips of space – a 'tartan grid' – to house service elements like showers and toilets. Enclosing walls can be on the outer or inner edges of the tartan zone, or on the centre line, or omitted entirely. A clever combination of these various options converts an unpromising brief into a sequence of dignified, even monumental spaces – a Roman bath complex in miniature. Kahn himself saw this building as

Yale University Art Gallery, New Haven, Connecticut, USA. Louis Kahn, 1953. Walls are either all brick or all glass, without compromise.

a turning point in the development of his architecture. In the typical Modernist 'free plan' structural elements like columns and space-defining elements like walls are independent of one another. But here they are congruent, combining to serve the inherent social form of the activity they house – the separation of men and women into different changing rooms, for example, but also their coming together in the central atrium and their moving forward up a wide flight of steps to the pool itself.

The architecture of services

A perfect square of flexible floor space was also the basic planning module of Kahn's next major building, the Richards Medical Research Laboratories at the University of Pennsylvania. Designed in 1957 and completed in 1961, it was the building that established his reputation internationally. In its first phase, three seven-storey laboratory towers, square on plan and mostly glazed, are linked to a fourth brick-clad tower containing vertical circulation and service rooms, including animal quarters. Kahn thought of the laboratories as 'studios', places of creative thought as well as experimental analysis. Their openness is emphasized by glass-to-glass joints at the column-free, cantilevered corners. Structurally this was achieved by an ingenious post-stressed, precast concrete frame devised by the engineer August Komendant. Further brick-clad service towers, containing escape stairs and exhaust stacks from fume cupboards, stand in the middle of the laboratory towers' free sides. The formal result is a picturesque cluster of elegant vertical forms in brick, concrete and glass, sharply detailed. Photographs of the building in international architectural magazines created a sensation among progressive architects. In Reyner Banham's *The Architecture of the Well-Tempered Environment*, first published in 1969, the Richards Laboratories were hailed as the building that forced architects and architectural critics to acknowledge the growing importance, and formal potential, of mechanical services. As Banham pointed out, Frank Lloyd Wright had shown the way half a century earlier in his Larkin Building (see page 69) – undoubtedly an influence on Kahn – but that building's brick-clad corner ducts and stair towers had been interpreted in purely sculptural terms.[1]

It is possible for a building to succeed architecturally but to fail as a practical answer to its client's needs, and the Richards Laboratories are a good example. Scientists found the square towers hard to inhabit. Though flexible in theory, they were difficult to plan and replan in practice, and the division between served and servant spaces soon broke down in a welter of ad-hoc adaptations. They also over-heated in the summer. In Kahn's mind they were mixed-use studios but the scientists wanted to separate their paperwork and their thinking space from the clutter of experimental apparatus. Kahn responded to this criticism in his next laboratory building, the Salk Institute at La Jolla, California.

Richards Medical Research Laboratories, University of Pennsylvania, USA. Louis Kahn, 1961. The buildings established Kahn's worldwide reputation.

Upper floor plan
1. Studio towers
2. Elevators and stairs
3. Animal quarters
4. Animal service rooms
5. Fresh air intake stacks
6. Air distribution shafts
7. Fume and exhaust stacks

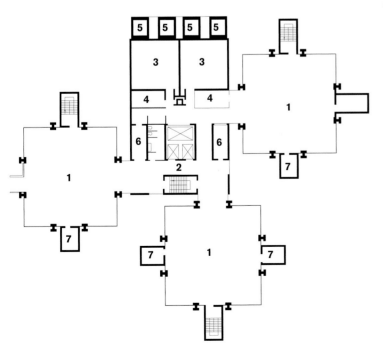

Salk Institute for Biological Studies, perspective of meeting house at La Jolla, California, USA. Louis Kahn, 1965. In this unbuilt project we see the first clear statement of Kahn's new monumental Modernism.

The Salk Institute

Like Kahn, Jonas Salk, the Nobel Prize-winning developer of the first polio vaccine, saw scientific research as a creative exploration. More than just a laboratory, his institute would be a monastery-like cultural community, bridging the gap between art and science. His brief to Kahn therefore included residences for research fellows and a 'meeting house'. In the event neither of these additional facilities was built, but in Kahn's final project for the meeting house we see the first clear statement of his new monumental Modernism. A cluster of simple, geometrical forms, unified by a level roofline, is perched on an Acropolis-like bluff overlooking the ocean. An open courtyard, like that of a Renaissance palace, is surrounded by a three-storey gallery serving a variety of subcomplexes, including visitors' overnight accommodation, a gymnasium, a restaurant and a library. Reading rooms and dining rooms become almost separate buildings, respectively circular and square on plan, shaded from the glaring Californian sun by solid but perforated wrap-around walls (respectively square and circular on plan). These protecting shells are clearly versions of the hollowed-out ancient ruins that Kahn had sketched obsessively in Rome.

The most important part of the La Jolla scheme, the part that was actually built, is equally formal and monumental, even though its function as working laboratories might be thought of as quasi-industrial. Kahn at first proposed towers on the model of the Richards Laboratories but this idea was soon abandoned in favour of four two-storey parallel blocks with semi-contained courts in between. The site, on high ground at the head of a ravine like a dry river inlet, commanded an uninterrupted view of the distant ocean horizon. Perhaps it was this theatrical setting (as well as the need to cut costs) that persuaded Kahn to condense the accommodation into two three-storey blocks on either side of a single courtyard. The whole development was now dominated by the open-ended court, its ocean view framed, proscenium-like, by the flanking laboratory buildings. This greatly enhanced the monumentality of the ensemble. A pair of courts is merely a spatial provision, but a single court invites historical comparison – with Michelangelo's Campidoglio on the Capitol in Rome, perhaps, or even, on a vastly larger scale, the forecourt of St Peter's – and that is exactly what has happened. The Salk courtyard has become one of modern architecture's most famous spaces, a place of pilgrimage and a proof that modern architecture and monumentality are not mutually exclusive. Early drawings and models show trees and other soft landscaping in the court, but Kahn seems to have been hesitant about this treatment. The story goes that when the Mexican architect Luis Barragán visited the site, he advised Kahn simply to pave it over. Kahn took the advice, but added a drainage channel in the middle, like a 'River of Paradise' in an Islamic garden, which falls into a pool in a lower terrace at the western end. The court's fame spread beyond the architectural cognoscenti when Kahn's son Nathaniel roller-skated round it in his 2003 documentary film *My Architect*.

Salk Institute for Biological Studies, La Jolla, California, USA. Louis Kahn, 1965. Scientists' study rooms are clustered in four-storey 'houses' with angled views over the ocean.

The court, then, is the main architectural event, but the buildings that define it are equally interesting. The conflict between thinking and working space that had become apparent in the Richards Laboratories is here solved by providing the scientists with separate study rooms in house-like buildings at the edge of the court, their main windows angled towards the ocean view. Behind them lie the bulky, quasi-industrial, open-plan laboratories. An early proposal for a folded-plate floor and roof structure was simplified to more conventional, almost storey-height, precast concrete trusses, post-tensioned with steel cables to improve earthquake resistance. August Komendant was once again the engineer. Services are accommodated in the fully accessible truss zone and fed down through the ceiling to the laboratory benches below. The served-and-servant principle is therefore maintained, this time not as towers but as a horizontal sandwich.

One more aspect of the Salk Institute should be noted: the relationship between its construction and its architecture. Kahn's love of Roman buildings was qualified: he preferred them ruined. Many would have been faced in marble and richly ornamented, which would not have been to Kahn's taste. He held an orthodox Modernist belief in truth to materials and the honest expression of construction. The main material at the Salk Institute is in-situ concrete, unfaced, but showing the traces of the smooth plywood panels that formed it, including their bevelled edges and the bolts that

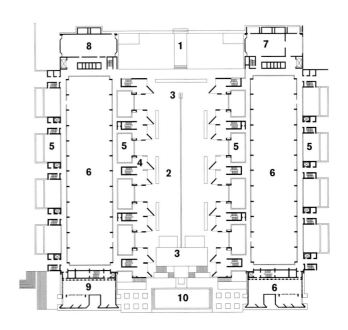

Ground floor plan at laboratory level
1. Entry from Torrey Pines Road
2. Central court
3. Fountain
4. Portico of studies

5. Light well
6. Laboratory
7. Mechanical services
8. Photo laboratory
9. Library
10. Terrace

tied them. Where Le Corbusier's *béton brut* makes a virtue of roughness and imprecision, Kahn's concrete is smooth and accurate, like dressed granite. The Californian climate helps to keep it that way. The technique was widely admired and imitated by other architects, notably Tadao Ando (see Chapter 27).

National Assembly Building, Dhaka

When Kahn secured the Salk commission in 1959 he was already 58 years old, had practised architecture all his working life, and had taught the subject at Yale University for more than 20 years. He had come to be regarded, by his colleagues, students and ex-students, and by serious-minded architects all over the world, as a master of his craft. In 1962, Ayub Kahn, the president of Pakistan, decided to build a

National Capital complex at Dhaka in the separate, eastern part of his country. Failing to secure the services of either Le Corbusier or Alvar Aalto, his advisors turned to Louis Kahn. Kahn accepted the commission gladly. Here was an opportunity to tackle a project on the scale of Le Corbusier's Chandigarh or Oscar Niemeyer's Brasília. There were many buildings to be designed – a hospital, a residential quarter, a market, schools and offices – but it was the National Assembly Building, the symbolic heart of what was to become the independent nation of Bangladesh, that stirred his deepest creative urges.

Making a virtue of the vast, flat site's tendency to flood, Kahn created a V-shaped artificial lake. Hostels and dining halls for delegates, built in local brick (there was a brickworks on the site), are ranged along its outer shores, flanking the assembly building itself, which stands in the water at the focal point. Basically octagonal, symmetrical in most aspects, freestanding, and isolated even from the ground it stands on by the reflective plane of water, the parliament

National Assembly Building of Bangladesh, Dhaka, Bangladesh. Louis Kahn, 1962–82. Forms are gathered around a single point like a group of people listening to an orator.

building could hardly be more remote from the informal functionalist norms of Modernism. Like any Beaux-Arts composition it is a collection of smaller objects, but here they are assembled not in military ranks and hierarchies but around a single point, like a group of people listening to an orator. Thus it illustrates its function as a meeting place for the Bangladeshi people and their representatives. Perhaps it is the presence of the reflecting pool that makes one think also of seventeenth-century Mughal architecture, and the Taj Mahal in particular. We know that Kahn visited and was deeply impressed by the Mughal monuments of Lahore, Jaipur and Agra.

If the overall composition of the National Assembly Building is simple, the spaces within and between its constituent forms are complex. In the centre is the chamber itself, octagonal on plan and, like Kahn's beloved Pantheon, as high as it is wide, but roofed by a concrete shell more like a Gothic vault than a dome. It is surrounded by public galleries that look into it through large openings in its walls, alternating with triangular light wells. A corridor ring, 16 sided, controls access to the galleries and defines the limit of the central block. Eight more distinct buildings surround this central block: at the cardinal points, a stair hall and entrance block (north), a prayer hall (south), members' lounges (east) and a cafeteria (west); and between these, on the diagonal axes, four practically identical rectangular office blocks. All of these are accessible from a high, wide ambulatory occupying the space between the outer buildings and the central block. This may sound like a rabbit warren but in reality it is made light and airy partly by a generosity of scale and partly by large openings carved out of the concrete walls to admit daylight and permit views in all directions. Each of the office buildings, for example, though a simple shoe box in outline, contains a pair of multi-storey atriums lit and ventilated by huge unglazed 'windows', rectangular, triangular and circular. The prayer hall is externally like a castle keep, square but with fat, round corner towers and rotated slightly to face Mecca (an irregularity that Kahn welcomed), but inside it is a perfect abstract cube, extended and inscribed by a logical sequence of circles, semi-circles and three-quarter-circles. The corner towers turn out to be light wells. This appendage to the National Assembly Building bears a striking similarity to another perfectly square, geometrically disciplined Kahn building, the library and dining hall at Phillips Exeter Academy in New Hampshire, completed in 1972. An early version of that design featured round corner towers, and in the finished building, the concrete walls of its cubic central atrium are perforated by circular openings, four storeys high.

In-situ reinforced concrete is the main material, inside and out, of the assembly building. The enormous strength of concrete and its potential fluidity can lead to formlessness

Phillips Exeter Academy Library, New Hampshire, USA. Louis Kahn, 1972. Space is governed by a strict geometry of squares, triangles and circles.

and scalelessness in the wrong hands. There are too few structural limitations to discipline the architect's ambitions. Kahn, however, was always attuned to the intrinsic qualities of materials. We have seen how, in the Salk Institute, he contrived to preserve a record of the building's construction in the finished building. The concrete at Dhaka is similarly disciplined by the inlaying of narrow strips of marble that stand out clearly – perhaps too clearly – as an all-enveloping linear grid. This might be taken as pure decoration, but it has a constructional logic: the horizontal strips, which occur at 1.5-metre (5-foot) intervals, are 'day joints' marking the extent of each 'pour'. When we reflect that most of the concrete was lifted into position on the backs of female labourers, we realize that the day joint is a measure of human scale in the fullest sense.

'Silence and light'

With the outbreak of the bloody Bangladesh Liberation War in 1971, Kahn's contract was terminated. The assembly

building was still unroofed. He continued to work on the project, however, and when a fragile, famine-sickened |peace was restored, he was reappointed. The building was finally inaugurated in 1982, eight years after his death. It had been expensive to build and was even more expensive to maintain, yet to this day the Bangladeshi people take pride in it as the symbol of their poor but dignified nation. Kahn is famous as much for his aphorisms as for his architecture. The gnomic utterance was his chief mode of expression as a teacher and theorist; for example: 'ask a brick what it wants to be' (answer – an arch), 'a street is a room by agreement', 'every building is a world of its own' and, most famously, 'architecture is silence and light'. Fundamentally, what they all mean is that architecture is a serious business, a primary aspect of humankind's relationship to nature and not to be supplanted by rival polities such as commerce or technology. For example, natural light, for Kahn, was always preferable to artificial light, and if it needed to be directed or controlled then architecture itself, not mechanical or electrical devices, should do the job.

Kimbell Art Museum, Fort Worth, Texas, USA. Louis Kahn, 1972. Parallel concrete vaults seem indeterminate, as if they might be extended ad infinitum in both directions.

This principle is best illustrated in this museum in Fort Worth, Texas, completed in 1972. In some ways the

Gallery in the Kimbell Art Museum. Daylight is immediately intercepted, reflected and softened by curved soffits.

building is untypical of Kahn's architecture. The parallel, linear concrete vaults that form its basic structure seem open ended and non-finite, like a system that could be extended horizontally in either direction. Contrast this with the singular, centralized compositions of, say, the Phillips Exeter library, the Bangladeshi parliament or even the Salk Institute, which, though composed of repetitive elements, is unified by the single paved court. At the Kimbell, there is no architectural centre, no spatial climax. The entrance hall is placed centrally and is accessible directly at ground level from the surrounding park, but internally the form of the roof is not altered or adjusted to accommodate it. Most of the design effort has been concentrated on this roof of what, though there is extensive semi-basement 'servant' accommodation, is essentially a single-storey building. The main problem was the one faced by all modern gallery designers: how to provide perfect picture-viewing conditions without exposing precious artworks to destructive ultra-violet rays. Daylight enters through continuous narrow slots in the apexes of the vaults, where it is immediately intercepted and reflected onto the curved

concrete soffits by fixed aluminium baffles. In fact these are not vaults in the true structural sense but are more like long-span prestressed concrete beams, engineered, of course, by August Komendant. The sectional profile is a cycloid, the curve traced by a point on a rolling circle. As always in a late Kahn building, mechanical and electrical services are integrated into the architectural form, occupying the valleys between the vaults. The spaces are rather low by traditional gallery standards, but the intimate scale, the soft light, the travertine-clad walls and wooden floors, the strategically placed light wells that offer glimpses of the sky, and the way that the vaulted form combines room-like enclosure with flexible openness, have led some experts to declare it the best modern gallery in the world. Kenneth Frampton called it the 'apotheosis' of Kahn's career.[2]

23 | 'NON-WESTERN' INFLUENCES 1937–1991

'Non-western' is a problematic term, which is why it arrives in inverted commas. Such a negative designation inevitably implies an inferior, or at least secondary, status. It is an implication that any truly objective historian would want to avoid. Surely northern, southern and eastern architectures ought to be looked at in their own terms, not in relation to a privileged home territory. But histories of architecture and other art forms are mostly based on preselected examples, some of which attained their canonical status as much by accident as by merit. Such histories are inevitably impure and partial. A relatively brief survey of more than 100 years of architecture would not be a practical proposition without some tolerance of such imperfections. So we must accept the term 'non-western' while remaining conscious of its problematic nature.

We might begin by recognizing that all of the four architects chosen here to represent 'non-western' influences were in fact thoroughly acquainted with western culture through education, travel and general intellectual orientation. The Egyptian architect Hassan Fathy was trained in the Beaux-Arts tradition by British teachers; the young Abdel-Wahed El-Wakil attended the British Victoria College in Alexandria and read Ruskin while at engineering college in Cairo; Balkrishna Doshi studied at North London Polytechnic before working with Le Corbusier in Paris; and Charles Correa studied under Buckminster Fuller at MIT. What these architects all shared, apart from their western schooling, was a worldliness and sophistication that allowed them to operate in two cultures at once. But it isn't quite as simple as that. 'Non-western' carries overtones of 'traditional' and 'vernacular', words that are equally applicable in a western context. So one might argue that the coming together of western and non-western perspectives was only one aspect of a more general reconciliation of Modernism with tradition. It was this changing ideological climate that allowed developments like Fathy's attempts to revive traditional mud-brick construction in the late 1940s to be celebrated by architectural history.

Hassan Fathy

Fathy was born into a wealthy, landowning Egyptian family. In 1926 he graduated from the engineering school at what was later to become Cairo University and for the first ten years of his architectural practice designed houses and other small buildings in an undistinguished western style. Then in 1937 he mounted an exhibition in Cairo of beautiful coloured drawings depicting designs for traditional houses with domes, courtyards and pointed arches. His westernized friends were shocked. It seemed a regressive step, but in some circles it caught the mood of rising Egyptian nationalism and in the years that followed several houses of this type were built, typically to accommodate landowners visiting their rural estates – the Nasr House at Fayyum, for example, of 1945, or the Stoppelaere House near Luxor of 1950. It is in these and later one-off houses, especially the house Fathy built for himself at Sidi Krier on the Mediterranean coast in 1971, that we can best perceive the subtlety of his art.

The Sidi Krier house is not a simple revival of a vernacular prototype but an artistic adaptation and recombination of traditional Islamic forms: the courtyard; the square main living space or *qu'a* roofed by a dome on squinches (diagonal corner arches); the *iwan* or deep alcove, arched or semi-domed; the loggia orientated to catch the evening breeze; the barrel vault, often parabolic, used to cover rectangular spaces such as storerooms and corridors; the claustrum, or perforated masonry gable; and the *mashrabiya*, or lattice-screened window. To the left of the entrance hall lies a square, high-walled courtyard with a fountain in the middle and a loggia on one side. Beyond the courtyard is the *qu'a*, flanked by two deep *iwans* serving as bedrooms. To the right of the entrance hall a short vaulted corridor leads to a bathroom like a miniature *qu'a*, domed with *iwans*, and beyond that to a kitchen opening onto a little yard from which steps lead up to the roof. These spaces are small – none is more than 3 metres (10 feet) wide – and though contained in a rectangular outline are fitted together asymmetrically in a balanced composition rather than mechanically ordered. Only the courtyard and the *qu'a* share an axis.

Looking back in his book *Architecture for the Poor*, first published in French in 1963, Fathy describes how the romantic vision of rural Egyptian life that he cherished as a youth was darkened by later encounters with the reality

House at Sidi Krier, Egypt. Hassan Fathy, 1971.
Not a vernacular building but an artistic adaptation and
recombination of traditional Islamic forms.

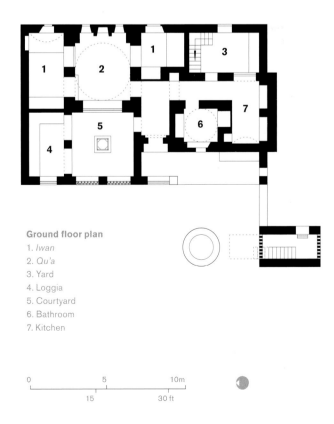

Ground floor plan
1. *Iwan*
2. *Qu'a*
3. Yard
4. Loggia
5. Courtyard
6. Bathroom
7. Kitchen

```
0              5              10m
 ——————————————————————————
       15             30 ft
```

of poverty, squalor and disease.[1] He wanted to improve
conditions by enabling peasants to build their own houses
but realized that modern materials and methods were
culturally inappropriate and too expensive. In the early 1940s,
wood, concrete and steel were in short supply in Egypt. The
only abundant and cheap building material was sun-dried
mud brick. Local builders could make satisfactory walls with
this material, but expensive timber was still required either for
roof beams or to make temporary formwork. Early attempts
to construct vaults and domes without formwork failed, but
then Fathy learnt of an ancient technique still practised by
Nubian craftsmen in villages around Aswan in upper Egypt.
The technique dispensed with formwork by means of various
geometrical subtleties such as the leaning of each new
section of a barrel vault against its predecessor so that newly
placed bricks would stay in place long enough for their arch
to be completed. The craftsmen were duly engaged and
brought north to build a demonstration farm at Bahtim in

the Nile Delta for the Royal Society of Agriculture. It was completed in 1941.

Fathy now commanded both the compositional and constructional means to begin his mission of improvement. The opportunity to apply it on a large scale came when the government was embarrassed internationally by the theft and attempted export of an important ancient Pharaonic basalt stone. The probable culprits were the inhabitants of the village of Qurna, or Gourna, in the Valley of the Kings on the west bank of the Nile opposite Luxor. It was decided that the villagers should be moved away from the temptation of the ancient tombs to a site further east, and that the construction of a new village – New Gourna – would be an opportunity to test Fathy's self-build principles. It is on the partial realization of this project, and the book that he wrote about it, that Fathy's international reputation mainly rests. His master plan envisaged a whole new life for the village based not on tomb-raiding but on a combination of agriculture and craft production. There was a craft school, an exhibition building and a theatre as well as more essential community facilities such as a market, a mosque, girls' and boys' primary schools, and a clinic. Two-storey houses with courtyards and domed *qu'as* were grouped

in contiguous blocks with a hierarchical network of streets and alleyways between. Everything was mud brick, and domed or vaulted. Larger buildings like the mosque were created by simple repetition of the domed square bay, with columns instead of walls – a form familiar in both Byzantine and Ottoman architecture. The beautiful dome of the mosque, with its elaborate squinches, stepped externally, bore a striking resemblance to that of the thirteenth-century ablution fountain at the Ibn Tulun Mosque in Cairo.

The New Gourna plan was only partly realized, largely, it seems, because the population refused to play the role assigned to them. They were not much interested in the house-building process and felt no need for the craft training and exhibition facilities, though the mosque and market functioned well enough. But there were perhaps deeper cultural misunderstandings, made apparent, for example, in the villagers' addition of decorative parapets to Fathy's plain walls. It is also said that the proliferation

---

New Gourna Village, Luxor, Egypt. Hassan Fathy, 1945–49.
An ambitious plan, only partly realized, to improve rural conditions by introducing self-build technologies.

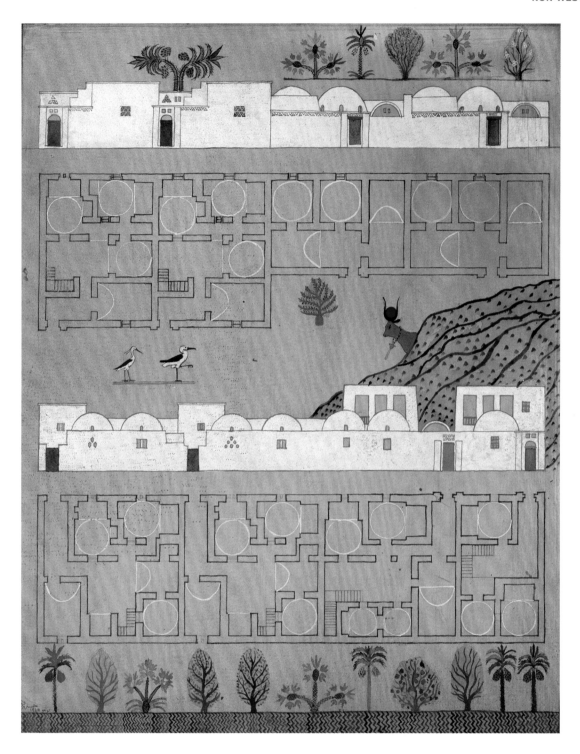

Plan for New Gourna Village. Hassan Fathy.
Fathy's artistic revival of traditional forms shocked
his cosmopolitan friends.

of domes was disliked because domes were associated
with tombs. What seemed to western eyes to be deeply
traditional architecture was alien to people who preferred
to live with their animals in the hovels and caves of their old
mountainside settlement. New Gourna is now dilapidated
and depopulated, its mud-brick walls crumbling and its public
buildings unused. There have been recent attempts to rescue
and restore it, largely because of the fame of its creator.

After a five-year sojourn in Athens working on research
projects for the urban theorist Constantinos Doxiadis, Fathy

returned to Egypt in 1962 and began work on another ill-
fated village project. New Baris in the Kharga Oasis was
part of a larger government plan to develop agriculture in
the central desert. The climate was less hospitable than
in the Nile valley and electricity would not be available for
some time. 'Passive' cooling had been one of the main

justifications for Fathy's revival of traditional forms: shady courtyards, thick masonry walls of high thermal mass, and various devices to encourage natural ventilation. At New Baris passive cooling was not just desirable; it was essential for survival. Fathy responded by extending his repertoire of forms while sticking to the basic principles of domed and vaulted masonry construction. The market, for example, was a large rectangular building divided into small repetitive units with a central courtyard; but it was also a giant wind catcher, with tiers of parabolic-vaulted and claustrum-gabled roofs scooping the wind into the shops and storerooms below. This was a new, invented form but also an extended version of the wind tower, a device that was common in various Middle Eastern architectural traditions and would become an inspiration to western architects in the years after the 1973 Arab oil embargo (see Chapter 30). New Baris, like New Gourna, was never completed. Construction stopped in 1967 at the outbreak of the Six Day War with Israel and was not resumed.

Abdel-Wahed El-Wakil

Fathy's built output was relatively modest, but his influence was widespread, east and west. One of the channels of that influence was Abdel-Wahed El-Wakil, an Egyptian architect born in 1943, who worked for Fathy in the late 1960s. Having established his own practice, he met early success with his Halawa House, which won the Aga Khan Award for Architecture. Completed in 1975 in the Egyptian Mediterranean resort of Agamy, its debt to Fathy is obvious and indeed it was constructed under the supervision of Aladdin Moustafa, the Nubian mason who had been Fathy's chief builder. Plastered loadbearing masonry, domes, vaults, claustrums and *mashrabiyas* are all present, but there is a new freedom and an air of luxury rather than austerity. The central courtyard – actually a clever way to meet a restricted allowable plot ratio – is large and eventful, with a loggia, a belvedere overlooking the beach, and a relaxed double-flight stair incorporating a little arched *iwan*. This is not architecture for the poor, but then Fathy himself produced

Market at New Baris, Kharga Oasis, Egypt. Hassan Fathy, 1967. The market building was a giant wind-catcher, scooping the cooling breeze into shops and storerooms.

Halawa House, Agamy, Egypt. Abdel-Wahed El-Wakil, 1975. Traditional forms now creating an air of luxury rather than austerity.

(Above) **Al-Ruwais Mosque, Jeddah, Saudi Arabia. Abdel-Wahed El-Wakil, 1989.** The structurally pure brickwork before receiving its stucco coating.

(Above right) **Corniche Mosque, Jeddah, Saudi Arabia. Abdel-Wahed El-Wakil, 1986.** The prayer hall is covered by a single dome on squinches.

Island Mosque, Jeddah, Saudi Arabia. Abdel-Wahed El-Wakil, 1986. A cubic prayer hall attended by elegant secondary forms.

several large expensive houses, including a retreat for President Sadat, never occupied.

In his subsequent career, El-Wakil became best known as a designer of mosques in Saudi Arabia. All are traditional in style and construction, drawing on a thousand years of Islamic architectural history, freely reinterpreted. Most satisfying to western architectural eyes are three small mosques on the Corniche at Jeddah. Each is a sculptural group of traditional forms. In the Island Mosque, so-called because it occupies its own artificial island, a cubic prayer hall is attended by elegant secondary forms – an off-centre octagon and dome, a forecourt defined by an L-shaped seven-bay domed arcade, and a minaret that raises its own cube, dome and octagon high on a cornice embellished with traditional *muqarnas*. The Corniche Mosque is more compact, its prayer hall completely covered by a dome on squinches and its entrance porch roofed by a parabolic arch. In the Al-Ruwais Mosque nearby, parabolic arches take over, ranged in two tiers over the prayer hall and acting as wind scoops – an obvious borrowing from Hassan

Fathy's market in New Baris. The *qibla* wall, the one facing Mecca, is distinguished by a row of three domes, the central one raised over the *mihrab*.

(Left) Oxford Centre for Islamic Studies, Oxford, UK. Abdel-Wahed El-Wakil, 1987. A reminder that Gothic and Islamic architecture share a common heritage.

(Below) Sangath architect's office, Ahmedabad, India. Balkrishna Doshi, 1981. Half buried in the ground, this office and studio complex is as much a landscape as a building.

Arguably, the most important aspect of El-Wakil's architecture is not its dependence on historic Islamic prototypes but its insistence on traditional loadbearing masonry construction – although the two cannot entirely be separated. Modernist architects revel in the strength and freedom offered by steel and reinforced concrete, but in El-Wakil's eyes the result is only an ugly scalelessness. He welcomes the limitations of brick and stone that 'naturally' create beautiful forms like the arch, the dome and the vault, though the masonry is routinely plastered over and painted white, a disappointment to western architects trained to appreciate 'materiality'. El-Wakil had strong connections with Britain, maintaining an office in southern England for many years. It is not surprising therefore that he should have come to the notice of the Prince of Wales, who found in him the non-western equivalent of favoured classical revivalists such as Quinlan Terry and Demetri Porphyrios. When Oxford University established a Centre for Islamic Studies, with the prince as its patron, El-Wakil was chosen to design the buildings. The result is a traditional Oxford college in a kind of anglicized Islamic style. There are courtyards, arcades, a dome and a tower, all in stone or brick just like the other, older colleges. One is reminded that Gothic and Islamic architecture share a common heritage, as indeed do western and Islamic scholarship.

It is not unreasonable to argue that Indian modern architecture, as a cultural field and a continuing tradition, was founded by Le Corbusier and Louis Kahn. While Le Corbusier was building the new city of Chandigarh in the 1950s (see pages 232–235) he was also developing aspects of his Indian style in commissions from the industrialists of Ahmedabad, the capital of Gujarat. The Mill Owners' Association Building, the Villa Shodhan and the Villa Sarabhai are almost as important to architectural history as the Palace of Assembly and the High Court at Chandigarh. Similarly, while Louis Kahn was building the National Assembly Building in Dhaka in the late 1960s (see pages 298–300) he was also building the Indian Institute of Management (IIM) in Ahmedabad, to be completed in 1974.

Balkrishna Doshi
A key figure in Indian architecture's reverse adoption, so to speak, of these two father figures was Balkrishna Doshi. After studying architecture in Mumbai and London, in 1951 he went to work in Paris for Le Corbusier, who soon sent him back to India to supervise the construction of the High Court in Chandigarh and other buildings. In 1956 he started his own practice in Ahmedabad, where he was offered the IIM commission but turned it down, persuading his would-be clients to offer it instead to Louis Kahn, whom he had met on a visit to the University of Pennsylvania. It was a shrewd move. An association with Kahn's international profile could do far more for the careers of Doshi and his young compatriots than a single commission, and besides they were keen to learn from the American master. Doshi's first buildings as an independent architect, including the Institute of Indology, completed in 1962, and the School of Architecture, completed in 1968, both in Ahmedabad, are accomplished and original compositions but also unmistakably descendants of Le Corbusier and Kahn. Concrete and brick are the main materials, combined in

elemental assemblages of strong, simple wall and floor slabs – India's version of Brutalism. The 'non-western' label is hard to justify in these cases. Hindu and Mughal references that some critics have detected are surely as much attributable to Kahn as to Doshi.

Later in his career Doshi developed a friendlier, more individual style, the best example of which is Sangath on the outskirts of Ahmedabad, an office and studio complex for his own Vastu Shilpa ('Design of the Environment') Foundation. As much a landscape as a building, the lower of its two storeys is half sunk into the ground, creating a new ground level on its roof. Thin, semi-circular concrete tunnel vaults rise above this new ground from high spaces below. At the north end another storey is added with its own pair of tunnel vaults, and on the west side the roof/ground steps down to a little tree-shaded amphitheatre through which flows a stream with waterfalls. Vaults and other external surfaces are covered in fragments of white ceramic tile, a less brutal and more weather-resistant alternative to exposed concrete and brick. Some critics have claimed that these parallel vaults were inspired by Indian vernacular forms but a more obvious source is Kahn's Kimbell Art Museum in Fort Worth (see page 300).

School of Architecture, Ahmedabad, India. Balkrishna Doshi, 1968. The influence of Louis Kahn, and of Doshi's ex-employer, Le Corbusier, is evident.

In the Husain-Doshi Gufa art gallery, also in Ahmedabad, all traces of Corb/Kahn influence have disappeared. According to Doshi the design was inspired by a dream in which Kurma, the turtle-like avatar of Vishnu, spoke to him in language reminiscent of Louis Kahn. 'What this Gufa wants to be is what you see in these forms: a building which is dynamic, difficult to describe yet great to experience.'[2] The forms in question, shown in what Doshi calls 'holograms', were all natural, like eggs, fruit, bones and shells – similar to the forms of Kurma's own body. Le Corbusier also played a part in the dream, in particular his wildly unconventional pilgrimage chapel at Ronchamp (see page 228). It was a dream of freedom, freedom from 'day-to-day notions of how to design an acceptable form' and also, paradoxically, freedom from the legacy of Corb and Kahn. *Gufa* means 'cave', so this is an artificial cave, dug into the ground and roofed over by a loose cluster of small, ribbed domes low enough for children to climb on. Like the vaults at Sangath they are covered in white ceramic fragments into which Doshi's artist collaborator, M. F. Husain, inlaid a black cobra, winding its way between roof-lights that look like eyes on stalks. Inside we find that the domes, of ferro-cement, are supported by columns like tree trunks, irregularly spaced, some of them leaning. Comparisons with cave-like, rock-cut Hindu temples are far fetched. Antoni Gaudi's Colònia Güell, combined with the mosaic-covered serpentine benches of his Parc Güell (see page 13), seems nearer the mark. The Gufa was completed in 1995.

Charles Correa

Doshi's contemporary and rival for historical recognition, Charles Correa studied at the University of Michigan and MIT before starting his own practice in Mumbai in 1958. Though inevitably influenced by Corb and Kahn, Correa's work leaves more scope for non-western interpretation. Nevertheless, his first major building, the Gandhi Memorial Institution in Ahmedabad, completed in 1963, seems almost pure Kahn. It is clearly a version of the Trenton Bathhouse (see page 294) but with a multiple array of square bays, some pyramid roofed, some open to the sky, instead of Kahn's single five-bay cross. It functions as a museum for Mahatma Gandhi's letters and personal possessions but it is also a place of study and meditation. A shallow pool fills a four-bay courtyard at its centre. Kahn would have approved of the austere materials: brick and concrete with clay-tiled roofs.

Correa was a problem solver as much as he was an artist, interested in mass housing and town planning as well as one-off buildings. From 1970 to 1974 he was chief architect and planner of the state of Maharashtra, having earlier led a proposal to expand the constricted peninsular city of Mumbai by developing land on the east side of the harbour.

Gandhi Memorial Institution, Ahmedabad, India. Charles Correa, 1963. Clearly a version of Kahn's Trenton Bathhouse, though housing a very different function.

The progress of the New Bombay or Navi Mumbai project was fitful and failed to fulfil its original aims, though it created a city that now serves a population of more than a million. Correa's designs for mass housing were practical planning exercises rather than architectural showpieces. The best example is Belapur in Navi Mumbai, completed in 1986, which provided houses for 100 families in a range of income groups. Each family was provided with a plot of about 50 square metres (540 square feet) containing, in the most basic version, an 'open to sky' space, a toilet and a rudimentary shelter that could be improved and extended by the family in their own time with the help of local builders. Seven such dwellings were grouped in a roughly square compound around a communal yard; this group was then combined with two similar groups around a larger public space, which in turn was combined with two others, and so on up a theoretically endless urban hierarchy.

The architecture of the houses was extremely modest – single or two storey with white-painted stucco walls and shingle-covered, shallow-pitched roofs. A few basic planning rules helped to preserve the individual identity of each house and guarded, for a while at least, against unneighbourly over-development. Early photographs show a dense but calm and informal arrangement of private, shared and public spaces, appropriately scaled. Now, more than 30 years later, the planning rules have been forgotten and many of the original houses have been replaced by new concrete villas, yet the mixed community survives and thrives. Trees have matured, walls have been repainted, often in bright colours, and the hierarchy of public and semi-public open space still functions. Correa himself would probably count it a success.

The key to Correa's art lies in Belapur's basic unit of composition, that cluster of seven houses contained in a notional square. Note that this is not a form – a box or a tower, a cylinder or a pyramid – but a demarcated territory, like a board on which to play a game. It might contain forms but mostly it contains space, divided by walls and floors and roofs that only occasionally combine to form enclosed rooms. Even in a tower block, such as the well-known Kanchanjunga Apartments in Mumbai, completed in 1983, Correa refuses to submit to the enclosed-room model. Instead he carves out the corners of the tower and allows the floors of the apartments to step up and down in free-flowing, single- and double-height, indoor and outdoor spaces. The overall plan, though, is a perfect square. In the many lectures that he gave to architects and students all over the world, Correa often spoke of western architects' natural tendency to think in terms of fully enclosed space and freestanding forms, and how his own architecture belonged to a different tradition. In Indian architecture, especially the Mughal architecture of the sixteenth and seventeenth centuries, 'rooms' are often either unroofed – platforms and courtyards 'open to the sky' in Correa's favourite phrase – or unwalled, like the traditional *chhatri*, a domed canopy supported on columns. There is of course a climatic reason for this openness. India has many climates but in very general terms it is wise to seek a breezy shade in the middle of the day and a space open to the cool depth of the sky in the evening.

None of this necessarily implies a square planning module, which derives from a different aspect of Indian culture – the mandala, or sacred symbol. Actually, *mandala* is the Sanskrit word for 'circle' but often circles and squares are combined in diagrams that represent the otherwise invisible structure of the cosmos. When Maharaja Jai Singh II built the new city of Jaipur in the eighteenth century he planned it on the basis of the Vashtu Purusha mandala, a square divided into nine equal smaller squares, but with one corner square displaced to

Kanchanjunga Apartments, Mumbai, India. Charles Correa, 1983. Correa's favourite square plan-form is here stacked up to form a tower with open corners.

avoid steeply sloping ground. Charles Correa's design for Jawahar Kala Kendra, a cultural centre in Jaipur dedicated to the memory of Jawaharlal Nehru, follows the same principle. Nine 30-metre (98-foot) squares are separated by high walls but connected by central openings that create a continuous route around the whole building. Each square contains a group of related functions, like a self-contained building, or perhaps a small settlement, with as much 'open to sky' space as enclosed space. Three of the squares are dedicated to museum displays of different kinds, including one that might be a small section of Belapur, with stuccoed houses, a fragment of a village street and a little look-out tower. Other squares accommodate a domed entrance plaza, a library, a research centre and a cafeteria. Following the precedent of Jai Singh's urban plan, a corner square containing two small theatres is pushed aside to form an angled entrance forecourt. The ninth, central square, is empty, symbolizing the void at the centre of existence, but

there are steps around its perimeter that faintly recall the great eleventh-century *kund* or water tank at Modhera in Gujarat. Such an overt evocation of Hindu myth might be thought suitable only for this particular building type, yet Correa had used a rather similar mandala plan in his government complex at Bhopal, designed a few years earlier. The love of symbolic order, and of the square plan in particular, seems to be fundamental to his architecture. In lectures and essays he referred to square and circular plans in other traditions – the Islamic paradise garden as interpreted in Mughal architecture, the solid mound of the Buddhist *stupa*, and the Jain 'cosmograph'. What the West contributed to this tradition according to Correa, was the 'tabula rasa', the clean slate, full of liberating energy and yet ultimately nihilistic: 'Quite soon, the rational becomes the merely commonsensical and eventually dwindles into the prosaic. In architecture, the frisson of the tabula rasa becomes the stupefying banality of one more high-rise glass box.'[3]

Jawahar Kala Kendra, Jaipur, India. Charles Correa, 1991. The central courtyard, one of nine 30-metre (98-foot) squares forming a mandala plan.

Geoffrey Bawa

Geoffrey Bawa came late to his profession. He first studied law in Cambridge and London, qualifying as a barrister, then travelled the world for two years before returning to his native Ceylon (today Sri Lanka) to buy an old rubber estate at Lunuganga and convert it into an Italian garden. Finding that he lacked the technical skills to carry his project forward, he apprenticed himself to a local architect and later enrolled at the Architectural Association in London. He finally qualified in 1957, at the age of 38, and returned to Ceylon to begin his practice.

Given his cosmopolitan upbringing and education, Bawa can hardly be described as a 'vernacular' architect. He designed a few buildings in a sophisticated Modernist style, for example the 13-storey State Mortgage Bank in Colombo, completed in 1978, which shows the influence of Alvar Aalto. But he is best known for his so-called Tropical Modernist buildings, in which tradition and modernity are combined. 'Sri Lankan vernacular' is not an easy tradition to define, being itself a combination of other traditions: Sinhalese and Kandyan with Portuguese, Dutch and British colonial admixtures. The traditional *walauwa* or manor house, though not uniform as a building type, is typically one or two storeys high, with courtyards, columned verandahs and shallow-pitched, hipped roofs. Bawa took these simple forms, with a few variations of his own such as the cantilevered verandah,

as his compositional raw material in buildings as different in function and scale as the Bentota Beach Hotel of 1969 and the Sri Lankan parliament complex of 1982. The result was a modern, functional architecture, without ornament, which nevertheless looked comfortably at home in the hot, wet Sri Lankan climate.

Bawa's own house in Colombo perfectly illustrates his relaxed architectural manner. Its slow development began in 1958 when he bought one of four bungalows in a row along a cul-de-sac. Over a ten-year period he acquired the other three as they became vacant, adding them to what had become an informal cluster of small courtyards, verandahs and enclosed rooms behind a surrounding wall. Then to finish it off he built a Corbusian wing at the street end, complete with pilotis and roof garden. In the rest of the house, behind this modern front, the distinction between inside and outside spaces is practically irrelevant, though there are some air-conditioned bedrooms. A side entrance passage terminates at a miniature pool framed by columns recycled from an old Chettinad house. Bawa enjoyed bricolage of this kind, incorporating works by his artist friends, such as doors decorated by Donald Friend and Ismeth Raheem. With its top-lit spaces, compact plan, artworks and bricolage, the Bawa House is perhaps the Sri Lankan equivalent of Sir John Soane's famous early nineteenth-century house-museum in London.

Sri Lankan Parliament, Colombo, Sri Lanka. Geoffrey Bawa, 1982.
Forms derived from the traditional *walauwa*, or manor house, form the basis of a 'tropical Modernism'.

24 | **POSTMODERNISM 1964–1990**

When Robert Venturi and Denise Scott Brown got married in 1967, they honeymooned in a Las Vegas casino hotel. Nothing unusual about that, of course, except that gambling seems an unlikely recreation for a couple of up-and-coming young architects and intellectuals. Were they perhaps making some kind of ideological point? Undoubtedly they were. Venturi had recently written an important theoretical book called *Complexity and Contradiction in Architecture*, and in 1972 the couple were to publish a kind of sequel called *Learning from Las Vegas*.

Learning from Las Vegas

The general idea was that Modernist architecture had lost its way and that a new Postmodernist architecture was needed to replace it. Whereas Modernist buildings were expected to be 'heroic and original', Postmodernist buildings would be prepared to respond to popular culture and might even turn out to be 'ugly and ordinary'. The idea that the function of a building should be the generator of its form was questioned. It was pointed out that in the real, non-architectural world, buildings were often multi-purpose shed-like structures decorated with simple signs. Spatially a bank, say, might not be that different from a clothing store or a restaurant or a marriage parlour, but its facade would have to be bank-like so as to signal its function clearly to the public. Architects, said Venturi and Scott Brown, could learn a lot from 'the decorated shed'. It was a radical manifesto and it initiated a new pattern of architectural thinking that became, for some years at least, as pervasive as Modernism itself.

In Part II of *Learning from Las Vegas*, Venturi and Scott Brown, with Steven Izenour, compare one of their own buildings, an old people's home in Philadelphia called Guild House, with Crawford Manor, a building of similar size and function in New Haven, Connecticut, designed by Paul Rudolph. The latter is presented as a typical product of the old Modernist orthodoxy. Its complex, articulated external form combines plain towers, somewhat reminiscent of the

'servant' towers of Louis Kahn's Richards Laboratories (see page 295), with vertical stacks of windows behind rounded projecting balconies. All this vigorous expressiveness, apparently carved out of solid concrete, turns out to enclose not a complicated laboratory building but a cluster of ordinary bed-sits and one-bedroom apartments. The servant towers contain stacks of small kitchens, and although the shapes of

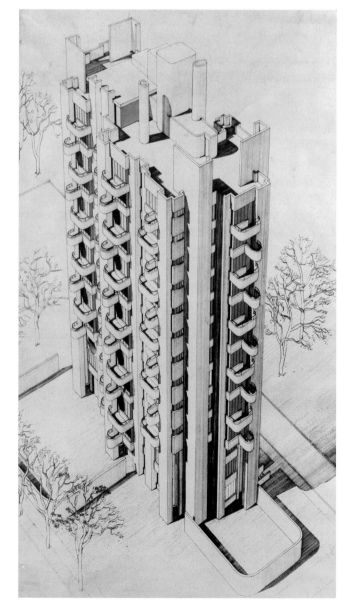

Crawford Manor, New Haven, Connecticut, USA. Paul Rudolph, 1966. Venturi and Scott Brown's chosen representative of an ailing Modernist orthodoxy.

Guild House, Philadelphia, USA.
Robert Venturi, 1963. Symmetrical
with remnants of classical detailing
and a jokey symbolism: popular, not
Modernist.

the balconies are varied, the living rooms behind them are all the same. A domestic interior is enclosed in a machine-like exterior in order to fulfil Modernism's requirement for 'heroic originality'.

It is hard to imagine many of the elderly occupants of the building responding positively to its over-assertive image. Guild House, on the other hand, according to its designers, is more modest and more sensitive to popular taste. It is symmetrical, with the main entrance in the middle, and its external walls are brick with mostly ordinary rectangular windows. There are even a few details indicating that this might be a traditional classical building. The centre section is pushed forward, as if presenting itself to the street, with recessed balconies above the main entrance suggesting a kind of portico. Above the balconies, a big shallow-arched window, lighting a communal lounge on the top floor, might be taken for a segmental pediment, and around the rest of the building runs a thin stone string course at classical cornice height, with a notional attic storey above. This is not, however, a straightforward piece of popular, or populist, architecture. Its classical details are abstracted, not literal. An architect might appreciate their subtlety, whereas a layperson will perceive only an inoffensive ordinariness. There are 'in-jokes' too, like the gilded non-functional television aerial on the roof, representing the main occupation of the residents, the single fat red column in the middle of the entrance, and the big brash 'Guild House' sign over it where one might have expected something more

discreet. So the architecture can be 'read' at different levels; it is 'multivalent', to use the jargon of the period.

Venturi and Scott Brown aimed to bring stylistic subtlety and communicativeness back into mainstream architecture, to create a new richness of meaning that would fill the cultural void left by an over-simplified Modernism. Their architectural heroes were the Mannerists of the seventeenth century, not the functionalists of the early twentieth century: Michelangelo and Giulio Romano, not Walter Gropius and Mies van der Rohe. Mies had said 'less is more'; Venturi and Scott Brown said 'less is a bore'. Underlying this new way of thinking was the basic idea that architecture is a language, a visual language. In architectural theory, concern shifted from function to meaning, from the 'shed' to its decoration, from what a building did to what a building said.

The architecture-as-language idea implies three assumptions. First, that architecture is a medium shared by everyone, consumers as well as producers, 'readers' as well as 'writers'. Architects can't complain when the general public interprets their buildings 'wrongly', when, for example, a housing estate is likened to a prison or a school to a factory. Buildings convey meaning whether you want them to or not, so popular taste has to be taken into account. Second, it means that history cannot be ignored. Language is not created from scratch by an individual, it grows and changes gradually and its ability to convey meaning depends on its long history. Modernism valued novelty more than tradition; it wanted to do away with the past and make a fresh start. But the language idea rules out fresh starts because a completely new world would be a completely meaningless world. Third, the old Modernist idea of honesty and truth to materials is questionable. If architecture is a visual language, then what a building looks like is more important than what it is made of. If, in the language of architecture, marble denotes quality and permanence, then whether the marble is real or not is irrelevant. Fake marble becomes allowable.

In 1977 *The Language of Post-Modern Architecture* by the critic and historian Charles Jencks was published. It was by no means the first time that architecture had been spoken of as a language (see, for example, John Summerson's still-popular book *The Classical Language of Architecture*, first published in 1963), but Jencks brought a new philosophical rigour to the idea, applying semiological concepts that he had developed in earlier essays (notably 'Semiology and Architecture' of 1969[1]) to the analysis of modern buildings. According to Jencks, most Modernist buildings, such as those designed by Mies van der Rohe for the IIT campus (see page 192), were either sullen and silent, refusing to communicate with users and passers-by, or else conveyed the wrong messages through insensitivity and ignorance. The boiler house, for example, with its clerestory windows and campanile-like chimney, looked like a chapel, whereas the 'dumb box' of the chapel looked like a boiler house.[2] On the other hand certain recent buildings by Robert Venturi and Denise Scott Brown, Robert Stern, Charles Moore,

Michael Graves, and in Europe, Ricardo Bofill, Hans Hollein and James Stirling were breaking the Modernist silence and beginning to communicate. Postmodernism had arrived, fully equipped with a manifesto and a set of examples.

Michael Graves and Peter Eisenman

As a student in the Harvard Graduate School of Design, Michael Graves had been a dutiful Modernist, continually poring over the eight volumes of Le Corbusier's *Œuvre Complète*. Then, like Louis Kahn before him, he became a scholar at the American Academy in Rome and began to have creative doubts about the nature of Modernism, and even of architecture itself. When he returned he became a teacher at Princeton and set up a small practice designing mostly domestic-scale projects in a style that was recognizably Corbusian but so refined and delicate that it was hard to connect it with any idea of 'functionalism'. The Hanselmann House in Fort Wayne, Indiana, for example, is an almost perfect cube, or rather two cubes, one of them invisible, its presence signalled only by the positioning of the entrance steps some distance away at the end of a long bridge. The three-storey built cube is also rather insubstantial, its horizontal and vertical planes (walls, floors and roof) eaten away in places so that space, conceived as a single continuum, can flow through and leak out in every direction.

Graves was a member of the so called New York Five with Peter Eisenman, Charles Gwathmey, John Hejduk and Richard Meier, whose work was exhibited at the Museum

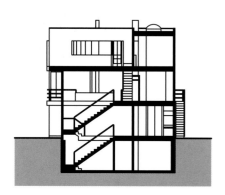

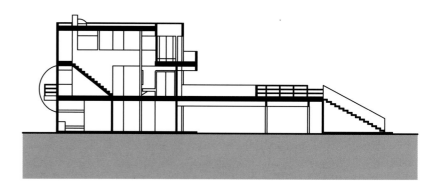

Hanselmann House, Indiana, USA. Michael Graves, 1967. A composition of two cubes, one of them invisible.

Sections and first floor plan
1. Entrance
2. Living room
3. Kitchen
4. Bathroom

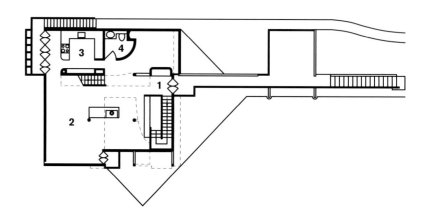

of Modern Art in 1969 and published in a book three years later. According to Arthur Drexler's preface, the Five had 'picked up where the thirties left off, before an architecture of rational poetry was interrupted by World War II and its subsequent mood of disenchantment, restlessness and resentment'.[3] In other words, this was an architecture devoid of any social or political programme. To this extent, though it was based on European precedents, it was typically American.

Eisenman was its most extreme exponent, designing 'houses' that were almost purely conceptual, not so much the outcome of a rational process of design as the record of a series of arbitrary formal transformations. The real clients of his House VI in Cornwall, Connecticut of 1973 (see page 382) were expected to live with such inconveniences as an upside-down staircase and an open slot in the middle of the bedroom floor (the clients dutifully exchanged their double bed for two singles). Perhaps it was this divorce of architecture from any social or functional context that paved the way for Postmodernism. The houses of Graves and Eisenman were meant to be looked at first and used only later; they were inspired by history – the Modernism of the 1930s; and they were indifferent to ethical notions like truth to materials. Although they looked like reinforced

concrete structures, usually they were mocked up in timber and plaster.

So some of the basic theoretical assumptions of Postmodernism were already in place. Only the esoteric nature of these buildings distanced them from the populism, or 'multivalency', of Venturi and Scott Brown. Houses for adventurous individual clients could afford to ignore popular taste, but what about public buildings? Should they also be made into intellectual puzzles? Probably not. Michael Graves's radical change of style around 1977 might have been a shrewd career move, an attempt to move on from frustratingly small domestic projects to larger, public commissions. Nevertheless, it was in a house, the Plocek House at Warren, New Jersey, designed in 1977 and completed in 1982, that the new style first appeared. In many ways the Plocek House is the opposite of the Hanselmann House: an additive rather than a subtractive form, not abstract but 'figurative', not pure and timeless but anchored in centuries of architectural tradition. 'Figurative' was a word that Graves himself used in his theoretical writings. He meant that the component parts of the building represented traditional architectural features – columns, arches, doors, windows – which everybody could recognize. Like Venturi and Scott Brown's Guild House, this is a classical building, but only approximately so. Sited on a steep slope, it stands on a solid, notionally rusticated base and its main entrance is axial, between a pair of columns. But those columns are magnified and simplified, with curious divided keystone-

Plocek House, Warren, New Jersey, USA. Michael Graves, 1982. An additive form, 'figurative' and anchored in tradition: the opposite of the Hanselmann House.

Municipal Services Building, Portland, Oregon, USA. Michael Graves, 1982. Big, flat, simplified motifs decorate an intrinsically economical cube.

shaped capitals that no Greek or Roman architect would recognize. The keystone shape became something of an obsession with Graves. In this building it occurs as a void in the plan of the side entrance court, and as a solid in the garden pavilion that terminates the main axis.

With hindsight, the Plocek House looks like a rehearsal for the main event: the Municipal Services Building in Portland, Oregon, completed in 1982, which was to become the most prominent representative of the early Postmodernist style. By 1979, when the design competition for the new building was launched, Portland had become a city of bland, curtain-walled Modernist towers. It may have been the decorative freshness of Graves's design that appealed to the jury, which was strongly influenced by Philip Johnson, but just as importantly the building's squat, 15-storey, deep-planned form was judged very economical to build. Like the Hanselmann House, it is basically a cube, not fragile and floating this time but solidly grounded on a stepped podium. Its square facades are like vast murals in which big, flat, simplified architectural features such as columns, wreaths, garlands and keystones, occasionally stepping out timidly into three dimensions, are set off against a cream background perforated by small, square windows.

Piazza d'Italia

If the Portland Building, as it came to be known, had simply been curtain walled in glass or thin stone, it would no doubt have been grumbled about locally as a dumb Modernist box and totally ignored by architectural history. But its bold

yet shallow ornament, either a brilliant or a desperate ploy according to your point of view, made it controversial in a more creative way. The message to outraged Modernists was: 'See? It can be done; ornament is possible and is not a crime.' Actually, this point had already been made, even more shockingly, in the semi-derelict downtown of New Orleans where Charles Moore, an influential teacher and theorist, had designed a piazza for the Italian community. Buried in the centre of a city block and approached by narrow alleyways, it was meant to deliver the kind of spatial surprise that tourists experience in Rome or Naples. Sadly, the perimeter blocks were never built so it was always an interior without an exterior, and in any case, it looked nothing like a real Italian piazza because it was made of metal and plaster, brightly coloured and lit by neon. Its basically circular plan was half enclosed by curved and stepped colonnades at various scales and in jokey versions of the traditional classical orders. A paved boot-of-Italy lay in a miniature Mediterranean to form its obligatory fountain. Otherwise, it had no particular function, but then, it might be argued, neither does a real Italian piazza; the question of function only arises because of the modern American context. As a local amenity the Piazza d'Italia, completed in 1978, was a flop. The development it was supposed to stimulate never arrived and it soon became the first Postmodern ruin, though it has not been bulldozed and there have been two attempts to restore it. A non-event locally, it nevertheless became a major event internationally. For a while its image became the routine accompaniment to every magazine article about the new Postmodernist architecture – and that is how architectural history is made.

Piazza d'Italia, New Orleans, Louisiana, USA. Charles Moore, 1978.
The piazza became the first Postmodern ruin, though there have been various restoration efforts.

It may have been Philip Johnson's influence that ensured the success of the Portland Building, which is surprising given that it had been he who, with Henry-Russell Hitchcock, had introduced European Modernism to America in the 'International Style' exhibition back in 1932 (see Chapter 15). Johnson's decisive conversion to Postmodernism was confirmed in the design of an office building in Manhattan for the telecommunications giant AT&T, then one of the richest companies in the world. The building was called, mockingly, the Chippendale skyscraper because it looked like a vertically stretched cabinet by the great eighteenth-century English furniture maker. Most of the tower's 37 storeys are straightforwardly clad in glass and plain brown stone, but at top and bottom the flat face of the monolith is carved away in simple geometrical shapes: an open colonnade with a seven-storey-high arched main entrance at street level, and the outline of a broken pediment at the top where it is visible to the rest of the city and to the architectural photographers of the world. Johnson's

Postmodernist statement, like those of Graves and Moore, was made with very simple means, as if all the Modernist raging against traditional ornament had been unnecessary. Ornament is inexpensive and easy to achieve, it seemed to say, so let's have more of it.

Strada Novissima

Meanwhile in Europe, where moralistic Modernism originated, Postmodernism was beginning to declare itself. In 1980, the Italian architect and academic Paolo Portoghesi lined up all the Postmodernist architects he could find along the so-called Strada Novissima, a mocked-up street of 'houses' in an old ropeworks at the Venice Biennale. The anti-Modernist sentiment of the exhibition, called 'The Presence of the Past', was already implied in the revival of the corridor street form itself, which Le Corbusier had tried to abolish. Each architect's contribution would inevitably be a formal rather than a functional statement. Robert Stern, Charles Jencks, Christian Norberg-Schulz and Vincent Scully were among Portoghesi's advisors. Kenneth Frampton withdrew from the project because of a disagreement over policy but also no doubt because of his squeamishness about the whole Postmodernist

---

AT&T Building, New York City, USA. Philip Johnson and John Burgee, 1984. A classical broken pediment converts a routine New York skyscraper into a herald of Postmodernism.

(Below) Strada Novissima, Venice Biennale, 1980.
A mocked-up street of Postmodernist and Neo-Rationalist 'houses' side by side.

Les Arcades du Lac, Saint-Quentin-en-Yvelines, France.
Ricardo Bofill, 1974. A Postmodernist Versailles to the west of
Paris, not far from the real Versailles.

enterprise. Exhibitors were of two main types: those who
treated their houses as illusionistic, ephemeral constructions,
and those who were more serious about the revival of solid
classical certainties. For example, Venturi, Rauch and Scott
Brown, in the first group, were content to paint a cartoon
version of a classical temple on a flat screen, whereas
Léon Krier, in the second group but right next door, built a
neo-primitive construction with plastered walls and a solid
wooden lintel. This difference of approach was the sign of
a widening ideological gap between the mainly American
Postmodernists and the mainly European Neo-Rationalists
(see Chapter 25).

Ricardo Bofill

The Catalan architect Ricardo Bofill, represented at the
Biennale by a kind of tomb with rusticated columns, holds
a special place in the history of Postmodernism because
of the unhesitating confidence of his revived classicism
and because he applied it to, of all unlikely building types,
public-sector housing. As early as 1974, he was building Les
Arcades du Lac, a kind of Versailles for the masses at Saint-
Quentin-en-Yvelines, not far from the real Palace of Versailles
to the west of Paris. Four-storey continuous terraces with
arcaded ground floors are arranged in formal squares,
circles and crescents. Nearby, a multi-storey inhabited pier

Les Espaces d'Abraxas, Marne-la-Vallée, France. Ricardo
Bofill, 1983. A crescent of giant glass columns, actually the bay
windows of ordinary living rooms.

stands in the adjacent lake, recalling the fifteenth-century
bridge-chateau of Chenonceau. At Les Espaces d'Abraxas,
built a few years later as part of the new town of Marne-la-
Vallée, the style has lost all restraint. The residential blocks
now rise to ten storeys and have become unambiguously,
bombastically classical. One crescent-shaped block is
adorned internally by a giant order of glass columns, actually

just stacks of bay windows lighting ordinary living rooms, and externally by Colosseum-like superimposed orders with paired pilasters, except that all are simplified Doric. This is kitsch image-making on a grand scale (Disneyland Paris is not far away, geographically and artistically) but it does at least create well-defined public spaces, in this case a version of a Roman theatre with a huge triumphal arch as its *scaenae frons*. Modernist functionalism has been forgotten completely – form and human use seem unconnected – but modern construction is a major theme. Precast concrete, of high quality, is the basic technology. Bofill's office in Barcelona, known as the Taller de Arquitectura, was, and still is, a large and competent multidisciplinary practice.

But Bofill is not the best representative of European Postmodernism. The Austrian Hans Hollein was a more sophisticated pioneer of figurative architecture. In his eclectic Vienna travel agency, for example, completed in 1978 but since destroyed, various destination types were represented by symbolic installations such as golden palm trees, broken columns and a Lutyens-style domed pavilion. It was symbolism of a literal kind but also wryly humorous. In England, Terry Farrell, having broken with High Tech partner Nicholas Grimshaw, enthusiastically proclaimed his newly adopted Postmodernism in the London headquarters of a new breakfast television company, TV-am. An unpromising 1950s garage in north London, between a back street and a canal, became a joyous declaration of independence from Modernism. The snaky metal- and stone-clad facade was enlivened by large, extruded letters – TVam – facing the busier main roads and each end, and by an open steel-framed arch with a deconstructed keystone over the vehicle

Travel agency, Vienna, Austria. Hans Hollein, 1978. Broken columns, palm trees and a Mughal dome unambiguously denote travel to far-off lands.

MI6 Headquarters, London, UK. Terry Farrell, 1994.
The building has since come to symbolize the secret but
possibly glamorous world of espionage.

entrance. Inside, a two-storey concourse was 'themed' like
a holiday hotel, with a Japanese garden for a hospitality
suite and a miniature Busby Berkeley film set for a main
staircase. On the canal side, the existing saw-tooth wall
was decorated not with urns or pineapples but with egg-
cups to symbolize breakfast. The popular Art Deco style
of the 1920s and 1930s (see Chapter 13) was an obvious
influence, and Farrell would go on to exploit it in more
prominent London buildings such as Embankment Place
and the MI6 headquarters, both Thames-side landmarks.

James Stirling

But the subtlest and most skilful of the European
Postmodernists was undoubtedly James Stirling. His alert,
agile architectural creativity might have been summed up
and dismissed in the pale word 'eclectic' had not each
of his stylistic career turns produced historic landmark
buildings. We saw in Chapter 17 how his mystification when
faced with Le Corbusier's new post-war style, especially
the enigmatic chapel at Ronchamp, was quickly turned to
creative use in the flats at Ham Common, completed in

1957, initiating a British 'brick Brutalist' style in residential
and university buildings. Stirling himself meanwhile wandered
restlessly away from Corb's influence and became interested
in Russian Constructivism. His Engineering Building at
Leicester University ignited unusual interest and enthusiasm
among British architects, perhaps because the Russian
references (Mel'nikov's Rusakov Workers' Club, for example,
see page 144) were at that time relatively obscure. Reyner
Banham immediately included the building in his book *The
New Brutalism*, though it displayed none of the normal
Brutalist characteristics, whether Miesian or Corbusian.
A slender tower with chamfered corners dominates a
cluster of facetted forms, including two lecture theatres,
their raked seating banks cantilevered out to show their
undersides as sloping soffits. Engineering laboratories are
housed in a low, compact industrial block with a crystalline,
diagonally structured glass roof. In this building, the versatile
combination of aluminium bars and glass sheets, then known
as 'patent glazing', becomes a medium for sculpture. Solid
parts are clad in red bricks and tiles, presumably thought
to be appropriate for the red-brick city of Leicester and its
'red brick' university, yet the materials palette remained the
same when Stirling was called upon to design a Faculty of
History library for the decidedly non-red-brick university of
Cambridge. Here are the facetted forms again but arranged

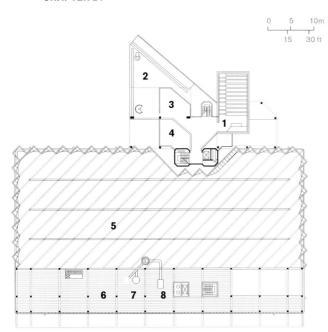

0   5   10m
15   30 ft

First floor plan and section

1. Small lecture theatre
2. Terrace
3. Lobby
4. Upper part of entrance hall
5. Upper part of laboratories
6. Paint shop/store
7. Upper part of boiler room
8. Boiler

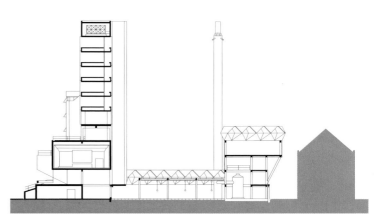

Engineering Building, Leicester University, Leicester, UK. James Stirling with James Gowan, 1963. Resemblance to Russian Constructivist projects of the 1920s is probably deliberate. Stirling knew his history.

as a quadrant-shaped reading room and book stack within an L-shaped office block – not unlike an open book, though the symbolism was certainly not intended to be literal. The plan arises from the 'panopticon' principle, with bookcases arranged radially so that they can be supervised from a single point. A cascading glass roof is double skinned, with air-handling machinery, painted in primary colours, visibly suspended between steel trusses. This is High Tech, surely; but the date is 1968, so too early. It may be no coincidence, however, that in 1962 Richard Rogers and Norman Foster, who were to become the chief exponents of the High Tech style, had studied at Yale University, where the well-connected and well-respected Stirling was a visiting critic. Years later, in 1986, the three would be reunited in a major exhibition at the Royal Academy called simply 'Foster, Rogers, Stirling'.

The Cambridge library subsequently suffered many technical failures, becoming notorious among university administrators and also among student users like Gavin Stamp, David Watkin and Roger Scruton who later became influential, anti-Modernist critics. Stirling continued his technically risky progress, nevertheless, in buildings for St Andrews University (ridged precast concrete), the Olivetti typewriter company (glass-reinforced plastic cladding) and the Southgate Estate at Runcorn New Town (uncompromising concrete with round windows, completed in 1977 and demolished in 1990). None of these buildings suggests Postmodernist leanings but, unlike the early work of Michael Graves, they show a restless willingness to experiment and to move beyond, rather than work within, Modernist precepts.

Stirling's openness to new architectural possibilities was matched by a personal openness to the influence of

(Top) History Faculty Library, Cambridge, UK.
James Stirling, 1968. Red tiles and 'patent glazing'
carried over from the Leicester Engineering Building
to a very different Cambridge context.

Southgate Estate, Runcorn New Town, Cheshire,
UK. James Stirling, 1977. Uncompromising concrete
with round windows, demolished in 1990 when only
13 years old.

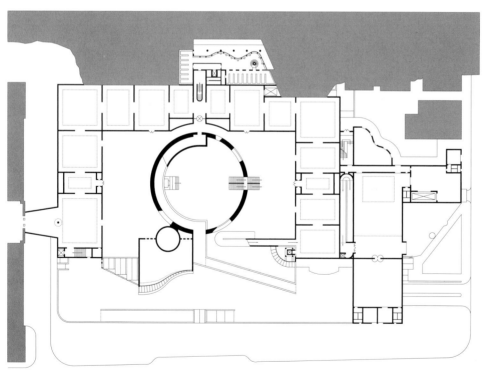

Neue Staatsgalerie, Stuttgart, Germany. James Stirling, 1984.
A Postmodernist collage, including the direct quotation of a tomb by Weinbrenner.

First floor plan

**Hotel, Lake Buena Vista, Florida, USA. Michael Graves,
1990.** Cartoon architecture on an epic scale. The roof ornaments
are six storeys high.

colleagues. From 1956 to 1963 he worked in partnership with James Gowan. In 1969 the young Léon Krier joined the office for a short time and may have encouraged a more intense focus on history and urban context, though we should bear in mind that Stirling's knowledge and love of architectural history had been profound since his student days. In 1971, Michael Wilford became a partner. That year a project for an arts centre at St Andrews University involved the creation of a formal forecourt dominated by a preserved eighteenth-century house. After this was published, invitations began to arrive to participate in design competitions for cultural projects in Germany. In 1977 the practice's entry for the Neue Staatsgalerie (New State Gallery) competition in Stuttgart was successful. The building was completed in 1984 and is now regarded as a high point in the development of European Postmodernism.

The Neue Staatsgalerie is a collage – its architect frankly described it as such – and collage is a Modernist medium, so right from the start the Postmodernist label seems doubtful. There is no question here of a straight revival of classicism or even of its transformation into an integrated new style in the manner of Venturi and Scott Brown or Graves. This is a composition of fragments stolen from various styles and periods, sometimes reinterpreted, like solid stone walls that turn out to be thin, mortarless

cladding, and sometimes quoted verbatim, like the copy of a nineteenth-century tomb by Friedrich Weinbrenner that marks the sunken entrance from the courtyard. The site is a fairly steep slope between two roads: a quiet street at the top and an urban almost-motorway at the bottom. The old nineteenth-century building next door provides the basic model: a U-shaped block of conventional top-lit galleries around a courtyard. But the courtyard of the new building contains a second, circular, sunken courtyard like the remains of a once-domed hall. Other functions, including a lecture hall, two small theatres, a music room, offices and a library, are grouped under and around this basic parti, some of them in separate pieces of architecture, like the tall, stripped classical theatre wing to the south and the Corbusian Modernist house at the top of the site that contains the library and offices. Colourful High Tech details, such as thick pink handrails, ship's deck cowls to ventilate the basement car park, and a warped glass foyer wall with bright green mullions, denote a playful modernity. The brief required a pedestrian right of way to be maintained across the site between the two roads. Stirling makes a virtue of this potentially destructive intrusion, threading

327

Team Disney Building, Burbank, California, USA. Michael Graves, 1986. Dopey and the other six dwarves supplant the ancient idols of classical architecture.

Fatal success

In the words of Charles Jencks: 'An architectural movement often finds it easier to survive persecution than success.'[14] Postmodernism's fatal success came in 1985 when Michael Eisner, the head of the Walt Disney empire, invited a number of prominent architects, including Robert Stern (himself on the Disney board of directors), Frank Gehry, Charles Moore, Robert Venturi and Denise Scott Brown, and

it right through the middle of the building where it skirts the courtyard on a ramp. Passers-by become passers-through who can enjoy the architectural experience free of charge and return another day for a proper visit. Whatever its stylistic allegiances, the Neue Staatsgalerie displays consummate compositional skill.

Michael Graves to design buildings for Disney in theme parks and elsewhere. James Stirling refused to participate. Graves participated eagerly, with a pair of hotels at Lake Buena Vista, Florida, completed in 1990. Two enormous symmetrical arrangements of flat, patterned and pastel-coloured forms face each other across an artificial lake. They are named the Dolphin and the Swan after their paired roof ornaments, which are approximately six storeys high. If this were a scene from a children's animated film, which it clearly resembles, these buildings would surely represent the evil empire over which the humble hero eventually triumphs. Graves's other major contribution to Disney real estate is the Team Disney Building in Burbank, California, a more obviously classical building featuring caryatids in the shape of six of the Seven Dwarves, with Dopey occupying the place of honour in the pediment above. It is hard to say who should be more offended, lovers of classical architecture or lovers of early Disney masterpieces such as *Snow White* and *Fantasia*.

The Vanna Venturi House

History has decided that the Vanna Venturi House, completed in 1964, was the very first Postmodern building. Frederick Swartz, an architect and writer who worked with Venturi, went so far as to call it 'the first Postmodern anything'. It was designed while Venturi was writing *Complexity and Contradiction in Architecture* and might be seen as the built analogue of that manifesto. All the supposed virtues of Modernism are called into question: its simplicity and consistency, its scientism and functionalism, its rejection of history and its aloof silences. Venturi preferred the mysterious subtleties of the sixteenth-century Mannerist architecture he had studied while on a fellowship at the American Academy in Rome. The commission from his mother for a house on a suburban site close to Louis Kahn's Esherick House (see page 292) gave him the opportunity to test the possibilities of a twentieth-century Mannerism.

This is not a silent but a communicative building. Its front elevation declares its identity by presenting a symmetrical, gabled outline with a chimney, like a child's drawing of a house. But immediately there are inconsistencies. This is not just a gable, but a pediment, a Mannerist broken pediment that, to the initiated, might faintly recall Michelangelo or Giulio Romano. The chimney is a symbol of domesticity – there is a welcoming fire somewhere inside – but it is right in the middle, it is bigger than it needs to be and it seems to have a window in it, visible through the break in the pediment.

The whole facade is symmetrical, except that it isn't: the recessed porch is in the middle but the three windows are all different and placed irregularly. Those on the left are square and traditional-looking, but the one on the right is a short ribbon that might be a quotation from Le Corbusier. Already the ambiguities are piling up and we haven't yet got past the front facade.

Inside, the plan is equally subtle. Rather than allocate a space to each function as a Modernist might, Venturi deliberately sets up conflicts and awkwardnesses that have to be resolved by what he called 'accommodations'. For example, the porch, the fireplace and the staircase all want to be at the centre of the composition and have to fight each other for priority. The result is complex and contradictory but with some surprising functional benefits. For example, the steps that find themselves stranded where the flight narrows to accommodate the chimney become handy shelves for things waiting to be taken upstairs. This is not an 'open', Modernist plan. A living room, a kitchen and three bedrooms, one on the first floor, are contained by conventional partitions, but there are ambiguous spaces too, like the external 'yard' tucked under the main roof like another room. Venturi spent a long time designing this small building, producing at least six fully worked-out designs (his indulgent client was in no hurry). The 'difficult whole' that resulted was a box of architectural tricks that made its Modernist contemporaries look tired and dull.

25 | NEO-RATIONALISM 1967–1991

When Modernism began to founder in the mid-1960s, American and European reactions were very different. In America, in 1966, Robert Venturi published *Complexity and Contradiction in Architecture*, the foundation text of Postmodernism; in Europe, in the same year, Aldo Rossi published *L'architettura della città* (*The Architecture of the City*), the foundation text of Neo-Rationalism. For a while the two movements were closely associated and sometimes confused with one another because of their shared anti-Modernism – for example, both were represented side by side in the Strada Novissima at the Venice Biennale of 1980 (see page 320) – but actually they had little in common. Postmodernism was at home in America, an enormous empty territory relatively recently populated by fast-built cities of a provisional and experimental nature. The impression of permanence and solidity in American architecture had mostly been achieved by the imitation of classical forms. Surface appearance and communicativeness were more highly valued than material integrity. Neo-Rationalism, on the other hand, was born in Italy, a country built among the ruins of the ancient empire that had bequeathed those classical forms. Actual permanence was what mattered to Rossi, not just the appearance of it. In Italian cities, 2,000-year-old structures were still the settings of daily life. For example, an old Roman amphitheatre survived in the oval plan of a public square in Lucca, and in Rome Piazza Navona, with its seventeenth-century Baroque fountains, maintained the outline of a first-century stadium.

Aldo Rossi

According to Rossi this continual adaptation of urban remains was a kind of collective architecture developing over time. Cities were works of art that had to be respected and maintained, like gardens or households. 'Contextualism' was what the Anglo-Saxon world called it. Why it came to be known as Neo-Rationalism is something of a mystery. It might have inherited a certain liking for simple, functional forms from pre-war Rationalists like Giuseppe Terragni (see page 182), and it certainly acknowledged allegiance to the rational philosophical tradition of the eighteenth-century Enlightenment, but the name is misleading because early in his book Rossi made it

very clear that he regarded Modernist 'functionalism' – the idea that the form arose from rational solutions to functional problems – as a naive concept.[1] For Rossi, a better way to think about architectural form was as a collection of 'types' – a 'typology'. Types are families of common forms such as streets, squares, towers, halls, apartment blocks, monuments, corridors, rooms, columns, beams and so on. They are families in two senses: because their members are similar but not identical, and because they have ancestors receding, generation by generation, into the remote past. The traces of that inheritance lay all around in the old cities of southern Europe. And it was from those cities, in which the activities of daily life were densely and richly mixed, and a street or a square might be 2,000 years old, that the Neo-Rationalist architects took their inspiration. The movement was delivering a counterblow to the Modernist urbanism of Le Corbusier, who thought that streets and squares were obsolete and that a city could be designed all at once, with different zones to accommodate its various functions.

Actually though, one of Rossi's earliest major works as an architect, the Gallaratese housing block on the outskirts of Milan, would not look out of place in Le Corbusier's Ville Radieuse. Though divided by a narrow gap about one-third of the way along, it is effectively a single linear block, four storeys high and 180 metres (197 yards) long. The ground floor is open, with a row of columns on one side and a row of concrete fins on the other. Access to the apartments is via continuous open balconies along the south-east side. All windows are square, their regular rhythm relieved only by larger square openings marking the lift and staircase lobbies. It is hard to see any connection between this isolated, diagrammatic Modernist composition and the inherited urbanism described in *L'architettura della città*, though Rossi claimed that the form of the building was based on the traditional tenements of the region. Gradually, his architecture moved from this very severe Rationalism to something more poetic, combining simple, traditional forms to make buildings that, though not literal imitations of pre-Modernist architecture, nevertheless evoked its memory. Rossi's poetic manner is nicely exemplified in the little floating theatre that he designed for the milestone Venice Biennale of 1980.

(Above) Housing, Gallaratese, Milan, Italy. Aldo Rossi, 1976. The square windows were to become a leitmotif of Neo-Rationalism.

(Right) Teatro del Mondo, 1980 Venice Biennale. Aldo Rossi, 1979. An apparently solid building that could not be relied upon to stay in one place.

The Teatro del Mondo was made in a boatyard at Fusina and towed across the lagoon to Venice where it was moored in the Giudecca Canal, near the Custom House and the church of Santa Maria della Salute. Apparently made of wood but actually supported by a hidden frame of steel scaffolding, it was essentially a tower, square on plan but flanked by thinner, taller stair towers and crowned by an octagonal lantern with a steep pyramid roof. Inside was a single-volume auditorium, full height, with two galleries. Perhaps it was the dream-like quality of this building that made it memorable, the fact that, though monumental in profile, it floated and could not be relied upon to stay in one place. The comparison is often made with surreal, faintly disturbing urban scenes in the paintings of Giorgio de Chirico.

In the hands of a different architect – Le Corbusier, say – such a combination of simple geometrical solids might have been purely abstract, but in Rossi's architecture the solids are reminiscent of traditional building elements and usually arranged in symmetrical compositions. There is an almost personal appeal to memory, a cultural or collective memory, distilled and made more potent by unexpected proportions. The secondary school at Broni, completed in 1979, for example, adopts the simplest possible courtyard plan, almost square with a cloister-like corridor. Single storey, with a shallow-pitched roof and square windows, it is utterly plain but saved from banality by monumental

(Above) Secondary school, Broni, Italy. Aldo Rossi, 1979. A dream-like monumentality achieved by simple means.

(Below) Aurora House, Turin, Italy. Aldo Rossi, 1987. The columns might have been salvaged from an ancient building and reused.

San Cataldo Cemetery, Modena, Italy. Aldo Rossi, 1976–85. Ranks and files of what might be windows create an uncertain sense of scale.

points of transition along the centre line: an entrance portico with a clock, an octagonal assembly hall on a circular base in the middle of the courtyard, and a narrow flight of steps under an extruded pediment on the other side.

In the early years of his career Rossi was enough of a left-wing radical to get himself suspended from his teaching post in Milan, but by no means all of his buildings are schools and social housing. Aurora House in Turin, completed in 1987, is an economical urban office building, five storeys high, on a corner site. This too is a combination of typical forms. Colonnades along the street frontages carry stone-clad 'attics' with trademark square windows. Above them, brick is the main material, as if the modern offices had been built on the remains of an older, more public building. A diagonal brick tower on the corner incorporates an entrance portico with a pair of columns that look too tall and fat, as if preserved from the imaginary older building and reused.

But the project that best represents Rossi's style and philosophy is the San Cataldo Cemetery at Modena, first designed as early as 1971, then redesigned in 1976 and under construction until 1985 but still not finished. Supposedly conceived as a city of the dead, it is hardly city-like in its spatial character – a vast flat field, bounded by narrow, linear buildings in which the remains of the dead are stacked in 'columbaria' on either side of straight walkways. The main architectural event is the red cube of the multi-storey ossuary at the centre of the composition. Here, once again, are those square windows, now reduced to plain, frameless openings arranged on a regular grid as though the dead occupants of the building had need of daylight but not of shelter. Externally there is no further elaboration, no base or cornice, no pilasters or architraves. Inside, we discover that the walls are lined by columbaria

House, Riva San Vitale, Switzerland. Mario Botta, 1973.
The light steel entrance bridge contrasts with the masonry of
the tower as if it were a later addition.

but the eight floors implied by the rows of 'windows' do
not exist. There are only steel-framed walkways on three
levels, almost industrial in character, and the central part
of the roof is open to the sky. This is a powerful piece of
architecture, or perhaps just a powerful image, especially
when viewed from a distance when its scale becomes
ambiguous and that surreal, dream-like quality is felt again.
The local residents, however, are said to hate it and to be
reluctant to think of it as their final resting place.

Mario Botta

Italy was the heartland of Neo-Rationalism. Other members
of the so-called *Tendenza* included Giorgio Grassi, whose
book *La costruzione logica dell'architettura* ('The Logical
Construction of Architecture') helped to establish the
theoretical foundations of the movement, and Vittorio
Gregotti, the designer of important university buildings
in Palermo, Florence and Calabria. But many of the most
committed and productive *Tendenza* architects worked
in Ticino, the Italian-speaking southernmost canton of
Switzerland. Among them, Luigi Snozzi, Aurelio Galfetti
and Livio Vacchini were well respected but the best known
was Mario Botta, who developed a distinctive personal
style and went on to establish a large international practice.
Botta was trained at the school of architecture in Venice,
where Rossi was a teacher, but he also worked briefly with
both Le Corbusier and Louis Kahn on unrealized projects
for that city. Le Corbusier instilled in him a lasting respect
for Modernist principles and Kahn showed how they
might be reconciled with the monumental Italian tradition.
Botta's style is best exemplified by a group of early houses,
which respond to the hilly Ticino landscape not by trying
to be part of it, in the manner of Frank Lloyd Wright, but
by declaring their independence as geometrically pure
objects. The first, completed in 1973 at Riva San Vitale,
is a tower of concrete blockwork standing at the foot of a
slope but accessible from the top via a steel-framed bridge.
It is five storeys high, including a semi-basement, and its
plan is a perfect square. The staircase within is also square
but placed slightly off centre to allow more choice in the
sizes and proportions of living spaces. A basic diagonal
symmetry is maintained nevertheless.

The Round House at Stabio, completed in 1982, is a squat
cylinder, again in grey concrete block – a formal contrast to,
and an implied criticism of, the eclectic villas that populate
the surrounding hillsides. Since it is impossible to extend
a cylinder sideways without destroying its purity, this one
has been developed and made habitable by subtraction,
by carving out the living spaces and the openings

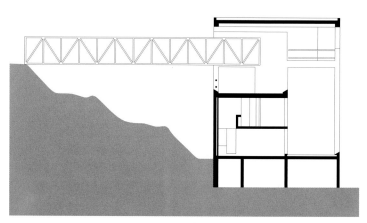

Entry level plan and section

0   5   10m
15   30 ft

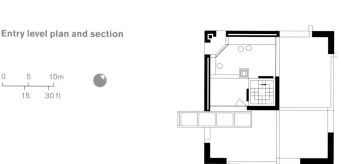

San Francisco Museum of Modern Art, San Francisco, USA. Mario Botta, 1995. A representative of European monumentality visits a west-coast American city.

necessary to light them. Outside, the object remains formal and symmetrical but inside spaces are divided or linked, both horizontally and vertically, in clever combinations. This is not a classical building in the traditional sense, but its rounded stair tower is nevertheless equipped with a corbelled top like a primitive capital. These smartly dressed, formal houses at first seem anti-urban but they are as much inspired by the traditional European city as Rossi's dream-like visions. In 2011, Botta said: 'The city is the most evolved form of human or social aggregation. And I believe that the European city is the best model we know.'[2] This view did not, however, deter him from working in non-European cities. His San Francisco Museum of Modern

Art, completed in 1995, a symmetrical, stepped brick mass pierced by a huge, angle-sliced cylindrical roof-light, has all the geometrical formality of the early houses and brings a European monumentality to the SoMa district of the city.

O. M. Ungers

Neo-Rationalism found allies elsewhere in Europe, especially in Germany where Oswald Mathias Ungers and Josef Paul Kleihues adapted the movement's principles to a German cultural context. Ungers's earliest works were influenced by British Brutalism, but in the 1960s he became an academic and concentrated on theoretical alternatives to Modernism, developing themes under headings such as 'transformation', 'assemblage', 'incorporation' and 'assimilation'.[3] Then in the 1980s he returned to practice and produced a clutch of important buildings in Germany such as the Baden Regional Library in Karlsruhe, opposite the early nineteenth-century church of St Stephan by Weinbrenner, and the Deutsches Architekturmuseum (German Architecture Museum) in Frankfurt. The latter perfectly illustrates the principle of 'incorporation'. A classical villa built in 1912 becomes the container of a second 'house' rising through four floors to emerge in the attic, complete with typical Neo-Rationalist pitched roof and square windows. The principle has wider analytical applications and, according to Ungers, is fundamental to architecture; he cites the Greek temple – a sanctuary within a 'cella', within a colonnade, within a sacred precinct. The appeal to ancient constancies is typical of Neo-Rationalist theory.

As director of planning for the International Building Exhibition (in German, Internationale Bauausstellung or IBA) in the early 1980s, Kleihues invited prominent Postmodernists and Neo-Rationalists to demonstrate their urban ideas in the reconstruction of neglected areas of

West Berlin. Rossi, Gregotti, Grassi and Ungers were all represented, as were James Stirling and Peter Eisenman. Rob Krier, who had worked with Ungers in the 1960s, helped to set the agenda with his Ritterstrasse apartments in Kreuzberg, completed in 1978 – a white-stuccoed, flat-roofed block that could almost be called Modernist but for its symmetry and the mutilated winged figure that looms over its shallow-arched gateway, perhaps symbolizing a ruined and divided Berlin. But Krier is best known for his contribution to theory in a book called *Urban Space*, first published in German in 1975 as *Stadtraum in Theorie und Praxis* ('Urban Space in Theory and Practice'). The basic tenet of the book is that cities have been destroyed by industrial culture and are in desperate need of reconstruction. For Krier this means mainly the re-establishment of defined and contained public spaces – streets and squares. The possibilities are illustrated in fragmentary, small-scale plans analyzing historical and invented examples in terms of solid and void, or 'figure and ground' in the contemporary jargon. It was left to Rob Krier's

German Architecture Museum, Frankfurt, Germany. O. M. Ungers, 1984. A house within a house – the principle of 'incorporation'. Note the models of Mendelsohn's Einstein Tower in the foreground.

younger brother, Léon, to forge these fragments into a series of visionary urban projects.

Léon Krier's anti-industrialism

Léon Krier's politics were ferociously anti-industrial and based, initially at least, on the Marxism of Theodor Adorno. In the introduction to a charter for the reconstruction of the European city, Krier said: 'The myth of unlimited technical progress and development has brought the most "developed" countries to the brink of physical and cultural exhaustion.'[4] Modernism had supported that myth, dividing the city into functional zones and dissolving the solid monumentality of traditional urban architecture. Krier wanted to re-establish the integrated life patterns of the traditional city by dividing it not into zones but into multifunctional 'quarters', each like a mini-city with its own public spaces and monuments. He had no time for advanced building technologies, believing that health and wholeness could only be restored to the city by a revival of classicism, which he saw as a symbol not of authority but of shared public worth. For Léon Krier, classical architecture was the timeless, symbolic elaboration of traditional building crafts. Later in his career he would even go so far as to praise the classicism of the Nazi architect Albert Speer (see page 187).

The most widely publicized and influential of Léon Krier's visionary projects was his 1976 plan for the La Villette district of northern Paris, which six years later was to be the site of the famous 'urban park for the twenty-first century' competition won by Bernard Tschumi (see page 378). Krier's project presents detailed proposals for a complete new urban quarter. His coloured drawings – plans and perspectives – are beautiful and seductive. A traditional,

rectangular street grid is applied to the site, its blocks filled by what look like uniformly plain three- or four-storey tenements but are possibly place holders for more varied mixed-use buildings as yet undesigned. The grid is relieved by larger public spaces, principally a roughly north–south double boulevard that bisects the site and creates a formal setting for major public buildings. The boulevard is crossed by a stretch of existing canal, which continues westward into the city where it is terminated by a late-eighteenth-century *barrière* or custom house by Claude-Nicolas Ledoux. Krier would certainly have admired this neo-classical building and perhaps meant it to be included, conceptually, in his monumental boulevard. On the site itself, the canal passes through two parks, one of which is fringed by a curious serpentine row of tower houses made into a single spatially porous building by a continuous pitched roof. Such clever inventions prove that Krier was more than just a classical revivalist.

But how real is this vision of a future restored urbanity? Motorized traffic seems to have been banished from its streets. At the time this assumption seemed pure fantasy but now, since the widespread introduction of congestion charges and road space rationing, it looks like common sense. Those non-specific tenement buildings, which presumably contain workshops as well as apartments, seemed quaint in 1976, but now seem not too different from the converted lofts of London, New York or San Francisco, which serve digitally transformed work patterns. And these

Urban Quarter project, La Villette, Paris, France. Léon Krier, 1976. An ordered urban hierarchy of well-defined public spaces and monumental buildings.

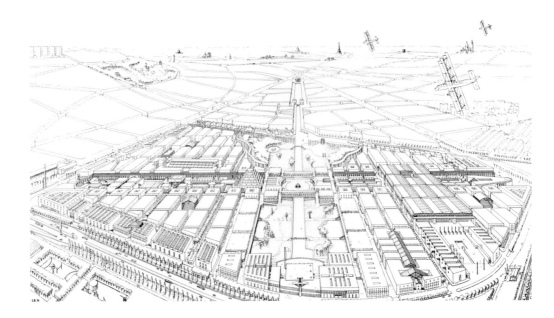

hierarchies of public spaces – streets and squares, paved, contained and furnished with monuments – now represent conventional planning wisdom, at least in city centres if not on the outskirts where retail sheds, car parks and urban motorways prevail. Krier's urban projects were visionary and perhaps also prophetic, but the transformation of industrial culture that actually took place was very different from the one he wished for. Though his theoretical position was in most respects the opposite of Le Corbusier's, both shared an idealism that shone out in dream-like drawings. As a young student (he studied architecture formally for only a few months) Krier was besotted with Le Corbusier, reading him, with his brother Rob, 'like revolutionaries'.[5] Despite his subsequent disillusionment, that old love lingers in certain graphic details like the biplanes flying over the big aerial perspective, and the café furniture in vignettes of local public squares.

Early in his career as a project maker Krier declared that he would build nothing as long as cultural conditions made the creation of true architecture impossible. But he was too much of an architect to hold out for long. In 1984 the Prince of Wales made a speech at Hampton Court Palace in which he revealed his anti-Modernist taste in architecture, describing a proposed extension to the National Gallery as 'a monstrous carbuncle on the face of a much loved and elegant friend'.[6] The extension was designed by the well-respected practice Ahrends, Burton and Koralek, though it is likely that the prince had confused their design with one by Richard Rogers. It was the beginning of a royal campaign

Sainsbury Wing, National Gallery, London, UK. Robert Venturi and Denise Scott Brown, 1991. Tentative, cerebral Postmodern classicism for an important site on Trafalgar Square.

that made villains of some of Britain's best architects and created a minor rash of insipid neo-classical projects such as the Richmond Riverside development by Quinlan Terry and Grand Buildings, a replica Victorian hotel on the south-east corner of Trafalgar Square by Sidell Gibson, but also the

Richmond Riverside, London, UK. Quinlan Terry, 1987. Ordinary commercial development built all at once but pretending to be an accretion of old buildings.

Fire station, Poundbury, Dorset, UK. Calderpeel Architects, 2008. A cartoon classical building said to have been designed by the Prince of Wales.

rather more interesting exercise in Postmodern Mannerism by Robert Venturi and Denise Scott Brown that was the eventual built outcome of the National Gallery extension saga.

Léon Krier became Prince Charles's expert guide in this campaign. Soon the prince, answering an implied suggestion from the profession that he try it himself if he thought he could do any better, was proposing the building of a new community on land that he owned in Dorset, to the west of the old market town of Dorchester. Krier prepared the initial master plan in 1988, construction started in 1993 and Poundbury, as it is known, has grown slowly ever since. Theoretically it embodies Krier's principles, such as mixed rather than zoned functions and the suppression of the motor car, but it looks nothing like La Villette. Its architecture is neither Postmodern nor Neo-Rationalist but a corny pastiche of cottage vernacular mixed with neo-Georgian, not too different from developers' suburbs elsewhere in

the country where local-authority planners insist on the maintenance of 'local character'. It is said that the prince himself designed the fire station, a risible combination of cartoon Roman temple with 1930s garage. But there is at least a village hall on a village square surrounded by useful shops, creating a rudimentary public realm and preventing a complete collapse into American-style motorized sprawl.

New Urbanism

Meanwhile in America a similar campaign against the destructive effect of the motor car was developing under the name 'New Urbanism'. Seaside, a 'resort community' on the Florida panhandle coast, planned by architects Andrés Duany and Elizabeth Plater-Zyberk, was its demonstration piece. Krier advised on the master plan in the early 1980s and contributed a wooden tower house with one classical temple on top and another at right angles sheltering a roof terrace lower down. It vaguely resembles the imaginary Tuscan houses he drew to amuse his friends in the 1970s, but American lightweight platform frame construction has sapped its vigour. New Urbanism and Neo-Rationalism share certain tenets – faith in the traditional city, distrust of the automobile, a natural leaning towards classicism – but the environments they produce are very different. What counts as 'urban' in an American context often looks like ordinary suburbia to European eyes. The example of Seaside probably improved the architectural quality of residential developments elsewhere in Florida, including the Disney town called Celebration, near the gates of Walt Disney World, which was developed from an approved set of architectural pattern books compiled by Urban Design Associates. Public buildings in the town were all designed by famous architects: a bank by Robert Venturi and Denise Scott Brown, a town hall by Philip Johnson, a cinema by Cesar Pelli, and a post office by Michael Graves. Architecture has become a 'theme' rather than a necessary craft. Seaside and Celebration are really not very different from countless other less famous developments in Florida, many of them gated and targeted at specific sectors of the community such as the over-sixties,

those with young families or those who play golf. All have to be fairly wealthy.

New Urbanism was one ideological crossroads at which European Neo-Rationalism and American Postmodernism met, but there had already, in the 1970s, been a good deal of transatlantic exchange at the level of teaching and theory. Oswald Mathias Ungers was chairman of the Department of Architecture at Cornell University from 1969 to 1975 and Aldo Rossi was a regular visitor to American architecture schools, including Yale and Cornell. A key figure was the British historian and theorist Colin Rowe, who held a professorship at Cornell from 1962 to 1990 and taught many famous architects, including James Stirling and Peter Eisenman. His book *Collage City*, written with Fred Koetter and first published in 1978, concurred with Rossi's *L'architettura della città* in its scepticism about Modernist urban planning

Tower House, Seaside, Florida, USA. Léon Krier, 1980. Krier's early dream-like drawings become somewhat less entrancing when realized in a Florida resort.

(Left) **Environmental Education Center, Liberty State Park, New Jersey, USA. Michael Graves, 1983.** A collage of European Neo-Rationalist motifs. Its architect called it a 'frog museum'.

(Below) **School, Saint Quentin-en-Yvelines, France. Léon Krier, 1978.** A typically seductive Krier drawing that exerted a world-wide influence.

but added a new concept, 'Bricolage', borrowed from the Structuralist anthropologist Claude Lévi-Strauss. What most architects took from the book, however, was the simple idea that Le Corbusier's 'City of Prophecy' had failed and it was time to re-examine the traditional 'City of Memory'.[7]

At the level of buildings, too, the Europeans made their mark in North America, both by influencing American architects and by direct export. Michael Graves was foremost of the American Postmodernists, but certain of his buildings clearly show the influence of Léon Krier. In its 'pavilion' planning and its classical-vernacular detailing, his Environmental Education Center at Liberty State Park, New Jersey, completed in 1983 (he called it a 'frog museum'), is similar to Krier's 1978 project for a school at Saint-Quentin-en-Yvelines, the French new town in which Ricardo Bofill built Les Arcades

**Mississauga Civic Centre, Toronto, Canada. Ed Jones and
Michael Kirkland, 1987.** The long pedimented block, probably
borrowed from Krier, is transported to a Canadian suburb.

du Lac (see page 321). Krier's project shows a miniature
city composed of separate buildings – assembly hall,
restaurant, library, gymnasium, headmaster's house, and
so on – each aspiring to be a perfect classical type. The
assembly hall is an astylar temple, the teacher's building
is a circular chapter house and the restaurants are housed
in a long, thin, sideways-pedimented building that doubles
as the site's main entrance portico. Graves's versions
of these types are simpler and cheaper, but the solid
stuccoed walls, carpentered roof trusses and strutted
wooden lintels are certainly derived from Krier and, beyond
him, from Karl Friedrich Schinkel's early nineteenth-century

Roman baths at the Charlottenhof Palace in Potsdam.
That sideways-pedimented form, somewhat reminiscent of
Gunnar Asplund's 1921 court house in Lister County in the
extreme south of Sweden, appears again on a larger scale
in the Mississauga Civic Centre near Toronto, designed by
Ed Jones and Michael Kirkland and completed in 1987. The
centre is surrounded by a suburban patchwork of low-rise
housing, shopping centres, parks and parking lots, with a
scattering of high buildings. Perhaps it was the complete
absence of anything resembling European urbanity that
persuaded the architects to create a little city of their own.
Here again we have a collection of separate, classical
buildings including a rotunda for the council chamber, a
forecourt flanked by colonnades and a tall clock tower.
Possible references to the local farmhouse vernacular are
misleading; it may be a long way from home, but this is
unmistakably an offshoot of European Neo-Rationalism.

Carlo Scarpa

The typical Modernist architect of the 1950s and 1960s was interested in mechanical abstraction rather than the qualities of natural materials, and in the reinvention of the city rather than its conservation. But by the mid-1980s the words 'materiality' and 'context' had crept into the conversation of teachers and students at the more progressive schools. Modernism was becoming sensitive to history and tradition. The work of the Venetian architect and teacher Carlo Scarpa provided an instructive example. He built very little and on a small scale, typically adapting old buildings for their new use as museums. But he was a Modernist, an admirer of Frank Lloyd Wright and Le Corbusier, and a friend of Louis Kahn. When he altered the fabric of a Venetian palace or a medieval fortress he never pretended new was old, never faked or copied. His interventions clearly represented the twentieth century's contribution to a composite work accumulated over time, like an Italian city.

Scarpa worked like a craftsman, with other craftsmen – masons, metalworkers, glass blowers, plasterers, joiners – designing details that were modern inventions but that understood the old techniques grounded in the nature of materials. Scarpa's details express a kind of creative fastidiousness. At the Querini Stampalia Palace in Venice, for example, new wall plaster stops just short of surviving medieval capitals, the junction between new floor and old walls is resolved in a gap that fills with water during the *acqua alta*, and a renewed flight of stone steps leaves the old steps exposed on either side. For Scarpa, the mounting and placing of works of art was a work of art itself. At the Abatellis Palace in Palermo, every painting, bust and statue is considered individually – the shape and material of its plinth or easel, its daylighting and background, its position and orientation in relation to the visitor's progress.

But the most famous Scarpa creation is the Museo Civico del Castelvecchio in Verona, on which he worked in various campaigns between 1958 and 1973. The fourteenth-century castle, incorporating an older section of the city wall, was used as a barracks by Napoleon in the 1790s. In the 1920s, Napoleon's extension, along the north wall facing the courtyard, was converted into a museum and provided with a fake Venetian Gothic facade. So already the building presented at least four different historical layers. Scarpa's fifth layer would pay attention to all of its predecessors as well as to the works of art on display. Early proposals envisaged a radical disruption of the inappropriately symmetrical 1920s facade. In the final version the interventions are more subtle. Window openings are backed by new glass walls, asymmetrically framed in steel and wood, and a new upper floor is constructed with an exposed steel beam running through all the galleries. The boldest intervention, however, was the complete demolition of the west end of the gallery wing, including a very solid Napoleonic staircase. The resulting gap is multi-levelled in both the physical and historical senses, exposing the old city wall and the openings that lead to the Mastio Tower and the Reggia wing beyond. And in this gap, at first-floor-level, angled slightly on its cantilevered concrete plinth, stands the museum's proudest asset: the equestrian statue of Cangrande della Scala, who ruled Verona at the beginning of the fourteenth century and was host and patron of the poet Dante.

Museo Civico del Castelvecchio, Verona, Italy. Carlo Scarpa, 1973. Equestrian statue of Cangrande della Scala, the museum's focal point and proudest asset.

26 | HIGH TECH
1967–1991

The application of new technologies to everyday building construction is a major theme in the history of twentieth-century architecture. Louis Sullivan and Auguste Perret used steel and reinforced concrete frames in otherwise traditional office blocks and apartment buildings (see Chapter 4), preparing the way for Mies van der Rohe and Le Corbusier to give these materials full expression in a new Modernist architecture. This was the architecture of what Reyner Banham called the First Machine Age, the age of the railway and the factory, the ocean liner and the power station. But by the mid century, machinery was taking on a new character. The typical machine was no longer a steam engine, but an automobile, no longer the exclusive concern of specialist engineers working for industry or government, but available on the open market for ordinary people to buy and use. Even the domestic environment was being transformed by small machines like refrigerators, electric cookers and vacuum cleaners.

Archigram

The Second Machine Age had dawned. How should architecture respond? In the early 1960s a group of

young architects recently graduated from London's Architectural Association (AA) school began publishing a small-circulation magazine called *Archigram*. It served as a justification for continued project-making of the free, futuristic kind that the group's members had enjoyed as students. Some of these projects have since become famous – Peter Cook's Plug-in City of 1964, for example, and Ron Herron's Walking City of the same year. No-one, least of all their authors, envisaged actually building these cities. They were pictorial provocations like scenes in a science fiction comic. But they were inspiring because they questioned the most basic assumptions about the nature of architecture, especially the assumption that it was an art of static formal composition. Plug-in City, despite its monstrous scale, was based on a dynamic and fundamentally individualistic idea: that dwellings would take the form of living 'pods', not too different from automobiles, that would be mass produced in factories, sold on the

Section of Plug-In City, Max Pressure Area. Peter Cook,
© Archigram, 1964. Not a static, formal composition but an ever-shifting urban configuration.

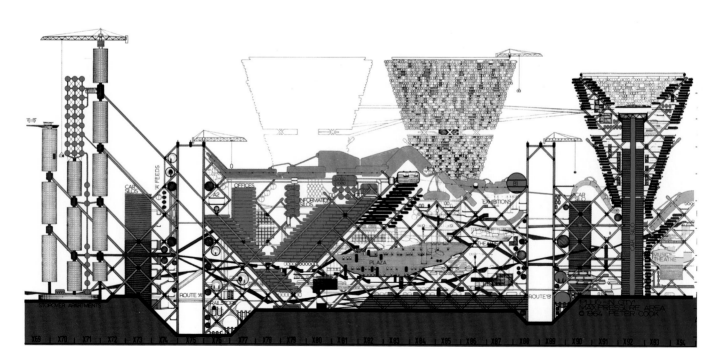

**Reliance Controls Factory, Swindon, Wiltshire, UK. Team 4,
1967.** Diagonal bracing, not strictly necessary in every bay, takes
the basically Miesian structure in a new direction.

open market and plugged into a three-dimensional service
infrastructure. Walking City was also dynamic, in a more
obvious and literal way.

So was the Archigram group showing the way forward for
an architecture of the second machine age? The irony is that
conceptually its projects were already a reality. American
trailer parks, for example, can be seen as examples of
dynamic urban form combining communal infrastructure
with factory-made living pods. And mobile cities had existed
for a long time in the shape of ocean liners. These existing
forms, however, did not count as architecture. They needed
to be brought into architecture's cultural orbit before they
could begin to influence actual buildings. This was the
service that Archigram performed. It encouraged practising
architects to look beyond the construction industry,
borrowing technologies from other fields and allowing those
technologies to influence the look of their buildings. In the
event, Archigram's influence would be as much aesthetic
as conceptual.

Among Archigram's approximate contemporaries at the
AA were Richard Rogers, Michael Hopkins and Nicholas
Grimshaw, who, for the next three decades, would inject
something of the spirit of those science fiction fantasies
into the real architecture that came to be known as High

Tech. But it was a fourth architect, Norman Foster, from a
less privileged background and trained at the Manchester
School of Architecture, who gave High Tech its steely
sense of purpose. It was not a 'movement' exactly, though
its protagonists were all known to one another and often
collaborated, especially in the early years of their careers.
It would be more accurate to say that High Tech was a
'style', though the superficial connotations of the word seem
inappropriate for an architecture that was based as much
on concepts and principles as on aesthetic preferences.

A definition

The main features of the style were as follows: the use of
synthetic materials like steel and glass rather than natural
materials like wood and brick; an almost moralistic code
of honesty of expression with no sham structures or false
facades; a preference for prefabrication rather than on-site
construction, and the expression of that preference in the
form of the building; and a tendency to ignore functional
and social distinctions, combining different human activities
in large, flexible spaces. Note that the High Tech style
had nothing to do with what we would now regard as high
technology – that is, digital technology. High Tech was
pre-digital, inspired by the physicality of machines, not the
virtuality of the internet. The typical High Tech building was a
factory on an open site, like Reliance Controls near Swindon
in Wiltshire, which is generally recognized as the first High
Tech building. Completed in 1967, it was designed by Team
4, a partnership between Richard Rogers and Norman Foster
with Su Rogers and Wendy Cheesman.

Reliance Controls did not look much like an Archigram fantasy. The direct influences on it were more mainstream, in particular the Cummins engine factory at Darlington in County Durham by Kevin Roche and John Dinkeloo, completed just a few years earlier. Roche and Dinkeloo had been associates of Eero Saarinen in the United States, but Mies van der Rohe was the underlying influence on their elegant glass-walled, flat-roofed factory with its exposed steel frame in pre-rusted Cor-Ten steel. One small technical detail of the building – the neoprene gaskets used in its glazing – was adopted by Team 4 and was to play an important part in the story of High Tech. But if Reliance Controls, like Cummins, was essentially Miesian, it was also a cheap and practical building, a simple shed combining production and office functions in the same space. Only the external cross-bracing of the steel frame gave any clue to the structural expressiveness that would later become a prominent feature of High Tech.

Another candidate for the title 'first High Tech building' is a glass-clad spiral of plastic bathroom 'pods' attached to the back of a Victorian house in London as part of its 1967 conversion into a student hostel. It was designed by Nicholas Grimshaw, then in partnership with Terry Farrell, who would eventually defect from the High Tech camp to become an important Postmodernist (see Chapter 24). The concept of a plug-in service tower that was itself an assemblage of plug-in units was like a small fragment of Peter Cook's urban vision.

Norman Foster

The partnership between Rogers and Foster did not last long. Soon each was designing simple sheds on his own

account in subtly different interpretations of the High Tech credo. Foster's earliest solo efforts were object lessons in the conversion of unpromising clients' briefs into high-class, not to say historic, architecture. The first of these was an office and amenity building in the London docks for Fred. Olsen Cruise Lines, built in 1971. London's dockers were used to insecure employment and poor working conditions. Clients and users alike might reasonably have expected some cheap temporary or portable buildings to accommodate the necessary toilets and showers. What Foster gave them was a two-storey building wedged between two warehouses that combined facilities for both dockers and office workers in unprecedentedly egalitarian juxtaposition. Its front wall was made entirely of storey-height mirror glass sheets held in structural neoprene gaskets. British architecture had never seen a wall like it. Foster had flown to America to discuss its detailed design with the specialist supplier, establishing the principle of collaboration between architect and manufacturer that was to characterize his practice in the years to come. In the same year, now working with Michael Hopkins, he converted a similar unpromising brief, this time from the giant computer company IBM, into a single-storey, deep-planned, glass-clad office and amenity building of extreme simplicity. It was meant to be a mere stop-gap before the completion of a new headquarters building on an adjacent site, but the 'temporary' building stands to this day at Cosham in Hampshire and is remembered as one of the milestones of early High Tech.

These early Foster buildings, for all their slickness, were rather calm, quiet presences. Richard Rogers was more willing to be expressive, adopting for a time a vehicle-like style with round-cornered windows fixed in lightweight panels by neoprene gaskets. In 1968 he designed a 'zip-up' house for a competition sponsored by Dupont. It took the form of a highly insulated yellow tube, like a big refrigerator, on pink telescopic legs. Its low-energy technologies were prophetic. The drawings indicate a roof-mounted wind-powered generator and a small electric car plugged into the house for recharging. Nicholas Grimshaw also saw the potential of lightweight panels and neoprene gaskets. The walls of his Herman Miller furniture factory at Bath, finished in 1976, could be dismantled and reattached in different configurations by unskilled labour in response to changing functional needs. In practice, this rarely if ever happened, but such flexibility and indeterminacy, even if only theoretical, were important principles of High Tech.

IBM Headquarters, Cosham, Hampshire, UK. Norman Foster, 1971. Utter simplicity: open planned and flat roofed with external walls of full-height glass in neoprene gaskets.

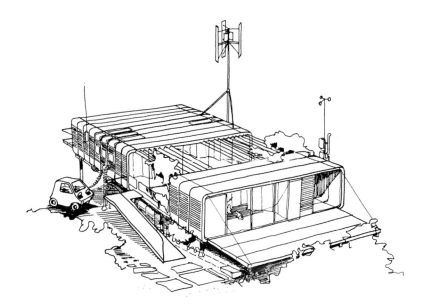

A 'yellow submarine' on pink legs, but the wind turbine and electric car were prophetic.

By the mid-1970s Norman Foster's 'simple shed' manner was being adapted to suit prestige buildings on sensitive sites. His headquarters building for the insurance company Willis Faber & Dumas, completed in 1975, was proof that High Tech and the city were not incompatible. The three-storey building in the centre of Ipswich has the expected open floor plans, unified by a central atrium and a cascade of escalators. In effect it is one large flexible volume. A rooftop restaurant and a basement swimming pool (now altered) complete Foster's vision of a new kind of workplace – open, collaborative and social. The continuous, serpentine, frameless-glass external wall, literally reflecting the urban context, is only the most visible innovation in a building that set a new standard in the design of office blocks. It was universally admired, won several architectural awards and is routinely listed among the most important British buildings of the century.

Herman Miller furniture factory, Bath, Somerset, UK. Nicholas Grimshaw, 1976. In theory, panels of glass and GRP can be unzipped and rearranged when replanning demands it.

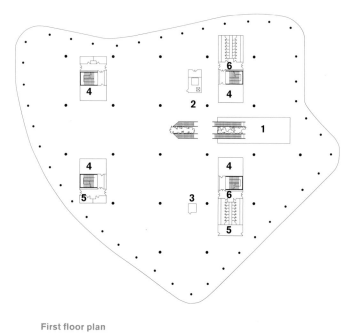

First floor plan

1. Escalator
2. Service lift
3. Document lift
4. Plant
5. Storerooms
6. WCs

0   10   20m
    30   60 ft

Willis Faber & Dumas exterior and interior, Ipswich, Suffolk, UK. Norman Foster, 1975. High Tech comes to town and solves the 'context' problem by reflecting the surroundings – literally.

While Willis Faber was being built, Foster was planning a prestige building of a different kind: the Sainsbury Centre for Visual Arts on the campus of the University of East Anglia. It was a bold step to imagine that a flexible, factory-style plan might be applicable to an art gallery, a building type traditionally organized as an enfilade of classical rooms. But there was some sense in the idea. A modern art gallery has to accommodate temporary exhibitions that are more like installations than traditional picture 'hangs'. This is not too different in principle from the periodic reorganization of a factory production line. But the Sainsbury Centre is not only factory-like in its plan, it actually looks like a factory – a big, open-ended shed on a grassy site near Denys Lasdun's famous 'ziggurat' student residences of ten years earlier (see Chapter 21). A Foster building is almost always unanalyzable into two basic categories of space: 'servant' and 'served'. The distinction is usually attributed to Louis Kahn (see Chapter 22). At the Sainsbury Centre, the servant spaces – plant rooms, toilets, air ducts, switch rooms and so on – are all contained in a thick external envelope formed by the side walls and roof combined. The served space is the plain, uninterrupted rectangle, 7 metres (23 feet) high, contained by this envelope. Aluminium and glass panels held in neoprene-gasketed frames form the outer layer of the envelope.

Willis Faber and the Sainsbury Centre mark the culmination of the first stage in the development of High Tech. It might have ended there with these proofs of the efficacy of flexible plans and demountable enclosures had not Richard Rogers, in partnership with the Italian architect Renzo Piano, won the 1971 international design competition for a new arts centre on the Beaubourg site in the centre of Paris. The completion of the Centre Pompidou in 1977, and its phenomenal success as a public attraction, boosted High Tech's credibility and took it into new territory. Pompidou is like a six-storey version of the Sainsbury Centre – a rectangular slab of served space flanked by linear servant zones. The building occupies only half of the site, the other half being left open as a sloping piazza, never without some kind of street entertainment. In early versions of the design, the elevation facing this piazza was an interactive electronic billboard; in the actual building, a flight of escalators in a glass tube snakes diagonally across it. On the other side of the building, facing the relatively narrow Rue du Renard, a close-packed row of brightly coloured service ducts explodes every preconception of what a street facade should look like. This is the Archigram comic-book vision made real, although it probably owes more to a 1961 paper project called Fun Palace by another denizen of London's Architectural Association, Cedric Price.

Sainsbury Centre for Visual Arts, University of East Anglia, Norwich, UK. Norman Foster, 1978. A big column-free space, not unlike a factory, ready to accommodate changing exhibitions and installations.

Sainsbury Centre exterior. Structure and services wrap around the space; factory-like in appearance as well as concept.

Section and second floor plan

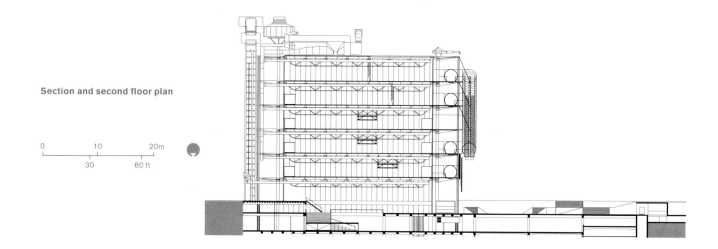

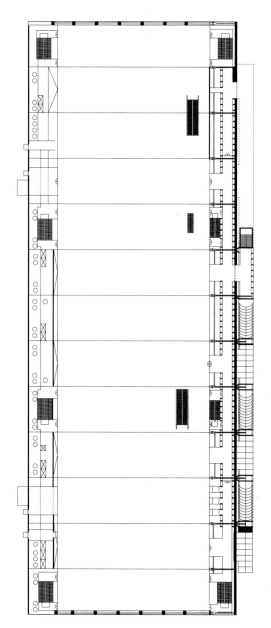

Centre Pompidou, Paris, France. Renzo Piano and Richard Rogers, 1977. Football pitches of flexible, fully serviced space created by an ingenious tensioned structure.

Centre Pompidou

High Tech's preference for flexible plans was taken to an extreme in the Centre Pompidou. The client's brief included a library, a museum of modern art, another of industrial design, a theatre and a cinema, not to mention all the cafés, restaurants and shops essential to any modern cultural venue. But the brief hardly mattered because, in principle, anything could happen anywhere. Every arrangement was to be provisional. Achieving this degree of flexibility required engineering on the scale of bridge-building. Steel trusses spanning the whole width of the building were too heavy to be supported on simple columns. Their weight had to be balanced by pivoting brackets known as 'gerberettes' (named after their inventor, Heinrich Gerber) anchored to the ground

who initiated this trend, in his Italian pavilion for Expo '70 in Osaka, which featured a tensioned external steel structure not unlike a miniature, single-storey version of the Pompidou frame. As we have seen, Norman Foster, and his then partner Michael Hopkins, had been content to tuck structure and services away neatly behind slick skins or louvred screens. But after Pompidou came a rash of otherwise straightforward industrial buildings made into eye-catching architecture by external steel frames, often painted in primary colours. Richard Rogers's 1982 Inmos microchip factory in Newport, south Wales (a convergence of 'High Tech' in the stylistic sense with 'High Tech' in the digital sense) is perhaps the best example. Its plan, naturally, is a plain rectangle, single storey, with external walls of square, detachable panels. These walls are hardly noticeable, however, in the glare of the elaborate apparatus that looms overhead. Structure, services and circulation are all combined in a central spine. Air-handling units, important to create extra-clean manufacturing conditions, are lined up on the roof of the spine between tall steel frames from which the exposed tubular roof trusses are

(Below) Renault Distribution Centre, Swindon, Wiltshire, UK. Norman Foster, 1982. Gothic High Tech: masts are anchored to the ground like reverse flying buttresses.

(Above) Centre Pompidou detail. Exposed pipes and ducts on the Rue du Renard side of the building.

by tension rods. The football pitches of fully serviced space that this structure created have proved over the years to be less a source of joyous freedom than of expensive awkwardness. Interior spaces still had to be created, suitable for human activities such as sitting in an audience, walking round an exhibition or drinking a cup of coffee, and this proved more difficult in practice than in theory. The heavy engineering was also problematic, requiring frequent renovation. Fireproofing, for example, was a headache from the start. In a road or railway bridge, steelwork can simply be painted to prevent corrosion, but the steel frame of a building must be covered in some form of insulation so that it doesn't weaken and collapse in a fire. A few years after completion of the Centre Pompidou, spray-on insulation could be seen slowly dropping off the building in great grey globs. An internal frame would have been easier to fireproof, but this frame was exposed to the weather; its 'expression' was an essential part of the architecture.

And here we come to an important aspect of the High Tech style, indeed the aspect with which it is most associated in the public eye: the exposure of structure and services – the bones and guts of the building – on the outside where everyone can see them. It may have been Renzo Piano

Hopkins House, London, UK. Michael Hopkins, 1976. The architect's own house, a homage to the Eames House in California of thirty years earlier.

(Above) Schlumberger Research Centre, Cambridge, UK. Michael Hopkins, 1985. A tent like a circus big top covers a winter garden at one end and a drilling test rig at the other.

suspended by tension rods. The whole arrangement is like a functional diagram – symmetrical and perfectly legible. All steelwork is painted blue.

Norman Foster's response to this challenge was the Renault Distribution Centre in Swindon, completed in 1982. Its steel frame is arranged in square bays with masts at the corners from which slightly domed roofs are suspended. This time the steelwork is painted bright yellow. Red was also a popular colour, for example in Richard Rogers's 1981 Fleetguard factory at Quimper in north-west France and Nicholas Grimshaw's Ladkarn factory in London of 1983. The bright colours soon went out of fashion but the roof suspension structures, now painted black, lived on in, for example, Grimshaw's Oxford Ice Rink of 1984 and Michael Hopkins's Schlumberger Research Centre in Cambridge of the following year.

Hopkins, leaving the Foster office in the mid-1970s to set up in practice with his wife Patty, produced some of the most inventive and refined High Tech buildings, beginning with his own London house of 1976. Essentially a homage to the Eames House in California of 1949 (see page 194) it is a rare example of a domestic application of the style.

Perhaps only architects can live comfortably in a box made of profiled metal and glass.

The Schlumberger Research Centre, built for an oil exploration company, is the most spectacular of Hopkins's industrial buildings. Two parallel, single-storey Miesian blocks with exposed roof trusses house offices and laboratories. Between them rises a tent like the big top of a three-ring circus. It shelters two drilling test pits and a 'winter garden' that serves as a meeting place for the researchers. The choice of a tent rather than a solid building to cover these quasi-external spaces was inspired. Its steel frame is external and equipped with all the raking struts and tension rods that had by the mid-1980s become de rigueur in a High Tech building. Fabric structures of this kind, sheltering inside/outside spaces, became something of a Hopkins trademark, even after he had undergone a mid-career metamorphosis, replacing steel and glass with brick and timber as his default materials.

This transformation began in the new Mound Stand at Lord's Cricket Ground, completed in 1987. For construction planning reasons, it made sense to preserve and renovate the old arcaded, brick base of the stand before erecting a steel superstructure crowned by a fabric canopy. Hitherto unfamiliar with brick as a material, Hopkins seems to have fallen in love with it. He proceeded to build a series of important buildings for British establishment clients, including the Glyndebourne opera house in Sussex, completed in 1994, and the new parliamentary building in Westminster, Portcullis House, completed in 2000 (see page 414). These can no longer be classified as High Tech, though they share at least one important characteristic of that style: its insistence on complete honesty. A brick wall in a Hopkins building is always a real, loadbearing structure, not just the facing of a steel or concrete frame.

Lloyd's Building

In 1978, perhaps reassured by the success of the Centre Pompidou, another British establishment client, the Lloyd's insurance market, engaged Richard Rogers to prepare a development plan for the organization's various premises. Unsurprisingly, this brief eventually turned into a proposal for a new building in the City of London. It was to be one of

(Above) Glyndebourne opera house, Sussex, UK. Michael Hopkins, 1994. The High Tech doctrine of truth to materials still applies. Brick arcades are genuinely loadbearing.

(Left) Mound Stand, Lord's Cricket Ground, London, UK. Michael Hopkins, 1987. The renovation of an existing brick arcade seems to have converted Hopkins into an enthusiast for natural materials.

the two culminating masterpieces of High Tech completed in 1986, the other being the Hongkong and Shanghai Bank (see below). Whereas Hopkins's style altered and softened as the establishment commissions began to arrive, Rogers stuck to his High Tech principles even for the bowler-hatted gentlemen of this 300-year-old institution. The basic idea was simple: the market or trading floor, traditionally known as the Room, would be accommodated in a single, multi-storey, rectangular space surrounding a central atrium with escalators. This would be the served space. Everything else – all the servant elements, including lifts, toilets, escape stairs, mechanical plant and ductwork – would be fitted to the outside. The complex visual outcome of this strategy is shockingly like a piece of pure engineering, an oil rig perhaps,

or a power station. The clarity of the underlying diagram is further obscured by the stepping down of the Room on the south side, exposing the glass barrel vault over the atrium like a fragment of every High Tech architect's favourite nineteenth-century building, the Crystal Palace. Every element conforms to High Tech principles: lift cars are fully glazed wall climbers; toilets are housed in separate metal-clad pods with round windows; escape stairs are boldly articulated; plant is contained in modular towers like stacks of containers; air ducts, both horizontal and vertical, are tubular, with dimpled silver casings. The main structural frame is concrete, not steel, to avoid the fireproofing problems of Pompidou, but it is nevertheless cast in steel-like profiles, with cylindrical columns, brackets and diagonal bracing.

(Left) Lloyd's of London, London, UK. Richard Rogers, 1986. A complicated exterior makes possible a simple multi-storey 'omniplatz'.

(Opposite) Lloyd's of London, interior. The atrium is animated by escalators. Note the concrete columns with steel-like profiles.

Hongkong and Shanghai Bank, Hong Kong, China. Norman Foster, 1986. Three multi-storey suspension bridges rise side by side to different heights, creating an indeterminate form.

Hongkong and Shanghai Bank

Meanwhile, in Hong Kong, Rogers's friend and rival Norman Foster was talking to another venerable institution, the Hongkong and Shanghai Bank. The bank had occupied its 1 Queen's Road Central site since 1865. Its current building, designed by Palmer and Turner

in the mid-1930s, was well loved, especially for its Art Deco banking hall, but was short of office space. The brief to Foster was simple, therefore: stay on the same site, keep the banking hall, and build a skyscraper to accommodate the offices. It is worth remembering this original brief when looking at the completed building. Why does it look like a multi-storey suspension bridge? Because it was originally designed to bridge over the preserved banking hall. At some stage in the development process it was decided that the banking hall could go after all, but it was too late to rethink the bridge idea.

But perhaps the bridge idea also appealed to Foster for other reasons. That preference among High Tech architects for open, flexible spaces is hard to satisfy in a conventional skyscraper because the central structural and service core leaves only a relatively narrow strip of usable floor around the perimeter. Foster therefore rejected a central-core plan and instead gathered the servant spaces and vertical structure on either side of the served space – an arrangement that naturally implied a bridge-like structure. Having created an open space on each floor, he then tackled the other unsatisfactory aspect of the conventional skyscraper: that every floor is spatially divorced from every other floor. To move from one floor to another, one must pass through an intermediate enclosed space, either a lift or an escape stair. Space, in other words, is discontinuous, and flexibility of use is compromised. Foster's solution was to unify the served space by means of escalators, as he had done on a smaller scale at Willis Faber, and indeed as Rogers was doing at Lloyd's. These two innovations – the bridge-like structure and local circulation by escalator – amounted to a reinvention of the skyscraper.

East–west section and plan at level 28/29

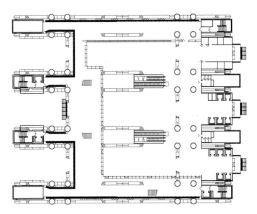

Many alternative designs based on these principles were produced during the development period, including the so-called Chevron scheme, which structurally treated every individual floor as a suspension bridge, resulting in a proliferation of diagonal tension members. The final building is less radical but revolutionary nevertheless. Bridge-like horizontal structural elements occur at intervals in the height of the building, with between seven and nine floors hanging from each one. Continuing the multi-storey suspension bridge analogy, there are really three of them, like three towers placed side by side, each rising to a different height. This creates the impression that the building is unfinished, that the two lower towers might one day be extended upwards to match the highest. The form is partly the result of local regulations to prevent overshadowing. Floors are also set back in the other direction, between the massive composite steel masts. But the indeterminate look is quite deliberate. It is as if the building were a system temporarily configured for a particular situation rather than a fixed, finite form. Nobody believes that the lower towers will ever actually be 'finished' or the missing sections of floor filled in, but the unfinished look is in tune with High Tech's flexibility principle.

Eden Project, Cornwall, UK. Nicholas Grimshaw, 2000.
More organic than High Tech, like frogspawn or some weirdly fruiting fungus.

So, if the structure is essentially a bridge, what does it now bridge over? The answer is nothing, just an open paved area, which, paradoxically, has become one of the building's best-loved features. Accessible to the public at most times, it is a popular shady picnic spot. It is also the very unconventional main public entrance to the building. Two angled escalators appear to have been lowered onto this pavement from above like gangplanks. Taking the up escalator, one rises through the glass 'underbelly' of the building into a cavernous ten-storey-high atrium that has been created by simply omitting the lower floors of the central multi-storey bridge. The 'front door' of the building is therefore a horizontal shutter closing off the escalator when not in use. It could hardly be more different from the grand classical portico that one traditionally associates with bank entrances.

In the design and construction of the Hongkong and Shanghai Bank, Foster's habit of collaborating with building component manufacturers became standard procedure. It was even given a name, though a rather dull one: 'design development'. Representatives of the Foster office were sent out to work with specialists all over the world. The structural steelwork came from Britain; the external cladding, including the very complex aluminium sheathing of the fireproofed external structure, came from the United States; the prefabricated toilet and plant modules stacked up in the service towers came from Japan. Every element of the

building was rethought from first principles. Almost nothing was taken from a standard catalogue. The result was one of the most technically advanced buildings of the twentieth century – and one of the most expensive.

In the Lloyd's Building and the Hongkong and Shanghai Bank the principles of High Tech were triumphantly vindicated. Those buildings marked a high point but also a change of direction. The style's main protagonists, now firmly established, began to explore new architectural territory. Already in the mid-1980s Norman Foster was designing a 'mediatheque' in Nimes in the south of France, for a site opposite the well-preserved Roman temple known as the Maison Carrée, in very un-High Tech materials: concrete, bronze and local stone. A note in Foster's handwriting on an early sketch states: 'No diagonals in structure – must not look industrial'. Richard Rogers began to take an interest in traditional urban form, a topic remote from the usual concerns of High Tech. Eventually, in 1997 he wrote an influential book on the subject called *Cities for a Small Planet*. Even Nicholas Grimshaw, most dogmatic of the group, showed signs of shifting his interpretation of High

Tech principles. The cluster of geodesic domes at the Eden Project in Cornwall, completed in 2000, suggest an organic rather than a technological inspiration. They appear to have grown spontaneously in their disused-quarry site, though in fact they were painstakingly constructed on a mass of temporary scaffolding.

Stansted airport

One late High Tech building, completed in 1991, deserves special mention because of its enormous international influence. Stansted Airport (London's third, after Heathrow and Gatwick) marks a turning point in the design of airport terminals. Norman Foster brought to the job a personal interest in flight (he is an experienced pilot) as well as his by-now formidable analytical design skills. The main idea, following the usual High Tech preference for spatial simplicity, was to house all of the public functions – departures and arrivals – in one big room. Passengers would be able to see where they were going and would no longer be completely reliant on stress-inducing signs and announcements. But the most influential aspect of the design was the lightweight, billowing roof. All mechanical plant is consigned to an undercroft, relieving the roof of the usual clutter of ducts, access walkways and suspended ceilings. Air, water, electricity and artificial light are supplied to the space via the four-strutted, tree-like steel columns. Following publication of the building, tree-like columns almost instantly

London Stansted Airport, Essex, UK. Norman Foster,
1991. A high, day-lit space, roofed by square domes and
cleared of the clutter of mechanical and electrical services.

Chek Lap Kok Airport, Hong Kong, China. Norman Foster, 1998. The design principles of Stansted applied at a much larger scale on an artificially extended island.

became an architectural cliché, cropping up in forecourts, bus stations, and railway platforms everywhere. But more importantly, the example of the big public hall with an unencumbered roof admitting daylight to the heart of the building was followed by airport designers around the world, from Richard Rogers in Madrid to Kisho Kurokawa in Kuala Lumpur and Renzo Piano in Kansai, Japan. Foster himself refined the form in Hong Kong's Chek Lap Kok airport, opened just after the colony was handed back

to China in 1997, and at Beijing's huge Terminal Three, completed before the opening of the 2008 Olympic Games (see Chapter 33). These later versions, with their flowing, computer-generated forms, make little Stansted look almost primitive, like a pre-war biplane.

By the turn of the century the High Tech style had lost its distinctive identity, but the architects associated with it – Rogers, Foster, Grimshaw and Hopkins – now fêted and honoured, continued to run large international practices. They were turning into the grand old men not just of British, but of world architecture. A 2014 BBC television series devoted to them was called *The Brits Who Built the Modern World*.

Jean Prouvé

Jean Prouvé was president of the jury that awarded Renzo Piano and Richard Rogers first prize in the Centre Pompidou competition of 1971. But this was by no means his only contribution to the progress of modern architecture. He had earned his place in its history long before he became an inspiration to High Tech architects.

Prouvé was not an architect but a creative metalworker who drew his inspiration from the constructive potential of the materials he knew – steel and aluminium, especially in the form of sheets, folded, pressed and welded. Though always a believer in the benefits of industrialization and mass production, he began by making crafted furniture and special components for architects, and arguably remained in that role for the rest of his career. In the 1920s and 1930s he collaborated with Le Corbusier's studio, including Pierre Jeanneret and Charlotte Perriand, with Robert Mallet-Stevens, and with the Beaudouin and Lods partnership, for whom he designed and made the innovative metal and glass external cladding of the House of the People in Clichy on the outskirts of Paris, completed in 1938. After the Second World War he experimented with prefabricated housing units as emergency accommodation and succeeded in building a small permanent development, which still exists, in the Paris suburb of Meudon. In the early 1950s his workshop at Maxéville employed 200 people, but he was a better craftsman than a businessman and, needing more investment, he allowed it to be taken over by L'Aluminium Français, who eventually wrested it from his control.

One of Prouvé's buildings has in recent years become something of a monument, though a prefabricated and portable one. His Tropical House, prototyped in 1949, was designed as a house suitable for colonial administrators in Africa. It vaguely resembled a bungalow on stilts, with a shallow, pitched roof and a surrounding balcony/verandah, but its legs were steel and its walls were aluminium panels, some of them with circular windows. In theory it could be made in France, packed neatly into the cargo hold of an aeroplane and erected quickly on its African site without much need for local labour or materials. In practice, the cost of manufacture and transport was far too high for the project to be viable. Three Tropical Houses nevertheless made it out to Africa, one to Niamey in Niger and two to Brazzaville in what is now the Republic of Congo. In 2001 the Brazzaville houses were 'rescued' and brought back to France for restoration and exhibition. Whether they served as demonstrations of Prouvé's creative genius or as symbols of late colonial hubris is a matter of debate. There is no doubting their value on the modern art market, however. One was sold at auction in New York in 2007 for almost $5 million.

Tropical House, Brazzaville, Republic of Congo. Jean Prouvé, 1949. Fabricated in France and assembled in Africa to house colonial administrators, in practice it proved too expensive.

27 | JAPAN
1945–2000

August 15 1945 was the day of the Japanese surrender and the end of the Second World War. Arata Isozaki was 14 years old. Fifty years later, he remembered it as 'an instance of total tranquillity, when everything seemed to have stopped … the houses and buildings that we had considered mainstays of our way of life, the established belief in the national state with the Emperor at its head, and the social system that controlled even the smallest daily activities, had been destroyed and had vanished, leaving behind only the void of the blue sky overhead.'[1] The history of modern architecture in Japan could never be presented as a straightforward account of technical and artistic progress. It is full of conflict and confusion caused by that country's ambivalent relationship with western industrial culture.

Kenzo Tange
During the war, Kenzo Tange, the father of modern Japanese architecture, entered and won government competitions for

the design of buildings in the traditional monumental style that appealed to the military authorities. Ten years later, he designed the Hiroshima Peace Memorial Museum as an elegant concrete box raised on pilotis in the best Corbusian manner. The arrival of western Modernism was one aspect of a wider political, cultural and economic domination, but it never completely suppressed the indigenous architectural culture. How could it? Traditional Japanese houses, shrines and temples had been revered by western architects ever since Frank Lloyd Wright had first set eyes on the reconstructed Japanese temple at the 1893 World's Columbian Exposition in Chicago. Early Modernist visitors to Japan, such as Walter Gropius and Bruno Taut, saw the Japanese house as a proto-Modernist paragon.

Hiroshima Peace Memorial Museum, Hiroshima, Japan. Kenzo Tange, 1955. Corbusian Modernism comes to post-war Japan loaded with symbolism.

The kind of industrialized architecture they were struggling to develop – modular, mass produced, lightweight, and spatially fluid – seemed to be prefigured in those fast-disappearing traditional wooden buildings.

In the 1950s, a hybrid style developed in Japan, part Brutalist, part traditional. For example, Tange's Kurashiki City Hall, completed in 1960 and now converted into an art museum, is made of rough concrete inside and out, like Le Corbusier's buildings at Chandigarh (see pages 232–235), but details such as the paired projecting beam-ends and the interlocking corners recall timber construction. In the sports stadiums for the 1964 Tokyo Olympics that sealed his international reputation, Tange managed to give innovative tensile structures a Japanese profile, vaguely suggestive of temple roofs (see pages 218–219).

Metabolism

The first truly indigenous post-war Japanese movement in modern architecture was founded at the 1960 World Design Conference in Tokyo by a group of architects including Kiyonori Kikutake, Kisho Kurokawa and Fumihiko Maki. Their programme was wildly over-ambitious but nevertheless essentially practical in intention: to design cities as integrated mechanisms that could grow and change like ecosystems. 'Metabolism' was the name they chose, unwisely given its confusing '-ism' suffix and the fact that it brought to mind the internal workings of a single organism rather than the more apt metaphor of a community of organisms. Still, it was a powerful idea that seemed in tune with an era of rapid economic growth, fast-expanding cities and confidence in the problem-solving efficacy of modern technology. Kenzo Tange and his then assistants Kurokawa and Arata Isozaki soon got involved and produced the movement's most famous project: a vast new extension to the city of Tokyo making use of the only available open space: Tokyo Bay itself. Its hierarchical, tree-like plan branched out from a central spine that stretched the full 30

Kurashiki City Hall, Kurashiki, Japan. Kenzo Tange, 1960.
A reinforced concrete building but borrowing certain details from a timber building tradition.

kilometres (19 miles) across the bay. But it was only one of several Metabolist urban visions, including Kikutake's floating Marine City and Kurakawa's Agricultural City, a grid of streets designed to grow and in-fill itself gradually until it became a perfect square like a Roman *castrum*. Louis Kahn's concept of 'served' and 'servant' spaces (see page 292) lay behind these projects but was combined with two additional ideas: that future growth and change in cities might be planned for and facilitated by clever design, and that served elements of the city, such as houses and office buildings, might be mass produced in factories.

Of course cities had always been composed of distinct elements with different life expectancies. In the traditional European city the 'infrastructure' of streets and squares might last for centuries while the buildings that it served were likely to be renewed on a shorter timescale. But now the distinction could be clarified and the process of change could be industrialized. Houses could be prefabricated in

(Above) **Yamanashi Press and Broadcasting Centre, Kofu, Japan. Kenzo Tange, 1966.** The Metabolist idea realized in a permanent, but in theory re-configurable, building.

(Left) **Tokyo Bay Project (unbuilt). Kenzo Tange, 1960.** A city on the water, branching out from a 30-kilometre- (19-mile-) long central spine.

factories and 'plugged into' a more permanent supporting network, forming a dynamic megastructure. The British Archigram group were thinking along similar lines. Peter Cook's Plug-in City project of 1964 (see page 344) is probably the clearest illustration of the idea, but the Metabolists were actually building it, or fragments of it. Tange's Yamanashi Press and Broadcasting Centre at Kofu, completed (if that is the word) in 1966, is a radically indeterminate eight-storey building, supported by 16 concrete towers, 5 metres (16 feet) in diameter, rising to different heights. Single-storey bridges span between them, stacked in twos and threes but with gaps left as if more bridges might soon arrive from the factory. The towers contain stairs, lifts, toilets and other servant functions, while the bridges contain usable space for studios and offices. More bridges were indeed added a few years after 'completion', proving that the indeterminacy was, at least to some extent, genuinely practical. But symbolism was as important as practicality; this is notionally a whole city in embryo, designed for systematic growth and change.

Nakagin Capsule Tower, Tokyo, Japan. Kisho Kurokawa, 1972. Living pods could be made in factories and simply clipped to a structural core – in theory, at least.

Kisho Kurokawa

An even more vivid illustration of Metabolist principles is the Nakagin Capsule Tower in Tokyo, designed by Kurokawa and completed in 1972. Two linked servant towers are encrusted with 140 prefabricated steel-and-concrete boxes – minimal living pods for single people. Each pod is visibly separate, with a single round window, and proud of its boxy character. Once again, a whole city of such towers can readily be imagined. The towers could be linked together at several levels and the pods, were they to fall into disrepair, could be replaced by new models. In 2006, when the building had indeed fallen into disrepair, pod replacement was proposed, but for sentimental rather than practical reasons. By then the building had become a historical monument.

Expo '70, the world exposition held in Osaka in 1970, was a celebration of Japan's phenomenal economic expansion since the war and of an almost religious faith in modern technology. Tange was the master planner and many of his Metabolist colleagues took part. Kikutake contributed a landmark tower, triangular and steel framed, from which an excrescence of geodesic spherical pods erupted half way up. Kurokawa's Takara Beautilion was an indeterminate cluster of cubic modules framed by bent steel tubes, and his Capsule was a single-storey prototype for the Nakagin Tower. Arata Isozaki, working with Tange, planned the exhibition's centrepiece: the Festival Plaza, sheltered by a huge space-frame canopy, in which various mobile robotic devices – cranes, decks, banks of seating and lighting gantries – created a 'cybernetic environment' reminiscent of Cedric Price's 1961 Fun Palace project. But already global faith in industrial technology was beginning to weaken,

Nakagin Capsule Tower interior. A spatially minimal, but richly equipped living space.

**Takara Beautilion, Expo '70, Osaka, Japan.
Kisho Kurokawa, 1970.** An indeterminate cluster
of modular forms held in a grid of bent steel nodes.

and in architecture the realization was dawning that the
inspirational power of technology was as much destructive
as constructive. Isozaki relates how, while completing
preparations for the Expo extravaganza, he suffered
a profound disillusionment: 'When everything was
as I wished, it was impossible for me to cry out that
everything was wrong – but it was wrong.'²

Arata Isozaki
Isozaki had begun to see Metabolism, and the technology
worship that it implied, as a betrayal of human and, more
specifically, Japanese values. It had interpreted Modernist
principles in purely instrumental terms, like a kind of
engineering, as if a cultural artefact as complex as a city
could be designed like a machine to serve not just the
present but also a predictable future. The concept of
time that this implied was alien to a culture that valued
the ephemeral and the fleeting. Brought up among
ruins, Isozaki knew that ruin was the ultimate fate of all
architecture. A building lived and grew in the mind of the
architect but as soon as it was built it began to die. In a
land of earthquake and fire, what survived into the future
were ideas and traditions, not material constructions.
Traditional Japanese architecture, so much admired by
European Modernists, had developed and endured not
because it was functional but because it was beautiful. It
produced uninsulated houses in a country of cold winters,
it ignored practical structural devices such as diagonal

cross-bracing, and its primitively organized spaces contained
no furniture. Yet so refined and delicate was it that it seemed
almost a product of nature. So it was to culture rather than
to technology that Isozaki and his colleagues in the second
generation 'new wave' – Kisho Kurokawa, Fumihiko Maki
and Tadao Ando among them – turned for inspiration in the
1970s and 1980s. Each adopted a different approach but
all sought justification in ideas and philosophical concepts.
Often these concepts arose from the peculiar character of
Japanese cities such as Tokyo, Osaka and Nagoya, which
spread and churned like volatile seas of humanity in the
over-heated economic climate. Distinctions that are taken
for granted in western cities – between inside and outside,
public and private, centre and periphery – are dissolved in
multi-centred cities like Tokyo, where public space is a three-
dimensional labyrinth, monumental buildings are rare and
everything changes all the time.

'Maniera' was the name Isozaki gave to the new style that
he developed after 1970. The name implies a kinship with
Mannerism, the refined, expressive personal style associated
with the sixteenth-century architecture of Michelangelo,
but in Isozaki's practice it mainly meant a reduction of the
elements of composition to simple geometrical forms: the
regular square grid and the so-called Phileban and Platonic
solids, such as cubes, cylinders and pyramids. Note that this
idea is borrowed from western, not Japanese philosophy
(except that, paradoxically, such borrowing is typically
Japanese). The style is fully developed in the Museum of
Modern Art at Gunma, completed in 1974. Eighteen 12-metre
(39-foot) cubes form the basis of the composition. They are
sometimes combined to make longer, rectangular forms,
and sometimes expressed separately. One double-cube
wing, designed to accommodate traditional Japanese art,
is set at an angle to the rest of the building. Cubes can be
in-filled with solid walls or fully glazed. Glass panes and
metal cladding panels are all either squares or half-squares,
and uniformly gridded with no implied hierarchy. Perhaps
the cubes are symbolic of the museum as a building type –
empty boxes or three-dimensional picture frames waiting to
be filled with art. They might be seen as essentially structural
elements, but this aspect is not emphasized or dramatized
as it might be in a Modernist composition. Neither do they
owe anything to historical precedents, whether western or
Japanese. This is a completely abstract architecture, a fresh
start from basic geometrical principles.

In later designs, this complete abstraction began to loosen
and include quotations from the western classical tradition.
Isozaki seems to have accepted this as an inevitable
development and come to terms with it. The Fujimi Country
Club building in Oita, completed in 1974, is a linear
barrel-vaulted building laid onto the site like a question
mark squeezed from a toothpaste tube. The concept is

Museum of Modern Art at Gunma, Takasaki, Japan. Arata Isozaki, 1974. The angled, double-cube wing accommodates Japanese art.

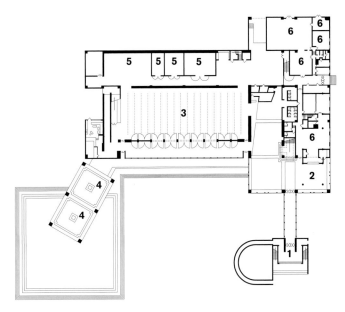

Ground floor plan

1. Entrance
2. Reception
3. Temporary storage
4. Aedicule
5. Storage
6. Offices

0   10   20m
30   60 ft

fundamentally abstract but the cut-off ends of the vault bear some resemblance to the entrance of Palladio's Villa Poiana, between Verona and Padua. This is not an accidental reference. We should bear in mind that Japanese architects at this time were participating fully in the international debate about the future of Modernism and the possible reintroduction of historical forms. They taught as guest professors in American architecture schools and won many important foreign commissions. In the 1980s Isozaki himself designed the Museum of Contemporary Art in Los Angeles and the Team Disney Building in Orlando, Florida. But the

building that best illustrates his developing style in the 1980s is the Tsukuba Center Building, completed in 1983. Tsukuba was a new 'science city' 64 kilometres (40 miles) from Tokyo that brought together various government and university research organizations. The centre included a hotel, a concert hall, a community centre and a mall of shops, all gathered around what Isozaki called a 'reverse Campidoglio', a sunken oval court paved in the pattern invented by Michelangelo for the Capitol in Rome. The buildings are cubic and gridded like the Gunma museum, but they also have rusticated lower walls, column-guarded entrances

Fujimi Country Club, Oita, Japan. Arata Isozaki, 1974. References to western architectural traditions are deliberate and knowing.

and, in the case of the multi-storey hotel, a segmentally pedimented top storey. The classical forms are approximate only, and deliberately unco-ordinated, but their origins are clear enough.

Kisho Kurokawa, like Isozaki, began to lose faith in technology as a ruling principle. He proposed a radical shift of viewpoint: the supplanting of the age of technology by the 'Age of Life'. Metabolism had been based on an over-simplified organic metaphor. His new philosophy would recognize that nature was infinitely subtle and complex, and that human culture was a part of nature. 'Symbiosis' was a key concept. It meant not just co-operation between organisms in an ecosystem, but also co-operation between human cultures. Western dualism (either–or, centre–periphery, figure–ground, public–private) would be replaced by a Buddhist 'grey area' of tolerance and acceptance.[3] It is hard to imagine precise architectural equivalents of these ideas, but then perhaps that is the point. The idea of vagueness and indeterminacy is alien to western thinking. In Kurokawa's architecture, it can be discerned in various 'in-between' spaces, often in between exterior and interior. For example, the Museum of Modern Art, Saitama, completed in 1982, is essentially a simple box, but one corner has been pushed out at an angle and its walls and roof dissolved, leaving only an open framework. A serpentine glass wall seals off the interior of the entrance hall behind. It is a porch of a kind, but big enough to contain a garden,

allowing the visitor to linger and hesitate, to be undecided and to enjoy that state rather than be troubled by it. The Nagoya City Art Museum, completed five years later, uses a similar combination of rigid framework with undulating wall, subverting classical norms with Buddhist ambiguity. But a concept as vague as Symbiosis is open to over-literal interpretations. Kuala Lumpur International airport, designed by Kurokawa (or his office) in the mid-1990s and completed in 1998, is often described as an example of Symbiosis. It is said, for example, that its mosque-like plan and silhouette represent a symbiosis between Modernism and Islamic architecture, or that its setting in reclaimed rainforest represents a symbiosis between civilization and nature. It would be more accurate to say that its services-free, timber-lined, hypar roof supported on a square grid of conical columns owes more to Norman Foster's seminal Stansted airport, completed at the beginning of the decade (see page 359), than to any subtle philosophy.

Fumihiko Maki

Among the 'second generation' or 'new wave' of Japanese modern architects, Fumihiko Maki was perhaps the most conversant with western culture and institutions, having studied at Harvard, worked for Skidmore, Owings and Merrill in New York and taught for six years at Washington University, St Louis. He was loosely connected with Team X (Aldo van Eyck also taught at Washington University) and he knew Louis Kahn's work well, having acted as translator

Museum of Modern Art, Saitama, Japan. Kisho Kurokawa, 1982. The 'dissolved' corner. A space in which to linger or hesitate before entering.

when Kahn lectured in Japan in 1955. In 1964 he published a little booklet called 'Investigations in Collective Form' in which he tackled the question of urban design in fresh terms.[4] According to his analysis there were three main types of urban form: 'compositional form', or western Modernist town planning, represented, for example, by Brasília or Chandigarh; megastructure (Maki possibly coined the term in this publication), represented by Metabolist projects such as Tange's Tokyo Bay or Kurokawa's Agricultural City; and 'group form', represented by European medieval hill towns, Greek islands, north African villages and other 'vernacular' creations. One of the accompanying illustrations was a striking aerial photograph of an unidentified linear Japanese village, its old, pitched-roofed houses curving like a crocodile

Hillside Terrace, Shibuya, Tokyo, Japan. Fumihiko Maki, 1969. An attempt to create the 'group form' typified by European hill towns and north African villages.

along the spine of a country road. Group form was presented not just as one of three possible alternatives, but as a clear criticism of the other two. Its main features were consistency of form and materials, human scale, a practical but sometimes daring response to topography and orientation, and what Maki called the 'sequential development' of building types and components – houses, porches, fences, gates, towers and so on. 'Sequential' meant two things: developed over time and subject to individual variation.

Like most architectural theories, group form was easier to describe than to put into practice, especially in a single building. But when Maki returned to Japan in 1965 and set up a practice in Tokyo, one of his first major projects was Hillside Terrace, a group of apartment buildings in Shibuya, and in it we can clearly see group-form principles in action on a limited scale. The development was built in several phases and consists of six separate apartment buildings. They are neither completely different nor completely similar, but are recognizably akin, sharing certain features like big square windows and recessed balconies but displaying them in different combinations, asymmetrically and with limited repetition. Each building occupies its part of the site with comfortable assurance – either along the street frontage or standing behind – yet all are loosely aligned geometrically and acknowledge each other's presence. Most importantly, it is in the in-between spaces – the street frontage and the courts and gardens within – that its distinctive spatial character emerges. Is it a village or a hill town? Not really, but it would be hard to find a better example of a 'modern vernacular'. To what extent this 'composition', or form, or space, is characteristically Japanese is open to question. The meaning of the word 'space' is slippery enough in English usage; in Japanese translation it becomes even harder to pin down. *Ma* is one possibility, but it means 'interval', 'gap' or 'pause' rather than a geometrically defined entity. Interestingly, it shares its written character with *ken*, which is sometimes translated as 'architecture' though it also refers to a standard dimension, roughly 1.8 metres (6 feet), in traditional Japanese building. Suffice it to say that the Japanese and western perceptions of space are subtly but profoundly different. The difference can be sensed in Japanese gardens or flower arrangements, in which elements seem to be freely juxtaposed rather than fitted into any system or hierarchy.

It can be sensed too in the nine-storey street elevation of the Wacoal Media Center in Tokyo, designed by Maki in the early 1980s. This is a functionally complex building, containing a theatre, video studios, bars, restaurants, offices, beauty salons and, at the back, a spiral ramp in a cylindrical atrium. The natural assumption is that the complexity of the elevation is a reflection of this inner complexity. But this is true only to a limited extent. There is a gap, a disconnect, a *ma*, between interior and exterior. The various materials, patterns, profiles, set-backs and angles of the elevation are composed freely like a Cubist collage that dissolves scale and perspective. Perhaps it is also a notional map of a city in which those familiar western dualities have been subverted and all monumentality has disappeared. Ironically, in view of his evident preference for asymmetry and fragmentation, the building for which Maki is best known is unified, isolated and symmetrical. The Tokyo Metropolitan Gymnasium, completed in 1990, has been likened to a spaceship and to a samurai warrior's helmet, but surely it is some species of crouching crustacean, its articulated carapace sheathed in shiny stainless steel.

Tadao Ando

For this most famous of all Japanese modern architects, nature and spirituality were more important sources of creativity than the chaos of the consumerist city, from which he sought refuge and protection. In-situ concrete, straight from the mould but smooth and precise in the

Wacoal Media Center, Tokyo, Japan. Fumihiko Maki, 1985.
The complex facade does not necessarily reflect the complexity of the plan.

manner of the Salk Institute by Louis Kahn (see page 295), was his main material. It is not too fanciful to say that his other main material was daylight. The Horiuchi House in Osaka, completed in 1979, illustrates in simple form the chief characteristics of his architecture. It is a two-storey rectangular concrete box, divided into three equal sections. The centre section is a courtyard that is open to the street at ground level on one side. Apart from a small access door, this is the only connection between the inner world of the house and the surrounding city. If it were a plain opening, it would be an invitation to enter, and the courtyard would become a semi-public space. Instead, the terms of exchange between city and house are regulated by a freestanding translucent screen of glass blocks. The message conveyed by the screen is hardly welcoming, but neither is it forbidding or defensive. Come in by all means, it seems to say, but know that you enter private territory. There are no views out of the house except the most important view of all, the view of the sky, unspoilt and unspoilable.

The Church of the Light, built in 1989 on a suburban street corner in Ibaraki, north of Osaka, is also a plain, triple-cube concrete box – and that is almost all it is. An angled wall slices a corner off the box to provide an entrance, but the only other embellishment of an interior that would otherwise be as plain as a water cistern is a cross carved out of the east wall. Full height, full width and full thickness, it would appear to compromise the wall's structural integrity but somehow it

(Top and above) **Tokyo Metropolitan Gymnasium, Tokyo, Japan. Fumihiko Maki, 1990.** A spaceship, a Samurai helmet or a crouching crustacean?

remains in place as the simplest possible representation of the Christian symbol – a cross of pure light. In the Church on the Water, a wedding chapel annexed to a hotel on the snowy northern island of Hokkaido, the cross theme is developed into a veritable symphony for concrete, steel, glass and water. Four crosses stand in a square on the roof of a concrete cube. They are fenced in by four glass walls, each divided into four by steel crosses. Guests entering at the top of the sloping site are required to walk up to, into and around this monument before descending via a half-spiral stair into the larger concrete cube of the chapel. The east wall of the chapel is all glass, once again divided into four by a steel cross. Outside, yet another steel cross stands dead centre in a reflecting pool that steps down the site over a series of shallow weirs.

But the cross theme, though insistent, is not the most important aspect of this composition, which, far from being focussed on an object of contemplation, looks outwards to the pool and beyond it to the trees – and beyond them to the distant hills. Here in this semi-rural environment, Ando has left behind his urban protective enclosures and embraced the natural landscape. The crucial detail is that the all-glass east wall can be made to disappear by sliding it sideways into a freestanding external concrete frame. Hills, trees, cross and water then become part of the chapel's interior. This controlled openness to nature becomes more expansive in the Chikatsu-Asuka Museum near Osaka, completed in 1994. The museum acts as an interpretation centre for the many ancient *kofun* burial mounds that lie in the surrounding park. The building is itself a kind of burial mound – a stepped concrete hill from which the tumuli can be viewed and under which the excavated remains can be found in deliberately gloomy, top-lit galleries.

Horiuchi House, Osaka, Japan. Tadao Ando, 1979.
The entrance to the courtyard is screened by a translucent wall. The only views out are of the sky.

Church of the Light, Ibaraki, Osaka, Japan. Tadao Ando, 1989. The carved-out cross evidently does not compromise the structural integrity of the wall.

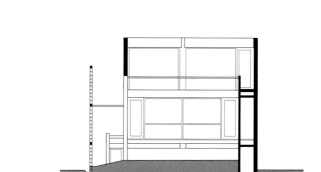

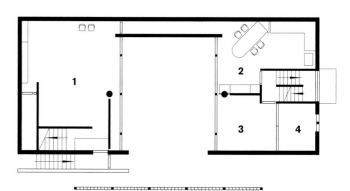

Section and first floor plan
1 Living room
2. Dining room
3. Bedroom
4. Cupboard

(Above) Church on the Water, Hokkaido, Japan. Tadao Ando, 1988. The glass wall overlooking the lake slides sideways into the frame on the left.

(Left) Chikatsu–Asuka Museum, Osaka, Japan. Tadao Ando, 1994. An interpretation centre for the *kofun* burial mounds that lie nearby.

Toyo Ito

While Ando sought security in solidly grounded concrete, his contemporary Toyo Ito sought freedom and fluidity in floating planes and veil-like walls. Mies van der Rohe was an acknowledged influence – the early glass skyscraper projects and the Barcelona Pavilion (see Chapter 10) rather than the later steel classicism. Ito's old people's home at Yatsushiro, completed in 1994, is structurally and diagrammatically very simple: a two-storey, flat-roofed building to accommodate 50 old people, with individual rooms between concrete cross-walls on one side and double-height communal spaces on the other. It is the thin plane of the corrugated steel roof deck that introduces the freedom and fluidity. On the communal side, where it breaks away from its supporting cross-walls and relies instead on spindly steel columns, sweeping curves and oval holes are profile cut into it as if it were a piece of thin card. In the Lyric Hall at Nagaoka, completed two years later,

new developments in computer-aided design and manufacture allow the curves of the thin roof, now concrete, to break into the third dimension, billowing and undulating like a just-thrown picnic blanket. Here too oval holes shine daylight onto focal points in the interior. One might expect a performing arts complex, including a theatre and a concert hall, to display a certain formality, even monumentality, but this building rests lightly on its open site, like a temporary visitor. The black box of the theatre and the white oval drum of the concert hall rise through the undulating blanket like insubstantial apparitions, particularly the concert hall, which is walled in corrugated translucent glass, lit from behind at night.

Old People's Home, Yatsushiro, Japan. Toyo Ito, 1994.
The thin corrugated steel roof deck is profile cut as if it were a sheet of card.

In the Mediatheque at Sendai, completed in 2000 and generally acknowledged to be Ito's masterpiece, freedom and fluidity become the ruling principle of the design, not in terms of its outline, which is a simple box, but in terms of its structure and services. If Ito was influenced by Le Corbusier, as he surely was, then the Maison Dom-ino sketch of 1914 (see page 57) might have been the key image. The Mediatheque is a seven-storey version of the Maison Dom-ino, with thin, flat, cantilevered floors and all-glass external walls. It is the columns that are different, 13 of them, not straight concrete posts but free-form baskets of tubular steel, sheathed in glass, forming continuous service and circulation ducts through the height of the building. This is a radically new and beautifully simple solution to the problem of the highly serviced urban building. Ito himself likened it to an aquarium in which

Lyric Hall, Nagaoka, Japan. Toyo Ito, 1996. Computer-aided design now allows the thin roof to billow and undulate like a thrown blanket.

the columns/ducts sway and writhe like seaweed. On 11 March 2011 at 2.46 in the afternoon, they literally swayed and writhed when Sendai was hit by the most powerful earthquake in Japanese history. Hundreds of thousands of buildings were ruined. Though apparently a fragile construction – a stack of separate concrete floors resting on crooked wicker baskets – the Mediatheque survived relatively unscathed. This was no miracle but a testament to Japanese expertise in earthquake-proof design and in particular to the knowledge and skill of Ito's consultant structural engineer, Mutsuro Sasaki.

Mediatheque, Sendai, Japan. Toyo Ito, 2000. An apparently fragile structure with basket-like columns, yet it survived the powerful March 2011 earthquake.

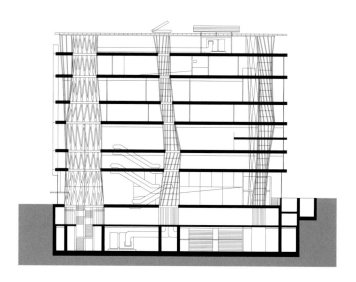

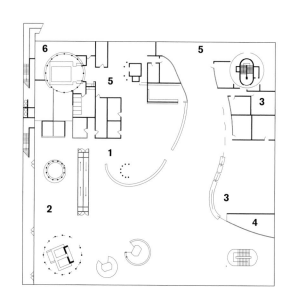

0   5   10m

15   30 ft

Section and first floor plan

1. Children's library
2. Meeting room
3. Offices
4. Voluntary workers' office
5. Service space
6. Deposit for children's library

Shigeru Ban

The architecture of Mies van der Rohe, especially his Farnsworth House, and of John Hejduk, a member of the New York Five, were among the early influences on the Japanese architect Shigeru Ban. But by his own account it was the models he made in special classes taken while still at high school that engendered his exceptional spatial and structural ingenuity. A relative ignorance of normal construction practice might also have helped. Several individual houses that he designed in the 1990s are named after the surprising ideas that dominate their designs. The flat roof of the Miesian Furniture House of 1995, for example, is supported not by walls or columns but by bookcases. A weekend retreat built in 1993 by Lake Yamanaka is roofed by thin corrugated steel sheets that are liable to deflect under snow load, but this doesn't matter because the roof is structurally independent of the ceilings below, hence it is known as the House with a Double Roof. And in the Curtain Wall House (Tokyo, 1995), a wide L-shaped terrace at first-floor level on a street corner is shaded, externally, by actual fabric curtains, two storeys high.

But it was Ban's use of cardboard as a structural material that made him famous. Returning to Japan in 1985 after graduating from Cooper Union in New York, he designed some fabric screens for an exhibition about the Argentinian architect Emilio Ambasz. The fabric was supplied in rolls round stout cardboard tubes. Ban kept the tubes, thinking they might one day come in useful. The following year, he designed an exhibition of Alvar Aalto's furniture. Wood was the natural choice of material for the display stands, but it

was too expensive. So out came the cardboard tubes, which, with others specially ordered, were used vertically to create serpentine walls and horizontally to create wavy ceilings. Here was a light, strong, cheap building component, available in a wide range of sizes and perfect for temporary buildings.

At this point, moral and ideological factors came into play. Uncomfortable with architecture's role as glorifier of the rich and powerful, Ban wanted to help the refugees from the Rwanda Civil War of 1994 who were in desperate need of shelter. Tents with metal frames were the standard UNHCR solution but the refugees sold the metal frames and used wood instead, causing local deforestation. Ban's cardboard-tube alternative was prototyped and proved effective. It was the first of a series of emergency housing projects all over the world. In Kobe, after the earthquake of 1995, Ban built Paper Log Houses for the Vietnamese community using beer crates as foundations and vertical cardboard tubes as external walls. Even the Catholic church was rebuilt using similar technology: 58 paper tubes, 4.9 metres (16 feet) high and 33 centimetres (13 inches) in diameter, arranged in a 'Baroque' ellipse with a fabric roof. More disaster relief projects followed: Turkey in 1999, India in 2001, Sri Lanka in 2004, China in 2008, Haiti in 2010 and the great eastern Japan earthquake and tsunami of 2011. In 2013 Ban's construction method reached its architectural apogee in the Cardboard Cathedral, built as a temporary replacement for the earthquake-damaged nineteenth-century Gothic original in Christchurch, New Zealand.

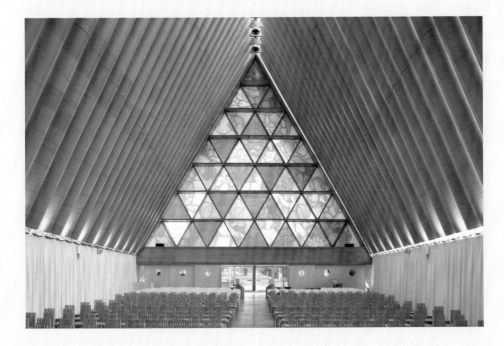

Christchurch Cathedral, Christchurch. New Zealand. Shigeru Ban, 2013.
A large, even monumental, public building made of cardboard.

28 | DECONSTRUCTIVISM
1982–1995

In 1982 the government of France ran a competition for the design of 'an urban park for the twenty-first century' on a large, semi-derelict site at La Villette in northern Paris. It was one of President Mitterrand's *Grands Projets*. The competition winner, Bernard Tschumi, had previously built almost nothing. He was a Swiss architect known mainly for his teaching at the Architectural Association in London and for his avant-garde conceptual projects. His design for La Villette was completely uncompromising. The common idea that a park should represent a natural landscape was rejected. This park would be more like an enormous, dismembered building. The functions required by the brief – playgrounds, exhibition spaces, concert venues, sports fields and so on – would be ordered by an architectural system. That system, however, would also be unusual. Spaces would not be allocated to specific functions and designed to suit them as they might be in a conventional building; instead,

functions would have to accommodate themselves as best they could to an abstract, triple-layered composition of points, lines and surfaces. The points, distributed on a regular 120-metre (131-yard) grid, were little red buildings called 'follies' and, as the name implies, they were designed without any particular function in mind. Some of the lines functioned straightforwardly enough as footpaths, but others were meandering routes like random scribbles. Surfaces conformed to a different geometry of simple figures surrounded by trees. These three layers were combined with each other and with the large existing buildings on the site – a converted abattoir and a nineteenth-century market building – in a studiedly accidental way so that, conceptually at least, a folly might find itself in the middle of a tennis court and a line of trees might cross a path at an oblique angle as if it were in a different world.

The design awarded second prize in the competition was the work of an almost equally inexperienced architect, Rem Koolhaas, who also taught at the Architectural Association. Koolhaas was Dutch and his practice was called Office for Metropolitan Architecture, or OMA. If anything, Koolhaas's design was even more unconventional than Tschumi's, though it resembled it in certain ways. Instead of three layers, there were five, and the main ordering principle was not points, lines and surfaces but parallel strips, like medieval farming or like the cross-section of a skyscraper laid flat on the site.

Within a few days of the unveiling of the La Villette winner, the result of another international competition was announced, for the design of a leisure club on Victoria Peak overlooking Hong Kong harbour. Once again, the winner was a teacher at the Architectural Association, a young Iraqi-born architect called Zaha Hadid. Hadid had only recently been a student in the teaching unit run by Rem Koolhaas. Not surprisingly, despite the very different briefs, her design for the Hong Kong club showed a kinship with

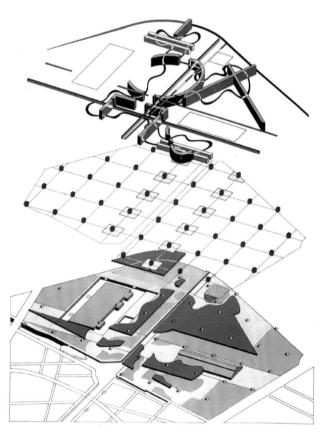

An Urban Park for the Twenty First Century, La Villette, Paris, France. Bernard Tschumi, 1982. Lines, points ('follies') and surfaces, overlayed but not aligned.

Parc de la Villette, Paris, France. Bernard Tschumi, 1982–98.
One of the red, neo-Constructivist follies, not specifically designed
for its function.

both of the La Villette projects. The published drawings
seemed at first unintelligible. What they depicted looked
more like a bunch of sticks thrown down on the hillside
than a buildable building. But close scrutiny revealed
order of a kind. The sticks turned out to contain rooms and
corridors, and they also functioned as beams spanning long
distances over the residual external voids. The voids were
also functional, accommodating recognizable elements
such as swimming pools and sunbathing terraces. Cut into
the hillside below, service spaces such as kitchens and car
parks were discernible.

Function and form redefined

A new style was emerging among these young, London-
based architects. It did not yet have a name, but certain
of its features were already apparent and it was beginning
to be taken seriously. Like all new styles, its first aim
was to distinguish itself from what had gone before. The
Postmodernism of the previous decade (see Chapter 24)
was rejected as shallow and regressive, but there was no
question of reviving the old Modernist orthodoxy summed up

in the phrase 'form follows function'. Tschumi's conceptual
projects, notably the one called Manhattan Transcripts, had
essentially been critiques of the over-simplified Modernist
concept of 'function', seeking to replace it with the richer,
more involving concept of 'narrative'. In both of the La
Villette projects 'function' was a dynamic, indeterminate
concept. Those 'layering' devices (the word, and what it
described, quickly became an architectural cliché) were
designed not so much to accommodate settled patterns
of use, such as playing a game of tennis or attending a
concert, as to encourage new combinations of uses by
random juxtaposition. In reality, human institutions are rather
resistant to such treatment. Staging a concert in a tennis
court creates certain practical problems. But the 'misuse'
of functionally defined space – a picnic in a farmer's field,
for example – is common enough and often pleasurable.
And this was another feature of the new style. It had a
hedonistic streak. In both the Paris park and the Hong
Kong leisure club, unusual spaces were there not just
to shock but to be enjoyed in creative, convivial ways.

The concept of form was being questioned as much as the
concept of function. Modernism, in its late, decadent phase,
was considered to have become mannered and formulaic.
The basically classical approach to form that had always

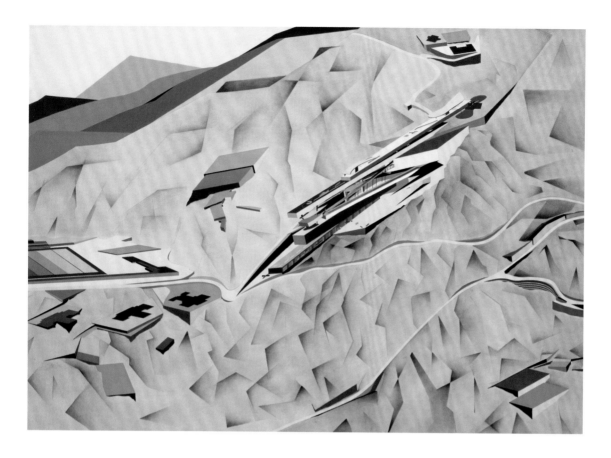

Hong Kong Peak Leisure Club project. Zaha Hadid, 1982. One of Hadid's eccentric paintings of the building on its hillside site.

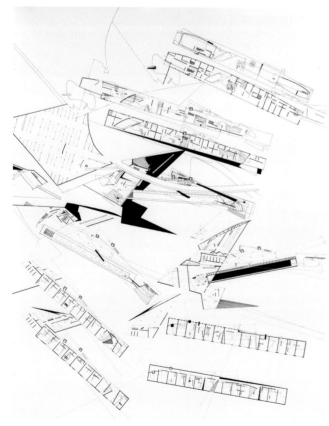

Hong Kong Peak Leisure Club plan, Zaha Hadid, 1982.
On close inspection, plans show recognizable sequences of spaces, including ordinary rooms and corridors.

lurked just beneath its plain white surfaces had become tiresome. It must be subverted, taken apart, exploded. Why should all floors be flat, all columns vertical, all corners right angles? Why shouldn't surfaces be warped, columns skewed, walls fragmented? And why should scale be consistent? The tired old hierarchies – architectural and perhaps, by implication, social – must be overthrown. As we shall see, this negative, iconoclastic aspect of the new style was to become its defining feature. It was a destructive more than a constructive force.

The destructiveness, however, was not naive or impetuous. Tschumi, Koolhaas and Hadid knew very well that there was a clear historical precedent for both the theoretical and the formal aspects of their style in the art and architecture of post-revolutionary Russia, in Constructivism and Suprematism (see Chapter 11). The bundle of sticks that was the Hong Kong club was reminiscent of the randomly positioned rectangles in one of Malevich's Suprematist paintings, Tschumi's follies at La Villette bore a family resemblance to Yakov Chernikhov's architectural fantasies of the late 1920s and early 1930s, and for Rem Koolhaas and his AA students, Ivan Leonidov was a common historical reference point.

Loyola Law School, Los Angeles, California,
USA. Frank Gehry, 1981. Four freestanding
columns seem to signify a missing classical portico.

The new style might therefore reasonably have been
called Neo-Constructivism, but there were other influences
at work and other contributors to its formation. Two
Americans, Frank Gehry and Peter Eisenman, had in their
different ways been undermining architectural convention
for some years. In Gehry's 1981 Law School building for
Loyola Marymount University in Los Angeles, for example,
a basically classical composition, appropriate for a law
school, is attacked, dismembered, even mocked by its very
creator. Its conventionally well-proportioned facade, with
Georgian windows, is rudely pushed apart by a staircase
that seems in a hurry to escape the interior. In the forecourt
stands a tetrastyle classical portico, except that it has lost
its pediment and its columns are plain aluminium cylinders.
This might be called Postmodern, but it contains the seed
of something more radical. The idea of strange forms
bursting out of ordinary buildings had already appeared
in Gehry's extensions to his own house in suburban Santa
Monica. The tilted cube that started the destruction in
about 1979 was followed by whole families of escaped
forms, gathering in the garden and leaving behind the
flayed structure of the original house.

Peter Eisenman's latent destructive tendencies went back
even further, to his membership of the New York Five, a
group of Neo-Modernist architects who had first exhibited

together in 1969 (see page 382). Eisenman had always
been the intellectual of the group. For him architecture
was an autonomous art, a game in which what he called
'formal universals' were manipulated in various ways
– division, duplication, subtraction, rotation, extension
– and transformed into something new. By such means,
the simple and recognizable was made complex and
unrecognizable. Often these transformations had nothing
to do with function in the normal sense of human use.
His House VI of 1973 is a good example (see page 382).

Jacques Derrida

But Eisenman contributed more than architectural
autonomy to the new style; he contributed the philosophy
of Jacques Derrida. Derrida was the hero of French critical
theory. His philosophy was called Deconstruction. Bernard
Tschumi too was a follower of Derrida. It is hard, if not
impossible, to sum up the philosophy of Deconstruction in a
few words and it originally had nothing whatever to do with
architecture. But there were perhaps crude parallels to be
drawn between, for example, Deconstruction's questioning
of the relationship between language and reality, and the
new style's questioning of the relationship between form
and function. Whether or not such parallels were valid, just
the name 'Deconstruction', with its obvious architectural
overtones, was enough to entice architects like Eisenman

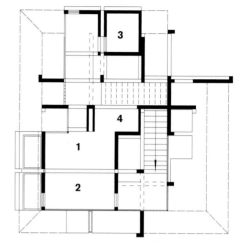

House VI, Cornwall, Connecticut, USA. Peter Eisenman, 1973. The composition, including an upside-down staircase, is the outcome of a sequence of formal transformations.

First floor plan (top)
1. Bedroom
2. Slot in floor
3. Bathroom
4. Wardrobe

Ground floor plan (below)
1. Entrance
2. Dining space
3. Kitchen
4. Living room

0   5m

15 ft

and Tschumi who were looking to justify their practice by reference to real philosophy. In 1988 Eisenman even went so far as to collaborate directly with Derrida himself in a project, never realized, for a small, themed park to be incorporated into Tschumi's master plan for La Villette. The theme was, approximately, the questioning of representation in architecture.

By this time, certain critics had begun to apply the name 'Deconstruction' to the new architectural style. But there was an alternative designation, 'Deconstructivism', in which historical and philosophical affiliations were neatly combined and it was this name that was finally sanctioned in a major exhibition held at the Museum of Modern Art in New York in 1988. The exhibition included buildings and projects (but mainly projects) by Tschumi, Koolhaas, Hadid, Gehry and Eisenman, plus Daniel Libeskind and Coop Himmelb(l)au. It was endorsed by Philip Johnson as co-curator, which prompted comparisons with the famous International Style exhibition of 1932 (see page 108). But the guiding light of the Deconstructivist exhibition was the critic Mark Wigley, who, five years later, was to write an influential book called *The Architecture of Deconstruction – Derrida's Haunt*. Wigley's essay in the exhibition

catalogue was packed with all those negative words that seem unavoidable in any description of the style: devious, deformed, distorted, disturbed, disquiet, uncanny, uncontrollable, unsettled, unfamiliar, uneasy, angst, nightmare, alien, slippery, subverted, suppressed – all these from the last three short paragraphs.[1] One would imagine from Wigley's essay that the Deconstructivist architects were all earnest intellectuals who despaired of any joy in human life. In fact they were nothing of the kind and, apart from Tschumi and Eisenman, they were not much inclined to intellectualize their work. Wigley's essay was a determined attempt to find a retrospective theoretical justification for a style that had arisen spontaneously on both sides of the Atlantic.

Daniel Libeskind

Libeskind was represented in the exhibition by a competition-winning project for the Tiergarten district of Berlin. Its most prominent feature was an enormous inhabited beam that reared up out of the ground to a height equivalent to ten storeys so that it could look over the Berlin Wall. Symbolically the beam *was* the Berlin Wall, freed from gravity and, by implication, freed from political oppression. The interior of the beam was represented as

Jewish Museum, Berlin, Germany. Daniel Libeskind, 1999. The zig-zag plan is notionally part of an enormous Star of David inscribed far beyond the boundaries of the site.

City Edge project, Tiergarten, Berlin, Germany. Daniel Libeskind, 1987. An enormous inhabited beam lifted up to look over the Berlin Wall.

an unintelligible jumble of straight lines and circles that looked very like the abstract pen-and-ink drawings for which Libeskind was at that time mainly known. The combination of literal symbolism with out-of-control geometry would continue to characterize his designs in later years. His first major commission also came in 1988 when he won the competition to design a Jewish museum for Berlin, though the building was not completed until 1999.

The symbolic programme of the Jewish Museum is complex. The zig-zag plan, for example, is conceived in relation to an enormous, distorted Star of David notionally inscribed on and beyond the site and extending over the Berlin Wall, which still stood at the time of the design. The Holocaust is signified by a linear space or void that penetrates the whole building and that visitors must cross repeatedly in their progress through the museum. Among the other themes mentioned in Libeskind's own account of the design are Schoenberg's incomplete opera *Moses und Aron*, the *Gedenkbuch* (memorial book), which lists the names of all those people deported from Berlin during the Holocaust, and Walter Benjamin's essay 'One-Way Street'.[2] Libeskind is himself a Jew who was born in Łódz in 1946. Many members of his family had perished in the Holocaust. He is also an accomplished musician. The building has been widely acclaimed, though it is in some respects a disappointment. Its built form, with level roof and vertical

walls, is a simplification of the original design, which had sloping walls, and the domestic displays that it houses look out of place in its strenuous architecture. Most of the available architectural photographs of the building show it before the exhibits were installed.

Coop Himmelb(l)au

The Austrian practice Coop Himmelb(l)au (the name means either Blue Sky Co-op with the 'l', or Sky Building Co-op without it), led by Wolf Prix and Helmut Swiczinsky, exhibited three projects in the Deconstructivism exhibition, the most interesting of which was a steel-and-glass, insect-like structure settled apparently insecurely on the roof of an ordinary Vienna apartment block. Its fragmented, asymmetrical form obeyed no obvious logic and might have been the result of a blind drawing exercise, but it was built, it stood up and it served its purpose in both an ordinary practical sense, as the office of a law firm, and in the sense that it brought this once-fringe practice, established in 1967, to the attention of clients with money to spend. In the years that followed, Coop Himmelb(l)au built substantial buildings in various European cities, sometimes taming their style to suit budgets and client expectations, as in the bent tower of their Gasometer B apartment building in Vienna, designed in 1995, and sometimes maintaining a degree of wildness, as in their museum building at Groningen in the Netherlands, completed in 1994.

(Above) Rooftop remodelling, Falkestrasse, Vienna, Austria. Coop Himmelb(l)au, 1988. The insect-like form might have been the result of a blind drawing exercise.

(Right) Gasometer B apartment building, Vienna, Austria. Coop Himmelb(l)au, 2001. The distorted tower is an early example of a form that later became commonplace as computer modelling spread.

Le Fresnoy Art Centre, Tourcoing, France. Bernard Tschumi, 1997. A new umbrella roof over an existing leisure complex creates an ambiguous intermediate space.

The Deconstructivism exhibition boosted the careers of all its participants. Eisenman and Gehry were already well established in practice and Koolhaas had built a handful of buildings, but Tschumi and Hadid had achieved fame solely on the basis of paper projects. Their aim now was to build. Tschumi's Parc de la Villette project went ahead: the follies were built (looking no more real than they had as drawings),

the surfaces were laid and the trees planted without departing too far from the spirit of the original design, but the public's attention was more drawn to the real buildings on the site – the City of Science and Industry in the converted abattoir and Christian de Portzamparc's City of Music – than to the virtual building of the park itself. Tschumi pursued an academic career, becoming dean of the Graduate School of Architecture at Columbia University in 1988, but continued to practise in the United States, France and Switzerland. In his Le Fresnoy contemporary arts studio at Tourcoing near Lille in France, ideas of layering, accidental juxtaposition and unpredictable use are kept alive in an economical design that covers an existing 1920s leisure complex with a shed-like umbrella roof. The space between the old and new roofs becomes a zone of indeterminate use accessed by elevated walkways. Tschumi compares this combination of new roof and old buildings to the Surrealist image of 'the chance encounter of a sewing machine and an umbrella on a dissecting table' but from the client's point of view it was probably more attractive as a money-saving strategy. Tschumi's most important commission was to come in 2001 with the Acropolis Museum in Athens.

Vitra Fire Station, Weil am Rhein, Germany. Zaha Hadid, 1993. Reinforced concrete stretched to the structural limit in Zaha Hadid's first important building.

Zaha Hadid had to wait until the turn of century before large commissions came her way and by then her jagged Deconstructivist style had turned into something smoother, slicker and more accommodating to corporate clients (see pages 448–451). Her influence on architects all over the world, and especially on architectural students, should not be under-estimated, however. She was an artist/architect of astonishing vision and her drawings and paintings form an impressive oeuvre even though most of the buildings they depict were never built.

In a Hadid painting, such as those that accompanied the Hong Kong club design, gravity has been abolished and buildings can fly. This essentially simple vision is the whole message of her early work. The sort of architectural drawings – plans, sections and elevations – that are normally used to fix and record the form of a building are boldly combined with the sort of drawings – perspective views – that are meant to give a visual impression. And both are slanted and foreshortened as if seen from a spaceship in low orbit. Real buildings, unfortunately, are subject to gravity, so weightlessness has to be simulated. In her only real building of the 1990s, a fire station for the Vitra furniture company at Weil am Rhein in Germany, ordinary reinforced concrete is stretched to the limit, as if straining to take off and almost succeeding. In 1994 it seemed that for Hadid the breakthrough to building had come with her winning of the Cardiff Bay Opera House competition against a field

of 267 architects from all over the world. A traditional opera house is the last building type that one would associate with an architect who is deeply sceptical about customs and laws, even the laws of nature, so this was a surprise result. But it was also an impressive demonstration of Hadid's ability to master a complex brief and inspire the confidence of an expert jury. The project had a stormy ride. It was distrusted by the local authorities, sniped at by the press and, amid accusations of elitism on one side and philistinism on the other, eventually it foundered. Hadid's reputation, though, suffered no harm.

Colliding grids
At the time of the Deconstructivism exhibition, Peter Eisenman's academically orientated practice was already beginning to tackle larger projects. The Wexner Center for the Arts at Ohio State University in Columbus might reasonably be thought of as the first large-scale Deconstructivist building, although, like Gehry's Loyola Law School, it also shows some affinity with 1970s Postmodernism. One simple way to achieve the kind of disjunction and disorientation that Deconstructivism demanded was to overlay one controlling grid on another at a slight angle. Building elements like walls or floors might

Cardiff Bay Opera House (unbuilt). Zaha Hadid, 1994.
The competition-winning project eventually foundered after encountering opposition from the press and local authorities.

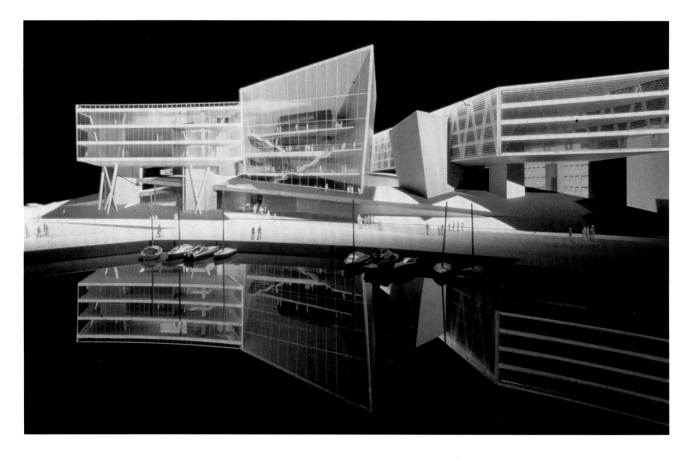

Wexner Center for the Arts, Ohio State University, Columbus, USA. Peter Eisenman, 1989. Campus grid and city grid overlap and combine to create unexpected, deconstructed forms.

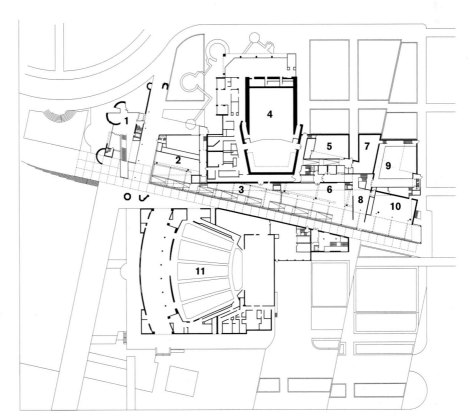

Ground floor plan
1. Upper lobby
2. Open to Ohio gallery below
3. Permanent collection gallery
4. Weigel hall
5. Instrumental hall
6. Main gallery
7. Choral hall
8. Performance space lobby
9. Open to performance space below
10. Experimental gallery
11. Mershon auditorium

obey either grid and clash satisfyingly with their neighbours of the other allegiance. At the Wexner the grids came with the site: one corresponded to the street plan of the city of Columbus and the other to the plan of the university campus. The new arts centre, which obeyed the city grid, was sited between and under two existing auditoriums that obeyed the university grid. To make the clash apparent, Eisenman introduced a new public walkway through the middle of the complex marked by an open framework like a pergola. The Postmodern element was the rebuilding of the old castle-like university armoury to form an entrance to the walkway. The new armoury roughly resembled the original except that its turrets and arches were sliced through – deconstructed – in an apparently arbitrary manner.

Greater Columbus Convention Center, Ohio, USA. Peter Eisenman, 1993. The street front reveals the ends of train-like roofs, though the space below is a simple hall.

Checkpoint Charlie housing, Berlin, Germany. Peter Eisenman, 1985. A very early deconstructed facade in a still-divided Berlin.

Eisenman had already explored the potential of overlapping grids in his Checkpoint Charlie housing in Berlin, completed in 1985, and he continued to explore it in buildings like the Aronoff Center for Design and Art in Cincinnati, Ohio, completed in 1996. But his restless intellect was moving into fresh conceptual territory in its search for a radically new architecture. In the Greater Columbus Convention Center, completed in 1993, he explores the curvilinear forms of roads and railways, the in-between spaces of the city. The site was an old rail yard and the exterior of Eisenman's building looks like the trains that once stood in it. Inside, though, the space mostly consists of a vast open area, ready to be configured for almost any combination of events.

Frank Gehry

If Eisenman soon moved on from Deconstructivism, it is doubtful that Frank Gehry ever really inhabited that territory in the first place. A Jewish Canadian working in Los Angeles, Gehry has always described himself as an outsider. His buildings are as much sculpture as architecture and are strongly influenced by artists such as Robert Rauschenberg and Claes Oldenburg. Gehry has always been alert to the surreal potential of large objects in city streets. His California Aerospace Museum building of 1984 is unambiguously signposted by the real Lockheed Starfighter bracketed off its facade, and in his 1991 headquarters for the advertising agency Chiat/Day in Venice, Los Angeles, a giant pair of binoculars serves as an entrance porch. But there are also

subtler, more sophisticated influences. The Winton Guest House of 1987, for example, is said to have been inspired by the art of Giorgio Morandi, who obsessively painted bottles and jugs on tabletops. Only one of the objects that combine to make the house looks like a bottle, but the composition is unmistakably a still life nevertheless.

Painting and sculpture inspire Gehry, but so does nature, especially fish, which are something of an obsession. For Gehry, the writhing, silvery forms of fishes represent an image of what architecture might become if only it could be freed from its traditional rectilinearity. Fish first appear in his work as simple signs or totems, like the grey scaly

Chiat/Day offices, Los Angeles, California, USA. Frank Gehry, 1991. The binoculars, designed by Claes Oldenburg and Coosje van Bruggen, frame the entrance to the car park.

Winton Guest House, Wayzata, Minnesota, USA.
Frank Gehry, 1987. A composition inspired by Giorgio
Morandi, obsessive painter of bottles on tabletops.

specimen that stands in front of the Fishdance Restaurant
in Kobe, Japan of 1987 or the more abstracted fish-form
that adorns the seafront of the Vila Olímpica in Barcelona.
But soon they begin to be inhabited. At one stage in the
ten-year-long and ultimately fruitless gestation of the
house he designed for Peter B. Lewis, a wealthy American
businessman, the design was dominated by a large,
whale-like form.

It is tempting to follow Gehry in his obsession and
begin to interpret all of his later work in terms of fish.
One begins to see the fish influence in even relatively
(for him) straightforward multi-storey buildings like the
Cinémathèque Française in Paris of 1994, or the well-
known 'Fred and Ginger' (Astaire and Rogers) building in
Prague of 1996. Gehry can't construct a straightforward
office building without giving it a biomorphic twist. His

Fishdance Restaurant, Kobe, Japan. Frank Gehry,
1987. One of several fishes and fish-like forms in Gehry's
idiosyncratic oeuvre.

clients would be disappointed if he did. But if the building is a museum or an art gallery – a one-off rather than a representative of an urban type – then biomorphism takes over completely and the dream of a liberated architecture is almost realized. The Weisman Art Museum at the University of Minnesota, completed in 1993, seems to be tripping over itself in its anxiety to struggle free, but in the Guggenheim Museum in Bilbao, completed four years later, the scale is more generous and the composition more assured. It has been hailed as one of the greatest buildings of the twentieth

'Fred and Ginger' building, Prague, Czech Republic. Frank Gehry and Vlado Milunic, 1996. Gehry's nickname is now deemed inappropriate in this culturally independent city.

century. When Philip Johnson first stood in the atrium of the Bilbao Guggenheim he was moved to tears, comparing it to Chartres Cathedral.[3] The comparison is hardly apt. This atrium is Gothic only in its height. Limestone, steel, glass and white-painted plaster are combined with the freedom of an action painting rather than in conformity with a strict

Guggenheim Museum, Bilbao, Spain. Frank Gehry, 1997. A filleted, titanium-scaled exterior but there are traditional, square, top-lit galleries inside.

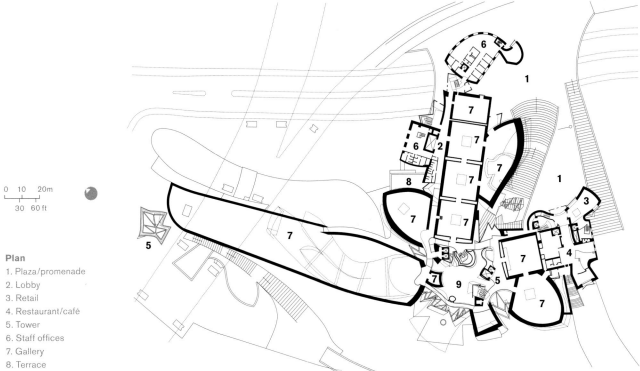

0 10 20m
30 60 ft

Plan
1. Plaza/promenade
2. Lobby
3. Retail
4. Restaurant/café
5. Tower
6. Staff offices
7. Gallery
8. Terrace
9. Atrium

Weisman Art Museum, University of Minnesota,
Minnesota, USA. Frank Gehry, 1993. Deconstructed
to an extreme degree, like a Cubist sculpture.

geometrical and structural system. And the atrium is a
special space even in this extraordinary building. Most of
the galleries in which paintings and sculpture are displayed
are perfectly conventional – square on plan and top lit. It is
as if the building occasionally goes quiet, suddenly aware
of its duty to step back and display the art, but then can
no longer contain itself and bursts out again, demanding
attention. Some of its most extravagant flourishes are pure
sculpture. The long East Gallery, for example, looks like
a three-storey structure but its fish-like upper levels are
floorless voids. Computer-aided design, in this case the
CATIA (Computer-Aided Three-dimensional Interactive
Application) system developed by the French aircraft
company Dassault and adapted for architecture in Gehry's
own office, has made geometrical discipline a thing of
the past. The rigid steel nets that support those writhing,
titanium-scaled bodies would have been almost impossible

to fabricate on such a scale before the coming of CAD/CAM
technology. It is important to note, though, that the forms
originated not in a computer but in Gehry's imagination. The
computer merely speeded up a design process that originally
involved repeated modifications to physical sketch models.
The forms are human inventions and their exuberance
delights architects, critics and the general public alike. In the
history of modern architecture such agreement is extremely
rare. Whether Gehry's personal method has any future as a
style to be developed and continued by others and applied
to building types other than art galleries is doubtful. But the
Guggenheim can be said to have engaged with twenty-first-
century urban reality in at least one respect: it 'put Bilbao
on the map', attracted droves of tourists and stimulated
the city's economic regeneration. It may not be Gothic,
but symbolically it is a cathedral.

Of the seven participants of the Deconstructivism
exhibition, only Rem Koolhaas remains to be discussed.
But his work and influence must be examined in more
detail in a separate chapter.

Deconstruction

Deconstruction is a linguistic theory or method invented by the French philosopher Jacques Derrida (1930–2004). Despite its obvious architectural overtones, the word originally had nothing to do with architecture. Derrida was what is now known as a Poststructuralist; that is to say he continued the semiotic and Structuralist tradition founded by Ferdinand de Saussure but disagreed with certain important aspects of it. In general terms, the idea is that every human communication, no matter how urgent or immediate it might be – a cry for help, perhaps – depends on an arbitrary, abstract system of 'differences' that exists independently of the communicating person. Language, especially written language, is such a system. Writing depends neither on the presence of the person that creates it nor on the presence of what it refers to. The meaning of a text is always provisional and approximate, always 'deferred'. And since human beings can only understand their world by means of language and other sign systems, which are kinds of text, they can never attain complete knowledge of anything in that world. Signs signify other signs, which in turn signify other signs in an endless chain. There can be no fixed, permanent, 'transcendent' reality to which language refers.

When Deconstruction is applied to the sign system called architecture, the argument becomes even more convoluted. Architecture and philosophy are, it turns out, related in rather fundamental ways. Often architecture provides metaphors for thought itself. We talk about the 'structure' of a philosophical system, about opinions that are 'well founded', about the 'embellishment' of an argument. It is as if architecture were itself a kind of philosophy – a set of ideas about the fixed, logical, stable relationships between things. It is the architectural aspect of philosophy that Derrida objects to most, the idea that it is possible to take an overview of reality, to see how one part relates to another and thereby to understand it. Even that word 'understand' has faint architectural resonances. Deconstruction dismisses all such notions as mere comforting illusions. It sounds like something architects should steer well clear of but in the 1980s certain architects, notably Peter Eisenman and Bernard Tschumi, adopted Deconstruction as the theory of a new kind of architecture that would question the 'common sense' notion that the form of a building might 'represent' the reality of its construction, its function, its context or the traditions of the society that produced it.

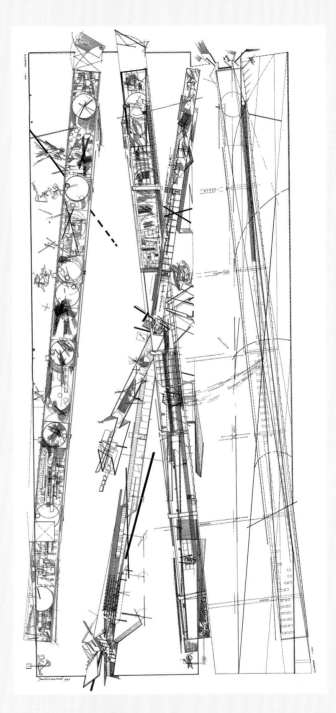

City Edge project, Berlin, Germany. Daniel Libeskind, 1987.
The drawing depicts a building proposal but is also designed to be appreciated as an abstract composition.

'Architecture disappeared in the twentieth century; we have been reading a footnote under a microscope hoping it would turn into a novel.'[1]

Can this really be true? Have books like the one you are reading become irrelevant? Let's hope not. It's a worrying thought – that architecture, as normally defined, has lost control of building – although actually we've known it for a long time. Most buildings are not designed by architects, and even some of those that are find themselves excluded from architecture's territory because they pay too little attention to its rules of etiquette. The Pritzker Prize – chief global arbiter of architectural etiquette – is never going to notice your local shopping centre, or the volume-built housing estate on which you live, or the industrial shed in which you work. So the idea isn't new; it's just that we don't like to be reminded of it. The quotation is from

'Junkspace', a now-famous essay published in 2001. It was designed to explode architectural complacency by pointing out what is obvious but unacknowledged – such as the probability that an architect visiting his or her local shopping centre will often feel like a visiting alien – and it is full of worrying thoughts. Here are a few more: 'The idea that a profession once dictated, or at least presumed to predict, people's movements now seems laughable.' Or: '[Junkspace] creates communities not out of shared interest or free association, but out of identical statistics and unavoidable demographics, an opportunistic weave of vested interests.' Or: 'Minimum is the ultimate ornament, a self-righteous crime, the contemporary Baroque. It does not signify beauty, but guilt. Its demonstrative earnestness drives whole civilizations into the welcoming arms of camp and kitsch.'

The author is Rem Koolhaas, a Pritzker Prize-winning architect who is also a brilliant writer and theorist. Comparisons have been made with Le Corbusier and Frank Lloyd Wright. He appears in Chapter 28 of this book as an entrant in the Parc de la Villette competition and a contributor to the 1988 Deconstructivism show in New York. More samples of his provocative wisdom can be found in *S,M,L,XL*, a 1,376-page book about the architectural and theoretical work of his Rotterdam-based architectural practice, the Office for Metropolitan Architecture, or OMA. It contains essays, most either too short or too long, on such subjects as globalization, 'bigness', the fate of urbanism, the city of Atlanta, the history of Singapore, the strange fate of the Palace of the Soviets site in Moscow, the 'typical plan', 'dirty realism', and much more, all shamelessly padded out with photographs and drawings that ignore the rules of conventional book design. It is hard to read and too big to carry round, but in 1995 when it was published, every serious architecture student bought a copy.

Koolhaas *provokes* like no other architectural writer, using descriptions of the real world, as he sees it, to demolish the false world of architects' deluded imaginings. Born in Rotterdam in 1944, he spent four years of his youth in Indonesia, where his father was chief cultural advisor to the government. Returning to the Netherlands, he pursued

Remment Lucas 'Rem' Koolhaas. Born in Rotterdam, the Netherlands, 1944.

Sections through the Villa dall'Ava

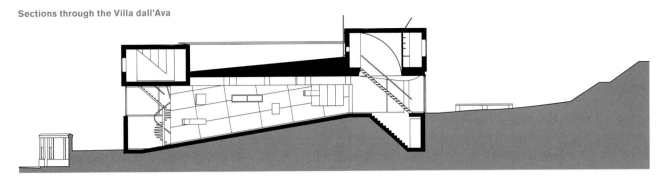

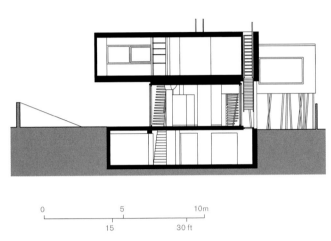

0   5   10m
   15   30 ft

Villa dall'Ava, Paris, France. Rem Koolhaas, 1991.
Spatial convention and structural common sense subverted:
a rooftop swimming pool with a view of the Eiffel Tower.

a career as a journalist and scriptwriter before becoming
a student at the Architectural Association in London in
1968. A period of study with Oswald Mathias Ungers at
Cornell University was followed by a visiting fellowship
at Peter Eisenman's Institute for Architecture and Urban
Studies in New York and the writing of a full-length book,
Delirious New York, published in 1978, by which time he
was teaching at the AA and had established OMA with his
wife, Madelon Vriesendorp, and Elia and Zoe Zenghelis. The
book was Koolhaas's first serious foray into architectural
theory. Or should that be 'anti-architectural theory'? Its
broad thesis is that the Manhattan the world knows and
loves was created not by architecture but by a combination
of technology, rigid planning and commercial logic. The steel
frame, the elevator, the electric light and the grid-iron plan
provided the means to maximize the profits of development,
resulting in a cityscape of extraordinary beauty and a new
way of life that Koolhaas called 'the culture of congestion'.
The breathless, almost evangelical tone of the book persists
in Koolhaas's later writings, but some of its observations
and insights have also been important in shaping his
architecture. One example is the concept of the Manhattan
skyscraper as a simple container with a 'deep', functionally
unspecific plan and a randomly layered section that mixes

ordinary office space with hotel rooms, apartments,
auditoriums, gymnasiums, ballrooms and bars. We shall
see how these features are reinterpreted in Koolhaas's own
public buildings and urban plans, but first let us consider
the houses, so often the test-beds of architectural ideas.

Villa dall'Ava
This villa on the outskirts of Paris, completed in 1991,
has been interpreted as a version of Le Corbusier's Villa
Savoye. The two buildings share certain features, such as
a roof terrace, ribbon windows, an integrated garage and
a ramp that rises from the entrance hall to a first-floor living
room, with a spiral staircase as an alternative short cut. But
no-one would describe this building as 'purist'. Its external
materials and finishes look practical rather than pristine –
mostly grey concrete and coloured corrugated metal with
anodized aluminium window frames.

The black, rubble-patterned stone that clads the lower
parts of the walls where they emerge from the sloping
ground might have been stolen from an ordinary pattern-
book suburban house. And whereas the layout of functions
in the Villa Savoye is almost conventional – main living
space on the upper floor with car and servant below –

the Villa dall'Ava ignores not only convention but structural common sense by putting a swimming pool on the roof. The arrangement is deliberately irrational but justified by an intensification of the hedonistic activity of private swimming. There is no room for poolside loungers, but imagine the thrill of swimming in an unfenced tank with a rooftop view of the Eiffel Tower in the distance. So, although the reference to the Villa Savoye is undoubtedly conscious, the message it conveys is ambiguous. It seems to say: yes, make the comparison with Le Corbusier by all means, but don't assume that this is any kind of homage; an awful lot has changed since 1931 and mainstream Modernism, with all its formal and functional assumptions, is just a memory.

Denial of the column

In the Bordeaux House, completed seven years later in 1998 on a hilltop overlooking the city, irrationality gets into its stride. Take the question of columns, the very symbols of Architecture itself. Indispensable? Not to Koolhaas and his colleagues. The Bordeaux House represents a determined denial of the column, and by implication of all architectural tradition. Convention assumes that buildings have solid bases and lighter superstructures: a temple of columns and beams, originally wooden, on a solid stone stylobate. Already, in the Villa dall'Ava, the convention has been subverted, but the row of fat columns that supports

the swimming pool is only partly concealed. At the Bordeaux House it is genuinely hard to see how the enormous concrete bar of the top storey is supported above the glass-walled main living space at ground level. Each of the building's three storeys offers a different spatial experience. The lowest, dug into the hillside, is cave-like, facing an entrance court that is accessed by driving under, rather than through a surrounding wall. A kitchen, a laundry and a television room push finger-like extensions back into the ground to form a larder, a wine store and three different staircases. Already, irrationality reigns. The retaining wall that encloses these spaces insists on following their complicated outline instead of cutting straight across as any engineer or builder would recommend. The mass of the retained ground no doubt helps to keep the spaces cool, but it seems an unnecessary complication, either pure or perverse according to your viewpoint.

The middle of the three staircases rises in a sculpted alcove like the inside of a shell and lands in the open ground floor under a slot in the hovering concrete mass above. We are now on the hilltop, with only glass walls to separate us from the view over the valley of the Garonne. One of these walls can slide out onto a terrace, simultaneously opening one space while sheltering the other. Above us looms the potentially crushing weight of the top storey with its flat,

Bordeaux House, Bordeaux, France. OMA, 1998.
A combined lift and study for the disabled client is only one of the building's many inventions and subversions.

Ground floor plan

1. Main entrance	4. Lift
2. Kitchen	5. Wine cellar
3. Laundry	6. TV room
	7. Staff quarters

Section

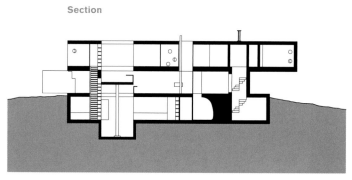

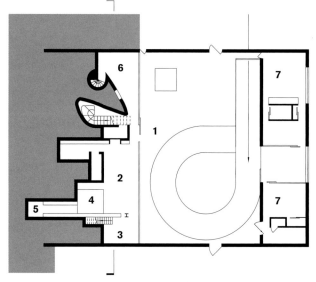

Kunsthal, Rotterdam, the Netherlands. OMA, 1992. The building is a single container, abutting a dike and bridging over a service road at the lower level.

beamless soffit of raw concrete. Climbing up into that storey via a cantilevered staircase we find ourselves in a mostly enclosed world of bedrooms and bathrooms. Only the master bedroom at the east end is open to the landscape, with a full-width balcony. The other, children's bedrooms are lit indirectly by tiny courtyards and by portholes in the concrete walls that seem randomly distributed at first but actually direct themselves at key points in the rooms such as desktops, pillows and baths.

How then is the mysterious hovering concrete box supported? At the east end a black-painted steel downstand that we hadn't noticed before turns out to be a kind of portal frame, its two vertical elements cunningly disguised, one of them standing some way off in the garden as if dissociating itself from the house proper. At the west end, the arrangement is truly perverse. A fat cylinder, dematerialized by a reflective chrome cladding lest it be mistaken for a column, is actually made of concrete and accommodates a spiral staircase. It rises through the concrete box to support a deep steel beam above the roof. The box seems to support the beam; actually the box is suspended from the beam. One last perversity: the concrete cylinder is placed off centre of the beam, which therefore has to be balanced by extending it over the courtyard and anchoring it to the ground with a tension rod. And this is not the house's most unusual feature. The client was disabled and in a wheelchair. A conventional lift would have been unsatisfactory – a mere adaptation of a house designed essentially for the able bodied. The lift therefore takes the form of a fully furnished platform that rises and falls on a hydraulic column like a car lift in a garage. Looked at another way, it is a three-storey room with a

moveable floor. One of its walls is a full-height bookcase. The Villa dall'Ava might have been inspired by Le Corbusier, but the Bordeaux House is totally original. Was Rem Koolhaas trying to design the last great house of the twentieth century? If so, he may have succeeded.

Kunsthal, Rotterdam

By 1998 the habit of undermining conventional architectural expectations was already an expected aspect of Koolhaas's architecture. The Kunsthal in Rotterdam, completed six years

Interior of the Kunsthal. The auditorium is incorporated into a stepped and ramped circulation system.

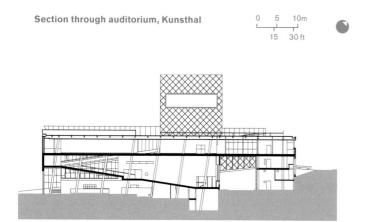

Section through auditorium, Kunsthal

0   5   10m
15   30 ft

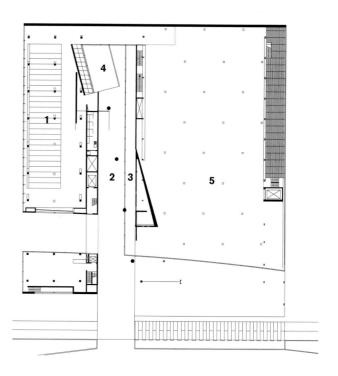

Dike level plan
1. Entrance/auditorium
2. Ramp outside
3. Ramp inside
4. Roof garden
5. Hall 2

earlier, had made it clear even to conservative architects and critics that the mainstream would have to shift course to accommodate a new mode of architectural composition. The building's programme was conventional enough: three flexible exhibition galleries, an auditorium and a restaurant, on a site at the edge of Museumpark, up against a major road raised on a dike, with a parallel service road at the lower level. The conventional element under attack in this design is the staircase. It is easy to imagine how a classical architect would have arranged the spaces: a suitably formal frontage on the road, with a foyer behind leading to a grand staircase from which the galleries on two or three levels could be reached directly. The auditorium would have been in the basement. Koolhaas's scheme ignores this obvious solution. Everything – including some open space – is accommodated in a single container: a big flat-roofed box. It faces the road and there is even a kind of Miesian portico. The main entrance, however, leads not to a foyer but to the top of a straight and quite steep public ramp that passes right through the building to the park beyond. Half way down the ramp on the left is the real main entrance, no more than a sidestep into a combined entrance hall and auditorium. This space is really just another ramp, going in the opposite direction, with a stepped area for the auditorium seating. It takes us either down to exhibition hall 1 or up to hall 2, passing either under or over the public ramp into the other half of the building. Or we can take another, angled 'ramp', actually a very shallow flight of steps, up to hall 3 over the auditorium. The restaurant is under the auditorium, facing the park. So this is a box well

packed, in which spaces have unexpected opportunities to communicate with one another.

We expect an art gallery to be either formal and well dressed or making do in a disused warehouse. This is neither. It is something new – a gallery that challenges expectations just as much as the modern art installations it exhibits. Materials are unexpected too, or used in unexpected ways: internal walls of translucent corrugated plastic, steel columns dressed up to resemble tree trunks, floor panels of steel mesh. Externally there is some stone facing, on the elevation facing the park, but it is a plain rectangle above the glass wall of the restaurant and it looks more like wallpaper. We have to get used to the idea that a piece of architecture by Koolhaas is also a piece of anti-architecture. It refuses to behave as architecture should.

On the S–M–L–XL scale, the Kunsthal is M for Medium. For a Large example, we will travel 170 kilometres (105 miles) south to Lille, an old town that became a long-distance rail hub when it was connected to the Channel Tunnel in the mid 1990s. But first it is worth pausing to look at a Large unbuilt project of the early 1990s, the Centre for Art and Media Technology (ZKM) at Karlsruhe in Germany, nicknamed 'the electronic Bauhaus'. The brief was complex

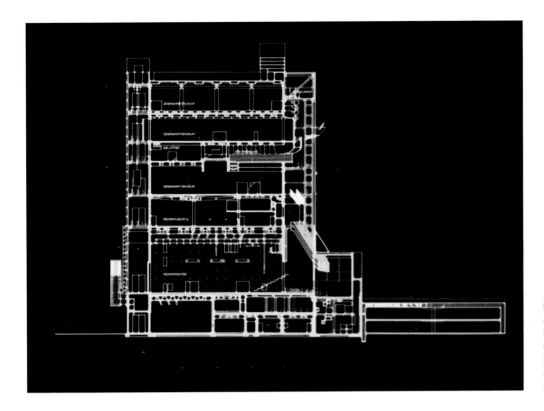

Section of the Centre for Art and Media Technology (ZKM), Karlsruhe, Germany (unbuilt). OMA, 1989. 'The electronic Bauhaus': a deep-planned box, ingeniously structured, housing a stack of disparate functions.

– music and film studios, computer laboratories, a theatre, a media museum, a library, a lecture hall, a contemporary art gallery and a restaurant, on a site right next to the railway station. The proposed solution, however, was simple: another deep-planned box, this time 58 metres (190 feet) high and 43 square metres (463 square feet) on plan, in which the various functions would be stacked, the more heavily serviced electronics-related spaces at the bottom and the simpler art galleries at the top.

In the Kunsthal, Koolhaas was content to solve structural problems in an ad-hoc manner, allowing columns where necessary but doing away with them whenever possible, for example in Hall 2 where there is only a lightweight roof to be supported. In the ZKM, with the help of his now famous engineering consultant, Cecil Balmond, he devised a consistent structural system designed to provide total planning freedom on alternate floors. Storey-height Vierendeel (unbraced) trusses span two parallel walls of black concrete. The storeys occupied by the trusses have to be planned around the struts (columns, in effect), but the floors above and below are completely column free. One of them is circular and surrounded by voids. A band of servant spaces wraps round this inner box, providing it with animated facades: a full-height atrium on the north side facing the town centre, an electronic billboard to the east, offices to the west and a goods- and scenery-shifting void to the south. This would have been an important building and a milestone in the development of the Koolhaas style. Almost for the first time we see him taking an interest in

structure and using it efficiently rather than rebelling against its constraining demands. Sadly, in June 1992, the city council cancelled the project, the political circumstances having been transformed by the reunification of Germany.

Congrexpo, Lille

And so to Lille, where a relatively inexperienced Koolhaas team was commissioned to design the biggest building of their career so far: a 'Congrexpo' containing a rock-concert hall to seat 5,000, a conference centre with three large auditoriums, and a 20,000-square-metre (4.9-acre) exhibition hall. It was to be linked to the proposed new Euralille development, of which more later. The team evidently relished the prospect, when they were not terrified by it. On a two-page spread in the *S,M,L,XL* book, an elevation of the Eiffel Tower is overlaid by an oval paragraph of text in which the scale of the project is indicated by amusing statistics, beginning with the fact that the piled foundations could support the world's heaviest aircraft carrier plus the world's biggest battle ship and still have spare capacity for 3,000 elephants. The Eiffel Tower is there because its height roughly matches the length of the building – 300 metres (1,000 feet). The text is oval because that is the plan-form of the building, not a box this time but a simple geometrical form nevertheless, like an element in a Suprematist painting.

Or is it three buildings? Koolhaas's own descriptions encourage an urbanistic interpretation, as if the three main elements had been built for different organizations on a

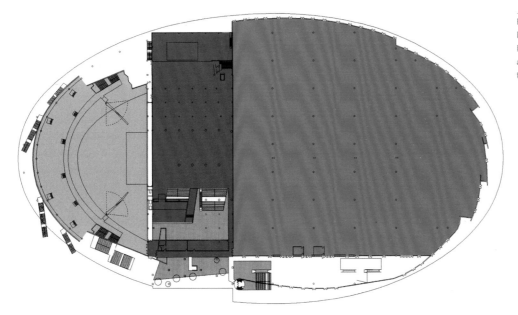

Lille Grand Palais (Congrexpo),
France. OMA, 1994. The exhibition
hall (red), can serve as a backstage
area for the concert hall (yellow)
through the conference centre (blue).

site that just happened to be oval. The single-big-container idea is combined with a different, parallel-strip strategy that goes right back to Koolhaas's entry in the La Villette competition in the early 1980s (see page 378). The oval plan might be said to be unified in its width but differentiated in its length. At the east end the concert hall is like half of a sports stadium, its seating arranged on an inward-facing fan of concrete, hoisted up on round columns that expose its underside to external view. At the other end, most of the rest of the oval is taken up by a vast, divisible emptiness waiting to filled by one or more trade shows. In between lies the conference centre, packed in a box like the Kunsthal and the ZKM, its separateness clearly signalled by a completely different external treatment. The exhibition hall and concert hall on either side are clad in different materials – the former in imitation dark grey cyclopean masonry, the latter in corrugated aluminium and plastic – but they nevertheless conform to the overall oval outline and therefore seem to belong together. The facetted-glass west facade of the conference centre, on the other hand, is straight and rectangular, with a higher roof, as if it had been designed by a different architect.

So is this one building or three? Well, both at once, of course. The three come together in a big foyer under the arch formed by the undersides of the back-to-back conference auditoriums – an arrangement that allows the exhibition centre to serve as an enormous backstage area for spectacular productions in the concert hall. Early versions of the design seemed to promise that the three buildings would be united by a single oval roof, but this is not the case in the building as built. The exhibition hall roof is supported by an almost pedestrian 24 square metres (258 square feet) grid of columns joined by braced steel beams, though the

secondary beams combine steel with timber in an interesting way. It is the edge of the roof that is least satisfactory: thin and weak, propped up by a seemingly ad-hoc arrangement of columns and struts. Materials are generally grey and dully economical. The look is no doubt deliberate and justified on artistic grounds, but cheapness is cheapness.

Euralille

With the Euralille master plan we arrive at XL, eXtra Large – frighteningly large, as Koolhaas freely admitted. The project arose because of a kind of space-time distortion represented by a warped map drawn to a temporal rather than a spatial scale. It indicated that, with the coming of the Channel Tunnel and the TGV, Lille was suddenly the centre of Europe – 70 minutes from London, 50 minutes from Paris, 18 minutes from Brussels. How should all the consequent infrastructural and commercial development be carried out without ruining the old town? Attention focussed on a triangle of land on the edge of town among the remains of a previous infrastructural project, Vauban's seventeenth-century fortifications. It lay between the old railway station and the new, buried TGV line, just north of the Congrexpo, on the other side of the tracks.

Master planning is architectural only up to a point. Traditionally it sees its task as the layout of a street plan and the imposition of massing restrictions, leaving the actual architects with sensible sites to build on and a rule book to follow without worrying too much about the neighbours. Koolhaas's beloved Manhattan might be one example; Léon Krier's La Villette (see page 337) might be another. But at Lille Koolhaas rejected this idea, preferring instead to explore the creative possibilities of complexity and interaction. As he put it: 'Montage of program and superimposition of

Euralille master plan, Lille, France. OMA, 1989–94.
The development occupies a triangle of land between
the TGV line, top left, and the old station, right.

building could restore both density and continuity.'[2] In other
words, even though other designers would be involved, the
development would essentially be a single building with a
floor area of a million square metres (250 acres). A key idea
was that the TGV station should be made visible so that the
local population could become acquainted with the powerful
agent of change that had arrived in their city. This was
achieved not by dragging it up out of its tunnel but by tilting
the triangle of land between it and the old station. Most of
the triangle is occupied by a vast, sloping, two-level shopping
centre under a single plane of metal-clad roof. Five office
towers are embedded in its southern side, facing the flank
of the old station, and a long thin hotel and housing block
stands against its western edge. Designed by Jean Nouvel, it
leaves room for a big plaza on the other side, next to the TGV
station, flowing under an elegant ring-road flyover into the
grass and trees of the Parc Henri Matisse.

The TGV station itself wears a wavy High Tech roof, one of
the last works of the great structural engineer Peter Rice,
but has to submit to the indignity of being straddled by three
office towers designed by different architects. One of them,
by Christian de Portzamparc for Crédit Lyonnais, is shaped
like a boot. To what extent Koolhaas and his colleagues
were pleased by the realization of their master plan might
be judged from the careful wording of their description in
S,M,L,XL: 'The status of the projects is ambiguous: we

defined levels, sections, relationships, interfaces – but not
architecture. No project is our project; we were working (with
different degrees of success) with/through other architects.'[3]

Rem Koolhaas's urbanism is the opposite of Aldo Rossi's
(see pages 330–334). For Rossi, the city represents memory
and continuity; for Koolhaas it is the engine of modernization.
Frustrated by architecture's passivity – that fact that an
architect must always await the instructions of a client with
money to spend – Koolhaas has tried over the years to gain
some influence on the direction of urban change through his
Project on the City initiative at Harvard University and AMO,
the think-tank offshoot of OMA. There have been studies
of Rome, Moscow, Beijing and China's Pearl River Delta
as well as *The Harvard Guide to Shopping*. Whether or
not these studies have had any effect on global policy, they
seem to have inspired Koolhaas's own work as a designer
of buildings. In 2002 he made a documentary film about
Lagos, directed by Bregtje van der Haak.[4] He found a city
modernized in the 1970s and equipped with tower blocks
and clover-leaf junctions but subsequently transformed by
population growth and a new culture – dangerous and poor
but also creative, productive and surprisingly well organized.

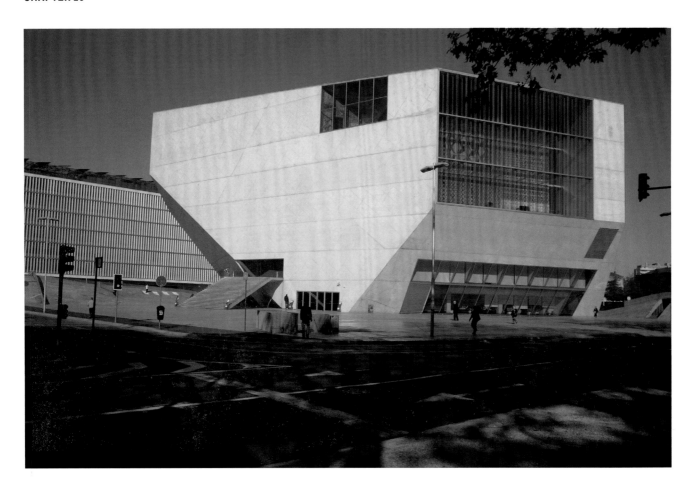

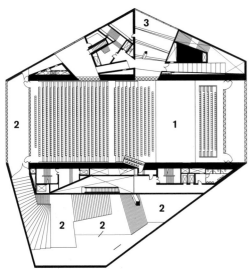
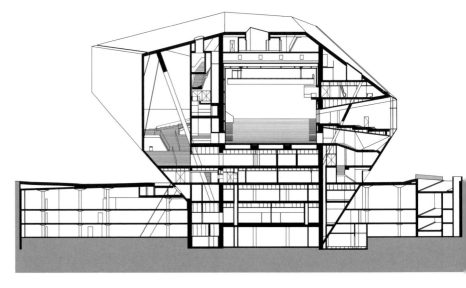

Casa da Música, Porto, Portugal. OMA, 2005.
A conventional shoe-box concert hall commands views over the city through a glass wall at the platform end.

Level 4 and section
1. Main auditorium
2. Foyer
3. Cyber music room

0   5   10m
15   30 ft

Casa da Música

When Koolhaas came to design a new concert hall in safely civilized Porto, Portugal, the improvisatory quality of Lagos life, the bricolage of unofficial markets and recycling yards, suggested the idea of adapting an existing, unrealized house design rather than dutifully analyzing requirements and constraints in the usual way. The house was called Y2K because of its client's anxiety about the possibly catastrophic effect of the millennium-turn on the world's computer systems. Its main feature, however, was a shoe-box-shaped living space with glass end walls designed to take maximum advantage of a view preserved at some cost by the acquisition of adjacent land. All other spaces – bedrooms, bathrooms, kitchens and so on – were wrapped around the four solid sides of the shoe box. Now, as every acoustic consultant knows – and much to the frustration of architects who might wish to emulate, for example, the valley landscape of Hans Scharoun's Berlin Philharmonie (see page 249) – the safest shape for any concert hall is a dull tunnel-like box, not likely to appeal to Koolhaas. Add in the glass end walls, however, and the space is transformed. The exclusive, elite world of the concert hall is opened to the city, suggesting a different social meaning. The site, beside a monumental traffic island called the Rotunda da Boavista, seemed to call for a degree of continuity with its neighbours. Koolhaas ignored this suggestion, instead creating a continuous travertine pavement that rises here and there like a rucked carpet to accommodate various ancillary functions underneath. The facetted form of the concert hall itself is embedded in the middle of the pavement like a fallen meteorite. This is another building that refuses to do

Seattle Central Library, Washington, USA. OMA, 2004.
Thorough functional analysis resulted in a complicated profile wrapped like an awkward parcel in diamond-gridded glass.

conventional things with staircases. Its main entrance is a single, high and steep flight of steps seemingly hinged down like the cargo door of an aeroplane. Inside is a wheelchair user's nightmare of wide, vertiginous flights with fan-like winders taking up acres of circulation space. Foyers and smaller performance spaces flow under, over and around the main hall, which, when entered, delivers a double surprise: its conventional sumptuousness, with a gold wood-grain pattern on the walls, and its views over the city through doubled, corrugated glass walls.

A built diagram

But bricolage is not, in fact, a dominant theme in Koolhaas's work, which often involves a great deal of systematic analysis. Modernist architecture is sometimes criticized for its 'diagrammatic' quality, implying that simple, cubic forms are translations of tidy spatial diagrams rather than responses to subtle human preferences. Koolhaas happily embraces the idea of the translated diagram while cleverly avoiding the accusation of inhumanity. Seattle's Central Library, completed in 2004, is a good example. The public library is a problematic building type in the age of digital media and privatization, but in 1998 the people of Seattle voted overwhelmingly in support of a $198 million 'libraries for all' project, including a new downtown library. The most revealing image of the new library is not a photograph or a

floor plan but a chart that translates the client's brief into a set of coloured bars. The first bar represents about 100 different functional spaces – book storage, administration, teaching spaces, reading rooms and so on. In the second bar this complex spectrum is simplified to show that there are in fact only 11 basic functions. In a third bar, these functions are 'reshuffled' into mixed groups according to their necessary connectedness, and divided into two types: 'stable' – parking, staff, meeting, spiral (book stack), and 'hq'; and 'unstable' – kids, living room, mixing chamber and reading room. This diagram can be read directly in the building as built. Each of the stable groups is allocated a rectangular 'platform', including the spiral ramp that accommodates the books. The platforms are offset from one another and separated vertically so that the 'unstable' functions can be inserted between them. Finally the whole thing is wrapped like a particularly awkward parcel in a diamond grid of steel

and glass. Nothing, it seems, is done for visual effect; everything emerges from the analysis of function. And yet the resulting jagged form and bright, eccentric spaces, bearing no reference to any kind of architectural tradition, are apparently pleasing to passers-by and well loved by the library's users.

There is a paradox at the heart of Koolhaas's architecture. On the one hand, it denies any connection with Architecture as an established cultural field. In Aaron Betsky's words, the buildings are not allowed to 'locate themselves anywhere in a consensus of good taste or acceptability'.[5] And yet it is in the field of Architecture, not politics or film-making or anthropology or Freudian psychology or construction or 'junk space', that Koolhaas strives and succeeds. In the end, it seems, even anti-architecture becomes part of architectural history.

Section through Seattle Central Library

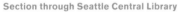

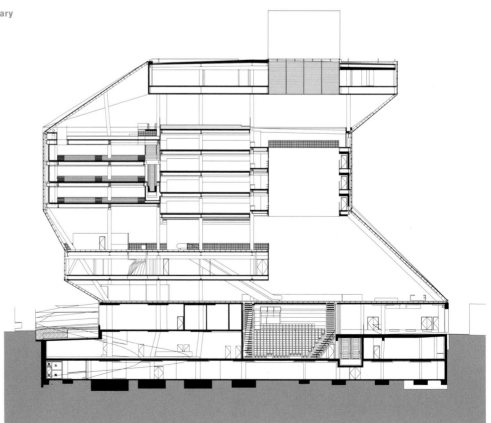

The Architectural Association School

Founded in 1847 by articled pupils in London architectural practices, the Architectural Association became the most important force in the development of British architectural education. It was pressure from the AA that persuaded the Royal Institute of British Architects to initiate its Voluntary Examination in 1862, establishing for the first time the possibility of a structured and monitored course in architecture. The AA's own school was established in 1901. It always valued its independence and was often a supporter of the avant-garde. In the mid-1930s it became Britain's first Modernist school, teaching by what is now known as the 'unit' or studio system. In the 1960s teachers like Cedric Price and Peter Cook made it the centre of a new approach to architecture that fused technology with fashion and popular culture, and was typified by the projects of the Archigram group. By the early 1970s, the AA was under pressure, both financial and political, to conform to the profession's policy of establishing architecture courses in universities. Negotiations were initiated with Imperial College but terms for a merger could not be agreed. Closure seemed inevitable but the students took matters into their own hands and elected Alvin Boyarsky, a lecturer at the University of Chicago and the organizer of an international summer school, as chairman and head of the school. It was

a wise choice. Over the next ten years, Boyarsky transformed the AA into one of the most influential architectural institutions in the world, a publishing house and an exhibition promoter as well as a school. By 1983 there were 450 students in the school, recruited from all over the world. The newly refurbished Georgian premises in central London's Bedford Square became an urban institution including a public lecture theatre, a gallery, libraries, a bookshop, a bar and a café. Unit teachers worked on one-year contracts and had to sell their educational wares competitively to the students. In return they were given almost complete freedom in the setting of projects and the exploring of fresh architectural territory. It was this environment that attracted intellectual and iconoclastic architectural thinkers such as Dalibor Vesely, Daniel Libeskind, Léon Krier, Elia Zenghelis, Rem Koolhaas, Zaha Hadid, Bernard Tschumi and Charles Jencks. Boyarsky died in 1990 but the AA school has since continued to grow and flourish on the principles that he established.

Architectural Association School alumni. Design Research Laboratory presentation at the AA, with Rem Koolhaas, Mohsen Mostafavi and Zaha Hadid, 1999.

30 | 'THE ARCHITECTURE OF THE WELL-TEMPERED ENVIRONMENT' REVISITED 1973–2007

In the final pages of the book from which this chapter's title is borrowed, Reyner Banham compares two recent buildings (the book was published in 1969) to represent the extremes of what he calls 'the range of choice in environmental method' available to architects.[1] One is the United States Atomic Energy Commission Portable Theater, a bubble-like air-supported enclosure; the other is St George's School in Wallasey in the north of England, a two-storey concrete-framed teaching block heated by a combination of electric lights, the body warmth of teachers and students, and a south-facing glass wall. The first relies completely on mechanical plant, even for its structural integrity; the second does away with the need for mechanical plant altogether.

Note that Banham wants to unite these buildings by putting them on the same scale, rather than separate them into different categories. The twenty-first-century reader is puzzled: no, surely they must be separated; the first is 'active', the second 'passive'; the first uses lots of energy and creates pollution; the second saves energy and prevents pollution. It did not occur to Banham that a strategic design decision like the degree of reliance on mechanical plant might have consequences beyond the field of architecture and building, or that the continued health of planet Earth itself might depend on the saving of energy and the minimizing of pollution. He didn't realize that 'active' was bad and 'passive' was good.

The book is still worth reading nevertheless. It was a kind of catching-up exercise. Banham saw that architectural history had largely ignored technical developments in mechanical services, especially the rise of air conditioning, and had failed to appreciate their effect on architectural form. Modernist historians had been concerned mainly with structure, with the static physicality of the building, and had ignored more dynamic qualities such as lighting, the movement of air, temperature and humidity, all of which were now routinely controlled mechanically. He looked again at famous works like Frank Lloyd Wright's Larkin Building (see page 69), Le Corbusier's Cité de Refuge (page 121) and Louis Kahn's Richards Laboratories (page 295), and found a new story about architecture's struggle to accommodate mechanical services.

In America the story was well advanced. Banham cites Eero Saarinen's General Motors Technical Center (see page 200), with its open-plan offices, its long-span steel structure leaving space for air-conditioning ducts, and its sophisticated suspended ceilings with fully integrated light fittings. In Europe, where air conditioning was still confined mainly to cinemas and luxury hotels, this degree of architectural integration was rare, but young architects like Norman Foster and Richard Rogers were learning fast and applying their knowledge in buildings such as the temporary IBM building at Cosham with its deep plan and roof-mounted air-conditioning units (see page 346). By the end of the decade Renzo Piano and Rogers's Centre Pompidou (see page 350) had exploited the architectural potential of mechanical services to the full, forging a new aesthetic out of the pipes and ducts themselves.

Economic crisis and ecological concern

In the 1970s, technology was seen as a positive benefit to be celebrated architecturally; 'active' was still good and 'passive' was a minority interest among services engineers and clients who needed to minimize running costs. But the global outlook was changing. In October 1973, OPEC (the Organization of the Petroleum Exporting Countries), prompted by American support for Israel in the Yom Kippur War, imposed an oil embargo on western countries. Over the next six months, the price of oil quadrupled. It was the resulting economic crisis that first clarified in the public mind the idea that the earth's natural resources were finite and that energy-hungry western industrial culture might have a limited life-span. By the early 1980s concern about resources had been overtaken by concern about pollution. Most scientists agreed that the emission of carbon dioxide in the burning of fossil fuels was the cause of potentially disastrous global warming of the 'greenhouse effect'. Public concern grew and the 'Green' movement was established, most solidly in Germany and the Netherlands but with offshoots all over the world. Architecture could hardly ignore these shifts of global perspective. It was estimated that in developed countries like the United States buildings consumed almost half of the nation's energy and emitted almost half of its carbon dioxide. To make matters worse, in 1974 it had been discovered that the chlorofluorocarbons (CFCs) commonly used in air-conditioning systems were the cause of holes appearing in the ozone layer of the atmosphere, further contributing to global warming. If buildings could be made more energy-efficient, relying less on mechanical equipment, then resources would be conserved, pollution contained, and the day of doom postponed.

The concept of 'green architecture' is problematic, more so even than the stylistic labels in which architectural history commonly deals. 'Greenness' is, to some extent at least, an objective rather than a subjective quality. Energy consumption and pollution can be measured, and while that measurement is crucial to the economics of building, its relevance to the craft of architecture is inconstant and indirect. For example, a 100-year-old house in a temperate climate zone can be made 'green' by a few simple energy-saving modifications – draught-proofing, double glazing, extra insulation, low-energy light bulbs, better heating controls and perhaps a couple of solar panels on the roof – without noticeably affecting its architecture. And it is often argued that the construction of a new building, rather than the adaptation of an old one, is an essentially ungreen act. The principle of recycling applies as much to building as to industrial and household waste. So rather than construct another artificial category and give it a label, it might be more useful to observe the general effect on architecture of a growing concern with energy conservation, just as Banham observed the effect on architecture of developments in mechanical engineering.

Daylight, natural ventilation, heating and cooling by passive means, and the reappearance of natural materials like wood and stone with low 'embodied energy': these are the main themes in the post-Banham architecture of the well-tempered environment.

For a few early post-oil-crisis pioneers the imagined green future entailed a complete dismantling of industrial culture and a return to the simple life lived in harmony with nature. The British architect and sculptor Christopher Day built several houses and schools in the 1970s and 1980s entirely by hand on remote sites using only materials found in the immediate vicinity. The Nant-y-Cwm Steiner kindergarten at Llanycefn in west Wales, completed in 1989, is typical: single storey with curved and battered walls roughly plastered, womb-like interiors, and a turf roof supported by unwrought tree branches. Inevitably buildings like this became 'Hobbit houses' in the popular imagination, though Day's ecological design principles, as set out in his book *Places of the Soul* (1990), were humanistic rather than fantastical. He was more interested in the psychological benefits of organic form and natural materials than in quantifiable energy conservation. His buildings were occasionally featured in architectural magazines, but he was never interested in expanding his practice and becoming famous.

Nant-y-Cwm Steiner kindergarten, Llanycefn, Wales, UK. Christopher Day, 1989. Organic form, natural materials and a cosiness that appeals to the hobbit in all of us.

Magney House, Bingie Point, New South Wales, Australia. Glenn Murcutt, 1984. Corrugated metal is the material that roofs the typical Australian suburban house, but rarely as elegantly as this.

Glenn Murcutt

The same might be said of the Australian architect Glenn Murcutt, who throughout his career worked as a 'one-man-band', designing mainly single houses and refraining from collaboration even with his architect wife. The difference is that while Day remained a relatively obscure figure, Murcutt became world famous despite himself. In fact, he became the most famous of all Australian modern architects and in 2002 was awarded the Pritzker Prize, generally regarded as architecture's Nobel. Day and Murcutt would probably have agreed on certain architectural principles, such as the intimacy of a building with its natural setting and a holistic rather than an abstract concept of human comfort, but the former was working in damp Welsh woodland and the latter in the Australian semi-desert. Their buildings are consequently very different. Where Day insists on natural materials like timber and stone, Murcutt is master of the very unnatural material that roofs most Australian suburban houses – corrugated metal. In his hands it becomes the symbol of a society and a landscape. The thin, curved roof of the Magney House, completed in 1984 at Bingie Point on the coast of New South Wales, seems to have settled on its supports like a bird rather than been lifted up laboriously. A generous overhang on the north side, propped up on angled struts, shades the upper part of an all-glass wall at an angle calculated to keep out the summer sun but admit the less searing winter sun. The lower part of the wall is shaded by adjustable external louvres.

The site of the Marika–Alderton House, completed in 1994 in the far north of the continent, at Yirrkala in the Northern Territory, presented environmental problems of a different order. Here air temperatures never fall below 25 degrees Celsius (77 degrees Fahrenheit) and often soar into the 40s. And then there are the poisonous spiders and snakes to consider. An air-conditioned sealed box would have been the obvious solution, but this was not Murcutt's way and not what his clients – Aboriginal artist Banduk Marika, her English partner and their children – wanted. That old Aboriginal injunction to 'touch the ground lightly' was taken almost literally. The house is basically a long wooden platform raised on stubby steel columns. There are no walls or windows in the conventional sense, only arrays of wooden shading devices – grilles, baffles, fins and flaps. The double-pitch roof is of corrugated metal, of course, on a steel frame, with very generous overhangs. Through-ventilation is maintained even at night when the house is securely closed against animal intruders. Swivelling roof vents draw the warm air out and continuous screened slots at low level let the cool air in. This is a perfect example of the 'passive' approach to heating and cooling, which needs no energy other than the force of the wind and the warmth of the sun. There is, however, a qualification to be noted in this building's green credentials. Ideally, its materials, either natural or recycled, would have been gleaned from the immediate surroundings. In fact the whole thing was prefabricated 3,200 kilometres (2,000) miles away in Gosford near Sydney and brought to the site in sections by truck and boat. Strictly speaking, the oil consumed on that journey should be factored into the energy account.

Thomas Herzog

Murcutt's early houses were admired just as houses before it occurred to anyone that they might be 'green', but in the work of the Munich architect and academic Thomas Herzog, energy conservation was a conscious theme from the start. His house in Regensburg, completed in 1979, was one of the first to give novel architectural expression to the passive energy principle. Its overall form is a simple triangular prism with a long mono-pitch roof – the hypotenuse of the triangle – reaching right down to the ground. The lower part of this roof is either glazed to promote solar heat gain or, in two of the six bays, omitted entirely, in one case to accommodate an existing tree and in the other to create a patio next to the dining space. When the roofline has risen sufficiently, a first floor is introduced, accessible by a couple of spiral staircases, but again bays are left out, three this time, to create double-height living spaces. So this is an

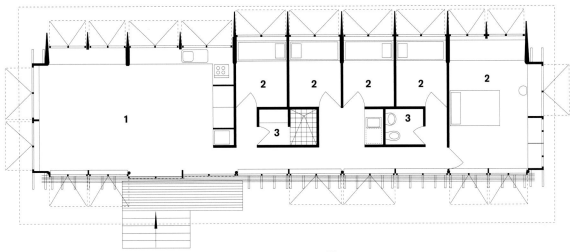

Marika–Alderton House, Yirrkala, Northern Territory, Australia. Glenn Murcutt, 1994. A tropical architecture of grilles, baffles, fins and flaps.

Plan
1. Living room
2. Bedroom
3. Bathroom

0   5m
        15 ft

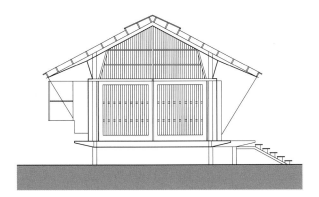

East elevation

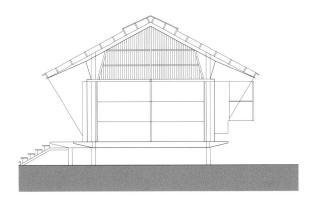

West elevation

House at Regensburg, Germany. Thomas Herzog, 1979.
Cross-sections with wavy arrows became essential tokens of
environmental respectability.

indeterminate spatial and structural system typical of the
progressive architecture of the 1980s. Only its choice
of materials – various kinds of wood including laminated
beams and columns – saves it from being High Tech.
Published drawings of the house always include a series
of cross-sections in which wavy arrows indicate solar
radiation and the flow of fresh air at different times of day
and in different seasons. Drawings of this kind have since
become essential tokens of environmental respectability.

Herzog's house and its many successors were new
inventions, logical designs owing more to science than
sentiment, but vernacular architecture has often been a
fruitful source of ideas and imagery for would-be green
architects. Building traditions that have grown over
centuries in rural communities have usually developed
ingenious forms to exploit or withstand whatever the land
and the seasons inflict. But there is a kind of contradiction
in the phrase 'vernacular architecture'. Professional

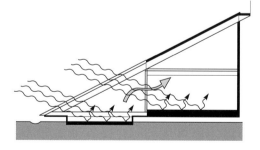

Winter day

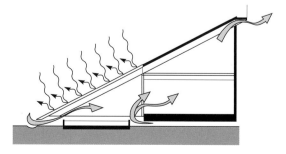

Summer day

architects cannot, by definition, produce vernacular architecture; they can only imitate it. Often this means imitating its forms and outlines, its colours and textures, rather than its functional logic. Sometimes such imitations can be real works of art, like the country houses of Lutyens and Voysey (see Chapter 2) or the quiet but strong churches designed by the British architects Robert Maguire and Keith Murray in the 1960s, of which St Paul's, Bow Common, London, is a particularly tough example; but more usually they lapse into dull routine, not vernacular but 'neo-vernacular'.

Amid the general slackening of confidence in Modernism that was felt in Britain and other western countries in the 1970s, the neo-vernacular style flourished, especially in the housing schemes and community buildings that followed the fall of system building (see Chapter 19). Bricks and tiles replaced concrete and steel, creating a superficially village-like scene. Friars Quay in Norwich, designed by Feilden and Mawson and completed in 1974, is an untypically high-quality example. 'Conservation' was the word on every responsible architect's lips but the green potential of the truly vernacular was seldom exploited.

High Tech to Eco Tech

Meanwhile, partly in reaction to neo-vernacular, the style known as High Tech was building its case for a new kind of Modernism, inspired not by traditional building but by the aerospace industry (see Chapter 26). In its 1980s maturity it mostly ignored the passive energy principle, keener to show off the technology of air conditioning than to abolish it. But then in the 1990s, as the climate change consensus grew, High Tech found itself a new job. Its belief in science and love of technology would be brought to bear on the question of energy conservation. High Tech became 'Eco-Tech', the title of a 1997 book by Catherine Slessor. The building that most clearly signalled this transformation was the British pavilion, designed by Nicholas Grimshaw, at Expo '92 in Seville. It was like a collection of low-energy cooling devices assembled to make a building. Every face of what was basically a steel-framed box was cooled by a different method. On the east side a continuous curtain of water fell

British Pavilion, Expo '92, Seville, Spain. Nicholas Grimshaw, 1992. The sunny side of the building is walled by stacks of water-filled containers to increase thermal mass.

against a frameless glass wall into a linear pool from which it was raised to high level again by solar-powered pumps. The flat roof was shaded by an array of big S-curved louvres fitted with solar panels. North and south walls were ultra-light: single layers of fabric stretched like sails between bowed masts, with extra sails as 'fly-sheets' on the south wall. For the west wall, the principle of thermal mass was brought into play. Heavy buildings such as those with thick stone walls are always cooler than light ones on hot days because it takes the sun a long time to heat them up. Massive walls become, as it were, reservoirs of coolness. But for an architect like Nicholas Grimshaw stone walls were ruled out because they represented the antithesis of High Tech's lightweight, factory-made ideal. His solution was ingenious: the weight and mass would be provided by a stack of metal tanks full of water. An additional benefit was that, in theory at least, the tanks could be recycled

when the building was dismantled. Air conditioning was not completely eliminated from the building; it was still required for the pod-like internal enclosures that contained cinemas and artificially lit exhibitions. But the demonstration was effective enough, proving that High Tech and low energy were not necessarily incompatible.

Even Richard Rogers, who in the 1980s had been besotted by the paraphernalia of mechanical heating and cooling (see Lloyd's of London, page 354), was soon converted to the passive-energy principle and was keen to exploit its architectural potential. In his Bordeaux Law Courts, completed in 1998, he even went so far as to experiment with natural materials like stone and wood. Law courts, like cinemas and concert halls, tend to be solid, enclosed buildings. How can they be made open and airy, perhaps even welcoming? Rogers's answer was to treat the courtrooms themselves as freestanding, flask-like objects, lifting them up on legs and standing them in a row on an open, limestone-clad platform. An administrative block, concrete framed but clad in metal, stands next to the platform

Bordeaux Law Courts, Bordeaux, France.
Richard Rogers, 1998. Flask-like courtrooms stand on an open platform sheltered by a wavy umbrella.

and shares with it a lightweight, wavy roof on separate spindly steel columns. The flasks, made of wood with dished concrete bases, poke their heads through the roof for light and ventilation. All but one of them is sheltered behind a glass curtain wall forming a kind of 'conservatory', an intermediate internal/external space with adjustable natural ventilation that reduces the heating and cooling load on the fully internal spaces. Energy consumption is thus reduced and at the same time that wished-for openness and friendliness is achieved. The old neo-classical law court building next door, though elegant, seems sternly formal by contrast.

In 2000 Rogers's old sparring partner Norman Foster wrote: 'From my first days in practice environmental issues and a concern for economy of means have been a fundamental part of our thinking.'[2] He went on to imply that buildings like the Willis Faber & Dumas offices (see page 347) and Stansted airport (page 359) were really low-energy buildings all along. There may be some justification for this claim, but it was not until the early 1990s and the winning of several big commissions in Germany, including the rebuilding of the Reichstag in Berlin, that energy conservation became a specific theme in Foster's ideology. A key project was, of all things, a skyscraper, the tallest in Europe. Sceptics will immediately scoff. A skyscraper is a major engineering project. Its inevitably heavy construction will already have consumed vast amounts of energy before its first users move in and turn on the air conditioning. Even so, energy conservation was declared to be a major determinant of the form of the Commerzbank headquarters in Frankfurt, completed in 1997.

The skyscraper reinvented

Reimagining the skyscraper had been an ongoing Foster project since the late 1970s when the Hongkong and Shanghai Bank design (see page 357) began its long gestation. The aim had always been to find an alternative to the usual 'kebab' arrangement, with floors skewered on a central core making a stack of spatially unconnected horizontal spaces. At Century Tower in Tokyo, completed in 1991, a full-height atrium had been attempted for the first time, but it was little more than a narrow slot and its unifying effect was limited. The Commerzbank's full-height atrium is a generous triangle on plan and effects a complete spatial transformation. In most skyscrapers, office workers at their desks enjoy only one view of the outside world, and probably a distant one at that. In the Commerzbank Tower, all workers are close to windows and most have a second direction of view, inwards across the atrium to other offices,

opposite, above and below. This might sound like a doubtful benefit, a view over a vertiginous pit, but the building's other new invention makes all the difference: four-storey-high gardens, richly landscaped, break through the surrounding offices at intervals on all sides, stepping up around the atrium like a giant spiral staircase and letting in floods of daylight. Lifts, escape stairs, toilets and vertical ducts, which would normally be where the atrium is, are moved into the building's three corners. All offices are naturally ventilated most of the time, a very rare occurrence in skyscrapers. It is this concern for the comfort and welfare of the workers, giving them fresh air, a sense of their place in the building, a local hanging garden in which to take their lunch breaks, and some control over the environment at their workstations, that justifies the building's green credentials.

Commerzbank headquarters, Frankfurt, Germany.
Norman Foster, 1997. Recognizably a descendant of Century Tower, Tokyo, and the Hongkong and Shanghai Bank.

Commerzbank headquarters, interior. Four-storey-high internal gardens occur at regular intervals in the height of the building.

Michael Hopkins, fourth member of the famous High Tech quartet of British architects, was not slow to conform to the new low-energy consensus. His architecture, however, had already undergone a different kind of transformation. It could no longer be described as High Tech. Though it continued to be ruled by certain High Tech principles such as the 'honest' expression of structure, its characteristic materials had changed utterly from lightweight metal to heavyweight masonry. This preference was instinctive rather than rational, partly a rediscovery of an earlier passion for the blunt but beautiful nineteenth-century industrial buildings photographed by Eric de Maré for J. M. Richards's classic book, *The Functional Tradition in Early Industrial Buildings* (1958). Hopkins had become the British establishment's favourite architect and in 1989 he was commissioned to design a new office building for members of Parliament

on a super-sensitive Thames-side site. Despite, or perhaps because of, its eccentricity, the building seems comfortable in the company of its distinguished neighbours – the Gothic-curtained Houses of Parliament on one side, and Norman Shaw's New Scotland Yard on the other.

Portcullis House is a solid, orderly building, seven storeys high, with a central courtyard. Chimneys are its most striking external feature, 14 of them, regularly spaced along the ridge of its steeply pitched roof. They are finished in aluminium-bronze, or 'gunmetal', but apart from this extravagant choice of material there is no attempt to disguise their nature, to make them 'architectural' in the way that Augustus Pugin disguised rather similar vertical vents as Gothic pinnacles in the Palace of Westminster next door. Hopkins's chimneys are simple pipes such as one might find on a power station or a chemicals factory. Not since Elizabethan times have undisguised chimneys played such a prominent part in a piece of architecture of national importance. They are functional, of course, removing stale air from the offices, but they are also symbolic, proclaiming that this is a new kind of modern office block, not air conditioned but naturally ventilated. To the knowledgeable observer they convey a great deal more. It is possible, by close scrutiny of the building's exterior, to understand exactly how its structural and ventilation systems work and how they are integrated one with the other.

The chimneys rest on structural ducts like spiders' legs, the outlines of which are traced by seams in the gunmetal roof covering. Each leg rests on a loadbearing stone pier and also delivers or removes fresh or exhaust air from vertical ducts on either side of that pier. This is a functionally perfect combination. The piers become narrower storey by storey as they rise up the building and the load they have to carry decreases; conversely the ducts get wider as they rise and the volume of air they carry increases. A similarly dogged functional expressiveness characterizes other features of the building, such as the big concrete arches around the courtyard that support the inner walls over the deep, square pit of Westminster Underground station, also designed by Hopkins; or the geodesic glazed roof of the courtyard, framed not in thin metal but in chunky laminated timber. An eccentric building, then, and almost painfully honest.

Greenness in the USA

In the United States, the land of free enterprise, cheap oil and widespread climate change denial, the idea that buildings should be environmentally 'responsible' was slow to catch on. The US Green Building Council was set up in 1993 and soon afterwards established a rating system for new buildings called LEED (Leadership in Energy and Environmental Design). By the year 2000, however, a New York exhibition of mainly European buildings called 'Ten Shades of Green' could still excite enough curiosity to send it on a tour of the whole country.[3] Whereas in Britain and Germany, greenness had become mainstream, in the US it was still a novelty. Morphosis, the west coast architectural practice founded in the 1970s by Thom Mayne, provides two examples of a freer, less resolved approach to energy-saving forms and facades. The District 7 headquarters of Caltrans (California Department of Transport) in Los Angeles, completed in 2005, and the San Francisco Federal Building, completed two years later, both combine tallish office blocks with social amenities and public open space on city-centre sites.

Portcullis House, London, UK. Michael Hopkins, 2000.
A blunt, honest building that makes architecture out of its structural and ventilation systems.

Morphosis had worked in Europe (on the Hypo Alpe-Adria Center in Klagenfurt, Austria, for example) and had imbibed a European feeling for public space and the quality of a working environment. The office blocks are shallow planned, allowing workers a view out and a measure of natural daylight, and there is some attempt to enrich their spatial experience of the building as a whole by modifications to the circulation system. At Caltrans lifts work on a 'skip stop' principle to encourage physical exercise and random social encounters, and at San Francisco, three-storey-high 'sky lobbies' are provided with enormous projecting windows. But the most striking innovation in both cases is the separate perforated metal skin that wraps loosely around the office block to shade it from the sun, but then peels off like folded paper at the lower levels to shelter ancillary buildings such as cafés, shops and kindergartens. On the east and west sides of the Caltrans office block there are top-hung flaps in the metal skin that can be opened by office workers to improve their view over the city when the sun has gone down. The whole facade is therefore constantly changing, as if it were transmitting messages in some kind of Morse code. All this is, of course, as much ineffable art as measurable technology (on the LEED scale, the Caltrans building achieved only a Silver rating – Gold and Platinum are possible) but then this might also be said of its more earnest-seeming European counterparts.

What would a truly green architecture look like? Perhaps like the conical timber-and-grass huts of the Kanak people of New Caledonia in the south Pacific. In 1984 Jean-Marie Tjibaou, the western-educated son of a tribal chief, became leader of the Kanak movement for independence from France. In 1988 he negotiated the Matignon Accords, which postponed independence (valuable nickel is extracted from ruinous open-cast mines on the main island) but promised greater respect for Kanak culture. Tjibaou was assassinated in 1989 but is remembered in the naming of a French-financed cultural centre designed by Renzo Piano

Caltrans District 7 headquarters, Los Angeles, California, USA. Morphosis, 2005. Hand-operated top-hung flaps in the metal cladding facade create an ever-changing pattern.

(Top) San Francisco Federal Building, San Francisco, California, USA. Morphosis, 2007. The external wall peels off at the lower levels to shelter ancillary buildings.

(Above) Tjibaou Cultural Centre, Nouméa, New Caledonia. Renzo Piano, 1998. Tall wooden wind-scoops, called 'cases', look like many-fingered hands.

and completed in 1998. It occupies a narrow peninsula, between a lagoon and the open sea, 8 kilometres (5 miles) from New Caledonia's capital, Nouméa.

Piano's first idea was to adapt the form of those traditional conical huts and thereby reconcile western and indigenous architectures. But this was to be a big building providing classrooms, exhibition spaces, libraries and theatres. Its resemblance to a Kanak village would be superficial at best and wrongly scaled. In the final version the huts have become not cones but more like huge, many-fingered hands, raised and cupped as if to catch the wind. There are ten of them in a curving line, the biggest 28 metres (92 feet) tall, equal to a nine-storey office building. Mono-pitch roofs lean against their concave sides, reaching to about half their height, but the tall gathering and exhibition spaces thus formed account for only a small fraction of the functional space in the whole complex, most of which is flat roofed, stepping out and down from the main circulation spine. A conventional, western-style theatre, with seating for 400 people, rakes down into a three-storey concrete basement served by an underground delivery road. So what are the cupped hands, called 'cases', for exactly? The obligatory cross-sectional drawings with arrows show how they control air flow through the building in different conditions, including cyclone winds. But their real function, surely, is symbolic. They are framed in laminated timber with steel joints and their slatted wooden cladding looks, from a distance, like a kind of weaving. So, although in their size and substance they are nothing like Kanak huts, there is nevertheless a vague resemblance. They represent a bridge between cultures and an acknowledgement that there might be lessons to be learnt on both sides.

Kanak village hut. The vernacular form that inspired Piano's 'cases', though in the end the resemblance is slight.

Ken Yeang

The Malaysian architect Ken Yeang has devoted his career to what he calls 'bioclimatic architecture' and in particular the development of the bioclimatic skyscraper. His Mesiniaga Tower for IBM in Kuala Lumpur is a 15-storey cylindrical office tower supported by four pairs of metal-clad columns, exposed externally in the High Tech manner and tied together by circular beams at irregular intervals. This armature supports an episodic arrangement of floors with missing segments, external cladding that steps in and out, and bracketed, discontinuous sunshades. The service 'core' is on the east side where it can contribute to shading and cooling of the building. But the most original feature is the landscaped gardens, sometimes double height, that spiral around the outside of the building like a giant staircase. They are open to the external air and there is no central atrium, but the idea is strongly reminiscent of Norman Foster's much bigger Commerzbank Tower (see page 413) – except that this building was finished five years earlier, in 1992.

Yeang's own house in Kuala Lumpur, known as the Roof-Roof House, completed in 1984, is a purposeful demonstration of passive energy-saving principles in a truly tropical climate. Its most prominent feature is the big, curved, concrete pergola that casts stripy shadows on the cluster of vaguely Corbusian, white-stuccoed forms below. The pergola is only one of several modern versions of traditional features. There is a louvred upstand in the middle of the roof terrace that works like a traditional Middle Eastern wind tower, and the swimming pool, close up against the house on the breezy side, acts as a cooling fountain. A raised walkway surrounds and partly shades the pool, forming a two-storey cloister. On the other side of the house, a generous projecting balcony shared by two bedrooms is big enough to shade a parked car. Floor plans look fairly conventional at first, with small, enclosed rooms on two levels, but in fact they combine two very different categories of space: air-conditioned bedrooms and non-air-conditioned living areas. The split-level living and dining room itself looks small until we realize that it is conceived as a corner of the poolside patio. Architects brought up in a temperate climate tend to think of gardens and terraces as extensions of indoor spaces but in the heat and humidity of Kuala Lumpur the priority is reversed. It is better to live outside, provided the shade and the breeze have been properly managed.

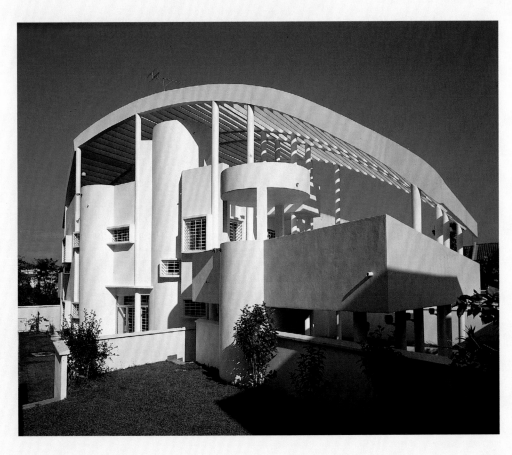

Roof-Roof House, Kuala Lumpur, Malaysia. Ken Yeang, 1984.
Passive energy features dominate, including a big, curved pergola.

31 | 'CONTEXT' AND 'MATERIALITY' 1963–2012

Architecture's role in the world of twenty-first-century global capitalism is perhaps not so different from its role in the world of the ancient empires, or of medieval Christianity, or Baroque absolutism; that is to say it mainly serves rich and powerful institutions. It provides them with buildings that may be useful functionally but are often valued more for their symbolic meaning. Buildings of no special symbolic importance – houses for ordinary people, for example – do not usually count as 'Architecture'; they fall outside a cultural field that is hard to define but easy to recognize. In hindsight, early Modernism's social project, its aim to bring architecture to the masses, failed and is now passing into historical oblivion. The world is not full of radiant workers' cities; it is full of shameless skyscrapers surrounded by shanty towns in which architecture is powerless. More than a century ago, Walter Gropius prepared a comprehensive programme for the mass production of well-designed prefabricated houses. That programme failed and, we must now admit, so did most of the similar architect-led programmes that followed it down the years. The architecture of mass housing has been unpopular, while popular housing, like factory-building, warehousing and mass retailing, has mostly managed very well without architecture.

A relationship with the past

But architecture's symbolism is not always a simple glorification of political and economic power. It can denote subtler social allegiances and orientations, one of the most fundamental of which is a special relationship with the past. Buildings often endure for long periods and take on a 'monumental' function in the strict sense of the word (*monumental* from the Latin *monere*, 'to remind or warn'). We preserve them because they represent a reassuring past, a past that we survived, and we sometimes follow their example in our new buildings. In very broad terms, architects either respect and learn from older architectures, or reject them as irrelevant to new conditions. This chapter will examine some examples in the former category, though sometimes its boundaries will be stretched almost to

City Hall, The Hague, the Netherlands. Richard Meier, 1995. Early Modernists rejected revivalism, but 'Neo-Modernist' is an appropriate designation for much of Meier's work.

breaking point. Tradition and modernity are not necessarily mutually exclusive. Even Modernism itself can now be regarded as a tradition. Take, for example, the American architect Richard Meier, who as a member of the so-called New York Five in the late 1960s revived the early Modernism of Le Corbusier in a collection of one-off houses. He went on to build a global practice designing important public buildings such as the city hall of The Hague in the Netherlands, completed in 1995, notable for its 12-storey atrium and its Neo-Modernist formal language. The spirit of the Dutch Constructivist Mart Stam (see page 101) is somewhere close by.

Museums were a Meier speciality, culminating in his masterpiece, the Getty Center at Brentwood, Los Angeles, a hilltop gallery on the scale of a small university campus, housing the art collection of the oil magnate J. Paul Getty. The mainly two-storey, flat-roofed buildings are arranged around a paved court like temples on a slightly over-crowded Acropolis. A grid of 76-centimetre (30-inch) squares, or rather a pair of such grids overlaid at an angle of

22.5 degrees, governs the arrangement. Individual buildings conform to one or other grid, though here and there serpentine walls break free of both. Externally, two materials dominate: white enamelled steel panels – each 760 mm (30 inches) square, naturally – and honey-coloured travertine stone, regularly coursed but 'riven' or 'cleft' to create a rough-textured surface. The entrance building is a drum, full height inside and brightly day-lit. Galleries for paintings are on the upper levels of the other buildings, where they enjoy the benefit of roof-lighting. Drawings, manuscripts and other items of decorative art are accommodated in the darker rooms below. This, then, is like a traditional art museum that has been sliced up and spread out. The gaps between the galleries are opportunities for visitors to take a break from the concentrated close-up scrutiny of art and enjoy its opposite – long views over the city to the distant horizon.

More than one critic has argued that the city of Los Angeles is itself meant to be viewed as a work of art, a 'found object' representing the modern art that is excluded by the collection's artificial cut-off date of 1900. Perhaps the architecture of the gallery too represents a missing modernity but if so, it also shows respect for an older tradition. Like his Beaux-Arts-trained American predecessors, Louis Kahn among them, Meier draws inspiration as much from the ancient world as from early Modernism. The travertine was not chosen purely for its colour and texture; it represents the past and a willingness to submit to its influence. In a letter to his client, Meier wrote: 'In my mind, I keep returning to the Romans – to Hadrian's Villa, to Caprarola – for their sequences, their spaces, their thick-walled presence, their sense of order, the way in which building and landscape belong to each other.'[1]

Rafael Moneo

In one of the best-known buildings by the Spanish architect Rafael Moneo, ancient Rome is not merely recalled but is materially present. The National Museum of Roman Art at Mérida in Extremadura, completed in 1986, is sited directly over excavated Roman ruins, including houses, tombs, an early Christian basilica and part of an aqueduct. New brick arcades, stepping carefully through the remains, support the concrete floor of the museum. Above the floor they rise and align themselves to form a magnificent high nave of transverse arches with multi-storey side chapels to accommodate special exhibits such as statues, marble columns and mosaic floors. The arcades are made of thin Roman bricks. Critics have been keen to point out that this brickwork, which is attached to a reinforced concrete core, is mortarless and creates a distinctive modern smoothness.

National Museum of Roman Art, Mérida, Spain. Rafael Moneo, 1986. A nave of Roman arches rises from the excavated ruins in the basement.

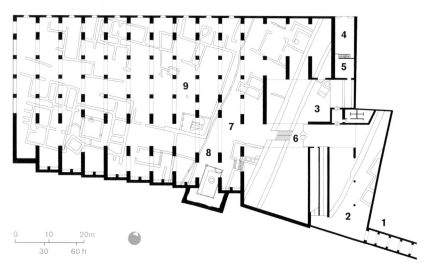

Excavation level plan
1. Entrance to theatre and amphitheatre ruins
2. San Lázaro aqueduct remains
3. Cafeteria
4. Storage and garage access
5. Cafeteria storage
6. Access to archaeological precinct
7. Paleochristian basilica remains
8. Roman house remains
9. Tombs

But it would be foolish to deny that this is an imitation of ancient Roman construction and that Moneo relished the monumental opportunity.

Moneo's willingness to acknowledge and learn from the past is restricted neither to the museum as a building type nor to his love of Roman ruins, a love strengthened by a two-year sojourn at the Spanish Academy in Rome in the early 1960s. The western Islamic tradition, best exemplified by the Great Mosque at Córdoba, has directly influenced several Moneo buildings including a railway station and an airport. This is not as surprising as it may at first seem. Historians have often commented that the low, rectangular, mat-like form of early Umayyad mosques (Córdoba dates back to the eighth century) seems, in its abstraction and repetition, its lack of hierarchy and its necessary disregard

of immediate context, to prefigure modern building types such as factories and car parks. There are similarities too with the work of 'Structuralists' like Aldo van Eyck and Herman Hertzberger (see Chapter 21).

When Moneo roofs over the tracks at Madrid's Atocha station with a skewed grid of flat, steel-framed platforms, each supported, mushroom-like, on a single slender concrete column, we can be sure that he had ancient mosques in mind. The hypnotic repetition and the impression of infinite extendibility were learnt in Córdoba. Nearby, the perfect drum of the ticket hall, with its shallow dome supported on angled brick piers, might be a reference to a later Islamic style, and the freestanding brick clock tower might be a kind of minaret. Even if these references were not intended, there is no mistaking the general willingness to conform to ancient

Madrid Atocha Train Station, Spain. Rafael Moneo, 1988. The many-columned canopy over the tracks is like an ancient mosque, with the clock tower as its minaret.

tower and dome precedents. These extensions to Atocha station were completed in the early 1990s. The airport at Seville, finished a few years earlier, compares interestingly with Norman Foster's roughly contemporary Stansted airport. Both have departure halls roofed by grids of square domes, but whereas Foster's are supported by tubular steel trees, Moneo's are solid concrete on squat columns with massive splayed capitals. These are pendentive domes, painted dark blue with contrasting white arch soffits. It is as if Moneo is insisting that this old Byzantine/Islamic form is still valid even amid the various lightweight technologies associated with flight.

Sometimes the attempt to preserve ancient forms in modern contexts strains credibility. Moneo is considered a great architect in America. From 1985 to 1990 he was chairman of the Harvard Graduate School of Design and he won the Pritzker Prize in 1996. But European respect for tradition does not always sit comfortably in the relatively ahistorical context of an American city like Los Angeles. His Roman Catholic Cathedral of our Lady of the Angels, completed in 2002 on the Hollywood Freeway not far from Frank Gehry's Disney Concert Hall, somehow fails to provide the city with a convincing symbol of community and spirituality even though, in theory, it is equipped with all the necessary architectural components.

In Europe the west fronts of cathedrals often face public squares and thus symbolize the connection between church and city. Here the arrangement is similar, except that it is the east front that faces the square, which is raised high above street level and accessible from the carillon-adorned main gate via two broad flights of steps. The small act of pilgrimage implied by these steps is unconvincing because everyone knows that most worshippers arrive by lift from the underground car park. And that east front is also curiously hesitant in its gesture of welcome – asymmetrical, with the main entrance on one side leading to the ambulatory that is necessary to take the visitor to the correct end of the nave. Big bronze doors surmounted by a statue of the Virgin do little to offset the awkwardness of the arrangement. Inside, the 3,000-seat nave is huge and impressive, with walls of polished concrete, a floor of Spanish stone, a facetted wooden ceiling and an angled, extruded cross high over the altar, surrounded by a window of translucent alabaster. A 46-metre (150-foot) campanile on the north-west corner of the site completes the picture.

Cathedral of Our Lady of the Angels, Los Angeles, California, USA. Rafael Moneo, 2002. A hesitant gesture of welcome: the entrance is on the far left.

Hedmark Museum, Hamar, Norway. Sverre Fehn, 1971. A fourteenth-century bishop's fortress lies around and beneath the renovated farmhouse.

Moneo's Roman museum at Mérida was not the first to be built directly over an archaeological dig. In 1971 the Norwegian architect Sverre Fehn built a museum in the U-shaped footprint of an old eighteenth-century farmhouse at Hamar on the shore of Mjøsa, Norway's largest lake. A new pitched roof supported by heavy timber columns and trusses is fitted to what remains of the farmhouse walls, with glass and wooden boarding to close the gaps. The main exhibit, however, is not the farmhouse but the ruins of the early fourteenth-century bishop's fortress that lies around and beneath it. Visitors inhabit a third, modern building – a suspended apparatus of concrete ramps, bridges, platforms and stairways from which the older structures are viewed, both internally and externally.

Fehn designed several museums, including the Norwegian Glacier Museum at Fjærland of 1991 and his last work, the National Museum of Architecture in Oslo, completed in 2008, which is an extension to a nineteenth-century classical building. But arguably all of his buildings express a contemplative relationship with the past, sometimes the mythical past. The Villa Busk of 1990, for example, which crowns a rocky outcrop overlooking Oslo's fjord, is provided with an almost freestanding look-out tower, square on plan under a pyramid roof, that might be an illustration in a fairy tale. Appropriately it houses children's bedrooms.

Álvaro Siza

The Portuguese architect Álvaro Siza is often described, in Kenneth Frampton's phrase, as a 'critical regionalist', though the basis of his design method is an extreme sensitivity to physical and cultural context wherever he happens to be working. His earliest buildings show the influence of Portuguese vernacular architecture, of Alvar Aalto and perhaps also of Frank Lloyd Wright. The Boa Nova seaside

Boa Nova Restaurant, Leça da Palmeira, Portugal. Álvaro Siza, 1963. Alvar Aalto, Frank Lloyd Wright and Portuguese vernacular architecture were early influences.

restaurant at Leça da Palmeira, not far from Siza's home city of Porto, affects to be an ad-hoc arrangement of pan-tiled mono-pitch roofs propped up over a rocky shore that has been roughly modified by in-situ concrete walls. On the landward side the walls are smartened up with white stucco and the ground is tamed by paved terraces, but every plane and profile is angled and articulated to maintain the impression of spontaneous shelter-building. A few hundred metres along the shore, Siza has modified the rocks differently to create a swimming pool right next to the sea with a linear strip of showering and changing rooms backed up against the sea wall. Here the mono-pitch roofs, at road level, are shallower, and the concrete walls unpainted, as if they were a natural geological occurrence. It was in these two early projects, completed in 1963, that Siza, by his own account, learnt the importance of topography – the thoughtful modification of the ground to receive a building so that it belongs in its place.

We see the same care and consideration in later mature works. The Faculty of Architecture at the University of Porto, completed in 1995, sits on a terraced hillside overlooking the river Douro. Siza's first act was to strengthen and clarify the terracing, creating three big steps for the buildings to sit on. A long, continuous block occupies the top step, forming a visual and acoustic barrier against the road to the north. Its roofs and walls are angled and folded to fit a complex plan that includes lecture halls, offices and a library. The next step down is an open yard with a straight southern edge against which three separate, squat towers abut themselves, standing on the third step below and linked to

the northern block by corridors under the yard. They look like early Modernist town houses but with gaps between to allow views from the yard over the river estuary. All are basically white stuccoed boxes, with identical footprints, evenly spaced, and they contain similar collections of architectural studios. Each, however, is differently arranged. Windows, roof-lights and projecting sunshades vary according to the nature of the spaces and their orientation. It is easy to see these buildings as people standing in a line but such symbolism is actually untypical of Siza, whose buildings are almost all completely abstract.

Siza's architecture is perhaps best defined negatively, by the clichés from which it refrains. It is not interested in stylistic imitation, or novelty for its own sake, or personal expression, or any rules of composition that might be carried over from one project to another. It has no preconceptions. Each project is a unique response to circumstances: brief, site and context – the constraints that they impose and the opportunities that are latent in them. Many architects would see a commission to design a museum in their home town as an occasion to build a monument, but not Siza. The Serralves Museum of Contemporary Art in Porto, completed in 1999, is a low, white, facadeless groundscraper that seems anxious not to disturb its mature parkland setting. Even its main entrance is hard to find, hidden away behind the crouching bulk

Faculty of Architecture, University of Porto, Portugal. Álvaro Siza, 1995. Separate blocks, like early Modernist town houses, contain architectural teaching studios.

of a sunken auditorium. But within this inexpressive form the double-height, top-lit galleries are well proportioned, the circulation route is easy to use and there are elegant, comfortable spaces like the glass-walled restaurant and roof terrace on the top level.

Jean Nouvel

'Unique responses to circumstances' they may be, but Siza's buildings, wherever they are, all speak a basically Modernist formal and material language. The same cannot be said of the French architect Jean Nouvel, who came to prominence in the 1980s with the completion of his Institut du Monde Arabe in Paris, one of François Mitterrand's *Grands Projets* (see page 378). His buildings all seem to speak different languages, calling into question the consistency of his personal authorship. How can, say, the opera house in Lyons, completed in 1993, which preserves the nineteenth-century classical facades of the old building but then dwarfs them with a thumping multi-storey barrel vault like an inflated attic storey, come from the same architectural mind as the roughly contemporary Cartier Foundation in Paris, which is a delicate layering of glass, all shifting reflections, refractions

(Above) Serralves Museum of Contemporary Art, Porto, Portugal. Álvaro Siza, 1999. The understated restaurant and roof terrace overlook mature parkland.

(Below) Institut du Monde Arabe, Paris, France. Jean Nouvel, 1987. The library, patterned by sunlight shining through the *mashrabiya* of the south wall.

and transparencies? A possible answer emerges in Nouvel's theoretical writings, such as the so-called 'Louisiana Manifesto', written for an exhibition in the Louisiana Museum of Modern Art at Humlebæk in Denmark. In it he says: 'Let us reclaim the architectures of the improbable! Those that unite praxis and poetry to leave their imprint on a place, to throw in their lot with that place.'[2] The point seems to be that globalization is imposing a new kind of uniformity that architecture must resist by remaining sensitive to place, custom and climate.

So Nouvel's buildings are all different because they belong to different places, geographically and culturally. At the Institut du Monde Arabe, on the bank of the Seine not far upstream from Notre-Dame, two moderately tall slabs, the northern one slightly lower with a curved taper to accommodate the riverside road, are linked by a narrow, recessed atrium. It is an elegant sculptural form with some unexpected spatial complexities, such as a courtyard that sits between the two blocks at the upper levels. But the feature most visitors remember is the south-facing elevation, of gridded glass, each square division of which is fitted internally with a symmetrical array of adjustable metal irises like those that alter the aperture of a camera lens. Inside, especially on a sunny day, every surface is patterned by sunlight that comes and goes and is never still. Any resemblance to the traditional

Islamic *mashrabiya* or lattice-screened window is, of course, deliberate. This is a building that belongs to two places at once: Paris and *le monde arabe*.

A prominent corner of land projecting into a lake at the hinge point of a city surrounded by hills is the kind of site an architect might either relish or dread. Whatever is built there is going to be on show and obliged to perform. There is nowhere to hide. In 1989, faced with such a site in Lucerne, Switzerland, Nouvel's first idea was to meet the challenge head on and put the new Culture and Congress Centre in the lake itself. It soon became clear, however, that this would offend local sensibilities so instead he brought the lake into the site in the form of narrow channels like docks for small ships, dividing the building into its three main components: two concert halls and a conference centre with offices and catering facilities. A long service bay connects the three blocks on the landward side, facing the forecourt of the city's main railway station. (Note that compositionally this is similar to the atrium-divided blocks of the Institut du Monde Arabe. Every Nouvel building may look different, but certain planning habits are detectable nevertheless.) So what

Culture and Congress Centre, Lucerne, Switzerland. Jean Nouvel, 1998. The thin, blade-like roof cantilevers out an impossible-looking 20 metres (65 feet).

kind of performance does the building give? A bold one, is the answer. It makes its entrance, so to speak, sporting an enormous square roof that unites the three blocks and cantilevers out a full 20 metres (65 feet) towards the lake's edge. From most angles the projecting portico seems to be made only of a thin sheet of silky grey aluminium. Of course this cannot be: 20-metre cantilevers require structural depth. We assume there must be big, tapered steel beams somewhere above the sightline, and so there are. But the effect of weightlessness, and the way the form gestures towards the lake and the landscape, gives the building a certain sense of command. It takes its place confidently.

Herzog & de Meuron

In this grouping together of architects who respect 'context', whether physical or historical, it is hard to justify the inclusion of the Swiss architects Jacques Herzog and Pierre de Meuron (Herzog & de Meuron), whose buildings are self-referential works of art depending on no obvious precedents. In their own pronouncements they have been reluctant to make any acknowledgement of influence from the past other than a polite nod to their teacher, Aldo Rossi. Yet their architecture, in the early buildings at least, has a 'grounded' quality that distinguishes it from other, more futuristic or fantastic creations. It is grounded not in architectural history but in aeons of bodily human experience. 'Phenomenological' would be the fancy philosophical term for it. Phenomenologists are concerned with reality as perceived by human beings, not reality as conceived, 'objectively', by science. Herzog & de Meuron's buildings are meant to appeal to human perception in a rich sense, not merely to the eyes but to the whole body and to the memories alive in that body. This is achieved by the use of unusual materials that, by association, stimulate all of the senses at once. It may not be possible to touch them, but we can nevertheless tell what they feel like; we might hear the echo of their hardness or the silence of their softness; and we might even be able to imagine what they taste and smell like. For a while in the 1990s the clumsy word 'materiality' was on every thinking architect's lips. Painted

Railway signal box, Auf dem Wolf, Switzerland. Herzog & de Meuron, 1994.
1990s 'materiality': copper strips have been twisted to admit light to the offices behind.

429

or polished surfaces, clear like glass or arbitrarily coloured and textured, were out of fashion. A new depth of colour and texture was sought and Herzog & de Meuron provided it.

It is rare that a railway signal box enters architectural history, but the one at Auf dem Wolf near Basel, completed in 1994, has become the perfect illustration of 1990s 'materiality'. It is a six-storey-high concrete building, containing mainly electronic signalling equipment with a few workstations for signal operators. It would be completely unremarkable but for its external cladding made of horizontal copper strips 200 millimetres (8 inches) wide, some of which are twisted to admit daylight to the inhabited rooms behind. The strips create a strangely silky texture when viewed from a distance. A material common in traditional construction here finds an unusual application but one that seems appropriate to its thinness and malleability.

The warehouse at Laufen completed in 1987 for the Ricola herbal sweet company (an equally unlikely subject for historical celebration) wears a similarly simple but subtle external cladding, this time using Eternit, a manufactured fibrous board. The boards, arranged in courses and slightly angled like big overlapping tiles, form a 'rain-screen' over the galvanized metal of the wall proper. The subtlety is in the details. Boards get deeper as they rise up the building,

creating a deliberately uncertain sense of scale. On close inspection it turns out that they rest on narrow cantilevered shelves, as if 'stored' like the merchandise inside. Foundation beams are exposed at the base of the wall and a kind of cornice made of delicate timber struts finishes it off at the top.

This exposure of structure, with its faint echo of a classical order, is actually an exception in Herzog & de Meuron's work, as we shall see. The manufactured smoothness of the cladding material is emphasized by its contrast with the rough cliffs of the limestone quarry in which the building is sited. At the Dominus Winery in Napa Valley, California, completed in 1998, the idea of a plain but materially rich exterior attains a new purposefulness. The building is a long, flat-roofed rectangle, conforming to the linear geometry of the vineyard in which it sits. It accommodates the whole wine-making process, from the tank room at one end through the oak fermentation vats in the middle to the bottling and storage section at the other end. External walls are completely screened by gabions – those wire-mesh containers filled with rock rubble that are sometimes used

Ricola warehouse, Laufen, Switzerland. Herzog & de Meuron, 1987. There is a faint echo of a classical order in the base-shaft-capital arrangement of the lightweight cladding.

(Left) Dominus Winery, Napa Valley, California, USA. Herzog & de Meuron, 1998. A long, flat-roofed box conforming to the cultivated geometry of the vineyard.

(Below) Library of the Eberswalde Technical School, Germany. Herzog & de Meuron, 1999. Friezes of repeated photographs, chosen by the artist Thomas Ruff, cover the whole building.

as retaining walls in river and motorway engineering. Their purpose here, or perhaps one should say their 'functional justification', is to moderate the temperature inside the building by passive means. They are heavy and therefore heat up and cool down slowly, creating what is sometimes called a 'thermal flywheel' effect. But there is no doubt that it is their tactile texture and the way that they filter the daylight inside the building that excited the architects.

Enhanced materiality was the main theme of these three early Herzog & de Meuron buildings, but it was not their only innovation. There was also a new simplicity, an insistence on the solving of planning problems by obvious means, for example by putting everything into a plain box. This was an implied criticism of those celebrations of complexity that flourished in the 1980s, including Postmodernism, High Tech and, later, Deconstructivism. It is tempting to reach for the vaguely defined and widely applied adjective 'minimalist' but it doesn't quite cover Herzog & de Meuron's architecture, which is more sensuous and less moralistic than the tidy-minded designs of, say, John Pawson or Alberto Campo Baeza. Herzog & de Meuron's buildings are not meant to disappear into nothingness, nor are they designed to promote any particular social or political ideology. They are meant to move their users like works of art with 'a hint of memory and association'. In their second major building for Ricola, a factory and warehouse on a wooded site at Mulhouse-Brunstatt in France completed in 1993, Herzog & de Meuron introduced a new and unexpected feature: surface decoration in the form of a repetitive leaf motif screen

printed onto translucent polycarbonate cladding panels. The fully phenomenological enjoyment of unusual materials and textures seems suddenly to have changed into its opposite: a shallow, purely visual diversion. But this was no aberration.

In the library of the Technical School at Eberswalde near Berlin, another simple shoe box completed in 1999, repetitive pictorial decoration completely covers the whole building. Photographs chosen by the artist Thomas Ruff are screen printed onto concrete cladding panels and also onto the continuous bands of high-level windows that light the interiors of the three storeys. The pictures are thematically various – a skull, a stag beetle, an old aeroplane, a running race – but repeated along each 'course' of blocks or windows so that the effect is rather monotonous. This is a deliberate challenge to a long-established tradition in which elements of structure and construction such as columns and beams, either real in the Modernist version or representational in the classical version, provide the 'subject matter' of architectural ornament. Here the subject matter is random, or at least personal, and unconnected with architecture. Structure and construction are suppressed.

In the early years of the new century, Herzog & de Meuron, along with other Pritzker Prize winners such as Rem Koolhaas and Renzo Piano, joined forces with the global

Walker Art Center, Minneapolis, Minnesota, USA. Herzog & de Meuron, 2005. The tall block is clad in shiny metal panels like pieces of paper that have been scrunched up and straightened out.

(Opposite and below) Prada shop, Tokyo, Japan. Herzog & de Meuron, 2003. The enveloping grid is abstract and weightless, with no differentiation between parts that bear differing loads.

fashion industry. Their Prada shop in Tokyo, completed in 2003, might be said to display a new interest in structure, housed as it is in a diagrid steel cage in-filled with a mixture of concave, convex, transparent and translucent glass panels. But the grid has that simplified quality characteristic of Herzog & de Meuron, with no visible differentiation between parts that bear differing loads. It is a patterned polygon, deliberately abstract and scaleless, angled and facetted to fill the maximum allowable volume once a small European-style piazza has been subtracted from the site. Inside, the old boxiness has been superseded by a three-dimensional 'landscape' with many an angled balcony overlooking double- or triple-height spaces. About half way up, a continuous tube, diamond-shaped in section, spans right across the building providing a less public area in which to try on clothes.

In the two American art galleries completed in 2005 – an extension to the Walker Art Center in Minneapolis and the de Young Museum in San Francisco's Golden Gate Park – the new, spectacular, global style has fully matured. Forms are angled in all directions and interiors are spatially complex. At the Walker, Edward Larrabee Barnes's rectilinear, brick, pinwheel-planned gallery of 1971 now shares the site with four other volumes set at angles and overlapping each other within a straight glazed concourse. The tallest of the four, which houses a theatre for the performing arts, is clad in shiny metal panels like pieces of paper that have been screwed up and straightened out. The interest in surface texture persists, therefore, as does the refusal to emphasize, or even to acknowledge, any joint or junction or structural member. All is flush and weightless.

Peter Zumthor

The personification of Herzog & de Meuron's architectural conscience is Peter Zumthor. He too comes from Basel and made his name in the 1980s designing simple, materially rich buildings. The first to become internationally famous, in 1988, was a tiny hillside chapel for the Alpine village of Sumvitg in the eastern canton of Graubünden. The old Baroque chapel had been swept away by an avalanche, which may be one of many possible explanations for the streamlined 'teardrop' plan-form of the new chapel. In other ways it is rather traditional. A unified group of unvarnished wooden pews, shaped to fit the curve of the walls, faces a communion table at the rounded, apse-like end of the teardrop. A wooden roof like a boat is supported on thin columns, slightly distanced from the walls as if implying notional aisles. The only daylight is provided by a continuous clerestory.

Outside, the cladding is natural wooden shingles, and there are bells high up on what looks like a campanile from which everything but the access ladder has been removed. These forms are fresh and original, but are nevertheless based on conventional prototypes. The thermal baths at Vals, another remote Alpine village in Graubünden, is an altogether stranger and more powerful work. Stone, not wood, is the predominant material – a local grey quartzite used in narrow strips to face concrete walls. Turf roofed and entered from above, the building is like a strangely ordered quarry carved out of the hillside, or perhaps like the excavated remains of some alternative Rome that failed to invent the arch but was adept in the arrangement of flat, cantilevered planes. External and internal swimming pools are surrounded by smaller, specialized spaces housed in stone-clad boxes. These support the roof, the component slabs of which are separated by narrow glazed slots admitting lines of light that wiggle on the surface of the water. This is Zumthor's masterpiece and a clear statement of his philosophy. He wrote: 'The world is full of signs and information which stand for things that no-one fully understands because they too turn out to be signs for other things. The real thing remains

Chapel, Sumvitg, Graubünden, Switzerland. Peter Zumthor, 1988. Everything but the access ladder seems to have been removed from the campanile.

Chapel, Sumvitg, interior. The roof, like an upturned boat, is supported on thin columns attached to, but distanced from, the walls.

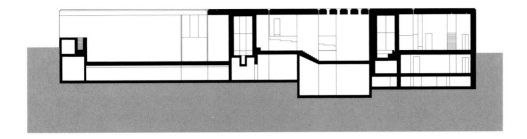

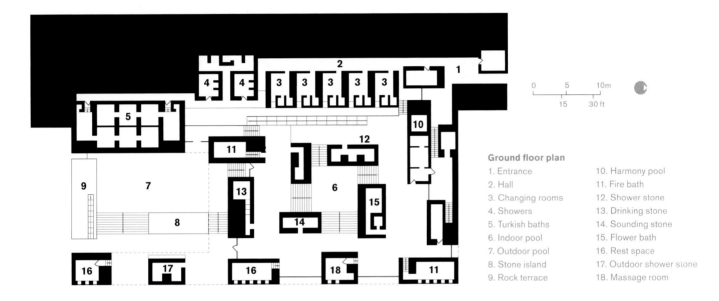

0   5   10m
15   30ft

Ground floor plan

1. Entrance	10. Harmony pool
2. Hall	11. Fire bath
3. Changing rooms	12. Shower stone
4. Showers	13. Drinking stone
5. Turkish baths	14. Sounding stone
6. Indoor pool	15. Flower bath
7. Outdoor pool	16. Rest space
8. Stone island	17. Outdoor shower stone
9. Rock terrace	18. Massage room

Thermal Baths, Vals, Graubünden, Switzerland. Peter Zumthor, 1996. Cantilevered roof slabs are separated by narrow slits that draw lines of light on the walls and water below.

hidden … Nevertheless, I am convinced that real things do exist.'[3] Completed in 1996, the baths have become famous in Switzerland and a place of pilgrimage for architects from all over the world.

In Zumthor's Kunsthaus Bregenz in the extreme west of Austria, completed in 1997, the label 'minimalist' is harder to avoid. This is another box-like building, four storeys high, and clad entirely in translucent glass – simple, but also spatially and technically ingenious. The cladding is not a curtain wall of the old kind but an unsealed rain-screen with its own ground-borne support system occupying a wide vertical cavity. The building inside is made of concrete, its floor slabs supported by just three straight walls set back from the floor edges to demarcate circulation spaces. Other, non-loadbearing, upstand walls rise only to the height of the suspended ceilings, which are of translucent glass, like the rain-screen. The space between the ceiling and floor above is therefore a 'light plenum', borrowing filtered daylight from the rain-screen cavity and spreading it evenly over the gallery spaces below. This is a museum of contemporary art with no permanent collection to accommodate. Exhibits are often installations that respond creatively to the strange effect of filtered daylight in planar voids cleansed of all ornament and completely cut off from the outside world.

Having won his Pritzker Prize in 2009 and become world famous, Zumthor was asked to design a new building for the Los Angeles County Museum of Art on Wilshire Boulevard. His proposal was anything but austere and constrained. It showed a horizontal slab of enclosed space, shaped like a Matisse cut-out or a blob of ink, raised off the ground over a shady plaza. The total freedom of the form was completely unexpected, yet it had a rather obvious source: the nearby La Brea tar pits in Hancock Park, which are almost real blobs of ink. Representation, fought against so fiercely in earlier projects, had at last asserted itself, calling into question all that had gone before. It seems that even Zumthor's monastic intensity is vulnerable when exposed to more ambitious American expectations.

Steven Holl

The transatlantic traffic in phenomenological ideas about architecture has not always travelled from east to west. In the 1990s the United States had its own committed phenomenologist in Steven Holl, a New York architect trained at the University of Washington and the Architectural Association in London. In 1991 he met the Finnish architect and theorist Juhani Pallasmaa at an Alvar Aalto symposium

Kunsthaus, Bregenz, Austria. Peter Zumthor, 1997. The structure creates horizontal and vertical 'light plenums', producing a soft, even glow.

in Jyväskylä. A year later the two met again in Helsinki, where Holl was preparing to enter a competition for a new museum of contemporary art on a site close to Aalto's Finlandia Hall. These meetings initiated a theoretical discussion that, with help from Alberto Pérez-Gómez, became Pallasmaa's

Kunsthaus, Bregenz. A separate administration building, in the foreground, preserves the purity of the translucent gallery block.

Kiasma Museum of Contemporary Art, Helsinki, Finland.
Steven Holl, 1998. The main block is curved in plan and section.
The lower, straight block can be seen on the right.

short phenomenological treatise *The Eyes of the Skin* – essentially a questioning of the way western culture tends to favour sight over all the other human senses. Holl won the museum competition with a design he called 'Chiasm' (*Kiasma* in Finnish), meaning, roughly, 'intertwining'. The word was borrowed from the phenomenological philosopher Maurice Merleau-Ponty, who used it to describe the peculiarly involved, multisensory quality of human perception – the 'intertwining' of the human body with its surroundings.

This idea is represented, or 'enacted', in the museum's divided form. Two linear blocks, one straight and square, the other higher and curved in both plan and section, are placed side by side with a narrow atrium between. At the north end the second block expands and bends round as if to eat the first. This is not really an intertwining, but the idea begins to make sense when we ascend the long, switchback pedestrian ramp that takes us from the main entrance at the south end of the atrium up into the ranges of galleries on either side. Perhaps more important than the

intertwining metaphor is the idea that it is only in the body's movement through space that perception is fully activated. The static, objective, predominantly visual tradition of western art (and perhaps of science and technology too) is called into question by a building that asks to be explored and experienced actively in four dimensions.

So Holl is a committed phenomenologist; or is he? More recent products of his growing international practice seem to suggest an ideological shift. Simmons Hall, a dormitory for MIT undergraduates in Cambridge, Massachusetts completed in 2002, looks like an enormous artificial sponge, a single, contained block but perforated and with chunks bitten out of it. External walls are regular square grids of loadbearing precast concrete (an 'exo-skeleton') bearing no obvious relationship to floor levels and therefore creating an uncertain sense of scale and distance. The plan is based on a central corridor with rooms either side, but this default pattern is continually interrupted by larger, communal spaces carved like caves out of the interior or excised from the external mass to make balconies and roof terraces.

'Porosity' was the general name given to this method of composition. It was later adapted and applied to two large-scale urban projects in China, both named after versions of

437

the concept: Linked Hybrid in Beijing, completed in 2009, and Sliced Porosity in Chengdu, completed three years later. The former is the more daring and original. It is founded on three basic ideas: that high-rise buildings should be multi- rather than unifunctional (hence 'Hybrid'); that it ought to be possible to alleviate the isolation of high-rise living by building bridges between the upper floors of adjacent towers (hence 'Linked'); and that towers should be arranged in groups to contain and define public spaces.

Holl is a New Yorker and Rockefeller Center (see page 173) is acknowledged as a precedent, but Linked Hybrid is more direct and literal in its translation of concept to form. There are nine towers, one a hotel, the others mostly residential, with public functions such as shops, restaurants, a cinema and a school at the lower levels relating to the big watery

plaza between the blocks. Up above, at levels 12 to 18, bridges between the towers contain additional public functions, including a café, a gallery, an auditorium and a fitness centre. One of the bridges contains a swimming pool. In a sense the whole development is a single multifunction megastructure, but spatial relationships – of bridges to towers, towers to podium, and podium to the surrounding city streets – are legible enough to maintain a traditional urban clarity. So how does it relate to Holl's phenomenology? It seems the philosophy no longer applies. In a 2013 interview with the *Architectural Review* Holl said: 'I definitely believe in ideas driving a design, and that makes me different from the people who pretend to be phenomenologists. I am very different from them: you must have an idea to drive a design. I am much closer to Peter Eisenman or Zaha Hadid than I am to Zumthor.'[4]

'Linked Hybrid' development, Beijing, China. Steven Holl, 2009. Towers are multifunctional, arranged to define public spaces and linked by high-level bridges.

The Neues Museum, Berlin

Any architect called upon to restore an important old building must first ask a basic question: to what stage in the building's life should it be restored? Should the intentions of the original architect be faithfully recreated or should later additions and alterations, which might themselves be of some artistic value, be preserved? When in 1997 the British architect David Chipperfield won the competition to restore the Neues Museum in Berlin he was faced with a bewilderingly complicated version of this question.

The original building was designed by Friedrich August Stüler in a handsome neo-classical style and completed in 1855 using advanced construction techniques such as bowstring iron trusses and lightweight shallow domes made of hollow pots. In the Second World War it suffered extensive bomb damage and was left as a ruin until the late 1980s when some repairs were carried out to prevent further decay. Now it was to become the centrepiece of Berlin's 'Museum Island', a collection of five museums including the famous Altes Museum by Karl Friedrich Schinkel.

Ideas about museum display had changed since Stüler's time so it seemed inappropriate to restore large murals originally designed as pictorial backdrops for ancient exhibits. The past that History had pictured 150 years earlier was no longer convincing. On the other hand some fragments of those murals survived and it seemed wrong to destroy them. They themselves had become historic. This was a museum, after all; its whole purpose was to preserve and display historic fragments. There were other problematic 'contextual' features too, not least the classical columns and friezes that were intrinsic to the building's architecture. Where they were damaged or missing, should they be reproduced or replaced with modern versions? And in a sense wasn't the bomb damage itself an important part of the building's history? Removing all traces of it would create a false past, as if the war had never happened.

Chipperfield and his colleagues, including the specialist restoration architect Julian Harrap, decided that no single principle – repair, restoration, reproduction or renewal – could solve their problem. They would need a mixture of all of them, approaching each room, gallery and courtyard

on its own terms. They wanted to restore the whole life of the building, not just one stage in its history. Repair would blend seamlessly into restoration; reproduction – of a missing column, perhaps – would be permitted but not insisted upon; where new, modern interventions were made, they might either declare themselves openly or recede tactfully into the colours and textures of their immediate surroundings; and where underlying structure, such as a brick wall or a hollow-pot dome, had been exposed, it could be cleaned up and left on show or even reproduced in new work using secondhand materials. In the central hall, for example, the grand, straight-flighted staircase was renewed completely in pristine marble-aggregate concrete, but preserving the overall form of Stüler's ornamented original. Surrounding walls are of old and new brick, with fragments of painted plaster, and the steel-beamed ceiling is new, but on the main landing stand four dignified Ionic columns, chipped, patched and still blackened by the smoke of war. In 2009 the Egyptian, prehistoric and early historic exhibits moved in, including the famous bust of Queen Nefertiti, and the building opened to general acclaim.

Neues Museum restoration, Berlin, Germany. David Chipperfield, 1997–2009. Central hall, guarded by four Ionic columns still blackened by the smoke of war.

32 | DIGITAL FUTURES
1994–2012

Computers have been helping architects, engineers and builders to cope with the complicated business of constructing buildings for 60 years or more now. 'Building information models' or BIMs have supplanted physical drawings as the medium in which detailed designs are recorded and shared. In theory, this development has nothing to do with the progress of architecture. A BIM might as easily be made of a completely traditional design as of some ground-breaking new concept. But in practice the computer does influence architecture, just as it influences every other aspect of modern life. The strength of that influence grew in the early 1990s when CAD (computer-aided design) in the architect's studio moved up a gear from two to three dimensions and began to be linked to CAM (computer-aided manufacturing) in the factories that made building components.

Three-dimensional CAD suddenly increased the range of thinkable building forms. The old tectonic assumptions – that buildings should have level floors, upright walls and either flat or pitched roofs – were brought into question. Dynamic, curved forms, like the bodies of animals, could

be 'made' in the computer and called 'architecture'. They could even be published in magazines and become the basis of an architectural reputation.

For example in 1997 Greg Lynn, one of many talented architects to emerge from the New York office of Peter Eisenman, designed the Embryological House, which was theoretically available in many 'mass-customized' versions but was hard to imagine anywhere outside the virtual environment of the computer. Similarly Lars Spuybroek and his Rotterdam-based practice NOX struggled to convert virtual form into material reality. Their 1993 Water Experience Pavilion for the Dutch ministry of transport emerged sleek and slug-like from the computer only to be mocked up crudely in profile-cut formers and longerons like an old-fashioned aeroplane. Soon, however, with the help of CAM, genuinely complex curved forms began to appear

Water Experience Pavilion, Rotterdam, the Netherlands. Lars Spuybroek and NOX, 1993. Converting virtual reality into actual reality can sometimes look awkward.

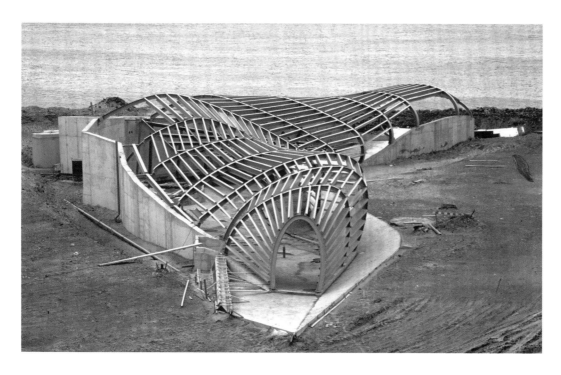

in the real world as buildings or parts of buildings. Norman Foster's remodelling of the British Museum, completed in 2000, included a new glass roof over the Great Court, formerly occupied by the old British Library. It was an awkward space to roof, square but with the drum and dome of the old reading room in the middle of it. A pre-CAD/CAM solution might have involved a radial arrangement of heavy steel trusses that would have crushed, visually, Robert Smirke's stately classical porticos below. But Foster's roof is gentle and delicate, like a hanging net but inverted so that it swells rather than sags. It is a complex type of geodesic dome made possible by the simple fact that the steel rods forming the net are all different in length and weight.

This is the sort of thing that computer-controlled machinery can do easily. The old Fordist rule used to be that in order to mass-produce complicated objects like cars you had to standardize them. In architecture, it was a principle that was often cited in order to excuse the disappointingly slow development of mass-produced housing. Houses could never be completely standardized, it was argued, because of the necessity to suit them to unique sites. Fordism had an effect on the development of architecture nevertheless, if only at a symbolic level. Early Modernist buildings were not actually mass produced in factories, but they looked as if they had been. They were hand-crafted symbols of

a machine age. The coming of CNC (computer numerical control) machines, which could make a hundred different things in not much more time than it took to make a hundred identical things, changed the rules, both practically and symbolically. One-off adaptations – to suit a building to its site, say – could now be made efficiently in the factory. But equally a different symbolic language was required. Mechanical repetition was out of date; the coming of the digital age would be heralded by a parade of unique, curvaceous forms.

(Above) Kunsthaus, Graz, Austria. Colin Fournier and Peter Cook, 2003. The stomach of a butchered animal perhaps, though locals call it 'the Friendly Alien'. Tubes like cut-off veins or intestines are revealed inside as roof-lights.

(Left) Great Court, British Museum, London, UK. Norman Foster, 2000. An elegant early example of CAD/CAM form – the bars in the glass roof are all different.

441

'Blobism'

A shorter way of saying 'unique curvaceous form' is 'blob'. For a while around the turn of the new century 'Blobism' and 'Blobitecture' became popular stylistic labels. They were applied to buildings like the Kunsthaus Graz in Austria, a modern art museum completed in 2003 and designed by Colin Fournier with Archigram pioneer and veteran architectural educationalist Sir Peter Cook (see page 441). Locals call it 'the Friendly Alien' and alien it certainly is to the modest old buildings that it shoulders aside on its riverside site, and the historic nineteenth-century iron house to which it attaches itself. But more than a visitor from outer space, it looks like the bluish-black stomach of a butchered animal with the stubs of its veins and intestines still waving in the air. Actually they serve as tubular roof-lights. A hidden geodesic steel frame is clad in double-curved, heat-formed acrylic panels. Those on the side facing the river are equipped with circular fluorescent lights that can be switched or dimmed by a computer program, becoming a screen of big pixels, able to form crude moving images. All of this technology is rather primitive compared with the 'mylar film incorporating anisotropic carbon threads and kevlar/Nomex aramid honeycomb struts'[1] that was originally envisaged, but it marks a definite first step towards the realization of an organic, cellular, responsive skin. The two-storey arrangement of the main galleries, with an intermediate floor supported on ordinary columns, somewhat dilutes the experience of being 'inside the stomach' but the outer integrity of the form is maintained by raising it up above a glass-walled entrance floor.

It was the shift in computing from two to three dimensions that made Blobism possible. Architects couldn't resist testing the potential of 3D CAD/CAM. They designed blobs because they could. But another development in computing was already well advanced that would have more important consequences, at least in theory. It went by various names, such as 'scripting', 'algorithmics' and 'parametrics'. The idea was that computers could do more than just help with the manipulation of forms in three dimensions. They could actually design the forms themselves, automatically, as long as they were fed with the right data, such as space requirements, microclimate, strength of materials and so on – all the 'parameters' that architects and engineers routinely grappled with. 'Morphogenesis' was another popular term, giving the concept an almost biblical resonance. Patrik Schumacher, who, as we shall see, worked with Zaha Hadid on some of the most fluidly futuristic buildings of the new century, coined another, even more radical term: 'autopoiesis', meaning automatic creation – 'poetry' in the ancient sense of the word.[2]

But autopoeisis is still, in the second decade of the century, more a dream than a reality. Designing a large building

without the help of a computer may have become almost as unthinkable as designing without drawings and models, but architecture remains a human activity. No real physical buildings have yet been designed entirely by machines. Schumacher sees 'Parametricism' as the successor to Modernism and, like Modernism, it is as much a style as a method of production; it symbolizes the freedom of the digital world just as Modernism symbolized the repetitive order of the machine age. Actual computers are perhaps less important than the idea of an infinitely flexible, capable, digital-organic technology. That word 'organic' is a reminder that in the history of modern architecture flexible curved forms are nothing new. We saw them, for example, in the writhing iron tendrils of Hector Guimard's Art Nouveau Métro stations (see page 12), in the sculpted concrete of Erich Mendelsohn's Einstein Tower (see page 77) and in the sails of Jørn Utzon's Sydney Opera House (see page 212). Two precursors of the modern digital-organic style, Antoni Gaudí (see page 12) and Frei Otto (see page 219), are especially important, and are acknowledged as pioneers by theorists such as Lynn, Spuybroek and Schumacher. Their importance is encapsulated in the idea that they did not so much *create* form as *find* it. The physical models that they made – Otto's propped nets and Gaudí's inverted tensile vaulting – were the equivalents of computer models. Like nature itself, they automatically adopted the most efficient structural forms; they were participating in nature rather than standing apart from it. There are some fundamental philosophical objections to the idea that architecture can somehow become 'natural', but it is a powerful idea nevertheless, though an old one.

Building-as-landscape

Classical buildings – Palladio's Villa Rotonda, for example – distinguish themselves deliberately from the landscape in which they sit. Static uprightness is set against rolling horizontality. One consequence of the new interest in organic form, prompted by digital technology, was the emergence of the radically anti-classical building, the building-as-landscape. In their international ferry terminal at Yokohama, completed in 2002, Farshid Moussavi and Alejandro Zaera-Polo, known as Foreign Office Architects, designed a rectangular pier that looks more like a site for a building than the building itself. There is no uprightness, no columns and beams, only an artificial landscape of hillocks and caves formed by a folded steel plate structure. The young husband-and-wife team, who had worked in Rem Koolhaas's office on the ZKM project in Karlsruhe (see page 399), beat a field of more than 700 to win the design competition (Koolhaas was on the jury, with Arata Isozaki and Toyo Ito). It was their first job – a £150 million building that would symbolize a nation's relationship with the rest of the world, for it was right here that American sailors

International Ferry Terminal, Yokohama, Japan. Foreign Office Architects, 2002. Building as landscape, the opposite of a basically classical norm.

International Ferry Terminal, detail. Interior and exterior are one folded and flowing space.

first landed in 1853, bringing to an end Japan's 200-year isolation from the west. Irénée Scalbert, writing in 1995 about the winning design, said: '[It] clarifies and redefines the aspirations of a generation.'[13] Zaera-Polo spelt out one of those aspirations as 'the hybridization of infrastructure, landscape and architecture' – in other words the abolition of all conventional types and categories. Is the ferry terminal a building or a landscape? A park or a border post? A barrier or an entrance? A zone of officialdom or a field of freedom? The building-as-landscape symbolizes freedom because it is one continuous, interleaved space rather than a collection of functionally specific enclosures. Uprightness and enclosure are provided by the visiting ocean liners and cruise ships that moor at its sides.

The Yokohama terminal is not a blob, of course, not a moulded mass or an inflated bladder, but a folded sheet. 'The fold' was for a while an influential concept among intellectual architects. *The Fold: Leibniz and the Baroque* by Gilles Deleuze was the relevant philosophical text. Those few practically minded architects who bothered to read it were mostly baffled, but there did seem to be something important and graspable in the idea that natural structures were more like continuous sheets – folded, pleated, layered and enveloping – than like the elemental constructions familiar to architecture. There was a realization that traditional plans, sections and elevations, which were fine for representing columns, beams, walls and floors, might have blinded architects to the potential of forms suggested by nature, folds as well as blobs.

Conceptual models

The Moebius House in Utrecht, designed by Ben van Berkel and Caroline Bos, who later called themselves UNStudio, illustrates the new interest in folded forms. Its design is supposedly based on a Moebius strip, that well-known trick that, by twisting a strip of paper and gluing its ends together, seems to create a sheet with only one side. But the picture is confused by the architects' statement that the design is also based on a 'double-locked torus', which looks like a knotted loop of intestine. Actually, the built house bears little resemblance to either of its conceptual models, but the general idea of replacing traditional spatial arrangements with something more organic is clear enough. The house is conceived as a continuous loop of space corresponding to the daily routines of its inhabitants, although there are some almost-conventional rooms along

the route. The Moebius-strip idea applies to the space-enclosing elements as much as to the space itself. Stiff ribbons of concrete and glass fold over and around each other to create views through, under, over and across. There are no windows, only glass walls, so the sparsely wooded surroundings are notionally continuous with the internal landscape. For a couple of progressive architects, this was a dream commission. The clients reportedly asked for 'a house that would be acknowledged as a reference for the renovation of the architectural language' – which is what they got.

Moebius House, Utrecht, the Netherlands. Ben van Berkel and Caroline Bos, 1998. Moebius strip or 'double-locked torus'? A continuous loop of space corresponds to daily routines.

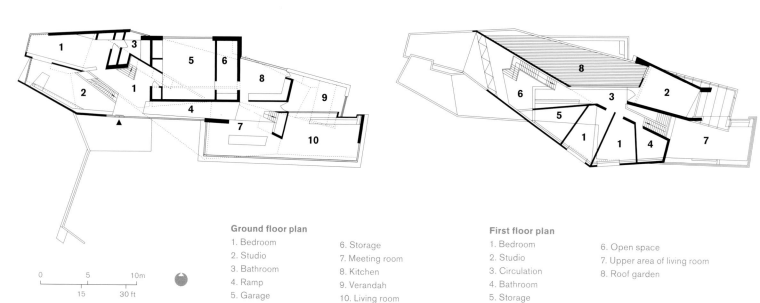

Ground floor plan
1. Bedroom
2. Studio
3. Bathroom
4. Ramp
5. Garage
6. Storage
7. Meeting room
8. Kitchen
9. Verandah
10. Living room

First floor plan
1. Bedroom
2. Studio
3. Circulation
4. Bathroom
5. Storage
6. Open space
7. Upper area of living room
8. Roof garden

0   5   10m
15   30 ft

The argument of this chapter so far would seem to be that developments in computing led inevitably to a new, free-form architecture, but in fact this is a distortion of the truth. The 'aspirations of the generation' grew from deeper historical roots. Peter Cook and his Archigram colleagues were designing blob-like buildings decades earlier – David Greene's Living Pod of 1966, for example, which was in turn inspired by Friedrich Kiesler's Endless House project of the 1950s. One of the most shocking blobs of the 1990s was the Media Centre at Lord's Cricket Ground, an alien's eye balanced on two stalks to overlook a strip of turf held sacred for 200 years. It was designed by Future Systems, led by Jan Kaplický and Amanda Levete. In 2003 they produced a bigger blob in the centre of Birmingham, a fairly conventional multi-storey department store for Selfridges, loosely wrapped in a sprayed concrete blanket painted blue and studded with aluminium discs. Once again, 'alien' is the word that comes to mind. But Jan Kaplický was no young computer wizard. He had been a pioneer of High Tech in the early 1970s and had worked with Richard Rogers and Renzo Piano on the Centre Pompidou (see page 350). His original 'future systems' idea, illustrated in influential paper projects like the House for a Helicopter Pilot of 1979, had belonged to the mostly pre-digital high technology of the aerospace industry. Kaplický died in 2009.

(Right) **Selfridges Department Store, Birmingham, UK. Future Systems, 2003.** Blob-like outside, but inside a fairly conventional multi-storey department store.

Media Centre, Lord's Cricket Ground, London, UK. Future Systems, 1999. A futuristic eye on legs to survey a strip of turf hallowed for 200 years.

Kansai International Airport, Osaka, Japan. Renzo Piano,
1994. The 1.7-kilometre- (1.1-mile-) long wave- or wing-like roof
slopes down gently towards its extremities.

A shift from machine-like High Tech to organic
curvaceousness can be detected in the work of Renzo
Piano's now global practice as early as the 1980s. The
shopping centre at Bercy, near a big junction on the Paris
Périphérique where it crosses the Seine, is wrapped in a
single envelope, like Future Systems' Selfridges, but here
the skin is made of aluminium panels organized with a
view to economical standardization of the old, Fordist kind.
Piano's Kansai airport, on its vast artificial island in Osaka

Bay, might reasonably be described as late High Tech
(it was completed in 1994). Its wrap-around, wing-like
enclosure, 1.7 kilometres (1.1 miles) long, was designed to
promote efficient natural ventilation and get rid of unsightly
ducts. Wavy steel trusses and a double-curved skin seem
to anticipate the coming CAD/CAM freedom, but in fact
the 82,000 stainless steel panels are all identical and the
very gradual slope of the 'wing' down to its extremities is
accommodated in the 'tolerances' of the joints.

Norman Foster designed a similar wrap-around enclosure to
shelter the Sage music centre in Gateshead from the cold
north wind that scours its riverside site. Three concert halls
– one medium sized, one large and, sandwiched between
them, a small, box-like rehearsal hall – are conceived as
separate, self-contained buildings. Left exposed they would
look like exercises in old-fashioned white Modernism, their
rounded forms weakly reminiscent of Mendelsohn, but
the glass and stainless steel wave that rears up on the
inland side, easily clears their flat roofs and breaks over
the riverside promenade places the whole complex firmly
in the Blobist avant-garde of the time. It creates a relaxed
shared foyer, overlooked by the halls' access galleries,
with the rhyming steel-arched form of the nearby Tyne
Bridge visible through the glass. The local music school
is buried under the foyer, rather awkwardly adapting itself
to the plan-profiles of the auditoriums above.

Sage concert hall, Gateshead, UK. Norman Foster, 2004.
A metal and glass wave breaks over an otherwise fairly
conventional set of three concert halls.

In 2002, two years before the completion of the Sage, Foster had built City Hall in London, an almost perfect blob and a clear demonstration of the principle of automatic building design. Its Thames-side site could hardly be more prominent, just west of Tower Bridge on the tourist route between Tate Modern and the Tower of London. In theory part of a large office development called More London, master-planned by Foster, the building nevertheless stands alone on a wide, paved expanse, perhaps symbolizing free public access to the democratic processes taking place within. Its overall form is approximately a sphere, the most efficient form possible if the aim is to minimize an expensive enclosing envelope. But this is a sliced sphere, each slice a storey, and the slices step back from the riverfront, creating a slightly mad look, like a windswept head.

The reason for the strange shape is that it minimizes the area of external surface directly exposed to the sun's rays. Leaning the building southwards allows the sun to deliver, as it were, only glancing blows, lightening the load on the air conditioning or, in this case, allowing it to be dispensed with altogether. Of course, it was computer modelling that revealed this shading principle and suggested the leaning-sphere form. It is not a form that any human designer would ever think of spontaneously, so, in a limited sense at least, this is a building designed by a computer. Even the type and transparency of the cladding is dictated by the computer model, creating a distinctive clear-glass keystone pattern on the north side, facing the river.

Inside, certain features of Foster's renovation of the Reichstag in Berlin, completed in 1999, are reprised on

a smaller scale. In the Reichstag a public spiral ramp rises up into the glass dome over the heads of the assembled democratic representatives below. In City Hall the arrangement is similar, but squeezed into the north side of the 'sphere' so that the diminishing ramp, lit by the glass keystone, can also serve the office floors above.

City Hall, London, UK. Norman Foster, 2002.
The spiral ramp might be inherited from the Reichstag in Berlin, remodelled by Foster.

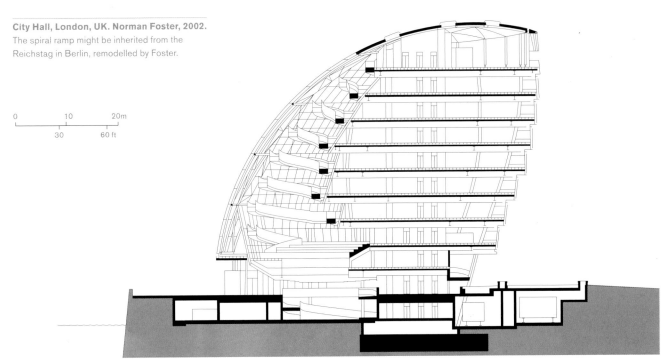

0   10   20m
  30   60 ft

Parametricism

But if old-timers like Piano and Foster took naturally to the new digital-organic mode, the true leader of the style was surely Zaha Hadid, ably assisted by Patrik Schumacher, who joined her office in 1988. It may have been Schumacher's computer expertise that supercharged Hadid's creativity and helped it over the barrier between project-making and real building. Schumacher himself, however, was insistent that the origins of 'parametricism' lay not in computer software but in Hadid's imagination. The big paintings that took the place of buildings during her ten-year wait for real commissions were more radical and convention busting than anything prompted by advanced 3D software.

Early projects like the Hong Kong leisure club (see page 379) and her entry in the 1985 Grand Buildings competition for Trafalgar Square were represented not by any single projection type such as plan and section, or isometric, or perspective but by a mixture of all of them, spontaneously distorted, fragmented and overlaid as if space itself were undergoing some apocalyptic alteration. It was not completely without precedent. The Cubism of Picasso and

Painting: Grand Buildings competition, Trafalgar Square, London, UK. Zaha Hadid, 1985. The London of Hadid's imagination – space itself undergoing some apocalyptic transformation.

Braque, and the Suprematism of Malevich – with which, we can be sure, Hadid was well acquainted – had done something similar 70 years earlier but that was in pure painting, not in the representation of supposedly buildable buildings. Hadid was exploiting to the full the traditional alliance between architecture and fine art in order to conquer the gravitational inertia of actual materials. And in a sense that is what she continued to do, in constructed reality, with the help of computers and the ingenuity of engineers.

The last place you expect to find a Zaha Hadid building is on the site of a car factory. What could the wild visions of Cubism and Suprematism possibly contribute to such a fortress of realism and practicality? It was perhaps for this reason that the BMW Central Building at Leipzig, completed in 2005 – not a gallery or a museum or an exhibition pavilion but a functioning part of an advanced manufacturing operation – finally confirmed Hadid's graduation from project maker to real-world builder. The whole factory was new, on the outskirts of the city, a statement of confidence in the economic revival of this part of former East Germany. Assembly lines are housed in big, plain sheds, as one would expect, but on the north-west corner of the site three of those sheds – designated Body in White (the jargon term for a basic car body), Assembly and Paint Shop – are linked by Hadid's Central Building, which houses various shared functions: main entrance, offices, canteen, kitchen, recreation areas and café for visitors.

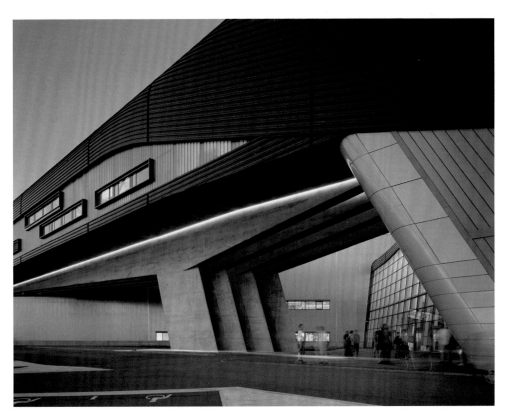

(Left and below) BMW Central Building, Leipzig, Germany. Zaha Hadid, 2005. An assembly line carrying car bodies travels at high level through the office wing of the building.

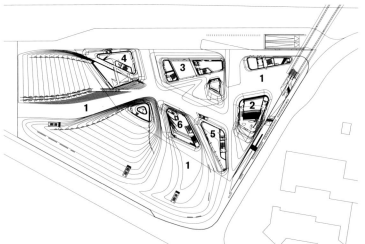

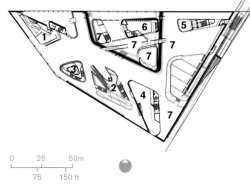

Ground floor plan

1. Landscape
2. Auditorium
3. Event space
4. Workshop
5. Bistro
6. Main entrance

Concourse plan

1. Shop
2. Main entrance
3. Group entrance
4. Restaurant
5. Laboratory/Loading
6. Laboratory
7. Exhibition

Phaeno Science Centre, Wolfsburg, Germany.
Zaha Hadid, 2005. Under the raised building the site
is paved and sculpted like a skateboard park.

There is a social agenda at work here. All visitors and
employees, white collar and blue collar alike, use the
same entrance and the same facilities. One is reminded
of Norman Foster's early industrial buildings, which
similarly ignored social distinctions (see page 346).
Offices take up most of the open interior, in two stepped
terraces arranged scissor-fashion on either side of a long
tapering well. It is not this landscape-like arrangement
that characterizes the building as a whole, however, but the
essentially linear plan that zig-zags between the three big
sheds. Movement is the theme, emphasized by a phalanx
of raking columns near the entrance and rhomboidal
or trapezoidal openings in the long concrete walls that
divide up the interior. But there is real as well as imaginary
movement here, and this is what clinches the idea of a link
building that is part of the manufacturing process. The
car assembly lines travel right through the building. While
employees eat their lunch or work at their workstations,
bodies in white glide silently along narrow suspended
tracks overhead.

Hadid completed the Phaeno Science Centre in the same year, within sight of another car factory, the Volkswagen plant in Wolfsburg. Unusually, authorship of the building is attributed to Zaha Hadid with Christos Passas, not Patrik Schumacher. Whereas BMW Central is linear, like a railway junction, Phaeno rises and spreads like a fruiting concrete fungus. Surprisingly, it develops an old Corbusian device, the piloti, but in a more fluid form. The site, at the north end of Porschestrasse, where town and factory face each other across the railway and the Mitelland Canal, is paved and sculpted like a skateboard park. Eight fat, roughly conical mushroom stalks grow out of this prepared ground to support the main body of the building. One of these stalks is the entrance, in which visitors rise to a kind of indoor adventure playground offering a range of experiments and demonstrations set up like a science teacher's dream.

Everything is moulded in curvaceous concrete, either plastered or 'fair face', except the ceiling, which is a disappointingly straightforward steel space-frame. This occupied internal landscape is less beautiful, because less materially consistent, than the external landscape beneath it, which might be called cave-like were it not so open and free flowing. But perhaps the comparison with Corbusian pilotis (those of the Unité d'Habitation, for example;

see page 224), and the general idea of a lifting up, is misleading. If the interior is a landscape then its floor is notionally solid ground and the conical pilotis are excavated pits. External walls present a problem. Landscapes do not have walls so they must be disguised. Actually they are straight and vertical, but with enormous angled and curved slices taken out of them and in-filled with glass. There are ordinary windows too, which slope as if distorted by some invisible dynamic thrust. A pedestrian bridge shoots off from the east side of the building to connect to Volkswagen's popular Autostadt exhibition centre on the other side of the railway and the canal.

The third major Hadid building of these years is the Museo Nazionale delle Arti del XXI Secolo (National Museum of Twenty-First-Century Arts) in Rome, known as the MAXXI – a more expected building type in a more visited city, though some distance from the centre, among the old barracks of the Flaminio district. Though it was not completed until 2009, it was designed at about the same time as BMW Central and in collaboration with Schumacher, so the reappearance of the linear method of composition is no surprise. A view from the air best reveals the building's overall form, which is like a handful of square concrete snakes, writhing in existing courtyards. One snake slithers over and across the others, thrusting out its head as if to look more carefully at the dignified old buildings around it.

Essentially this is a building of multiple walls in parallel sets that intersect and are constantly disappearing round bends. These walls are full-height versions of smaller, closer-spaced longitudinal roof beams between which daylight falls. There are multiple levels too, with long snaky staircases at points of intersection, painted black in an otherwise mainly white interior. Concrete is once again the main material, special self-compacting concrete that can be finished smoothly and accurately. 'Fair-face' concrete is one thing that Hadid shares with the Modernist tradition, and here and there imprints of the formwork are faintly visible, but there is no sense of the enjoyment of 'concreteness' that one finds in Corb or Kahn or Ando. Concrete's essentially fluid nature is, of course, well suited to continuous convoluted forms but it has become a universal rather than a specific material. In the years immediately after its opening the MAXXI came close to being abandoned because of budget cuts and doubts about its artistic role, but it survived and will no doubt continue to be visited for the sake of its architecture if not its exhibitions.

Museo Nazionale delle Arti del XXI Secolo (MAXXI), Rome, Italy. Zaha Hadid, 2009. A handful of square concrete snakes, one of which slithers over the others to stare at the old buildings around it.

Guangzhou Opera House, Guangdong, China.
Zaha Hadid, 2010. A conventional auditorium but
unified, as if carved from a single semi-precious stone.

These three buildings represent Hadid's mature style well enough, though they can hardly be said to be typical of an oeuvre that is surprisingly varied when surveyed as a whole. The Guangzhou Opera House, completed in 2010, looks externally like a couple of rounded, river-worn pebbles of glass and granite, although plans and sections reveal that, in their basic anatomy, these are conventional theatres. The Art Museum at Michigan State University on the other hand, sponsored by the billionaire architecture patron Eli Broad and completed in 2012, is a piece of stainless steel origami, pleated and folded, leaning and angular, its galleries cleverly lit by strip windows buried in the pleats.

Hadid could design relatively economical, workaday buildings too, such as the Evelyn Grace Academy in London and the Maggie's Centre cancer care clinic at Kirkcaldy in central Scotland. What these all have in common is an open attitude to the design process. For Modernists, design proceeded

(Right) Guangzhou Opera House. The exterior is like two enormous, river-worn pebbles.

(Below) Art Museum, Michigan State University, USA. Zaha Hadid, 2012. Not rounded this time but folded, like stainless steel origami.

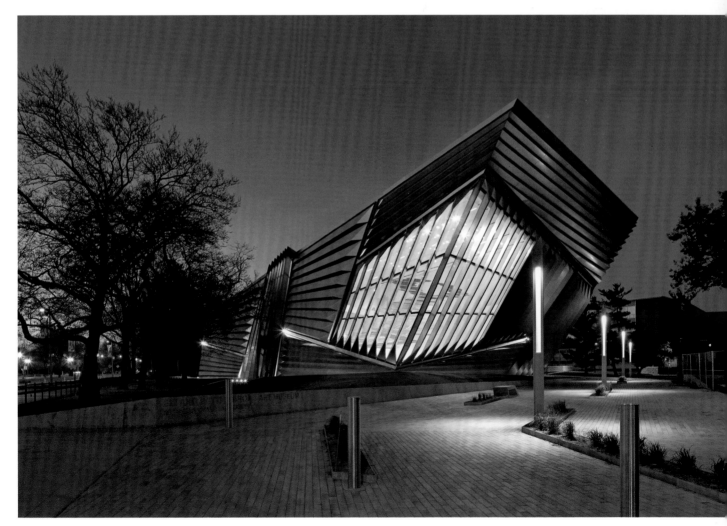

rationally, step by step, from the analysis of brief and site to the synthesis of the final building. But even they knew that what was subsequently presented as rational had often been instinctive or accidental in the moment of creation. Hadid and Schumacher embraced instinct and accident from the start, identifying parameters but ignoring precedent, stabbing in the dark, taking short cuts, welcoming the free association of analogy and resemblance, gesturing in the air or on paper, and then, with the help of computers, converting the gestures into material reality. Zaha Hadid died aged 65 in 2016, at the height of her career.

If the free, physical gesture has an opposite, then it might be the fixed, intellectual concept; and if the MAXXI in Rome is the architectural representation of the former, then the 21st Century Museum of Contemporary Art in Kanazawa, Japan, completed five years earlier in 2004, stands for the latter. Its architects were Kazuyo Sejima and Ryue Nishizawa, founders of the Tokyo-based international practice called

Evelyn Grace Academy, London, UK. Zaha Hadid, 2010.
A relatively economical, workaday building by Hadid's standards.

SANAA. The floor plan bears a vague resemblance to certain paintings by Mondrian, though the echo is probably accidental. An ordered grouping of rectangles (and one circle), differently sized and proportioned but similarly oriented, is contained in a perfect circle on an open site. The rectangles are all separate and most are undivided. Introducing the third dimension reveals that the containing circle is a glass wall under the edge of a flat roof, and that the rectangles are boxes (and the circle a cylinder) – in effect one-room buildings – rising to different heights and either penetrating the roof or cutting out a section of it to create a courtyard open to the sky.

There is formality in this composition, but also freedom; most of all there is complete clarity, both of concept and of detail: no accidents or impurities, no ornament and very little evidence of any construction process. Materiality seems a secondary consideration. The essence of the building might as well be expressed in a cardboard model as in actual concrete, steel and glass. And yet the concept is essentially human, not abstract. Openness is the main aim, a museum accessible from all sides to all people and not just for serious art appreciation but for everyday enjoyment. There is a café, a library, a lecture theatre and spaces for children as well as the galleries themselves, each of which creates a world of its own with different proportions and lighting to suit different works of art. This is a miniature city, the boxes like urban blocks and the spaces between like public streets. Kazuyo Sejima is not given to philosophical pronouncements but it is clear from interviews that for her city streets are as much places of solitude as of community. 'Alone in a crowd' can be a creative condition.

Faced with a constricted site in lower Manhattan and a brief for yet another museum of contemporary art, SANAA's conceptual clarity was severely tested. In the New Museum boxes are once again the main theme of the composition, but this time stacked up to make a small tower, clean and white amid the scruffy and mostly (for New York) low-rise buildings of the Bowery. But there is cleverness here too in the way the boxes are offset from one another so as to make space for terraces or for roof-lights at gallery edges. External walls are covered in an expanded metal mesh that continues over office windows, hiding them in the daytime but revealing them at night as a softly glowing strip. The building was completed in 2007.

Boxes play no part in the composition of the Rolex Learning Center at the Ecole Polytechnique Fédérale in Lausanne, Switzerland, although the site is once again open and expansive (Rolex was the sponsor, not the client). Completed in 2010, this is SANAA's best-known building, and for good reason: for once that over-used adjective 'innovative' is justified. In her early career, Sejima worked for Toyo Ito and this building can be seen as a continuation of developments that began in his office in the early 1990s (see page 374): first the fondness for thin roof planes (the old people's home at Yatsushiro), then, with the coming of CAD and CAM, the curving and flexing of those planes (the Lyric Hall at Nagaoka). SANAA's innovation is simple but radical: to curve and flex the floor as well as the roof. The Learning Center is basically a single-storey building, a vast rectangle 166 metres (545 feet) by 122 metres (400 feet), but rucked like a carpet, or perhaps like a slice of cheese – Emmental, it must be, because of the free-form oval courtyards that account for about a third of its area. Pedestrians, approaching from any direction, walk under the undulating floor slab to reach the main entrance in a courtyard near the centre.

Inside, the space is unified and continuous, a hilly terrain in which to wander freely and find a place to settle alone or gather in a group. Unity is not in fact complete but the space is so extensive and free flowing that occasional curved enclosing walls, many of glass, are hardly noticed. Here and there a flat floor is required for a range of bookshelves or a cluster of café tables, and some of the 'hillsides' are too steep to meet disabled-access regulations, but the resulting terraces, ramps and handrails seem only to reinforce the impression of an adapted park-like landscape. Space is divided not by walls but by contours and horizons: a restaurant occupies a hilltop with views, an auditorium

nestles in a valley like a Greek theatre. It all has a specific meaning, of course. Spatial freedom represents academic freedom, the freedom of researchers and students to mix informally with their colleagues from other disciplines and find creative combinations.

Computer modelling was essential to the development of the design, but not in the sense of automatic problem-solving or of merely increasing the range of available expressive forms. Mutsuro Sasaki, the engineer who worked with Ito on the earthquake-defying Sendai Mediatheque (see page 375), was the computer's interpreter. He and SANAA collaborated in a to-and-fro process of proposal, testing, modification and retesting. For example, where increased stresses in the concrete floor slab threatened to make it too thick and heavy, the problem could be solved spatially by carving a hole to make a courtyard. The final configuration thus emerged gradually from a respect for structural realities combined with other functional considerations such as access, day-lighting, ventilation and acoustics. It was parametrics of the old kind, guided not by technological or artistic ambition but by simple human pleasures – an informal meeting, a lunch with friends, a walk in the park or a moment of thoughtful solitude.

Rolex Learning Center, Lausanne, Switzerland. SANAA, 2010. Why should floors be flat? The hilly terrain inside is like a park in which to wander freely.

Santiago Calatrava

Félix Candela, Pier Luigi Nervi, Robert Maillart, Antoni Gaudí, Viollet-le-Duc, and behind them the manifold, fertile abundance of the Gothic tradition – these are the historical associations awakened by contemplation of the buildings and bridges of the Spanish architect and engineer Santiago Calatrava. Organic nature is his inspiration, not in any abstract, conceptual sense but directly, from the physical, articulated bodies of animals and plants. His structures are not just visible, they put on a show like acrobats or ballet dancers. They are bodies in tension, holding, straining, spanning. A Calatrava bridge, of which there are many, is never a subdued presence; always its structure rears up above deck level, often in the form of steel arches, like those of the 1987 Bac de Roda Bridge in Barcelona, in pairs on either side of the roadway, the outer arches leaning in against their upright companions. In the Alamillo Bridge at Seville, built to serve Expo '92, structural tension is dramatized to an extreme degree. Roadways are suspended from a pylon 58 metres (190 feet) high at one end, which leans far back to take the strain like the anchor man in a tug-of-war. Conventional suspension bridge design leads one to expect some kind of balancing steel guy to prevent the forward collapse, but the weight of the concrete-filled steel pylon itself and the strength of its footing on the bridgehead are apparently enough to do the job.

In buildings, as in bridges, structure is paramount but with an added complexity. Canopies and roofs lend themselves readily to organic shaping as leaves or wings supported by branches or skeletons. In Stadelhofen railway station in Zurich, a relatively early work completed in 1990, Calatrava deals capably with the complex section of a stepped and warped ground fissure, marshalling a varied repertoire of steel and concrete columns and canopies that lean and curve and taper. But often his buildings are single objects, or animals, or parts of animals, like the planetarium in Valencia, completed in 1996, which shelters its spherical night-sky dome under an eye-shaped concrete and glass outer case. And like an eye, the case has a lid that can be folded up to reveal its inner 'iris'. Motion is often implied in Calatrava's structures; sometimes, as here, it becomes actual. The glazed atrium, completed in 2001, of Milwaukee Art Museum is equipped with wing-like *brises-soleil* that are so large they seem likely at any moment to carry the building off over Lake Michigan, yet they fold away neatly when high winds threaten. There is at least some functional justification for this display. The Tenerife Auditorium of 2003 is a crustacean, cupped and shielded by concrete shells, one of which breaks free as a great overarching claw with no apparent function other than to excite expressions of awe. Puritans will prefer the glass canopy over the platforms at Oriente station in Lisbon, completed in 1998. Its regularly spaced supports – upright for once – are tree-like but not exaggeratedly so. It might have been designed by a nineteenth-century engineer, but an artistically gifted one. Viollet would have approved.

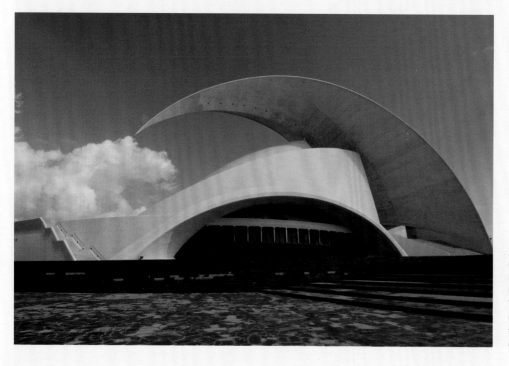

(Left) Auditorium, Tenerife, Canary Islands. Santiago Calatrava, 2003. One of the building's concrete shells becomes an enormous, and apparently functionless, claw.

(Opposite) Quadracci Pavilion, Milwaukee Art Museum, Wisconsin, USA. Santiago Calatrava, 2001. The *brise-soleil* comprises 72 steel fins, ranging from 8 to 32 metres (26 to 105 feet) long. Its wingspan is similar to that of a Boeing 747 aircraft.

33 | CHINA 1911–2012

Modern architecture is a western concept. The very phrase 'Chinese modern architecture' implies a relationship between Chinese and western traditions. Any study of Chinese modern architecture must therefore give an account of that relationship. The main features of traditional Chinese architecture – its courtyard planning and its timber-framed, hipped-roofed halls with their elaborate eaves structures – remained unchanged over many centuries; there was no Chinese equivalent of the Italian Renaissance or the Industrial Revolution to deflect the tradition from its narrow course. Construction details codified in illustrated books like the twelfth-century *Yingzao Fashi* were still being used in the nineteenth century, and indeed are used to this day in traditional houses.

By the time the child emperor Pu Yi had abdicated and left the Forbidden City in 1912, bringing to an end the 268-year rule of the Qing dynasty, there were already many western-style buildings in China. The metropolitan architecture of port cities like Hong Kong and Shanghai, which were dominated by British, French and American commercial interests, was

thoroughly western, a direct transplant that completely ignored any indigenous architectural tradition. The buildings were designed by western architects for western clients and their location in China was architecturally irrelevant.

The famous 'Bund' in Shanghai (*bund* is a colonial English word that simply means 'embankment') is a mile-long line of handsome classical buildings – banks, office blocks, clubs and hotels – built in the 1920s and 1930s on the western bank of the Huangpu River. Many of these buildings were designed by Palmer and Turner, a Hong Kong-based practice founded by an English architect, William Salway, in 1868. Now called the P&T Group, it is still the largest architectural and engineering practice in south-east Asia. Typical of Palmer and Turner's contributions to the Bund is the Customs House, completed in 1927, an 11-storey, reinforced-concrete-framed building in a stripped-down classical style with a bold cornice, an attic storey and clock tower. But the centre of Shanghai is full of buildings like this, conservative in style but modern in their construction, which would have been just as well suited to London or Liverpool.

The Bund, Shanghai, in the 1930s.
A display of thoroughly western architecture. The clock tower in the middle distance belongs to the Customs House.

458

Mainstream architectural history has always favoured the European Modernist or International style but Art Deco, its brasher, less intellectual cousin, was far more popular and successful. It spread all over the globe in the 1920s and 1930s and there are many fine examples in Shanghai. The Hungarian architect László Hudec, who worked in Shanghai from 1918 to 1945, was a fluent and productive Art Deco designer. His Park Hotel in Nanjing Road was the tallest building in the Far East when it was built in 1934, and the nearby Grand Theatre of 1933, which still survives in good condition, is as slick an exercise in 'Cinema Moderne' as anything in Europe or America. Hudec's 1938 house for the Chinese industrialist D. V. Wu might have been influenced by Erich Mendelsohn. Whether it is Art Deco or Modernist is hard to decide.

(Right) House for D. V. Wu, Shanghai. László Hudec, 1938. Hudec was stylistically versatile. This house is more Modernist than Art Deco.

(Above) Grand Theatre, Shanghai. László Hudec, 1933. A fine example of 'Cinema Moderne', well preserved and still in use.

(Left) Park Hotel, Shanghai. László Hudec, 1934. For some years this was the tallest building in the Far East.

Hybrid style

There is, then, no shortage of early-twentieth-century modern architecture in China but most of it is purely western. There was, however, a hybrid Chinese/western style that produced buildings of high quality throughout the twentieth century. Its practitioners were sometimes European or American, sometimes Chinese. The Peking Union Medical College, built in 1918 and still beautifully preserved in a turning off Beijing's main shopping street, was designed by the Chicago practice Shattuck and Hussey. Its two- and three-storey buildings combine western Beaux-Arts planning principles with traditional Chinese features, most obviously the upward-curving hipped roofs. But the courtyard layout, the insistent symmetry, the stepped and balustraded forecourt, and the little red-columned porches are obviously the result of close study and appreciation of traditional Chinese architecture.

Peking Union Medical College, Beijing. Shattuck and Hussey, 1918. Designed by a Chicago practice, combining Beaux-Arts planning principles with Chinese roofs.

Another American architect, Henry K. Murphy, competed with Shattock and Hussey to design buildings in China for American universities and charitable foundations. Murphy adopted the admirably modest aim of preserving as much as possible of traditional Chinese architectural form, introducing western adaptations only when absolutely necessary. He wanted to do for Chinese architecture what the Renaissance had done for western classicism, making it more adaptable without losing its spirit and essence.

Murphy built the Ginling College for Girls in Nanjing and important parts of the campus of Beijing University but his influence extended beyond his actual building commissions. Many native Chinese architects learnt their craft in his office and went on to form the nucleus of the emerging Chinese architectural profession. Almost all of them had attended European or American architecture schools. The University of Pennsylvania was the most popular. It offered a traditional Beaux-Arts training, which proved peculiarly sympathetic to would-be architects wanting to preserve something of the

discipline and dignity of traditional Chinese architecture. The few western scholars who have studied early twentieth-century Chinese architecture mostly agree that there is a hidden kinship between western neo-classicism and traditional Chinese architecture. They share certain characteristics – regularity, axiality, monumentality and a preference for tripartite single-storey elevations: base, column, roof. Perhaps these characteristics arise from the nature of traditional building materials such as wood and stone, the first suggesting a lightweight frame, the second massive walls. The western classical habit of building frame structures, or imitations of them, in stone is where the two traditions part company. But at a time when new materials like steel and reinforced concrete were becoming common, both traditions could enjoy a certain freedom in the relationship between style and construction.

Sun Yat-sen Mausoleum, Nanjing. Lu Yanzhi, 1929.
Lu Yanzhi was a graduate of Cornell University and had worked in the office of Henry K. Murphy.

The social and political turmoil of the 1920s in China produced a surprising number of large-scale architectural projects even outside the territories of the foreign concessions. In 1927 a new Nationalist government was established with its capital in Nanjing and the promotion of a Chinese modern architecture was part of its political agenda. A competition was held for the design of a mausoleum for Sun Yat-sen, the revolutionary leader and first president of the republic. The competition was won by Lu Yanzhi, a graduate of Cornell University who had worked in Murphy's office. His design combined a traditional Chinese memorial hall with a western classical-style domed tomb chamber. These buildings were placed on high ground above a wide, sloping assembly space designed to accommodate 50,000 people. Such openness was unknown in the Chinese tradition, which always favoured closed courtyards. The roof of the memorial hall, however, was unmistakably Chinese.

Henry K. Murphy was chief architectural advisor to the Nanjing government and it was one of his assistants, Dong Dayou, who in the early 1930s took charge of an ambitious project to create a new civic centre for Shanghai, to the north east of the foreign concessions. It was planned on Beaux-Arts principles with a cruciform layout of tree-lined boulevards, parks and monumental freestanding buildings, including a municipal administration building, a museum, a library and a stadium. The administration building at the head of the cross adopts the outline of a traditional Qing dynasty hall but converts it into a four-storey office block with unlit longitudinal corridors. Its structure is reinforced concrete, not timber. The library and museum are even freer in their use of Chinese forms. Traditionally the timber-framed hall is the primary element, resting on a masonry base, but in these buildings the priorities have been reversed. Their bases have grown tall and house most of the accommodation while the hall has shrunk to a token pavilion crowning the central section.

The brick and stone-clad structures that surround the stadium are thoroughly western in their general form but with Chinese details, such as the bracketed eaves between the buttresses of the main entrance. A strict Modernist might sneer at these attempts to adapt traditional Chinese architecture to modern purposes, but they are no less logical, and no less handsome, than mainstream western classical buildings of the period – Charles Holden's buildings for London University, for example, or the architecture of Paul Cret, head of the Department of Architecture at the University of Pennsylvania. The marriage of Beaux-Arts and Chinese traditions was in fact remarkably successful. Over 80 years on, these Shanghai buildings are all still in use, incorporated into various local institutions.

National Art Museum of China, Beijing. Dai Nianci, 1962. Multiple eaves and delicate colonnades grace a fundamentally modern plan.

Various versions of the hybrid 'National' style, often simply called 'Chinese roofs', continued to appear right up to the end of the twentieth century. In 1962, for example, Dai Nianci designed the National Art Museum of China in Beijing with multiple eaves and delicate colonnades. Fifty years later, the contents of the gallery are strictly censored, but the building, recently restored, has grown old gracefully.

Municipal Administration Building, Shanghai. Dong Dayou, 1932. Outwardly a Qing dynasty hall but actually an office building with a reinforced concrete frame.

In the 1930s Modernist buildings were rare even in Europe but there were already a few in China and not all of them designed by European immigrants. Chinese architects trained in America tended to regard Modernism not as a new direction for architecture but simply as a stylistic option. Dong Dayou, for example, built a thoroughly Modernist concrete house for himself in 1935. Yang Tingbao, who had made friends with Louis Kahn when they were both students at Penn, mixed Modernism with more traditional styles throughout his long and distinguished career. His Shenyang railway station of 1927 was a Beaux-Arts masterpiece, while his Sun Ke residence of 1948 was thoroughly Modernist.

In 1951 Yang Tingbao designed the Peace Hotel in Beijing, a plain but elegant Modernist composition that became the focus of a debate about the meaning of Modernism in the new communist state. As the influence of Soviet Socialist Realism grew, Modernism began to be regarded with suspicion. Even so, the Faculty of Architecture at Shanghai University in Beijing ran a Bauhaus-influenced course and was housed in a Modernist building by Ha Xiongwen and Huang Yulin completed in 1953. Chinese and western modernism may have looked the same, but they did not have the same meaning. It was not until the 1990s that a 'critical' Modernism, with all of its social, technological and ethical overtones, became established in China.

Faculty of Architecture, Tongji University, Shanghai. Ha Xiongwen and Huang Yulin, 1953. Full-blown Modernism – a style chosen from a number of options.

Discovered architectural heritage

If the concept of modern architecture is essentially western, then so too is the concept of architectural history. In China architecture was not considered a subject worthy of scholarly study until the mid-twentieth century. Its forms were developed by artisan craftsmen working in an ancient tradition passed down directly from master to apprentice. Innovation and progress were not valued or encouraged. There was no development to trace, no story for the historian to tell. But when those first few privileged members of the nascent Chinese architectural profession returned from their training in foreign universities, they realized that the architecture of their homeland was a vast unexplored territory.

In 1931, Liang Sicheng, who had studied with Paul Cret at the University of Pennsylvania from 1924 to 1928, set about exploring that territory systematically. His wife, Lin Huiyin, who would also have studied architecture at Penn had the course admitted female students, was his partner in the enterprise. They studied ancient building handbooks, especially the *Yingzao Fashi*, but more importantly they studied the buildings themselves, travelling around the country in often difficult and dangerous conditions, measuring, drawing, photographing and writing about the old buildings that they found. The oldest was a Buddhist temple, Foguang Si, in Shanxi province, built in 857AD. The fruits of this research were published in the quarterly *Bulletin of the Institute for Research in Chinese Architecture* and finally collected together as *A History of Chinese Architecture* in 1944. This book, of which Liang wrote an English version published many years later as *A Pictorial History of Chinese Architecture*, is completely western in spirit – an accurate, scientific analysis including plans, sections, elevations and construction details. It owes an obvious debt to Sir Banister Fletcher's famous *History of Architecture on the Comparative Method*, first published in 1896, which Liang had studied at Penn.

Political imperatives

Liang went on to become an influential figure in the development of mid-twentieth-century Chinese architecture. When the People's Republic of China was founded under Mao Zedong in 1949, Liang was called upon to design the new national emblem, which included an architectural elevation of the fifteenth-century Tiananmen building. He helped to formulate a policy for the development of Beijing as the new nation's capital, and to establish guidelines for a new architectural style appropriate to the communist state. In 1953 he visited Moscow and became the main channel of Soviet influence on government architectural policy. But it was a delicate balancing act.

In practice, the important policy decisions were taken by party officials untrained in architecture. Subtle theoretical arguments about tradition and modernity, style and appropriateness, were often ignored. In the matter of style, Liang's instinct was to promote a version of the National style favoured by the Nanjing regime, but the political colouring that this implied had to be very carefully shaded. A combination of traditional Chinese architecture with French/American neo-classicism was likely to be dismissed as mere bourgeois revivalism. On the other hand, abstract European Modernism was also regarded with suspicion.

Great Hall of the People, Beijing, China. Zhang Bo, 1959. A huge complex, including an auditorium that seats 10,000, stretches to match the vastness of Tiananmen Square.

It seemed to deny any possibility of monumentality or cultural celebration, and increasingly it was being identified with western capitalist institutions. When the necessary Soviet Socialist Realist ingredient was added to the mix the ironies and contradictions became almost comical. This 1957 statement of party policy is typical: 'We oppose revivalism, but not ideas of national form … we should develop new national forms that are not disconnected with history.'[1] These seem to be flat contradictions, but it had become dangerous to make unambiguous statements.

This kind of woolly thinking had tangible consequences nevertheless. As the tenth anniversary of the revolution approached, it was decreed that ten large public buildings would be built to prove the nation's maturity. Stylistically,

they were varied, reflecting the general ideological confusion. Some adopted a version of the National style. The Cultural Palace of Nationalities in Beijing, for example, by Liang's ex-student Zhang Bo, graced its well-proportioned central tower with Chinese roofs in a completely convincing manner. But the two most important buildings of the ten, the Great Hall of the People and the National Museum of China, on either side of Tiananmen Square, were inspired by western totalitarian architecture, from the Palace of Versailles to the Palace of the Soviets. The Great Hall, designed by a team including Zhang, is a huge complex containing a three-tier auditorium that seats 10,000. The museum opposite, designed by Zhang's friend and rival Zhang Kaiji, is slightly smaller but no less imposing. What dictated the scale and external appearance of these

(Opposite) Cultural Palace of Nationalities, Beijing. Zhang Bo, 1959. The Chinese roof, seen here undergoing renovation in 2012, seems a perfectly appropriate termination of the central tower.

(Right) National Museum of China, Beijing. Zhang Kaiji, 1959. No less imposing than the Great Hall on the other side of the square.

**The Forbidden City, the Imperial Palace, Beijing,
1420–1912.** The largest of its many courtyards is
dominated by the Hall of Supreme Harmony.

buildings was not their internal spaces and functions but the vastness of the square, measuring 880 by 500 metres (962 by 547 yards). And what dictated the size of the square was the whim of the party leader, who, looking out over the square from the Tiananmen building on the day of the inauguration of the People's Republic ten years earlier, had demanded that it should be big enough to accommodate a million people. Realistically it will accommodate perhaps a tenth of that number, but Mao's other ambition – that it should be the largest public square in the world – was comfortably realized. As an exercise in the manipulation of apparent scale, the two buildings are remarkably successful. Though only three or four storeys high they nevertheless command the open space like fearsome, crouching animals. Without them the square would be a mere blank; with them it becomes a recognizable urban form. There is a paradox inherent in this urban form. On the one hand it is freely accessible to everyone and therefore public. The actual use of the space,

however, is anything but free, as the protests of 1989 proved. But in 1959 this openness, formal if not political, was a powerful symbol of the nation and of its emergence into world politics.

Tiananmen Square is not a Chinese space but a Chinese version of a western space. It lies immediately south of the old imperial palace known as the Forbidden City, and is aligned with the axis of that vast complex, but is completely different in character. The Forbidden City, built by the Ming dynasty in the early fifteenth century, is the epitome of traditional Chinese architecture and planning. Its open spaces are all courtyards – enclosed, symmetrical, and orientated north–south in line with the main axis. Each courtyard is surrounded by a group of timber-framed halls, the biggest and most important standing in the middle of the north side. Every hall is conceived as part of its courtyard, not as a freestanding object. The largest courtyard, on the main axis, is dominated by the Hall of Supreme Harmony, which houses the emperor's throne. This is the epicentre of the complex, and of the whole city of Beijing. In imperial times, the heart of the city was inaccessible, a void. It symbolized the power of the emperor but it also symbolized the powerlessness of his subjects.

In its basic plan, the Forbidden City is no more than a very large version of a traditional Beijing house or *siheyuan*. These single-storey courtyard houses were ranged along narrow streets and alleyways known as *hutongs*, creating a uniform, carpet-like urban texture. The houses were inward looking, turning blank walls to the street. Many *hutong* districts survive today even in the central zone of the city, though almost all are under threat from voracious commercial development. Old Beijing was quite different from equivalent western capitals. It was low, uniform and non-hierarchical; its buildings had no facades, its streets were featureless alleyways and its centre was a void. Its plan was controlled by a rigid axis that extended far beyond the Forbidden City, but it was a conceptual rather than a visual axis. The palace from which it originated kept itself hidden.

Mao Zedong's Tiananmen Square supplied what the old city lacked. It was an open square, not a closed courtyard, and the palaces that flanked it were freestanding objects with facades designed to be seen. The Monument to the People's Heroes at the centre of the square was a gigantic version of a traditional Chinese stele, but its spatial effect was the same as the Egyptian obelisk in Piazza del Popolo or Nelson's Column in Trafalgar Square. Tiananmen Square symbolized

Mei Lanfang Memorial Hall, Beijing. A stately and well-preserved *siheyuan*, or courtyard house, the basic planning unit of old Beijing.

the arrival in the new China of the concept of a 'public', a population to be served rather than placed in servitude, whatever the underlying political reality.

By 1959, large parts of old Beijing had been destroyed, including its city walls and many of its ancient gates. The advice of conservatives like Liang Sicheng was ignored. Liang wanted to preserve the old city and build a new government centre in a western suburb; Mao wanted to fill the city with factories. Roads fit for motor vehicles had already been sliced through the old *hutong* districts in the early years of the century. Now they were straightened and widened, the main ones becoming multi-lane highways 100 metres (109 yards) wide. New radial roads and ring roads were built, cutting against the grain of the old city. Chang'an Avenue, which runs east–west between the Forbidden City and Tiananmen Square, was wide enough to accommodate a long but not interminable procession of 700,000 people on 1 October 1959, the tenth anniversary of the revolution.

A threatened discipline

In the 1960s it became increasingly difficult and dangerous to be any kind of intellectual in China. Architecture, especially architectural history and theory, became a threatened discipline. Even before Mao's declaration of the Great Proletarian Cultural Revolution in 1966, it was impossible to be 'critical' in any sense of the word as tolerance of free thought ebbed away. In 1965 history and theory were effectively abolished in architecture schools and the following year posters appeared denouncing Liang as a 'reactionary'. If there had been any opportunity for debate, 'functionalism versus monumentality' might have been an apt topic, but as it was the very concept of architecture was under suspicion because of its bourgeois roots. Some buildings were built, especially those that were essential to the maintenance of China's relationship with the outside world: airports, hotels and sports facilities. A few of them were undoubtedly works of architecture – a new airport for Nanjing, for example, by Yang Tingbao, and a new wing for the Beijing Hotel by Zhang Bo. Their style might be described as quietly Modernist, simple and austere.

The Cultural Revolution officially ended in 1969 but it was not until Mao's death and the arrest of the Gang of Four in 1976 that reform could begin in earnest under Deng Xiaoping. The 'functionalism versus monumentality' debate was resumed, although the difficult marriage of Chinese and western architectural traditions was too complicated to be summed up in a simple dichotomy. Peter G. Rowe and Seng Kuan put it succinctly: 'The Chinese, unlike those in the west, could never entirely accept the idea of an architecture constituted by its own substance, function and making.'[2] The idea was perhaps not entirely accepted in the west either, but it was at least understood as an ideal. In China, disbelief in abstract functionalism could never quite be suspended. There was a new richness of argument nevertheless. Western architectural theory was itself entering an expansive phase as Postmodernism and French critical theory began to question the limits of orthodox Modernism. Chinese architects and teachers now became aware of this development and began learning how to handle new ideas, even applying them tentatively in buildings. But the question of Chinese identity could not be ignored. In 1982 the famous Chinese-American architect I. M. Pei indicated a possible direction to follow in the Fragrant Hill Hotel near Beijing. Its abstract, linear ornament was Chinese in spirit and so was its general plan – two- to four-storey buildings linked together by arcades to form courtyards. It was greeted with great excitement and a conference was organized to discuss its implications.

Fragrant Hill Hotel, Beijing. I. M. Pei, 1982. A Chinese-American architect shows a possible way forward for Chinese modern architecture.

The response of native Chinese architects was cautious, especially in important public buildings like the National Library of China in Beijing, completed in 1987 and one of the largest libraries in the world. Many well-known designers were involved, including Yang Tingbao, Dai Nianci and Zhang Bo. Its plan is symmetrical and its profile is traditional, including shallow, hipped roofs, but its massing is well handled and clearly expressive of its function. A cluster of low blocks on the street frontage contains the reading rooms; behind rises a double tower, 17 storeys high, containing the book stacks. By the late 1980s housing design was being treated as architecture rather than merely pragmatic space packaging, and it was an architecture that acknowledged the tradition of the *siheyuan* and the *hutong*. The Ju'er Hutong housing project in Beijing by Wu Liangyong – a tight, three-storey apartment complex grouped around courtyards with white rendered walls and traditional tiled roofs – won a World Habitat Award in 1993. The architecture of the emerging commercial sector was perhaps less thoughtful but was keen to use up-to-date western technologies, especially the glass curtain wall, the first of which appeared on the Great Wall Hotel in Beijing, designed by Becket International and completed in 1983.

Deng Xiaoping

The Tiananmen Square protests of 1989, and their brutal suppression on 4 June, were a sign of the social and political consequences of Deng Xiaoping's attempt to combine a communist administration with a market-based economy. The architectural consequences were more benign but no less convulsive. Foreign investment and economic expansion in the 1990s triggered a building boom of ferocious intensity. Whole new cities were built

Hutong **in central Beijing.** New traditional housing for middle-class professionals and government officials.

in just a few years. Shenzen, one of five 'special economic zones', was a small village in 1979. By the end of the century its population was more than three million. Ten years later it was ten million. Its instant crop of skyscrapers, like a cartoon Manhattan, seemed to western observers to be completely devoid of architectural merit, but perhaps the sheer quantity of buildings made it impossible to appreciate any individual examples. In their book *Great Leap Forward*, published in 2001, Rem Koolhaas and his students at Harvard summed up the situation in a set of startling statistics. China, they

National Library of China, Beijing. Yang Tingbao, Dai Nianci and Zhang Bo, 1987. A traditional, symmetrical plan but competently handled in its massing.

(Above) Shenzen skyline. A small village in 1979, by 2010 a city of ten million people, and growing.

(Right) Shanghai Museum. Xing Tonghe, 1995. Maybe inspired by an ancient bronze cauldron, with handles at the cardinal points.

calculated, had one-tenth as many architects as the United States, but they were responsible for five times as much building. This made them 'the most important, influential and powerful architects on earth'.[3]

In architecturally mature cities like Shanghai, new public buildings seemed to strive more earnestly for architectural quality. The People's Park (the old racetrack) was provided with two museums and a theatre, all of them symmetrical, freestanding objects. The Shanghai Museum of 1995 by Xing Tonghe takes the form of a wheel hovering horizontally over a subdivided square base. It is said to have been inspired by an ancient bronze cauldron such as might be found among the museum's exhibits, and indeed it does appear to have four handles at the cardinal points.

Shanghai Grand Theatre. Jean-Marie Charpentier, 1998. A vague evocation of traditional Chinese forms by a French architect.

Placed on the north–south axis of the city hall, its heavy, pink-granite-clad form is a commanding presence in the park, but inside its symmetry is rather dull.

To the west of the city hall, the Shanghai Grand Theatre, completed in 1998, was designed by the French architect Jean-Marie Charpentier. Whether it is French or Chinese in spirit is hard to say. The huge upward-curving roof under which it shelters is vaguely reminiscent of traditional Chinese roof forms, but the building would not look out of place in La Défense or Montparnasse. The Grand Theatre's opposite number to the east of the city hall is the Shanghai Urban Planning Exhibition Center by the East China Architectural Design and Research Institute (ECADI), which records and celebrates the recent building of the new Shanghai in a combination of vast models and wordy wall displays. The building that houses it is provided with yet another interesting roof, this time in the form of four upside-down pyramids, whose function seems to be mainly decorative. The city hall itself is an austerely symmetrical 19-storey tower by the Shanghai Institute of Architectural Design and Research (SIADR).

But Shanghai also has its quota of meaningless, shape-making skyscrapers. Some are obviously inspired by western styles like Postmodernism or Deconstructivism, others look like spaceships, or propelling pencils, or bottle openers. The replanning of the Pudong district of the city, across the river from the Bund, was the subject of an international competition that attracted entries from Richard Rogers and Toyo Ito among others. In the event, none was adopted, or rather all were adopted in an amalgamated, compromise scheme.

Shanghai Urban Planning Exhibition Center. ECADI, 2000. Another umbrella roof, decorative but of uncertain function.

(Above) Pudong district of Shanghai. A sparse forest of skyscrapers competing for attention.

(Top right) Jin Mao Tower, Pudong. Skidmore, Owings and Merrill, 1999. The terrifyingly vertiginous hotel atrium. Each ring is a floor.

The result is a kind of sparse forest of skyscrapers, all competing for attention, none quite succeeding in capturing it. At 420 metres (1,380 feet), the Jin Mao Tower by Skidmore, Owings and Merrill, completed in 1999, is one of the highest. It tries hard to look Chinese by dressing itself in an approximation of the form of the Kaifeng pagoda in Henan. The upper part of the tower is a Hyatt hotel, which wraps itself round a nightmarish 34-storey circular atrium. The building would be awe-inspiring if it stood alone, but in 2008 its record height was topped by its very close neighbour, the Shanghai World Financial Center, designed by Kohn Pederson Fox. This is the skyscraper with a top like a bottle opener.

There was a danger in the 1990s that amid the commercial glitz and bombast all those attempts from 1911 onwards to reconcile the western and Chinese traditions would be forgotten. The 'Chinese roof' style continued, however, in important public buildings like Beijing West railway station of 1996 by Zhu Jialu, which crowns a gigantic multi-storey stone arch with traditional Chinese pavilions designed originally to accommodate a railway museum. The work of Zhang Jinqiu, China's most important female architect, is

Jin Mao Tower (right), Skidmore, Owings and Merrill, 1999, and Shanghai World Financial Center. Kohn Pederson Fox, 2008. Two big American architectural practices with different ideas about the appropriate form for a Chinese skyscraper.

more thoroughgoing and convincing. Zhang was a student of Liang Sicheng in Beijing in the 1950s. In 1966 she was sent to work at the North-Western Institute of Architectural Design in Xi'an and has remained there, becoming chief architect in 1987. Her Shaanxi History Museum of 1991 is a scholarly reinterpretation of Tang dynasty architecture in modern materials, while her Bell and Drum Tower Plaza project in Xi'an integrates the two Ming dynasty structures with a new park on the roof of an underground shopping centre.

(Above left) Shaanxi History Museum, Xi'an. Zhang Jinqiu, 1991. A scholarly interpretation of Tang dynasty architecture by a student of Liang Sicheng.

National Grand Theatre, Beijing. Paul Andreu, 2007. The enveloping dome sits in the middle of an artificial lake behind the Great Hall of the People (left).

Beijing Olympics

If the relationship between Chinese and western architecture in the twentieth century was a long engagement then the Beijing Olympics of 2008 was the marriage ceremony. But first there was a dress rehearsal: the 1998 competition for the design of the National Grand Theatre, on the block immediately to the west of Tiananmen Square. The competition was won by the French architect Paul Andreu, working in collaboration with Tsinghua University.

The building, completed in 2007, hides an opera house, a concert hall and a theatre under a huge flattened glass-and-titanium-clad dome. The dome sits in the middle of a small lake, like a treacle pudding on a plate, and is entered via a long, axial, glass-roofed, underwater corridor. The auditoriums themselves are relatively conventional. The design was controversial and work was halted for a while in 2000 by a protest from the Chinese Academy of Sciences. But this was just the beginning of a long-term global image-building project the point of which would become clear after 2001, when China joined the World Trade Organization and won the Olympic bid. More international competitions were announced for an array of big projects. The most important of these

were the Olympic stadium, won by Herzog & de Meuron, the China Central Television (CCTV) headquarters, won by Rem Koolhaas and OMA, and the Beijing Capital airport extension, won by Norman Foster. Of these three, Foster's airport is the most conventional, though this is perhaps an odd word to describe what is said to be the largest covered structure ever built. But it is clearly a development of earlier designs – Hong

Beijing Capital International Airport. Norman Foster, 2008. Maybe the largest covered structure ever built, it was completed in only four years.

Kong's Chek Lap Kok airport of 1998 (see page 360), and before that the enormously influential Stansted airport of 1991. The basic idea is to hide all the messy mechanical services under the floor, leaving the roof unencumbered and free to express itself. At Beijing the roof is a vast but delicate space-frame, 3 kilometres (2 miles) long, rising and falling like the swell of the sea as it accommodates itself to the double-Y plan shape. The approved metaphor is not marine, however, but mythological. This is meant to be a Chinese dragon, complete with scales in the form of triangular roof-lights. The colour scheme is Chinese too: red and gold like the Forbidden City. These Chinese features may be superficial but they are important nevertheless as polite acknowledgements of deep-seated cultural preferences. And although Foster must take credit for the uplifting architecture, the speed and efficiency of its construction was entirely Chinese. To build an airport bigger than Heathrow in only four years was an epic technical and managerial achievement.

Olympic stadium, Beijing. Herzog & de Meuron with Ai Weiwei, 2008. The structure of the bird's nest is not as random as it looks. There are hidden regularities.

The design of the Olympic stadium was a collaboration between Herzog & de Meuron and the Chinese artist Ai Weiwei. The Swiss practice had some experience of stadium design, notably their Allianz football stadium in Munich completed in 2005, but their reputation was based on sober, serious-minded buildings, mainly art galleries (see Chapter 31). The collaboration with Ai was therefore a genuine partnership rather than a mere politic arrangement. In any case, Ai was hardly an establishment figure and his dissident tendencies would eventually lead to his arrest in 2011. It was Ai that contributed the 'bird's nest' idea – a tangle of external steel members supporting the roof over the concrete amphitheatre. It represented that disorderly aspect of Chinese culture that surfaces in its garden design, its ceramics and perhaps in the spontaneity of its calligraphy. In fact, the bird's nest is not as disorderly as it looks. There are regularly spaced vertical and diagonal supports hidden in the apparently random texture. But it could not have been designed without the help of new computer software developed by the engineers Ove Arup and Partners, who were the consultants on all of these big projects. The bird's-nest image was perfectly judged, conveying a message of relaxed, friendly innovation to

balance the militaristic order of the spectacular opening ceremony of the Olympics.

Rem Koolhaas and OMA's CCTV building, sited out on the third ring road to the east of the city centre, did not form part of the Olympic image but it was probably the most important of these buildings in the eyes of the global architectural community. Whereas the airport was the child of known parents and the stadium was recognizably a stadium, the CCTV building was like nothing anybody had seen before. It was neither skyscraper nor groundscraper, it owed allegiance to no recognizable architectural tradition and it was curiously scaleless, as if it could as well be a personal trinket as an urban monument. Its looped form, like a clunky Moebius strip, suggests a connectedness and

continuity quite different from the simple layered stack of the conventional skyscraper. But looked at another way it is really no more than two skyscrapers linked by a podium at the bottom and a bridge at the top. The podium contains studios and production facilities, the smaller 44-storey tower contains the news departments, the larger 54-storey tower contains the business departments, and the cantilevered L-shaped bridge contains the administrative departments. Whether the loop form actually facilitates communication between these departments is doubtful but perhaps just the knowledge that it is possible to travel continuously round the building without changing direction is enough to transform the experience of its interior. The apparently abstract patterns made by the external curtain wall are meant to reflect the varying stresses in the underlying structure, but no-one

China Central Television (CCTV) building, Beijing. Rem Koolhaas, 2008. The possibility of continuous travel around the building without changing direction may change users' perceptions.

would guess. They are perhaps meant as compensation for the building's scalelessness and complete lack of tectonic expression. It was officially opened on 1 January 2008 but its full occupation was delayed by a fire in the Television Cultural Centre next door, also designed by OMA, and it remained empty until 2012.

These four buildings, including the National Grand Theatre, all have one thing in common: they are simple, unified forms and therefore easily recognizable. Metaphorically they are objects you could pick up and move around: a pudding, a dragon, a bird's nest and pair of boxer shorts (the Beijing taxi drivers' name for the CCTV building). One might argue that this bold simplicity is essentially Chinese. Could they have been built at any other time and in any other place? But the one-off form is a comparative rarity in architecture, whether western or Chinese, classical or modern, and it is a poor basis for any architectural style or tradition. In the long run it is the everyday modern architecture of China that will affect people's lives most profoundly.

Many Chinese architectural practices are large state-sponsored organizations such as ECADI (East China Architectural Design and Research Institute), CAG (China Architecture Design and Research Group) and SIADR (Shanghai Institute of Architectural Design and Research). But since the early 1990s it has been possible to set up independent small practices and many talented young architects have grasped the opportunity. Some, but not all, were trained in the West and like their counterparts in

Europe and America have adopted 'critical' and artistic rather than commercial values. A few, such as Cui Kai, Ma Qingyun and Yung Ho Chang, have begun to develop a truly Chinese modernism and to establish international reputations.

Wang Shu, whose practice, called Amateur Architecture Studio, is based in Hangzhou, is a leader of this new tendency. He trained at the Nanjing Institute of Technology in the late 1980s before undertaking research into the renovation of old buildings. He then worked for ten years with builders and craftsmen rather than purely in design. His architecture shows the effect of these experiences – by no means historicist but often making use of traditional materials and modern interpretations of traditional forms. One of his biggest projects is the China Academy of Art's Xiangshan campus in Hangzhou, the second phase of which was completed in 2007. There are 21 new buildings on the campus, including a library, a museum, studios and student residences. Forms and materials vary from building to building. There are big, upward-curving tiled roofs, Le Corbusier-inspired *brises-soleil*, perforated concrete walls of which Kahn might have approved, and external ramps and stairs that faintly recall Aalto. But the eclecticism that this description suggests is tempered by a limited range of skilfully handled materials and the result is a confident, craftsman-like architecture of a kind that is beginning to be recognized and admired the world over. In 2012 Wang won the prestigious Pritzker Prize. Chinese modern architecture had arrived at last.

China Academy of Art, Xiangshan campus, Hangzhou. Wang Shu, 2007. Chinese modern architecture at last attains its 'critical' maturity.

Chinese traditional architecture

The indigenous architecture of China is the longest continuous building tradition in existence. From a western point of view its static nature is puzzling. In the western way of thinking, progress is taken for granted; circumstances change, technologies improve, taste and fashion are hungry for newness. But traditional Chinese architecture has not changed in any important respect for more than a thousand years. This does not mean that it is primitive. It is a highly sophisticated art. But its social and intellectual foundations do not include a concept of technological progress. And where there is no progress, there can be no history.

Another important difference between Chinese and western traditions concerns the question of function. One might argue that even in western architecture the concept of function in the sense of 'human use' emerged relatively recently, but it is nevertheless central to our idea of what 'architecture' means. For example, we often categorize buildings by their function: churches, palaces, factories, railway stations, houses. They take different forms because they house different functions. But in traditional Chinese architecture, a temple, a house and a palace are formally very similar. Buildings are distinguished from one another by size and rank rather than by function. The Forbidden City in Beijing is a large and lavish version of the ordinary houses that surround it.

The third important difference between Chinese and western traditions concerns the question of authorship. The designers of traditional Chinese buildings were not 'architects' in the western sense. Perhaps we should not even call them 'designers' if 'design' means the rational ordering of form for a specific purpose. The men in charge of building projects worked within the narrow confines of a tradition that was handed down from master to apprentice and codified in government regulations. Innovation was not part of their job. They had no personal reputations to build or protect. They were anonymous craftsmen.

Apart from special religious buildings such as pagodas, Chinese architecture is mainly horizontal. Its typical form is the single-storey hall, with a modular timber frame, a hipped roof and, on high-ranking buildings, an elaborate bracketed eaves painted in bright colours. Halls are almost always grouped round an inward-looking courtyard or *siheyuan*, which is the basic planning unit. Courtyards are usually orientated north–south in accordance with *feng shui* (literally 'wind and water'), a set of half-practical, half-mystical rules for the positioning of buildings. Although the entrance to a *siheyuan* is often at the south-east corner, the overall plan is usually symmetrical about a north–south axis, like the Forbidden City.

The Forbidden City, Beijing. The Hall of Supreme Harmony at the centre of the Forbidden City is the building that dictated the plan and architecture of old Beijing.

NOTES

Chapter 1

1 Nikolaus Pevsner, *Pioneers of Modern Design,* Yale University Press, 2005, p.92.
2 Robert Schmutzler, *Art Nouveau,* H. N. Abrams, 1962, pp.102–104.
3 Charles Jencks, *The Language of Post-modern Architecture,* Rizzoli, 1977, p.98.
4 Nikolaus Pevsner, *Pioneers of Modern Design,* Yale University Press, 2005, p.137.
5 Robert Schmutzler, *Art Nouveau,* H. N. Abrams, 1962, p.244.
6 Otto Wagner, *Modern Architecture: A Guidebook for Students to This Field of Art,* Diane Publishing Company, 2003.
7 Richard Weston, *Plans, Sections and Elevations: Key Buildings of the Twentieth Century,* Laurence King, 2004, p.28.
8 Ulrich Conrads, *Programmes and Manifestoes on 20th Century Architecture,* MIT Press, 1970, p.19.
9 Reyner Banham, *Theory and Design in the First Machine Age,* MIT Press, 1980, p.89.
10 Kenneth Frampton, *Modern Architecture, a Critical History,* Thames & Hudson, Fourth Edition, 2007, p.92.

Chapter 2

1 Hermann Muthesius, Dennis Sharp, ed., *The English House,* BSP Professional Books, 1987, p.10.
2 In a letter to *the Architects' Journal,* quoted in Thomas Sherrer Ross Boase, *English Art 1870–1940,* Clarenden Press, 1978, p.121.
3 C. F. A. Voysey, *Ideas in Things,* in Thomas Raffles Davison, *The Arts Connected With Building,* Batsford, 1909 and Forgotten Books, 2013, p.108.
4 Reyner Banham, *Theory and Design in the First Machine Age,* MIT Press, 1980, p.47.
5 *Country Life,* Volume 28, 1910, p.60.
6 Quoted in Alan Crawford, *C. R. Ashbee: Architect, Designer and Romantic Socialist,* Yale University Press, 2005, p.98
7 Bruce Brooks Pfeiffer, ed., *The Essential Frank Lloyd Wright: Critical Writings on Architecture,* Princeton University Press, 2008, p.38.
8 Quoted in Alan Crawford, op. cit., p.155.
9 Gustav Stickley, *More Craftsman Homes,* Craftsman Publishing Company, 1912, p.2.

Chapter 3

1 Henry-Russell Hitchcock, *Architecture: Nineteenth and Twentieth Centuries,* Yale University Press, 1977, p.533.
2 Quoted in Marja-Riitta Norri, Elina Standerskjöld, Wilfried Wang, *Finland: 20th-Century Architecture,* Prestel, 2000, p.125.
3 Quoted in Reyner Banham, *Theory and Design in the First Machine Age,* MIT Press, 1980, p.141.
4 Ibid. p.24.

Chapter 4

1 Adrian Forty, *Concrete and Culture: A Material History,* Reaktion Books, 2013.
2 Louis Sullivan, Robert Twombly, *The Public Papers,* University of Chicago Press, 1988, p.111.
3 The entire 'Messagio' is quoted in Reyner Banham, *Theory and Design in the First Machine Age,* MIT Press, 1980, p.128.
4 Ibid. p.135.
5 Kenneth Frampton, *Modern Architecture, a Critical History,* Thames & Hudson, Fourth Edition, 2007, p.86.

Chapter 5

1 Quoted in W. Hawkins Ferry, *The Legacy of Albert Kahn,* Wayne State University Press, 1970, p.19.
2 Reyner Banham, *A Concrete Atlantis,* MIT Press, 1986, p.86.
3 Quoted in W. Hawkins Ferry, op. cit., p.21.
4 Henry Jonas Magaziner, 'Working for a Genius: My Time with Albert Kahn', *APT Bulletin,* Vol. 32, No. 2/3 (2001), pp.59–64.
5 See Reyner Banham, *Theory and Design in the First Machine Age,* MIT Press, 1980, Chapter 5.

Chapter 6

6 Tom Wolfe, *From Bauhaus to Our House,* Bantam Books, 1999.
7 Stanford Anderson, 'Deutscher Werkbund – The 1914 Debate: Hermann Muthesius versus Henry van de Velde', in Ben Farmer, Hentie J. Louw, *Companion to Contemporary Architectural Thought,* Taylor and Francis, 1993, pp.462–467.
8 The memorandum is quoted in full in *Gropius at Twenty-Six, Architectural Review,* July 1961, pp.49–51.
9 Reyner Banham, *A Concrete Atlantis,* MIT Press, 1986, pp.194–215.

Chapter 6

1 Quoted in Maristella Casciato, *The Amsterdam School,* 010 Publishers, 1996, p.142.
2 Quoted in Tim Benton, Charlotte Benton, Dennis Sharp, *Expressionism,* Open University Press, 1975, p.62.

Chapter 7

1 Sigfried Giedion, *Space, Time and Architecture,* Harvard University Press, 2008, p.426.
2 Reyner Banham, *Theory and Design in the First Machine Age,* MIT Press, 1980, p.164.
3 Tom Wolfe, *From Bauhaus to Our House,* Bantam Books, 1999, p.53.
4 Quoted in Richard Weston, *Plans, Sections and Elevations: Key Buildings of the Twentieth Century,* Laurence King, 2004, p.52. See also: K. Beekman, Jan de Vries, *Avant-Garde and Criticism,* Rodopi, 2007, p.31.

Chapter 8

1 Quoted in Kenneth Frampton, *Modern Architecture, a Critical History,* Thames & Hudson, Fourth Edition, 2007, p.126.
2 Quoted in Franz Schulze, Edward Windhorst, *Mies van der Rohe: A Critical Biography,* University of Chicago Press, 2012, p.99.
3 Sigfried Giedion, *Space, Time and Architecture,* Harvard University Press, 2008, p.696.
4 Henry Russell Hitchcock, Philip Johnson, *The International Style: Architecture Since 1922,* W. W. Norton, 1932, p.95.

Chapter 9

1 The title of the latest edition in English is *Toward an Architecture,* a new translation edited by Jean-Louis Cohen, Getty Publications, 2007.
2 Colin Davies, *The Prefabricated Home,* Reaktion Books, 2005.
3 See Colin Rowe, *The Mathematics of the Ideal Villa and other Essays,* MIT Press, 1982.

Chapter 10

1 From 'The New Era', an essay written by Mies van der Rohe in 1930, quoted in Kenneth Frampton, *Modern Architecture, a Critical History,* Thames & Hudson, Fourth Edition, 2007, p.166.
2 The memories were prompted by a Frank Lloyd Wright exhibition at the Museum of Modern Art in 1940. Quoted in Vincent Scully, Neil Levine, *Modern Architecture and Other Essays,* Princeton University Press, 2003, p.57.
3 The account of Behrens's remark is usually attributed to Philip Johnson. See Alan Windsor's review of Wolf Tegethoff's book, *Mies van der Rohe: Die Villen und Landhausprojekte* in *Burlington Magazine,* Vol. 125, No. 964, July 1983, p.430.

Chapter 11

1 Selim Khan-Magomedov, *Pioneers of Soviet Architecture,* Thames & Hudson, 1987, pp.260–264.

Chapter 12

1 *Frank Lloyd Wright: An Autobiography,* Pomegranate, 2005, p.187.
2 Neil Levine, *The Architecture of Frank Lloyd Wright,* Princeton University Press, 1996, p.124.
3 *Frank Lloyd Wright: An Autobiography,* Pomegranate, 2005, p.234.

Chapter 13

1 See Bevis Hillier, *Art Deco of the 20s and 30s,* Studio Vista, 1973.
2 Le Corbusier, *The Decorative Art of Today,* MIT Press, 1987.

3 See Charlotte Benton, Tim Benton, Ghislaine Wood, *Art Deco 1910–1939,* Harry N. Abrams, 2015.
4 Quoted in David Ward, Oliver Zunz, *The Landscape of Modernity: New York City, 1900–1940,* Johns Hopkins University Press, 1987, p.172.

Chapter 14
1 See Léon Krier, 'Albert Speer: Architecture, 1932–1942', Archives d'Architecture Moderne, 1985.
2 Quoted in Robert Grant Irving, 'Architecture for Empire's Sake: Lutyens's Palace for Delhi', *Perspecta,* Vol. 18, 1982, p.9.
3 Nikolaus Pevsner, Bridget Cherry, *The Buildings of England: London, Vol. I,* Penguin Books, 1973, p.182.
4 Albert Speer, *Inside the Third Reich,* Simon and Schuster, 1970, p.102.

Chapter 15
1 Strictly speaking, the title of the exhibition was *Modern Architecture: International Exhibition. The International Style* was the title of the accompanying publication.

Chapter 17
1 James Stirling, 'Garches and Jaoul: Le Corbusier as Domestic Architect in 1927 and 1953', *The Architectural Review,* September 1955, p.145.
2 Colin Davies, *The Prefabricated Home,* Reaktion Books, 2005, pp.90–94.
3 Beatriz Colomina, *Privacy and Publicity: Modern Architecture as Mass Media,* MIT Press, 1996, pp.82–100.

Chapter 18
1 See Demetri Porphyrios, *Sources of Modern Eclecticism: Studies on Alvar Aalto,* Academy Editions, 1982.
2 Alvar Aalto, *Synopsis,* Birkhäuser, 1970, p.16.
3 See, for example, Kenneth Frampton, *Modern Architecture, a Critical History,* Thames & Hudson, Fourth Edition, 2007, p.197.
4 Reyner Banham, *The Age of the Masters: A Personal View of Modern Architecture,* Architectural Press, 1975, p.136.
5 Richard Weston, *Alvar Aalto,* Phaidon, 1997, p.224.

Chapter 19
1 Nikolaus Pevsner, *An Outline of European Architecture,* Pelican, 1981, p.15.

Chapter 21
1 Reyner Banham, *The New Brutalism: Ethic or Aesthetic?,* Architectural Press, 1966, p.10.
2 Ibid. pp.45–46.
3 Alison and Peter Smithson, 'Robin Hood Gardens, London E14', *Architectural Design,* No. 9, 1972, p.569.

Chapter 22
1 Reyner Banham, *The Architecture of the Well-Tempered Environment,* Architectural Press, 1969, p.12.
2 Kenneth Frampton, John Cava, *Studies in Tectonic Culture: The Poetics of Construction in Nineteenth and Twentieth Century Architecture,* Graham Foundation, 1995, p.238.

Chapter 23
1 Hassan Fathy, *Architecture for the Poor: An Experiment in Rural Egypt,* University of Chicago Press, 2010.
2 James Steele, Balkrishna V. Doshi, *The Complete Architecture of Balkrishna Doshi: Rethinking Modernism for the Developing World,* Whitney Library of Design, 1996, p.153.
3 Charles Correa, *A Place in the Shade: The New Landscape and Other Essays,* Penguin Books India, 2010, p.35.

Chapter 24
1 Charles Jencks, George Baird, *Meaning in Architecture,* G. Brazilier, 1970, pp.11–25.
2 Charles Jencks, *The Language of Post-Modern Architecture,* Rizzoli, 1977, p.17.
3 MoMA, *Five Architects,* Wittenborn, 1972, p.1964.
4 Charles Jencks, *The New Paradigm in Architecture: The Language of Post-Modernism,* Yale University Press, 2002, p.151.

Chapter 25
1 Aldo Rossi, Peter Eisenman, *The Architecture of the City,* MIT Press, 1982, pp.46–48.
2 'Mario Botta in conversation with Laurent Stalder', *AA Files,* No. 63, Architectural Assocation, 2011, p.113.
3 Oswald Mathias Ungers, *Architecture as Theme,* Electa, 1982.
4 Léon Krier, 'The Reconstruction of the European City: Outline for a Charter', in 'Léon Krier Drawings 1967–1980', Archives d'Architecture Moderne, 1980, p.XXV.
5 'Léon Krier Talks to Colin Davies', in 'Léon Krier Drawings 1967–1980', Archives d'Architecture Moderne, 1980, pp.XVII–XXIV.
6 The full text is available at www.princeofwales.gov.uk.
7 Colin Rowe, Fred Koetter, *Collage City,* MIT Press, 1983, p.49.

Chapter 27
1 Arata Isozaki, David B. Stewart, *Arata Isozaki: Four Decades of Architecture,* Universe, 1998, p.34.
2 Ibid. p.72.
3 See Kisho Kurokawa, *The Philosophy of Symbiosis,* Academy Editions, 1994.
4 Available to download from the library of Washington University in St Louis: http:/library.wustl.edu/wp-content/uploads/2015/04/maki-entire.pdf

Chapter 28
1 See Philip Johnson, Mark Wigley, *Deconstructivist Architecture,* Museum of Modern Art, 1988.
2 Daniel Libeskind, *Jewish Museum, Berlin,* G+B Arts International, 1999.
3 Matt Tyrnauer, 'Architecture in the Age of Gehry', in *Vanity Fair,* August 2010.

Chapter 29
1 Rem Koolhaas, *Junkspace,* 2001, available at: www.readingdesign.org/junkspace
2 Rem Koolhaas, Bruce Mau, Jennifer Sigler, Hans Werlemann, *S,M,L,XL,* Monacelli Press, 1998, p.1174.
3 Ibid. p.1184.
4 *Lagos Wide and Close: An Interactive Journey into an Exploding City,* available at: http:/lagos.submarinechannel.com/
5 Veronique Patteeuw, ed. *Considering Rem Koolhaas and the Office of Metropolitan Architecture,* NAi Publishers, 2005, p.31.

Chapter 30
1 See Reyner Banham, *The Architecture of the Well-Tempered Environment,* Architectural Press, 1969, Chapter 12.
2 David Jenkins, ed., *Norman Foster: Works 4,* Foster and Partners and Prestel Verlag, 2004, p.344.
3 See: Peter Buchanan, *Ten Shades of Green: Architecture and the Natural World,* Architectural League of New York, 2005.

Chapter 31
1 Richard Meier, *Building the Getty,* University of California Press, 1999, p.39.
2 Jean Nouvel, Michael Juul Holm, *Louisiana Manifesto,* Louisiana Museum of Modern Art, 2008, p.183.
3 Peter Zumthor, *Peter Zumthor,* a+u Publishing Company, 1998, p.14.
4 Emmanuel Petit, 'Interview: Steven Holl', *Architectural Review,* 4th March 2013.

Chapter 32
1 From the text that accompanied Cook and Fournier's original Kunsthaus Graz competition entry.
2 See Patrik Schumacher, *Parametricism 2.0: Rethinking Archtecture's Agenda for the 21st Century AD,* John Wiley and Sons, 2016.
3 Irénée Scalbert, 'Foreign Office Architects: Yokohama International Port Terminal', *AA Files,* No. 30, Autumn 1995, pp.86–87.

Chapter 33
1 Quoted in Jianfei Zhu, *Architecture of Modern China: A Historical Critique,* Routledge, 2013, p.93.
2 Peter G. Rowe, Seng Kuan, *Architectural Encounters with Essence and Form in Modern China,* MIT Press, 2004, p.124.
3 Chuihua Judy Chung, Jeffrey Inaba, Rem Koolhaas, Bernard Chang, Sze Tsung Leong, *Great Leap Forward,* Harvard Design School, 2001, p.161.

BIBLIOGRAPHY

General histories of modern architecture

Banham, Reyner, *Age of the Masters: A Personal View of Modern Architecture,* Architectural Press, 1975.

Banham, Reyner, *Theory and Design in the First Machine Age,* Architectural Press, 1962.

Benevolo, Leonardo, *History of Modern Architecture,* Routledge & Kegan Paul, 1971.

Blundell Jones, Peter, *Modern Architecture Through Case Studies,* Architectural Press, 2002.

Blundell Jones, Peter, and Eamonn Canniffe, *Modern Architecture Through Case Studies 1945–1990,* Routledge, 2012.

Cohen, Jean-Louis, *The Future of Architecture Since 1889,* Phaidon, 2012.

Colquhoun, Alan, *Modern Architecture,* Oxford University Press, 2002.

Conrads, Ulrich, ed., *Programmes and Manifestoes on 20th Century Architecture,* Lund Humphries, 1970.

Curtis, William J. R., *Modern Architecture Since 1900,* 3rd Revised Edition, Phaidon, 1996.

Davies, Colin, *Plans, Sections and Elevations: Key Houses of the Twentieth Century,* Laurence King, 2006.

Frampton, Kenneth, *Modern Architecture 1851–1945,* Rizzoli, 1983.

Frampton, Kenneth, *Modern Architecture: A Critical History,* 4th Revised Edition, Thames & Hudson, 2007.

Frampton, Kenneth, edited by John Cava, *Studies in Tectonic Culture: The Poetics of Construction in Nineteenth and Twentieth Century Architecture,* MIT Press, 1995.

Giedion, Sigfried, *Space, Time and Architecture: The Growth of a New Tradition,* 5th Revised Edition, Oxford University Press, 1967.

Hitchcock, Henry Russell, *Architecture 19th and 20th Centuries,* 3rd Revised Edition, Penguin, 1968.

Pevsner, Nikolaus, *Pioneers of Modern Design,* 4th Revised Edition, Yale University Press, 2005.

Scully, Vincent, *Modern Architecture: The Architecture of Democracy,* Revised Edition, Brazilier, 1974.

Weston, Richard, *Plans, Sections and Elevations: Key Buildings of the Twentieth Century,* 2nd Edition, Laurence King, 2010.

Wolfe, Tom, *From Bauhaus to Our House,* Cape, 1982.

Chapter 01

Benton, Tim and Charlotte, eds., *Architecture and Design, 1890–1939: An International Anthology of Original Articles,* Whitney Library of Design, 1975.

Crawford, Alan, *Charles Rennie Mackintosh,* Thames & Hudson, 1995.

Davey, Peter, *Arts and Crafts Architecture,* Phaidon, 1997.

Dernie, David and Alastair Carew-Cox, *Victor Horta,* Academy Editions, 1995.

Descharnes, Robert and Clovis Prévost, *Gaudi, The Visionary,* Viking Press, 1982.

Geretsegger, Heinz, *Otto Wagner 1841–1918,* Pall Mall Press, 1970.

Gresleri, Giuliano, *Joseph Hoffmann,* Rizzoli, 1985.

Howarth, Thomas, *Charles Rennie Mackintosh and the Modern Movement,* Routledge, 1997.

Latham, Ian, *Joseph Maria Olbrich,* Rizzoli, 1980.

Long, Christopher, 'The Origins and Context of Adolf Loos's Ornament and Crime', *Journal of the Society of Architectural Historians,* Vol. 68, No. 2 (June 2009), pp.200–223.

Macleod, Robert, *Style and Society: Architectural Ideology in Britain, 1835–1914,* RIBA, 1971.

Rheims, Maurice, *Hector Guimard,* H. N. Abrams, 1988.

Russell, Frank, *Art Nouveau Architecture,* Rizzoli, 1979.

Schmutzler, Robert, *Art Nouveau,* H. N. Abrams, 1962.

Wang, Wilfried, Yahuda Safran, *The Architecture of Adolf Loos,* Arts Council of Great Britain, 1985.

Rainer Zerbst, Gaudi: The Complete Buildings, Taschen, 1988.

Chapter 02

Amery, Colin, Margaret Richardson, Gavin Stamp, *Lutyens* (exhibition catalogue), Hayward Gallery, 1981.

Crawford, Alan, C. R. Ashbee: *Architect, Designer and Romantic Socialist,* Yale University Press, 2005.

Crawford, Alan, 'Ten Letters from Frank Lloyd Wright to Charles Robert Ashbee', *Architectural History,* Vol. 13, 1970, pp.64–76, 132.

Creese, Walter, Parker and Unwin, 'Architects of Totality', *Journal of the Society of Architectural Historians,* Vol. 22, No. 3, October 1963, pp.161–170.

Davies, Colin, *The Prefabricated Home,* Reaktion, 2005.

Futagawa, Yukio, text by Bruce Brooks Pfeiffer, *Frank Lloyd Wright: Prairie Houses,* A. D. A. Edita Tokyo, 2002.

Hitchcock, Henry Russell, *In the Nature of Materials 1887–1914: The Buildings of Frank Lloyd Wright,* Da Capo Press, 1942.

Hitchmough, Wendy, *Charles F. A. Voysey,* Phaidon, 1997.

Morse, Edward, *Japanese Homes and their Surroundings,* Courier Corporation, 2012.

Muthesius, Hermann, translated by Janet Seligman, *The English House,* BSP Professional Books, 1987.

Saint, Andrew, *Richard Norman Shaw,* Yale University Press, 2010.

Skelton, Tim, *Lutyens and the Great War,* Frances Lincoln, 2008.

Stickley, Gustav, *Craftsman Homes and More Craftsman Homes,* Courier Corporation, 2012.

Turner, Paul Venable, 'Frank Lloyd Wright and the Young Le Corbusier', *Journal of the Society of Architectural Historians,* Vol. 42, No. 4, December 1983, pp.350–359.

Weaver, Laurence, 'Houses and Gardens by E. L. Lutyens', *Country Life,* 1914.

Winter, Robert, Alexander Vertikoff, *Craftsman Style,* Harry N. Abrams, 2004.

Wright, Frank Lloyd, *The Essential Frank Lloyd Wright: Critical Writings on Architecture,* Princeton University Press, 2010.

Chapter 03

Caldenby, Claes, Jöran Lindvall, Wilfried Wang eds., *Sweden: 20th Century Architecture,* Prestel, 1998.

Cret, Paul P., 'The Ecole des Beaux-Arts and Architectural Education', *Journal of the American Society of Architectural Historians,* Vol. 1, No. 2, April 1941, pp.3–15.

Davey, Peter, 'Holland House: Born in the USA', *Building Design Magazine,* December 2009.

Drexler, Arthur, ed., *The Architecture of the Ecole des Beaux-Arts,* Museum of Modern Art, 1977.

Grossman, Elizabeth G., *The Civic Architecture of Paul Cret,* Cambridge University Press, 1996.

Lawrence, Jeanne Catherine, 'Steel Frame Architecture versus the London Building Regulations: Selfridges, the Ritz and American Technology', *Construction History,* Vol. 6, 1990, pp.23–46.

Middleton, Robin, ed., 'The Beaux Arts', *Architectural Design,* Vol. 48, Nos. 11–12, 1978.

Norri, Marja-Riitta, Elina Standertskjold, Wilfried Wang eds., *Finland: 20th Century Architecture,* Prestel, 2000.

Plummer, Henry, *Nordic Light: Modern Scandinavian Architecture,* Thames & Hudson, 2012.

Polano, Sergio, et al., *Hendrik Petrus Berlage: Complete Works,* Random House, 1988.

Rovinelli, H. Paul, 'H. P. Berlage and the Amsterdam School, 1914–1920', *Journal of the Society of Architectural Historians,* Vol. 43, No. 3, October 1984, pp.256–264.

Stamp, Gavin, 'London 1900', *Architectural Design,* Vol. 48, Nos. 5–6, 1978.

Treib, Mark, Lars Sonck, 'From the Roots', *Journal of the Society of Architectural Historians,* Vol. 30, No. 3, October 1971.

White, Samuel G., *McKim, Mead and White: The Masterworks,* Rizzoli, 2003.

Wickman, Mats, translated by Melody Favish, *Stockholm City Hall,* Sellin, 2003.

Searing, Helen, ed., *In Search of Modern Architecture: A Tribute to Henry Russell Hitchcock,* MIT Press, 1982.

Saarinen in Finland: Gesellius, Lindgren, Saarinen 1896– 1907, Saarinen 1907–1923, Exhibition Catalogue, Suomen Rakennustiteen Museo, 1984.

Chapter 04

Banham, Reyner, *Theory and Design in the First Machine Age, Section 2,* Architectural Press, 1960.

Britton, Karla, *Auguste Perret,* Phaidon, 2001.

Billington, David P., *Robert Maillart: Builder, Designer and Artist,* Cambridge University Press, 1997.

Billington, David P., 'An Example of Structural Art, The Salginatobel Bridge of Robert Maillart', *Journal of the Society of Architectural Historians,* Vol. 33, No. 1, March 1974, pp.61–72.

Caramel, Luciano, *Antonio Sant'Elia: The Complete Works,* Rizzoli, 1988.

Collins, Peter, *Concrete: The Vision of a New Architecture: a study of Auguste Perret and his Precursors,* Faber, 1959.

Forty, Adrian, *Concrete and Culture: A Material History,* Reaktion, 2013.

Frampton, Kenneth, 'Auguste Perret and Classical Rationalism', Chapter 5 of *Studies in Tectonic Culture,* MIT Press, 1995.

Rowe, Colin, 'Chicago Frame: Chicago's Place in the Modern Movement', *Architectural Review,* November 1956.

Saint, Andrew, 'Some Thoughts About the Architectural Use of Concrete', *AA Files,* Nos. 21 and 22, Spring and Autumn 1991, pp.3–12 and 3–16.

Sullivan, Louis, Robert Twombly, *The Public Papers (including The Tall Office Building Artistically Considered),* University of Chicago Press, 1988.

Twombly, Robert, *Louis Sullivan: His Life and Work,* University of Chicago Press 1987.

Wiebenson, Dora, *Tony Garnier: The Cité Industrielle,* Studio Vista, 1969.

Chapter 05

Anderson, Stanford, *Peter Behrens and a New Architecture for the Twentieth Century,* MIT Press, 2000.

Banham, Reyner, *Theory and Design in the First Machine Age,* Chapters 5 and 6, Architectural Press, 1960.

Bucci, Federico, *Albert Kahn: Architect of Ford,* Princeton Architectural Press, 2002.

Hawkins Ferry, W., *The Legacy of Albert Kahn,* Wayne State University Press, 1987.

Hildebrand, Grant, *Designing for Industry: The Architecture of Albert Kahn,* MIT Press, 1974.

Hildebrand, Grant, 'Albert Kahn: The Second Industrial Revolution', *Perspecta,* Vol. 5, 1975, pp.31–40.

Jaeggi, Annemarie, 'Modern Matters: Gropius and Meyer at Fagus', *Architecture Today,* No. 113, November 2000, pp.78–84.

McCarter, Robert, *Unity Temple: Frank Lloyd Wright,* Phaidon 1997.

McLeod, Mary, 'Architecture or Revolution: Taylorism, Technocracy and Social Change', *Art Journal,* Vol. 43, No. 2, Summer 1983, pp.132–147.

Magaziner, Henry Jonas, 'Working for a Genius: My time with Albert Kahn', *APT Bulletin,* Vol. 32, No. 2/3, 2001, pp.59–64.

Pevsner, Nikolaus, 'Gropius at Twenty-Six', *Architectural Review,* July 1961, pp.49–51.

Quinan, Jack, *Frank Lloyd Wright's Larkin Building: Myth and Fact,* MIT Press, 1987.

Chapter 06

Benton, Tim, *Expressionism,* Open University Press, 1975.

Blundell Jones, Peter, *Hans Scharoun,* Phaidon, 1995.

Blundell Jones, Peter, *Hugo Häring: The Organic Versus the Geometric,* Menges, 1999.

Boyd Whyte, Iain, *Bruno Taut and the Architecture of Activism,* Cambridge University Press, 1982.

Boyd Whyte, Iain, *The Crystal Chain Letters: Architectural Fantasies by Bruno Taut and his Circle,* MIT Press, 1985.

Casciato, Maristella, *The Amsterdam School,* 010 Publishers, 1996.

Conrads, Ulrich and Hans G. Sperlich, *Fantastic Architecture,* Architectural Press, 1963.

James, Kathleen, *Erich Mendelsohn and the Architecture of German Modernism,* Cambridge University Press, 1997.

Pehnt, Wolfgang, *Expressionist Architecture,* Thames & Hudson, 1973.

Posener, Julius, *Hans Poelzig: Reflections on his Life and Work*, MIT Press, 1992.

Schirren, Matthias, *Bruno Taut: Alpine Architektur*, Prestel, 2004.

Zevi, Bruno, *Erich Mendelsohn: The Complete Works*, Birkhäuser, 1999.

Chapter 07

Blau, Eve, *The Architecture of Red Vienna, 1919–1934*, MIT Press, 1999.

Bergeijk, Herman van, ed., *W. M. Dudok*, 010 Publishers, 2001.

Broekhuizen, Dolf, ed., *Robert van 't Hoff: Architect of a New Society*, NAi, 2010.

Doesburg, Theo van, translated by Charlotte I. Loeb and Arthur L. Loeb, *On European Architecture: Complete essays from Het Bouwebedrijf 1924–1931*, Birkhäuser, 1990.

Doig, Alan, *Theo van Doesburg: Painting into Architecture, Theory into Practice*, Cambridge University Press, 1986.

Janssen, Hans, Michael White, *The Story of De Stijl: Mondrian to van Doesburg*, Lund Humphries, 2011.

Jelles, E. J., C. A. Alberts, *Duiker 1890–1935*, de Boer, 1972.

Jones, Jesse, 'Karl Marx-Hof, Vienna', *Building Material*, Autumn 2009, pp.28–33.

Mulde, Bertus, and Ida van Zijl, *The Rietveld Schroder House*, Princeton Architectural Press, 1999.

Swenarton, Mark, *Homes Fit for Heroes: the Politics and Architecture of Early State Housing in Britain*, Heinemann Educational, 1981.

Wagenaar, Ed, Taverne Cor, Martien de Vletter, *J. J. P. Oud 1890–1963: Poetic Functionalist: The Complete Works*, NAi, 2001.

Zijl, Ida van, *Gerrit Rietveld*, Phaidon, 2010.

Chapter 08

Barry Bergdoll, Leah Dickerman, *Bauhaus 1919–1933: Workshops for Modernity*, Museum of Modern Art, 2009.

Blijstra, Reinder, *Mart Stam: Documentation of his Work 1920–1965*, RIBA Publications, 1970.

Fehl, Gerhard, 'The Niddatal Project, Frankfurt', *Built Environment*, Vol. 0, No. ¾, 1983, pp.185–197.

Giedion, Sigfried, *Walter Gropius*, Dover, 1992.

Gropius, Walter, *The New Architecture and the Bauhaus*, Faber, 1935.

Gropius, Walter, *Scope of Total Architecture*, Allen and Unwin, 1956.

Hays, K. Michael, *Modernism and the Post Humanist Subject: The Architecture of Hannes Meyer and Ludwig Hilberseimer*, MIT Press, 1992.

Henderson, Susan R., *Ernst May and the New Frankfurt Initiative, 1926–1931*, Peter Lang, 2013.

Isaacs, Reginald, *Gropius: An Illustrated Biography of the Creator of the Bauhaus*, Bullfinch, 1991.

Lane, Barbara Miller, *Architecture and Politics in Germany 1918–1945*, Harvard University Press, 1968.

Naylor, Gillian, *The Bauhaus Reassessed: Sources and Design Theory*, Herbert Press, 1985.

Pommer, Richard, Christian F. Otto, *Weissenhof 1927 and the Modern Movement in Architecture*, University of Chicago Press, 1991.

Wilk, Christopher, ed., *Modernism 1914–1939: Designing a New World*, Victoria and Albert Museum, 2006.

Chapter 09

Benton, Charlotte, 'From Tubular Steel to Bamboo: Charlotte Perriand, the Migrating "Chaise-longue" and Japan', *Journal of Design History*, Vol. 11, No. 1, 1998, pp.31–58.

Benton, Tim, *The Villas of Le Corbusier, 1920–1930*, Yale University Press, 1987.

Curtis, William J. R., *Le Corbusier: Ideas and Forms*, Phaidon, 2015.

Eliel, Carol S., Francoise Ducros, Tag Gronberg, *L'Esprit Nouveau: Purism in Paris, 1918–1925*, Los Angeles County Museum of Art with Harry N. Abrams, 2001.

Jencks, Charles, *Le Corbusier and the Tragic View of Architecture*, Allen Lane, 1973.

Le Corbusier, Jean-Louis Cohen, *Toward an Architecture*, Getty Publications, 2007.

Le Corbusier: Architect of the Century (Centenary Exhibition, Hayward Gallery London), Arts Council

of Great Britain, 1987.

Le Corbusier, *The City of Tomorrow and its Planning*, Architectural Press, 1971.

Le Corbusier et Pierre Jeanneret: Oeuvre Complete, Volumes 1–3, Birkhäuser, 1999.

McLeod, Mary, ed., *Charlotte Perriand: An Art of Living*, Harry N. Abrams, 2003.

Moos, Stanilaus von, *Le Corbusier: Elements of a Synthesis*, MIT Press, 1979.

Rowe, Colin, *The Mathematics of the Ideal Villa and Other Essays*, MIT Press, 1982.

Chapter 10

Bergdoll, Barry, *Mies in Berlin*, Museum of Modern Art, 2002.

Blake, Peter, *Mies van der Rohe: Architecture and Structure*, Harmondsworth, Pelican, 1960.

Cohen, Jean-Louis, *Ludwig Mies van der Rohe*, Birkhäuser, 2007.

Evans, Robin, 'Mies van der Rohe's Paradoxical Symmetries', *AA Files*, No. 19, Spring 1990, pp.56–68.

Hammer-Tugendhat, Daniela, Ivo Hammer, Wolf Tegethoff, *Tugendhat House*, Walter de Gruyter Inc., 2014

Hilberseimer, Ludwig, *Mies van der Rohe*, Theobald, 1956.

Honey, Sandra, ed., *Mies van der Rohe: European Works*, Academy Editions, 1986.

Johnson, Philip, *Mies van der Rohe*, Museum of Modern Art, 1978.

Riley, Terence, Franz Schulze and Edward Windhorst, *Mies van der Rohe: a Critical Biography*, University of Chicago Press, 2012.

Sola-Morales, Ignasi de, Cristian Cirici, Fernando Ramos, *Mies van der Rohe: Barcelona Pavilion*, Gili, 1993.

Snodin, Michael, ed., *Karl Friedrich Schinkel: A Universal Man*, Yale University Press, 1991.

Tegethoff, Wolf, *Mies van der Rohe: The Villas and Country Houses*, MIT Press, 1985.

Chapter 11

Building the Revolution: Soviet Art and Architecture 1915–1935, (Exhibition Catalogue, including photographs by Richard Pare), Royal Academy of Arts, 2011.

Cooke, Catherine, *Russian Avant-Garde: Theories of Art, Architecture and the City*, Academy Editions, 1995.

Cooke, Catherine, ed., 'Chernikov: Fantasy and Construction', AD Profile 55, *Architectural Design*, Vol. 54, No. 9/10, 1984.

Ginzburg, Moisei, *Style and Epoch*, MIT Press, 1982.

Jakovljevic, Branislav, 'Unframe Malevich!: Ineffability and Sublimity in Suprematism', *Art Journal*, Vol. 63 No. 3, Autumn 2004, pp.18–31.

Khan-Megomedov, Selim Omerovich, *Pioneers of Soviet Architecture: the Search for New Solutions in the 1920s and 1930s*, Thames & Hudson, 1987.

Khan-Megomedov, Selim Omerovich, *Alexandr Vesnin and Russian Constructivism*, Lund Humphries, 1986.

Ivan Leonidov, (introduction by Vieri Quilici, essay by Selim Omerovich Khan-Megomedov), Rizzoli, 1981.

Lodder, Christina, *Russian Constructivism*, Yale University Press, 1983.

Pare, Richard, Jean-Louis Cohen, *The Lost Vanguard: Russian Modernist Architecture 1922–32*, Monacelli, 2007.

Shatskikh, Aleksandra, 'The Cosmos and the Canvas: Malevich at Tate Modern', *Tate Etc.*, Issue 31, Summer 2014.

Starr, S. Frederick, *Melnikov: Solo Architect in a Mass Society*, Princeton University Press, 1978.

Chapter 12

Carter, Brian, *Johnson Wax Administration Building and Research Tower: Frank Lloyd Wright*, Phaidon, 1998.

Frampton, Kenneth, 'Frank Lloyd Wright and the Text-Tile Tectonic', Chapter 4 of *Studies in Tectonic Culture*, MIT Press, 1995.

Gebhard, David, *Romanza: The California Architecture of Frank Lloyd Wright*, Chronicle, 1988.

Hines, Thomas S., *Architecture of the Sun: Los Angeles Modernism 1900–1970*, Rizzoli, 2010.

Hines, Thomas S., *Richard Neutra and the Search for Modern Architecture: A Biography and History*, Oxford University Press, 1982.

Levine, Neil, *The Architecture of Frank Lloyd Wright*, Princeton University Press, 1996.

McCarter, Robert, *Fallingwater: Frank Lloyd Wright*, Phaidon, 1994.

Neutra, Richard, *Survival Through Design*, Oxford University Press, 1969.

Sergeant, John, *Frank Lloyd Wright's Usonian Houses*, Whitney Library of Design, 1976.

Sheine, Judith, *R. M. Schindler*, Phaidon, 2001.

Smith, Kathryn, *Frank Lloyd Wright: Hollyhock House and Olive Hill: Buildings and Projects for Aline Barnsdall*, Rizzoli, 1992.

Smith, Kathryn, *Frank Lloyd Wright's Taliesin and Taliesin West*, Harry N. Abrams, 1997.

Wright, Frank Lloyd, *An Autobiography*, Horizon Press, 1977.

Wright, Frank Lloyd, *Modern Architecture, Being the Kahn Lectures for 1930*, Southern Illinois University Press 1987.

Chapter 13

Balfour, Alan, *Rockefeller Center: Architecture as Theatre*, McGraw Hill, 1978.

Bayer, Patricia, *Art Deco Architecture: Design, Decoration and Detail from the Twenties and Thirties*, Thames & Hudson, 1992.

Benton, Charlotte, Tim Benton, Ghislaine Wood, *Art Deco 1910–1939*, Harry N. Abrams, 2025.

Eyles, Allen, *Odeon Cinemas: Oscar Deutsch Entertains Our Nation*, Cinema Theatre Association, 2002.

Ferriss Leich, Jean, *Architectural Visions: The Drawings of Hugh Ferriss*, Whitney Library of Design, 1980.

Goldberger, Paul, *The Skyscraper*, Allen Lane, 1982.

Hitchmough, Wendy, *Hoover Factory: Wallis Gilbert and Partners*, Phaidon, 1992.

Hillier, Bevis, Stephen Escritt, *Art Deco Style*, Phaidon, 1997.

Hillier, Bevis, *Art Deco of the 20s and 30s*, Studio Vista, 1973.

Irish, Sharon, *Cass Gilbert Architect: Modern Traditionalist*, Monacelli, 1999.

Karol, Eitan, *Charles Holden, Architect*, Shaun Tyas, 2007.

Le Corbusier, *The Decorative Art of Today*, Architectural Press, 1987.

Scarlett, Frank, Marjorie Townley, *Arts Decoratifs 1925: A Personal Recollection of the Paris Exhibition*, Academy Editions, 1975.

Solomonson, Katherine, *The Chicago Tribune Tower Competition: Skyscraper Design and Cultural Change in the 1920s*, Cambridge University Press, 2001.

Stern, Robert A. M., Thomas P. Catalano, *Raymond Hood*, Institute for Architecture and Urban Studies, 1982.

Ward, David, Olivier Zunz, eds., *Landscape of Modernity: New York City 1900–1940*, John Hopkins University Press, 1992.

Chapter 14

Ahlin, Janne, *Sigurd Lewerentz, Architect*, MIT Press, 1987.

Antliff, Mark, 'Fascism, Modernism and Modernity', *The Art Bulletin*, Vol. 84, No. 1, March 2002, pp.148–169.

Barker, Michael, 'International Exhibitions at Paris Culminating with the Exposition Internationale des Arts et Techniques dans la Vie Moderne, 1937', *Journal of the Decorative Arts Society 1850– the Present*, No. 27, 2003, pp.6–21.

Blundell Jones, Peter, *Gunnar Asplund*, Phaidon 2006.

Borsi, Franco, *The Monumental Era: European Architecture and Design, 1929–1939*, Lund Humphries, 1987.

Caldenby, Claes, Jöran Lindvall, Wilfried Wang eds., *Sweden: 20th Century Architecture*, Prestel, 1998.

Ciucci, Giorgio, Jessica Levine, 'The Classicism of E42: Between Modernity and Tradition', *Assemblage*, No. 8, February 1989, pp.78–87.

Cooke, Catherine, 'Beauty as a Route to "The Radiant Future": Responses of Soviet Architecture', *Journal of Design History*, Vol. 10, No. 2, 1997, pp.137–160.

Eisenman, Peter D., 'From Object to Relationship II: Giusseppe Terragni, Casa Giuliani Frigiero, Casa Del Fascio', *Perspecta*, Vol. 13/14, 1971, pp.36–65.

Hays, K. Michael, 'Tessenow's Architecture as National Allegory: Critique of Capitalism or Protofascism?' *Assemblage*, No. 8, February 1989, pp.104–123.

Heskett, John, 'Art and Design in Nazi Germany', *History Workshop*, No. 6. Autumn 1978, pp.139–153.

Irving, Robert Grant, 'Architecture for Empire's Sake: Lutyens's Palace for Delhi', *Perspecta*, Vol. 18 (1982), pp.7–23.

Krier, Leon, *Albert Speer: Architecture 1932–1942*, Monacelli, 2013.

Lane, Barbara Miller, *Architecture and Politics in Germany 1918–1945*, Harvard University Press, 1968.

Lewerentz, Sigurd, *The Dilemma of Classicism*, Architectural Association, 1989.

Speer, Albert, *Inside the Third Reich*, Hachette UK, 2015.

Stamp, Gavin, *Sir Giles Gilbert Scott (1880–1960)*, Oxford Dictionary of National Biography, 2004.

Tarkhanov, Alexei, Sergei Kavtaradze, *Stalinist Architecture*, King, 1992.

Udovicki-Selb, Danilo, 'Facing Hitler's Pavilion: The Uses of Modernity in the Soviet Pavilion at the 1937 Paris International Exhibition', *Journal of Contemporary History*, 2012, 47:13.

Ward, William, 'Rationalism: Architecture in Italy Between the Wars', *The Thirties Society Journal*, No. 6, 1987, pp.32–41.

Chapter 15

Adams, Nicholas, *Skidmore, Owings and Merrill: SOM since 1936*, Electa, 2006.

Adamson, Paul, *Eichler: Modernism Rebuilds the American Dream*, Gibbs Smith, 2002.

Brooks Pfeiffer, Bruce, *Frank Lloyd Wright: Master Builder*, Thames & Hudson, 1997.

Friedman, Alice T., *American Glamour and the Evolution of Modern Architecture*, Yale University Press, 2010.

Fox, Stephen, *The Architecture of Philip Johnson*, Bullfinch, 2002.

Gordon, Alastair, *Naked Airport: A Cultural History of the World's Most Revolutionary Structure*, Metropolitan Books, 2004.

Hines, Thomas S., *Architecture of the Sun: Los Angeles Modernism 1900–1970*, Rizzoli, 2010.

Hitchcock, Henry-Russell, Philip Johnson, *The International Style*, Norton, 1995.

Hunting, Mary Anne, *Edward Durell Stone: Modernism's Populist Architect*, Norton, 2013.

Lambert , Phyllis, ed., *Mies in America*, Canadian Centre for Architecture, 2001.

McCallum, Ian, *Architecture USA*, Architectural Press, 1959.

McCoy, Esther, *Case Study Houses 1945–1962*, Hennessey and Ingalls, 1977.

Merkel, Jayne, *Eero Saarinen*, Phaidon, 2005.

Millard, Charles W., 'Lincoln Center', *The Hudson Review*, Vol. 20, No. 4, Winter 1967–1968, pp.657–663.

Saliga, Pauline, Mary Woolever, eds., *The Architecture of Bruce Goff 1904–1982: Design for the Continuous Present*, Prestel, 1995.

Steele, James, *Eames House: Charles and Ray Eames*, Phaidon, 1994.

Stern, Robert A. M., *New Directions in American Architecture*, G. Braziller, 1977.

Wright, Gwendolyn, *Modern Architectures in History: USA*, Reaktion, 2008.

Yamasaki, Minoru, *A Life in Architecture*, Weatherhill, 1979.

Chapter 16

'Airport Terminal with Barrel-Arch Concrete Roof at St Louis Mo., Architects: Hellmuth, Yamasaki and Leinweber', *Architectural Record*, April 1956, pp.195–202.

De Long, David G., C. Ford Peatross, *Eero Saarinen: Buildings for the Balthazar Korab Archive*, Norton, 2008.

Drew, Philip, *Frei Otto: Form and Structure*, Crosby Lockwood Staples, 1976.

Drew, Philip, *Tensile Architecture*, Crosby Lockwood Staples, 1979.

Faber, Colin, *Candela the Shell Builder*, Architectural Press, 1963.

Frampton, Kenneth, 'Jørn Utzon: Transcultural Form and the Tectonic Metaphor', Chapter 8 of *Studies in Tectonic Culture*, MIT Press, 1995.

Fromonot, Francoise, *Jørn Utzon: the Sydney Opera House*, Gingko, 1998.

Garlock, Maria E. Moreyra, David P. Billington, *Felix Candela: Engineer, Builder, Structural Artist*, Princeton University Art Museum, 2008.

Huxtable, Ada Louise, *Pier Luigi Nervi*, Mayflower, 1960.

Krausse, Joachim, Claude Lichtenstein eds., *Your Private Sky, R. Buckminster Fuller: The Art of Design Science*, Lars Müller, 1999.

Marks, Robert W., *The Dymaxion Word of Buckminster Fuller*, Southern Illinois University Press, 1960.

Nervi, Pier Luigi, *New Structures*, Architectural Press, 1963.

Pawley, Martin, *Buckminster Fuller*, Taplinger, 1990.

Saint, Andrew, 'Some Thoughts About the Architectural Use of Concrete', *AA Files*, Nos. 21 and 22, Spring and Autumn 1991, pp.3–12 and 3–16.

Chapter 17

Benton, Caroline, *Le Corbusier and the Maisons Jaoul*, Princeton Architectural Press, 2009.

Colomina, Beatriz, *Privacy and Publicity: Modern Architecture as Mass Media*, MIT Press, 1996.

Crippa, Maria Antoinetta, Francoise Caussé, *Le Corbusier: The Chapel of Notre Dame du Haut, Ronchamp*, Harry N. Abrams, 2015.

Curtis, William J. R., 'On Re-reading Le Corbusier', *AA Files*, No. 58, 2009, pp.50–55.

Evenson, Norma, *Chandigarh*, University of California Press, 1966.

Jenkins, David, *Unité d'Habitation, Marseilles: Le Corbusier*, Phaidon, 1993.

Le Corbusier et Pierre Jeanneret, Oeuvre Complete, Volumes 4-8, Birkhäuser, 1999.

Le Corbusier, *The Modulor: A Harmonious Measure to the Human Scale Universally Applicable to Architecture and Mechanics*, Birkhäuser, 2000.

Le Corbusier: Architect of the Century (Centenary Exhibition, Hayward Gallery London), Arts Council of Great Britain, 1987.

Le Corbusier: The Art of Architecture, Vitra Design Museum, 2007.

Matossian, Nouritza, *Xenakis, Kahn and Averill*, 1986.

Rowe, Colin, 'Dominican Monastery of La Tourette', *Architectural Review*, June 1961, pp.400–410.

Stirling, James, 'Ronchamp: Le Corbusier's Chapel and the Crisis of Rationalism', *Architectural Review*, March 1956, pp.155–161.

Stirling, James, 'Garches and Jaoul: Le Corbusier as Domestic Architect in 1927 and 1953', *Architectural Review*, September 1955.

Chapter 18

Aalto, Alvar, *Synopsis: Painting, Architecture, Sculpture*, Birkhäuser, 1970.

Blundell Jones, Peter, *Hans Scharoun*, Phaidon, 1995.

'Continental Prefabrication', *Architectural Review*, May 1963, pp.321–332.

Hitchcock, Henry-Russell, G. E. Kidder Smith, 'Aalto: The Other Finland', *Perspecta*, Vol. 9, 1965, pp.131–166.

Miller, William C., 'Furniture, Painting and Applied Designs: Alvar Aalto's Search for Architectural Form', *The Journal of Decorative and Propaganda Arts*, Vol. 6, Autumn 1987, pp.6–25.

Pallasmaa, Juhani, ed., *Alvar Aalto Furniture*, Museum of Finnish Architecture, 1984.

Pearson, Paul David, *Alvar Aalto and the International Style*, Whitney Library of Design, 1978.

Porphyrios, Demetri, *Sources of Modern Eclecticism*, Academy Editions, 1982.

Schildt, Gora, ed., *Sketches: Alvar Aalto*, MIT Press, 1978.

Schildt, Goran, *Alvar Aalto: His Life*, Alvar Aalto Museum, 2007.

Schildt, Goran, *Alvar Aalto: Masterworks*, Thames & Hudson, 1998.

Weston, Richard, *Alvar Aalto*, Phaidon, 1995.

Weston, Richard, *Town Hall, Säynätsalo: Alvar Aalto*, Phaidon, 1993.

Weston, Richard, *Villa Mairea: Alvar Aalto*, Phaidon, 1992.

Chapter 19

Bauer, Catherine, *Modern Housing*, Houghton Mifflin Company, 1934.

Brumfield, William Craft, *Russian Housing in the Modern Age: Design and Social History*, Cambridge University Press, 1993.

Bullock, Nicholas, '4000 Dwellings from a Paris Factory: The Procédé Camus and State Sponsorship of Industrialised Housing in the 1950s', *Architectural Research Quarterly*, Vol. 13, No. 1, 2009, pp.59–72.

Bullock, Nicholas, '"20,000 Dwellings a Month for 40 Years", France's Industrialised Housing Sector in the 1950s', *Construction History*, Vol. 23, 2008, pp.59–76.

Carolin, Peter, 'Sense, Sensibility and Tower Blocks: The Swedish Influence on Post-War Housing in Britain', *Twentieth Century Architecture*, No. 9, 2008, pp.98–112.

Coleman, Alice, *Utopia on Trial: Vision and Reality in Planned Housing*, Shipman, 1990.

Finnimore, Brian, *Houses from the Factory: System Building and the Welfare State 1942–74*, Rivers Oram Press, 1989.

Glendinning, Miles, Stefan Muthesius, *Tower Block: Modern Public Housing in England, Scotland, Wales and Northern Ireland*, Yale University Press, 1994.

Glendinning, Miles, ed., 'Post-War Mass Housing', *Docomomo Journal*, No. 39, September 2008.

Hanley, Lynsey, *Estate: An Intimate History*, Granta, 2007.

Harris, Graham, 'Ove Arup and Box Frame Construction', *Construction History*, Vol. 22, 2007, pp.61–73.

Herman, Leon M., 'Urbanisation and New Housing Construction in the Soviet Union', *American Journal of Economics and Sociology*, Vol. 30, No. 2, April 1971, pp.203–219.

Hunt, D. Bradford, *Blueprint for Disaster, The Unravelling of Chicago Public Housing*, University of Chicago Press, 2009.

Jane, Jacobs, *The Death and Life of Great American Cities*, Modern Library, 1993.

Lizon, Peter, 'East Central Europe: The Unhappy Heritage of Communist Mass Housing', *Journal of Architectural Education*, Vol. 50, No. 2, November 1996, pp.104–114.

Morton, Henry W., 'Housing in the Soviet Union', *Proceedings of the Academy of Political Science*, Vol. 35, No. 3, The Soviet Union in the 1980s (1984), pp.69–80.

Newman, Oscar, *Creating Defensible Space*, Diane Publishing, 1966.

Partridge, John, 'Roehampton Housing', *Twentieth Century Architecture*, No. 9, 2008, pp.114–120.

Radford, Gail, *Modern Housing for America: Policy Struggles in the New Deal Era*, University of Chicago Press, 2008.

Venkatesh, Sudhir, *American Project: The Rise and Fall of a Modern Ghetto*, Harvard University Press, 2002.

Chapter 20

Ahlberg, Hakon, 'Sigurd Lewerentz 1885–1975: The Dilemma of Classicism', *AA Files* No. 19, 1989.

'Architecture in Mexico', Special Issue, *A+U*, No. 2, February 2003.

Brillembourg, Carlos, ed., *Latin American Architecture 1929–1960: Contemporary Reflections*, Monacelli, 2004.

Carranza, Luis E., 'Juan O'Gorman', *Casabella*, Vol. 65, No. 689, May 2001, pp.6–21, 82–85.

Eliovson, Sima, *The Gardens of Roberto Burle Marx*, Thames & Hudson, 1991.

Franck, Klaus, *The Works of Affonso Reidy*, Tiranti, 1960.

Fraser, Valerie, *Building the New World: Studies in the Modern Architecture of Latin America 1930–1960*, Verso, 2000.

Gonzales de Canales, Francisco, 'Juan O'Gorman 1905–1982', *Architectural Review*, June 2015, pp.18–19.

Philippou, Styliane, *Oscar Niemeyer: Curves of Irreverence*, Yale University Press, 2008.

Rispa, Raul, ed., *Barragán: The Complete Works*, Princeton Architectural Press, 2003.

Salas, Armando, *Portugal: Photographs of the Architecture of Luis Barragán*, Rizzoli, 1992.

Underwood, David Kendrick, *Oscar Niemeyer and the Architecture of Brazil*, Rizzoli, 1994.

Lima, Zeuler R. M. de A., *Lina Bo Bardi*, Yale University Press, 2013.

Chapter 21

Banham, Reyner, *Megastructure: Urban Futures of the Recent Past*, Thames & Hudson, 1976.

Banham, Reyner, *The New Brutalism: Ethic or Aesthetic?* Architectural Press, 1966.

Banham, Reyner, 'The New Brutalism', *Architectural Review*, December 1955, pp.855–861.

Blundell Jones, Peter, 'Reframing Park Hill', *Architectural Review*, October 2011, pp.83–93.

Curtis, William J. R., *Denys Lasdun: Architecture, City, Landscape*, Phaidon, 1994.

Dunnett, James, Gavin Stamp, *Ernö Goldfinger*, Architectural Association, 1983.

Heuvel, Dirk van den, Max Risselada, eds., *Alison and Peter*

Smithson: From the House of the Future to a House for Today, 010, 2004.

A Language and a Theme: The Architecture of Denys Lasdun and Partners, RIBA Publications, 1975.

Lewerentz, Sigurd, *Two Churches,* Arkitektur Förlag, 1997.

McCarter, Robert, *Aldo van Eyck,* Yale University Press, 2015.

McCarter, Robert, *Herman Hertzberger,* NAi010, 2015.

McKean, John, *Royal Festival Hall: London County Council, Leslie Martin and Peter Moro,* Phaidon, 2001.

Rohan, Timothy M., 'Rendering the Surface: Paul Rudolph's Art and Architecture Building at Yale', *Grey Room,* No. 1 (Autumn, 2000), MIT Press, pp.84–107.

Rudberg, Eva, 'Building the Welfare of the Folkhemmet, 1940–1960', in Claes Caldenby, Jöran Lindvall, Wilfried Wang eds., *Sweden: 20th Century Architecture,* Prestel, 1998, pp.110–141.

Smithson, Peter, 'Reflections on Hunstanton', *Architectural Research Quarterly,* Vol. 2, No. 8, Summer 1997, pp.32–43.

Saint, Andrew, *Park Hill: What Next?,* Architectural Association, 1996.

Smithson, Alison and Peter, 'Robin Hood Gardens, London E14', *Architectural Design,* No. 9, 1972, pp.559–573.

Webb, Michael, *Architecture in Britain Today,* Hamlyn, 1969.

Whiteley, Nigel, 'Banham and "Otherness": Reyner Banham and his Quest for an Architecture Autre', *Architectural History,* Vol. 33, 1990, pp.188–221.

Chapter 22

Ashraf, Kazi K., *National Capital of Bangladesh, Dhaka, Bangladesh, 1962–83, Louis I. Kahn* (Global Architecture 72), A.D.A. Edita, 1994.

Brawne, Michael, *Kimbell Art Museum: Louis I. Kahn,* Phaidon, 1992.

Brownlee, David B., and David G. De Long, *Louis I. Kahn: In the Realm of Architecture,* Rizzoli, 1991.

Burton, Joseph, 'Notes from Volume Zero: Louis Kahn and the Language of God', *Perspecta,* Vol. 20, 1983, pp.69–90.

Goldhagen, Sarah Williams, *Louis Kahn's Situated Modernism,* Yale University Press, 2001.

Komendant, August E., *18 Years with Architect Louis I. Kahn,* Aloray, 1975.

Kries, Mateo, Jochen Eisenbrand, Stanislaus von Moos, *Louis Kahn: the Power of Architecture,* Vitra Design Museum, 2012.

Latour, Alessandr, ed., *Louis I Kahn: Writings, Lectures, Interviews,* Rizzoli, 1991.

McCarter, Robert, *Louis I. Kahn,* Phaidon, 2005.

Maki, Fumihiko, *Richards Medical Research Building, Pennsylvania, 1961; Salk Institute for Biological Studies, California, 1965, Louis I. Kahn* (Global Architecture 5), A.D.A. Edita, 1971.

Scully, Vincent, 'Louis Kahn and the Ruins of Rome', *MoMA,* No. 12, Summer 1992, pp.1–13.

Solomon, Susan G., *Louis I. Kahn's Trenton Jewish Community Center,* Princeton Architectural Press, 2000.

Steele, James, *Salk Institute, Louis I. Kahn,* Phaidon, 1993.

Chapter 23

Abel, Chris, 'Work of El-Wakil', *Architectural Review,* November 1986, pp.52–60.

Al-Asad, Mohammad, 'The Mosques of Abdel-Wahed El-Wakil', *Mimar,* No. 42, March 1992, pp.34–39.

Çelik, Zeynep, 'New Approaches to the 'Non-Western' City', *Journal of the Society of Architectural Historians,* Vol. 58, No. 3, September 1999, pp.374–381.

Correa, Charles, *A Place in the Shade: the New Landscape and Other Essays,* Hatje Cantz, 2012.

Correa, Charles, 'The Public, the Private and the Sacred', *Daedalus 118,* No. 4, 1989.

Fathy, Hassan, *Architecture for the Poor: An Experiment in Rural Egypt,* University of Chicago Press, 1973.

Murray, Irene, ed., *Charles Correa: India's Greatest Architect,* RIBA Publications, 2013.

Nalbantoglu, Gülsüm Baydar, 'Beyond Lack and Excess: Other Architectures, Other Landscapes', *Journal of Architectural Education,* Vol. 54, No. 1, September 2000, pp.20–27.

Richards, J. M., Ismail Serageldin, Darl Rastorfer, *Hassan Fathy,* Architectural Press, 1985.

Robson, David, *Geoffrey Bawa: the Complete Works,* Thames & Hudson, 2002.

Steele, James, *The Complete Architecture of Balkrishna Doshi: Rethinking Modernism for the Developing World,* Thames & Hudson, 1998.

Steele, James, 'The Translation of Tradition: A Comparative Dialectic', *Traditional Dwellings and Settlements Review,* Vol. 7, No.2, Spring 1996, pp.19–34.

Steele, James, 'The Hassan Fathy Collection, A Catalogue of Visual Documents' at the Aga Khan Award for Architecture, The Aga Khan Trust for Culture.

Tarragan, Hana, 'Architecture in Fact and Fiction: The Case of the New Gourna Village in Upper Egypt', *Muqarnas,* Vol. 6, 1999, pp.169–178.

Chapter 24

Canty, Donald, 'AT&T: The Tower, the Skyline and the Street: Philip Johnson and John Burgee', *Architecture (AIA),* Vol. 74, No. 2, February 1985, pp.46–55.

Farrell, Terry, Stephen Dobney, *Terry Farrell: Selected and Current Works,* Images Publishing Group, 1994.

Five Architects: Eisenman, Graves, Gwathmey, Hejduk, Meier (Preface by Arthur Drexler, Introduction by Colin Rowe), Oxford University Press, 1975.

Graves, Michael, 'Referential Drawings', *Journal of Architectural Education,* Vol. 32, No. 1, Working Drawings, September 1978, pp.24–27.

James, Warren A., ed., *Taller de Arquitectura: Buildings and Projects 1960–1985,* Rizzoli, 1988.

Jencks, Charles, *The Language of Post-Modern Architecture (fourth edition),* Academy Editions, 1984.

Jencks, Charles, George Baird, *Meaning in Architecture,* Cresset Press, 1969.

Jencks, Charles, *Kings of Infinite Space: Frank Lloyd Wright and Michael Graves,* (based on a BBC film), Academy Editions, 1983.

Jencks, Charles, *The New Paradigm in Architecture: the Language of Post-Modernism,* Yale University Press, 2002.

Johnson, Eugene J., ed., *Charles Moore: Buildings and Projects 1949–1986,* Rizzoli, 1986.

McKean, John, *Leicester University Building: James Stirling and James Gowan,* Phaidon, 1994.

von Moos, Stanislaus, *Venturi, Rauch and Scott Brown: Buildings and Projects,* Rizzoli, 1987.

Shwartz, Frederic, ed., *Mother's House: The Evolution of Vanna Venturi's House in Chestnut Hill,* Rizzoli, 1992.

Stern, Robert A. M., 'From the Past: Strada Novissima', *Log.* No. 20, Curating Architecture, Fall 2010, pp.35–38.

Stern, Robert, (introductory essay by Vincent Scully), *Robert Stern,* Architectural Design, 1981.

Stirling, James, *Michael Wilford and Associates: Buildings and Projects 1975–1992* (introduction by Robert Maxwell), Thames & Hudson, 1994.

Venturi, Robert, *Complexity and Contradiction in Architecture,* Museum of Modern Art, 1977.

Venturi, Robert, Denise Scott Brown, Steven Izenour, *Learning from Las Vegas* (revised edition), MIT Press, 1977.

Vogel Wheeler, Karen, Peter Arnell, Ted Bickford, eds., *Michael Graves: Buildings and Projects 1966–1981,* Architectural Press, 1983.

Vogel Nichols, Karen, Patrick J. Burke, Caroline Hancock eds. (essays by Robert Maxwell, Christian Norberg-Schulz), *Michael Graves: Building and Projects 1982–1989,* Architecture Design and Technology Press, 1990.

Chapter 25

Adjmi, Morris ed., *Aldo Rossi: The Complete Buildings and Projects 1981–1991,* Thames & Hudson, 1992.

Aymonino, Carlo, Aldo Rossi, Pierluigi Nicolin, Yukio Futagawa, *Housing Complex at the Gallaratese Quarter, Milan Italy, 1969–74,* A.D.A. Edita, 1977.

'Berlin: Origins to IBA', Special Issue, *Architectural Review,* April 1987, pp.22–106.

'Mario Botta in Conversation with Laurent Stalder', *AA Files,* No. 63 (2011) pp.111–117.

Dal Co, Francesco, *Mario Botta: Architecture 1960–1985,* Architectural Press, 1987.

Duany, Andres, Elizabeth Plater-Zyberk, *Suburban Nation: The Rise of Sprawl and the Decline of the American Dream,* North Point Press, 2000.

Economakis, Richard, ed., *Leon Krier: Architecture and Urban Design 1967–1992,* Academy Editions, 1992.

Jones, Edward, 'The Genesis of Mississauga City Hall', *RIBA Transactions,* Vol. 5, No. 2, 1987, pp.20–31.

Klotz, Heinrich, *O. M. Ungers: Bauten und Projekte 1951–1984,* Vieweg, 1985.

'Leon Krier: Drawings 1967–80', Archives d'Architecture Moderne, 1980.

Krier, Rob, *Urban Space,* Academy Editions, 1979.

McCarter, Robert, *Carlo Scarpa,* Phaidon, 2013.

Ockman, Joan, 'Form without Utopia: Contextualising Colin Rowe', *Journal of the Society of Architectural Historians,* Vol. 57, No. 4, December 1998, pp.448–456.

Pizzi, Emilio, *Mario Botta,* Gili, 1997.

Rossi, Aldo, *Architect,* Academy Editions, 1994.

Rossi, Aldo, *Architect,* Electa, 1987.

Rossi, Aldo, *A Scientific Autobiography,* MIT Press, 1981.

Rossi, Aldo, *The Architecture of the City,* MIT Press, 1982.

Rowe, Colin, Fred Koetter, *Collage City,* MIT Press, 1978.

Ungers, Oswald M., *Architettura Come Tema – Architecture as Theme,* Electa, 1982.

Vidler, Anthony, Leon Krier, Massimo Scolari, *Rational Architecture: The Reconstruction of the European City,* Editions des Archives d'Architecture Moderne, 1978.

Chapter 26

Amery, Colin, *Architecture, Industry and Innovations: The Early Work of Nicholas Grimshaw and Partners,* Phaidon, 1995.

Appleyard, Bryan, *Richard Rogers: A Biography,* Faber, 1986.

Davies, Colin, *High Tech Architecture,* Rizzoli, 1988.

Davies, Colin, *Hopkins: The Work of Michael Hopkins and Partners,* Phaidon, 1993.

Gössel, Peter, *Nils Peters, Jean Prouvé: 1901–84: The Dynamics of Creation,* Taschen, 2013.

Huppatz, D. J., 'Jean Prouvé's Maison Tropicale: The Poetics of the Colonial Object', *Design Issues,* Vol. 26, No. 4, Autumn 2010, pp.32–44.

Jenkins, David, ed., *Norman Foster: Works, 6 Volumes,* Prestel, 2002–2012 (see Volume 2 for Hong Kong and Shanghai Bank).

Moore, Rowan, ed., *Structure, Space and Skin: the Work of Nicholas Grimshaw and Partners,* Phaidon, 1993.

Powell, Kenneth, Robert Torday, *Richard Rogers: Architecture of the Future,* Birkhäuser, 2006.

Powell, Kenneth, *Richard Rogers: Complete Works (1961–88),* Volumes 1–3, Phaidon, 2008.

Powell, Kenneth, *Stansted: Norman Foster and the Architecture of Flight,* Fourth Estate, 1992.

Rabeneck, Andrew, 'Building for the Future: Schools Fit for our Children', *Construction History,* Vol. 26, 2011.

Sadler, Simon, *Archigram: Architecture without Architecture,* MIT Press, 2005.

Sudjic, Deyan, *Norman Foster: A Life in Architecture,* Weidenfeld and Nicolson, 2010.

Sudjic, Deyan, *Norman Foster, Richard Rogers, James Stirling: New Directions in British Architecture,* Thames & Hudson, 1986.

A Guide to Archigram 1961–74 (Exhibition Catalogue), Academy Editions, 1994.

Chapter 27

Bettinotti, Massimo, *Kenzo Tange 1946–1996: Architecture and Urban Design,* Electa, 1996.

Bognar, Botond, *Contemporary Japanese Architecture: Its Development and Challenge,* Van Nostrand Reinhold, 1985.

Drexler, Arthur, *The Architecture of Japan,* Museum of Modern Art, 1955.

Ito, Toyo, Dana Buntrock, Taro Igarashi, Riken Yamamoto, *Toyo Ito,* Phaidon, 2009.

Jodidio, Philip, *Ando: Complete Works 1975–2014,* Taschen, 2014.

Koshalek, Richard, David B Stewart, *Arata Isozaki: Four Decades of Architecture,* Thames & Hudson, 1998.

Kurokawa, Kisho, *Metabolism in Architecture,* Studio Vista, 1977.

Kurokawa, Kisho, *The Philosophy of Symbiosis,* Academy Editions, 1994.

Luna, Ian and Lauren A. Gould eds., *Shigeru Ban: Paper in Architecture,* Rizzoli, 2009.

Maki, Fumihiko, *Investigations in Collective Form,* School of Architecture, Washington University, 1964.

Maki, Fumihiko, David Stewart, Mark Mulligan, Kenneth Frampton, *Fumihiko Maki,* Phaidon, 2009.

Morse, Edward, *Japanese Homes and Their Surroundings,* Courier Corporation, 2012.

Salat, Serge, Francoise Labbe, *Fumihiko Maki: An Aesthetic of Fragmentation*, Rizzoli, 1988.

Sharp, Dennis, ed., *Kisho Kurokawa: From the Age of the Machine to the Age of Life*, Book Art Ltd., 1998.

Stewart, David B., *The Making of a Modern Japanese Architecture: 1868 to the Present*, Kodansha International, 1987.

Tanizaki, Junichiro, *In Praise of Shadows*, Vintage Books, 2001.

Witte, Ron, Hiroto Kobayashi, eds., *Toyo Ito: Sendai Mediatheque*, Prestel, 2002.

Chapter 28

Balfour, Alan, et al. Special Issue 'AR Reviews AA', *Architectural Review,* October 1983.

Dal Co, Francesco, Kurt W. Forster, Hadley Arnold, *Frank O. Gehry: The Complete Works*, Monacelli, 1998.

Damiani, Giovanni, ed., *Bernard Tschumi*, Thames & Hudson, 2003.

Davidson, Cynthia, ed., *Tracing Eisenman: Peter Eisenman Complete Works*, Thames and Hudson, 2006.

Deconstructivist Architecture (Exhibition Catalogue), Museum of Modern Art/Thames & Hudson, 1988.

Eisenman, Peter, *Eisenman Inside Out: Selected Writings 1963–1988*, Yale University Press, 2004.

Eisenman, Peter, *Written into the Void: Selected Writings 1990–2004*, Yale University Press, 2007.

Zaha Hadid: Vitra Fire Station (Exhibition Catalogue), Aedes, 1992.

Hardingham, Samantha, Kester Rattenbury, *Bernard Tschumi: Parc de la Villette*, Routledge, 2012.

Libeskind, Daniel, *Breaking Ground: Adventures in Life and Architecture*, Murray, 2004.

Libeskind, Daniel, *Chamber Works: Architectural Meditations on Themes for Heraclitus*, Architectural Association, 1983.

Libeskind, Daniel, *Jewish Museum, Berlin,* G+B Arts International, 1999.

Noever, Peter, ed., *Architecture in Transition: Between Deconstruction and New Modernism*, Prestel, 1991.

Norris, Christopher, *Deconstruction: Theory and Practice,* New Accents, 1982.

Rahgeb, J. Fiona, ed., *Frank Gehry, Architect,* Guggenheim Museum Publications/Abrams, 2001.

Schneider – Bernhard, *Daniel Libeskind: Jewish Museum Berlin – Between the Lines*, Prestel, 1999.

Stein, Karen D., 'Over the Edge: Rooftop Remodelling, Vienna; Architects: Coop Himmelblau', *Architectural Record*, Vol. 177, No. 9, August 1989, pp.82–91.

Tschumi, Bernard, *The Manhattan Transcripts,* Academy Editions, 1994.

Vidler Moneo, Rafael and Anthony, *Wexner Center for the Visual Arts*, The Ohio State University, Rizzoli, 1989.

Wigley, Mark, *The Architecture of Deconstruction: Derrida's Haunt*, MIT Press, 1993.

Wilson, Peter, 'The Park and the Peak: Two International Competitions. 1. Parc de la Villette, Paris. 2. The Peak, Hong Kong'. *AA Files*, No. 4, July 1983, pp.76–87.

Chapter 29

Cuito, Auror, ed., *Rem Koolhaas/OMA*, teNeues, 2002.

Godlewski, Joseph, 'Alien and Distant: Rem Koolhaas on Film in Lagos, Nigeria', *Traditional Dwellings and Selttlements Review*, Vol. XXI, No. 11, 2010.

Jaques, Michel, ed., *OMA, Rem Koolhaas: Living*, Birkhäuser, 1998.

Koolhaas, Rem, 'Junkspace', available at: www.readingdesign.org/junkspace.

Koolhaas, Rem, Bruce Mau, Jennifer Sigler, Hans Werlemann, *S,M,L,XL*, Monacelli Press, 1998.

Koolhaas, Rem, *Content: Triumph of Realisation*, Taschen, 2004.

Koolhaas, Rem, *Delirious New York*, 010, 1994.

OMA/Rem Koolhaas, 1987–1998, El Croquis Editorial, 1998.

Lootsma, Bart, *SuperDutch: New Architecture in the Netherlands*, Thames & Hudson, 2000.

Lucan, Jacques, ed., *OMA Rem Koolhaas: Architecture 1970–1990*, Princeton Architectural Press, 1991.

Moore, Rowan, '*The Best House in the World, Ever (Bordeaux House)*', Blueprint, No. 153, September 1998, pp.32–36.

Pateeuw, Veronique, ed., *What is OMA? Considering Rem Koolhaas and OMA*, NAi Publishers, 2005.

Ramus, Jahua, 'Seattle Central Library', *GA Document*, No. 80, June 2004, pp.8–61.

Chapter 30

Adler, Gerald, *Robert Maguire and Keith Murray: Twentieth Century Architects*, RIBA Publishing, 2012.

Banham, Reyner, *The Architecture of the Well Tempered Environment*, Architectural Press, 1969.

Buchanan, Peter, *Ten Shades of Green: Architecture and the Natural World*, Architectural League of New York, 2005.

Buchanan, Pete, *Renzo Piano Building Workshop: Complete Works*, Volume 4, Phaidon, 2000.

Day, Christopher, *Places of the Soul: Architecture and Environmental Design as a Healing Art*, Routledge, 2014.

Davies, Colin, *British Pavilion, Seville Exposition 1992: Nicholas Grimshaw and Partners*, Phaidon, 1992.

Davies, Colin, 'Uncommon Law: Palais de Justice, Bordeaux; Architects: Richard Rogers Partnership', *Architecture* (New York), Vol. 88, No.1, January 1999, pp.64–73.

Davies, Colin, Ian Lambot, *Commerzbank Frankfurt: Prototype for an Ecological High-Rise*, Watermark, 1997.

Davies, Colin, *Hopkins 2: The Work of Michael Hopkins and Partners*, Phaidon, 2001.

Fromonot, Francoise, *Glenn Murcutt: Buildings and Projects, 1962–2003,* Thames & Hudson, 2003.

Hagan, Susannah, 'Five Reasons to Adopt Environmental Design', *Harvard Design Magazine*, No. 18, Spring/Summer 2003.

Slessor, Catherine, *Eco-Tech: Sustainable Architecture and High Technology*, Thames & Hudson, 1997.

Special Issue 'Thinking Green', *Architectural Review*, July 2005.

Wang, Wilfried, 'Sustainability is a Cultural Problem', *Harvard Design Magazine*, No. 18, Spring/Summer 2003.

Yeang, Ken, *The Skyscraper Bioclimatically Considered: A Design Primer*, Academy Editions, 1996.

Chapter 31

Campbell, Hugh, 'Zumthor's Trousers: A Critical Guide'**,** *Building Material*, No. 12, Autumn 2004, pp.48–51.

Carrier, David, 'The Art Museum as a Work of Art: The J. Paul Getty Museum', *Notes in the History of Art*, Vol. 22, No. 2, Winter 2003, pp.36–44.

Drake, Scott, 'The "Chiasm" and the Experience of Space: Steven Holl's Museum of Contemporary Art, Helsinki', *Journal of Architectural Education*, Vol. 59, No. 2, November 2005, pp.53–59.

Frampton, Kenneth, *Alvaro Siza: Complete Works*, Phaidon, 2000.

Gonzales de Canalez, Francisco, Nicholas Ray, *Rafael Moneo: Building, Teaching, Writing*, Yale University Press, 2015.

Leatherbarrow, David, 'Working Materials: or, Architecture Shows What Materials Do', *Building Material*, No. 17, Winter 2007, pp.37–47.

Lorenz, Werner, 'Classicism and High Technology: The Berlin Neues Museum', *Construction History*, Vol. 15, 1999, pp.39–55.

Mack, Gerhard, *Herzog and de Meuron: The Complete Works* (4 volumes), Birkhäuser, 1997–2009.

Marovánszky, Ákos, 'My Blue Heaven: The Architecture of Atmospheres', *AA Files*, No. 61, 2010, pp.18–22.

McCarter, Robert, *Steven Holl*, Phaidon, 2015.

Meier, Richard, *Building the Getty*, Knopf, 1997.

Meier, Richard, *Architect* (6 volumes, Vol. 3 for The Hague City Hall and The Getty Centre), Rizzoli, 1984–2013.

Moneo, Rafael, *Rafael Moneo: Remarks on 21 Works*, Thames & Hudson, 2010.

Morgan, Conway Lloyd, *Jean Nouvel: The Elements of Architecture*, Thames & Hudson, 1998.

Moore, Rowan, 'Two Decades of Herzog & de Meuron', *Architectural Review*, March 2015, pp.79–89.

Murphy, Orla, 'Zumthor's Baths: A Sensual Guide', *Building Material*, No. 12., Autumn 2004, pp.44–47.

Nouvel, Jean, *Jean Nouvel* (Vol. 1: 1970–1992, Vol. 2: 1993–2008), Taschen, 2008.

Nouvel, Jean, Michael Juul Holm, *Louisiana Manifesto*, Louisiana Museum of Modern Art, 2008.

Nys, Rik, ed., *David Chipperfield Architects*, Thames & Hudson, 2013.

Pallasmaa, Juhani, *The Eyes of the Skin*, Wiley, 2012.

'Upon a Peak in Brentwood', *The Burlington Magazine*, Vol. 140, No. 1138, January 1998, pp.3–4.

Zumthor, Peter, *Thinking Architecture*, Birkhäuser, 2006.

Zumthor, Peter, *Thermal Baths at Vals*, Architectural Association, 1996.

Zumthor, Peter, *Peter Zumthor Works: Buildings and Projects 1979–1997*, Lars Muller, 1998.

Chapter 32

Betsky, Aaron, *The Complete Zaha Hadid*, Thames & Hudson, 2013.

Buchanan, Peter, *Renzo Piano Building Workshop: Complete Works* (5 volumes), Phaidon, 1993–2008.

Blundell Jones, Peter, 'Alien Encounter: Art Museum, Graz, Austria, Spacelab Cook-Fournier', *Architectural Review*, March 2004.

Ferre, Albert, Tomoko Sakamoto, Michael Kubo eds., *Yokohama Project: Foreign Office Architects*, Actar, 2002.

Gregory, Rob, 'Rolex Learning Centre, Lausanne, Switzerland: Architects SANAA', *Architectural Review*, May 2010, pp.42–49.

Jenkins, David, ed., *Norman Foster: Works*, 6 Volumes, Prestel, 2002–2012.

Jodidio, Philip, *Santiago Calatrava: Complete Works 1979–Today*, Taschen, 2015.

Lynn, Greg, *Animate Form*, Volume 1, Princeton Architectural Press, 1999.

Lynn, Gre, ed., *Folding in Architecture*, Wiley, 2004.

Saunt, Deborah, 'SANAA's Rolex Learning Centre in Lausanne', bdonline.co.uk, 5 March 2010.

Scalbert, Irénée, 'Foreign Office Architects: Yokohama International Port Terminal', *AA Files*, No. 30, Autumn 1995, pp.86–87.

Schumacher, Patrik, *The Autopoiesis of Architecture: Vol. 1: A New Framework for Architecture; Vol. 2: A New Agenda for Architecture*, Wiley, 2011, 2012.

Schumacher, Patrik, *Digital Hadid: Landscapes in Motion*, Birkhäuser, 2004.

Slessor, Catherine, '"Top Gear": BMW Central Building by Zaha Hadid, Leipzig, Germany', *Architectural Review*, June 2005.

Spuybroek, Lars, *NOX; Machining Architecture*, Thames & Hudson, 2004.

Sudjic, Deyan, *Future Systems*, Phaidon, 2006.

Washida, Merur, ed., *Kazuyo Sejima + Ryue Nishizawa/SANAA: 21st Century Museum of Contemporary Art, Kanazawa*, Toto, 2005.

Chapter 33

Chung, Chihua Judy, et al. eds., *Great Leap Forward*, Taschen, 2001.

Cody, Jeffrey W., *Building in China: Henry K. Murphy's 'Adaptive Architecture', 1914–1935*, Chinese University Press, 2001.

Cody, Jeffrey W., Nancy S. Steinhardt, Tony Atkin, eds., *Chinese Architecture and the Beaux Arts*, University of Hawaii Press, 2011.

Cody, Jeffrey W., *Exporting American Architecture 1870–2000*, Routledge, 2003.

Denison, Edward, Guang Yu Ren, *Modernism in China: Architectural Visions and Revolutions*, Wiley, 2008.

Lai, Delin, 'Searching for a Modern Chinese Monument: the Design of the Sun Yat-Sen Mausoleum in Nanjing', *Society of Architectural Historians Journal*, Vol. 64, No. 1, March 2005, pp.22–55.

Liu, Laurence G., *Chinese Architecture*, Academy, 1989.

Murray, Christine, ed., Special Issue 'China', *Architectural Review*, November 2015.

Rowe, Peter G., *Seng Kuan, Encounters with Essence and Form in Modern China*, MIT Press, 2002.

Sicheng, Liang, edited by Wilma Fairbank, *A Pictorial History of Chinese Architecture: A Study of the Development of its Structural System and the Evolution of its Types*, MIT Press, 1984.

Steinhart, Nancy S., ed., *Chinese Architecture*, Yale University Press, 2002.

Webb, Michael, ed., Special Issue 'China', *Architectural Review*, July 2008.

Wenjun, Zhi, Xu Jie, *New Chinese Architecture*, King, 2009.

Xue, Charlie Q. L., *Building a Revolution: Chinese Architecture Since 1980*, Hong Kong University Press, 2006.

Zhu, Jianfei, *Architecture of Modern China: A Historical Critique*, Routledge, 2009.

INDEX

PICTURE CREDITS

The author and publisher would like to thank the following institutions and individuals for permission to reproduce images in this book. In all cases, every effort has been made to credit the copyright holders, but should there be any omissions or errors the publisher would be pleased to insert the appropriate acknowledgment in any subsequent edition of this book.

P.6 Alamy Stock Photo/Martin Bond
P.7 Getty Images/Richard Bryant
P.8 Getty Images/Alan Copson
P.10 Alamy Stock Photo/Granger Historical Picture Archive
P.11 © Victoria and Albert Museum, London
P.12 RIBA Collections/Martin Charles/© DACS 2016
P.13 Alamy Stock Photo/Angelo Hornak
P.14 Alamy Stock Photo/John Kellerman
P.15 Alamy Stock Photo/Jordiphotography
P.16 top Alamy Stock Photo/Marek Poplawski
P.17 Getty Images/Leemage
P.18 top Alamy Stock Photos/LOOK Die Bildagentur der Fotografen GmbH
P.18 bottom Alamy Stock Photos/Stock Photos/londonstills.com
P.19 Getty Images/Imagno
P.20 Getty Images/Imagno
P.21 Getty Images/Florian Monheim
P.22 Colin Davies
P.23 Alamy Stock Photos/Florian Monheim
P.24 Alamy Stock Photos/Angelo Hornak
P.25 Getty Images/Print Collector
P.26 RIBA Collections
P.27 Bridgeman Images/©Country Life
P.28 left RIBA Collections/Cloud 9 Leeds
P.28 Right Colin Davies
P.29 The Frank Lloyd Wright Foundation Archives (The Museum of Modern Art | Avery Architectural & Fine Arts Library, Columbia University, New York)/©ARS, NY and DACS, London 2016.
P.31 Getty Images/Patrick Grehan
P.32 Getty Images/Richard Bryant
P.32 ©ARS, NY and DACS, London 2016
P.33 Getty Images/Frank Lloyd Wright Preservation Trust/©ARS, NY and DACS, London 2016
P.34 Colin Davies
P.35 Alamy Stock Photos/ClassicStock
P.36 Alamy Stock Photos/Jan Sandvik Editorial
P.37 iStock/Getty Images/Hannu Mononen
P.38 Alamy Stock Photos/nobleIMAGES
P.39 top left Alamy Stock Photos/imageBroker
P.39 top right Getty Images/Ulf Borjesson
P.39 bottom CC photo take by Udo Schröter
P.40 Alamy Stock Photos/Ivan Vdovin
P.41 Alamy Stock Photos/Arcaid Images
P.42 Getty Images/View Pictures
P.43 Getty Images/Library of Congress
P.44 top Alamy Stock Photos/Sean Pavone
P.44 bottom Getty Images/Bettmann
P.45 top Colin Davies
P.45 bottom Alamy Stock Photos/F1online digitale Bildagentur GmbH
P.46 Getty Images/Oli Scarff
P.47 Alamy Stock Photos/godrick
P.48 Alamy Stock Photos/Granger Historical Picture Archive
P.49 Alamy Stock Photos/Angelo Hornak
P.50 Getty Images/GE Kidder Smith
P.51 Alamy Stock Photos/Vespasian
P.52 Getty Images/Bettmann
P.53 left Alamy Stock Photo/Prisma Archivo/©DACS 2016
P.53 right ©DACS 2016
P.54 left Getty Images/Roger Viollet/©DACS 2016
P.54 right Alamy Stock Photos/Eden Breitz/©DACS 2016
P.55 Getty Images/AFP/©DACS 2016
P.56 Getty Images/Ullstein bild
P.57 right Le Corbusier Foundation/©FLC/ADAGP, Paris and DACS, London 2016
P.58 Getty Images/DEA/G. Cigolini
P.59 Scala, Florence/DeAgostini Picture Library

P.60 Library of Congress
P.61 Collection Centre Canadien d'Architecture/Canadian Centre for Architecture, Montréal; Gift of Federico Bucci
P.62 top Getty Images/Universal Images Group
P.62 bottom Collection Centre Canadien d'Architecture/Canadian Centre for Architecture, Montréal Gift of Federico Bucci
P.63 top Mark Hall for Historic Detroit
P.64 top Alamy Stock Photos/Agencja Fotograficzna Caro
P.65 akg-images/Sputnik
P.66 Alamy Stock Photos/Bildarchiv Monheim GmbH
P.67 Harvard Art Museums/Unidentified Artist/Factory and Office Building for Werkbund Exhibition, Cologne, 1914: Office and factory building, c. 1914 Gelatin silver print; sheet: 65.4 x 97 cm (25¾ x 38⅜ in.) Harvard Art Museums/Busch-Reisinger Museum, Gift of Walter Gropius, BRGA.6.5. Photo: Imaging Department © President and Fellows of Harvard College
P.68 Collection Centre Canadien d'Architecture/Canadian Centre for Architecture, Montréal Gift of Federico Bucci
P.69 top ©ARS, NY and DACS, London 2016
P.69 bottom left image Courtesy of The Buffalo History Museum
P.69 bottom right image Courtesy of The Buffalo History Museum/©ARS, NY and DACS, London 2016
P.70 Getty Images/Chicago History Museum
P.71 Getty Images/Print Collector
P.72 Getty Images/ullstein bild
P.73 RIBA Collections
P.74 Fotopolska
P.75 Topfoto/ullstein bild
P.76 top Collection Het Nieuwe Instituut archive (code): KLER inv.nr.: 1429
P.76 bottom Scala, Florence/bpk, Bildagentur fuer Kunst, Kultur und Geschichte, Berlin
P.77 right Getty Images/Hulton Archive
P.78 Scala, Florence/bpk, Bildagentur fuer Kunst, Kultur und Geschichte, Berlin
P.79 akg-images/Peter Weiss
P.80 top Getty Images/View Pictures
P.80 bottom Getty Images/Universal Images Group
P.81 Alamy Stock Photos/FP Collection
P.82 ©DACS 2016
P.83 Alamy Stock Photos/Bildarchiv Monheim GmbH
P.84 akg-images
P.85 top left Alamy Stock Photos/Loop Images Ltd
P.85 top right ©DACS 2016
P.85 bottom ©DACS 2016
P.86 top Scala, Florence/© 2016. Digital image, The Museum of Modern Art, New York
P.86 bottom Alamy Stock Photos/Picture Partners/©DACS 2016
P.87 CC Rijksdienst voor het Cultureel Erfgoed
P.88 Collection Het Nieuwe Instituut archive (code): DUDO inv.nr.: 42FG.7
P.89 Alamy Stock Photos/Bildarchiv Monheim GmbH
P.90 Getty Images/ullstein bild
P.91 © foto Bart van Hoek
P.92 Collection Het Nieuwe Instituut archive (code): TJUB inv.nr.: 5_1-1
P.93 © Hans Sibbelee/Nederlands Fotomuseum
P.94 Collection Het Nieuwe Instituut archive (code): LEPP inv.nr.: d28-4
P.95 Alamy Stock Photos/Angelo Hornak
P.97 top Scala, Florence/© 2016. Digital Image, The Museum of Modern Art, New York/©DACS 2016
P.97 bottom akg-images/ullstein bild/©DACS 2016
P.98 top Alamy Stock Photos

P.98 bottom left and right/©DACS 2016
P.99 top Alamy Stock Photos/Bildarchiv Monheim GmbH
P.99 bottom left /©DACS 2016
P.99 bottom right Alamy Stock Photos/Bildarchiv Monheim GmbH
P.100 top Bildnachweis: Bauhaus-Archiv Berlin
P.100 bottom Alamy Stock Photos/Frans Lemmens
P.101 Bridgeman Images/The Art Institute of Chicago, IL, USA/Gift of George E. Danforth
P.102 Getty Images/Joan Woollcombe Collection
P.103 Alamy Stock Photos/imageBROKER
P.104 top Colin Davies/©FLC/ADAGP, Paris and DACS, London 2016
P.104 bottom ©FLC/ADAGP, Paris and DACS, London 2016
P.105 top agk-images/Imagno
P.105 bottom Alamy Stock Photos/Julie G. Woodhouse
P.106 akg-images/Stefan Diller
P.107 Institut für Stadtgeschichte, S7A1998/21814
P.109 Scala, Florence/©2016. Digital image, The Museum of Modern Art, New York.
P.110 left Fondation Le Corbusier
P.110 right Fondation Le Corbusier/©FLC/ADAGP, Paris and DACS, London 2016
P.111 top Alamy Stock Photos/Arcaid Images/©FLC/ADAGP, Paris and DACS, London 2016
P.111 bottom/©FLC/ADAGP, Paris and DACS, London 2016
P.112 Scala, Florence/©2016. Digital Image, The Museum of Modern Art, New York/©FLC/ADAGP, Paris and DACS, London 2016
P.113 Fondation Le Corbusier/©FLC/ADAGP, Paris and DACS, London 2016
P.114 Fondation Le Corbusier/©FLC/ADAGP, Paris and DACS, London 2016
P.115 Fondation Le Corbusier/©FLC/ADAGP, Paris and DACS, London 2016
P.116 top Fondation Le Corbusier/©FLC/ADAGP, Paris and DACS, London 2016
P.116 bottom Fondation Le Corbusier/©FLC/ADAGP, Paris and DACS, London 2016
P.117 View Pictures/© Stephane Couturier/Artedia/©FLC/ADAGP, Paris and DACS, London 2016
P.118 left Fondation Le Corbusier/©FLC/ADAGP, Paris and DACS, London 2016
P.118 right Fondation Le Corbusier/©FLC/ADAGP, Paris and DACS, London 2016
P.118 bottom ©FLC/ADAGP, Paris and DACS, London 2016
P.119 left Colin Davies/©FLC/ADAGP, Paris and DACS, London 2016
P.119 right ©FLC/ADAGP, Paris and DACS, London 2016
P.120 Fondation Le Corbusier/©FLC/ADAGP, Paris and DACS, London 2016
P.121 Scala, Florence/©2016. Andrea Jemolo/©FLC/ADAGP, Paris and DACS, London 2016
P.122 top Fondation Le Corbusier/©FLC/ADAGP, Paris and DACS, London 2016
P.122 bottom Fondation Le Corbusier/©FLC/ADAGP, Paris and DACS, London 2016
P.123 Fondation Le Corbusier/©ADAGP, Paris and DACS, London 2016
P.124 akg-images/ullstein bild
P.125 top Scala, Florence/©2016. Digital image, The Museum of Modern Art, New York
P.125 bottom Scala, Florence/©2016. Digital image, The Museum of Modern Art, New York/©DACS 2016
P.126 top Scala, Florence/©2016. Digital image, The Museum of Modern Art, New York/©DACS 2016
P.126 bottom Alamy Stock Photos/Odyssey-Images
P.127 Scala, Florence/©2016. Digital image, The Museum of Modern Art, New York/©DACS 2016

P.128 Scala, Florence/©2016. Digital image, The Museum of Modern Art, New York./©DACS 2016
P.129 top Scala, Florence/©2016. Digital image, The Museum of Modern Art, New York./©DACS 2016
P.129 bottom Scala, Florence/©2016. Digital image, The Museum of Modern Art, New York./©DACS 2016
P.130 top ©DACS 2016
P.130 bottom akg-images/Bildarchiv Monheim/Florian Monheim
P.131 Alamy Stock Photos/Petr Svarc
P.132 top Scala, Florence/2016. Digital image, The Museum of Modern Art, New York
P.132 bottom ©DACS 2016
P.133 top/©DACS 2016
P.133 bottom Colin Davies
P.134 Scala, Florence/© 2016. Digital image, The Museum of Modern Art, New York/©DACS 2016
P.135 Alamy Stock Photos/imageBROKER
P.136 Alamy Stock Photos/The Print Collector
P.137 left Getty Images/Sovfoto
P.137 right Getty Images/Sovfoto
P.138 right Getty/DEA Picture Library
P.139 RIBA Collections/Roland Halbe
P.140 Alamy Stock Photos/Mikhail Chekalov
P.141 CC ©Alex 'Florstein' Fedorov
P.142 akg-images/Bildarchiv Monheim/Jochen Helle
P.143 Alamy Stock Photos/Heritage Image Partnership Ltd
P.144 top left Alamy Stock Photos/ITAR-TASS Photo Agency/©DACS 2016
P.144 top right ©DACS 2016
P.144 bottom Alamy Stock Photos/Arcaid Images
P.145 Getty Images/Sovfoto
P.146 Collection Centre Canadien d'Architecture/Canadian Centre for Architecture, Montréal
P.147 Alamy Stock Photos/SPUTNIK
P.148 top Alamy Stock Photos/Hedrich Blessing/Chicago Historical Society
P.149 top Getty Images/Layne Kennedy
P.149 bottom Alamy Stock Photos/Mary Evans Picture Library
P.150 Colin Davies
P.150 bottom left ©ARS, NY and DACS, London 2016
P.150 bottom right Alamy Stock Photos/Kayte Deioma/©ARS, NY and DACS, London 2016
P.151 Alamy Stock Photos/Arcaid Images
P.153 top Alamy Stock Photos/Robert Harding
P.153 bottom Getty Images/Permissions courtesy Dion Neutra, Architect © and Richard and Dion Neutra Papers, Department of Special Collections, Charles E. Young Research Library, UCLA
P.154 Top & centre permissions courtesy Dion Neutra, Architect © and Richard and Dion Neutra Papers, Department of Special Collections, Charles E. Young Research Library, UCLA
P.154 bottom Photo ©Michael Freeman/Permissions courtesy Dion Neutra, Architect © and Richard and Dion Neutra Papers, Department of Special Collections, Charles E. Young Research Library, UCLA
P.155 Alamy Stock Photos/Nick Higham
P.156 ©ARS, NY and DACS, London 2016
P.157 Getty Images/FPG/©ARS, NY and DACS, London 2016
P.158 top Arcaid Images/Alan Weintraub/©ARS, NY and DACS, London 2016
P.158 bottom ©ARS, NY and DACS, London 2016
P.159 Julius Shulman photography archive/© J. Paul Getty Trust. Getty Research Insitute, Los Angeles (2004. R. 10)
P.161 top Getty Images/Roger Viollet
P.161 bottom Getty Images/adoc-photos

498

PICTURE CREDITS

P.347 bottom Grimshaw/Richard Bryant/ Arcaid Images
P.348 top left Getty Images/View Pictures
P.348 top right Getty Images/View Pictures
P.349 Colin Davies
P.350 right Alamy Stock Photo/Arcaid Images
P.351 top Alamy Stock Photo/Valery Voennyy
P.351 bottom Alamy Stock Photo/Arcaid Images
P.352 top Alamy Stock Photo/David Jackson
P.352 bottom Hopkins Architects © Matthew Weinreb
P.353 left Hopkins Architects © Dave Bower
P.354 Colin Davies
P.355 Alamy Stock Photo/Archimage
P.356 Colin Davies
P.358 Alamy Stock Photo/Greg Balfour Evans
P.359 Getty Images/View Pictures
P.360 Getty Images/View Pictures
P.361 Scala, Florence/© 2016. BI, ADAGP, Paris/©FLC/ADAGP, Paris and DACS, London 2016
P.362 Alamy Stock Photo/Ei Katsumata
P.363 RIBA Collection/John Barr
P.364 top www.japan-photo.de
P.364 bottom Kawasumi Kobayashi Kenji Photograph Office Co.,Ltd.
P.365 left Alamy Stock Photo/Arcaid Images
P.365 right © KISHO KUROKAWA architect & associates Photo: Tomio Ohashi
P.366 RIBA Collection/Architectural Press Archive
P.367 top and bottom Photo by Yasuhiro Ishimoto, © Kochi Prefecture, Ishimoto Yasuhiro Photo Center
P.368 Photo by Yasuhiro Ishimoto © Kochi Prefecture, Ishimoto Yasuhiro Photo Center
P.369 top CC Wiiii
P.369 bottom Paco Valderrama. a+t research group
P.370 Courtesy of Maki and Associates/ photo by Toshiharu Kitajima
P.371 top Colin Davies
P.371 bottom Courtesy of Maki and Associates/photo by Toshiharu Kitajima
P.372 left CC Bujatt
P.373 top designed by Tadao Ando Architect & Associates, photo by Tadao Ando
P.373 bottom RIBA Collections/John Barr
P.374 Toyo Ito & Associates, Architects/ photo by Naoya Hatakeyama
P.375 Toyo Ito & Associates, Architects/ photo by Naoya Hatakeyama

P.376 top Alamy Stock Photo/Arcaid Images
P.377 Alamy Stock Photo/View Pictures Ltd
P.379 Colin Davies
P.380 top and bottom courtesy Zaha Hadid Architects
P.381 Getty Images/©Roger Ressmeyer/ Corbis/VCG
P.382 top left Paul Rocheleau photographer
P.382 right LKP plans
P.383 top courtesy Studio Libeskind /©Guenter Schneider
P.383 bottom courtesy Studio Libeskind/©Studio Libeskind
P.384 left courtesy COOP HIMMELB(L) AU/©Duccio Malagamba
P.384 right courtesy COOP HIMMELB(L) AU/©Duccio Malagamba
P.385 top View Pictures/©Robert Cesar/ Artedia
P.385 bottom courtesy Zaha Hadid Architects/©Christian Richters
P.386 Courtesy Zaha Hadid Architects
P.387 top Alamy Stock Photo/Mark Burnett
P.388 top left Alamy Stock Photo/ RSBPhoto
P.388 right www.japan-photo.de
P.388 bottom Colin Davies
P.389 top Mike Ekern/University of St. Thomas
P.389 bottom Getty Images/Yoshikazu Tsuno
P.390 Alamy Stock Photo/Profimedia. CZ a.s.
P.391 top Alamy Stock Photo/ap-travel
P.392 Alamy Stock Photo/Steve Skjold
P.393 Courtesy Studio Libeskind/©Studio Libeskind
P.394 Getty Images/Lars Niki
P.395 top © OMA/DACS 2016
P.395 left © OMA/DACS 2016
P.395 bottom right OTTO/Peter Aaron for Rem Koolhaas (OMA)
P.396 left courtesy OMA/Photo by Hans Werlemann
P.396 right top and bottom © OMA/DACS 2016
P.397 top Alamy Stock Photo/View Pictures Ltd
P.397 bottom Alamy Stock Photo/View Pictures Ltd/© OMA/DACS 2016
P.398 left and right © OMA/DACS 2016
P.399 ©OMA
P.400 ©OMA
P.401 courtesy OMA/photo by Frans Parthesius
P.402 Colin Davies
P.403 Alamy Stock Photo/Ron Buskirk
P.404 © OMA/DACS 2016
P.405 Architectural Association Photo Library
P.407 Rex/Shutterstock/Photofusion

P.408 Antony Browell courtesy Architecture Foundation Australia
P.409 top Glenn Murcutt courtesy Architecture Foundation Australia
P.410 top courtesy Thomas Herzog Architekten/photo by Richard Schenkirz
P.411 Grimshaw Architects LLP/Jo Reid & John Peck
P.412 Alamy Stock Photo/Paul Thompson Images
P.413 Alamy Stock Photo/Bildagentur-online/Schoening
P.414 Alamy Stock Photo/Arcaid Images
P.415 Alamy Stock Photo/Justin Kase z12z
P.416 Getty Images/Ted Soqui
P.417 top Getty Images/ART on FILE, Inc.
P.417 bottom Alamy Stock Photo/Andre Seale
P.418 CC ©Fanny Schertzer
P.419 Copyright T. R. Hamzah & Yeang Sdn. Bhd. (2015)
P.420 Colin Davies
P.421 Getty Images/Robbin Goddard
P.422 top Alamy Stock Photo/Hemis
P.423 Colin Davies
P.424 Alamy Stock Photo/Jamie Pham
P.425 top Richard Weston
P.425 bottom Colin Davies
P.426 Colin Davies
P.427 top Colin Davies
P.427 bottom Alamy Stock Photo/age footstock
P.428 View Pictures/©Luc Boegly/ Artedia
P.429 Getty Images/View Pictures
P.430 ARTUR IMAGES/©Reiner Lautwein
P.431 top Alamy Stock Photo/Cephas Picture Library
P.431 bottom Alamy Stock Photo/Julie G Woodhouse
P.432 Alamy Stock Photo/Batchelder
P.432 top Getty Images/Art on FILE, Inc
P.432 bottom Alamy Stock Photo/View Pictures
P.434 left Alamy Stock Photo/Johann Hinrichs
P.434 right Alamy Stock Photo/Arcaid Images
P.435 bottom Alamy Stock Photo/Arcaid Images
P.436 top Alamy Stock Photo/View Pictures
P.436 bottom Alamy Stock Photo/Agencja Fotograficzna Caro
P.437 Alamy Stock Photo/Hannu Mononen
P.440 NOX/Lars Spuybroek
P.441 top Alamy Stock Photo/ imageBROKER
P.441 bottom left Colin Davies
P.441 bottom right Alamy Stock Photo/ LOOK Die Bildagentur der Fotografen GmbH

P.443 top Alamy Stock Photo/View Pictures
P.443 bottom Alamy Stock Photo/View Pictures
P.444 top UNStudio/photo Christian Richters
P.445 top Alamy Stock Photo/lovethephoto
P.445 bottom Alamy Stock Photo/View Pictures
P.446 top Alamy Stock Photo/Yooniq Images
Ph 446 bottom Colin Davies
P.447 top Colin Davies
P.448 courtesy: Zaha Hadid Architects
P.449 top courtesy: Zaha Hadid Architects/ photo Helene Binet
P.449 bottom courtesy: Zaha Hadid Architects/photo Helene Binet
P.450 top courtesy: Zaha Hadid Architects/ photo Werner Huthmacher
P.451 Colin Davies
P.452 courtesy: Zaha Hadid Architects/ photo Hufton + Crow
P.453 top courtesy: Zaha Hadid Architects/photo Hufton + Crow
P.453 bottom courtesy: Zaha Hadid Architects/photo Hufton + Crow
P.454 courtesy: Zaha Hadid Architects/ photo Luke Hayes
P.455 Alamy Stock Photo/Nick Higham
P.456 Alamy Stock Photo/Robert Harding
P.457 Alamy Stock Photo/Stan Gregg
P.458 Getty Images/Popperfoto
P.459 top Shanghai Daily/Imaginechina
P.459 bottom left Colin Davies
P.459 bottom right Colin Davies
P.460 Colin Davies
P.461 Alamy Stock Photo/Henry Westheim Photography
P.462 Colin Davies
P.463 Colin Davies
P.464 Colin Davies
P.465 Colin Davies
P.466 Alamy Stock Photo/View Stock
P.467 Colin Davies
P.468 CC ©Gislin
P.469 top Colin Davies
P.469 bottom Getty Images/View Stock
P.470 top Alamy Stock Photo/Sean Pavone
P.470 bottom Colin Davies
P.471 Colin Davies
P.472 top Colin Davies
P.472 bottom Alamy Stock Photo/acppix_ shanghai
P.473 top left Alamy Stock Photo/Dorling Kindersley Ltd
P.473 top right Colin Davies
P.473 bottom Alamy Stock Photo/BSTAR IMAGES
P.474 Colin Davies
P.475 Colin Davies
P.476 ©Edward Denison
P.477 Getty Images/Macduff Everton